PAULINE CHURCHES AND DIASPORA JEWS

Pauline Churches and Diaspora Jews

John M. G. Barclay

William B. Eerdmans Publishing Company
Grand Rapids, Michigan

Wm. B. Eerdmans Publishing Co.
2140 Oak Industrial Drive N.E., Grand Rapids, Michigan 49505
www.eerdmans.com

First published 2011 in Germany by
Mohr Siebeck, Tübingen

Eerdmans edition published 2016
Printed in the United States of America

22 21 20 19 18 17 16 1 2 3 4 5 6 7

Library of Congress Cataloging-in-Publication Data

Names: Barclay, John M. G., author.
Title: Pauline churches and diaspora Jews / John M. G. Barclay.
Description: Grand Rapids : Eerdmans Publishing, 2016. |
Originally published: Tübingen : Mohr Siebeck, c2011. |
Includes bibliographical references and index.
Identifiers: LCCN 2016027592 | ISBN 9780802873743 (pbk. : alk. paper)
Subjects: LCSH: Pauline churches. | Jewish diaspora—History. |
Jews—History—168 B.C.–135 A.D. | Jews—Mediterranean Region—History. |
Mediterranean Region—Ethnic relations.
Classification: LCC BS2545.P47 B37 2016 | DDC 270.1—dc23
LC record available at https://lccn.loc.gov/2016027592

To Wayne A. Meeks
Inspiration and Friend

Contents

Foreword

There are many reasons to welcome this collection of essays and I am deeply honoured to have been invited to contribute a foreword in which I can express my sense of appreciation, which I am sure will be shared by very many others. Like many collections of essays, this one gathers together pieces by a single author otherwise scattered in a wide range of publications, some not very widely available. That is one good reason to welcome it, especially in an affordable edition, accessible to students. But there are other, more substantial, reasons to welcome this collection of John Barclay's essays in particular — even while one is conscious of other important 'Barclay essays' not included here (perhaps we may hope for a further volume . . .).

First, some of these essays have made unusually incisive and influential contributions to major debates in the field of New Testament studies. Perhaps the best example is Barclay's paper on Paul's stance towards the Roman Empire, published here for the first time (Ch. 19), but presented initially in one of those SBL sessions which everyone seems to talk about afterwards (and which I have a peculiar talent for missing: I did not attend the Annual Meeting in 2007!). This paper posed sharp and telling questions concerning the popular and influential view of Paul as an anti-imperial figure, and it offered a different reading of the Apostle. For Barclay, Paul is indeed profoundly political, but the political significance of his message is expressed not through coded oppositions between Christ and Caesar but through a theological narration of history that simply does not see the Emperor as a significant figure. This has already proven a landmark contribution which cannot be avoided in future discussions of 'Paul and Empire'.

Second, some of these essays, in outlining new perspectives and social reconstructions, have proven programmatic for further research, not least research carried out with notable success by Barclay's doctoral students, as well as others who sought his input and advice. Here I think of an essay like 'Thessalonica and Corinth: Social Contrasts in Pauline Christianity' (Ch. 9 here), which helped to stimulate a range of socio-historical analyses of the diversity of the different 'Pauline communities', the letters addressed to them, and their construal of relations with the wider world. Notable examples include Edward Adams's *Constructing the World* (2000), Craig De Vos's

Church and Community Conflicts (1999), and Todd Still's *Conflict at Thessalonica* (1999) – in this last case, Barclay's essay on 'Conflict in Thessalonica' (1993), not included in this volume, is also a significant precursor.

Third, these essays contain some of the wider research and intellectual underpinning for the major works John Barclay has published during this period, most notably *Jews in the Mediterranean Diaspora* (1996) and his commentary on Josephus' *Contra Apionem* (2006). The first of these books was originally intended to contain a major section on Paul, but in the end grew so substantially in size and scope that it became primarily a book on Diaspora Judaism, with just a single chapter on Paul. Consequently, it is especially good to have in this collection some of the essays which explore in more detail the comparisons between Paul and other Diaspora Jewish writers, especially Philo and Josephus – though the promise to deliver a major study of Paul set firmly in the context of other Jewish perspectives has now been fulfilled in Barclay's magisterial volume *Paul and the Gift* (2015). Barclay's commentary on Josephus' *Contra Apionem*, while rich in historical, textual, and philological detail, is unusual among works of the genre in that it also draws creatively on postcolonial perspectives to illuminate Josephus' writing. Again, since the more extended analysis and discussion could not all be included in the commentary itself, it is enormously valuable to have some of the detailed studies which articulate and explore that perspective on Josephus gathered together here.

Taken together these essays represent – to use Barclay's own archaeological metaphor – a series of 'exploratory trenches' dug deeply and carefully into the extant historical evidence for early Christianity and Diaspora Judaism, set firmly in the context of the wider Greco-Roman world. Barclay dedicates his study to Wayne Meeks, author of the ground-breaking and landmark study, *The First Urban Christians* (1983), a study which paints a rich and compelling portrait of the early Pauline communities in their socio-historical setting, drawing both on a wide range of historical evidence and on social-scientific theory. Barclay's studies continue in this vein, not least in their creative and nuanced use of contemporary theoretical perspectives, from deviance theory to postcolonial studies. Yet they are also concerned – again following Meeks's example – to deploy these theoretical perspectives in a sensitive and discerning way, always attentive to the details and features of the ancient evidence. As any reader of these essays will discover, they are immensely rich in detailed engagement with primary historical evidence, yet their use of contemporary theory and concepts makes the analysis and arguments much more stimulating and significant than is often the case in such work.

For all these reasons and more, students of the social history of earliest Christianity and Diaspora Judaism will warmly welcome the opportunity to have access to the riches of John Barclay's research in this one volume. As

I said at the outset, I feel very honoured and privileged to have been given the opportunity to express my appreciation for the wealth of creative and patient scholarship here displayed. If these few words of commendation help to promote this new edition I will be pleased — though I am confident that John Barclay's work needs no such additional commendation given the immense respect and global influence it has already acquired.

David G. Horrell
University of Exeter, UK
September 2015

Preface

The following essays were composed over a period of 20 years (from 1992 to 2011), during which my research interests focused on the social history of early Christianity and the life of Jews in the Mediterranean Diaspora. The two interests were from the start entwined. In the urban Roman world of the first century the early churches and the Diaspora synagogues were closely parallel and sometimes overlapping social phenomena: they have enough in common to make them obvious candidates for comparison, but also sufficient differences for the comparison to reveal the distinct characteristics of each. In the opening introductory essay I have described the rationale and the agenda for this comparison, placing these essays in the context of contemporary research. They constitute, of course, only probes into a very large research field, but their combination and their interconnections offer a composite vision of social realities in the first century which I hope will stimulate new research.

Three of the essays in this volume were new, or substantially new, when published in the Mohr Siebeck edition in 2011: the first chapter, which introduces the collection; chapter 18, which substantially adds to a recently published essay; and chapter 19, which is a wholly rewritten version of an oral presentation (a debate with N. T. Wright) at SBL in November 2007. All the rest had been previously published, but in some cases in relatively out-of-the-way locations. I have used the introduction to place all the essays in a contemporary research context, and I have not updated the previously published pieces except with the addition of cross-references and select recent bibliography in footnotes (in square brackets). Otherwise they have been kept unaltered, apart from the standardization of bibliographical and referencing systems.

I am grateful to all the original publishers for permission to reprint (for details, see pp. 419–20), and record here my thanks to the British Academy for an overseas conference grant which enabled the SBL presentation on which chapter 19 is based. I am extremely grateful to Dr. Henning Ziebritzki of Mohr Siebeck for the invitation to publish a collection of my essays on these themes, and for the patience and professionalism of his team in helping me bring this to fruition. That process would have been impossible but for the immensely valuable assistance of Dr. Ben Blackwell, who offered helpful advice on all the new essays, and has spent an enormous amount of time standardizing (and in some cases, recovering) the essays, compiling the bibliography and indices, and preparing the materials for publication. I am highly honoured to have these essays now reprinted by Eerdmans, and thereby made more accessible, and I am most grateful to Michael Thomson for initiating this project, and to Andrew Knapp for its execution. The only changes are the correction of some typographical errors (with thanks to N. T. Wright for bringing them to my attention).

I dedicate this volume to the person who has been my chief inspiration throughout these years: Wayne Meeks. He played a decisive role in opening up this research field, and has always set the highest standards in scholarly rigour, clear thinking and felicity of style. He has also become a friend, and I owe much to him for stimulating conversation, quiet encouragement and personal support.

John M. G. Barclay
January 2016

Abbreviations

Josephus

Ant.	*Antiquities of the Jews*
c. Apion.	*Against Apion*
Bell.	*Jewish War*
Vita	*Life*

Philo

Abr.	*On the Life of Abraham*
Aet.	*On the Eternity of the World*
Agr.	*On Agriculture*
Anim.	*Whether Animals Have Reason*
Conf.	*On the Confusion of Tongues*
Contempl.	*On the Contemplative Life*
Decal.	*On the Decalogue*
Det.	*That the Worse Attacks the Better*
Deus Imm.	*That God Is Unchangeable*
Ebr.	*On Drunkenness*
Flacc.	*Against Flaccus*
Fug.	*On Flight and Finding*
Gig.	*On Giants*
Heres	*Who Is the Heir?*
Hyp.	*Hypothetica*
Jos.	*On the Life of Joseph*
Leg. All.	*Allegorical Interpretation*
Legatio	*On the Embassy to Gaius*
Migr. Abr.	*On the Migration of Abraham*
Mos.	*On the Life of Moses*
Op. Mund.	*On the Creation of the World*
Plant.	*On Planting*
Praem.	*On Rewards and Punishments*
Prob.	*That Every Good Person is Free*

Prov.	*On Providence*
Quaest. Gen.	*Questions and Answers on Genesis*
Quaest. Exod.	*Questions and Answers on Exodus*
Sob.	*On Sobriety*
Somn.	*On Dreams*
Spec. Leg.	*On the Special Laws*
Virt.	*On the Virtues*

Other

CIJ	J.-B. Frey, *Corpus Inscriptionum Iudaicarum* (Rome: Pontifical Institute of Biblical Archaeology, 1936, 1952; vol. 1 revised with prologue by B. Lifschitz, New York: Ktav, 1975).
CIL	*Corpus Inscriptionum Latinarum* (Berlin: de Gruyter, 1863–).
CPJ	V. Tcherikover and A. Fuks, *Corpus Papyrorum Judaicarum* (3 vols.; Jerusalem: Magnes Press; Cambridge, Mass.: Harvard University Press, 1957, 1960, 1963).
GLAJJ	M. Stern, *Greek and Latin Authors on Jews and Judaism* (3 vols., Jerusalem: The Israel Academy of Sciences and Humanities, 1974, 1981, 1984).
ILCV	E. Diehl, ed., *Inscriptiones Latinae Christianae Veteres* (2 vols.; Zürich: Weidmann, 1925, 1961).
OGIS	W. Dittenberger, *Orientis Graeci Inscriptiones Selectae* (2 vols.; Leipzig: Hirzel, 1903, 1905).
RIT	G. Alföldy, *Die römischen Inschriften von Tarraco* (2 vols; Berlin: de Gruyter, 1975).
SEG	*Supplementum Epigraphicum Graecum* (Amsterdam: Gieben, 1923–).

I. Introduction

1. Pauline Churches, Jewish Communities and the Roman Empire

Introducing the Issues

The essays collected in this volume constitute exploratory trenches in the excavation of early Christianity. In particular, they seek to unearth how the 'assemblies' (churches) of 'believers' within Paul's orbit constructed their identity 'in Christ', using as the chief point of comparison the communities of Jews/Judeans in the Diaspora.[1] Gathering them in this book makes me acutely aware of how much of this corner of the archaeological site is here left untouched. Readers will find next to nothing on gender, ritual, social status, or scriptural interpretation, while the comparison with Diaspora Judeans is not complemented by comparisons with other types of urban group. The limitation in scope allows a corresponding depth in focus: there is much to be learned by placing Pauline assemblies alongside Diaspora synagogues, and the comparison has thus far received less attention than it deserves. In order to situate these essays within ongoing debates, and to reflect on their research agenda, I will here first sketch their context in scholarship, and then introduce each of the following main sections of this

[1] As is already clear, nomenclature is a complex (and contested) dimension of research in this field. Although the adjective 'Christian' is a convenient, and sometimes unavoidable, anachronism when speaking of the first generations of 'believers', I use the term sparingly, not only because it was an outsider-imposed label absent from Pauline literature and very rare in first-century documents (1 Pet 4.16; Acts 11.26; 26.28), but also because it threatens to distort social reality in at least two ways. It implies that the widely differing groups of Christ-believers early recognised themselves as a single distinct community (with a distinctive common label); and it fosters the impression of a social identity distinct from 'Jews' and 'Judaism', thus subtly constructing 'Christianity' as a Gentile phenomenon. On the use of the label 'Christian' in New Testament texts, see now D. G. Horrell, 'The Label Χριστιανός: I Pt 4:16 and the Formation of Christian Identity', *JBL* 126 (2007) 361–81; C. K. Rowe, *World Upside Down: Reading Acts in the Graeco-Roman Age* (Oxford: Oxford University, 2009) 130–35. Because the translation of ἐκκλησία as 'church' can evoke anachronistic images (of buildings and organisational structures), I will use that term interchangeably with another, 'assembly'. On early Christian self-labels, see P. Trebilco, *Self-Designations and Group Identity in the New Testament* (Cambridge: Cambridge University, 2011). For the interchangeable synonyms 'Jews' and 'Judeans', see below, note 19.

volume: Pauline Churches and Diaspora Jews; the Invention of Christian Identity in the Pauline Tradition; and Josephus, Paul and Rome.

I. Contemporary Social-Historical Research into the Early Christ-Movement

The present phase of research into the social history of early Christianity was initiated in the 1970s, enabled by a number of shifts in the context and content of historical investigation.[2] Reacting against earlier tendencies to treat 'ideas' in abstraction, historical study is now focused on social and economic realia, with emphasis on the particular (not the general) and the communal (not the individual). Scholars of early Christianity have ridden the wave of a vast new output of research on the social life of the non-elite in the Roman empire, informed by new non-literary evidence. Since it is now recognised that 'religion' in antiquity was integral to every other dimension of life, scholars from outside the traditional 'theological' milieux have been drawn to the study of early Christianity, posing fresh questions from different angles of vision. Enhanced by the influence of the social sciences on Western intellectual culture, this 'social turn' was brought into Pauline studies in the ground-breaking work of Malherbe, Theissen and Meeks in the late 1970s/early 1980s, and has continued to develop and expand ever since.[3]

---

[2] For a sociological analysis of the waves of (German) research in this field, see G. Theissen, 'Sociological Research into the New Testament', in *Social Reality and the Early Christians: Theology, Ethics and the World of the New Testament* (Edinburgh: T & T Clark, 1993) 1–29. For a fuller description, see R. Hochschild, *Socialgeschichtliche Exegese. Entwicklung, Geschichte und Methodik einer neutestamentlichen Forschungsrichtung* (NTOA 42; Göttingen: Vandenhoeck & Ruprecht, 1999). For an illuminating personal account by a key player, see W. A. Meeks, *In Search of the Early Christians* (New Haven: Yale University, 2002) xi-xxviii.

[3] A.J. Malherbe, *Social Aspects of Early Christianity* (Philadelphia: Fortress, 1977); G. Theissen, *Studien zur Soziologie des Urchristentums* (WUNT 19; Tübingen: Mohr Siebeck, 1979); idem, *The Social Setting of Pauline Christianity* (trans. J.H. Schütz; Edinburgh: T & T Clark, 1982); W.A. Meeks, *The First Urban Christians: The Social World of the Apostle Paul* (New Haven: Yale University, 1983). An early pioneer (appropriately, an ancient historian) was E.A. Judge, *The Social Pattern of Christian Groups in the First Century* (London: Tyndale, 1960), reprinted in D.M. Scholer, ed., *Social Distinctives of the Christians in the First Century: Pivotal Essays by E.A. Judge* (Peabody, MA: Hendrickson, 2008) 1–56. Among the many critical surveys of research since those beginnings, note especially B. Holmberg, *Sociology and the New Testament* (Minneapolis: Fortress, 1990); D.G. Horrell, 'Social Sciences Studying Formative Christian Phenomena: A Creative Movement', in A.J. Blasi, J. Duhaime and P.-A. Turcotte, eds., *Handbook of Early Christianity: Social Scientific Approaches* (Walnut Creek: Altamira, 2002) 3–28; and T.D. Still and D.G. Horrell, eds., *After the First Urban Christians: The Social-Scientific Study of Pauline Christianity Twenty-Five Years Later* (London: T & T Clark, 2009).

Among the beneficial characteristics of this generation of research, two are of particular relevance to the essays gathered here: the use of social comparisons and the deployment of theory from the social sciences. In earlier research into Christian origins (e. g., the *religionsgeschichtliche Schule*), it was common to foreground genetic questions, investigating the roots of ideas, practices or terms which the early believers borrowed or adapted. This is a perfectly legitimate inquiry (of which elements appear in these essays), but it is easily influenced by (theological) anxieties to minimize 'pagan borrowings' and to preserve Christian 'uniqueness'.[4] The last generation of research has seen strenuous efforts to break down the artificial division of cultures into 'Jewish' and 'pagan' (or 'Graeco-Roman'), exploring, for instance, how Diaspora Jews developed their Judean identity precisely by creative engagement with Hellenistic/Roman culture, not by isolation from it.[5] But at the same time we have learned that comparisons can be illuminating quite apart from questions of origin: early Christian communities may be placed alongside contemporary social groups for the purpose of analogy whatever one might decide regarding genealogy. All such comparisons are of course partial, capable of illuminating some features, not all; they are also non-exclusive, allowing more than one 'close' point of comparison. Research has shown that Pauline communities have important features in common with ancient philosophical schools, but also with household-based networks, with voluntary associations or clubs, and with the synagogues of Diaspora Judeans (a species of ethnic association).[6] The categories are inex-

[4] For analysis of these tendencies, see J. Z. Smith, *Drudgery Divine: On the Comparison of Early Christianities and the Religions of Late Antiquity* (London: School of Oriental and African Studies, 1990).

[5] See, in general, T. Engberg-Pedersen, ed., *Beyond the Judaism/Hellenism Divide* (Louisville/London: Westminster John Knox, 2001). On the Diaspora: E. Gruen, *Heritage and Hellenism: The Reinvention of Jewish Tradition* (Berkeley: University of California, 1988); J. M. G. Barclay, *Jews in the Mediterranean Diaspora from Alexander to Trajan (323 BCE–117 CE)* (Edinburgh: T & T Clark, 1996).

[6] The four categories (household; club; philosophical school; synagogue) were suggested by Meeks, *First Urban Christians*, 75–84. Cf. the survey of research in intervening years by E. Adams, 'First Century Models for Paul's Churches', in Still and Horrell, eds., *After the First Urban Christians*, 60–78). R. S. Ascough, *What Are They Saying about The Formation of Pauline Churches?* (New York: Paulist, 1998), drew comparisons with synagogues, philosophical schools, mystery religions and voluntary associations. For the Diaspora Jewish communities as an ethnic association, one of the hugely diverse forms of city clubs and associations, see J. S. Kloppenborg and S. G. Wilson, eds., *Voluntary Associations in the Graeco-Roman World* (London: Routledge, 1996). The point has been fruitfully illustrated by P. Harland, *Associations, Synagogues, and Congregations* (Minneapolis: Fortress, 2003); idem, *Dynamics of Identity in the World of the Early Christians: Associations, Judeans and Cultural Minorities* (New York/London: T & T Clark, 2009); cf. A. Gutsfeld and D.-A. Koch, eds., *Vereine, Synagogen und Gemeinden im kaiserzeitlichen Kleinasien* (Tübingen: Mohr Siebeck, 2006). For a close comparison of the Corinthian church with local associations, see E. Ebel, *Die Attraktivität früher christlicher Gemein-*

act and overlapping; but each is potentially illuminating to the extent that it can clarify structurally significant features of social life. As Stowers notes in this connection, 'comparison is a complex, multitaxonomic activity'.[7]

The social sciences have proved particularly valuable for such social comparisons. Every comparison places one entity alongside another in relation to some comparable feature, and it is the more illuminating the more individual items can be connected in clusters or patterns. But to configure social activities or forms in clusters one needs some framework for understanding society, that is, some (simple or elaborated) social theory. Even historians of early Christianity who eschew engagement with the social sciences operate with implicit social theories.[8] Disputes over the use or non-use of social-scientific 'models' have alerted us to the danger of predetermining results,[9] and the necessary criteria for the successful use of sociology or anthropology in the analysis of antiquity seem to be the presence of sufficient 'data', the cross-cultural applicability of the theories / models deployed, and a willingness to allow the ancient evidence to modify theories / models honed in different contexts. It is no longer popular to analyse the Pauline movement as a 'sect', and for good reason: the category arises out of a social history largely peculiar to the Christian tradition, and neither its binary structure nor the modern sub-classifications of sect fit the complex relations between Pauline communities and their multifaceted environment.[10] But there are plenty of

den: Die Gemeinde von Korinth im Spiegel griechisch-römischer Vereine (WUNT 2.178; Tübingen: Mohr Siebeck, 2004).

[7] S.K. Stowers, 'Does Pauline Christianity Resemble a Philosophical School?', in Engberg-Pedersen, ed., *Beyond the Judaism / Hellenism Divide*, 81–102, at 89. This essay and that by L. Alexander in the same volume ('Ipse Dixit: Citation and Authority in Paul and in the Jewish and Hellenistic Schools', 63–80), remain among the best comparisons between communal life in Pauline churches and the aims and outcomes of philosophical schools. See also T. Schmeller, 'Gegenwelten: Zum Vergleich zwischen paulinischen Gemeinden und nichtchristlichen Gruppen', *Biblische Zeitschrift* 47 (2003) 167–85.

[8] E.A. Judge is amongst those historians who criticise the use of social-science theory in this field: see his critique of 'the sociological fallacy' in 'The Social Identity of the First Christians: A Question of Method in Religious History', in Scholer, ed., *Social Distinctives of the Christians*, 117–36. But even his seminal book, *The Social Pattern of Christian Groups*, contains implicit social theories: for instance, the statement that 'with regard to public obligations, the attitudes [of the early Christians] change with changing circumstances' (73) implies a structural correlation between social contexts and social attitudes.

[9] See the debate between D.G. Horrell and P.F. Esler in *JSNT* 78 (2000) 83–113; for the use of 'models' in the social sciences, in critical dialogue with the 'Context Group', see D.G. Horrell, 'Whither Social-Scientific Approaches to New Testament Interpretation? Reflections on Contested Methodologies and the Future', in Still and Horrell, eds., *After the First Urban Christians*, 6–20.

[10] The general features of sectarian analysis with regard to Pauline churches and Diaspora synagogues were deployed by F. Watson in *Paul, Judaism and the Gentiles: A Sociological Approach* (Cambridge: Cambridge University, 1986). The sect typology developed by B. Wilson was influential on many, including M.Y. MacDonald, *The Pauline Churches:*

other resources in the social sciences suited to research into the patterns of early Christian life, and even those with functionalist or structuralist roots need not lead to reductionist or mechanistic models of causation.[11] Indeed, since no theoretical framework can 'explain' all aspects of society, and since different facets of the evidence require diverse theoretical tools, a pragmatic eclecticism seems entirely justified.[12]

From the start, my own research was influenced by this new intellectual context: in studying Galatians it seemed important to analyse not only the clash of theologies (between Paul and his opponents) but also the social factors that induced Paul's Galatian converts to adopt circumcision and Torah-practice.[13] Inspired by Theissen and Meeks to conduct a closer study of the social life of Paul's churches, I was intrigued by Meeks' suggestion that 'because Christianity was an offshoot of Judaism, the urban Christian groups obviously had the diaspora synagogue as the nearest and most natural

---

A Socio-Historical Study of Institutionalisation in the Pauline and Deutero-Pauline Writings (Cambridge: Cambridge University, 1988). For critical questions on the use of this analytical tool, see Holmberg, *Sociology and the New Testament*, 77–117. For parallel reasons I am sceptical of the value of the form of 'social identity theory' developed by H. Tajfel and utilised by P.F. Esler in relation to Galatians (*Galatians* [New Testament Readings; London/New York, 1988]) and Romans (*Conflict and Identity in Romans* [Minneapolis: Fortress, 2003]). This form of social analysis is based on necessarily artificial experiments on modern subjects, and its applicability across time and culture is extremely uncertain.

[11] Meeks' functionalism, designed to trace the social function of early Christian practices, was tempered by a Weberian interest in correlations ('elective affinities'), and was not intended to reduce the meaning of those practices to their social effects. A. Giddens' modification of the structuralist tradition (in the direction of 'structuration') gave greater scope to human agency and diachronic change and was valuably deployed by D.G. Horrell, *The Social Ethos of the Corinthian Correspondence: Interests and Ideology from 1 Corinthians to 1 Clement* (Edinburgh: T & T Clark, 1996) and S. Chester, *Conversion at Corinth: Perspectives on Conversion in Paul's Theology and the Corinthian Church* (Edinburgh: T & T Clark, 2003).

[12] Note the diverse social-scientific tools employed by G. Theissen in *Social Reality and the Early Christians*, and in his broad-ranging *Theorie der urchristlichen Religion* (Gütersloh: Gütersloher Verlag, 1999; trans. J. Bowden, *A Theory of Primitive Christian Religion* [London: SCM, 1999]). Cf. the variety of methods and theories deployed in J.H. Elliott, *Social-Scientific Criticism of the New Testament* (London: SPCK, 1993) and J. Neyrey, *Paul in Other Words: A Cultural Reading of his Letters* (Louisville: Westminster John Knox, 1990).

[13] J.M.G. Barclay, *Obeying the Truth: A Study of Paul's Ethics in Galatians* (Edinburgh: T & T Clark, 1988) 36–74. The social context and social implications of Paul's Gentile mission had been highlighted by a number of scholars during the 1970s (K. Stendahl; M. Barth; N. Dahl). Cf. Meeks, *First Urban Christians*, 223, n. 41: 'The social implications of continuing or abandoning Jewish ritual practices must have been at least as important, both for the various opponents of Paul and for Paul himself, as theological and Christological beliefs.' Enquiry into these implications was an important aspect of the 'new perspective' on Paul advanced by J.D.G. Dunn and N.T. Wright.

model'.[14] This was among the reasons why I undertook a long-term study of the Jewish Mediterranean Diaspora, which was initially intended as the first half of a comparative study with Pauline churches.[15] During this period I tested the value of a range of social theories (the sociology of knowledge; deviance theory; anthropological analysis of the diaspora condition and of cultural assimilation), as fitted the source material.[16] From my study of the Diaspora I became fascinated by Josephus' apologetic work, *Contra Apionem*, and while working on that text and its relationship to Rome, found aspects of 'postcolonial theory' particularly useful.[17] Throughout this period I have continued to investigate the social formation of identity in the Pauline stream of early Christianity, and the following essays respond to a set of research questions, which may be grouped as follows:

1. How do the assemblies within the Pauline tradition compare as social groupings with the communities of Diaspora Judeans in the Mediterranean basin? How, across this comparison, was social identity created and maintained? What constituted the most socially significant practices in the respective communities, and how were frontiers with 'outsiders' defined and negotiated?
2. To what degree was the social identity formed and practised in Pauline assemblies compatible with the social expression of Jewish identity in Diaspora communities? What structural components of social identification were shared between these sometimes overlapping groups, and where did points of tension arise?
3. How did Pauline churches invent and maintain a durable identity, despite deploying a smaller repertoire of differentiating practices compared to Diaspora Jews? What distinct 'Christian' practices emerged, or how were practices apparently identical to those of non-believers invested with distinctively Christian meanings?
4. How did Diaspora Jews and early Christian assemblies negotiate their potentially awkward relationship with Roman power and Roman religion? In particular, what stances and strategies can we discern in two contemporary but contrasting figures, Josephus and Paul?

---

[14] *First Urban Christians*, 80; I am now less inclined to identify a 'nearest' model.

[15] *Jews in the Mediterranean Diaspora*.

[16] The eclecticism of Gerd Theissen was a particular inspiration; as he writes, 'different perspectives are both an expression of our complex social situation and an adaptation to a complex subject, which cannot be sufficiently elucidated from any single angle' (*Social Reality*, 24).

[17] J. M. G. Barclay, *Flavius Josephus, Translation and Commentary, Volume 10: Against Apion* (Leiden: Brill, 2007).

These four groups of question set a large research agenda to which all of the essays in this volume respond; they may now be further and more precisely introduced section by section.

II. Pauline Churches and Diaspora Jews[18]

a) The Rationale for the Comparison

Because the churches within the orbit of the Pauline mission could trace their social origins to Jews in Jerusalem (Rom 15.26–27), because many of their leaders and some of their members were themselves Jews / Judeans, because their Scriptures were shared with and derived from Jews, and because in common with Jews they were socially peculiar in refusing to participate in normal religious practices ('idolatry'), it makes sense to put Pauline believers and Diaspora Jews / Judeans into a comparative framework.[19] Since our concern here is not genetic (what the churches *derived from* Jewish

[18] The term 'Pauline churches' is shorthand for those communities which were founded or addressed by Paul, together with those represented in later documents which appeal to the Pauline heritage. The extent of Paul's authority over these churches was of course varied: some may have considered him a marginal or even negative influence (see chapter 9). Moreover, while networked through Paul, such churches had contact with (and influence from) other early Christian networks; the Pauline tradition was far from hermetically sealed. Thus, the phenomena we study here are united less by their ideology than by their appearance in 'Pauline' literature – that is, as objects of the efforts of Paul and his successors to mould the social identity of early Christian communities. For critical reflection on the label 'Pauline churches', see D. G. Horrell, 'Pauline Churches or Early Christian Churches? Unity, Disagreement, and the Eucharist', in A. Alexeev et al., eds., *Einheit der Kirche im Neuen Testament* (WUNT 218; Tübingen: Mohr Siebeck, 2008) 185–203. For the relations between different streams of Christian tradition within a single location, see P. Trebilco, *The Early Christians in Ephesus from Paul to Ignatius* (WUNT 166; Tübingen: Mohr Siebeck, 2004).

[19] The translation of the term Ἰουδαῖοι (and Latin, *Judaei*) has become hotly contested in recent years. S. Mason has argued that the term has the same ethnic (and therefore geographical) connotations as similar terms in antiquity ('Egyptians', 'Syrians', etc.), and is given a one-sided ('religious') interpretation by the translation 'Jews'; he therefore advocates the consistent use of the alternative 'Judeans' ('Jews, Judeans, Judaizing, Judaism: Problems of Categorization in Ancient History', *JSJ* 38 [2007] 1–56, reprinted in his *Josephus, Judea, and Christian Origins* [Peabody: Hendrickson, 2009] 141–84). His conclusions have elicited objections, for different reasons, from A. Runesson ('Inventing Christian Identity: Paul, Ignatius and Theodosius I', in B. Holmberg, ed., *Exploring Early Christian Identity* [WUNT 226; Tübingen: Mohr Siebeck, 2008] 59–92, at 64–70) and D. R. Schwartz ('"Judean" or "Jew": How should we translate *ioudaios* in Josephus?', in J. Frey, D. R. Schwartz and S. Gripentrog, eds., *Jewish Identity in the Greco-Roman World* [Leiden: Brill, 2007] 3–28). Since I consider neither translation entirely adequate (the connotations in Greek / Latin do not match those in English), I have opted here to use both interchangeably, although most of the following essays employ the translation 'Jew'. Where the term 'Jew' seems to underplay the contextual implications of geographi-

communities) but analogic (in what respects they were *socially similar*), this comparison entails no claim that the Pauline churches were primarily 'Jewish' in ethos.[20] The historical relations (positive or negative) between Pauline communities and local Diaspora Jews are of course relevant to our enquiry, but the comparison conducted here is primarily structural, and thus remains possible even where precise local evidence is lacking. Given what we know about Diaspora communities in the Roman world, what can we learn about the social strategies and challenges of the believer-assemblies in the Pauline tradition?[21]

The last generation has witnessed a surge of fresh research on Diaspora Judaism, some driven by new evidence, some by new ways of understanding familiar material. The study of 'synagogues' as buildings and institutions has been stimulated by continuing archaeological discoveries,[22] and Jewish inscriptions from the Diaspora have been newly unearthed or re-edited.[23] At

cal loyalty, there is reason to opt for 'Judean' as a better alternative, as in Josephus' *Contra Apionem* (see my *Josephus, Translation and Commentary: Against Apion*, lxi).

[20] The genetic question determines the study conducted by J.T. Burtchaell, *From Synagogue to Church: Public Services and Offices in the Earliest Christian Assemblies* (Cambridge: Cambridge University, 1992); his conclusions suffer from over-generalisation and from a narrow concentration on only one feature of social structure.

[21] For one of the few attempts to approach this question in the round, see K.-W. Niebuhr, 'Identität und Interaktion: Zur Situation paulinischer Gemeinden im Ausstrahlungsfeld des Diasporajudentums', in J. Mehlhausen, ed., *Pluralismus und Identität* (Gütersloh: Chr. Kaiser/Gütersloher Verlagshaus, 1995) 339–59.

[22] See especially D. Urman and P.V.M. Flesher, eds., *Ancient Synagogues: Historical Analysis and Archaeological Discovery* (Leiden: Brill, 1995); D.D. Binder, *Into the Temple Courts: The Place of the Synagogues in the Second Temple Period* (Atlanta: Society of Biblical Literature, 1999); L.I. Levine, *The Ancient Synagogue: The First Thousand Years* (New Haven: Yale University, 2000); L.M. White, *Building God's House in the Roman World* (Baltimore: Johns Hopkins University, 1990) 60–101; A. Runesson, *The Origins of the Synagogue: A Socio-Historical Study* (Stockholm: Almqvist & Wiksell International, 2001); C. Claussen, *Versammlung, Gemeinde, Synagoge: das hellenistisch-jüdischer Umfeld der frühchristlichen Gemeinden* (Göttingen: Vandenhoeck & Ruprecht, 2002). Runesson's book grew out of a collaborative project on the synagogue at Lund University (1997–2001), whose other publications are listed, together with conference papers, in B. Olsson and M. Zetterholm, eds., *The Ancient Synagogue from its Origins until 200 C.E.* (Stockholm: Almqvist & Wiksell International, 2003). For an analysis of recent research, see S.K. Catto, *Reconstructing the First-Century Synagogue: A Critical Analysis of Current Research* (London: T & T Clark, 2007). Although many of the archaeological sites relate to buildings of a date later than our period of interest, the history and significance of the first-century synagogue at Ostia has elicited much debate (see Catto, *Reconstructing*, 52–61).

[23] See the new definitive editions by W. Horbury and D. Noy, eds., *Jewish Inscriptions of Graeco-Roman Egypt* (Cambridge: Cambridge University, 1992); D. Noy, ed. *Jewish Inscriptions of Western Europe* (2 vols.; Cambridge: Cambridge University, 1993, 1995); D. Noy, W. Ameling et al., eds., *Inscriptiones Judaicae Orientis* (3 vols.; Tübingen: Mohr Siebeck, 2004). For a convenient source-book relating to synagogues, see A. Runesson, D.D. Binder and B. Olsson, eds., *The Ancient Synagogue from its Origins to 200 C.E:*

the same time the social and cultural life of Jewish communities in the western Diaspora has been re-examined from a number of angles: the extensive literary sources have been re-assessed,[24] the history of Diaspora communities re-evaluated,[25] and attitudes to Jews among non-Jews re-examined.[26] Numerous studies have been devoted to the interface between Diaspora Judeans and their social and political environment.[27] There have also been specific studies, of special interest to our project, of the relations between Christ-believers and Jewish communities in Antioch, Rome and Ephesus.[28]

Although our evidence is occasionally rich, it is also scattered and often ambiguous. There are many significant sites of Pauline groups where the evidence for Jewish communities is miniscule or non-existent,[29] just as, conversely, the one location where we know most about Diaspora Jews

A Source Book (Leiden: Brill, 2008); for discussion of key epitaphs, P.W. van der Horst, *Ancient Jewish Epitaphs* (Kampen: Kok Pharos, 1991). A variety of sources is collected by M.H. Williams, *The Jews among Greeks and Romans: A Diasporan Sourcebook* (London: Duckworth, 1988).

[24] Barclay, *Jews in the Mediterranean Diaspora*; J.J. Collins, *Between Athens and Jerusalem: Jewish Identity in the Hellenistic Diaspora* (2nd edition; Grand Rapids: Eerdmans, 2000); E. Gruen, *Heritage and Hellenism*. The fragmentary texts have been re-edited by C.R. Holladay, *Fragments from Hellenistic Jewish Authors* (3 vols; Chico/Atlanta: Scholars, 1983, 1989, 1995), and a new series of commentaries on the works of Josephus and Philo is underway, published by Brill.

[25] Barclay, *Jews in the Mediterranean Diaspora*; E. Gruen, *Diaspora: Jews Amidst Greeks and Romans* (Cambridge, Mass.: Harvard University, 2002).

[26] P. Schäfer, *Judeophobia: Attitudes Towards the Jews in the Ancient World* (Cambridge, Mass.: Harvard University, 1997); B. Bar-Kochva, *The Image of the Jews in Greek Literature: The Hellenistic Period* (Berkeley: University of California, 2009).

[27] See, e.g., J. Lieu, J. North and T. Rajak, eds., *The Jews among Pagans and Christians in the Roman Empire* (London/New York: Routledge, 1992); M. Goodman, ed., *Jews in a Graeco-Roman World* (Oxford: Oxford University, 1998); J.R. Bartlett, ed., *Jews in the Hellenistic and Roman Cities* (London/New York: Routledge, 2002); T. Rajak, *The Jewish Dialogue with Greece and Rome: Studies in Social and Cultural Interaction* (Leiden: Brill, 2001).

[28] M. Zetterholm, *The Formation of Christianity at Antioch: A Social-Scientific Approach to the Separation between Judaism and Christianity* (London: Routledge, 2003); K.P. Donfried and P. Richardson, eds., *Judaism and Christianity in First-Century Rome* (Grand Rapids: Eerdmans, 1998); P. Trebilco's book *The Early Christians in Ephesus* builds on his earlier study, *Jewish Communities in Asia Minor* (Cambridge: Cambridge University, 1991); cf. M. Tellbe, *Christ-Believers in Ephesus* (WUNT 242; Tübingen: Mohr Siebeck, 2009).

[29] For instance, Corinth, Thessalonica and Philippi; for attempts to conduct comparisons in such sites, see C.S. de Vos, *Church and Community Conflicts: The Relationships of the Thessalonian, Corinthian and Philippian Churches with the wider Civic Communities* (Atlanta: Scholars, 1999); M. Tellbe, *Paul between Synagogue and State: Christians, Jews, and Civic Authorities in 1 Thessalonians, Romans, and Philippians* (Stockholm: Almqvist & Wiksell International, 2001). Even in Rome the best archaeological evidence regarding Jews comes from a period much later than the first century: L.V. Rutgers, *The Jews in Late Antique Rome: Evidence of Cultural Interaction in the Roman Diaspora* (Leiden: Brill, 1995).

in the first century, Alexandria, constitutes a blank in our knowledge of first-century Christianity. There are also many features of Diaspora life in relation to which the life-patterns of early Christ-believers are practically unknown: to what extent, for instance, did Jewish believers in Paul's churches participate in the annual temple tax, and what became of Jewish and non-Jewish believers who were associated with the local synagogue communities when this tax was transferred and expanded by the Romans after 70 C.E. to become the *fiscus Judaicus*?[30]

Given our inability to conduct local thick comparisons, we normally need to employ a degree of generalisation concerning the social life of Diaspora Jews, based on a collation of evidence from many sites. This is of course hazardous since Diaspora Jews negotiated their identities in different ways, depending on context, circumstance and social level, and Pauline churches differed amongst themselves, and developed variously in the following generations. But generalisations can still be of value if they illuminate the structural characteristics of each community-type, including its social strengths and weaknesses. Indeed, one persistent theme in the essays gathered in this section of the book (chapters 2–8) concerns the relative fragility of the Pauline churches in comparison with Diaspora synagogues. Here I take the opportunity to reflect further on this fragility in relation to structural features of the two types of community.

b) Ethnic and Non-Ethnic Communities

As I have argued elsewhere, 'the ethnic bond' (a combination of kinship and shared 'ancestral' customs) constituted the core of the identity of Jews/Judeans in the Diaspora: in their use of ethnic terminology, their concern for endogamy, their investment in the raising of children, and their resocialization of proselytes, Diaspora Jews wove their communal bonds around this central thread.[31] Of course, as recent studies have emphasised, ethnicity is always in some respects a constructed (rather than a 'natural' or 'primordial') phenomenon: its combined components represent creative acts of

---

[30] On the *Fiscus Judaicus*, see M. Goodman, 'Nerva, The *Fiscus Judaicus* and Jewish Identity', *JRS* 79 (1989) 40–44; idem, 'The *Fiscus Judaicus* and Gentile Attitudes to Judaism in Flavian Rome', in J. Edmondson, S. Mason and J. Rives, eds., *Flavius Josephus in Flavian Rome* (Oxford: Oxford University, 2005) 167–77. For the question of its impact on Christ-believers, see M. Zetterholm, *The Formation of Christianity in Antioch*, 185–201; M. Tellbe, 'The Temple Tax as a Pre-70 CE Identity Marker', in J. Ådna, ed., *The Formation of the Early Church* (WUNT 183; Tübingen: Mohr Siebeck, 2005) 19–44; M. Heemstra, *The* Fiscus Judaicus *and the Parting of the Ways* (WUNT 2.277; Tübingen: Mohr Siebeck, 2010).

[31] See my *Jews in the Mediterranean Diaspora*, 402–13.

rhetorical or social persuasion.[32] For philosophical or rhetorical reasons Diaspora Judeans could parade or downplay their identity as an *ethnos*, but it was generally in their legal and political interest to present themselves as bound together by ties of ancestry and kinship: this made the greatest sense, to themselves and to others, of their international unity and their shared bond to the 'homeland' and to its unique Temple.[33]

Paul is fully at home in this construction of Jewish ethnicity, and uses standard Jewish antitheses between 'Jews/Judeans' and 'the nations' (or 'Greeks') on numerous occasions (e.g., Gal 2.15; 3.28; 1 Cor 1.18–25; Rom 1.16). In establishing communities consisting of both Jews and non-Jews, he sometimes appears to cancel out the previous ethnicity of non-Jewish believers (1 Cor 12.2) and to graft them into a Jewish lineage: as 'children of Abraham' (Gal 3.6–9; Rom 4.10–12), they are encouraged to look to biblical history as the story of 'our fathers' (1 Cor 10.1; cf. Rom 2.29). That linguistic move has a theological rationale, and bears some similarities to proselyte resocialisation, but it is not carried through consistently and, most importantly, is not reinforced by social practice. The context in which Paul's Gentile converts undergo resocialisation 'in Christ' is not the Jewish community, whose ethnicity is practised within kinship-households and through shared ancestral customs, but the house-assemblies, whose strong social ties cross over (without erasing) ethnic differentials. Paul acknowledges believer-communities to be made up of both 'Jews' and 'Greeks', but also distinguishes them from both (1 Cor 1.22–24; 10.32). His strong relativising statements (Gal 3.28) do not eradicate ethnic identities, but they place them within a new orientation where inherited ethnicity is variously valorised and no longer determinative of practice (1 Cor 9.20–21; Gal 2.11–21). Thus, Paul's letters utilise a variety of social metaphors for members of his assemblies ('brothers and sisters'; 'assemblies'; 'the holy ones') alongside a new social dialect ('believers'; 'the spiritual'), but they do not employ the ethnic terminology characteristic of Diaspora Jews (ἔθνος, γένος, λαός, τὰ πάτρια, etc.).[34] The Deutero-Paulines similarly use a variety of familial,

[32] For the application of ethnicity theory to antiquity, see, e.g., J. Hall, *Ethnic Identity in Greek Antiquity* (Cambridge: Cambridge University, 1997); in relation to early Christianity, see D. Kimber Buell, *Why This New Race: Ethnic Reasoning in Early Christianity* (New York: Columbia University, 2005).

[33] For Jewish legal and political rights in the Diaspora, based on their ethnic identity, see M. Pucci ben Zeev, *Jewish Rights in the Roman World* (Tübingen: Mohr Siebeck, 1998).

[34] Cf. C. Johnson Hodge, *If Sons, Then Heirs: A Study of Kinship and Ethnicity in the Letters of Paul* (Oxford: Oxford University, 2007). Hodge rightly insists that Paul does not erase the ethnic identities of believers, and that he sometimes speaks as if Gentiles are affiliated to Israel without becoming Jews. But she fails to analyse sufficiently the character of the 'ethnic' language used by Paul (e.g., 'children of the promise'; 'sons of God'), which is made up of metaphors that do not match social practice in relation to birth, marriage or inheritance. The construction of ethnicity through metaphor is not the same as its

sacral and political metaphors (e.g. Eph 2.11–21), but not the language of 'race' (contrast 1 Pet 2.9–10).

This difference is by no means merely linguistic. *Jewish* members of Paul's assemblies might well retain their ethnic identity, but *Gentile* believers received their social formation in contexts where they had no ancestral roots, where their connection to other Christian communities bore no relation to kinship, where the homeland of Jews/Judeans had only a symbolic Scriptural resonance, and where the Jerusalem Temple could never belong to them, nor they to it.[35] Although some believers brought into the assembly a whole 'houseful' (e.g., 1 Cor 1.16), for others their Christ-allegiance cut across family loyalties (1 Cor 7.12–16), and for the first generation at least (and for converts in subsequent generations) their newly gained identity was at odds with their ancestral traditions. At a later period, some early Christian authors will deploy the language of ethnicity, depicting Christians as a (third) race, but such language corresponded properly to social practice only where Christian communities became self-propagating, through Christian marriages and households.[36]

As we have noted, Jewish communities in the Diaspora constituted a form of ethnic 'association', an organised minority community similar to other ethnic communities in their urban environment.[37] Pauline assemblies, in their communal activities, bore some resemblance to Jewish associations, for instance in their use of Jewish texts, their meetings for prayer and meals, and their aversion to normal ('pagan') cultic practice. But since their common identity was not constituted by ethnicity, they can hardly be classified as an ethnic association. In fact, we might say, they are most like Diaspora synagogues at the point where both assemblies and synagogues were most like philosophical schools.[38] The focus of philosophical schools on a comprehensive life-ethic, their demand for radical life-changes ('conversion'), their emphasis on knowledge, text and discourse, and their ability to undergird counter-cultural life-styles are traits shared with both Diaspora synagogues and Pauline churches. If, in this respect, Diaspora communities constituted

construction through the selection or manipulation of birth relations and kinship practices (even where the latter are supplemented by metaphorical extensions or additions).

[35] For this difference and its significance, given the interconnection of Temple, sacrifice, land and people, see Stowers, 'Pauline Christianity', 83–89.

[36] On the language of 'race', see Kimber Buell, *Why This New Race* and J. Lieu, *Christian Identity in the Jewish and Graeco-Roman World* (Oxford: Oxford University, 2004) 239–68.

[37] See Harland, *Dynamics of Identity*.

[38] Both Philo and Josephus make play of the 'school' character of synagogue meetings: Philo, *Legatio* 156–57, 312–13; *Somn.* 2.127; Josephus, *c. Apion.* 2.175. On this topic see the seminal essay by E.A. Judge, 'The Early Christians as a Scholastic Community', in idem, *The First Christians in the Roman World: Augustan and New Testament Essays* (ed. J.R. Harrison; WUNT 229; Tübingen: Mohr Siebeck, 2008) 526–52.

'ethnic schools', Pauline churches look most like Diaspora synagogues in their 'philosophical' mode, or most like a 'Judean school' whose membership was not characterised by an ethnic bond.

c) Social Practices and their Meaning

If, in including non-Judeans, the common identity of Pauline assemblies was crucially different from that of Judean synagogues, even those practices which they had in common with Diaspora synagogues acquired a different social meaning. The Jewish abstention from non-Jewish, pluralist and iconic cult was explicable (and generally excusable) in the Roman world because it represented an ancient ethnic tradition; it was generally known that Jews practised this peculiarity, and resentment was largely confined to cases where they drew non-Jews (sympathisers or proselytes) into this idiosyncratic behaviour.[39] For *Jewish* believers in Pauline assemblies, the continuation of this custom was probably unproblematic, but for *non-Jews* to 'turn from idols to the true and living God' (1 Thess 1.9) was to behave like Jews without any justification for doing so. Although disagreements might arise about what constituted 'idolatry' (1 Cor 8–10), it was hardly possible for Gentile believers who observed the strong prohibition of 'idolatry' to be considered other than 'atheists'. Thus, at the point where the practice of Gentile Pauline believers had the most distinctively Jewish ideological foundation, it lacked the necessary Jewish social rationale. Paul strives to give his converts' religious exclusivity a Christological foundation (1 Cor 8.4–6) and places the 'Lord's Supper' in ideological antithesis to meals dedicated to δαιμόνια (1 Cor 10.14–22), but it would take an unusual degree of ideological reinforcement for Gentile converts to remain robust on this matter – and clearly not all did.[40]

In other respects, also, the practice of Judean traditions in Pauline Jew-Gentile communities differed from the parallel practice in Diaspora synagogues. The Greek Scriptures which informed Diaspora Jewish life were also used within Pauline assemblies (to the extent to which they were accessible), but their applicability was much less certain. Some disputes within Pauline communities (e.g., in Galatia) turned on the authority of the Torah within the Scriptures, and the relative weight to be accorded to 'the gospel' and 'the archives' (Ignatius, *Phil.* 8) continued to be problematic for as long as a Christian hermeneutic of the Jewish Scriptures remained disputed. Of course, Jewish interpretation of these Scriptures was hardly uniform,

[39] See my *Jews in the Mediterranean Diaspora*, 428–34.

[40] On the difficulties for Gentile believers in realigning their 'practical consciousness', see Chester, *Conversion at Corinth*.

but the range of Christian questions regarding the validity of the Torah stretched well beyond the Jewish spectrum. Even where the Scriptures were granted authority, their moral rhetoric was harder to embody in practice in a non-ethnic setting. Pauline assemblies shared with Jewish communities an aversion to 'idolatry' and 'immorality' (e.g., Rom 1.18–32; Gal 5.19–21), but abstention from such entities was harder to clarify or enforce without the support of other social differentiations, such as meal-regulations, circumcision and endogamy. It was, for instance, more difficult to draw the line between what was sexually 'proper' and 'improper' when that line was not also scored by other distinctions between 'insiders' and 'outsiders'.

In this connection it is important to consider the range of Jewish practices which were integral to Jewish social identity in the Diaspora but not definitive for believer-identity in Pauline assemblies, notably circumcision, Sabbath-observance and food-regulations (see chapters 2–4).[41] For *Jewish* members of these assemblies, who maintained their identification with local Jewish groups, such practices might continue to mould their identities 'in Christ'. But for *non-Jewish* believers such socially significant practices did not constitute their Christian identity nor could they represent, for mixed *Jew-Gentile assemblies*, a common or shared identity. Paul's refusal to allow that circumcision be required of Gentile converts was of immense social significance. Since circumcision was (in most contexts) a distinct marker of Judean ethnicity, its non-adoption ensured that male Gentile believers lacked the clear sign of difference that characterised Jewish males. Among other things, circumcision played a decisive role in enforcing endogamy, limiting the marriage-choices of Jewish girls; by granting permission for marriage 'in the Lord' (1 Cor 7.39) without regard to this marker, Paul suggested a definition of Christian identity unsupported by ethnic differentiation.[42] With regard to the Sabbath, which through its highly visible abstention from work stamped the distinctive identity of Jews onto the weekly rhythm of life, the Pauline policy was socially indecisive. While Jewish believers were encouraged to observe this 'day' as special (Rom 14.5), it was neither legally nor socially possible for non-Jewish believers to cease work on the Sabbath or any other day they might choose. Even where they organised activities 'on the first of the sabbath' (1 Cor 16.2), these had to take place alongside normal patterns of work, and were liable

[41] For reflexion on these three topics, from the perspective of Paul's relation to the Torah, see K.-W. Niebuhr, 'Offene Fragen zur Gesetzespraxis bei Paulus und seinem Gemeinden (Sabbat, Speisegebote, Beschneidung)', *Berliner Theologische Zeitschrift* 25 (2008) 16–51.

[42] For the social significance of circumcision in the Diaspora see my *Jews in the Mediterranean Diaspora*, 411–12, 438–39.

to have little impact on outsiders.[43] Thus, the identity of Gentile believers and of the Jew-Gentile assemblies as a whole was not clearly, communally or publicly marked by the interruption of time to the same degree as in Diaspora synagogues.[44]

Food rules were similarly indecisive in the Pauline communities. Although Jewish practice in the Diaspora was no doubt uneven, the frequency with which Jews were noted by others as socially awkward indicates that distinctions were sufficiently commonly practised to set limits on the meal company Jews could accept.[45] Paul can encourage Jewish believers to maintain this tradition, and Gentile believers to support them if necessary (Rom 14), but he makes it clear that this is a matter of opinion not necessity (Rom 14.14), and he encourages his converts normally to eat with non-believers (1 Cor 5.10; 10.26; see chapter 2). This policy had its limits at the point where meals constituted acts of 'idolatry' (1 Cor 10.14–22), and in this respect Paul's communities shared with Diaspora synagogues a public boundary in the matter of food. But since this boundary failed to include other dimensions of Judean food-rules its social effect was far less comprehensive. With regard to Jews, Josephus insists that Moses carefully regulated the mode of life in the household 'even in relation to food, what they should refrain from and what they should eat, the company they keep in their daily lives, as well as their intensity in work and, conversely, rest' (*c. Apion.* 2.174). We could hardly ask for a clearer statement of the social significance of Jewish practice with regard to food, endogamy and Sabbath-observance, and if the believer-communities did not share such markers of difference it was harder for them to define what Josephus calls in this context their 'boundary' (ὅρος) and 'rule' (κανών).

d) Overlapping but Differentiated Communities

Paul's assemblies thus overlapped with Diaspora synagogues in two senses: a) they contained Jewish believers who also belonged to synagogue com-

[43] Pliny discovered only during the trial of Christians that they met before dawn (i. e. before work) *stato die* (*Ep.* 10.96).

[44] For the significance of Sabbath and festivals in the Diaspora, see my *Jews in the Mediterranean Diaspora*, 415–17, 440–42; L. Doering, *Schabbat: Sabbathalacha und -praxis im antiken Judentum und Urchristentum* (TSAJ; Tübingen: Mohr Siebeck, 1999) 283–386. The Pauline polemics against the observance of days (Gal 4.10; Col 2.16) hardly encouraged the adoption of a new Christian marking of time, while the transition from the Sabbath to 'the Lord's day' (Ignatius, *Mag.* 9) could not be matched (before Constantine) by an equivalent disruption of daily routines.

[45] *Jews in the Mediterranean Diaspora*, 434–37. Even if outsider comments reflect their own interests or prejudices (Lieu, *Christian Identity*, 122–26), there is no reason to doubt that they also reflect social practice.

munities (and probably for the most part continued their Jewish practices), and b) the practice of Gentile and Jewish believers matched that of Jewish communities at certain points, notably in their refusal to practise what they commonly labelled 'idolatry'. But as mixed Jew-Gentile communities their boundaries did not correspond to those of Diaspora Jews: they were neither co-extensive with nor incorporated within Diaspora synagogues. To speak of the Pauline assemblies as a 'sect within Judaism' makes little sense in ancient terms, since it fails to correspond to social realities.[46] Similarly, to define Paul's strategy as 'the social opening of Judaism for non-Jews' is misleading to the extent that 'Judaism', as the ethnic tradition of the Jewish/Judean people, is a tradition socially defined by *not* being 'opened' to non-Jews.[47] To speak of Paul 'judaizing the nations' is only partly justifiable, and it is no accident that Paul did not describe his strategy thus.[48] In demanding the abandonment of 'idolatry', Paul requires more from his Gentile converts than was expected of the Gentile 'sympathisers' who in various ways supported or associated with Diaspora Jewish communities. Yet, in relation to other traditional and constitutive features of Jewish identity, Paul did not expect his Gentile converts to behave like proselytes (e.g., in male circumcision). One could describe the Gentile members of Paul's communities as defective proselytes or as hyper-committed 'sympathisers', but in terms of their ethnic loyalties, their meal-practices, their relationship to the Jerusalem Temple and their rhythms of time, their social practices did not correspond to those of Diaspora communities – with the great and prominent exception that they refused to honour the pagan Gods.[49]

---

[46] Nanos' thesis that Paul's churches formed sub-groups within Diaspora communities appears to have no warrant in the text: nothing Paul says to his converts suggests such a social affiliation; see M. Nanos, *The Irony of Galatians: Paul's Letter in First-Century Context* (Minneapolis: Fortress, 2002). Campbell leaves open whether Pauline communities were separate from Jewish communities, and concludes, 'It was their liminal social location, on the borders of the Jewish world, but not quite part of it, and yet retaining significant aspects of its self-understanding and identity that constituted the peculiar problem of Paul in the guidance and development of his communities' (W.S. Campbell, *Paul and the Creation of Christian Identity* [London: T & T Clark, 2006] 67).

[47] *Pace* G. Theissen, 'Judaism and Christianity in Paul', in *Social Reality and the Early Christians*, 221; he places this model (de-restricted, open Judaism) alongside two others, parallelism and transformation.

[48] See P. Fredriksen, 'Judaizing the Nations: the Ritual Demands of Paul's Gospel', *NTS* 56 (2010) 232–52. Her note that 'common usage' prohibited Paul from employing 'Judaizing' in any positive way (cf. Gal 2.14) concedes that her categories are etic and not emic, i.e., dependent on *our* definitions of 'Judaism' and 'Judaizing', not those current in antiquity.

[49] As Fredriksen notes ('Judaizing the Nations', 244–49), there are features of Paul's thought that draw on the purity-ideology of the Temple, and he himself (with other Jewish believers) may have continued to honour its sanctity; but Gentile believers are not oriented to the Temple in any practical way (through pilgrimage or financial contribution), and the Pauline tradition develops Temple-concepts in a metaphorical not a literal

Of course Gentile believers could, and sometimes did, 'judaize' to a further degree. Paul resists the tendency towards full proselytism in his Galatian churches, and the adoption of Jewish practices is at least one element criticised by the letter to the Colossians (Col 2.16–23). In social terms, one can understand the desire of Gentile believers to justify their anomalous abstention from pagan cult by incorporation into the Jewish community: although such proselyte recusants were the target of criticism in the Roman world, they were at least a socially recognisable phenomenon.[50] Throughout the first Christian centuries Jewish practices (circumcision, Sabbath-rites, and food-laws) and Jewish communal events (synagogue meetings, festivals and new moons) continued to attract Gentile believers in a way that church leaders criticised but could do little to prevent.[51] In truth, the early Christian movement was underdeveloped in its own practices in such social domains, and constitutionally disinclined to define itself in culturally specific ways. By insisting that 'the kingdom of God is not a matter of food and drink' (Rom 14.17), believers could not define themselves by their food practices, but neither could they readily make this a matter of disqualification: such leeway made it difficult to offer good reasons why Gentile believers should *not* adopt *kashrut*.

Diversity in early Christian practice was unproblematic unless and until it caused internal division; and diversity in meal-regulations was an obvious point of difficulty. Given the significance of meals in the formation of the earliest assemblies, it is not surprising that this was a cause of tension already in the Antioch incident (Gal 2.11–14).[52] The more the early assemblies developed a distinct identity, through an intensity of social interaction, the more it became problematic for any sub-group to maintain practices that entailed social segregation. As the theological exclusivity of the Christian movement became increasingly reflected in comprehensive forms of communal life, the central features of Christian identity were defined by social interaction among believers, and their social coherence was threatened by competing social allegiances. The weight of Christian polemics against Gentile 'Judaizing'

---

mode (1 Cor 3.16; 6.19–20; Eph 2.11–21). The collection for 'the poor among the saints' in Jerusalem (Rom 15.26) is unconnected to the Temple and thus socially distinct from the Temple-contributions of Diaspora Jews (and sympathisers) at this critical point (see chapter 5).

[50] Roman criticism: Juvenal, *Sat.* 14.96–106; Tacitus, *Hist.* 5.5.1. On the phenomenon, L.H. Feldman, *Jew and Gentile in the Ancient World* (Princeton: Princeton University, 1993).

[51] For a survey of the first two centuries, see M. Murray, *Playing a Jewish Game: Gentile Christian Judaizing in the First and Second Centuries CE* (Waterloo, Ontario: Wilfrid Laurier University, 2004). Her discussion effectively answers the historical scepticism of M. Taylor, *Anti-Judaism and Early Christian Identity* (Leiden: Brill, 1995).

[52] For the significance of meals, see H. Taussig, *In the Beginning was the Meal: Social Experimentation and Early Christian Identity* (Minneapolis: Fortress, 2009).

(from Paul, through Ignatius, to Chrysostom) is a reflex of this anxiety to define the Christian movement as a socially complete and self-sufficient whole.

e) The Location of Jewish Believers

This social dynamic was bound to impact Jewish believers, though its effects were subtle and perhaps unforeseen. To speak of 'the parting of the ways' between 'Christianity' and 'Judaism' is unhelpful: it implies a definitive, singular moment of 'parting', and is apt to confuse different forms of 'parting' (theological, social and institutional). Since Christian ideological repudiation of 'Jews' was often out of kilter with social reality, the rhetoric of Christian texts is particularly unreliable as an indication of historical fact.[53] In the earliest period (the focus of these essays) the critical question concerns the degree to which Jewish believers could belong to a community of believers and a Jewish community, both at the same time. Our evidence from the Pauline tradition suggests that Jewish believers in mixed (Jewish and non-Jewish) assemblies faced the greatest pressures here not in their beliefs but in their social practices. Second Temple Judaism was certainly diverse, and lacked any strong form of *ideological* normativity, but Diaspora communities certainly observed limits in their tolerance of diversity in *practice*.[54] Of course, deviance is always in the eye of the beholder, and perceptions can vary over time and place, but we know that Jews did and

[53] In addition, the locally variable expressions of Jewish and Christian community make it impossible to generalise about such a 'parting', and what we now call 'Christianity' and 'Judaism' are to some degree constructs of this division rather than preconstituted entities that pulled apart. For discussion of such 'partings' see J. D. G. Dunn, *The Partings of the Ways* (London: SCM, 1991) and idem, ed., *Jews and Christians: The Parting of the Ways AD 70–135* (WUNT 66; Tübingen: Mohr Siebeck, 1992); S. G. Wilson, *Related Strangers: Jews and Christians 70–170 CE* (Minneapolis: Fortress, 1995). For critiques of the 'parting' model, see D. Boyarin, *Dying for God: Martyrdom and the Making of Judaism and Christianity* (Stanford: Stanford University, 1999) and J. Lieu, *Neither Jew nor Greek: Constructing Early Christian Identity* (Edinburgh: T & T Clark, 2002) 11–29. For a variety of ways in which it might be modelled see M. Goodman, 'Modeling the "Parting of the Ways"', in his *Judaism in the Roman World: Collected Essays* (Leiden: Brill, 2007) 175–8. Defining the phenomenon as the formation of non-overlapping cultural identities, D. Boyarin offers a revisionist thesis in *Border Lines: The Partition of Judaeo-Christianity* (Philadelphia: University of Pennsylvania, 2004), arguing that the second-century Christian definition of 'heresy' played a decisive role in creating a border between 'Christianity' and 'Judaism'.

[54] See my *Jews in the Mediterranean Diaspora*, 400–1: after taking full account of the rich diversity in Diaspora Judaism, we have still to explain 'what held Jews in the Diaspora together and what linked them to other Jews elsewhere and across time. Diversity is not the only characteristic of the Diaspora, and some explanation is required for the way that Jewish communities survived *as coherent and enduring entities*. What bound Jews together and prevented the disintegration of their communities? ... If Judaism is defined – as it should be – as a *social* and not just an *intellectual* phenomenon, it is hard to see how the plural 'Judaisms' could apply to the Diaspora.'

could define 'apostasy' and acted accordingly (see chapters 6 and 7). Thus the critical question is whether the social implications of belief in Christ drew Jewish believers into customary practices which could be regarded (by their fellow Jews) as compromising their Jewishness.[55]

It appears that in most circumstances Paul was content to allow Jewish believers to continue their Jewish practice – certainly with regard to circumcision (1 Cor 7.18–19) and Sabbath- and food-regulations (Rom 14) – and there is no reason to consider this merely a first-generational phenomenon. There were, however, some circumstances where Paul considered that Jewish practice should be suspended by Jews, in mission among non-Jews (1 Cor 9.20–21) and in commensality with non-Jewish believers (Gal 2.11–14): in these contexts Torah-observance would either divide the believer community or would make Jewish cultural practice a pre-requisite for belonging to Christ (Gal 2.11–14). In such circumstances Paul became 'as if without the law to those without the law' (τοῖς ἀνόμοις ὡς ἄνομος, 1 Cor 9.21), and he expected Peter and other Jewish believers in Antioch to live (with regard to food or meal-company) 'in a Gentile fashion' (ἐθνικῶς, Gal 2.14). For Paul, commitment to Christ is of higher priority than the maintenance of Jewish practice (even if in most circumstances the two need not clash) – or, to put this in social terms, bonds with fellow believers (Jewish *and* non-Jewish) were more important than bonds with fellow Jews.[56] As I argue in chapter 2, precisely in allowing difference of practice within his assemblies, Paul requires Jewish believers to recognise that service to the Lord can take place in terms outside the Torah: this categorises their Jewish practices as culturally sanctioned customs, which may normally be maintained but must also be considered non-essential for allegiance to 'the Lord'.[57]

---

[55] On deviance and apostasy, see now S.G. Wilson, *Leaving the Fold: Apostates and Defectors in Antiquity* (Minneapolis: Fortress, 2004).

[56] For analysis of the Antioch episode, see especially B. Holmberg, 'Jewish *versus* Christian Identity in the early Church?', *Revue Biblique* 105 (1998) 397–425. Cf. his further comments on the Antioch dispute, on the role of 'feedback' from the experience of commensality, and on 'reciprocal identity displacement' for Jews and non-Jews in his essays 'Understanding the First Hundred Years of Christian Identity' and 'Early Christian Identity – Some Conclusions', in B. Holmberg, ed., *Exploring Early Christian Identity* (WUNT 226; Tübingen: Mohr Siebeck, 2008) 1–32, 173–78. Johnson Hodge (*If Sons, then Heirs*, 117–35) rightly insists that for Paul being a Christ-follower does not erase Jewish ethnic identity, but she dismisses the boundary-crossing phenomena mentioned above as merely temporary accommodations made by Jewish believers with a special calling as teachers of Gentiles. The critical question (which she does not consider) is how common meals with reciprocal hospitality can continue over time in a believer community (such as that in Antioch) made up of both Jews and non-Jews. For an alternative reading of the Antioch incident, which downplays Paul's commendation of Peter for living ἐθνικῶς (Gal 2.14), see Zetterholm, *Formation of Christianity at Antioch*, 129–66.

[57] These Pauline texts render problematic the now common assertion that Paul took the relation of Jewish believers to the Torah to be unchanged by the Christ-event; see, e.g.,

Paul knew that his stance on circumcision, and his daring redefinition of what constitutes a 'Jew', were unlikely to win acceptance in the Jewish community (Rom 2.28–29), and in response he radicalised the principle that what counts is not human opinion, but God's (see chapter 3). It was this willingness to flout the opinions of local Jewish communities that made Paul liable to synagogue punishments (2 Cor 11.25) and it was such experiences, interpreted as 'persecution for the cross of Christ' (Gal 5.11; 6.13), which reduced the authority of the Torah in Paul's eyes, compared to the authority of Christ. From such experiences of 'hostility' Paul occasionally launches fierce attacks on 'the Jews', in terms partly derived from inner-Jewish polemics but gaining different meanings when spoken to non-Jews (1 Thess 2.14–16; see chapter 8). Where Paul was successful in winning Gentile converts, he also created trouble, both for the converts themselves and for local Jewish communities. As a Jew who caused widespread offence by turning pagan converts from their traditional cultic practices, he threatened to undermine the tolerance enjoyed by the Jewish community in its local environment.[58] In such light we can understand how Jewish communities might repudiate Paul and the assemblies he founded, making it difficult for Jewish believers to belong to both communities at once.

Such experiences of conflict may not have been typical for Jewish believers as a whole (we have few concrete examples), but we may make the following general deductions regarding their social location:

1. Although the boundaries of the Jewish community did not coincide with those of the believer-assemblies, Jewish believers could generally participate in both 'synagogue' and 'church' communities at the same time.
2. This 'dual belonging' was likely to be strained in circumstances where it could appear that allegiance to Christ required the overriding of commitment to the Torah.
3. This clash of loyalties was most likely to arise in ethnically mixed assemblies with a majority of non-Jews who did not conform to essential elements of the Torah, and where strong bonds of association caused Jewish

J.G. Gager, *Reinventing Paul* (Oxford: Oxford University, 2000) and M.D. Nanos, *The Mystery of Romans: The Jewish Context of Paul's Letter* (Minneapolis: Fortress, 1996). As a reaction to an older view that Paul expected Jewish believers to abandon their Jewish identities (to become 'Christians') and to repudiate the Torah, this is understandable. But Paul's presentation of his paradigmatic stance in Gal 2.14–21, climaxing in his claim that, being crucified with Christ, he had 'died to the law in order to live to God' (Gal 2.19) indicates that his allegiance to the Torah was now subordinate to his new identity in Christ – and if subordinate, either adhered to *or suspended* depending on the situational demands of serving Christ (Gal 1.10).

[58] See M. Goodman, 'The Persecution of Paul by Diaspora Jews', in his *Judaism in the Roman World*, 145–52.

believers to prioritise their commitment to fellow non-Jewish believers over their commitment to fellow Jews.

4. Apart from situations of communal hostility, the most regular condition in which this choice of priorities might occur was the practice of common meals. The choice of a Gentile marriage partner would also make a decisive difference.
5. In general, the extent to which believer-assemblies drew Jewish believers into deep social intimacy with non-Jews was the extent to which, over time, their behaviour was likely to be viewed by non-believing Jews as deviant.

The opinions of outsiders on the identity of believer-assemblies may also have played a part. At several points in Acts (with whatever accuracy) believers are regarded as a sub-species of 'Jew' (e.g., Acts 18.14–15; 24.5), but in second-century Roman literature 'Christians' are treated as a distinct category (e.g. Tacitus, *Ann.* 15.44, although the 'superstition' originated in Judea; Suetonius, *Nero* 16.2; Pliny, *Ep.* 10.96; Lucian, *Peregrinus* 11) or are ambiguously related to 'Jews' (Galen, *Puls. Diff.* 2.4; 3.3; Epictetus 2.9.19–21?). Opinions perhaps varied in different locations, but it may have been Paul's own trial in Rome that alerted Roman officials and Nero himself to the distinction between Jews and the 'Christians' they repudiated – with the result that, in seeking scapegoats for the fire of Rome, Nero picked on 'Christians' but did not also implicate the local Judean population.[59]

III. The Invention of Christian Identity in the Pauline Tradition

The prominence of the category 'identity' in the social sciences is reflected in the volume of research into the formation of 'early Christian identity'.[60] Although all identities are constructed and malleable over time, in the case of believers who formed the new assemblies we may speak not just of the construction, but of the invention of Christian identity. This was especially so, of course, for Gentile believers, but everywhere in the Pauline tradition – in the texts and behind them – we find strenuous efforts to construct, define and secure the identity of believers, which was often in practice unclear,

[59] See R. Lane Fox, *Pagans and Christians* (London: Penguin, 1986) 432–34.

[60] See, among many others, Lieu, *Christian Identity*; Esler, *Conflict and Identity in Romans*; Holmberg, ed., *Exploring Early Christian Identity*; B. Holmberg and M. Winninge, eds., *Identity Formation in the New Testament* (WUNT 227; Tübingen: Mohr Siebeck, 2008); M. Tellbe, *Christ-Believers in Ephesus: A Textual Analysis of Early Christian Identity Formation in a Local Perspective* (WUNT 242; Tübingen: Mohr Siebeck, 2009). For an overview of social identity theory, see R. Jenkins, *Social Identity* (London: Routledge, 2004).

underdetermined or fragile. What is remarkable here is not only the invention of their identity, but its maintenance over time: the survival of the early Christian movement is one of its most puzzling features. The essays in the third section of this book (chapters 9–13) explore the invention of identity from a number of different angles. There are many dimensions of identity formation not here discussed – for instance, ritual, labelling, gender, space, and institutionalisation – but the following remarks reflect on some of the issues here discussed.

a) The Demarcation of Difference and the Experience of Hostility

The discourse of the Pauline tradition is strongly marked by oppositional pairings. 'Believers' are demarcated from 'unbelievers' (2 Cor 6.15), as sharply as 'light' from 'darkness' (1 Thess 5.1–11; Eph 5.6–14); the 'spirit-people' (πνευματικοί) understand what the 'soul-people' (ψυχικοί) cannot (1 Cor 2.6–16), and the 'new creation' is set over against 'the world' (Gal 6.14–15). This strong discursive demarcation has its clearest social correlate in the believers' refusal to take part in 'idolatry': for Jewish believers this mapped onto their pre-formed ethnic differentiation from non-Jews, but for Gentiles this was a novelty with significant social impact. Since honouring the Gods was integral to the life of the household, and to major events in the life-cycle, and since sacrifice, festivals and the cultivation of divine images were central to the social and political life of the city, the Gentile believers' withdrawal from such activities fundamentally altered the pattern of their lives.[61]

This demarcation, and the disdain with which believers learned to speak of their past 'idolatry', could cause deep social offence. Gentile converts here broke with their ancestral customs and fractured the familial habits which united their households; and since their own religious customs entailed no sacrifices and associated them with no temples (not even the

[61] This element in the daily lives of Gentile believers seems under-acknowledged in the fine discussion of identity and ethos in Paul by M. Wolter ('Identität und Ethos bei Paulus', in his *Theologie und Ethos im frühen Christentum* [WUNT 236; Tübingen: Mohr-Siebeck, 2009] 121–69; for comments on an earlier version of his argument, see chapter 4). Wolter is right that the transcending of cultural and social differences in the Pauline assemblies made it impossible to determine the particularity of the Christian ethos with as much specificity as one might expect from its exclusive rhetoric. But some regular practices were taken to be incompatible with belonging to Christ, and even if Gentile believers' abstention from 'idolatry' was not distinctively 'Christian' in origin (it was inherited from the Jewish tradition), Paul gives it a distinctively Christian rationale (1 Cor 8.5–6; 10.14–21); and for Gentile believers who were not associated with local Jewish communities this peculiar practice must have seemed, to themselves and to others, a *novum* directly derived from their faith in Christ.

Judean Temple in Jerusalem), they were easily characterised as irreligious or adherents of a new and dangerous superstition.[62] But hostility from outsiders contributed in vital ways to the formation of Christian identity. As I have traced in chapter 9, this hostility was not experienced by every Pauline church, but where it was, it reinforced the dualistic ideology of the Pauline gospel and made 'difference' a ready-made social fact. In sharing hostility, members of beleaguered communities were likely to draw closer together, and from what we can observe in the Thessalonian and Corinthian churches we may suggest that the more believers experienced friction in their interactions with non-believers the easier it was to generate a pervasive sense of social difference. It is not surprising that tales of ostracism, persecution and martyrdom were to become integral to the narratives through which believers articulated their Christian identity.[63]

b) The Intensity of Christian Communal Life

We can catch only glimpses of the inner life of Pauline churches – their meetings and rituals, their meals and social bonds. While degrees of commitment no doubt varied, material contribution to the community was probably significant in bonding members to the community. Meetings in homes needed hosts, and common meals required both space and food: the greater the 'service', the greater the investment in the group (cf. chapter 5). Financial resources could also foster sociality: gifts might be given to travellers and community representatives (1 Cor 9; Phil 2.25–30; 4.10–20; Rom 12.13; 16.1–2), or to whole communities in another city, linking assemblies in networks of benefaction (1 Cor 16.1–4; 2 Cor 8–9). Locally, support for teachers or 'elders' (Gal 6.6; 1 Tim 5.17–18) created and expressed bonds of reciprocity, while the support of poorer members helped define the obligations of believers amongst themselves (Gal 2.10; 1 Tim 5.3–16).[64] The greater the degree of institutionalisation, the more those in leadership were identified with the community, their honour acquired and maintained within this new circle of reference.

Our snapshots of meetings in Pauline assemblies are embedded in texts and thus coloured by their authors' ideals. But they suggest what we might in any case have guessed, that in the absence of altars, priests and sacrifices

[62] On the social background of the hostility experienced by believers in Thessalonica, see my 'Conflict in Thessalonica', *CBQ* 55 (1993) 512–30; T.D. Still, *Conflict at Thessalonica: A Pauline Church and its Neighbours* (Sheffield: Sheffield Academic, 1999).

[63] See, e.g., J. Lieu, 'I am a Christian: Martyrdom and the Beginning of Christian Identity', in her *Neither Jew nor Greek*, 211–32.

[64] See now B.W. Longenecker, *Remember the Poor: Paul, Poverty and the Greco-Roman World* (Grand Rapids: Eerdmans, 2010).

a heavy emphasis is placed on *speech* as the medium by which Christian identity is articulated and maintained. In 1 Corinthians 14 Paul carefully regulates speech (from God to the community, and from the community to God) as the prime activity of the assembly.[65] It seems that Pauline believers invested considerable effort in speaking to each other about the Christ-event and its implications, drawing their language from an amalgam of Scripture, oral tradition, their own Christian texts, common parlance, and newly inspired speech. The letter to the Colossians gives a flavour of this activity:

> Let the word of Christ dwell in you richly; teach and admonish one another in all wisdom; and with gratitude in your hearts sing psalms, hymns and spiritual songs to God. And whatever you do, in word or deed, do everything in the name of the Lord Jesus, giving thanks to God the Father through him (3.16–17).

Here speech of several sorts (from God, to God, and amongst themselves) forms the ethos of the community, and there is a striking drive towards totalisation – performing *every* word and deed in the name of Jesus. The emphasis on gratitude hints at the significance of emotion in the formation of Christian identity: in their communal life, and especially in their highly charged meetings for worship, believers talked themselves enthusiastically into being.

Out of such intimate and emotional interaction there emerged new vocabulary and new linguistic patterns, constituting a form of Christian social dialect. Thus believers developed special in-house meanings for terms already in use, though otherwise found rarely or in different senses. The Christian use of 'the faith' (ἡ πίστις) and of the labels 'believers' (οἱ πιστεύοντες) and 'unbelievers' (ἄπιστοι) are cases in point; the adjective πνευματικός ('spiritual') is another (see chapter 10). Such special language bound believers together whilst marking their difference from others: it both expressed and produced their distinct Christian identity.

c) The Development of a Christian Habitus

Several decades ago Pierre Bourdieu developed the notion of the *habitus* to explain how cultural practice is governed by deep assumptions about the 'proper' or the 'reasonable', assumptions located beneath the level of

[65] As Averil Cameron says (of a later era), 'Christians built themselves a new world. They did so partly through practice ... and partly through a discourse that was itself constantly brought under control and disciplined ... As Christ "was" the word, so Christianity *was* its discourse or discourses.' (A. Cameron, *Christianity and the Rhetoric of Empire: The Development of Christian Discourse* [Berkeley: University of California, 1991] 21, 32.)

articulated rules or norms, even below the level of the conscious.[66] These structured dispositions themselves structure a vast array of practices, norms, bodily gestures, social values and cultural products, providing classificatory systems with an objectivity that makes them appear natural and normal. Since the *habitus* is the product of history and of material conditions (political, social, climatic and economic), it is not easily altered by conscious moral choices; moreover, it is in most cases too deeply inculcated (by upbringing and early socialisation) to be changed. At the same time, it endures by continual reinforcement through practice: it both produces practice and is itself reproduced by the confirmatory habits which normalise its orientations and perceptions. This relationship to practice makes it possible (though rare) for a *habitus* to change, if a new set of social practices and formative conventions effects a comprehensive alteration in the dispositions which govern social life.

We may appreciate how difficult it was for believers in the Pauline tradition to develop a Christian *habitus*. Paul, drawing on ingrained Judean assumptions, expected his converts in Corinth to alter their *habitus* far more than they found possible: as Chester has shown, they carried over into their new life most of their previous dispositions in their social, sexual and discursive practices.[67] Within the Judean tradition a set of interlocking practices embodied and confirmed distinctive ethnic convictions and taboos. Josephus, aware of the importance of childhood formation, speaks of a 'training in character' (ἄσκησις τῶν ἤθων) produced through distinctive practices and reinforced by regular instruction (*c. Apion.* 2.171–74; see chapter 4). Gentile believers in the Pauline tradition, as noted above, did not adopt many of the most socially significant Judean customs (Sabbath, circumcision, food laws), such that it became difficult to define and thus to inculcate a distinctively Christian *habitus*. In the second century both outsiders and insiders remarked on the relative rarity of Christian differences in practice. Trypho, noting the lack of Jewish marks of distinction, complains that 'you are not in any way distanced from them [non-believers], and do not alter your way of life from the Gentiles' (*Dialogue with Trypho*, 10); as insiders, Tertullian (*Apology* 42) and the *Epistle to Diognetus* emphasised that believers were *not* distinct in their food, clothing, speech or most other social habits. Certainly, compared with Diaspora Judeans, the early believers had a far smaller repertoire of distinctive practices through which their

[66] In English translation, see P. Bourdieu, *Outline of a Theory of Practice* (Cambridge: Cambridge University, 1977) esp. 72–95; idem, *The Logic of Practice* (Stanford: Stanford University, 1990) esp. 52–65. For an introduction, see R. Jenkins, *Pierre Bourdieu* (London: Routledge, 1992).

[67] Chester, *Conversion at Corinth*, drawing on the parallel notion of 'practical consciousness'.

special identity could be expressed, rendering the development of a distinctively Christian *habitus* both fragile and incomplete.

This is not to suggest that there were *no* distinctively Christian practices that could help form a Christian *habitus*. The major fault-line between Gentile believers and their environment was marked in religious practice, and however 'Jewish' this was in origin, both to themselves (e.g., 1 Cor 10.14–22) and to outsiders it appeared integral to their distinctive loyalty to Jesus. The practice of shared Christian meals ('love-feasts'), focused on the 'Lord's Supper', also inculcated new social practices and attitudes. There are signs of an attempt to mark Christian distinction also in death (see chapter 11), although here exhortations concerning the suppression of grief were perhaps rarely matched in practice. The practice of celibacy (not discussed in this volume) is an even more striking example of Christian self-differentiation; with its roots in Paul's letters (1 Cor 7), this policy was strongly favoured in some Pauline circles (e.g., *The Acts of Paul and Thecla*) and formed one of the most dramatic mechanisms by which believers declared themselves comprehensively at odds with 'the world'.[68]

But there was another way in which believers could meet the demand to 'do everything in the name of the Lord Jesus Christ' (Col 3.17). By a kind of hidden transaction, they could turn every practice, however 'ordinary' and indistinct, into a form of service to Christ. This is perhaps best illustrated by the household codes (see chapter 12). The attempt to embed a Christian ethos into the life of the household was of huge importance to early Christianity, as many studies have shown,[69] but most significant for our purposes was the capacity to make the routine relations and common practices of the household a site of service to Christ. While believers might regard themselves as qualitatively different from others in their 'superior' observance of common moral norms, the crucial step was the development of a life-hermeneutic which could frame even undifferentiated behaviour as an act of Christian self-expression.

In time, the household would develop into a significant medium of Christian socialisation: as believer households brought up children 'in the discipline (or training, παιδεία) and admonition of the Lord' (Eph 6.4) they could inculcate an alternative *habitus* far more easily than for adult converts. Even so, we find the early churches in many respects adopting the *mores*

---

[68] P. Brown, *The Body and Society: Men, Women and Sexual Renunciation in Early Christianity* (New York: Columbia University, 1988).

[69] See, e.g., H. Moxnes, *Constructing Early Christian Families: Family as Social Reality and Metaphor* (London: Routledge, 1997); C. Osiek and D.L. Balch, *Families in the New Testament World: Households and House Churches* (Louisville: Westminster John Knox, 1997); C. Osiek and M.Y. MacDonald, *A Woman's Place: House Churches in Earliest Christianity* (Minneapolis: Fortress, 2006).

of their contemporaries. I have traced one example of this phenomenon in relation to their age-assumptions (chapter 13), which reflect conventional perceptions of age and youth. Perhaps we should not be surprised: despite the totalising claims of their Christian ethos, believers whose social and economic lives were embedded in households (and thus in the social structures of the Roman world) did not have the social conditions necessary to generate a radically different vision of the 'normal'. It was only if their social practice disrupted and realigned their lived experience that it was possible to alter the inculcated assumptions and taxonomies that made up the *habitus* of their culture: hence the 'social conservatism' that pervades much of the early Christian movement. The option for celibacy was the most striking exception to this phenomenon, for the simple reason that it broke with the structure of the household.

IV. Josephus, Paul and Rome

The last section of this book is focused on two Diaspora Jews, Josephus and Paul, in their relationship to the Roman empire. The location of Jews/Judeans within the political and legal context of the empire is a large and complex topic: varied experience in different local contexts, differing treatment under successive emperors, and a largely peaceful relationship punctuated by the Judean War (66–70 CE), the Diaspora Revolt (115–17 CE) and the Bar Kochva Revolt (132–35 CE), make generalisations impossible.[70] Judeans in the Diaspora claimed and often enjoyed civic rights that protected their cultural traditions,[71] but it is another matter how individual Jewish authors negotiated the political realities of Roman power. No figure can be considered 'typical', although comparisons may draw out distinctive traits.

Josephus is an obvious candidate for political analysis, given his life history (as rebel commander, then aid to Titus and imperial protégé in Rome) and his literary output (written in Rome in the wake of the Judean War). Roman military control over most of the known world is the reality to which all Josephus' works respond; within that framework he explains the history of the Judean people and glorifies his cultural tradition, its Scriptures, heroes

[70] For large-scale surveys, with bibliographies, see E.M. Smallwood, *The Jews under Roman Rule from Pompey to Diocletian* (Leiden: Brill, 1981); Barclay, *Jews in the Mediterranean Diaspora*; Gruen, *Diaspora: Jews amidst Greeks and Romans*; S. Schwartz, *Imperialism and Jewish Society, 200 B. C. E. to 640 C. E.* (Princeton: Princeton University, 2001); M. Goodman, *Rome and Jerusalem: The Clash of Ancient Civilizations* (London: Allen Lane, 2007).

[71] Pucci ben Zeev, *Jewish Rights in the Roman World*; K.-L. Noethlichs, *Das Judentum und der römische Staat:Minderheitenpolitik im antiken Rom* (Darmstadt: Wissenschaftliche Buchgesellschaft, 1996).

and values. In works addressed partly to non-Jews, including Roman officials, Josephus utilizes the tools of his Greek education to defend, explain and extol his native tradition. The four essays on Josephus gathered here (chapters 14–17) explore various dimensions of Josephus' engagement with Rome in his last and most complex work, his *Contra Apionem*.[72]

In several of these essays I read Josephus with the aid of postcolonial theory, which is a diverse set of reading practices 'preoccupied principally with analysis of cultural forms which mediate, challenge and reflect upon the relations of domination and subordination – economic, cultural and political – between (and often within) nations, races or cultures'.[73] Among its objects of study are the forms of self-representation practised by those under the cultural domination of a colonising (or neo-colonial) power, and the ways in which these reproduce, but also subtly (and not always intentionally) alter the dominant forms of discourse. Under the influence of Derrida, postcolonial analysis (especially in its articulation by Bhabha) delights to identify the ambivalence of the postcolonial condition: the response of the postcolonial subject is typically unstable and destabilizing, its 'hybridity' not simply a fusion of two cultures, but a 'third space', which reproduces both the 'native' and the 'hegemonic' culture in ways that deform and reform them both.[74] Even where the discourse of the 'subaltern' writer may seem most compliant, the way it mirrors the terms and categories of the dominant culture may be, ironically, a mode of self-empowerment, even defiance; in some cases its 'mimicry' may result in a form of mockery. By the same token, even its most strident forms of cultural resistance may contain elements of capitulation to the terms dictated by the dominant power. From this angle of vision, every form of postcolonial discourse is slippery, eluding categorisation or simple alignment to a political cause; readers who deploy this mode of analysis should be prepared to find every text shifting equivocally from apparent complicity to subtle subversion, and back again from

---

[72] These essays accompany my commentary on this work, *Flavius Josephus, Translation and Commentary: Against Apion*.

[73] B. Moore-Gilbert, *Postcolonial Theory: Contexts, Practices, Politics* (London: Verso, 1997) 12. The literature within and on this theoretical field is vast, but for good introductions, besides Moore-Gilbert, see B. Ashcroft, G. Griffiths and H. Tiffin, *Post-Colonial Studies: The Key Concepts* (2nd edition; London: Routledge, 2001); A. Loomba, *Colonialism/Postcolonialism* (London: Routledge, 1998); R.J.C. Young, *Postcolonialism: An Historical Introduction* (Oxford: Blackwell, 2001); idem, *White Mythologies: Writing History and the West* (London: Routledge, 1990). An exceptionally clear explication (with annotated bibliography) may be found in S.D. Moore, *Empire and Apocalypse: Postcolonialism and the New Testament* (Sheffield: Sheffield Phoenix, 2006).

[74] See H.K. Bhabha, *The Location of Culture* (London: Routledge, 1994); for analysis, Moore-Gilbert, *Postcolonial Theory*, 114–51; D. Huddart, *Homi K. Bhabha* (London: Routledge, 2006); Moore, *Empire and Apocalypse*, 86–96.

apparent resistance to subtle implication in the structures of the system it seems to subvert.

Many features of Josephus' work invite postcolonial analysis. Writing under Roman patronage in the metropolis itself, he endeavours to represent his people's story in terms which honour their distinctive traditions, but in a form persuasive to a Romanized audience. Roman power remains the central reality in his work, not least since his nation and his own life have been shaped by recent, bruising encounter with it. To read his work through a postcolonial lens is to be alert to its potential ambivalence, the subtle ways in which it may absorb and reshape Roman cultural tropes in order to position the Judean tradition as its equal, even superior, on the world stage. In these essays I trace how Josephus uses the Roman negative image of 'Egyptians' to the cultural advantage of his own people (chapter 14), how he hints at alternative ways of reading the Roman destruction of the Temple (chapter 15), how he skilfully deploys Roman admiration of Sparta to present Jewish martyrs (under Roman torture) as the epitome of toughness (chapter 16), and how he defends Jewish non-iconic cult, with a mix of complicity and aggression even in relation to the emperor (chapter 17). Each of these essays involves close readings of particular Josephan texts, the sort of literary exercise where postcolonial analysis has proved most illuminating.

Turning to Paul, we are struck by a difference in theme and focus. Like all his contemporaries in the eastern Mediterranean, Paul writes under the conditions of Roman rule, but these political, military and economic realities feature on the surface of his discourse only obliquely or in passing (Rom 13.1–7; 1 Thess 5.3; Phil 1.13; 4.22; cf. 2 Thess 2.1–12): Rome is never the focus of discussion as it is, frequently, in Josephus. At one level, this is not especially surprising: unlike Josephus, Paul was not writing in the aftermath of a military clash with Rome, nor was he writing in Rome to a Romanized audience in a mode (historiography) where Roman power was necessarily a central topic. It is another matter how to interpret this virtual silence. Was Paul simply apolitical, quietly accepting the favourable conditions of the *pax Romana* which enabled him to conduct his mission in peace, preaching a gospel of individual salvation? Such has been a common Western interpretation of Paul. Or was Paul, to the contrary, intensely but covertly political, subtly counteracting 'the imperial cult' and Rome's claim to provide benefactions for its subjects? This latter reading, drawing on parallelisms in vocabulary, a new appreciation of 'the imperial cult', and an ideological critique of empire, has recently won significant advocates.[75]

---

[75] See, for instance, R.A. Horsley, ed., *Paul and Politics: Ekklesia, Israel, Imperium, Interpretation* (Harrisburg: Trinity Press International, 2000); N. Elliott, *The Arrogance of Nations: Reading Romans in the Shadow of Empire* (Minneapolis: Fortress, 2008); B. Kahl, *Galatians Re-Imagined: Reading with the Eyes of the Vanquished* (Minneapolis:

In the final two essays of this volume I offer a third way of reading Paul's stance in relation to Rome, which is neither 'apolitical' nor covertly but directly opposed to the Roman empire. Even in the most Romanized environments, his critique of Roman religion is not focused on its character as Roman, because his angle of perception views *any* worship not directed to the 'living God' through Christ as erroneous in principle: even 'the imperial cult' is not to him any special phenomenon because it fits within this larger framework – just as it formed only part of a larger symbol-system in the Roman empire (see chapter 18). Against recent attempts to unearth hidden references to the emperor or the Roman empire throughout Paul's text (chapter 19 critiques one exemplar, N. T. Wright), I draw attention to Paul's peculiar epistemology which views the world in terms very different from both ancient and modern political categories: in this light Paul's theology is certainly political, but not in the straightforward 'anti-empire' forms now frequently proposed.

This analysis makes it much harder to apply postcolonial forms of analysis to Paul, at least in anything like the way they fit Josephus. Among some biblical interpreters the term 'postcolonial' has become shorthand for a critique of *any* form of hierarchy, domination or exclusion; the connection with specifically *Roman* forms of domination becomes tenuous, since most forms of social, sexual and economic hierarchy in antiquity were in place well before, and outside, the Roman empire.[76] Among others, the term 'postcolonial' opens the way to what might be called 'Empire studies' – a study of Paul's relations to the Roman empire in particular.[77] There would indeed be straightforward ways of applying postcolonial theory to Paul if it was clear that he was specifically engaged with the cultural, political and military fact of Roman rule – as was Josephus. Other New Testament texts clearly are: the book of Revelation confronts the imperial claims of Rome, while in the gospels the most extended drama revolves around the Roman

---

Fortress, 2010), and D.C. Lopez, *Apostle to the Conquered: Reimagining Paul's Mission* (Minneapolis: Fortress, 2008). For further bibliography, see chapter 19.

[76] This extended sense of 'postcolonial' has the advantage of linking the discourses of politics, ethnicity, gender and economics, in a critique of all forms of domination; it has the disadvantage of foregoing the precise analysis of the power relations between cultures or people groups, which is where postcolonial analysis was born and has flourished in other fields. See for instance, J. A. Marchal, *The Politics of Heaven: Women, Gender, and Empire in the Study of Paul* (Minneapolis: Fortress, 2008).

[77] For the term and the distinction, see Moore, *Empire and Apocalypse*, 17–19. Among the contributors on Pauline letters in F. F. Segovia and R. S. Sugirtharajah, eds., *A Postcolonial Commentary on New Testament Writings* (London: T & T Clark, 2007), those who focus specifically on Paul and Rome (Elliott; Horsley; Wan; Agosto) use surprisingly little of the rich store of postcolonial theory. Some of these essays, however, evidence a whole other dimension of postcolonial theory, which is the critique of (Western) 'colonial' interpretation and employment of the Bible over the past few centuries.

trial and execution of Jesus and the narrative itself impels one to place the story of Jesus on a Roman map.[78] By comparison, Paul makes very little reference to Roman authorities (even in relation to the crucifixion and his own punishments), and recent attempts to interpret his language as coded, with hidden reference to the Roman empire, have proved unconvincing (see chapter 19). Thus the kind of postcolonial analysis that suits Josephus seems inappropriate to Paul – which is not to say that Paul's theology bears no relation to politics or to the play of power within his world, but that it would be better analysed with tools rather different than those deployed in postcolonial theory.[79]

What emerges from our study is that Paul's relation to Rome is subsumed under his relation to what he provocatively calls 'the present evil age' (Gal 1.14), on an apocalyptic stage newly configured by the Christ-event. He thus views and names political realities in accordance with taxonomies very different from the straightforward political categories employed by Josephus. Paul's form of 'theopolitics' is thus intellectually challenging precisely because it does not conform to our normal understandings of politics. But to pursue that challenge would take us beyond the social history of Pauline communities into Pauline theology – a task for another day.[80]

---

[78] For postcolonial readings of Revelation, Mark and John, see e. g., Moore, *Empire and Apocalypse* (chapters 2, 3 and 5). For Matthew's relation to Rome, see J. Riches and D. Sim, eds., *The Gospel of Matthew in its Roman Imperial Context* (London: Continuum, 2005). The case for using postcolonial theory in relation to 1 Peter has been advanced by D.G. Horrell, 'Between Confirmity and Resistance: Beyond the Balch-Elliott Debate: Towards a Postcolonial Reading of 1 Peter', in R.L. Webb and B. Bauman-Martin, ed., *Reading First Peter with New Eyes* (London: Continuum, 2007) 111–43.

[79] Since Paul writes as a Jew in Greek within the Roman empire, one could use postcolonial theory to examine the transformation of Jewish culture under the hegemony of Hellenism, which was then iself brought under Roman military and economic control; cf. studies of the Second Sophistic in S. Goldhill, ed., *Being Greek Under Rome: Cultural Identity, the Second Sophistic and the Development of Empire* (Cambridge: Cambridge University, 2001). But the power relations here are so diffuse that the interpretative gains for a figure such as Paul may prove meagre. Another alternative would be to treat Paul's understanding of the power of 'sin' as a misrecognition of the power of Rome; but that would be to substitute one configuration of 'truth' for another, and might do little more than confirm already established understandings of reality.

[80] For further comparison of Josephus and Paul, see D.L. Pinter, 'Divine and Imperial Power: A Comparative Analysis of Paul and Josephus' (Ph.D. thesis, Durham University, 2009).

II. Pauline Churches and Diaspora Jews

2. 'Do we undermine the Law?'

A Study of Romans 14.1–15.6

In the history of scholarship on 'Paul and the Law' by far the greatest attention has been paid to Paul's theoretical statements on our topic, with numerous attempts to plot the location of the law in relation to faith, Christ, grace and works on the complex map of Pauline theology. How Paul's thoughts on this matter were translated into practice, what he actually observed of the law's regulations and what he expected others to observe are matters which have been comparatively neglected or else relegated to an appendix on 'ethics'. Such an imbalance is not, in itself, surprising: most of the passages where the term νόμος appears are couched in abstract theological language, and as readers of his letters we, of course, encounter Paul only in his word, not his practice. Yet there is a strong case to be made that an historical understanding of Paul requires much greater attention to the social functions of his theological views, and that *for his contemporaries* what he did or encouraged others to do counted for much more than what he said. It is an important feature of some recent scholarship that the practical ramifications of Paul's theology of the law have begun to attract serious investigation, enabling Paul in his actual life-choices to come much clearer into focus.[1]

In line with this determination not just to *hear* but to *see* Paul in relation to the law, I have chosen to discuss a passage whose significance for our topic has not been sufficiently exploited. I will argue that in Romans 14.1–15.6 we are given a valuable insight into the practical effects of Paul's stance on the law, even though the term νόμος does not appear in this passage. Paul's discussion of law-observance in relation to food and sabbath is to be discussed in the context of their social significance for Jews in Rome, and by examining how Paul directs the Roman Christians to behave we will be able to measure the practical (and paradoxical) effects of his instructions. In answer to our

[1] The social implications of observance or non-observance of the law have been consistently emphasized by J. D. G. Dunn, for instance in his *Jesus, Paul and the Law* (London: SPCK, 1990). The practical options in some aspects of the food laws have been discussed recently by, e. g., P. J. Tomson, *Paul and the Jewish Law* (Compendia Rerum Iudaicarum ad Novum Testamentum III.1; Assen/Maastricht: Van Gorcum, 1990) and A. F. Segal, *Paul the Convert* (New Haven/London: Yale University, 1990).

title question νόμον οὖν καταργοῦμεν διὰ τῆς πίστεως; Paul had responded μὴ γένοιτο· ἀλλὰ νόμον ἱστάνομεν (Rom 3.31). From Romans 14.1–15.6 we may assess to what extent Paul lives up to that claim in practice.

I. The Situation Addressed in Romans 14.1–15.6

Two presuppositions undergird this study and here require some clarification:

1. I take it as probable that here, perhaps more than anywhere else in this letter, Paul has in view live issues in the Roman churches. The motivations for the writing of Romans are complex and multiple, but I support what is now the dominant opinion that Paul's composition of the letter is at least partly related to the prevailing conditions in the Roman churches.[2] While the degree of relevance to issues in Rome might vary through the letter, there is good reason to believe that in our passage Paul had Roman conditions in mind. There are, of course, some similarities with 1 Corinthians 8–10 in vocabulary, theme and general stance, but these should not lead us to conclude that Romans 14–15 is merely a generalized reprise of a common paraenetic theme.[3] Our passage differs from 1 Corinthians 8–10 not just in omitting certain items specific to Corinth (such as reference to εἰδωλόθυτα) but in adding certain specifics, such as the eating of vegetables (Rom 14.2) and the observance of days (14.5), which limit rather than widen the applicability of the instruction. Moreover, the space which Paul devotes to this theme, his careful description of opposing positions and the prominence of this passage at the end of the paraenesis all suggest its immediate applicability in Rome.[4] The fact that Paul can confidently number himself among 'the strong' (15.1) also indicates that he knows the issues involved. If he can predict his allegiance with one of the two groups in the debate, he must know where they stand: he would hardly donate his authority as a blank cheque cashable by any Pauline group claiming to be 'the strong'.

---

[2] The question is well discussed in K.P. Donfried, ed., *The Romans Debate* (rev. ed.; Edinburgh: T & T Clark, 1991), and A.J.M. Wedderburn, *The Reasons for Romans* (Edinburgh: T & T Clark, 1988). Among recent commentators Wilckens, Dunn and Stuhlmacher have all found Roman relevance in some aspects of the letter.

[3] As was argued by R.J. Karris, 'Romans 14:1–15:13 and the Occasion of Romans', reprinted in *The Romans Debate*, 65–84. W. Meeks regards this passage as a 'paradigmatic address to the scrupulous and the enlightened', 'Judgment and the Brother: Romans 14:1–15:13', in G.F. Hawthorne and O. Betz, eds., *Tradition and Interpretation in the New Testament. Essays in Honor of E. Earle Ellis* (Grand Rapids: Eerdmans, 1987) 290–300, here at 293.

[4] So, for instance, E. Käsemann, *An die Römer* (HNT 8a, 4th edition; Tübingen: Mohr Siebeck, 1980) 353; U. Wilckens, *Der Brief an die Römer* (EKK VI / 3; Neukirchen-Vluyn: Neukirchener, 1982) 79–80, 109–115.

To be sure, the theme is discussed with a degree of generality and obliqueness (e. g. 14.5, 15, 21), but this is easily explained on rhetorical grounds. In relation to a church he has neither founded nor visited, and in which his reputation is mixed, Paul has to proceed with tact. It would be presumptuous to write with instructions so specific as to give the appearance that he thought himself entitled to regulate their affairs in detail. The same diplomacy that requires Paul to insist that all he has written was only a reminder (15.15) demands that his instructions are couched in terms of apparent generality. Like a visiting preacher who knows the problems of a congregation but dares not presume to pronounce directly upon them, Paul frames his advice in generalized terms, yet with enough specific detail to hint to whom his advice applies.[5] Thus there is good reason to believe that Paul aims his words at actual disputes in the Roman churches. Any knowledge of local conditions in Rome could help illuminate those disputes and clarify the options open to the parties involved.

2. My second presupposition is that the issues Paul addresses in this passage concern the observance or non-observance of the Jewish law. The obliqueness of the passage and the variety of interpretations it has spawned have led some investigators to doubt that it is possible to discover its referents.[6] But there are good reasons to take the Jewish law as the central issue, as in fact most recent analysts do. The two topics directly referred to are the restriction of diet to vegetables (as opposed to eating 'everything', i. e. meat as well, Rom 14.2; cf. 14.21) and the observance of certain days in preference to others (14.5). A third, the drinking of wine (14.21; cf. 14.17), may be a purely hypothetical addition (since 'drinking' is naturally combined with 'eating'), but our case will be stronger if it is possible to incorporate this as well. In common with many others, I take these verses to refer to Jewish scruples (which could be held by Jews or Gentiles) concerning the consumption of meat considered unclean and the observance of the sabbath and other Jewish feasts or fasts; the wine, if it is relevant, is also a matter of Jewish concern, relating to its use in 'idolatrous' worship. There are four strong arguments to support this interpretation:[7]

---

[5] The illustration derives from a class discussion on the reasons for Romans in Glasgow University, in particular from a remark by my student Rolf Billes.

[6] Karris declares 'History of Religions' investigation of the passage to be 'bankrupt' (in *The Romans Debate*, 66–70). More positively, Wilckens carefully lists the problems of reconstruction, but presents a strong thesis of his own, *Der Brief an die Römer*, 3.109–15.

[7] Cf., among others, P.S. Minear, *The Obedience of Faith* (London: SCM, 1971); W. Schmithals, *Der Römerbrief als historisches Problem* (Gütersloh: Gütersloher Verlagshaus Gerd Mohn, 1975) 95–107; O. Michel, *Der Brief an die Römer* (KEKNT VI, 14th edition; Göttingen: Vandenhoeck & Ruprecht, 1978) 419–21; C. E. B. Cranfield, *The Epistle to the Romans* (ICC; Edinburgh: T & T Clark, 1979) 2.690–98; Wilckens, *Der Brief an die Römer*, 3.109–15; F. Watson, *Paul, Judaism and the Gentiles* (SNTSMS 56; Cambridge:

i) *Paul describes the issue as concerning 'purity' and 'impurity'*. At the heart of the passage is Paul's affirmation of his conviction that 'nothing is impure of itself' (οὐδὲν κοινὸν δι' ἑαυτοῦ, 14.14), or conversely, that 'all things are pure' (πάντα καθαρά, 14.20). These terms are characteristic of Jewish purity concerns, and κοινός is used here in this specialized Jewish sense unattested in non-Jewish Greek (where it means 'common' in the sense of 'shared', not 'common' in the sense of 'impure'). Paul takes this term to express not only his own perception of the issues, but also the perception of those he calls the weak (τῷ λογιζομένῳ τι κοινὸν εἶναι, ἐκείνῳ κοινόν, 14.14). While abstention from meat might be considered 'purifying' in non-Jewish asceticism, the peculiarly Jewish use of κοινός and the parallel use of such vocabulary in other NT passages (e.g. Mark 7.15–23; Acts 10.9–15; 11.5–9) strongly suggest that both the Roman Christians and Paul have Jewish purity issues in mind.[8]

ii) *The literary context of Romans 14.1–15.6 suggests that Jewish issues are under discussion.* It is now generally recognized that the theme of Romans is the 'righteousness of God' with specific reference to 'both the Jew, first, and the Greek' (1.16). The impartiality of God in relation to Jew and Gentile is a theme which permeates the letter, in which Paul both affirms and relativizes the priority of the Jew in relation to law, circumcision, promise and election (Rom 2–3, 9–11). It is therefore natural to interpret the paraenesis as related to such ethnic and cultural issues, which were indeed central to Paul's mission. Since some other aspects of the paraenesis cohere with the earlier chapters, and since a leading motif in our passage is the same term, πίστις, which has dominated earlier chapters, we are entitled to expect some connection with Paul's intercultural ecclesiology, unless the evidence points decisively in another direction.[9] The fact that 15.7–13 returns to the topic of Jew and Gentile united in Christ gives further support to our position, though this is not in itself as decisive as some interpreters have made out.[10]

Cambridge University, 1986) 88–98; Wedderburn, *The Reasons for Romans*, 30–35; J. D. G. Dunn, *Romans 9–16* (WBC 38B; Waco: Word, 1988) 795–806. [Alternative interpretations have been advanced in recent years: M. Reasoner, *The Strong and the Weak: Romans 14.1–15.13 in Context* (SNTSMS 103; Cambridge: Cambridge University Press, 1999); M. Nanos, *The Mystery of Romans: The Jewish Context of Paul's Letter* (Minneapolis: Fortress, 1996) 85–165. I confess I find neither convincing.]

[8] Dunn, *Romans 9–16*, 818–20; Wilckens, *Der Brief an die Römer*, 3.112–13.

[9] Dunn, *Romans 9–16*, 704–5, 800.

[10] E.g. Watson, *Paul, Judaism and the Gentiles*, 96–97 and Wilckens, *Der Brief an die Römer*, 3.113. It is possible to hold that 15.7–13 constitutes a summary of the whole epistle which illustrates the principle of mutual welcome urged in 14.1–15.6 (15.7 obviously mirrors 14.1) but does not identify precisely the parties involved; see Schmithals, *Römerbrief*, 95–96. For this reason I will refrain from employing 15.7–13 in the exegesis of 14.1–15.6, but will draw it in to the wider conclusions.

iii) *The controversies reflected here are easily imagined among Christians with differing perceptions of the Jewish law.* The main objection to our thesis that Paul here refers to Jewish concerns is that a general abstinence from meat and wine is not characteristic of Judaism.[11] But this objection can be met if it is recognized that Paul is discussing here not the general practices of the Christians concerned but their specific behaviour when they meet and eat together. The disputes arise when they do (or do not) welcome one another to meals (14.1–3), and their debates are given urgency not as general discussions of lifestyle but as specific arguments about the food set before them on such occasions. It is hard to see why the strong should despise the weak or the weak judge the strong with such strength of feeling unless their different behaviour made immediate impact on their lives, and this would occur, of course, when they attempted to share common meals.

One does not therefore have to speculate about the general ease or difficulty in acquiring kosher meat in Rome:[12] the question is simply whether or not the meat on the table in a Christian's house was considered pure by those observing the Jewish law on this matter.[13] There is no reason to take this passage as referring to principled vegetarianism or dietary asceticism, or a specially stringent form of Jewish practice as found, for instance, among the Therapeutae.[14] The issue that arises here is a typical problem of commensality – how observant Jews (and perhaps law-observant Gentiles) can participate in a meal hosted by those who do not scruple to observe the law. As has often been pointed out, there were well-known precedents in which faithful Jews like Daniel and Esther restricted their diet to vegetables and water when eating meals prepared by Gentiles, and there are first-century parallels to this solution in the behaviour of priests in captivity in Rome.[15] Here we have simply to imagine some Christians, who were influenced by the prohibitions of the law, refusing to eat the meat (or, perhaps, drink the wine) which had been provided by those whose law-observance they had reason to doubt. Whether the meat was from an impure animal, or an animal incorrectly slaughtered, or was suspected of idolatrous connections, it

---

[11] E.g. Käsemann, *An die Römer*, 355: 'Provenienz aus jüdischer Orthodoxie ist ausgeschlossen … Generelle Enthaltsamkeit von Fleisch und Wein gab es dort nicht.'

[12] *Pace* Dunn, *Romans 9–16*, 801 (exaggerating the significance of Claudius' expulsion of Jews in 49 CE in dialogue with C.K. Barrett, *A Commentary on the Epistle to the Romans* [London: A & C Black, 1971] 256); cf. Watson, *Paul, Judaism and the Gentiles*, 95, who suggests that Jewish Christians would be unwelcome customers in Jewish shops.

[13] This is rightly perceived by Schmithals, *Römerbrief*, 103–4 and Cranfield, *Romans* 2.695; cf. Minear, *The Obedience of Faith*, 10.

[14] Philo, *Vita Contemplativa* 37, 73. The references to the asceticism of Ebionites and of James (see Schmithals, *Römerbrief*, 98 n16 and Wilckens, *Der Brief an die Römer* 3.114) are intriguing but historically questionable and difficult to interpret.

[15] Daniel 1.8–16; Esther 14.17 LXX; Josephus, *Vita* 13–14; cf. 4 Macc 5.2–3; Judith 12.1–4; Josephus, *Ant.* 4.137.

was to such people in such circumstances κοινόν; the wine (if it is relevant) could also have been suspected of association with idolatry through its use in libation.[16]

It is natural to take the observance of days (14.5) as arising from the same set of scruples. It is easy to imagine the awkwardness in arranging Christian meetings if some did, and others did not, observe the Jewish sabbath. While Jewish feasts and fasts may enter the equation as well, that 'days' are the subject of significant controversy suggests that they are a *regular* problem, which the sabbath could most obviously become.

iv) *All the alternative reconstructions are highly implausible.* We have already seen that this passage is unlikely to be a generalized instruction unrelated to particular issues. Nor can its reference be restricted to the issue of 'food offered to idols',[17] though, as we have seen, the question of idolatry may be part of the wider Jewish concern with impure food (and wine). The most frequently canvassed alternative is that Paul is referring here to Christians who have adopted (or continued from their pre-Christian past) ascetic habits related to (neo-) Pythagorean or even Gnostic sensibilities. This thesis in its pure form was first advocated by Rauer,[18] but it has been partially adopted by Schlier, Barrett, and Käsemann who all suggest some form of Jewish-Pythagorean syncretism, possibly paralleled in Colossae (Col 2.16–23).[19]

I find this thesis implausible for three reasons: a) Paul's argument presupposes that 'the weak' consider their vegetarian practices and observance of days central to their Christian faith: their lifestyle is 'in honour of the Lord' (14.6) and if they are pressurized to drop such practices, Paul fears that they will lose their faith altogether (Rom 14.20). It is hard to imagine Pythagorean vegetarianism being so closely wedded to Christian faith as to be an issue on which believers could feel their loyalty to God depended. b) Secondly, if those who ate only vegetables *judged* (i. e. condemned) the meat-eaters (14.2), they must have considered their abstinence a universal requirement: for them, to eat the meat constituted a serious Christian sin. However, asceticism in the ancient world was a matter of personal choice; I know no parallels for vegetarians making their lifestyle a standard by

[16] On the problems (and possibilities) of commensality between Jews and Gentiles see E. P. Sanders, *Jewish Law from Jesus to the Mishnah. Five Studies* (London: SCM, 1990) 272–83, and *idem*, 'Jewish Association with Gentiles and Galatians 2.11–14', in R.T. Fortna and B.R. Gaventa, eds., *The Conversation Continues. Studies in Paul and John in Honor of J. Louis Martyn* (Nashville: Abingdon, 1990) 170–88.

[17] *Pace*, e.g., J. Ziesler, *Paul's Letter to the Romans* (TPINTC, London: SCM, 1989) 322–27.

[18] M. Rauer, *Die "Schwachen" in Korinth und Rom nach den Paulusbriefen* (Freiburg: Herder, 1923) 76–186.

[19] H. Schlier, *Der Römerbrief* (HTKNT VI, Freiburg: Herder, 1977) 403–6; Barrett, *The Epistle to the Romans*, 257–58; Käsemann, *An die Römer*, 355–56.

which to convict all others of sin. c) Thirdly, it is inconceivable that Paul should be so accommodating to scruples which derived from Pythagorean, Gnostic or other Gentile convictions. In our passage he urges the strong (including himself) to 'bear the weaknesses of the weak' (15.1) and cautions them severely against putting a 'stumbling-block' in their way (14.13, 21). Can we imagine him being so considerate of those who thought animal meat clogged the brain, or who observed 'pagan' fast days or considered certain days unpropitious? The author of Colossians, whether Paul or his disciple, is certainly less accommodating than this! Here in Romans Paul writes with a real sympathy for the views of the weak, as one who understands and appreciates their point of view, while personally differing from them. It is hard to imagine that he would do so if the basis of their viewpoint were some Gentile scruple or superstition.

However, all these characteristics – the centrality of the issue for the faith of the weak, their insistence that they stand for righteousness against sin and the accommodations required by Paul – make excellent sense on the hypothesis that Jewish scruples are at stake. We have no difficulty imagining in Rome the existence of those who continued their Jewish commitments after their adoption of Christian faith and who therefore judged Christian law-breakers as sinners. It is also easy to understand Paul's special concern here not to intimidate or antagonize such law-observant Christians. He knows very well how deeply rooted their convictions could be and what Scriptural support they could claim. He has just urged Gentile Christians not to boast over Jews (11.17–18) and he naturally turns that anxiety into a practical concern that Jewish (and any other) law-observant Christians should not feel intimidated or despised by their more aggressive brothers.

Thus we may conclude that the issue addressed in Romans 14–15 concerns the observance or non-observance of certain key aspects of the Jewish law. The 'weak' maintain Jewish kosher laws and observe the sabbath; the 'strong' do not. I have been careful not to describe the one party as Jewish Christians and the other as Gentile Christians, as we might be inclined to do. Although some of the 'weak' were probably Jewish, Paul, of course, is a Jew on the side of the 'strong' (15.1) and some of his Jewish Christian friends in Rome (e.g. Prisca and Aquila) may have agreed with him on these issues. Conversely, there may have been Gentile Christians among the 'weak' who found Jewish laws in this matter attractive. The letter itself indicates that the Roman Christians were of mixed ethnicity (11.13; cf. those listed in Romans 16) but the proportions, inclinations and relative power of Jews and Gentiles in the church are notoriously hard to discern. Fortunately for our purposes all that is necessary to know is that the issues Paul discusses here concern the observance or non-observance of Jewish law. We may therefore proceed to enquire into some practical aspects of the Jewish food and sabbath laws in Rome (2), before examining Paul's treatment of these issues (3) and assessing its effects (4).

II. Jewish Food and Sabbath Laws in Rome

If, as I have argued, Paul discusses real issues of dispute among Roman Christians concerning Jewish law-observance, it is worth gaining as full a picture as possible of the social context in which such disputes took place. Fortunately we are reasonably well informed from both Jewish and Roman sources about the practices and reputations of Jews in Rome concerning food and sabbath. Much of what we discuss here may also have been true elsewhere, but there are some unique features in the Roman environment which need to be taken into account.

a) Jewish Food Laws

It is evident from a number of sources that the Jews in Rome were particularly well known for their abstinence from pork. Macrobius (*Sat* 2.4.11) records a quip by Augustus that he would rather be Herod's pig than Herod's son,[20] a remark which suggests that Jews even at the highest social level were known to be faithful to the Jewish law on this point. The notoriety of Jews in abstaining from one of the most popular meats in Rome is evident from the comments of another emperor, Gaius, who is said to have challenged Philo's delegation to explain why they wouldn't eat pork (Philo, *Legatio* 361). According to Philo the question elicited laughter from Gaius' entourage; Jewish practice on this matter was a quirk which simply baffled the Romans and led to ill-informed discussions as to whether they abstained out of reverence or loathing for the pig.[21] The former theory made good sense on the analogy of the Egyptian animal cults and is entertained by Petronius (fragment 37 = *GLAJJ* #195: *porcinum numen*). Other Roman authors simply amuse their readers by reference to the Jewish *clementia* which allows pigs to live to an old age (Juvenal, *Sat* 6.160), and their equal abhorrence at eating human or swine's flesh (Juvenal, *Sat* 14.98–99). Tacitus' suggestion that the Jews abhorred the pig having once being plagued by its scabies (*Hist* 5.4.2) also suggests that some of the venom of Egyptian anti-Jewish sentiment influenced Roman perspectives on this issue.

[20] See M. Stern, *Greek and Latin Authors on Jews and Judaism* (Jerusalem: The Israel Academy of Sciences and Humanities, 1974, 1980) (= *GLAJJ*) #543, with notes supporting its historical accuracy; the joke of course is a play on the Greek υἱός and ὗς.

[21] See e.g. Plutarch, *Quaestiones Conviviales* 4.5–5.3 (669e–671b; *GLAJJ* #258), included in this discussion since the author had spent much time in Rome.

It is clear, then, that Jews in Rome were expected to abstain from pork. For that reason, among others, they were regarded as pernickety in their eating habits, the kind of people who would abstain from certain foods or decline to share a meal with non-Jews altogether. Seneca recounts a time when, under the influence of Pythagoreanism, he abstained from meat, but was persuaded to revert to a normal diet by his father since 'certain foreign rites' were becoming controversial, which required abstinence from some animal meats (*Epistulae Morales* 108.22). He dates this incident to the early years of Tiberius' rule, and it is very likely that the 'foreign rites' concerned were those of Judaism, which just at this time (19 CE) became the subject of public concern, issuing in the exile or conscription of many thousand Roman Jews (Josephus, *Ant.* 18.65–84; Tacitus, *Ann* 2.85.4; Suetonius, *Tiberius* 36; Cassius Dio 57.18.5 a). Seneca's anecdote confirms that Judaism was widely associated with eating peculiarities and that Jews were known as the sort of people who would decline to partake of certain meats when these were on offer. How Jews in Rome handled their distinction we do not know, but the tendency of such 'peculiarity' to lead to separatism at meals is clear from Tacitus' observation that the Jews were *separati epulis* (*Hist* 5.5.2).

Seneca's testimony also indicates that it was not only Jews in Rome who had unusual eating habits. Some Romans (chiefly philosophers) became vegetarian under Pythagorean influence and other ethnic groups (e. g. Egyptians) had their own taboos concerning animal meats (Philo, *Legatio* 361–62; Erotianus, fragment = *GLAJJ* #196). Josephus' comment about non-Jews observing 'our food prohibitions' (*c. Apion.* 2.282) *may* indicate that some Jewish food practices were imitated by Gentiles, but his vagueness perhaps indicates that others' practices were merely similar to Judaism, not copied from it. However, Juvenal indicates that Gentiles sympathetic to Judaism were known to abstain from pork (as well as resting on the sabbath, *Sat* 14.96–99), though in his eyes they would thereby be tarred with the same brush as the Jews themselves. Considering the mixed reputation of Jews in Rome in the first century CE, this is a factor which we will have to bear in mind when we consider what Paul requires of the 'strong' Roman Christians in their accommodation to the 'weak'.

In any case, we may safely conclude from this evidence that:

1. Jews in Rome of all social classes were generally careful to preserve their food laws (most noticeably, abstention from pork). These laws were indeed one of the chief means by which they were publicly identified as Jews.
2. Any Jews in Rome who did not observe the Jewish law on this point (who ate pork, for instance) would constitute a serious affront to the Jewish

community. They would also cause confusion among non-Jews if they still claimed to belong to the Jewish community.

3. Any Gentiles who observed Jewish food laws (or what appeared to be such) were likely to be identified with Jews, for good or ill.

b) Jewish Sabbath Laws

Jews were well known in Rome for their observance of the sabbath and for their gatherings on that day in their synagogues. The Jewish community in Rome was sufficiently well organized already in Cicero's day to constitute a political caucus and to send regular contributions to the Jerusalem temple (*Pro Flacco* 28.66–69). The basis of their organization seems to have been the regular meeting in 'associations' which Julius Caesar exempted from his general ban on *collegia* (cf. Suetonius, *Divus Julius* 42.3). According to a slightly dubious text (Josephus, *Ant.* 14.213–16), the Jews in Rome were given permission to meet, to collect contributions of money and to share common meals.[22] Such license seems to have been preserved by Augustus (Philo, *Legatio* 155–57) who also gave special permission that those Jews who were Roman citizens could collect their corn handout on the following day if the distribution happened to fall on the sabbath (*Legatio* 158). This is in many respects a striking concession. Clearly a significant number of Jews were entitled to such corn handouts but were also scrupulous enough in their observance of the sabbath not even to collect their dole on that day. It would be hard to find clearer testimony to the significance of the sabbath and its faithful observance in Rome. Nor could such a measure have gone unnoticed by the general public in Rome.[23]

Synagogue meetings and sabbath observance were of course closely integrated in Jewish community life. Philo talks of the Roman Jews' προσευχαί and their meetings in them 'especially on the sabbaths, when they receive as a body their education in the ancestral philosophy' (καὶ μάλιστα ταῖς ἱεραῖς ἑβδόμαις, ὅτε δημοσίᾳ τὴν πάτριον παιδεύονται φιλοσοφίαν, *Legatio* 156). A key function of the sabbath, therefore, was communal: it not only publicly identified the Jews as Jews, it also enabled them to gather and

[22] There are textual and historical oddities in this text, but its general thrust is plausible (and explains the Jews' special grief at Caesar's death, Suetonius, *Divus Julius* 84.5); see Z. Yavetz, *Julius Caesar and his Public Image* (London: Thames and Hudson, 1983) 85–96.

[23] It is possible that the Jews' refusal to collect their dole on the sabbath contributed to the impression that Jews fasted on the sabbath (e.g. Suetonius, *Divus Augustus* 76.2; Pompeius Trogus, epitome 36.2.14; Martial 4.4). [See now M. Williams, 'Being a Jew in Rome: Sabbath Fasting as an Expression of Romano-Jewish Identity', in J.M.G. Barclay, ed., *Negotiating Diaspora: Jewish Strategies in the Roman Empire* (London: T & T Clark, 2004) 8–18. On the Sabbath in the Diaspora see L. Doering, *Schabbat: Sabbathalacha und -praxis im antiken Judentum und Urchristentum* (TSAJ: Tübingen: Mohr Siebeck, 1999) 283–386.]

to reaffirm their communal identity in recommitment to their ancestral customs. It also reinforced their link with the Jerusalem temple, for it was probably at such gatherings that the collections of 'holy money' were made for Jerusalem (*Legatio* 156).

Among Roman writers, impartial observers note the 'sabbath rites' of the Jews (*cultaque Iudaeo septima sacra Syro*, Ovid, *Ars Amatoria* 1.76). More hostile voices, however, regard the Jews' well-known sabbath rest as a sign of their laziness; Seneca, for instance, complains that Jews lose a seventh of their lives by idleness (*apud* Augustine, *De Civitate Dei* 6.11 = *GLAJJ* #186), while Juvenal and Tacitus, those jaundiced commentators on Roman life, complain about the Jewish custom of dedicating each sabbath to sloth (Juvenal, *Sat* 14.105–6; Tacitus, *Hist* 5.4.3–4). The Roman spirit of duty and hard work, as expressed by these upper-class representatives, was clearly incompatible with such regular cessation of activity.

In fact, however, there is evidence that many ordinary Romans were inclined to observe Jewish sabbaths, at least to the degree of ceasing work. Horace, for one, indicates the influence of the Jewish custom in the Augustan era (*Sermones* 1.9.60–78). Here his friend Fuscus declines to rescue him from a bore, claiming his inability to converse on the grounds that 'today is the thirtieth sabbath; do you want me to insult the circumcised Jews?'.[24] When Horace replies that he has no such scruples, Fuscus teases by responding that he, however, has, since he is 'somewhat weaker, one of the many' (*sum paulo infirmior, unus / multorum*, 69–72). Fuscus is being mischievous, of course, but the joke would fail if there were not some general perception that the sabbath was a superstition observed by many ordinary and less educated Romans. (We shall return to the link between Horace's *infirmior* and Paul's ἀσθενῶν).

That this was indeed the case is confirmed by several references to the sabbath in Ovid (cf. *Remedia Amoris* 219–20). Particularly fascinating is the assumption underlying *Ars Amatoria* 1.413–16. Here Ovid is discussing good days on which to court a girl and, in a fine inversion of tradition, recommends the Allia (a mournful commemoration of Roman defeat by the Gauls) and the sabbath. The reason for noting such days is that the shops will be shut and one will therefore avoid impoverishment by the girl's demands for presents! Ovid considers the sabbath to have such general effect as to cause a significant closure of shops and businesses on that day (*quaque die redeunt rebus minus apta gerendis*, 415), presumably Gentile as well as Jewish.[25]

[24] The reference to the *thirtieth* sabbath remains obscure; see Stern ad loc. (=*GLAJJ* #129).

[25] The implication is noted by A.S. Hollis, *Ovid*: *Ars Amatoria Book One* (Oxford: Clarendon, 1977) 108, who remarks on the impact of Judaism on the social and economic

It is probable that the observance of such sabbath rest was more common among the lower social ranks, as Horace's *infirmior* and *unus multorum* suggest. The phenomenon may in fact be linked to the unofficial observance of the seven-day planetary week, which was coming into vogue at just this time. For the Jewish sabbath coincided with Saturn's day, known to be specially inauspicious. The two systems of counting, the planetary week and the sabbath week, thus reinforced each other and it is likely that, as Colson comments,

> the existence of the planetary week and the fact that the day on which the Jew abstained from work coincided with the day of the planet most adverse to enterprise promoted Sabbatarianism, and served to confirm many outsiders in the belief that it and Judaism in general deserved their respect and imitation.[26]

We may add further evidence of Roman imitation of the Jewish sabbath. Both Seneca (*Epistulae Morales* 95.47) and Persius (*Sat* 5.180–84) rue the fact that some Romans light lamps on the Jewish sabbath, a custom which from his side Josephus is proud to mention, alongside abstention from work (*c. Apion.* 2.282). It thus seems that many non-Jews observed the sabbath in Rome, at least to the extent of lighting lamps and shutting up shop. Their legal entitlement to cease work was another matter (the dole and any other legal concessions were extended only to Jews) and the Jews' complete rest from labour must have been impractical for most non-Jews.[27] It was also another question whether any of these 'sabbatarian' Gentiles attended Roman synagogues. For the Jews, synagogue and sabbath were closely connected, but it was probably only a minority of Gentiles who used their opportunity of rest in the same way as the Jews (cf. Juvenal, *Sat* 14.105–6). It is in this light that we will have to consider the varying practices of the Roman Christians and the options open to them and suggested (or ignored) by Paul.

Again we may draw three conclusions:

1. The observance of the sabbath was, in general, carefully maintained by Jews in Rome, for whom abstention from work and attendance at synagogue was an essential element of their Jewish identity.

---

life of Rome.

[26] F.H. Colson, *The Week* (Cambridge: Cambridge University, 1926) 41; cf. J.P.V.D. Balsdon, *Life and Leisure in Ancient Rome* (London: The Bodley Head, 1969) 59–65. Cf. the connection between the sabbath and Saturn suggested by Tacitus, *Hist* 5.4.4 and firmly asserted by Dio (37.16–19), by whose day (2nd–3rd century CE) the 7-day cycle had become traditional among Romans.

[27] Decrees from some Asian cities indicate the difficulties Jews themselves sometimes had in defending their legal rights on this matter (e.g. Josephus, *Ant.* 14.262–64; 16.45); a Gentile would not be able to appeal to 'ancestral custom'.

2. Any Jews in Rome who regularly ignored the sabbath would not only undermine the Jewish stance on this matter (over which they had won official recognition) but also forfeit an important means of maintaining their position in the Jewish community. To forego the social and educational opportunities of the synagogue meetings was to jeopardize the maintenance of one's Jewish identity.
3. Many Gentiles in Rome, especially in the lower social classes, appear to have observed Jewish sabbaths to the extent of ceasing work on that day. But in most cases the influence of Judaism seems to have been minimal (Saturn's day being at least as significant). Sabbath observance and attendance at a synagogue did not necessarily go together for such sabbatarian Romans.

We have now gained a clearer conception of the social realities of Jewish food and sabbath laws in Rome and the options open to the members of the Roman churches. Precisely what influenced the Roman Christians to take differing stances on these matters it is hard to assess. Our fragmentary evidence suggests that Jewish Christians in Rome had already been at the centre of controversy in certain Roman synagogues, if we may match Suetonius' famous *impulsore Chresto* (*Claudius* 25.4) with the reference in Acts 18.2 to the expulsion of Aquila and Priscilla.[28] The extent of this expulsion should not be exaggerated: Luke's 'all the Jews' is a manifest exaggeration, and the event does not merit mention either in Tacitus or in Josephus.[29] Thus it is hard to assess precisely how serious were the difficulties for Jewish Christians in Rome in their relations with the synagogue communities. We need to bear in mind the possibility of tensions here, while recognizing that the situation may have varied in different synagogues. We should also note that, if the example of Paul is anything to go by, Jewish Christians may have been anxious to maintain their place in the Jewish community even if they met opposition in that context.[30] How Gentile Christians viewed Jewish

[28] Suetonius probably indicates a Christian element in the Roman Jewish troubles, but not certainly so; see S. Benko, 'The Edict of Claudius of A. D. 49 and the Instigator Chrestus' *TZ* 25 (1969) 406–18.

[29] Tacitus' account of affairs in 41 CE is missing, so if the 'expulsion' is to be dated in that year, his silence is easily explained. However, it is more likely that Claudius' attempts to repress Jews in 41 CE (Cassius Dio 60.6.6) were not followed up with expulsion until 49 CE. Such at least is the 'harmonizing' solution of our conflicting evidence advanced by, e. g., A. Momigliano, *The Emperor Claudius and His Achievement* (rev. ed.; Oxford: Oxford University, 1961) 31–38, and E. M. Smallwood, *The Jews Under Roman Rule: From Pompey to Diocletian* (2nd ed., Leiden: Brill, 1981) 210–16. [Cf. J. M. G. Barclay, *Jews in the Mediterranean Diaspora from Alexander to Trajan (323 BCE–117 CE)* (Edinburgh: T & T Clark, 1996) 303–6; H. D. Slingerland, *Claudian Policymaking and the Early Imperial Repression of Judaism in Rome* (Atlanta: Scholars Press, 1997).]

[30] Observance of 'days' does not alone prove synagogue attendance, but it is likely that Roman Christians who observed sabbaths did attend synagogues given a) the importance

customs in relation to food and sabbath must have varied according to their previous contact with Jews and their personal convictions; as we have seen, there may have been Gentiles on both sides of the dispute between weak and strong in the Roman churches.

Having explored the relevant social context of Romans 14.1–15.6, we may turn now to examine Paul's advice in these verses.

III. The Key Elements of Paul's Instruction

Paul's response to these disputes concerning law-observance is composed of three main elements:

A. Paul counts himself among the strong (15.1) and shares with them the conviction that the Christian believer may eat 'anything' (14.2). Although there was no particular need in this context to declare his own position in the debate, he is in fact quite unashamed to declare that 'I know and am persuaded in the Lord Jesus that nothing is unclean of itself' (οἶδα καὶ πέπεισμαι ἐν κυρίῳ Ἰησοῦ ὅτι οὐδὲν κοινὸν δι' ἑαυτοῦ, 14.14). A few verses later he echoes this with the summary statement that 'all things are clean' (πάντα καθαρά, 14.20). This constitutes nothing less than a fundamental rejection of the Jewish law in one of its most sensitive dimensions. One may hesitate to join Käsemann in reckoning that Paul here 'removes for Christians the basic distinction of all antiquity, which is still influential today, between the cultic sphere and the profane';[31] the context here only concerns food, and Paul can still use purity language in other contexts (e.g. 1 Cor 5.6–8). But this strong denial of the Scriptural distinction between 'clean' and 'unclean' food should not be watered down.[32]

It is important to observe that Paul does not base his judgment here on an appeal to a 'higher principle' in the law or on an allegorical interpretation of the law. The law's regulations on this matter and the long history of interpretation of those regulations are here so summarily dismissed as not even to receive mention. Earlier in this letter Paul relativizes the significance

of the sabbath as the opportunity for synagogue meetings, b) the example of Paul (and Matthean and Johannine Christians) in remaining in synagogue communities until forced out, and c) Paul's respect for their observance of the sabbath as 'in honour of the Lord' (14.6).

[31] *An die Römer*, 362, as translated by G. Bromiley in *Commentary on Romans* (London: SCM, 1980) 375.

[32] Tomson, *Paul and the Law*, 247–48 considers such radicalism 'very unlikely', but is unable, in my view, to provide a satisfactory alternative interpretation. If the total effect of Paul's advice is a relativization of the food laws, that still entails a denial of the absolute value they are accorded in the Scriptures, even for Jews like Paul himself. That denial is what is articulated here.

of circumcision by appeal to the Scriptural tradition of 'circumcision of the heart' (Rom 2.25–29), but no reference is made here to an 'inner purity' which renders unnecessary the 'visible purity' of abstention from foods. Nor does Paul attempt an allegorical explanation of the law (cf. 1 Cor 9.8–11). Hellenized Jews from at least the time of Aristeas (2nd century BCE) had developed sophisticated means of interpreting the Jewish food laws in line with the Greek virtues (*Aristeas* 128–71), and Paul might have appealed to the exercise of such virtues (through the Spirit) as the proper 'fulfilment' of the law. But in fact he makes no such effort to explain or excuse himself, as if the relationship between his convictions and the law is no longer of central concern. The basis of his judgment is unashamedly non-legal: simply a 'knowledge' and 'conviction' in the Lord Jesus (14.14), or, as he puts it elsewhere, 'faith' (14.2, 22–23). It is possible that there lies behind the assertion of 14.14 some awareness of a saying of Jesus (later interpreted in Mark 7.15–19);[33] but Paul makes no attempt here to present Jesus as an interpreter of the law. He here expresses views which indicate that he is no longer ὑπὸ νόμον (Rom 6.14–15; 7.1–6), but he makes no attempt to 'legalize' his position by a claim to be ἔννομος Χριστοῦ (cf. 1 Cor 9.19–21).

The certainty and candour with which Paul here expresses his freedom from the law is thus quite breathtaking. In principle, it appears, he could see no objection to eating shellfish, hare or pork. Do we have reason to doubt that his diet was sometimes as scandalously 'free' as his principles? As regards the allied topic of sabbath observance, his own convictions and practices are less clear. He recognizes (14.5–6) that different believers have different practices in this regard, but he does not declare his own hand. His identification with the strong would suggest that here too he had no objection to the principle that the special observance of days (i. e. sabbaths) was unnecessary. But it may be that he declined to make so explicit his own convictions on this matter since it was known that he often in fact attended synagogues (i. e. observed sabbath days).

B. While holding his own opinion, Paul accepts an element of subjectivity in the definition of proper conduct relating to diet and calendar. As soon as he has expressed his own opinion in 14.14 a, he adds that food is unclean to anyone who considers it such (εἰ μὴ τῷ λογιζομένῳ τι κοινὸν εἶναι, ἐκείνῳ κοινόν, 14.14 b).[34] This allowance for individual perception is also strikingly portrayed in 14.5–6 where the issues of days and food are paral-

---

[33] See, e. g., Dunn, *Romans 9–16*, 819–20.

[34] The same point may be made after the πάντα καθαρά statement in 14.20, ἀλλὰ κακὸν τῷ ἀνθρώπῳ τῷ διὰ προσκόμματος ἐσθίοντι. But it is difficult to know whether the 'man' mentioned here is a representative of the weak or the strong. Wilckens, *Der Brief an die Römer*, 3.95 sees a reference to the weak; Dunn, *Romans 9–16*, 826 regards the phrase as ambiguous, but probably referring to the strong.

leled. On the matter of days, each individual is to act according to his / her own individual conviction: ἕκαστος ἐν τῷ ἰδίῳ νοῒ πληροφορείσθω (14.5). Thus each Christian can act, even if with opposite effect, 'in honour of the Lord': 'he who eats, eats to the Lord, for he gives thanks to God; he who abstains from eating, abstains to the Lord and gives thanks to God' (14.6). The individual definition of morality could hardly be more plainly stated, and is further reinforced towards the end of the discussion: 'the faith that you have, keep to yourself before God' (14.22). Paul refuses to allow matters of diet or sabbath to function as part of the defining structure of the Christian community. Within this sphere, which he is bold enough to claim for 'the kingdom of God', food and drink cannot define the legitimate bounds of the community: what counts rather is 'righteousness, peace and joy in the Holy Spirit' (14.17; cf. Rom 5.1–5). Precisely by refusing to allow food and drink (or sabbath observance) to enter into the definition of 'righteousness' (δικαιοσύνη), Paul indicates that the norms of the Christian churches will be decisively different from the defining values of the Jewish community.

This does not mean, of course, a lack of moral seriousness in Paul's depiction of Christian conduct. Each individual is to conduct his / her life as the household slave (οἰκέτης) of the κύριος (14.4) and in anticipation of the final judgment, in which a personal account will be rendered to God (14.10–12). In this sense a Christian morality outside the law is no less rigorous than one operating according to its structures (cf. Rom 6.1–15). But the shift in values requires that what was the basis of social unity and persuasion in the Jewish community could not operate as such in the church. Law-abiding members of the synagogue would be entitled to 'judge' (i.e. condemn) other members of the synagogue who failed to observe sabbath or food laws. As members of the church, however, they are instructed to 'welcome' and tolerate fellow believers even if they do not observe such rules. The mutual tolerance demanded by Paul in the Roman churches requires that neither side allow their strongly-held convictions to determine the contours of Christian commitment. We shall consider below the effects of this requirement on those with a double loyalty to synagogue and church.

C. Having stated the basic principle of mutual toleration (14.1–12, summed up in 14.13 a: μηκέτι οὖν ἀλλήλους κρίνωμεν), Paul goes on to require of the strong that they refrain from activity which would cause the weaker Christians to stumble or fall. Applying the same principle he had employed in 1 Cor 8–10, Paul warns the strong against putting a stumbling-block in the path of the weak (14.13), which could result in their injury (14.15 a) or even destruction (14.15 b). Whatever was the numerical balance between the weak and strong, it appears that the power relations between the two groups were such that the weak were considerably more vulnerable than the strong. It is implied that the strong, through 'despising' (ἐξουθενεῖν, 14.3) the weak, were liable to pressurize them to act contrary to their own convictions and thus undermine their Christian commitment. Such social disparities are also implicit in the labels 'weak' and 'strong': Horace's *infirmior* (see above) suggests that they could represent differential social locations.[35] Thus within the Roman churches the law-observant Christians were socially vulnerable and more easily induced to adopt the practices of the strong than vice versa. Paul's instruction here requires that they be protected in their law observance, both for their own sakes and for the sake of Christ who redeemed them (14.15; cf. 14.20).

Paul requires such accommodation to the practices of the weak specifically in relation to food (14.15, 20). His instruction seems to imply that to avoid the 'disputes' (14.1) liable to lead to the overpowering of the weak, the strong should refrain from offering food at the communal meals which the weak were unable to consume: hence the advice that 'it is good not to eat meat or drink wine or do anything by which your brother is made to stumble' (14.21). This suggests that, in this context, the communal meal should consist only of food (and drink) concerning which the weak could have no scruples, either limited to vegetables or, if meat, perhaps what they themselves provided. There is no good reason to take this advice as applying outside the particular context of the Christian communal meals. In 1 Cor 8–10 Paul talks of the strong eating meals in various public contexts, but here the specific context is the occasion when they 'welcome one another' (14.1), i.e. the community meals. In other words, Paul is requiring the strong to allow for Jewish scruples at their common meals, but not necessarily suggesting a complete change in their dietary habits.

It is intriguing that, although he mentions the parallel case of 'days' in his appeal for tolerance (14.5–6), Paul does not return to this issue when urging accommodation to the scruples of the weak. He does not require the strong to observe the sabbath. Presumably this matter was less immediately threatening to the convictions of the weak: if the church gathered on another day of the week, that did not prevent them observing the sabbath or attending synagogue, and if their meeting was on a sabbath, it could presumably be arranged not to clash with the synagogue meetings. Thus Paul leaves the matter of sabbath-observance as a standing difference between the different groups in the Roman churches and makes no attempt to 'judaize' those who did not observe the law in this respect.

---

[35] Compare Paul's use of such labels in Corinth, as discussed by G. Theissen, *The Social Setting of Pauline Christianity* (Edinburgh: T & T Clark, 1982) 121–43.

IV. The Social Effects of Paul's Advice

We may now assess the social effects of Paul's advice concerning these aspects of law-observance, bearing in mind the social and cultural realities in Rome. We may summarize our conclusions here under three heads:

a) Paul protects Law-observance and Jewish Christianity

By insisting that the strong should neither despise the weak nor pressurize them to change their convictions, Paul is careful to preserve the legitimacy of law-observance among Roman Christians. His requirement that the strong adapt their diet at the communal meals is a measure of how seriously he takes this matter. This certainly means that those Jewish Christians in Rome who wished to retain their links with the Jewish community in Rome were enabled to do so. As we have seen, a Jew in Rome who was found eating pork or otherwise infringing well-known Jewish food laws would destroy his Jewish identity in the eyes of both Jews and non-Jews. The effect of Paul's advice is to protect Jewish Christians from this danger. Similarly the acceptance that some in good conscience honour sabbath days grants permission to such Jewish Christians (and any Gentile sympathizers of Judaism) to attend the all-important synagogue gatherings and thus maintain their place in the Jewish community. On these two sensitive issues, Paul allows Jewish Christians to maintain their social base in the Jewish community and to preserve their Jewish identity. There is no reason why they should not also circumcise their sons, pay their temple dues and otherwise continue their Jewish life-style.[36]

To be sure, the tone in which Paul grants this permission is somewhat condescending. By employing the terms 'weak' and 'strong' and by openly declaring his position on the side of the 'strong', Paul endorses the perspective of the strong. 'Weak in faith' (14.1) is not the most complimentary phrase Paul could have used (cf. Rom 4.19)! It is only of the strong that he requires the application of love (14.15) and only to them that he applies the example of Christ (15.2–3). In all these ways Paul patronizes the weak and tips the theological balance in favour of the strong, even while attempting to make the scales even. Nonetheless, his genuine concern to protect the legitimacy of the weak cannot be overlooked, nor its social effects in

[36] Compare Justin's stance in *Dialogue with Trypho* 46–47, where, unlike some other Christians, he accepts that Jewish Christians may practise circumcision, keep the sabbath and observe other Jewish laws. But he considers such 'ceremonies' as instituted only because of the Jews' 'hardness of heart', and he strongly opposes any attempt to persuade Gentile Christians to follow suit. I am grateful to Graham Stanton for drawing this passage to my attention.

enabling them to maintain their Jewish (or Jewish-sympathetic) identity and their honour within whatever Roman synagogue they attended. Just as Christ was a διάκονος of the circumcised (Rom 15.8), so Paul attempts to serve the social and cultural needs of the Jewish-oriented members of the churches in Rome.[37]

b) Paul allows Law-neglect and a Gentilized Christianity

As we have seen, Paul makes clear his own conviction 'in the Lord Jesus' that the Jewish food laws may be abandoned, even by Jewish Christians like himself. In principle he supports the strong, though he here requires from them accommodation in certain practical respects with the scruples of the weak. In their common meals – though probably, as we have suggested, only there – the strong are to observe Jewish laws in relation to food and drink. It is not entirely clear how this limited adaptation of their behaviour would affect their reputations in Roman society. It may be that the Christian meals were sufficiently private for this accommodation to be of no social significance, though it is possible that Paul subtly acknowledges here the potential damage to their social standing. We may recall how, in some circles at least, Romans who gave the impression of 'judaizing' in their diet were subject to criticism: Seneca's anecdote certainly indicates sensitivity on this point and Juvenal lashes out in criticism of the pork-abstaining Gentile. When Paul talks of the strong bearing the weaknesses of the weak and not pleasing themselves (15.1–2), he appeals to the example of Christ and cites from Psalm 68.10 LXX: οἱ ὀνειδισμοὶ τῶν ὀνειδιζόντων σε ἐπέπεσαν ἐπ' ἐμέ (15.3). Beyond the general appeal to the self-sacrifice of Christ, why should this particular verse be cited here? Perhaps Paul intended to indicate a quite specific application to the case in point: the slanders and reproaches levelled at Jews in Rome would be shared by the strong to the extent that they were willing to adopt Jewish eating habits in their common Christian meals.[38]

---

[37] To this extent I would take issue with the thesis of Watson, *Paul, Judaism and the Gentiles*, that 'Paul's purpose in writing Romans was to defend and explain his view of freedom from the law (i. e. separation from the Jewish community and its way of life), with the aim of converting Jewish Christians to his point of view so as to create a single 'Pauline' congregation in Rome' (98). Watson's thesis has been criticized by W. S. Campbell, *Paul's Gospel in an Intercultural Context* (Frankfurt am Main: Peter Lang, 1992). [Cf. now F. Watson, *Paul, Judaism, and the Gentiles: Beyond the New Perspective* (2nd edn.; Grand Rapids: Eerdmans, 2007) 175–82; P. F. Esler, *Conflict and Identity in Romans: The Social Setting of Paul's Letter* (Minneapolis: Fortress Press, 2003) 339–56.]

[38] The psalm would thus be refracted through a double lens: it applies in the first instance to Christ absorbing the blasphemies directed against God, and by transference to the strong in Rome sharing the anti-Jewish sentiment which was suffered by Torah-observers. This is perhaps a clearer reading of the relevance of the quotation than that offered by Dunn, *Romans 9–16*, 839. The following reference to the teaching of the Scriptures and

As we saw above, Paul does not require of the strong similar accommodation in relation to sabbath-observance. At first sight, this is surprising. As we have seen, even among the non-Jewish population in Rome the Jewish sabbath was in part imitated and it would not have been culturally inappropriate for Paul to request the Gentiles in the Roman churches to make some gestures towards sabbath-observance. But further reflection suggests why he did not advocate this compromise. Paul's Jewish heritage indicated that the purpose of the sabbath was not just to rest from work but to gather in worship, prayer and communal education in the synagogues. If anyone honoured this day, it had to be 'to the Lord' (14.6). Paul cannot encourage Gentile Christians to enter the ambit of the synagogue and he cannot encourage the celebration of the sabbath except in this social and liturgical context. Thus the alternative to sabbath-and-synagogue has to be not some partial sabbath of lighting lamps or shutting up shop, but treating every day alike.

Thus, despite the partial 'judaizing' of the common Christian meals, Paul does not require Law-observance of the Roman Christians in these crucial respects. He permits the Roman Christian community to welcome and retain members who, in general, pay no heed to the Jewish law in relation to food and sabbaths.

c) Paul effectively undermines the social and cultural integrity of the Law-observant Christians in Rome

This final point is crucial and is stated in full awareness of the paradox it creates in juxtaposition with Conclusion a) above. For it seems to me that while, *on the surface* and *in the short term*, Paul protects the Law-observant Christians, in the long term and at a deeper level he seriously undermines their social and cultural integrity. This conclusion deserves a fuller explication than is possible here, but it may be presented in outline under two heads.[39]

---

their encouragement of 'endurance' (ὑπομονή, 15.4; cf. Rom 5.3–4) seems to underline the specific applicability of the quotation.

[39] The fundamental issues here have been addressed from a wider perspective by D. Boyarin, *A Radical Jew. Paul and the Politics of Identity* (Berkeley / London: University of California, 1994). Boyarin's claim that Paul 'erases' or 'annuls' cultural difference, in a universalizing drive towards 'sameness', does not, in my view, accurately represent Paul's theology. But he is right to detect that in (as I would say) relativizing the Jewish cultural tradition Paul challenges certain claims which lie *at the core of Jewish identity*. Thus there is an important measure of truth in Boyarin's statement (p. 32) that 'what will appear from the Christian perspective as tolerance, namely Paul's willingness – indeed insistence – that within the Christian community all cultural practice is equally to be tolerated, from the rabbinic Jewish perspective is simply an eradication of the entire value system which insists that our cultural practice is our task and calling in the world and must not be abandoned or reduced to a matter of taste' (cf. pp. 9–10, 290 n10).

a) *Social Integrity*. While permitting Law-observant Christians to keep the food laws, observe sabbaths and thus maintain their social base in the Jewish community, Paul *also* requires of them that they associate regularly and at the deepest inter-personal level with 'brothers and sisters in Christ' who are not bound by the regulations of the Jewish law. The weak Roman Christians have to accept that non-kosher and non-sabbatarian Christians are nonetheless living 'in honour of the Lord', and they are requested to associate with them intimately, on the basis of their common faith in Jesus as Lord. In prayer and worship (15.7–13), in common meals (14.1 ff.), in the sharing of prophecy and teaching (12.6–7), financial resources (12.8) and the common kiss (16.16), they are required to express a deep bond of unity with people fundamentally neglectful of the law. They are even expected to welcome Paul and to pool their spiritual gifts with his (1.11–12), just as they are now asked to pray for his visit to Jerusalem (15.30–32). In all these ways, while accepting their right to remain attached to the Jewish community, Paul requires from the weak a deep social commitment to their fellow Christians, even if they do not respect the Jewish law in their conduct.

The question is whether such dual loyalties can be maintained in the long term. Some comments of Josephus are relevant at this point. While rebutting charges of 'anti-social' behaviour in *Contra Apionem* book 2, Josephus is concerned to insist that Judaism is not an exclusive code, but he admits that there are limits to the associations allowed to Jews. 'He [Moses] graciously accepts all those who desire to come and live under the same laws with us, considering that relatedness is not a matter of race alone, but of choices taken in one's way of life. But he did not admit casual visitors (τοὺς ἐκ παρέργου προσιόντας) to join in our common life (ἀναμίγνυσθαι τῇ συνηθείᾳ)' (*c. Apion.* 2.210). Later in the same work Josephus admits the charge of Apollonius Molon that Jews 'do not wish to associate with those who choose to live according to a different mode of life' (μηδὲ κοινωνεῖν ἐθέλομεν τοῖς καθ' ἑτέραν συνήθειαν βίου ζῆν προαιρουμένοις, *c. Apion.* 2.258).[40] Yet Paul here requires of Christian members of the Jewish community a very significant depth of 'association' with those declining to live according to the same mode of life. Is this transcultural Christian φιλαδελφία (Rom 12.10) and κοινωνία (Rom 12.13; cf. 15.26–27) compatible with continued membership in a Jewish community, which is naturally

[40] The application of this principle in Rome is attested from another angle by Juvenal and Tacitus, although their evidence is biased by hostility. Juvenal remarks that the Gentiles incorporated into the Jewish community flout the laws of Rome and decline to indicate the way to any 'not worshipping the same rites' (*nisi sacra colenti*, *Sat* 14.103). Tacitus complains that the Jews *separati epulis, discreti cubilibus ... alienarum concubitu abstinent*; those who 'cross over to their ways' reject the gods, their homeland and their families, *Hist* 5.5.2.

concerned to preserve its social integrity? Can a law-observant synagogue member associate at the deepest level with a law-neglectful 'brother' or 'sister'? Paul's instructions, though palliative in the short term, created tensions which were likely to grow to the point when a difficult social choice would have to be made between the Jewish and Christian community.

b) *Cultural Integrity*. As we have seen, Paul accepts that law-observant Christians may continue to observe Jewish food and sabbath regulations and protects their rights to do so. But the way he discusses the matter makes it clear that, within his frame of reference, such conduct is not a foundational but merely an optional aspect of a life lived in honour of God.[41] By refusing to allow that the weak condemn the strong, Paul requires of them the acceptance of an alternative, non-observant lifestyle as *equally valid* in the sight of God. He who eats (even pork!), eats in honour of the Lord, serving God as worthily as he who abstains in honour of the Lord (14.6). Sabbath and food are removed from the sphere of 'righteousness' and made peripheral to 'the kingdom of God' (14.17). Thus the Jewish cultural heritage in these matters is no longer regarded as the divinely sanctioned norm, but as merely one option, one preference among others. In other words, while allowing the expression of the Jewish cultural tradition, Paul relativizes its significance and undermines key aspects of its theological and intellectual foundation.

The weak Roman Christian who observed the sabbath and attended his/her synagogue, would receive instruction there in the Jews' 'ancestral philosophy' (πάτριος φιλοσοφία, Philo, *Legatio* 156). The religious basis of that philosophy lay in the conviction that the law was uniquely God-given and therefore sacrosanct. Its intellectual claim was that the Jewish way of life represented the most pious and the most virtuous mode of conduct ever conceived. Such is the claim, explicit or implicit, of all Jewish literature from this period, not least of Josephus' apology, *Contra Apionem*, which therefore properly claims that Jews are utterly committed to the observance of the law. What Paul demands of these weak Christians is their commitment to a church in which the Jewish mode of life is tolerated but not required, in which credence is given to the claim that men and women can honour God as effectively by ignoring the sabbath as by observing it. Such toleration of each individual's conviction would surely have been castigated by Josephus as a crude example of τὸ αὐτεξούσιον, that self-defined liberty which he considered the root of apostasy (*Ant.* 4.145–49). In demanding this toleration, Paul subverts the basis on which Jewish law-observance is founded and precipitates a crisis of cultural integrity among the very believers whose

[41] Cf. Watson, *Paul, Judaism and the Gentiles*, 97.

law-observance he is careful to protect. Such is the fundamental paradox of the passage we are studying.

It is important to observe that the laws here discussed cannot be dismissed, from the Jewish perspective, as merely 'ceremonial' or 'ritual'.[42] As we have seen from the evidence of Jewish life in Rome, they are of central significance in defining the social and cultural identity of the Jewish community.[43] However Paul may extol the law as 'holy, righteous and good' (Rom 7.12, 14), law-observant Christians in Rome would want to know more precisely whether he actually observed it and encouraged others to do so. His claim that those who walked in the Spirit would fulfil the law (Rom 8.4; 13.8–10) would inevitably be subject to the litmus test of praxis. Josephus, in common with other Jews, was not impressed by words alone: it was his special boast that Judaism combined words and deeds (ἔργα) to a degree unparalleled in other cultural traditions (*c. Apion.* 2.171–78).

As we have seen, on the surface Paul supports the weak Christians in their right to observe the Jewish food and sabbath laws. In response to our title question, Paul had insisted that he upheld the law (Rom 3.31) and in this passage he fulfils his claim in the limited sense that he protects the right of others to uphold it. But he himself regards key aspects of the law as wholly dispensable for Christian believers and, more subtly, his theology introduces into the Roman Christian community a Trojan horse which threatens the integrity of those who sought to live according to the law. In this respect, Jewish Christians were right to fear Paul *et dona ferentem*.

---

[42] *Pace* Cranfield, *Romans* 2.697; Käsemann, *An die Römer*, 362 and many others.

[43] The point is rightly emphasized by Dunn, *Romans 9–16*, 800–2, 805–6.

3. Paul and Philo on Circumcision

Romans 2.25–29 in Social and Cultural Context

As contemporary Jews operating in (different parts of) the Diaspora, Paul and Philo invite comparison on a number of levels. Both classify as Jewish theologians variously influenced by their social and cultural environments, who reflected deeply on the Jewish Scriptures with innovative results. However, placing each on the map of first-century Judaism is a complex business, not least because our maps of Judaism contain ever-increasing detail and presently display boundaries less clearly defined than ever before. Out of the range of themes on which Paul and Philo may be compared, I choose to focus here on circumcision, a topic of importance to Philo as a token of Jewish identity and of massive significance to Paul in his redefinition of that identity.[1] Thus a study of these two figures on this topic promises to reveal much about their respective reformulations of the Jewish tradition, indicating where they stand in comparison with each other and in relation to other Jews.

My choice of this topic is also stimulated by the provocative thesis of Daniel Boyarin in *A Radical Jew: Paul and the Politics of Identity*.[2] Boyarin suggests that 'Pauline religion should itself be understood as a religio-cultural formation contiguous with other Hellenistic Judaisms' (13) and especially comparable to that of Philo: 'the congruence of Paul and Philo suggests a common background to their thought in the thought-world of the eclectic middle-platonism of Greek-speaking Judaism in the first century' (14). Paul's theology and practice was driven, according to Boyarin, by 'a Hellenistic desire for the One, which among other things produced

[1] For a broad comparative survey see H. Chadwick, 'St. Paul and Philo of Alexandria' *BJRL* 48 (1966) 286–307; anthropology and allegory are frequent topics for comparison. On our topic of circumcision see P. Borgen, *Philo, John and Paul. New Perspectives on Judaism and Early Christianity* (Atlanta: Scholars, 1987) 61–71, 233–54. The present essay follows up my fuller analysis of Paul and Philo, among other Diaspora Jews, in *Jews in the Mediterranean Diaspora from Alexander to Trajan (323 BCE–117 CE)* (Edinburgh: T & T Clark, 1996).

[2] D. Boyarin, *A Radical Jew: Paul and the Politics of Identity* (Berkeley: University of California, 1994). His thesis is partly adumbrated in *Carnal Israel: Reading Sex in Talmudic Culture* (Berkeley: University of California, 1993) 1–10, 231–35.

an ideal of a universal human essence, beyond difference and hierarchy … predicated … on the dualism of flesh and spirit' (7). There is thus a deep homology between Paul's dualistic anthropology (of flesh and spirit) and his allegorical treatment of Judaism, whose story and customs are spiritualized to identify their inner and universal meaning. This is significantly the case with regard to the custom of circumcision, whose literal physical performance is crucial to Jewish identity, but which, according to Boyarin, Paul universalizes under the influence of Hellenism (25–29, 69–81, 86–97). Thus Pauline Christianity is identified as a radically Hellenized Judaism, taking its spiritualizing tendencies to their reductive conclusion by doing away with the 'signifiers' (Jewish customs and history) in favour of the 'signified' (universal truths, revealed in Christ).

I consider Boyarin's reading of Paul subtly mistaken, but important enough to require discussion and re-examination of his evidence. The two passages to which Boyarin directs particular attention are indeed the two most significant for our broader purposes: Philo's famous rebuke of 'pure allegorists' in *Migr. Abr.* 89–93, and Paul's redefinition of circumcision as a 'hidden' phenomenon 'in the Spirit' in Rom 2.25–29. While other passages in Philo and Paul must also be taken into account, these two encapsulate their authors' cultural strategies with peculiar clarity. I shall use their juxtaposition, however, to argue against Boyarin's Hellenistic reading of Paul and to suggest that Paul's paradoxical reformulation of Judaism stands socially and ideologically in striking contrast to that of Philo.

I. Philo, Allegory and Circumcision

Philo's voluminous works give us ample opportunity to assess his hermeneutical strategy in relation to Jewish scriptures and laws.[3] His characteristic hermeneutic is allegory: he is heir to a long tradition of Jewish allegorical interpretation in Alexandria but the depth and coherence of his efforts probably surpassed his predecessors and contemporaries. Although allegory serves some apologetic functions, it is for Philo no mere rhetorical ploy: it represents his fusion of Jewish tradition with Platonic philosophy, according to which the surface of the text, like all visible things, is but an invitation to the soul to penetrate to the inner, invisible truths of the conceptual world (see e.g. *Contempl.* 78). The tendency of this hermeneutic is to dehistoricize the text, to cut its particular anchorage to time, place and people (the Jewish

[3] I have summarized my assessment in *Jews*, 158–80. See also P. Borgen, 'Philo of Alexandria: A Critical and Synthetic Survey of Research since World War II', in *ANRW* II.21.1, 98–154.

nation), such that Philo's allegories bear the potential to 'dejudaize' Judaism, dissolving its distinctiveness in the sea of timeless truths, universal realities and generalized human conditions. However, Philo did not allow his allegorical method to bear this dangerous fruit, since his ultimate commitment lay not with Hellenistic philosophy but with his Jewish community. As David Dawson has argued, Philo's allegorical scheme actually subordinates the achievements of the Greek philosophical tradition to the greater authority of Moses, finding in the Pentateuch not a pale reflection of Hellenistic truths and virtues, but their finest and most original expression.[4] Thus allegory is employed to Jewish advantage, pressed into service even to justify Jewish particularity in the terms of the dominant philosophical culture.

This cautious accommodation of Hellenism is well exemplified by Philo's treatment of circumcision. We may note first the special section devoted to this topic at the beginning of *De Specialibus Legibus* (1.1–11). Here Philo confronts those who mock circumcision (1.2), and lists six reasons for the custom (which he rightly notes is also Egyptian, and not just Jewish). The first two reasons are medical and practical: circumcision prevents infection of the penis (e.g. anthrax, 1.4) and the collection of dirt (1.5). The third is the assimilation of the penis to the heart: if the heart, which generates thought, is to be circumcised, so must be the member which generates physical offspring (1.6). This is an interesting redeployment of the biblical metaphor of the circumcision of the heart (alluded to elsewhere in *Spec. Leg.* 1.305; *Quaest. Gen.* 3.46–47), to which we will return below: but we may note in passing how for Philo the circumcision of the heart does not render superfluous the circumcision of the flesh, but positively requires it, since the unseen generator of thought should have assimilated to it what is visible and apparent (τὸ ἐμφανὲς καὶ ὁρατόν, 1.6). The fourth reason for circumcision is again pragmatic: the removal of the foreskin facilitates the delivery of sperm, thus explaining why the circumcised nations are the most prolific in offspring (1.7)!

These four explanations are those Philo has received 'from divinely gifted men' (παρὰ θεσπεσίοις ἀνδράσιν, 1.8); that is, they are long-established among Jews as explanatory devices. None of them is allegorical, though the third depends on a metaphorical transfer from heart to penis, probably a reversal of the process by which the biblical metaphor of heart circumcision was coined. But after listing these four, Philo adds two more of his own, both allegorical in nature. Firstly, circumcision is a σύμβολον of the cutting away

[4] D. Dawson, *Allegorical Readers and Cultural Revision in Alexandria* (Berkeley: University of California, 1992) 73–126. Cf. I. Christiansen, *Die Technik der allegorischen Auslegungswissenschaft bei Philon von Alexandrien* (Tübingen: Mohr Siebeck, 1969): Philo used allegory to discover the general in the particularity of the Scriptural text (42–46), but regarded Scripture as a uniquely trustworthy guide to the truth (152–71).

of pleasures: since sex is the most pleasurable human activity, a 'cut' here signifies the moral requirement to excise superfluous pleasures (the point here depends partly on word-play: περιτομή symbolizes the περιττῆς ἐκτομὴ ἡδονῆς, 1.9). Secondly, circumcision signifies the excision from the mind of the notion that human beings are able to generate from their own capacities: we are not gods in this matter, and the cutting of the generative organ matches the excision of conceit at this dangerous point (1.10–11).

These last two explanations are certainly allegorical: the lawgivers (*sic*) used circumcision to signify (αἰνίττεσθαι) the correct moral posture (1.9). Would it be possible, then, to adopt the right attitude to pleasure and to God without the inconvenience of circumcision? Everything about Philo's presentation of this matter suggests not. He has taken care to show how literal, physical circumcision is a *peculiarly appropriate* symbol of these moral and religious attitudes: sex is the greatest of the pleasures and the penis is precisely the organ by which men might imagine that they have creative power. But he has also offered these allegorical explanations only after listing other more pragmatic reasons, which he has indicated to be of traditional significance for Jews (1.3). There is little chance, then, that the abstract potential of allegory could subvert the literal practice. In fact, Philo introduced all six explanations *as reasons for retaining and performing* the custom (1.3). Allegory explains circumcision, but does not explain it away.[5]

This careful control of allegory is finely illustrated in the famous passage, *Migr. Abr.* 89–93. Here Philo criticizes a category of people who read the laws allegorically as symbols of noetic truths but are, in his view, 'over-punctilious' about the allegorical sense and 'lax' about the literal. This is the only time when Philo suggests that one can have too much (ἄγαν) of allegory, but the reason for his caution is plain. Nowhere does he deny the truth, even the value, of the allegorical explanations of the law, but he is deeply concerned about a 'pure' allegorical programme which omits, or seriously downgrades, the literal practice.[6] In *Migr. Abr.* 91–92 Philo lists three customs which have allegorical meanings – the Sabbath, the cel-

[5] Note the close parallel in *Quaest. Gen.* 3.48, where the same six explanations are offered (with slight variation in order) and the same distinction is drawn between the first four (as 'widely known facts') and the last two (as 'symbolical things'). In 3.47 Philo explains why for Jews it is only males who receive circumcision: because the male derives more pleasure from sex and because the male provides the 'art and cause' of the offspring (pleasure and pride in causation are what need to be checked). This affirms still more the appropriateness of male circumcision and ties the allegorical meanings still tighter to the literal practice. See the comparison of these passages by R. D. Hecht, 'The Exegetical Contexts of Philo's Interpretation of Circumcision', in F. E. Greenspahn et al., eds., *Nourished with Peace. Studies in Hellenistic Judaism in Memory of Samuel Sandmel* (Chico: Scholars, 1984) 51–79.

[6] Philo's targets here are usually dubbed 'extreme' allegorists, but that is to adopt his partisan perspective; it is preferable to term them 'pure' in that they are devoted purely

ebration of Feasts and circumcision – but insists that the appreciation of their allegorical meaning should not result in the neglect of their literal observance. In relation to circumcision, Philo acknowledges two allegorical explanations of the custom, the same that he offers in *Spec. Leg.* 1.8–11, but he refuses to allow that these could justify the abrogation of a law laid down on this matter. Philo does not disagree with the pure allegorists on an intellectual level (he too looks for the law's invisible inner truths), but he parts company with them in relation to practice and thus with regard to their social commitments.

The way in which Philo argues his case here is particularly fascinating since his argument is directed against facets of his own philosophical stance.[7] In *Migr. Abr.* 89 he suggests that the allegorical and the literal are of equal weight: one should take care of both, the careful investigation of the 'invisible' and irreproachable stewardship of the 'visible'. Similarly in section 93 he likens the allegorical to the soul and the literal to the body: if the body needs to be tended, as the abode of the soul, so must the literal be observed as affording a necessary expression, indeed a clearer conception, of the allegorical. But this is a strange argument for Philo to use. Elsewhere, like a good Platonist, he regards the soul as infinitely more important than the body. In *Det.* 32–34 he *castigates* those who, like Joseph, confuse the various kinds of good and suggest that the body is as important as the soul, to be cared for as the soul's abode: such people require full and careful refutation! Elsewhere, too, he regards the allegorical meaning of the text as far more interesting than the literal: the latter will do for the masses, but the élite are distinguished precisely by their ability to contemplate truths stripped of the body (cf. *Abr.* 147, 236). Such are the natural preferences of Philo as platonist philosopher, whose soul yearns to escape from the confines of the body (e.g. *Leg. All.* 1.105–8; *Heres* 82). In our passage, however, it becomes necessary to 'take thought for the body'; clearly much is at stake in the literal observance of the law.

The other reason Philo offers for observing the law in its literal sense is equally surprising: the opinion of the masses (οἱ πολλοί, *Migr. Abr.* 90, 93). Philo's earlier reference to 'irreproachable stewardship' (ταμιεία ἀνεπίληπτος, 89) had already indicated his prime concern for the preservation of tradition in accordance with the community's expectations. To have regard only to the invisible realities of the law is, Philo suggests, like living a wholly recluse life, without social connection or commitment, and without reference to τὰ δοκοῦντα τοῖς πολλοῖς (90). Philo insists that one should

to the allegorical sense of the law. See further D.M. Hay, 'Philo's References to Other Allegorists' *Studia Philonica* 6 (1979–80) 41–75, at 47–49.

[7] See also D.R. Schwartz, *Studies in the Jewish Background of Christianity* (Tübingen: Mohr Siebeck, 1992) 15–19.

pay regard to these opinions, since 'the sacred word' teaches us to care about a good reputation: it is right to avoid the censure (μέμψεις) of the masses and their accusations (κατηγορίαι, 93). He clearly has in mind here the *Jewish* masses, since only they would criticize the non-observance of the law.

But this is an extraordinary stance for Philo to adopt. Elsewhere he cultivates a lofty disdain for 'the masses' (both Jewish and Gentile). He considers their way of life despicable (*Agr.* 23–25) and advises keeping clear of cities, which are full of turmoil and vulgar crowds devoted to vice (e.g. *Ebr.* 26; *Decal.* 10–13; *Contempl.* 19–20). Why should he now urge paying attention to their normally worthless opinions? And why is he so concerned here with 'reputation'? In other contexts where he adopts his typical Stoic posture, Philo classes fame alongside wealth and public office among the 'external goods' which are not properly so called, since the only true 'good' is that of the soul (e.g. *Det.* 7–9, 122; *Jos.* 54–79; *Sob.* 67–68). Admittedly, he does not always maintain this strict Stoicism and on occasion follows the milder Peripatetic view that all three classes of good (of the soul, of the body and of external things) are of value (e.g. *Leg. All.* 3.86–87; *Conf.* 16–20; *Fug.* 25–38).[8] But to place so high a priority on the maintenance of honour, as something to be positively sought, not merely accepted when offered, and to castigate those who disregard the opinions of the masses for their antisocial tendencies – such are remarkable sentiments for a man who derides those who chase after pleasure, wealth and fame, and who wishes *he* could be alone in some deserted spot, away from the crowds and free to contemplate 'naked truth' (*Spec. Leg.* 3.1–6; *Ebr.* 101–3).

The emphasis on 'reputation' in our passage is partly explicable from its exegetical context. In *Migr. Abr.* Philo is commenting on Gen 12.1–6 and at this point (86) has reached the fourth gift there promised to Abram: μεγαλυνῶ τὸ ὄνομά σου. Hence the reference to the teaching of 'the sacred word' (90): if it was God's gift that Abram have a great name, then clearly reputation is a precious commodity. In a sense, then, the very materiality of the patriarchal stories kicks back against Philo's preferred (though perhaps somewhat posed) Stoic austerity. But Philo could have interpreted this 'great name' in a refined sense, or confined it to the honour one receives from the like-minded élite. It is the very plebeian emphasis in this passage – the concern for the opinion of the masses – which is so remarkable. And for this there can be only one explanation: for all his intellectual élitism, Philo is ultimately committed to the Jewish community, the whole community of all social ranks.

---

[8] Philo's inconsistency is often caused by the variant demands of the biblical text on which he comments; see J. Dillon, *The Middle Platonists: A Study of Platonism 80 B. C. to A. D. 200* (London: Duckworth, 1977) 146–48.

Thus this passage is peculiarly revealing of the social commitments which control Philo's use of allegory. He emerges as a fundamentally conservative figure, concerned to 'steward' inherited traditions and with a profound respect for customs fixed by 'divinely gifted men, who were better than those of our generation' (90). Jewish tradition is sacrosanct, and nothing in Philo's allegorical programme can be allowed to threaten it (cf. *Somn.* 2.123–32 on Sabbath observance).[9] With his faithfulness to tradition goes Philo's deep loyalty to the Jewish community, a loyalty displayed in his willingness to head the delegation of Alexandrian Jews in their dangerous mission to Gaius. Just as the soul needs a body, Philo's allegories needed a social location, and he makes his home without regret among the Jewish ἔθνος, both the Alexandrian community of Jews and the worldwide τὸ Ἰουδαϊκόν whose interests he struggled to protect in Rome (*Legatio* 184). Philo would not flout the conservative instincts of this community or risk their censure for failure to observe the law. A universalizing allegory was acceptable for him only insofar as it supported the particularities of the law, not if it threatened to undermine them.[10]

---

[9] It has sometimes been suggested, on the basis of *Quaest. Exod.* 2.2, that Philo was not rigorous about circumcision in relation to proselytes (e.g. H.A. Wolfson, *Philo* [Cambridge, Mass.: Harvard University, 1948] 2.369–71; N.J. McEleney, 'Conversion, Circumcision and the Law' *NTS* 20 [1974] 319–41, at 328–30; P. Borgen, *Philo, John and Paul*, 61–71, 217–24). But a close reading of the text reveals otherwise. Philo is explaining how the Scriptures (Exod 22.20; 23.9 LXX) can refer to the Israelites in Egypt as 'proselytes' although they were not circumcised (the end of the section confirms that this question is its central theme). The reference to the ψυχὴ τοῦ προσηλύτου (Exod 23.9) helps him to find the answer in the common 'circumcision of pleasures and desires'. But this explanation is required only because Philo knows that proselytes *are* circumcised and thus *prima facie* not comparable to the Israelites in Egypt. The 'not ... but' structure of the statement (προσήλυτός ἐστιν οὐχ ὁ περιτμηθεὶς τὴν ἀκροβυστίαν ἀλλὰ ὁ τὰς ἡδονὰς καὶ τὰς ἐπιθυμίας καὶ τὰ ἄλλα τῆς ψυχῆς) shifts the weight of the meaning of 'proselyte' onto ethical discipline, but only for tactical, exegetical reasons which presuppose that, in its normal sense, 'proselyte' means 'one who has been physically circumcised'. There is thus no justification for finding here a programmatic denial that bodily circumcision was necessary for entry into the Jewish community (*pace* Borgen, 65, 221, proposing a partial parallel with Rom 2.28–29). See also J. Nolland, 'Uncircumcised Proselytes?' *JSJ* 12 (1981) 173–94, at 173–79.

[10] Thus I cannot agree with J.J. Collins' assertion that 'Philo's allegorical understanding of the significance of circumcision inevitably detracts from the importance of the physical rite, even though he defends that too' ('A Symbol of Otherness: Circumcision and Salvation in the First Century', in J. Neusner and E.S. Frerichs, eds., *"To See Ourselves as Others See Us". Christians, Jews, "Others" in Late Antiquity* [Chico: Scholars, 1985] 163–86, at 173). His claim (*ibid.*) that Philo could have agreed with Paul at Rom 2.28–29 is what I wish to contest in this essay.

II. Paul and the Hidden Circumcision of the Heart

In relation to Paul, our main object of scrutiny will be Rom 2.25–29 since these verses take us to the heart of his redefinition of Judaism. They have been taken by Boyarin to exemplify Paul's allegorical hermeneutic, but I shall argue that the comparison with Philo indicates a very different phenomenon. With regard to circumcision Paul is, we shall find, far more radical than Philo in terms of his relationship to the Jewish community; but his hermeneutic is far less acculturated to Hellenism in its intellectual framework. After a preliminary survey of the passage, I will explore both these social and conceptual aspects of Paul's stance.

Romans 2 is a notoriously difficult passage on many counts, but its general line of thought is tolerably clear. Paul is out to destabilize a Jewish sense of confidence that Jews were in a different category from Gentiles in their obedience to the law, or at least in their possession of it. In a series of rhetorical moves, Paul pulls this rug from under the feet of his Jewish dialogue partner stage by stage.[11] Do Jews look down smugly on Gentile immorality? All will answer to God on the day of judgment and on precisely the same terms (2.1–11). But will not Jews inevitably come off better since they have the advantage of possessing the law? Possession is useless without obedience and, in any case, Gentiles have the law written on their hearts, with the internal witness of conscience (2.12–16; see below n. 31). But do not Jews have a superior moral sensibility, since they are instructed in the will of God and capable of instructing others? The Jewish instructor had better watch his own behaviour, since to do those things which you preach against is the ultimate hypocrisy and brings the greatest dishonour on God (2.17–24). Finally, then, what about circumcision (2.25)? Is this not a mark of Jewish distinction which Gentiles, however righteous, simply lack?

Rom 2.25–29 deals with this last question and by the end reaches the most radical conclusion of the whole chapter. Paul starts by applying the conclusions of the argument so far. Jewish privilege is valid only if it is matched by obedience. The mark of circumcision is of benefit only if one keeps the law; otherwise it is, as it were, cancelled out (your circumcised glans becomes foreskinned, 2.25).[12] 2.26 then looks at this matter from the point of view of the Gentile, just as 2.14–15 had done in relation to the law: here, as there, the uncircumcised ('the Gentiles') are represented as capable of keeping the demands of the law. But in the second part of the verse Paul makes a subtle

[11] Since the identity of the partner is made explicit only in 2.17, it is possible that the earlier verses have wider reference (to any 'righteous' persons), while subsequently proving to be of specific relevance to Jews.

[12] On the use of terms here, and their likely polemical nuances in Rome, see J. Marcus, 'The Circumcision and the Uncircumcision in Rome' *NTS* 35 (1989) 67–81.

and extremely important move, suggesting that by this means the Gentile state of uncircumcision could be counted as circumcision. The boldness of this claim is signalled by the fact that it is put in the form of a rhetorical question, οὐχ ἡ ἀκροβυστία αὐτοῦ εἰς περιτομὴν λογισθήσεται; (cf. the equally bold rhetorical questions in 2.21–22). In fact, as Paul well knew, circumcision could hardly count as simply equivalent to law observance. While it entailed commitment to the law (2.25; Gal 5.3), circumcision meant far more than that for Paul's Jewish contemporaries: it was the physical sign of belonging to the covenant of Abraham, the fleshly inscription of genealogical identity marking the ancestral heritage of every male Jew (cf. Phil 3.5).[13] Thus to suggest that non-Jews could be counted as 'circumcised' merely on the basis of 'keeping the just requirements of the law' is an astonishing claim.[14] Most Jews would have agreed with Paul (2.25) that law-observance is a *necessary* condition for the validity of circumcision: without law-observance circumcision will not count. But Paul here suggests that 'keeping the just requirements of the law' is actually a *sufficient* condition as well: with this alone a Gentile may count as if circumcised. It is this slide from necessary to sufficient condition which makes Rom 2.26 so radical, questioning Jewish definitions of identity at their most fundamental level.[15]

Thus the rhetorical question of 2.26 paves the way for the climactic statement of 2.28–29. 2.27 gives the revolutionary notion just mooted a polemical twist: uncircumcised lawkeepers would be judged superior to circumcised lawbreakers, and would themselves have a hand in judging the disobedient Jew! But it is in 2.28–29 that Paul shows just how radical is the conclusion his argument has reached: 'For the Jew is not one evidently so, nor is circumcision evident and in the flesh. The Jew is the hidden Jew and circumcision is of the heart, in the Spirit not in the letter; his praise comes not from humankind but from God'. The Greek here is elliptical, with several missing verbs and nouns, but, given the dangers of interpretative paraphrase, it is as well to use as few additions as possible. Paul boldly takes the terms 'Jew' and 'circumcision' and gives what he considers their

[13] For the Diaspora see Barclay, *Jews* 411–12, and for rabbinic Judaism, L. Hoffman, *Covenant of Blood. Circumcision and Gender in Rabbinic Judaism* (Chicago: University of Chicago, 1996). Josephus considered circumcision essential for ethnic continuity (*Ant.* 1.192).

[14] Of course, circumcision is normally regarded as one of the requirements of the law (e.g. Josephus, *Ant.* 20.44–45; cf. Lev 12.3), so that Paul's argument here (and in 1 Cor 7.19) must have sounded doubly strange.

[15] To take a Christian analogy, all Christian churches would assert that faith is a necessary condition for valid baptism (faith of the parents or sponsors, if not of the baptizand); but few would accept that, so long as one believes, it matters not at all whether one is physically, literally baptized. The physical sacrament represents, among other things, a publicly recognizable sign of belonging to a specific community, just as circumcision signified membership of a discrete ethnic group.

proper definition: to be a Jew is a hidden reality, not an evident one, and to be circumcised is a matter of the heart, not a matter of flesh. In 2.25 fleshly circumcision was of value if accompanied by law-observance. Now it is nothing at all: the 'both ... and' has been transformed into a 'not ... but'. Of course, it is not now an 'either ... or': flesh-circumcision is not excluded by heart-circumcision. But it is simply not worth counting as a circumcision; it has become an entirely superfluous phenomenon.

That we have properly grasped the radical movement of thought in 2.25–29 is confirmed by its sequel. It is because Paul has finally removed *all* the supports on which his Jewish interlocutor can stand that the questions of 3.1 arise: 'Then what is the advantage of the Jew and of what value is circumcision?' As C.H. Dodd observed, 'The logical answer on the basis of Paul's argument is, "None whatever!"'.[16] That Paul does not answer like this, but insists 'Much in every way', is a genuine surprise to the faithful reader of Rom 2. Like Rom 11.17ff., which it prefigures, 3.1–8 introduces a counterpoint which stands in tension with the previous direction of Paul's thought. In any full assessment of Pauline theology, both sides of that dialectic must be taken with full seriousness. Paul's remaining grip on Jewish election privilege must not be allowed to obscure the fact that what he argues in 2.25–29 thoroughly redefines the terms 'Jew' and 'circumcision' in a way which preserves their honorific status but cancels their normal denotation.

Having now surveyed our passage, we may explore in further depth its social ramifications and its conceptual underpinning. In both cases, our comparison with Philo will shed considerable light on Paul.

a) Circumcision and Social Reputation

We noted above that Philo's insistence on the literal, physical practice of circumcision was connected to his concern for the opinion of the Jewish 'masses' and the need to avoid their 'censure'. By contrast, it is striking that Paul, having defined the only circumcision that counts as a matter of heart, not flesh, closes his redefinition of such a 'Jew' with the comment, 'his praise comes not from humankind but from God' (2.29). This statement appears to be the mirror-image of Philo's concern with social regard. If Philo reflects the social pressure from the Jewish community to preserve physical circumcision, Paul insists that the non-literal circumcision he advocates is acknowledged by God, even if it wins no praise from the community.

This final clause in Rom 2.29 has long puzzled commentators. Some have suggested that Paul here plays with etymology and takes the term Ἰουδαῖος

[16] C.H. Dodd, *The Epistle of Paul to the Romans* (London: Hodder & Stoughton, 1932) 43.

to be derived ultimately from the name Judah, which is related to the Hebrew noun הודה (praise).[17] The Hebrew root can be turned both ways (Judah as a token of praise to God, or as the recipient of praise, Gen 29.35; 49.8), but the pun is not transferable into Greek and, to my knowledge, no Greek Jewish text connects the term Ἰουδαῖος to the name Judah, nor either to the notion of being praised.[18] But it is just this sense of receiving praise which is the point in 2.29, and one would have to imagine that Paul here effected an etymological tour de force (including transference from Hebrew to Greek) and somehow hoped his Roman readers might follow his thought. As Ernst Käsemann rightly notes, 'Sollte Pls das wirklich im Sinne haben, dürfte es der römischen Gemeinde kaum verständlich geworden sein'.[19]

Can we suggest an interpretation that *would* make sense to the Roman Christians? Anton Fridrichsen compared our phrase in 2.29 with the Stoic sentiment that one should fulfil one's tasks without regard to human approbation, since fame is not one of the wise man's true goods.[20] Given the religious tinge of Stoicism, it is not surprising to find some Stoics remarking that one should act not with a view to others' opinions but with a view to oneself *and to God* (πάντα ἐμαυτῷ καὶ θεῷ, Epictetus 4.8.17, citing Euphrates); one should be concerned only to do what God will praise (μὴ ποιεῖν ἄλλο ἢ ὅπερ μέλλει ὁ θεὸς ἐπαινεῖν , Marcus Aurelius 12.11). However, Paul's phrase can be given even closer definition if it is regarded not merely as a Stoic commonplace but as reflecting the social reality arising from his redefinition of 'Jew' and 'circumcision'. We found Philo suspending his Stoic disdain for 'reputation' in his desire to keep the respect of the Jewish community. Here Paul takes the moral high-ground (God's approval is more important than human honour) because he knows that his devaluing of fleshly circumcision is extremely unpopular in the Jewish community: those who espouse his redefinition will receive no praise from (Jewish) humanity and will have to look to God alone.

---

[17] C.K. Barrett, *A Commentary on the Epistle to the Romans* (London: A & C Black, 1962) 60; C.E.B. Cranfield, *The Epistle to the Romans* (ICC; Edinburgh: T & T Clark, 1975) 1.175, claiming the word-play is well-known in Judaism, but with no supporting evidence.

[18] Philo associates Judah with praise to God (e.g. *Plant* 135), but not with 'being praised'; cf. Josephus, *Ant.* 1.304; T Jud 1.4; L.L. Grabbe, *Etymology in Early Jewish Interpretation: The Hebrew Names in Philo* (Atlanta: Scholars, 1988) 170.

[19] E. Käsemann, *An die Römer* (HNT 8a; Tübingen: Mohr Siebeck, 1980) 73. J.D.G. Dunn, *Romans 1–8* (WBC 38A; Waco: Word, 1988) 1.123, considers Paul may be using word-play 'even though he could not expect it to be grasped by all or many of his Greek-speaking hearers'. An alternative explanation is preferable if we take Paul to be a purposeful communicator.

[20] A. Fridrichsen, 'Der wahre Jude und sein Lob' *Symbolae Arctoae* 1 (1922) 39–49, with many illustrations from Epictetus.

That this phrase 'whose praise comes from not from humankind but from God' has a concrete social correlation is suggested by the parallel in 1 Cor 4.5, where Paul dismisses the Corinthian opinion of him by appeal to God's (final) judgment: καὶ τότε ὁ ἔπαινος γενήσεται ἑκάστῳ ἀπὸ τοῦ θεοῦ. There an apparently generalized remark about 'praise' is very closely related to social conflict. In our case, however, the 'human' praise with which Paul dispenses is not that of the church, but of the Jewish community, since it is they alone whose praise would be forfeited by his redefinition of Jewish identity.[21] Indeed, two other passages in the NT employ the same motif precisely when referring to the requirement that Christians forfeit honour in the Jewish community. In Matt 6, the hidden practice of prayer, almsgiving and fasting is contrasted with the publicity gained by those who seek to be 'seen' (Matt 6.5, 16) or to be 'honoured' by their fellows (ὅπως δοξασθῶσιν ὑπὸ τῶν ἀνθρώπων, 6.2). When Matthew commends the secret practice which will be honoured by God, it is clear that his Christian addressees are learning to care less about their reputation in the Jewish community: their 'secret piety' is of a piece with their ability to stand independent of the opinion of the 'synagogue'.[22] Secondly, John 12.42–43 narrates that many of the 'leaders' believed in Jesus, but did not confess him publicly because of the Pharisees, lest they be expelled from the synagogue. John comments: ἠγάπησαν γὰρ τὴν δόξαν τῶν ἀνθρώπων μᾶλλον ἤπερ τὴν δόξαν τοῦ θεοῦ (12.43; cf. 5.44). Here, as in Rom 2.29, an apparently general remark about human motivation is intimately linked to social reality, since it is the ability, or inability, to forego the approval of the Jewish community (or 'Pharisees') which is at stake. Those who are concerned for 'human praise' are those who set much store by their social standing in the Jewish community.

[21] Clearly non-Jews would find nothing reprehensible about Paul's non-physical redefinition of 'Jew' and 'circumcision', since the physical rite was an object of ridicule among both Greeks (e.g. Philo, *Spec. Leg.* 1.1–2) and Romans (e.g. Petronius, Frag 37; Martial 9.94). Perhaps there also lies behind Paul's phrase consciousness of an accusation that he has abandoned literal circumcision in order to gain honour (for himself and his converts) from non-Jews (cf. Gal 1.10; 1 Thess 2.4–6). If so, his implied defence is that his redefined Jew is not interested in human praise, only in God's.

[22] This point stands however one views the precise stage of the relationship between 'the Matthean community' and the Jewish synagogues; see G.N. Stanton, *A Gospel for a New People. Studies in Matthew* (Edinburgh: T & T Clark, 1992) 113–68. The parallel between Rom 2.29 and Matt 6 was discussed by E. Schweizer, '"Der Jude im Verborgenen ..., dessen Lob nicht von Menschen, sondern von Gott kommt." Von Röm 2,28f und Mt 6,1–18', in J. Gnilka, ed., *Neues Testament und Kirche. Für Rudolf Schnackenburg* (Freiburg: Herder, 1974) 115–24. However, Schweizer overlooked the social correlation of these phrases and detected only a putative common critique of Judaism as concerned with gaining merit in the eyes of one's neighbours; cf. U. Wilckens, *Der Brief an die Römer* (EKK; Neukirchen-Vluyn: Neukirchener) 1.156.

In the case of John 12 we can see precisely what is at stake: membership in, or expulsion from, the synagogue.[23] Paul's remark in Rom 2.29 has an equally clear social location. Philo, we noted, was concerned to maintain the literal sense of circumcision (and other customs) lest he incur the 'censure' or the 'accusations' of the Jewish community. Elsewhere, in *Quaest. Gen.* 3.52 he discusses why it says of the uncircumcised male in Gen 17.14 that 'his soul shall be destroyed from its kind'. Since this is excessively harsh on an 8-day-old child, Philo notes that the law is popularly considered to apply to the parents: 'those adults who disregard and violate the law are deserving of punishment without regret or remission'. The tone of his remark is reminiscent of the harsh verdict in Jub 15 against those who fail to circumcise their sons: 'There is therefore for them no forgiveness or pardon so that they might be pardoned or forgiven from all of the sins of this eternal error' (15.34). The passage in Jubilees perhaps echoes the Maccabean fury against those who failed to circumcise their children or covered up their circumcision by epispasm (1 Macc 2.42–48), but Philo's comment indicates that Jewish feelings still ran high on this question, even in the Diaspora.[24]

How might this apply to Paul? He was himself circumcised and nowhere states that Jews should *not* circumcise their sons. But he does imply that his views on circumcision have got him into trouble: 'If I still preach circumcision, why am I still persecuted?' (Gal 5.11).[25] That trouble could only derive from the Jewish community and it is not hard to see why. If Paul insists that Gentile converts, whom he treats like proselytes, should not be circumcised, if he thus so relativizes circumcision that for him having a foreskin or not makes no difference at all (Gal 5.6; 6.15; 1 Cor 7.19), if he can state in our passage that flesh circumcision counts for nothing, only heart circumcision, and if he can even equate circumcision on occasion with mutilation (Gal 5.12; Phil 3.2), it is easy to appreciate why he could be regarded as undermining the seriousness with which Jews regarded the custom. If the absence of a foreskin really means nothing, what reason is there, beyond mere convention, for Jews to continue circumcision? It is hardly surprising that, according to Acts, Paul was represented as an apostate who taught

[23] J.L. Martyn, *History and Theology in the Fourth Gospel* (Nashville: Abingdon, 1968), showed that this question underlay many of the Johannine disputes with Jews. His thesis stands, even if the precise correlation with the *birkath ha-minim* is problematic to some degree. [Cf. now J. Marcus, '*Birkat Ha-Minim* Revisited' *NTS* 55 (2009) 523–51.]

[24] See further T. Seland, *Establishment Violence in Philo and Luke. A Study of Non-Conformity to the Torah and Jewish Vigilante Reactions* (Leiden: Brill, 1995).

[25] It is not clear whether 'if I still preach circumcision' represents a current claim about Paul's preaching and, if so, whence it springs. Borgen's thesis (*Philo, John and Paul*, 233–54) that Paul's moral teaching could be understood in a Philonic sense as 'ethical circumcision' is unconvincing; see my *Obeying the Truth. A Study of Paul's Ethics in Galatians* (Edinburgh: T & T Clark, 1988) 50–51.

Diaspora Jews not to circumcise their sons or to follow Jewish customs (Acts 21.21). To pronounce and to adopt the radical view on circumcision advocated in Rom 2.25–29 would certainly elicit a hostile reaction from the Jewish community: such a hidden Jew as Paul advocates would have to reckon on getting his praise from God, not from fellow Jews.

Would difficulties arise also for Jewish and Gentile believers in Rome? This nonchalant attitude to physical circumcision would gain them no critics among Gentiles, but, as for Paul himself, it is the opinion of the Jews which is at issue. We know that circumcision was well-known as a peculiarity of the Jewish community in Rome, and we may guess they were as scrupulous on this matter as they were about Sabbath-observance.[26] Elsewhere Paul indicates that Jewish Christians who associated closely with uncircumcised Gentile converts could come under criticism from fellow Jews on this matter (Gal 6.12; cf. Acts 11.3). The fact that circumcision is not an issue in Rom 14 might indicate that it was not such a flashpoint among the Roman Christians, but it can hardly have been irrelevant to their relations with non-Christian Jews, especially if Joel Marcus is right in his suggestion that ἀκροβυστία and περιτομή were pejorative labels in this context (see n. 11). Thus male Gentile Christians might be made to feel embarrassment, if not shame, at their uncircumcised state, and Jewish Christians find themselves under pressure to reassure their Jewish families and friends that they still cared deeply about one of their key tokens of identity. For both, Paul's radical redefinition of 'Jew' and 'circumcision' could be adopted only at some social cost: they too would have to be content with praise from God.

b) Paul's Hermeneutical Framework

Paul's interpretation of circumcision is thus far more radical in its social effect than that of Philo. But how did Paul reach this position? Is he just a more consistent allegorizer than Philo and has he, like the pure allegorizers whom Philo attacks, simply driven allegory through to its radical conclusions? Or has his hermeneutic a different foundation altogether?

As we noted at the outset, Boyarin considers Rom 2.25–29 a prime example of Paul's Hellenization. There are three main antitheses in 2.28–29:

ἐν τῷ φανερῷ	ἐν τῷ κρυπτῷ
περιτομὴ ἐν σαρκί	περιτομὴ καρδίας
(ἐν) γράμματι	ἐν πνεύματι

[26] Circumcision: Suetonius, *Domitian* 12.2; Petronius, *Satyricon* 102.14; Tacitus, *Histories* 5.5.2; Juvenal, *Sat* 14.99. Sabbath-observance: Philo, *Legatio* 155–58; Ovid, *Ars Amatoria* 1.76; Juvenal, *Sat* 14.105–6 etc.

Boyarin recognizes that the second of these is of Biblical provenance, but he considers the other two 'purely Hellenistic': the first expresses the Hellenistic opposition between inner and outer, and the third must be taken here in a hermeneutical sense, contrasting the 'literal' and the 'spiritual' meaning of circumcision. Thus for Boyarin 'we have an absolutely marvellous syncretism of biblical and Hellenic notions' in which 'the ethical dualisms of the Bible are mapped onto hermeneutical, anthropological, and ontological dualisms of Plato in a way that often seems almost seamless'.[27]

I believe that Boyarin is right to insist that Paul here goes beyond the biblical notion of the circumcision of the heart, but wrong in his identification of the intellectual framework of Paul's radicalism. We may examine each of the antitheses in turn, starting with the least controversial.

a) *Circumcision in the Flesh / of the Heart*. This antithesis clearly reflects the biblical metaphor, found most prominently in the Deuteronomic literature (Deut 10.16; 30.6; Jer 4.4; 9.25–26) but also in priestly sources (Lev 26.41 and Ezek 44.7, 9) and in subsequent Jewish literature (e.g. Jub 1.23; 1QpHab 11.13; cf. Odes of Sol 11.1–3). The sense of the metaphor is not immediately obvious, but the parallel notion of uncircumcised ears (Jer 6.10; 1QH 18.20) and lips (Ex 6.12; 1QH 2.18) suggests the removal of matter which prevents the proper operation of the organ, in this case the receptivity of the heart to God.[28] Thus the metaphor relates to Israel's stubbornness and disobedience (LXX translates 'the foreskin of your heart' as σκληροκαρδία, Deut 10.16; Jer 4.4; cf. 1QS 5.5). To be circumcised in the heart is not a matter of interiority or motivation, but of obedient response to God.[29] Thus it is an appropriate image for Paul to use in a context where he has repeatedly called for obedience, not just knowledge or possession of the law.

Where Paul departs from his biblical predecessors, however, is in the sharpness of the antithesis between the two sorts of circumcision and in the implication that circumcision of the heart, the only sort that matters, is possible for Gentiles just as much as for Jews. While the two circumcisions were sometimes explicitly juxtaposed (Jer 9.25–26; Ezek 44.7, 9), they were never played off against one another, as Paul does here, where the metaphorical sense is allowed to efface the significance of the circumcision of the flesh. Paul's statement is verbally most reminiscent of Jer 9.24–25 (LXX), where God's judgment is announced on the 'circumcised foreskins': ὅτι

[27] *A Radical Jew*, 78–79; Rom 2.25–29 is discussed twice, 78–81 and 93–97.

[28] See R.P. Carroll, *Jeremiah* (OT Library; London: SCM, 1986) 158. The circumcision of fruit trees (Lev 19.23–25) seems to be a different matter, perhaps reflecting an early association of the rite with fertility; so H. Eilberg-Schwartz, *The Savage in Judaism* (Bloomington: Indiana University, 1990) 141–76.

[29] To define its meaning as 'the interior motivation of human actions' (J.A. Fitzmyer, *Romans* [AB 33; New York: Doubleday, 1993] 322) seems to represent an unwarranted idealizing.

πάντα τὰ ἔθνη ἀπερίτμητα σαρκί, καὶ πᾶς οἶκος Ισραηλ ἀπερίτμητοι καρδίας αὐτῶν.[30] This seems to bring both Jew and non-Jew down to the level of the 'uncircumcised' – the Gentile as to the penis, the Jew as to the heart. That is radical enough, from the Jewish point of view, but Paul turns this over into its opposite, declaring that Jew and Gentile can equally count as circumcised before God, provided they are circumcised as to the heart (2.26–29). Theologically, this is consonant with his insistence that both Jew and Gentile are 'under sin' (3.9), but that God, who justifies the ungodly, thus justifies both by his righteousness, through faith (3.27–4.5). Hence, in utilizing the biblical metaphor of heart circumcision, Paul radicalizes its import, not by superimposing some other discourse concerning 'interiority', but by prioritizing the metaphorical sense over the literal and expanding its field of reference to include heart-circumcised Gentiles.

The antithesis here is not the Hellenistic contrast between body and soul, but the old biblical contrast between 'flesh' (penis) and heart. If Paul does not mean by 'heart' what we call the organ which pumps blood, neither would he take it in the abstract sense we give to terms like 'mind' or 'soul'. He shares neither our Cartesian dualism between body and self, nor the Platonic dualism of body and soul. The 'heart' is not some 'inner self' in principle separable from the body, but the willing and thinking person.[31] A circumcised heart is a transformed person, turned towards obedience (cf. Rom 6.17) and faith (Rom 10.8–10). Paul has not altered the biblical metaphor conceptually, but expanded its reference (to apply to Gentiles) and accorded it prior significance over physical circumcision.

b) *Circumcision (ἐν) γράμματι / ἐν πνεύματι.* At first sight, this antithesis appears to support Boyarin's contention of the influence of Hellenistic allegorizing dualism. There has indeed been a lengthy interpretative tradition which finds here (and in 2 Cor 3.6) a reference to contrasting hermeneutical principles, a 'literal' and a 'spiritual' interpretation of circumcision. But this reading is now rightly rejected by most Pauline interpreters, at least with regard to Rom 2.29.[32] Although Paul's use of γράμμα is puzzling, it seems to be shorthand for the Jewish τὰ ἱερὰ γράμματα and thus draws atten-

---

[30] For this complex passage see Carroll, *Jeremiah*, 249–52. The immediately preceding verses concern boasting (cited in 1 Cor 1.31), a theme of obvious relevance to Rom 1–4. That might suggest that this whole passage exercised some direct influence on the paragraph we are considering.

[31] See R. Bultmann, *Theology of the New Testament* (London: SCM, 1952) 220–27 and, for a critique of inappropriate anthropological models, D. Martin, *The Corinthian Body* (New Haven: Yale, 1995) 6–15.

[32] For discussion see, e.g., E. Käsemann, 'The Spirit and the Letter', in *Perspectives on Paul* (London: SCM, 1971) 138–66 and S. Westerholm, 'Letter and Spirit: The Foundation of Pauline Ethics' *NTS* 30 (1984) 229–48. On 2 Cor 3.6, see R. Hays, *Echoes of Scripture in the Letters of Paul* (New Haven: Yale, 1989) 122–53.

tion to the Scriptures as *written* word. In any case, this is not the standard terminology used of 'literal' meanings in relation to allegorical interpretation (cf. Philo, *Migr. Abr.* 89, οἱ ῥητοὶ νόμοι, *Abr.* 236, αἱ ῥηταὶ γραφαί). The use of the same antithesis later in Romans gives us the necessary clue to its meaning, for Christian existence is described in Rom 7.6 as service ἐν καινότητι πνεύματος καὶ οὐ παλαιότητι γράμματος. Here is it absolutely clear that πνεῦμα refers not to some abstract theological principle nor to the anthropological 'spirit' but to the Spirit of God (the phrase anticipates Rom 8.9–17 with its contrast between flesh and the Spirit of God / Christ).[33] In the same way, Phil 3.3 associates the (true) circumcision with 'the Spirit of God'. Correspondingly, γράμμα is not 'the literal', but the law as 'script', inscribed on paper (or stone).

Thus, in Rom 2.28–29 the contrast is not between the literal and the spiritual meanings of circumcision, but between circumcision of the penis as obedience to the written law and circumcision of the heart as effected by the Spirit of God. Paul was not in fact the first to associate the Spirit with circumcision of the heart (see Jub 1.23), a concatenation no doubt facilitated by the association of heart and Spirit in Ezek 36.25–27. His antithesis is allusive, requiring clarification in subsequent chapters, but in the light of the letter as a whole it is clear enough that heart circumcision is here linked to the new eschatological activity of the Spirit.[34]

c) *Evident and Hidden Circumcision.*[35] Does Paul in this emphatic antithesis invoke the Platonic contrast between 'the outer' and 'the inner', the visible world of seeming and the invisible world of truth? Again I think not. It is important to note the precise terms Paul uses: he does not say that the Jew is one 'inwardly' (despite many translations to this effect) nor does he use precisely the 'inner' – 'outer' contrast. His antithesis is between what is ἐν τῷ κρυπτῷ and what is ἐν τῷ φανερῷ. This might seem close enough to the contrast of 'invisible' and 'visible', but a distinction can be maintained.

---

[33] 'Flesh' and 'Spirit' appear in 2.28–29 in indirect, but not direct, antithesis; on the roots and meaning of this word-pair in Pauline theology see my *Obeying the Truth* 178–215 (esp. 185–87 with reference to E. Brandenburger's strained Philonic reading of the Pauline antithesis).

[34] Thus one may say that 2.28–29 refers implicitly to Christian believers (both Jewish and Gentile), although the rhetorical flow of the letter prevents Paul from doing more than set up the category into which he will subsequently fit them. It is just possible that Gentile Christians are in view in 2.14–16; so, e.g., Cranfield, *Romans*, 1.155–63; N.T. Wright, 'The Law in Romans 2', in J.D.G. Dunn, ed., *Paul and the Mosaic Law* (Tübingen: Mohr Siebeck, 1996) 131–50. But the position of φύσει in 2.14 and the lack of definitely Christian vocabulary argue against this; so, e.g., Dunn, *Romans 1–8*, 98–107.

[35] Strictly speaking, 2.28–29 contains the antithesis between 'evident' and 'hidden' Jew, but only 'evident' circumcision. However, the close parallel between 'Jew' and 'circumcision' in 2.28 implies that the 'evident' / 'hidden' antithesis is applicable to circumcision as well, the 'hidden' corresponding to 'the circumcision of the heart'.

In Platonic thought the word-pair 'invisible' and 'visible' were integral to an axiomatic contrast between noetic, incorporeal truths and sensible, corruptible matter. Paul does not adopt that conceptual or linguistic framework. What is 'hidden' for Paul is not what is, by constitution, invisible and incorruptible, but simply what is not (presently) accessible to human eyes. In 2.16 he had referred to human κρυπτά being revealed by God on the Last Day, and elsewhere uses the term in relation to human realities not known to other human beings (cf. 1 Cor 4.5; 14.25). It is a well-known biblical theme that God can see the 'heart' which humans cannot (1 Sam 16.7; 1 Kings 8.39; Prov 15.11 etc.), while the final revelation of 'secrets' is a familiar apocalyptic motif. There is no reason to suspect here some Hellenistic conceptual grid: the hidden circumcision (circumcision of the heart) and the hidden Jew are not noetic entities in some Platonic sense but simply truths not straightforwardly verifiable by other human beings.

Thus in all three cases Boyarin's 'hermeneutical, anthropological and ontological dualisms' turn out to be a mirage (and if so in this test case, probably also elsewhere in Paul). 'Circumcision of the heart' is metaphorical, not literal, but that does not make it *allegorical*; as we noted, Philo used this metaphor among the non-allegorical explanations of circumcision. In truth, Boyarin uses the term 'allegorical' in an extremely wide sense, covering any interpretation which tends towards the 'spiritual', 'ahistorical', 'universal' or 'non-material'.[36] But even on such terms, Paul's language does not fit this definition. His redefined circumcision is not 'spiritual' in a general sense, but effected by the Spirit of God; it is not 'ahistorical' but an eschatological phenomenon. It is not 'universal' in the sense of a universal human condition, only universalizable for Jew and non-Jew; nor yet is it 'non-material' in a Cartesian sense, since it affects the heart, the core of the human being which is all eventually to be redeemed (Rom 8.11, 23).

III. Conclusion

Thus our comparison with Philo sheds significant light on Paul's social and cultural stance. Paul emerges as socially far more controversial than Philo, willing to face Jewish unpopularity where Philo wished to avoid 'censure'. But this is not because Paul has gone beyond Philo in acculturation, accommodating himself (like the pure allegorists) to his cultural milieu. He has not here mapped his biblical themes onto a Hellenistic conceptual grid. However, he *has* radically redefined and reprioritized his inherited tradi-

[36] E.g. *A Radical Jew*, 7–8, 67–68, 74, 80, where even baptism and the Christian community are regarded as 'spiritual' and therefore 'allegorical'.

tion, effecting a fundamental shift in Jewish discourse. In Rom 3.1–8 Paul can still find some place for literal circumcision and the visible Jew, but only on the basis of historical priority (note the past tense in 3.2; cf. 9.3–5) and as bearers of the promises of God. Nothing can be said for them in terms of heart, Spirit and hidden reality, the values of 2.28–29. Even Abraham's circumcision is merely a seal of his prior justification by faith (4.11) and a disposable phenomenon for justified Gentiles. Nothing can hide the fact that the stretching of biblical language in 2.28–29 threatens to subvert the historical continuity of the Jewish tradition.

The source of this hermeneutical revolution lies not in an intellectual programme, the Hellenistic drive for 'universal human essence', but in a whirlwind of events and experiences (the death, resurrection and revelation of Jesus, the Gentile mission and the experience of the Spirit) which have reshuffled all Paul's Jewish convictions. He has neither the consistency nor indeed the intellectual equipment to translate his new experiences and still crystallizing convictions into a Hellenizing programme, although he left enough polysemous statements to encourage several early Christian successors to do just that (e.g. on circumcision, Barn 9.1–9; *Letter of Ptolemy* 5; Justin, *Dial* 41.4; *Gospel of Thomas* logion 53). His radicality lies not in any commitment to 'spiritualization' as such, but in his outrageously novel applications of biblical terms and categories to a new multi-ethnic community which had yet to position itself on the intellectual landscape. Herein lies Paul's innovative genius, or cultural vandalism. His statements and practices were to fascinate and puzzle but generally to scandalize his Jewish contemporaries, precisely because they fitted no recognizable mould and matched no contemporary form of Judaism.[37]

[37] An early draft of this paper was read in a NT graduate seminar at Duke University in November 1996; I am grateful for the advice of those present and the supplementary suggestions of the convener and host, Professor Richard Hays. [On the end of Romans 2, see now T. W. Berkley, *From a Broken Covenant to Circumcision of the Heart: Pauline Exegesis in Rom 2:17–29* (Atlanta: Society of Biblical Literature, 2000).]

4. Matching Theory and Practice

Josephus' Constitutional Ideal and Paul's Strategy in Corinth

I. Comparing Josephus and Paul

It is no surprise that Paul's letters to the church in Corinth continue to attract the interest of historians and theologians. The issues which Paul addresses in these letters reveal so much in detail about the social realities of an early Christian community that they invite historical and sociological reconstructions of Corinthian church life from many different angles. But they also reveal much about Paul. Precisely because he faced so many and such disparate difficulties in Corinth, Paul was forced here to reinscribe the contours of the Christian community in both theoretical and practical terms. By their very nature, Paul's letters represent follow-up, rather than initiatory, activity: they show us how he built on foundations which he and others had already laid. Yet, in these letters to Corinth, Paul feels himself forced so often to return to basics that we are given here a rare glimpse of his strategic priorities in the forging and forming of a Christian community. Here he is not so much nurturing the mature as feeding the new-born with their baby milk (1 Cor 3:1–4). Thus, although some of the issues addressed in these letters may be peculiar to the Corinthian church, the principles with which Paul responds are more general than the case to which he applies them. Hence these letters provide a rich insight into Paul's social and symbolic construction of a Christian community (in theological terms, his ecclesiology).

Paul's strategies for the establishment of his socially anomalous 'assemblies' (ἐκκλησίαι) are not easy to analyse. Comparison with contemporary social phenomena, such as the vastly diverse 'clubs' and 'associations', can be illuminating to a degree, but it is difficult to identify the key structuring elements which should form the focus of comparison between a 'church', on the one hand, and the numerous varieties of club, society, synagogue, or religious association on the other: they are always alike in some respects and unlike in others, but it is hard to establish which of these is socially most significant. It is perfectly proper to sharpen this historical analysis with the aid of perspectives developed in sociology and anthropology, as has sometimes been achieved to great effect. But these latter perspectives can be distorted by their refinement in cultural and social conditions (whether Western or pre-industrial) which are very remote from the world inhabited by the earliest Christians. Thus, the question arises: are there any useful analytical tools for social analysis available in the cultural matrix of the first Christians? In particular, can Paul's strategies in the formation of his churches be illuminated with the aid of culturally contiguous analyses of social formation?

One obvious candidate here is the Graeco-Roman tradition of political philosophy focused on civic constitutions. This came to its full flowering in Plato's *Republic* and *Laws*, and in Aristotle's *Politics*, though it continued to develop in derivative ways in later Greek and Roman political analysis.[1] At first sight this tradition appears less than pertinent, since these constitutional analyses cover topics such as political systems of government, suitable terrain for cities, appropriate terms for citizenship, and proper systems of education, all of which seem far removed, in scale and function, from Paul's house-churches. Although Paul can give these churches a quasi-political label (ἐκκλησίαι), and can utilize other political *topoi* in battling against their endemic disunity, the structures and goals of his communities are very different from the 'city-states' discussed in the classical tradition, and if they have a πολίτευμα it is, he says, in heaven (Phil 3:20).[2]

Nonetheless, some forms of 'constitutional' analysis are less remote than we might imagine. The term πολιτεία was elastic, ranging in meaning all the way from 'form of government' to something as loose as 'pattern of social life'; and the ancient Greek tradition of 'political' analysis was correspondingly adaptable. Thus, if we could identify examples of such 'constitutional' analysis which are broad enough to apply to societies less extensive and less complex than states, they might suggest fruitful questions for the analysis of Paul's community-formation.

The example which I wish to use in this essay is found in Josephus' apologetic work, *Contra Apionem*. Josephus is clearly conversant with the Greek political tradition, and at several points may be drawing more or less directly on Plato's *Laws*.[3] Earlier, in his *Antiquities*, he had presented his summary of the laws as Moses' 'constitution' (4.196–301), and at several

[1] Examples include Cicero, *De legibus* and Plutarch, *De tribus rei publicae generibus*. See T. A. Sinclair, *A History of Greek Political Thought* (London: Routledge & Kegan Paul, 1951). [Cf. C. Rowe and M. Schofield, eds., *The Cambridge History of Greek and Roman Political Thought* (Cambridge: Cambridge University Press, 2000).]

[2] The political aspects of Paul's church-formation have received only sporadic discussion; see e.g. E. Judge, 'Contemporary Political Models for the Inter-Relations of the New Testament Churches' *RTR* 22 (1963) 65–75; M. Mitchell, *Paul and the Rhetoric of Reconciliation* (Louisville: Westminster/John Knox, 1991).

[3] See C. Schäublin, 'Josephus und die Griechen' *Hermes* 110 (1982) 316–41; C. Gerber, *Ein Bild des Judentums für Nichtjuden von Flavius Josephus. Untersuchungen zu seiner Schrift Contra Apionem* (Leiden: Brill, 1997) 226–43.

points referred to Israel's political system with reference to the debate about the best system of government (e.g. *Ant.* 4.223–224).[4] However, in *Contra Apionem* Book 2, the specifically political dimensions of this topic are reduced, and Josephus utilizes the tradition for a broader depiction of the structural characteristics of the Jewish 'way of life'. This partially depoliticized version of the 'constitutional' tradition might, therefore, be of greater value for our purposes than its original application to city-states or nations.

Josephus' use of this tradition is slanted by his apologetic interest in demonstrating that Jews have the best and most balanced constitution of all. In one respect this makes his material all the more interesting for our comparison with Paul, since Jewish communities (at least those in the Diaspora, where Josephus writes) were in many respects the closest social analogue to the churches founded by Paul, and the histories of synagogue and church were in many places intertwined. In another respect allowing Josephus to set our agenda may be problematic if it does not raise some of the questions relevant to Paul, or raises them in ways which place undue emphasis on distinctively Jewish features. Nonetheless, I believe the experiment is worth conducting as a heuristic exercise which at least helps us see how others might analyse and assess Paul's church-forming strategies.

Such an experiment also raises some of the questions concerning Paul's cultural placement which permeate current research. On one side of our comparison we have a Diaspora-resident Jew whose loyalty to his Jewish tradition is expressed precisely in his creative use of an ancient Greek tradition (a use which is also perhaps slanted specifically for Roman readers): such a cultural mix clearly defies neat categorizations such as 'Hellenism' and 'Judaism'. On the other, we have another Diaspora-resident Jew whose social policy, I shall argue, differs from Josephus' at that point where he strives to enable a community of both Jew and Gentile, and attempts to forge them together into a new and culturally indeterminate (or at least, under-determined) 'church'.

II. Josephus and the Jewish Constitution

Josephus' *Contra Apionem* is the last of his extant works, written at the very end of the first century CE. It is designed to make up for the less than enthusiastic reception of his *Antiquities* and to refute, in a systematic manner, some of the most influential critics of Jews and their culture. After the lengthiest of these refutations, directed against Apion (2.1–144), Josephus

[4] See D.R. Schwartz, 'Josephus on the Jewish Constitutions and Community' *SCI* 7 (1983–84) 30–52.

turns to face 'Apollonius Molon, Lysimachus and certain others' (2.145), but changes tactic from a point-by-point defence to a positive portrayal of Moses and the 'constitution' he founded. It appears that Apollonius had engaged in derogatory comparisons between Jewish customs and the laws or constitutions of other nations (*c. Apion.* 2.150, 238, 270), so Josephus takes the opportunity to engage in a comparative exercise of his own. In this context he can afford to abstract this analysis from the historical vicissitudes of Jewish history and he here provides a generalized and idealized portrait whose focus is less on political governance, and not only on the content of the Jewish laws, but also on the structure or framework in which the constitution operates.[5]

When Josephus outlines the accusations levelled at Moses and the laws, he announces his plan to defend the latter by describing in brief both 'the whole structure of our constitution' (ἡ ὅλη ἡμῶν κατάστασις τοῦ πολιτεύματος) and its individual parts (2.145).[6] Thus, after a short presentation of Moses' virtues (2.151–163) and before his summary of the particular laws (2.190–218), Josephus outlines the 'structure' of the Mosaic constitution in terms which are of particular importance to our enquiry (2.164–189).[7]

The most famous feature of this outline is Josephus' coinage of the term θεοκρατία (2.165), which is clearly intended to trump all other constitutions, pure or mixed. The term is often taken to signify the rule of the priests ('hierocracy'), and Josephus does finish this section with reference to their putative political control (2.185–188). Its primary meaning, however, is something far more abstract and philosophical. Ascribing the sovereignty and power (τὴν ἀρχὴν καὶ τὸ κράτος) to God (Josephus' *definition* of 'theocracy', 2.165) means recognizing God's universal (and particular) providence (2.166), and acknowledging his omniscience (2.166), oneness and transcendence (2.167). Hence, Josephus claims, the chief and central virtue in Judaism is piety (εὐσέβεια, 2.170–171). This already indicates that Josephus' primary interest here is not political theory in the narrow sense

[5] On the relationship between this utopian depiction of the constitution and the emphases of Josephus' earlier works, see T. Rajak, 'The *Against Apion* and the Continuities in Josephus's Political Thought', in S. Mason, ed., *Understanding Josephus. Seven Perspectives* (Sheffield: Sheffield Academic, 1998) 222–46. [See now my commentary on this text, J. M. G. Barclay, *Flavius Josephus, Translation and Commentary: Volume 10, Against Apion* (Leiden: Brill, 2007); cf. F. Siegert, ed., *Flavius Josephus, Über die Ursprünglichkeit des Judentums: Contra Apionem* (2 vols.; Göttingen: Vandenhoeck & Ruprecht, 2008).]

[6] Josephus appears to use the terms πολιτεία and πολίτευμα as synonyms; their usage is intertwined throughout the second half of Book 2 (πολιτεία: 2.188, 222, 226, 256, 264, 273, 287; πολίτευμα: 2.145, 164–165, 184, 250, 257).

[7] As well as κατάστασις (2.145, 184), Josephus uses τρόπος (2.170) and τάξις (2.250) to refer to this 'structure'; cf. *Ant.* 1.10: ἡ διάταξις τῆς πολιτείας.

(the distribution of power within the Jewish 'state'), but the shape of Jewish life as governed by its monotheistic beliefs and God-given laws.[8]

Josephus was conversant enough with Greek philosophy to recognize that Judaism was hardly unique in affirming the providence and transcendence of God. He accepts that Pythagoras, Anaxagoras, Plato and the Stoics held similar views on the nature of God, though he hints (following an old Jewish contention) that they borrowed such truths from Moses (2.168). However, he immediately identifies the locus of Jewish superiority in this matter: where others kept their philosophical discoveries to the élite, Moses embedded such truths in the lives of the masses. The statement Josephus makes at this point skilfully combines the themes he will develop in the rest of this section of his discourse, and is worth quoting in full:[9]

> (169) But our legislator, by making practice conform to the laws,[10] not only convinced his contemporaries but also implanted this belief about God in their descendants of all future generations, such that it could not be shaken (ἀμετακίνητον). (170) The reason is that the very shape of the legislation makes it long-lasting and continually accessible to everyone. For he did not make piety (εὐσέβεια) an element of virtue, but viewed and established the other virtues together as elements of piety – that is, justice, moderation, endurance and harmony (συμφωνία) among citizens in all affairs. (171) All activities and occupations, and all speech, have reference to our piety towards God: he did not leave any of these unscrutinized (ἀνεξέταστον) or imprecise (ἀόριστον).

There are several points made here at once: that Moses ensured a match between the theory enshrined in the law and the practice of that law, that his legislation was transmitted to future generations, and that it remained permanently unalterable. The last two are dependent on the first, in that the embedding of belief or rule in action is what ensures its transferability and permanency. Josephus himself unpacks these intertwined claims in the

---

[8] On Josephus' coinage see Y. Amir, 'Θεοκρατία as a Concept of Political Philosophy: Josephus' Presentation of Moses' *Politeia*', *SCI* 8–9 (1985–88) 83–105. The common but false assumption that Josephus refers primarily to the rule of priests is evidenced, for instance, in H. Cancik, 'Theokratie und Priesterherrschaft: Die mosaische Verfassung bei Flavius Josephus, c. Apionem 2,157–198', in J. Taubes, ed., *Religionstheorie und politische Theologie* (München/Paderborn/Wien/Zürich: Wilhelm Fink/Ferdinand Schöningh, 1987) 3.65–77.

[9] All translations are my own. [For a slightly modified translation, with commentary, see now Barclay, *Flavius Josephus, Translation and Commentary: Against Apion*, 265–67.]

[10] ἅτε δὴ τὰ ἔργα παρέχων σύμφωνα τοῖς νόμοις. This is the text quoted in Eusebius, *Praep. evang.* 8.8.6, and adopted in the edition by S. A. Naber (Leipzig: Teubner, 1896); the editions by B. Niese (Berlin: Weidmann, 1889), H. St. J. Thackeray (LCL; Cambridge, Mass.: Harvard University, 1926) and T. Reinach (Budé; Paris: Société d'édition "Les belles lettres", 1930) follow L and the 6th century Latin translation in reading τοῖς λόγοις for τοῖς νόμοις. [Cf. now Siegert, ed., *Flavius Josephus, Über die Ursprünglichkeit des Judentums*, 1.189.]

paragraphs which follow (2.170–183), whose logical interconnection may be set out as follows:

The Principle:	Matching Theory and Practice
The Mechanisms:	1. Thorough Education in the Laws
	2. Comprehensive Application of the Laws
	3. Unquestioning Adherence to the Laws
The Result:	Harmony in Belief and Practice

It is clear that Josephus is describing an ideal, which we know, even from his own writings, was hardly realized in practice: the Josephus who here claims total harmony in belief and practice elsewhere describes fundamental differences in both spheres between the four Jewish 'philosophies' (e.g. *Ant.* 18.11–25)! Nonetheless, it is worth examining in more detail how he thinks this ideal is enshrined in the Jewish 'constitution', so that we can compare it with the structural ideals to be found in Paul's letters to Corinth. Our aim is certainly *not* to contrast Josephus' ideal with Paul's problems in the church in Corinth, but to juxtapose the aims and characteristics of Josephus' Jewish constitutional ideals with the comparable ideals expressed or implied in Paul's letters. If the constitutional shape of Paul's churches is different in theory and/or practice, it is important to perceive how and why this is so.

1. The foundational principle of *matching theory and practice* is explained immediately by Josephus in 2.171–174. There he distinguishes two possible modes of παιδεία (education) or κατασκευὴ περὶ τὰ ἤθη (moral formation): one utilizes λόγος (verbal instruction) and the other ἄσκησις τῶν ἠθῶν (practical moral training, 2.171).[11] Following a well-established topos in Greek literature, he illustrates this distinction by contrasting Spartans and Cretans on the one hand, with Athenians and 'almost all the rest of the Greeks' on the other. Spartans and Cretans employ ἔθη (customs), not λόγοι (words) in their education, while Athenians and the rest give instructions about what one must or must not do through laws (νόμοι) but neglect accustoming people to these requirements through deeds (τοῦ δὲ πρὸς αὐτὰ διὰ τῶν ἔργων ἐθίζειν ὠλιγώρουν, 172).

'Word' and 'deed' are a standard pairing in Greek, as in many other traditions (elsewhere in *c. Apion.* at 2.233, 241, 292). The contrast 'in word but not in deed' was a common way of expressing unreality (e.g. 2.241), while the harmony of word and deed was a recognized sign of a fully rounded character.[12] Josephus here combines two aspects of a hackneyed contrast be-

[11] It is not easy to decide between the textual variants at this point (between ἤθη and ἔθη), which in any case make little difference to the sense.

[12] Philo praises Moses' character (though not precisely his constitution) for its harmony of λόγος and βίος, especially the way Moses exemplified his philosophical creed in his daily life (διὰ τῶν καθ' ἑκάστην ἡμέραν ἔργων, *Mos.* 1.29); cf. Iamblichus, *Vita Pyth.* 170. At *Praem* 80–84 Philo utilizes the threefold 'mouth, heart and hand' of Deut 30:14 (LXX)

tween Spartans and Athenians. In the first place, the Spartans were famous for their pithy but unsophisticated style of speech; their image was as people of deeds (especially military deeds) but few words.[13] On the other hand, the unique system of Athenian democracy fostered an image of Athens as the scene of continual debate and intense competition in rhetorical prowess. The contrast could be variously evaluated: were the Spartans simply uneducated, or were they admirably short on words and long on disciplined obedience?[14] Secondly, Josephus builds on the contrast between the Spartan lack of written laws and the Athenian fetish for the recording and publication of theirs. Plutarch sums up a long line of commentators in insisting that Lycurgus (the Spartan legislator) did not put his laws in writing, since 'he reckoned that the guiding principles of most importance for the happiness and excellence of a state would remain securely fixed if they were embedded in the citizens' character and training' (ἀγωγή, *Lycurgus* 13).

Josephus' exploitation of these clichés is rhetorically effective, since he can combine the near universal admiration of the Spartan constitution with the widespread assumption that laws are more secure if fixed in writing (cf. 2.155). On the one side he lines up λόγος (word, speech, articulation) and νόμος (law); on the other, ἔργα (actions), ἄσκησις (practice/training) and ἔθη (customs). Jews, he claims, are guilty of neither form of one-sidedness since Moses took great care to combine both features (2.173): he did not leave ἄσκησις 'dumb' (κωφή, that is, without verbal support), nor did he leave the verbal articulation of the law (ὁ τοῦ νόμου λόγος) 'ineffectual' (ἄπρακτος, that is, without practical instantiation). Thus the Jews' constitution avoids the pitfalls of other constitutions while combining their strong points.[15]

Josephus' rhetoric artfully exploits the breadth and ambiguity of his terms, but his main point is clear enough: that the theory which Jews embrace (about God, themselves or their moral norms) is not merely talked or written about, but enmeshed in the practices and customs of Jewish life. This principle of matching theory with practice is, for Josephus, the foundation of all that follows: it is because the Jews have an articulated system of

---

to extol the Jewish unity of word, thought and action. On such as an ideal combination see Schäublin, 'Josephus und die Griechen', 334–5.

[13] βραχυλόγος, Plato, *Laws* 641 e etc.; the epithet λακωνικός is already proverbial in Plato. See the classic statements on this Spartan characteristic in Plutarch, *Lycurgus* 19–20.

[14] 'Uneducated' Spartans (Isocrates); disciplined obedience (Xenophon, Plutarch and many others).

[15] Josephus' skill in deploying these contrasts in this context is clear from the fact that elsewhere he can put them to rather different use. Thus at 2.292 he claims that Jews are unsophisticated in verbal tricks, while always supported by actions (ἀσόφιστοι λόγων παρασκευαῖς, τοῖς ἔργοις ἀεὶ βεβαιούμενοι); the latter, in fact, constitute clearer testimony than any document (τῶν γραμμάτων ἐναργέστερα).

'theory' (the laws / Scriptures) that it can be thoroughly learned; it is because they are concerned to apply it that it is practised with comprehensive range; it is because it is fixed both in writing and in custom that it remains unalterable; and it is because of their commonly-agreed doctrine and commonly-practised norms that Jews enjoy such harmony. Indeed, Josephus ties theory with practice even more securely by showing that the *content* of the 'theory' (the belief that God watches over everything) provides, in Jewish piety, the strongest sanction and the ultimate goal for every detail of Jewish practice. As he puts it at 2.181 (cf. 2.171, cited above):

> Nor will anyone see any difference in our living habits: we all share common practices and all make the same affirmation about God, in agreement with the law, that he watches over everything. As for the habits by which we live, that everything is geared towards piety one could gather even from the women and slaves.

2. If theory and practice are to match, it is clearly essential that the practitioners should know the theory, and Josephus thus devotes a paragraph to the topic of Moses' laws as the focus of a *thorough education* (2.175–178). As we saw, Josephus' programmatic statement presented Moses' achievement as 'implanting' the law in the lives of his people (ἐνέφυσεν, 2.169), and Josephus can go on to claim that Jews need no legal experts since everyone knows the laws 'more readily than his own name': they are so thoroughly learnt from the very first moment of consciousness as to be 'engraved on our souls' (ἐν ταῖς ψυχαῖς ὥσπερ ἐγκεχαραγμένους, 2.178). The reference in this sentence to the first moment of consciousness (ἀπὸ τῆς πρώτης αἰσθήσεως) indicates that Josephus is thinking in the first place of those crucial stages of primary socialization which take place in childhood. Later, in his summary of the law, he boasts of the Jews' concern for the reading ability of children, with its twin focus on 'the laws and the exploits of our forebears': the latter are to be imitated, while the former are the basis of an education which guarantees against transgression or ignorance (2.204; cf. 1.60).

All constitutional theorists were concerned, of course, with the education of citizens, especially of those who were to take leading political roles.[16] It was here that the virtues necessary for the good functioning of the state were to be learnt. Josephus' reference to the education of children in the exploits of the 'forebears' (οἱ πρόγονοι) reflects the importance of ethnic continuity, by which the 'ancestral customs' (τὰ πάτρια, 2.182, 237) are passed down from generation to generation, especially within the household (2.169).[17]

---

[16] See, e.g., Plato, *Republic* 376e–412b, *Laws* book 7 (788a–824c), Aristotle, *Politics* books 7–8 (1323a–1342b). Josephus himself notes the importance of this topic to Plato (*c. Apion.* 2.257).

[17] On the significance of this theme in Josephus see B. Schröder, *Die 'väterlichen Gesetze'. Flavius Josephus als Vermittler von Halachah an Griechen und Römer* (Tübingen: Mohr Siebeck, 1996).

But if in this respect the Jews had much in common with non-Jews (Josephus refers to the Athenians' πάτριος πολιτεία at 2.264), Josephus wishes to claim superiority in another. At 2.175 he boasts in the Jewish use of the law as teaching-material (παίδευμα) which is heard, not just on an occasional basis, but every week, since the Sabbath affords freedom from work for the purpose of gathering to hear and accurately learn the law (ἀκριβῶς ἐκμανθάνειν, 2.175; the verb is repeated in 2.178).[18] Like Philo (e.g. *Legatio* 156–157, 312–313; *Spec. Leg.* 2.63–64), Josephus celebrates the Sabbath gathering as an educational institution, signalling the Jews' unique concern to internalize the laws of their constitution.[19]

Josephus' claim that this system of education means that 'it is rare to find a transgressor and impossible to excuse oneself from punishment' (2.178) is an obvious idealization. Bur our concern is to delineate his ideal, and the important point is that Josephus' ideal constitution contains educational instruments as routine events embedded in the rhythm of Jewish life.

3. The matching of theory with practice requires that, for Josephus, the internalization of the laws involves not just the acquisition of knowledge about them, but also their *comprehensive application* in daily life. We have seen him make a claim to this effect in general terms: that 'all activities and occupations, and all speech' have reference to piety (2.171, cited above; cf. 2.156). However, he also spells this out in revealing particularity in 2.173–174 where he illustrates the practical effect of the law from the earliest stages of infancy:

> Starting from the very beginning of our upbringing and from the mode of life practised by each individual in the home (ἀπο τῆς κατὰ τὸν οἶκον ἑκάστων διαίτης), he [Moses] did not leave anything, even the minutest detail, free to be determined by the wishes of those concerned. Even in relation to food, what we should refrain from and what we should eat, the company we keep in our daily lives, and our application to work and, conversely, rest, he himself set the law as the boundary and rule, so that we might live under it as if it were our father and master and commit no sin either wilfully or from ignorance.

---

[18] In *Antiquities* Book 4, Josephus had not attributed this custom to Moses. There mention is made only of the septennial reading of the law (4.209–211; based on Deut 31:10–13), though its effect is described in similar terms as an engraving on souls (ταῖς ψυχαῖς ἐγγραφέντας , 4.210). For Josephus' pride in the Sabbath readings cf. *Ant.* 16.43.

[19] K.-W. Niebuhr thus rightly characterizes the Sabbath gatherings for instruction in the law: 'Sie bilden den Kristallisationskern für die Bewahrung jüdischer Identität unter den Alltagsbedingungen der Diaspora' ('Identität und Interaktion. Zur Situation paulinischer Gemeinden im Ausstrahlungsfeld des Diasporajudentums', in J. Mehlhausen, ed., *Pluralismus und Identität* [Gütersloh: Chr. Kaiser, 1995] 339–59, esp. p. 346). See further, J. M. G. Barclay, *Jews in the Mediterranean Diaspora from Alexander to Trajan (323 BCE–117 CE)* (Edinburgh: T & T Clark, 1996) 412–13, 416–17.

The three items given special mention here are perhaps of particular importance: dietary rules, limits in social intercourse and the regular Sabbath rest.[20] These all concern aspects of domestic routine which, as regular and intimate features of everyday life, have a marked and pervasive influence on life-patterns. What is more, the effort required to maintain these (cf. 2.234–235), especially as a minority cultural tradition, would do much to enforce the social distinctiveness of the community which practices such rules. Their special function as 'boundary marks' is thus clear. Outsiders confirm, in their comments on Jewish food, marriage and Sabbath laws, that these distinctive Jewish practices made a considerable social impact.[21] Their significance is also recognized by Josephus when he affirms (against detractors) the readiness of Jews to show kindness to outsiders and to 'welcome those who wish to come and live under the same laws as us', but adds the significant proviso that 'he [Moses] does not want those who approach us on a casual basis to mix with us at an intimate level' (2.209–10).

It is its imprint on the regular intimacies of daily life which makes the law's comprehensive application of such importance. It is not just the detailed definition of the law which matters here, but its hold on features of life which determine the everyday lifestyle of a Jew. Josephus is thus right to say that, according to his ideal, the Jewish constitution contained the means by which it could be made broadly effectual.

4. An important supplement to the above is the significance which Josephus attaches to *unquestioning adherence to the law*. This theme was adumbrated in Josephus' programmatic statement that the law is ἀμετακίνητον (2.169; cf. 2.234, 254). The term seems to imply both that the laws cannot be altered over time and that it is not open to individuals to interpret or circumvent them at will. The first sense is taken up in the continual refrain of *Contra Apionem*, that the Jews are ever faithful to their laws, willing even to die rather than transgress them; they see no benefit in updating their constitution or abandoning their laws (e.g. 2.232–235, 271–275, 277; cf. Philo, *Mos.* 2.12–16). Indeed, Josephus uses this virtue to counter the otherwise damaging charge that Jews have been signally lacking in cultural creativity (the charge is mentioned in 2.148 and countered in 2.182–183). The second sense implies that the law cannot be subverted by individual choice or 'freedom of opinion'. We have seen this point spelled out in 2.173, where Josephus insists that Moses 'did not leave anything, even the minut-

[20] The same three recur, alongside others, in a later list of customs which Josephus regards as especially demanding (signalling that the Jews' capacity for endurance was even greater than that of the Spartans!): there he highlights simplicity of diet, restraint of greed and extravagance, care in matters of food and drink, restrictions in sexual relations and the Sabbath rest (2.234–235). [See below, chapter 16.]

[21] See Barclay, *Jews in the Mediterranean Diaspora*, 411–12, 434–42.

est detail, free to be determined by the wishes of those concerned' (οὐδὲν οὐδὲ τῶν βραχυτάτων αὐτεξούσιον ἐπὶ ταῖς βουλήσεσι τῶν χρησομένων κατέλιπεν, cf. 2.234).

The key term here, αὐτεξούσιον, is highly charged. Josephus uses it elsewhere for the failure of military discipline (*Bell.* 3.86; 5.556) and for the dangerous freedom of autocratic power (*Ant.* 15.266), but its most potent use is in his expanded analysis of the revolt of Zimri (Zambrias) concerning intermarriage with Midianite women (*Ant.* 4.131–55, based on Numbers 25). The space which Josephus gives to the seductions of the Midianite women, and the speech he accords to Zambrias justifying his revolt against Moses' laws, indicate the paradigmatic significance of this episode for Josephus, and we may surely detect here echoes of debates in Josephus' contemporary Judaism.[22] Zambrias accuses Moses of accumulating tyrannical power and taking away from his people 'the sweetness and independence of lifestyle, which is enjoyed by free men who have no master' (τὸ ἡδὺ καὶ τὸ κατὰ τὸν βίον αὐτεξούσιον, ὃ τῶν ἐλευθέρων ἐστὶ καὶ δεσπότην οὐκ ἐχόντων, *Ant.* 4.146). It is this independence ('self-determination') which Josephus sees as the polar opposite to submission to the law, and it is not surprising that in extolling the strict discipline of the Jews, Josephus should hail the law as κανών, πατήρ and δεσπότης (*c. Apion.* 2.174). His ideal Judaism does not accord value to individual freedom in interpretation or adaptation of the law: it binds the community together precisely by binding them all to a single authority.

5. Thus we reach Josephus' constitutional goal: *harmony in belief and practice*. The importance of this theme is indicated not only by the fact that Josephus here devotes a paragraph to its explication (2.179–181), but also by his subtle alteration of the list of virtues in 2.170, so that the last is not φρόνησις or its equivalent (as we might expect from the Greek tradition) but συμφωνία (harmony). The 'unanimity' which Josephus here describes (ὁμόνοια, 2.179, 283, 294) matches the traditional concern among constitutional theorists that the state not descend into discord or factionalism (στάσις), but is internalized to an extraordinary degree by his insistence that it is operative in belief as well as in practice. Tying together his twin themes of 'theory' and 'practice', Josephus locates the unity of Jews both in their shared affirmations about God (εἷς λόγος περὶ θεοῦ – e.g. his existence and providence) and in their common practices (κοινὰ ἔργα). Although it remains at a high level of generalization, the breadth of this claim is striking.

---

[22] See W.C. van Unnik, 'Josephus' Account of the Story of Israel's Sin with Alien Women in the Country of Midian (Num. 25.1 ff.)', in M.S.H.G. Heerma von Voss, ed., *Travels in the World of the Old Testament* (Assen: Van Gorcum, 1974) 241–61.

It is not difficult to trace how, on Josephus' account, such constitutional harmony comes to be. Because theory and practice match, both spheres are equally affected, and mutually reinforcing. Because all Jews are educated in the law, all have the same outlook. Because the law covers every department of life, the unanimity in practice is comprehensive. And because no freedom of will is allowed, all bear allegiance to a common authority. This is, of course, Josephus' utopian scenario. He gives no recognition here to the Jews who strayed from the law to varying degrees, or, more significantly, to the necessary role of interpretation with regard to the common authoritative tradition, which helped make Judaism in antiquity so diverse. But it is Josephus' ideal which is our present concern, and one may grant him at least this: that his portrait of the Jewish constitution is carefully and consistently worked out, and that he puts his finger on certain structural elements in the Jewish way of life which at least bear the potential to function in the ways he describes.

III. Paul and the Constitution of the Church in Corinth

In turning to Paul, we may recall that our purpose is not to contrast the difficulties Paul encountered in his church in Corinth with the ideal constitution delineated by Josephus: that would be manifestly unfair to Paul, or to his converts. Rather, our task is to place Paul's ideals alongside those of Josephus, to compare their aims and structural characteristics. It is clear, for instance, that Paul places as high a value on unity, even unanimity, as Josephus: his aim is that his converts be 'of one mind and one opinion' (1 Cor 1:10). As Margaret Mitchell has shown, this concern for concord within the church permeates not only 1 Corinthians 1–4, but also the rest of that letter, and is treated by Paul in terms closely resembling the discussion of this topic in politics.[23] Thus it is reasonable to ask: do Josephus and Paul agree about the means towards this shared goal, or are their constitutional ideals differently structured?

Since Paul is not writing a treatise on this subject, we will have to discern his intentions in rather more subtle ways than was necessary in the case of Josephus. For our purposes is it fortunate that, as noted above, the Corinthian church forced him to redescribe the basics of his ecclesiology and to define his ideals of church life on a wide range of topics. Thus we have many explicit comments from which to work and can view his social edifice from enough angles to gain an adequate view of its shape. On occasion we may wish to supplement the material from the Corinthian correspondence with

---

[23] Mitchell, *Paul and the Rhetoric of Reconciliation*.

insights from other Pauline letters, but we will take as our starting point in each case the blueprints, goals and programmatic statements which Paul offers to the Corinthian believers.

Where we find Paul differing from Josephus it is important to enquire whence this difference arises. Does Paul's constitution match that of Josephus in general shape, differing only in its departure from particular Jewish practices, like Sabbath readings of the law or dietary restrictions? Or do these surface differences represent deeper structural discrepancies? Comparing Paul with Diaspora Judaism in general, Michael Wolter has recently put forward an interesting argument for a fundamental difference in the way Paul matches (or fails to match) the 'ethos' of his communities with their 'identity'.[24] Whereas in Diaspora Judaism, the exclusive identity of Jewish communities is matched and instantiated in a range of practices (the ethos-defining 'works of the law'), whose function is to represent their distinctive Jewish identity, Wolter finds no such straightforward symmetry between ethos and identity in the case of Paul's prescriptions for his churches. Although Paul describes his converts as an exclusive social entity (with many terms borrowed from Judaism to emphasize their difference from 'Gentiles'), he does not develop an exclusive range of practices to match: although the ban on idolatry and sexual immorality is retained from Judaism, other boundary-defining Jewish practices are not expected of his Gentile converts. Moreover, Paul's moral prescriptions which correlate ethos with identity either are so general as to lack specific content or inculcate moral norms whose function is not exclusive but *inclusive*: they match general moral norms in the wider society, such as love, joy and peace, and provide no alternative habitualized lifestyle. Thus Wolter concludes that 'the correlation of ethos and identity in Paul and in his communities is on various levels asymmetrical and deficient' ('die Korrelation von Ethos und Identität bei Paulus und in seinen Gemeinden auf mehreren Ebenen asymmetrisch und defizitär ist', 438).

Wolter finds an explanation for this 'asymmetry' in the fact that Paul's communities united Jewish-Christians and Gentile-Christians whose unity could not be expressed in common practices, on which they continued to differ. What unites them rather is their faith in Christ, and here Wolter locates the role of Paul's doctrine of 'justification by faith' as a legitimating symbol-system. Since faith is the central qualifying and distinguishing attribute of those 'in Christ', Wolter argues that Paul detaches the discriminating

---

[24] M. Wolter, 'Ethos und Identität in paulinischen Gemeinden' *NTS* 43 (1997) 430–44. [This essay has been reworked and expanded in M. Wolter, *Theologie und Ethos im frühen Christentum* (WUNT 236; Tübingen: Mohr Siebeck, 2009) 121–69. For further discussion, see chapter 1 in this volume.]

function of ethos from the level of practice and transfers it to faith.[25] Because the Christians' exclusive ethos takes expression only in faith, the way they lead their lives can be freed from the burden of distinguishing themselves from outsiders through habitual practices; only the (inherited) concern to withdraw from 'idolatry' and 'sexual immorality' forms an exception to this general pattern.[26]

I find Wolter's analysis stimulating, and many of my own comments on Paul will run parallel to his. However, some important questions arise. Why do the bans on idolatry and sexual immorality stand out as exceptions in this pattern? Would Paul have recognized them as such? Since, as we shall see, Paul's arguments against immorality and idolatry are given a distinctively Christian foundation, can they be integrated into the structure of Paul's thought? And would Paul have drawn such a sharp distinction between faith on the one hand, and habitualized practice on the other? That is, if Paul relativizes the significance of many Jewish practices (ἔργα νόμου), does he also downgrade the importance of ἔργα in general, or does Christian faith have its own concomitant practices? If these are less socially discriminating than some Jewish practices, does that make them less significant *for Christians themselves* as distinctive expressions of their faith?

We will return to these and related issues as we proceed with our analysis of Paul.

1. We may start with *the matching of theory and practice*: in what ways was the articulation of Christian identity (in preaching, exhortation, regulation and confession) made consonant with social practice?

Josephus, we may recall, castigated 'constitutions' which left activity 'dumb' (unexplained or uninscribed in law) or which, alternatively, left speech unenshrined in practice (*c. Apion.* 2.173). As to the first potential fault, one of the most striking features of 1 Corinthians is Paul's extensive effort to offer explanations for the practices of the community. Although he can lampoon rhetoric (1 Cor 1:18–2:5; cf. *c. Apion.* 2.292) and claims to prefer power (δύναμις) to speech (λόγος, 1 Cor 4:19–20), he actually invests much in the articulation of the gospel, whether that be represented in his own preaching (λόγος and κήρυγμα, 1 Cor 2:4; 2 Cor 2:17 etc.), in the creedal formulae he cites (e.g. 1 Cor 8:6; 11:23; 15:3–5), or in the Scriptures he quotes (e.g. 1 Cor 1:30; 10:1–12; 15:54–55). Paul's 'constitution' thus has

---

[25] 'Von entscheidender Bedeutung ist in diesem Zusammenhang zunächst, dass Paulus die Abgrenzungsfunktion des Ethos von der Ebene des Handelns ablöst und auf das πιστεύειν überträgt' ('Ethos und Identität', 439).

[26] 'Weil die exklusive Identität der christlichen Gemeinden ihren Ausdruck allein im Ethos des Glaubens findet, kann deren Lebensführung davon entlastet werden, sich – mit Ausnahme des Verzichts auf πορνεία und εἰδωλολατρία – durch habitualisierte Handlungen nach außen abgrenzen zu müssen' ('Ethos und Identität', 444).

plenty of foundational documents and oral traditions on which to draw, and his letters themselves continue the provision of such resources. At several points in 1 Corinthians Paul is concerned to provide the rationale for practices which he does not (or cannot) leave to be learned simply by habit. Thus in 1 Cor 11:2–16 he provides elaborate justification for his insistence that women should pray or prophesy only with their heads covered, a practice which it seems he has hitherto taken for granted (as a cultural token of female modesty), but now has to buttress with multiple theological and cultural supports. Similarly in 1 Cor 6:12–20 his previously assumed prohibition of sex with prostitutes is given an explicit theological rationale, the ban made articulate in a form that links it to foundational Christian beliefs.

Here, then, one may say that Paul goes to some lengths to provide the λόγοι which Josephus considered necessary: the rules of the community are not just ingrained by habit but spelled out and explained. Of course, the novelty of the Christian community made particular demands in this regard, since for Gentile converts little if any reliance could be placed on inherited traditions. As Paul repeatedly found, Gentile converts could not be expected to assume his Jewish moral sensibilities, while the special revolutionary features of the movement could lead some converts to call into question even quite generally held cultural assumptions. Early urban Christianity needed considerable articulation in order to support, explain and rationalize its 'customs', and the Corinthian correspondence shows us how complex and controverted that discourse might be. It is not surprising, perhaps, that gifts of well-founded speech are so highly regarded by Paul (1 Cor 1:5; 12:8) and his instructions in 1 Corinthians 14 show him regulating but nonetheless encouraging an extraordinarily loquacious community. Of course, the bandying of words could have its own dangers (the sort of λογομαχία for which Athens was notorious, cf. 1 Tim 6:4; 2 Tim 2:14), but at least Josephus could not have complained that Paul's polity was 'dumb'.

What about the other side of Josephus' equation, the concern not to let the λόγος of the constitution remain ineffective (ἄπρακτος)? How successfully did Paul embed his verbal (oral or written) definitions of Christian identity in practical activity? Again, the Corinthian correspondence shows Paul's special concern to link gospel to conduct. The message of the cross should make a direct impact on the evaluation of rhetorical prowess and human boasting (1 Corinthians 1–4). The resurrection of Christ, and thus the resurrection of the body, have immediate and far-reaching implications for the use of the body in the present (1 Cor 6:12–20). The gospel of grace should inspire and channel the generosity which springs from faith (2 Cor 8:1–9). These and many other examples of the appeal to 'come to your right minds and sin no more' (1 Cor 15:34) indicate Paul's concern to channel the application of Christian symbols in particular directions, matching the desired practical outcome with the theoretical resources of the Christian community.

The fact that Paul has to work so hard at this task in the Corinthian correspondence might, however, give us pause. In these letters we find Paul combating not a wholly different set of symbols but *an alternative interpretation of the same*. There is no reason to think that the Corinthian Christians doubted or denied the common creedal confessions to which Paul draws attention in 1 Cor 8:4–6 and 15:3–5. But they clearly saw different practical consequences arising from these beliefs. Why not hold, on the basis of the resurrection of Jesus, that death is defeated, the richness of life begun and the fulness of Spirit acquired (1 Cor 4:8 etc.)? Why not celebrate the Lordship of Christ by bold forays into the territory of shadowy 'no-gods'? Thus although Paul continually draws connections between Christian master symbols and definite patterns of life, we may wonder whether the links were always logically or theologically persuasive. If not, does this merely represent a failure on the part of the Corinthians to carry through the constitutional ideal, or does it signal that the structural correlation between Christian convictions and actions was not as clearly defined as Josephus' ideal might require?

This question concerning the match of word and deed may be pressed at certain points. In 1 Cor 7:19 Paul claims that the Christian duty is 'keeping the commandments of God' (τήρησις ἐντολῶν θεοῦ), but makes that assertion in a context where he relativizes circumcision as a cultural token, though it was naturally regarded in the Jewish tradition as one of God's commandments. A Jewish reader of 1 Corinthians might also sense that in 10:23–26 Paul suggests an alarmingly casual attitude to the Jewish food laws, a suspicion which would be supported by close attention to 1 Cor 9:21 and 2 Cor 3:6–18 (cf. Rom 14:14). It might thus seem legitimate to complain that Paul's traditional Jewish language such as 'keeping the commandments of God' is belied by his practical neglect of key features of the law. According to its normal meaning, honed by Jewish tradition, Paul's claim (λόγος) at this point does not seem well matched by practice (ἔργα). On a more general level, Paul claims for his converts an identity very different from their former Gentile selves. They are no longer, in a certain sense, ἔθνη (1 Cor 12:2), they have been washed, sanctified and justified (6:11), they are righteousness in contrast to sin, light in contrast to darkness (2 Cor 6:14). Yet Jewish observers, conscious of what distinguished *them* from 'sin', 'darkness' and 'the Gentiles', would naturally voice the complaint raised by Trypho:

> This is what we are most at a loss about: that you, professing to be pious (εὐσεβεῖν λέγοντες), and thinking yourselves better than others, are not in any way distanced from them, and do not alter your way of life from the Gentiles (κατ' οὐδὲν αὐτῶν ἀπολείπεσθε, οὐδὲ διαλλάσσετε ἀπὸ τῶν ἐθνῶν τὸν ὑμέτερον βίον), in that you

observe neither festivals nor Sabbaths, and do not practise circumcision; and further, resting your hopes on a crucified man, you still expect to obtain some good from God, although you do not keep his commandments (μὴ ποιοῦντες αὐτοῦ τὰς ἐντολάς). (Justin, *Dialogue with Trypho*, 10)

How would Paul respond to this charge? In relation to the particulars mentioned here by Trypho, he would have to concede that he did not regard circumcision as a rite to be enjoined on all the people of God, although he would insist that even the uncircumcised could still be considered 'pious' (cf. Rom 2:25–29). Although he marks time by Jewish festivals (1 Cor 16:8), and expects his converts to know when it is the first day after Sabbath (1 Cor 16:2), he has given the Passover a new meaning by its association with Christ (1 Cor 5:7) and can hardly expect his Gentile converts, who seem unattached to synagogue assemblies, to celebrate Jewish festivals and Sabbaths in the proper Jewish manner.[27] Thus Paul would define 'piety' and 'obeying God's commandments' in terms confusing to a Jew, just as elsewhere he decouples the Jewish notion of 'righteousness' from its standard association with Jewish dietary laws (Rom 14:17).

Could Paul's strategy here be construed simply as a redefinition of terms? Does he differ from Josephus only in the content he gives to abstract terms like 'piety' or 'righteousness', or does the difference here suggest a more significant discrepancy? We must stress that Paul has *not* reduced Christian difference to faith alone, since it is important for him that faith is made effective in practical activity of many kinds ('work' as in 1 Cor 3:10–15; 2 Cor 5:10; 9:8 etc.). On the other hand, Paul's polity tends towards less cultural specificity in the 'practice' which he links with his 'theory', since his own mission, and the churches which he founds, cross the cultural boundaries between Jews and Gentiles. His programmatic statement on this matter in 9:20–21 is revealing: he can afford to live sometimes ὡς ὑπὸ νόμον and sometimes ὡς ἄνομος, since his true position is neither ὑπὸ νόμον nor ἄνομος θεοῦ but what he describes as ἔννομος Χριστοῦ. What this latter entails is left ill-defined, but it clearly cannot contain the cultural commitment of submission to the Jewish law, nor the absence of moral obligation which Paul associates with Gentile 'lawlessness'. This culturally adaptable morality is evoked as the paradigm for Paul's converts in 1 Cor 10:31–11:1, where their dietary practices are left deliberately undetermined, so long as they represent giving glory to God (cf. Rom 14:5–12). As in 9:19–23, Paul here refers to the varying cultural contexts in which his converts live (10:32), thus signalling (as Wolter rightly suggests) that the cross-cultural mission

[27] See W.A. Meeks, 'Breaking Away: Three New Testament Pictures of Christianity's Separation from the Jewish Communities', in J. Neusner and E.S. Frerichs, eds., *"To See Ourselves as Others See Us." Christians, Jews, "Others" in Late Antiquity* (Chico: Scholars Press, 1985) 93–115.

and multi-cultural identity of Paul's churches places a *structurally necessary* limit on the specificity with which Christian obligation can be detailed. We will return to this point below, but may note here that while Paul is indeed concerned to match theory and practice, in line with Josephus' constitutional ideal, the ways in which he does this may be necessarily different from those enshrined in the Jewish 'constitution' which Josephus describes.

2. If we turn now to the mechanisms by which the constitution operates, we may enquire first into the *educational* means by which the Pauline norms are to be learnt. The first thing which might strike us by comparison with Josephus is that Paul too refers to an 'engraving on the heart'. Josephus, we may recall, considered the laws to be engraved on the soul from the child's first moments of consciousness. Paul, on the other hand, uses this metaphor with reference to the work of the Spirit, by whose means the Corinthians constitute a letter ἐγγεγραμμένη ἐν ταῖς καρδίαις (2 Cor 3:2–3). What is more, he consciously *contrasts* this Spirit-operation with the inscribing of the law by pen on paper, or chisel on stone, evoking the biblical narratives of the giving of the law only in order to emphasize the *superior* glory of the 'new' covenant.[28] If this contrast is more than merely rhetorical, it suggests that Paul's strategy of moral formation depends greatly on the work of the Spirit, whose effect is not only to inspire and energize but also to bring about a 'transformation' of the believer (2 Cor 3:18). Paul makes comparable statements elsewhere in the Corinthian correspondence, claiming, for instance, access to 'the mind of Christ' and 'the deep things of God' through the Spirit (1 Cor 2:6–16). The expectation of instruction through Spirit-inspired prophecy (1 Corinthians 14) points in the same direction: that Paul's prime educational aid is the guidance and instruction of the Spirit, effective both in individual and in communal formation.

In order to assess how large a difference this constitutes from Josephus' educational strategy, we may examine if Paul has any equivalent to the two phenomena which Josephus identified as the prime agents in the internalization of Jewish norms: the raising of children and the Sabbath readings of the law. Since he was founding new communities made up largely of Gentile converts Paul could not rely, of course, on their 'ancestral traditions' or childhood training. In fact, he places a symbolic gulf between their past and present (1 Cor 6:9–11; 2 Cor 6:14–7:1), since he has endeavoured to wean them from what 1 Peter would call 'the futile life-pattern inherited from your ancestors' (ἐκ τῆς ματαίας ὑμῶν ἀναστροφῆς πατροπαραδότου, 1:18). In its place he grafts them into an alternative family tree (1 Cor 10:1) and,

[28] Among recent discussions of this complex passage see especially R. Hays, *Echoes of Scripture in the Letters of Paul* (New Haven/London: Yale University, 1989) 122–53 and S.J. Hafemann, *Paul, Moses and the History of Israel* (Tübingen: Mohr Siebeck, 1995). [Cf. F. Watson, *Paul and the Hermenueutics of Faith* (London: T & T Clark, 2004) 281–98.]

like Josephus, appeals to the exploits (or failings) of their adopted 'forebears' (10:1–16). But this adopted ancestry cannot reproduce the emotional and practical impact of a real one: the Corinthians' 'Israelite' identity is not genuinely inherited and was not a factor in their primary socialization. Thus the Corinthians, like all converts, lacked that childhood security of inherited norms.

Nonetheless, Paul might expect them to transmit their traditions and norms to the next generation. What is striking, however, is how little interest Paul shows in this matter. His instructions on marriage in 1 Corinthians 7 are famous for their higher evaluation of celibacy, and even if he regards marriage as 'no sin' and sex within marriage as proper and necessary, he shows remarkably little interest in the offspring of such marriages. Children are mentioned explicitly only in 1 Cor 7:14, and then as a subsidiary argument for something else. The theological context of this chapter reveals an important cause of this omission: the imminent collapse of 'the form of this world' (1 Cor 7:25–29). It appears that the short-termism generated by early Christian eschatology militated against embedding Christian socialization into the structure of family life: it is not until Ephesians that we find our first reference to children in relation to the παιδεία κυρίου (Eph 6:4).[29]

Josephus' other medium of instruction was the weekly reading of the law. Was there anything equivalent, or similarly effective, in Paul's constitutional provision? In relation to the law itself, Paul's frequent citations and allusions might presuppose that he expects his converts to be regularly exposed to its contents. However nothing is said on this topic even in 1 Corinthians 14, where prophecy, teaching, revelation and tongues are mentioned, but no reading of Scripture; even in 2 Corinthians 3, the 'reading of Moses' is associated only with 'them' (Jews), and the Spirit's unveiling is said to enable not a clearer or better reading of Moses but a perception and reflection of the glory of the Lord (2 Cor 3:14–18). In practical terms, it is not clear whether Paul could rely on the availability of a copy of the Scriptures in the Corinthian, or any other, house-church: the rolls were bulky, expensive and obtainable only from Jews. Thus he prescribes nothing equivalent to the weekly reading of the Scripture.

However, the Scriptures were not the only, or even the main, form of 'training' within the Corinthian church 'constitution'. Presumably Paul thought, as their 'father' (1 Cor 4:14–15; 2 Cor 12:14–15), that he had provided what education they needed, through his example and teaching; further reinforcement was provided by παιδαγωγοί, by his letters and by

---

[29] See further J. M. G. Barclay, 'The Family as the Bearer of Religion in Judaism and Early Christianity', in H. Moxnes, ed., *Constructing Early Christian Families* (London: Routledge, 1997) 66–80.

delegates such as Timothy, who could remind them of his 'ways in Christ' (1 Cor 4:16–17). Since he appeals repeatedly to his earlier instructions, 'as I teach them in every church' (1 Cor 4:17; 11:2, 16; 14:33 [?]; 15:1–5), Paul seems to think of early Christian 'catechesis' as a sufficiently authoritative and integrated body of material to enable his converts to find their moral bearings.

What is unclear is how these norms would be regularly and effectively instilled, especially as Paul cannot control their interpreters – the Corinthians' παιδαγωγοί and πνευματικοί. These latter in particular highlight the authority which Paul's constitutional ideal accords to the Spirit, and the problems which that authorization could entail. There is massive potential here for immediacy, creativity and adaptability, but the concomitant lack of fixity would certainly be judged by Josephus as a disadvantage.

3. As we saw, Josephus' constitutional ideal emphasized not only knowledge of the law, but also its *comprehensive application* in daily life. Does Paul expect the same in relation to the ethos of his communities?

On the one hand, it is clear that Paul expects his theological and moral norms to influence every dimension and every aspect of life. The range of moral and social topics dealt with in 1 Corinthians speaks eloquently for this conclusion: here we find the believers addressed on matters as diverse as the conduct of common meals, covering (or not covering) one's head, eating meals in non-Christian company, buying meat in the market, and even sexual relations between husband and wife. Indeed, 1 Corinthians 7 demonstrates Paul's attempt to apply Christian convictions to every form of sexual status (single, married, betrothed, divorced), and the illustration of his central point by reference to slave and free, Jew and Gentile (7:17–24) further confirms the comprehensiveness of his moral vision. Just as he is concerned to take *every thought* captive for the gospel (2 Cor 10:5), so he wants his converts equipped for *every* good *work* (2 Cor 9:8), so that *everything* they do is done for the glory of God (1 Cor 10:32). Correspondingly, Paul's central virtue, love, is of universal application: it πάντα στέγει, πάντα πιστεύει, πάντα ἐλπίζει, πάντα ὑπομένει (13:7), and without it every action is worthless (13:1–3). This singular virtue is given shape by the many related individual injunctions (*Einzelgebote*), covering such matters as sex, social etiquette (food offered to idols) and financial responsibility.[30] If Josephus' crowning virtue is εὐσέβεια, and Paul's is ἀγάπη, both could

[30] I have suggested elsewhere that some of Paul's converts may have practised only 'segmental' participation in the community, regarding certain spheres of life (e.g. their legal business) as beyond its purview (J. M. G. Barclay, 'Thessalonica and Corinth: Social Contrasts in Pauline Christianity' *JSNT* 47 [1992] 49–74, esp. 70–1; reprinted as chapter 9 in this volume); by contrast, it is Paul's specific contention that the Christian ethos is fully comprehensive.

claim that every feature of their respective 'constitutions' embodies the virtue to which the whole is dedicated.

It is important to observe the significance of this comprehensive vision from the viewpoint of believers. As we noted above, Wolter has emphasized that the most socially distinctive features of Paul's moral rules (the ban on idolatry and sexual immorality) actually derive from Judaism, while much else was held in common with outsiders and was not in their view distinctively 'Christian'; few, for instance, would find Paul's depiction of love morally peculiar. Yet from Paul's point of view, and from the point of view of the insider, all these practices are marked as distinctively 'Christian' by their connection to key features of Christian identity. Thus, while Paul's rules on idolatry and sexual practice may differ little from those in Judaism, it is noticeable and important that he connects them to specifically Christian beliefs and the special allegiance of the believer to Christ (1 Cor 6:12–20; 10:14–22). Thus, from the insider's perspective, these are not inherited Jewish practices but the expression of Christian faith. Similarly, the virtues of honesty and love, which were quite unobjectionable to outsiders, do not thereby necessarily function *for insiders* as links which include them in the wider society, but could serve as part of their specifically Christian commitment. Thus it is not impossible for Paul to build a complete moral universe founded on a distinctively Christian identity, even where the majority of its components are not in practice socially distinctive. In such a case what will be required is the continual affirmation of distinctive Christian identity, a discourse of difference which can persist despite obvious similarities with outsiders in moral norms and social practices. In other words, Christians had to be made to *feel* different even when they were doing exactly the same as everyone else [see below, chapter 12]. A good deal of 1 Corinthians consists of this rhetorical affirmation of difference even where its moral norms conform to generally accepted standards.

Thus, in general terms, Paul could justifiably claim that his constitution was comprehensively applied. Josephus, however, might press Paul on those areas where, as a Jew, he found his 'constitution' having particular effect. We may recall that Josephus referred especially to Jewish rules concerning diet, social intercourse and the regular Sabbath rest (*c. Apion.* 2.173–174). As we noted, the common characteristic of these practices is their regularity, their intimate connection to the natural, repeated processes of life. Paul's polity is different, and somewhat less defined, in each area. As regards food, he advocates a bold acceptance of anything sold in the *macellum* (1 Cor 10:25–26) and regards the consumption or non-consumption of food as a matter of less than central concern (1 Cor 8:8; cf. 6:13; Rom 14:17). Moreover, in 1 Corinthians 8–10 he allows for different perceptions of food offered to idols, giving the food itself less emphasis than one's obligations to the 'weak'. This suggests a complex and variable assessment of how, in such cases, one gives glory to God (1 Cor 10:32), rather than the more predictable reinforcement of social difference necessitated by Jewish dietary laws.

Paul's expectations regarding social intercourse are harder to compare with those of Josephus, since the latter does not clarify what aspects of social interaction he has in mind. Paul ridicules the notion of social isolation and sees no problem in Christians eating with sexually immoral, unscrupulous or idolatrous non-Christians (1 Cor 5:9–11). But as this passage makes clear, this apparent laxity is workable only because it presupposes a strong sense of differentiation between 'brothers' and 'outsiders'. Whatever social contacts are maintained with unbelievers (necessarily so in the case of mixed marriages, 1 Cor 7:10–16), an ideological differentiation requires that they be regarded quite differently from believers, as an alien entity on the outside of the circle (cf. 1 Cor 6:1–8). Thus Paul knows, as well as Josephus, that 'bad company ruins good manners' (1 Cor 15:33), and given a choice would always encourage a Christian form of endogamy (1 Cor 7:39). But the subtleties of his social policy require a repeated emphasis on the church's ideological boundaries, a constant reminder to believers of their identity and how they differ from the 'outsiders' with whom they continually mingle.

The regular Sabbath rest is, however, a significant point of difference from Josephus' constitution, at least for Paul's Gentile converts. Whatever Paul himself or his fellow Jewish converts may have practised, there is no reason to think that his Gentile converts either would or could observe the Jewish Sabbath in abstention from work.[31] While Paul may presuppose that they counted time in Sabbaths (1 Cor 16:2), it is not clear how Sabbaths (or other Jewish festivals) could be anything more than names of days, rather than real alterations in routine. The (regular?) celebration of the Lord's supper (cf. Pliny, *Letter* 10.96, 'on a fixed day' [stato die]) and the mention of 'the first day after Sabbath' (1 Cor 16:2) might signify the rudiments of an alternative time-structure, but by social necessity this could hardly have changed the patterns of daily life as significantly as Jewish observance of the Sabbath. Thus, while *every day* can be lived in honour of the Lord (Rom 14:5), it seems that Paul had nothing equivalent to Josephus' mechanism for routine reinforcement of social identity.

Paul's difference in this regard could be taken to represent his failure to supply adequate compensation for the loss of specifically Jewish customs as the common repertoire of the Christian community. Perhaps the accumulating body of Christian rituals, major and minor, could go some way to meet

[31] In many circumstances it was difficult enough for Jews in the Diaspora to gain permission to abstain from work on the Sabbath, and it is difficult to see on what grounds Gentile Christians could gain this right. It is this dramatic change in routine which made such an impact on Jewish life and social reputation.

this lack.[32] Yet it is doubtful that Paul intended the comprehensiveness of his moral vision to attain the specificity we might anticipate. In his treatment of 'food offered to idols', Paul appears to sanction, within limits, the different perspectives and different practices of the 'weak' and the 'knowledgeable', as if it was important to recognize that 'giving glory to God in everything' might mean variable dietary practice (1 Cor 10:32). The same passage indicates the importance of knowledge in this matter, as tempered by love (1 Cor 8:1–13). In other words, Paul's 'constitution' seems to leave some room for moral discernment, under the guidance of the Spirit, not as a necessary evil (since all rules require interpretation), but as an integral characteristic of the moral task. If, compared to Josephus' ideal, Paul's comprehensiveness appears less predictable in its effects, he might have regarded this as a strength rather than a weakness.

4. This suggestion might be further illuminated by asking how Paul's polity compares with Josephus' virtue of *unquestioning adherence to the law*. For Paul, the situation is complicated, of course, in relation to the law itself, since his emphasis on 'keeping the commandments of God' (1 Cor 7:19) and the slogan 'not beyond what is written' (1 Cor 4:6) must be balanced against his statement that he is no longer 'under the law' (ὑπὸ νόμον, 1 Cor 9:21) and his disparaging comments about Moses' ministry of death (2 Cor 3:6–10; cf. 1 Cor 15:56). I take these latter comments, which would have been unthinkable for Josephus, as a sign that the law, although at times a theological resource, is no longer the unquestioned point of departure for his theology or ethics. He has, of course, other norms to which he can appeal, such as the creeds he cites, his own traditions and the commands of Jesus (1 Cor 7:10; 9:14). But it is unclear whether any of these provide that fixity and non-negotiability for which Josephus looks, since Paul shows an extraordinary ability to modify or disregard even the commands of Jesus according to circumstance. Yet there clearly are certain fixed points for Paul on which he will not allow dispute: sexual immorality and participation in idolatry are obvious examples.

We may be able to gain some insight on this question by comparing Josephus' horror of τὸ αὐτεξούσιον (see above) with Paul's reception of the Corinthian (?) slogan 'all things are lawful for me' (πάντα μοι ἔξεστιν, 1 Cor 6:12; 10:23). As we noted above, Josephus introduced the motif of 'self-determination' into his depiction of the Midianite disaster, allowing Zambrias (Zimri) to offer his defence for exogamy and the worship of Midianite deities, only to applaud Phinehas' ruthless suppression of this rebellion against the law. At first glance this seems parallel to Paul's warn-

[32] See W. A. Meeks, *The First Urban Christians* (New Haven: Yale University, 1983) 140–63.

ing against sexual immorality and religious compromise, a warning he also illustrates by Israel's disasters in the wilderness (10:1–22), including the Midianite episode (10:8). Yet Paul does not refute the Corinthian slogan, nor deny that they have in this matter a large measure of 'freedom/authority' (ἐξουσία).[33] The question is not whether they have this authority/freedom, but what they do with it, and the initial modifications of the slogan in 6:12 and 10:23 look surprisingly weak. There Paul insists only that freedom is limited by a paradoxical danger of enslavement, or by expediency (οὐ πάντα συμφέρει), which seems to mean specifically what is expedient for the community (10:23–24: οὐ πάντα οἰκοδομεῖ). To this extent, Paul's notion of 'freedom' is not αὐτεξούσιος, since the individual's interests are subordinated to those of the church, here particularly with regard to the 'weak' (8:9–13).

As the broader context shows, Paul in fact had other grounds on which to limit the range of the Corinthians' ἐξουσία. When he illustrates from his own ministry what it means to forfeit (or apply) that freedom (9:1–23), he brings into play not just the interests of the community but also the purposes of the gospel (9:12), his concern to 'gain' converts (9:19–21), and above all his sense of obligation to God (μὴ ὢν ἄνομος θεοῦ) and Christ (ἔννομος Χριστοῦ, 9:21). It is here that Paul locates what Josephus would have called his κανών (*c. Apion.* 2.174; cf. Gal 6:14–16). Yet, within this framework, and subject to these limits, Paul not only allows but positively encourages a degree of 'polyphony' (Meeks), in which different Christian convictions, of the 'weak' and of the 'knowledgeable', can be heard, and the community can come to its decision not simply by the interpretation of a rule but through a process of moral discovery.[34] In other words, while sometimes Paul can allow only his own voice to determine the Corinthians' decision (1 Cor 5:1–5), at other times he seems to want his converts to take responsibility for their own ethical decisions (11:13, 28; 14:29), to come to their own right minds and 'sin no more' (15:34).

This conclusion tallies well with our observations on the other features of Paul's constitutional mechanisms. We have suggested above that certain aspects of Paul's strategy necessitated a limit on the degree of specificity with which Christian obligation could be detailed, and we have a found

[33] See the discussion of this topic by A.J. Malherbe, 'Determinism and Free Will in Paul: The Argument of 1 Corinthians 8 and 9', in T. Engberg-Pedersen, ed., *Paul in his Hellenistic Context* (Edinburgh: T & T Clark, 1994) 231–55.

[34] W. A. Meeks, 'The Polyphonic Ethics of the Apostle Paul' *Annual of the Society of Christian Ethics* (1988) 17–29 [reprinted in W. Meeks, *In Search of the Early Christians* (New Haven: Yale University Press, 2002) 196–209]. See further the important reflections on Paul's pattern of instruction and exhortation in T. Engberg-Pedersen, 'The Gospel and Social Practice According to 1 Corinthians' *NTS* 33 (1987) 557–84; *idem*, '1 Corinthians 11:16 and the Character of Pauline Exhortation' *JBL* 110 (1991) 679–89.

a concomitant emphasis on the direction of the Spirit, and an apparently conscious disinclination to spell out what purchase the gospel should have on some aspects of daily life. While faith clearly has important practical effects (cf. Paul's descriptions of conversion in 1 Cor 6:9–11 and 14:25), not all of these can be predictably fixed: some space is accorded to 'freedom' not simply as an interpretative necessity, but as a structural *desideratum*.

5. For these reasons, Paul's goal of *communal harmony* is more complex than that articulated in Josephus' ideal. As we noted earlier, the unity of the Corinthian church is one of Paul's prime objectives in 1 Corinthians, as he strives to eliminate the factionalism and self-regard which vitiate its life. The interdependence of the body and the 'upbuilding' of the community are thus among the leading themes of the letter. However, Paul's prescription for unity also allows for a measure of diversity in the church – not only the diversity of different spiritual gifts and different forms of marital status, but also the principled acceptance of cultural diversity such that 'neither circumcision nor uncircumcision counts for anything' (1 Cor 7:19; cf. 12:13). To put the matter in Josephus' terms, while Paul might endorse Josephus' goal of 'uniform speech' (εἷς λόγος), he might give less than complete support for the notion of 'common practices' (κοινὰ ἔργα, *c. Apion.* 2.181), not because he is concerned only with faith, rather than works, but because the instantiation of that faith in works is to a certain degree under-determined, and deliberately so (cf. the strategy of permitted difference in Romans 14). Paul's constitutional strategy has a built-in 'uncertainty principle' which allows for different expressions of a common faith.

The dangers inherent in this strategy are obvious. Its permission for difference could encourage fissure, and the effort which Paul has to invest in keeping the Corinthian church together, and in keeping his Gentile churches in fellowship with Jerusalem (1 Cor 16:1–4), is testimony to the difficulties he faces. Insensitivity and judgmentalism, as displayed by the 'knowledgeable' in Corinth and the 'strong' in Rome, are further and associated risks. At the same time, Paul's strategy allows a degree of flexibility and adaptability which could be important factors in the church's growth and cultural penetration.[35]

Josephus' constitutional ideal thus helps raise significant questions concerning the aims and characteristics of Paul's church-formation. Even if Josephus' ideal is artificially utopian and its characterization of Judaism exaggerated for apologetic purposes, it helps set a grid against which to place Paul. Our purpose has not been to identify 'deficiencies' in the Pauline constitution, but to submit it to analysis from a new perspective capable of

[35] The double-edged character of Paul's strategy is rightly noted by Wolter, 'Ethos und Identität' 443–4.

revealing its structural characteristics. We have discovered a social strategy which is culturally under-determined in certain aspects of the practical outworking of faith, a strategy which, to succeed, will need to rely on the repeated assertion of 'difference' from outsiders (in the face of extensive similarity), and which will require skilful negotiation to enable the community to hold together, despite permissible internal difference.

If Paul refuses to compel his Gentile converts to 'judaize' (cf. Gal 2:14), neither does his policy amount to a subtle 'hellenization' of his Jewish tradition. While conscious of this (simplified) social distinction between 'Jews' and 'Greeks', Paul places himself and his converts paradoxically both within their own cultural traditions and beyond them. Those who believe in Christ crucified inevitably distance themselves from the 'wisdom' valued by 'Greeks' and the 'signs' sought by 'Jews' (1 Cor 1:22–23), and yet they remain as the 'called' still properly labelled 'Jews and Greeks' (1:24). At certain points Paul appears to suggest that 'the church' constitutes a third category beyond 'Jew' and 'Gentile' (1 Cor 10:32), yet it is clear from his own example that this 'church' entails not some new cultural package of its own, but an 'obligation to Christ' which can be expressed in variant cultural forms (1 Cor 9:19–21).[36] We have found that Paul's constitutional strategy involves a commitment to allow this obligation to affect every dimension of life, even in everyday habits, but also a restraint against determining what this obligation will mean for diverse individuals, in diverse circumstances, under the differential guidance of the Spirit. In these respects Paul would have recognized his own policy in the description of the Christians' paradoxical πολιτεία found in the Epistle to Diognetus: although not distinguished by country, language and custom, and following local custom in their dress, food and life-style, whether Greek or non-Greek, Christians yet retain their sense of difference paradoxically as 'strangers' and 'sojourners' whose identity is based outside any specific culture (5:1–5). It is clear that the trans-cultural communities which Paul attempted to build required a similar degree of flexibility to accommodate their diverse members and to situate themselves appropriately in their various social contexts. If that rendered them sometimes unstable, and vulnerable to multiple 'distortions', it also made them peculiarly adaptable and creative environments for the development of moral discernment.

[36] For a discussion of 1 Corinthians which points in this same direction see J. T. Sanders, 'Paul between Jews and Gentiles in Corinth' *JSNT* 65 (1997) 67–83.

5. Money and Meetings

Group Formation among Diaspora Jews and Early Christians

Sometime around the turn of the era, the Jews of Delos appealed to the proconsul of Asia concerning the opposition they encountered in their attempts to gather common funds and share communal meals. In a decree cited by Josephus, the proconsul replied by appeal to precedent: when Julius Caesar had forbidden the meetings of θίασοι in Rome, he had specifically exempted the Jews of Rome, allowing them to collect money and share meals. By the same token, the proconsul prohibited other θίασοι but allowed Jews to assemble and celebrate feasts in accordance with their ancestral customs (Josephus, *Ant.* 14.213–16).

While the names of individuals and places in this document have been garbled in transmission, and although the text has probably been edited in the interests of Jews, most scholars find some kernel of authenticity in this report.[1] What it demonstrates is that, for certain purposes and in certain eyes, it was possible to regard the communal activities of Diaspora Jews as analogous to those multiform, and multi-labelled, 'associations' which were so common a feature of the urban landscape of the Roman empire. It is not necessary here to decide whether this was the typical understanding, or normal legal definition, of Diaspora Jewish communities:[2] all that counts is that it was not implausible to regard synagogue activities as in some respects comparable to the sorts of gatherings, feastings and money-collections which were considered to be the normal functions of the variously named 'associations' (θίασοι, συναγωγαί, *collegia* etc.).

It appears that Christian gatherings could also be viewed in this way, at least on occasion, when it was convenient to employ this categorisation.

---

[1] For the latest and fullest discussion see M. Pucci ben Zeev, *Jewish Rights in the Roman World* (Tübingen: Mohr Siebeck, 1998) 107–18; for discussion of the Caesar precedent see Z. Yavetz, *Julius Caesar and his Public Image* (London: Thames & Hudson, 1983) 85–96. Even if the decree is inauthentic, Josephus' use suggests that he did not consider this categorisation of Diaspora communities to be implausible.

[2] This was contested by J. Juster, *Les Juifs dans l'Empire Romain* (Paris: P. Geuthner, 1914) 1.413–24; see the response by S. L. Guterman, *Religious Toleration and Persecution in Ancient Rome* (London: Aiglon, 1951) 130–56; cf. G. la Piana, 'Foreign Groups in Rome during the First Centuries of the Empire' *HTR* 20 (1927) 183–403, at 348–51.

Pliny, in his famous letter on the Christians (*Letters* 10.96), reports that those in his province had obediently stopped meeting for communal meals when he had banned *hetaeriae*: both he and they seem to have regarded that label, or some equivalent, as applicable to these Christian associations.[3] Later in the second century, Tertullian compares Christian churches to the *factiones* feared by the government, but insists that they perpetrate no violence (except in intercessory 'wrestling' with God!), that they instill perfectly moral behaviour, and that their collected monies are spent not on drunkenness but on aid to the poor (*Apology* 38–39). Again we cannot tell whether it was common to regard Christian gatherings as a species of 'association', but such texts indicate that the comparison was not unreasonable.[4]

There is, therefore, some historical justification for discussing Diaspora Jews and early Christians within the framework of ancient 'voluntary associations' – a label of necessarily loose definition.[5] But we must be careful to ask what an analysis of this kind can be expected to yield. The greater our knowledge of ancient 'associations', the harder it proves to identify their 'essential' characteristics, since the evidence, scattered over several centuries and over a wide geographical area, points to an incredible variety of names, forms, memberships and purposes. Even rough typologies (trade, funerary, household, and cultic 'associations') are continually frustrated by the messiness or scantiness of the evidence, and we have learnt to beware that the titles, and even the rules, of such 'associations' may tell us less than

[3] The term *hetaeriae* seems to be a loaded alternative to the more 'neutral' label *collegium*; cf. Pliny's exchange with Trajan concerning permission for a *collegium* of firemen (*Letters* 10.33–34).

[4] Cf. Lucian, *De Morte Peregrini* 11, who calls Peregrinus θιασάρχης and ξυναγωγεύς of the Christians. Celsus denigrated Christian meetings as secret and illegal 'associations' (Origen, *Contra Celsum* 1.1 [συνθῆκαι]; 8.17 [κοινωνία]). On this perception of early Christians, see R. L. Wilken, *The Christians as the Romans Saw Them* (New Haven: Yale University, 1984) 31–47.

[5] On the terms and the problems of taxonomy see J. S. Kloppenborg, 'Collegia and *Thiasoi*: Issues in function, taxonomy and membership' in J. S. Kloppenborg and S. G. Wilson, eds., *Voluntary Associations in the Graeco-Roman World* (London: Routledge, 1996) 16–30. The volume as a whole indicates the value of placing Diaspora Jews in this context, thus breaking down the often artificial distinction between Jews and 'pagans' in their respective influences on early Christianity. [For further discussion of Pauline communities in comparison with 'associations', see, e.g., P. A. Harland, *Associations, Synagogues, and Congregations* (Minneapolis: Fortress Press, 2003); idem, *Dynamics of Identity in the World of the Early Christians: Associations, Judeans and Cultural Minorities* (London: T & T Clark, 2009); R. S. Ascough, *Paul's Macedonian Associations: The Social Context of Philippians and 1 Thessalonians* (WUNT 2.161; Tübingen: Mohr Siebeck, 2003); T. Schmeller, *Hierarchie und Egalität: eine sozialgeschichtliche Untersuchung paulinischer Gemeinden und griechisch-römischer Vereine* (Stuttgart: Katholisches Bibelwerk, 1995); E. Adams, 'First Century Models for Paul's Churches', in T. D. Still and D. G. Horrell, eds., *After the First Urban Christians: The Social-Scientific Study of Pauline Christianity Twenty-Five Years Later* (London: T & T Clark, 2009) 60–78.]

we think about their real functions. To ask, therefore, in what respects the Diaspora synagogues or early churches were like 'associations' is akin to asking whether churches today are like clubs: there are too many different kinds of church, and too many different kinds of club to make this vague and over-generalised comparison of much heuristic value. For this reason, we can hardly expect a comparison of this sort to yield explanations for specific features of synagogue or early church life. Edwin Hatch's famous thesis that the ecclesial title ἐπίσκοπος was derived from its use for financial officers in contemporary 'associations' was a classic case of over-reaching specificity: given the paucity of evidence and the wide range of ways in which ἐπίσκοποι might function in 'associations' and churches of varied types, we cannot trace plausible genetic connections of this type nor even expect that overlaps in terminology will mirror similarities in function.[6]

However, Hatch's enquiry was not entirely without merit. By pointing to the importance of finance within the ancient 'associations', and in asking about its roles in the early churches, he put his finger on an important social phenomenon. To place Diaspora synagogues and Christian churches within the analytical framework of ancient 'associations' might thus be productive, if we employ this analysis to identify those social forms and social processes which helped to determine the character and social significance of such groups. Thus it may be helpful to locate and compare, within these roughly comparable groups, such common activities as meals, meetings, instruction, religious rites and communal deliberations, and such common structuring features as patterns of benefaction and leadership, monetary collections and resource commitments. We may then ask from new angles what forms of solidarity, loyalty, social integration and social differentiation these activities and structures established.

In this essay I can touch on just two of these ingredients, but two which may be of particular diagnostic significance: money and meetings. In the first case I can only touch on a selection of relevant evidence and suggest how it might be significant, while in the second I can simply raise a few potentially fruitful questions. I believe that an analysis of these phenomena among Diaspora Jews and early Christians might shed some light on the ways in which they created and maintained their respective identities – indeed the ways in which their identities took *differentiated* shape.

---

[6] E. Hatch, *The Organization of the Early Christian Churches* (2nd ed., London: Rivingtons, 1882) 26–55; for a survey of responses to Hatch, see J. S. Kloppenborg, 'Edwin Hatch, Churches and *Collegia*', in B. L. McLean, ed., *Origins and Method: Towards a New Understanding of Judaism and Christianity* (Sheffield: Sheffield Academic, 1993) 212–38.

I. Money Matters

Within the great diversity of social groups we call 'associations', there is frequently some evidence of the gifting, collection or distribution of money. In general, the 'associations' only came into existence by the donation of money – whether from a single benefactor (living or dead), by the subscription of a number of founder-members, or by the collection of membership-dues from those who made up the 'association'.[7] Financial arrangements could take a great variety of forms, of course. Sometimes large-scale donors made the association and its meetings viable by loaning or financing property, providing materials for the meals (food, wine, oil) or distributing other benefits for the members. In other cases, we know of regular (usually monthly) dues, payable by all members as contributions for the feasts or for the communal 'chest', which might be needed to hire communal facilities or guarantee payment of members' burial expenses. Often such arrangements necessitated the appointment of a 'treasurer' (ταμίας), who might himself make special contributions, or receive special financial exemptions. The common chest (κοινόν, θησαυρός, *arca* etc.) was, in any case, of concern to the whole association.[8]

Finance is, of course, of profound social significance, especially in relatively small groups such as the associations, which were rarely more than 150-strong. The close tie between giving (or receiving) money and membership of the association meant that all such financial transactions served to solidify the social identity of the group, and clarify the boundaries between insiders and outsiders. The cost of monthly or annual dues must have reaffirmed the loyalty of the members and induced attendance at meetings (where the regular rewards of membership were received). The appointment of treasurers and other officials not only established an internal system of honour, but also placed administrative and even judicial power in certain hands (e.g. in the exaction of fines or fees). Where benefactors placed others significantly in their debt, power-hierarchies were created, and the social power and prestige of the 'association' was no doubt connected to its financial resources and their public display in architecture and/or epigraphy.

---

[7] Among well-known cases: the Philadelphia Zeus-association (second/first century BCE) seems to be been funded largely, if not entirely, by Dionysius himself (see discussion by S.C. Barton and G.H.R. Horsley, 'A Hellenistic Cult Group and the New Testament Churches' *JAC* 24 [1981] 7–41); the Lanuvium association (136 CE) was at least sustained, if not purely founded, by membership subscription (*CIL* XIV, no. 2,112). For classic discussions of the financial aspects of 'associations' see F. Poland, *Geschichte des griechischen Vereinswesens* (Leipzig: Teubner, 1909) 453–98; J.P. Waltzing, *Etude historique sur les Corporations professionelles chez les Romains* (reprint, Bologna: Forni, 1968) 1.449–515.

[8] See the recent discussion of 'communal chests' by J.A. Harrill, *The Manumission of Slaves in Early Christianity* (Tübingen: Mohr Siebeck, 1995) 129–57.

Indeed, its very legality as an association might be affirmed by its corporate control of financial resources, and its right to handle them as it willed. Thus both in internal social dynamics and in relations with others, finance was liable to play a key social role, although particular arrangements might differ greatly from one 'association' to the next.

What can we say, in this connection, about the role of money within Diaspora Jewish communities, and within the early Christian churches? Although our evidence is patchy, I believe a number of significant observations can be drawn.

a) Money among Diaspora Jews

Diaspora communities varied enormously in size, from small groups meeting in private houses (now largely unidentifiable) to very considerable communities, endowed with impressive synagogues like those we hear about in Alexandria and see in Sardis. We cannot therefore generalise about the financial arrangements of such diverse communities, but we do find traces of features comparable to those just noted in (other) 'associations'. The most obvious signs of financial power are the identifiable synagogue buildings and the associated inscriptions concerning donations to the building, maintenance, refurbishment or decoration.[9] As we might expect, these benefactions (from both Jews and non-Jews) are important signs of patronage; the inscriptions and honorific decrees for such benefactors confirm the status-hierarchy which helped shape the character of the community.[10] In many cases, it seems, such buildings (προσευχαί or, later, συναγωγαί) operated as communal resources with multiple purposes. Besides the 'prayers' which their original names suggest, there was Sabbath instruction in the Scriptures,[11] special festival occasions, and also communal meals. Our sources are tantalising: a papyrus indicates that the officers of the προσευχή of Jews in Thebes (Egypt) paid a substantial amount (128 drachmas) each month for the supply of water, while the εὐχεῖον in the same place paid the same amount (*CPJ* 432 [2nd century CE]): what sort of communal activities did this large volume of water supply? We have fragmentary evidence of some 'contributions' made by Jews in Apollinopolis Magna (Egypt), ap-

[9] See, in general, B. Lifschitz, *Donateurs et Fondateurs dans les synagogues juives* (Paris: Gabalda, 1967); famous examples include MAMA 6.264 (=*CIJ* 766), concerning the synagogue building at Acmonia, built by Julia Severa (a pagan benefactress), and restored by several named synagogue leaders from their own funds and from 'what had been deposited' (τὰ συνκαταθεμένα) – presumably accumulated communal funds.

[10] For an analysis of the synagogue in Sardis and related inscriptions, see P. Trebilco, *Jewish Communities in Asia Minor* (Cambridge: Cambridge University, 1991) 37–54.

[11] Attested by, e.g., Philo, *Legatio* 156–57, 312–13; *Spec. Leg.* 2.62–63 etc.; Josephus, c. *Apion.* 2.175.

parently for communal feasts (*CPJ* 139 [first century BCE]), and the decree cited above, concerning Jews in Delos, indicates that they gathered on a regular basis for common meals (σύνδειπνα, ἑστιᾶσθαι, Josephus, *Ant.* 14.215–16).

In most such cases, some arrangement for the holding of common funds must have been made, just as there must have been a common chest into which the fines could be paid which were liable to the Jewish community from those caught disturbing Jewish graves,[12] or from which the community could pay the manumission costs of a slave (*CPJ* 473 [third century CE]). The famous Aphrodisias inscription (third century CE) indicates the establishment of some sort of communal Jewish fund, to which Jews, proselytes and 'God-fearers' made contributions: frustratingly, it is not clear what this fund was for, but the public display of such a long list of names speaks volumes for the pride of the Aphrodisias Jewish community, its social networks among both Jews and non-Jews, and the loyalties which it could command.[13] If the fund had a 'charitable' purpose, it would fit the reputation of Jews in antiquity for 'looking after their own', a network of social support which was paraded by Josephus (c. *Apion.* 2.283), resented by Tacitus (*Histories* 5.5.1), and envied by Julian (*apud* Sozomen, *History* 5.16.5).

Thus financial commitments clearly bound local Jewish communities together, creating both vertical and horizontal social ties: in particular the establishment of institutions, and the expenses of communal activities, forged social links by which loyalties were both created and maintained. In many cases, of course, these reinforced already-existing familial and ethnic ties, and if non-Jews were also drawn into these networks, the institutions they supported were still distinctively Jewish. If we find no traces here of monthly (or annual) 'membership dues', that perhaps reflects the ethnic base of Diaspora communities: these were 'associations' which, for the most part, people were born into, rather than electing to join. (We may guess that, for this reason, the financial burdens of the local community fell predominantly on the wealthier members, who duly received honour in return.)

But in one respect, Diaspora Jews *did* pay a special kind of 'membership fee' – the half-shekel temple tax, payable in Jewish law by all males over the age of 20 (Exod 30.11–16). A large range of evidence from the Diaspora (papyri, ostraka, Roman decrees, and notices in Cicero, Josephus and Philo) indicates that this tax was taken with the utmost seriousness by Diaspora

---

[12] MAMA 6.335 (see Trebilco, *Jewish Communities*, 62), with reference to the 'most holy treasury' to which fines are to be paid.

[13] J. Reynolds and R. Tannenbaum, *Jews and Godfearers at Aphrodisias* (Cambridge: Cambridge Philological Society, 1987); the reading and interpretation of the first line of face *a* are extremely uncertain, and the editors' suggestion that the institution marked by this inscription was a charitable distribution centre for food is little more than a guess.

Jews, who made local collections of this money, gathered it at regional collection points and made elaborate arrangements to ensure its safe transportation to Jerusalem.[14] Individual wealthy Diaspora Jews (or proselytes) might make additional contributions to the temple in Jerusalem, or to the welfare of the people of Judaea,[15] but the social significance of this general tax on all Diaspora Jews can hardly be exaggerated. The local administration may have required a register of liable male Jews (cf. Exod 30.11–13); it certainly necessitated local 'treasuries' (ταμεῖα) where money could be stored before dispatch (Philo, *Spec. Leg.* 1.77–78; Josephus, *Ant.* 18.312). Adult males, and therefore heads of families, were thereby bound together in a shared and equal commitment, which seems to have had enormous symbolic significance for all concerned. The money thus collected was generally known as 'sacred money', and, according to Philo, it was known as λύτρα (*Spec. Leg.* 1.77; cf. Exod 30.12 LXX: λύτρα τῆς ψυχῆς). Philo reports, perhaps accurately, that this was interpreted in extremely concrete terms, liable to appeal to Diaspora Jews of all social levels: contributing such money might win release from slavery, the healing of disease, the preservation of freedom and general preservation from danger (*Spec. Leg.* 1.77). Thus huge hopes were invested in this annual payment, whose safe delivery to Jerusalem was a matter of intense communal concern. The gathering of such money at regional collection points (Josephus, *Ant.* 14.110–13; Cicero, *Pro Flacco* 28.66–69) must have helped tie Diaspora communities together across geographical boundaries, while its common delivery to Jerusalem annually reinforced the international links of Diaspora Jews with one another, and with the Jerusalem temple. The fact that this shipment of money was sometimes contested on legal grounds must have raised its significance for Diaspora Jews still more: as a right for which they fought, this annual temple contribution came to be publicly recognised and fiercely defended, part of the very essence of what it meant to belong, distinctively, to the Jewish community.[16]

---

[14] The evidence in surveyed in my *Jews in the Mediterranean Diaspora from Alexander to Trajan (323 BCE–117 CE)* (Edinburgh: T & T Clark, 1996) 238–39, 266–70, 417–18. [Cf. now M. Tellbe, 'The Temple Tax as a Pre-70 CE Identity Marker', in J. Ådna, ed., *The Formation of the Early Church* (WUNT 183; Tübingen: Mohr Siebeck, 2005) 19–44.]

[15] Additional contributions for the temple: Fulvia (Josephus, *Ant.* 18.82); Nicanor (b Yoma 38 a); Alexander the Alabarch (Josephus, *Bell.* 5.201–5). Relief for Judaeans suffering famine: Helena and Izates of Adiabene (Josephus, *Ant.* 20.51–53).

[16] The passage in *Pro Flacco* 28.66–69 indicates the problems of Asian Jews in gaining the necessary legal permission, and the concern of Roman Jews on their behalf. The issue was to recur in Cyrene (Josephus, *Ant.* 16. 169–70) and in Asia (*Ant.* 16.163–68) and Philo is anxious to indicate that it was *not* a problem for Jews in Augustan Rome (*Legatio* 156–57, 313). Tacitus mentions this tax, as a matter of resentment (*Histories* 5.5.1), and the destruction of the Jerusalem temple, and diversion of the tax into the *fiscus Iudaicus*,

b) Money among early Christians

Not surprisingly, there are no institutional structures concerning money apparent in the first generation of the Christian movement: without buildings to construct or maintain, and without a membership fee or annual dues to collect, there was no reason for the earliest Christians to handle money on other than an *ad hoc* basis. But that is not to say that money was irrelevant to the social formation of the Christian movement. Any group that holds common meals, as 'believers' did on a regular basis, will have to find some way of getting the food to the table. While other 'associations' managed this problem in various ways, Paul's church in Corinth seems to have relied on members bringing their own food, or on the wealthier supplying food for others.[17] Not surprisingly, this resulted in inequality (1 Cor 11.21–22), a problem avoided, or at least carefully regulated, by the fixed quotas (and fixed fees) common in pagan 'associations'. But as well as the regular expense of meals (Christian cultic activity, fortunately, cost next to nothing!), there were the occasional, but significant costs of travelling 'prophets' and 'apostles'. It is not surprising that controversies seem to have broken out often over such unpredictable economic burdens, or that some of our earliest texts, both Q (Matt 10//Lk 10) and Paul's letters (1 Cor 9), reflect the strenuous ideological work of justifying the support of such anomalous figures.[18] Already in such texts we can detect the power-claims which such financial support entails, and although neither 'prophets' nor 'apostles' were to become permanent features of the Christian movement, they foreshadowed the questions which were to determine much else in its future direction: who are the Christian communities bound to support financially, and who is to control the channelling of this money?

Our earliest hint of targetted financial support within the community may be Gal 6.6, with its instruction that those who are taught the word share in all good things with the one who teaches (ὁ κατηχῶν). This is unlikely to be a permanent arrangement for 'full-time' teachers, but it makes specific the general requirement for a practical κοινωνία which seems to have been a significant part of the early Christian ethos. Whatever we make of the idealised depictions of pooled resources in Acts 2 and 4, there is good reason to think that the ethic of generosity (Rom 12.8–10) was a significant

---

could be explained as an attempt to ensure that Jews never again collected this degree of money (and power).

[17] P. Lampe, 'The Eucharist: Identifying with Christ on the Cross' *Interpretation* 48 (1994) 36–49; G. Theissen, 'Soziale Integration und sakramentales Handeln. Eine Analyse von 1 Cor. XI 17–34' *NovT* 16 (1974) 179–206 (E.T. in *The Social Setting of Pauline Christianity* [Edinburgh: T & T Clark, 1982] 145–74).

[18] G. Theissen, 'Legitimation und Lebensunterhalt: Ein Beitrag zur Soziologie urchristlicher Missionare' *NTS* 21(1974/75) 192–221 (E.T. in *Social Setting*, 27–67).

feature of communities of 'brothers'. The fact that Paul has to turn his commendation of φιλαδελφία into a warning not to depend *overmuch* on other believers for financial support (1 Thess 4.9–12; cf. 2 Thess 3.6–13) indicates a general presumption that 'brothers' will look out for one another (the label connoted in antiquity the sharing of resources, not equality).[19] Hospitality for travelling fellow believers was no doubt one important manifestation of this concern (Rom 12.13). Everything here is, as we would expect, informal, but the practices are no less socially significant for that. We may notice in particular how these patterns of giving within the community create a solidarity. To practice φιλαδελφία one has to know who one's ἀδελφοί are; thus every act of charity within the community clarifies and reinforces its social boundary (cf. Gal 6.10). In their financial dealings the Christian communities thus begin to establish their own identities which, if reinforced by other practices and by strong ideological warrants, could begin to set these communities apart from all others.

Perhaps the most formal, and certainly the most elaborate, financial initiative in the Pauline churches was the collection for Jerusalem. This did not require the establishment of a common 'chest': 1 Cor 16.2 suggests that each person will store up money at home, and pool it only on Paul's arrival. But it did encourage some scrutiny of who was liable to this levy, and it did require some collective decision-making about joining this enterprise, maintaining it once begun, and authorising those responsible for transporting it to Jerusalem (1 Cor 16.1–4; 2 Cor 8–9). Thus its unintended results must certainly have been to clarify the membership of the churches concerned and the leadership-responsibilities within them. Since the gift was for 'the poor among the saints in Jerusalem' (Rom 15.26), was one-off and not connected with the temple-cultus, it was parallel not to the Jewish temple tax but to the payments for foodstuffs for famine-struck Judaea organised by Helena and Izates (46/47 CE; Josephus, *Ant.* 20.51–53; cf. Acts 11.27–30).[20] But in this case, revealingly, the money is not for all Jews in Jerusalem indiscriminately, and the sum is not given to 'the leading men' (οἱ πρῶτοι) among the Jerusalemites (*Ant.* 20.53): rather, the gift is very specifically for *the saints* in Jerusalem, the special group of believers, presided over not by the high-priests or Sanhedrin, but by the 'pillars' of the church. Thus the collection, while designed to bind together Jewish and non-Jewish believers

---

[19] Cf. the discussion of early Christian 'mutualism' in J. J. Meggitt, *Paul, Poverty and Survival* (Edinburgh: T & T Clark, 1998) 155–78.

[20] K. F. Nickle, *The Collection: A Study in Paul's Strategy* (London: SCM Press, 1966) 74–93, exaggerates the elements of similarity between the temple tax and Paul's collection. Cf. K. Berger, 'Almosen für Israel' *NTS* 23 (1977) 180–204, who, however, presses the *theological* significance of Gentile donations further than the evidence allows.

across huge geographical distances, also solidified the distinction between believers and 'the rest' among Jews in Judaea itself.[21]

In fact, for Paul's converts, who lived alongside Diaspora Jews in the cities of the empire, precisely their *non-participation* in the Jerusalem temple-tax might have been one of the most significant factors in clarifying their *non-membership* of local Diaspora communities. It is possible, of course, that Paul himself, and any Jewish converts in his churches, did continue to participate in the tax: although he says nothing about this in his letters, the pericope on this topic in Matt 17.24–27 may suggest a (reluctant?) willingness to contribute among some Diaspora 'believer' Jews. But it is hard to see how Paul's Gentile converts would have had any incentive, or any opportunity, to contribute to the temple-funds, either through this tax or by means of any other gifts.[22] Since the channelling of these funds was organised by the Diaspora Jewish communities, and was, as we have seen, a regular and public hallmark of Jewish belonging, the very fact that Paul's Gentile converts were not part of that financial network must have helped clarify, to themselves and to the Jews, that they were not socially connected to the synagogue communities. In other words, although 'the parting of the ways' was a complex, untidy and unstable phenomenon, the differential allocation of financial resources must have had a part to play in clarifying the differentiation between 'believers' and 'Jews'.[23]

In subsequent generations of the Christian movement, and as we enter the second century, a more formal financial organisation appears to have become common, together with a more precise sense of the responsibilities of believers *towards one another*. To touch on just a few examples, we may note how the Pastorals presuppose that widows will be supported after some formal recognition of their status (1 Tim 5.3–16), an enrolment

---

[21] Rom 15.31 indicates clearly enough the intended destination of the collection, and Paul's awareness that even his person (let alone his money) is unacceptable to non-believing Jews in Jerusalem. As a partial parallel, we may note how 'Messianic Jews' in America, while desiring to make contributions for Israel, have had their donations to common Jewish funds refused, and find themselves instead supporting specifically *Christian* Jewish causes (C. Harris-Shapiro, *Messianic Judaism* [Boston: Beacon, 1999] 108–9); thus finance reinforces the separate identity of Messianic Jews, whatever their original intentions.

[22] Paul, of course, considers the 'temple' to be the body of believers (1 Cor 3.16; 2 Cor 6.16) or even each believer's body (1 Cor 6.19); and what expectation of λύτρα could he imagine from the support of the temple cultus? There are no signs that members of his churches viewed such matters differently. [Cf. F. W. Horn, 'Paulus and der herodianische Tempel' *NTS* 53 (2007) 184–203.]

[23] After the destruction of the Temple, when the rigorous Roman collection of taxes for the *fiscus Iudaicus* clarified who was, and who was not, a Jew (see M. Goodman, 'Nerva, the *Fiscus Judaicus* and Jewish Identity' *JRS* 79 [1989] 40–44), there was a strong financial incentive for Christians *not* to have themselves considered 'Jews'. [See now, M. Heemstra, *The* Fiscus Judaicus *and the Parting of the Ways* (WUNT 2.277; Tübingen: Mohr Siebeck, 2010).]

(5.9) which suggests the emergence of some financial structures. In the same context the rich are urged to give with great generosity, storing up for themselves a good foundation for the future (1 Tim 6.17–19): one is tempted to find here a Christian equivalent to the λύτρα which Jewish donors to the temple tax were encouraged to expect.[24] The Didache, while reflecting continuing debates over the support of 'prophets', encourages giving for their support as the equivalent of first-fruits: they are, indeed, nothing less than 'your high-priests' (13.1–3). In the post-70 symbolic world of Christians, where the temple is spiritually superseded as well as physically destroyed (cf. Barnabas 16), the financial commitments of the community bespeak a clearly non-Jewish set of priorities. Exhortations abound for almsgiving, but the context often reveals that this is primarily exercised within the Christian community: there the poor and the rich support one another, like elm and vine (Hermas, *Sim.* 1–2). For this to work, it is clearly becoming necessary for funds to be centrally gathered, and centrally distributed. Justin expects almsgiving to go to widows and orphans *via the president* of the community (*First Apology* 67), while both Ignatius (*Polycarp* 4.3) and Tertullian (*Apology* 39) assume that Christian communities will have a common 'chest' (τὸ κοινόν, *arca*). Tertullian says that the *desposita pietatis* will go to sustain and bury the poor, to support the widows, the old and the shipwrecked – categories that could include non-believers; but he goes on immediately to list the support of Christians who have been sent to the mines, or banished, or put in prison for their fidelity to God, and is proud of the proverb, 'see how these Christians love one another' (*Apology* 39.7). He thus suggests that the community used its funds primarily to solidify and sustain its own membership, and created, through the ties of gift and receipt, a strong web of affiliation. While it may be over-idealising to apply here the label 'the economics of affection', we can hardly doubt that money mattered immensely in creating solidarities in a movement that cut across social, economic and cultural barriers.[25]

---

[24] Cf. 2 Clement 16.4 suggests that almsgiving 'covers a multitude of sins' (cf. Tobit 12.8–9).

[25] Cf. the general comments on 'common funds' by Harrill, *Manumission*, 129: 'Far from being a trivial matter of administration, a group's common fund had significant social meanings and functions in the ancient world. To insiders, it made cultic activities possible; contributions to the fund demonstrated loyalty to the group and showed where one placed his or her values … Contributions and disbursements made explicit and reinforced a hierarchy of group members, and hence made possible competing sources of authority. Donors provided funds to help poorer members, and in this way the common treasury bound members together across social orders'. [Cf. B.W. Longenecker, *Remember the Poor: Paul, Poverty and the Graeco-Roman World* (Grand Rapids: Eerdmans, 2010.]

II. Meetings

The topic of meetings is perhaps too large and too amorphous to handle in this context, other than by posing a number of questions. It is clear that all 'associations' in the ancient world, pagan, Jewish and Christian, constituted themselves, in some sense, by their meetings, formal and informal; but such social events took a great variety of forms, and took place in a great variety of contexts. The pagan 'associations' met at varying frequency, and for various purposes: often the rules specify monthly meetings, but there were sometimes additional annual meetings, besides festivals for the patron deities (or the birthdays of human patrons), and in some cases the group might be constituted by its collective presence at burials of members, in reserved theatre seats or in religious processions. Thus we can scarcely generalise about the frequency of *collegium*-meetings, or the significance of membership of such groups for their individual members. Nor can we be sure, often, what went on in their regular meetings, besides meals, presided over by officials.

Meetings, including meal-meetings, were, of course, of great significance within both Diaspora Jewish and early Christian communities. The social analysis of meals – what food is consumed, at whose invitation, in whose company, with what purpose – is a topic of rich significance which I cannot even begin to broach here.[26] But, in staying on a deliberately general level, I would like to suggest two questions which concern the role of meetings in relation to the establishment of group identity, and where I think a comparison across different kinds of 'association' could help clarify their different characteristics:

1. *How did the meetings of the 'association' relate to affiliation to that group?* Since most of the pagan 'associations' defined membership precisely by the payment of dues and attendance at meetings, one might say that affiliation is here very closely related to meeting-participation. 'Associations' ceased to function when no-one attended the meetings, and they sometimes levied fines on those who failed to attend the funerals of their associates. If membership was by payment of fees, and if the primary activity of the group was common eating, it would hardly make sense to be a member and choose not to attend: one thereby missed what one had paid for! Since the ideology of the group was convivial (sometimes legislating against altercations at meals), it was the social network created by the meetings themselves that constituted the 'association'.

---

[26] See the recent collection of essays edited by I. Nielsen and H.S. Nielsen, *Meals in a Social Context* (Aarhus: Aarhus University, 1998). [Cf. H. Taussig, *In the Beginning was the Meal: Social Experimentation and Early Christian Identity* (Minneapolis: Fortress Press, 2009).]

The 'associations' of Diaspora Jews perhaps had a rather different character. Although one might know, by and large, which families were to be considered Jewish, and which men paid the temple tax, the community was formed by its relatively stable ethnic affiliations, rather than by participation in meetings. We have no notion of what percentage of the local Jewish population would attend Sabbath gatherings of the συναγωγή; but no text reflects concern over non-attendance, and one could hardly challenge another's 'Jewishness' on such grounds. The annual feasts (and fasts) were perhaps the primary focus of community affiliation: Philo reports that the fast of the Day of Atonement is observed by some Jews 'who do nothing holy (εὐαγές) in the rest of their lives' (*Spec. Leg.* 1.186). Although both annual and weekly gatherings would reinforce the ethos of the Jewish population as a whole, the link between self-identification as a Jew and attendance at meetings is not necessarily strong: as an ethnic group whose bonds are based on ascribed ('natural') connections, Diaspora communities did not need to work to define or maintain their membership.

If we may generalise at all about Christian 'associations', we may place them nearer to the meal-focused 'pagan' associations than to Diaspora communities. Although, to our knowledge, churches had no membership lists, and exacted no set fees, their ideology was intensely communal, and they invested much in the sharing of worship. Although Paul's letters may be idealistic in this regard, the incidental evidence of Pliny's letter (that Christians met regularly *stato die* before dawn, and then reassembled to share a meal) strongly suggests a group-ethos where the intensity of interaction is crucial (10.96). Of course, not all Christians could, or did, attend meetings regularly, but the fact that this is a matter of *concern* (Heb 10.24–25; Barnabas 4.10) indicates how much is invested in 'coming together'. The relatively small size of Christian communities, in their house-environments, no doubt enhanced this sense of active community, but it appears that the maintenance of membership could never be taken for granted and that the emotional aspects of the meetings themselves were crucial in securing their future. It was precisely here, in baptism and Lord's supper, in shared worship and communal instruction, that the churches articulated their common identity.

2. *How did the meetings of the 'association' relate to other social affiliations*? Here again I must risk impossibly large generalisations. The various pagan 'associations', hugely varied though they were, generally seem to have operated within, and served to complement, already existing social networks, whether of trade, locality, ethnicity, household or patronage. If they cut across social levels, as they manifestly did, it seems this was generally by absorbing already-existent social cross-sections (e. g. households, or client-patron groupings). Thus, although the governing elite might some-

times fear *collegia* as foci of loyalty not directly under their control, they were potentially dangerous precisely in uniting common interests, not in creating new allegiances among previous strangers.

Jewish 'associations' also clearly reduplicated, and reinforced, wider social affiliations within the Jewish community. If the Sabbath instruction percolated through the Jewish community by means of household networks (so Philo, *Hyp.* 7.14), it clearly cut with, rather than against, the grain of Diaspora society. In relation to the rest of society, however, synagogue meetings were clearly an oddity, which could interfere badly with normal social and economic activity and were occasionally the targets of local malice.[27] However, as long-established ethnic associations, committed to maintaining ancestral customs, such meetings could normally gain the tolerance of the governing elite, and for the most part they seemed to have operated openly, without suspicion, in the cities of the Graeco-Roman world.

Church-meetings, perhaps, show the greatest tendency to cut across normal social affiliations. As novel associations, whose rationale was a shared religious experience rather than pre-existing social or ethnic ties, they were perhaps the most socially innovative of all the 'associations' in antiquity. Of course, Christians, too, sometimes incorporated previously-existing groupings, especially households who converted *en bloc*, and we can guess, but cannot usually trace, other links of family, trade or residence between believers. Nonetheless, the ideology of Christian meetings was self-consciously socially innovative (Gal 3.28; Col 3.11), and the lines of distinction between 'believers' and 'the rest' often went precisely *through* households, neighbourhoods, and previous friendships. The offence caused by converts in *breaking* with past associations seems to have continued right through the pre-Constantinian period, and Christian meetings were regarded with suspicion precisely because their ideology was presumed to be so *anti-social*.

Although my answers to these questions may be hopelessly over-generalised, I believe the questions themselves are not unhelpful, and could in fact be supplemented by several more.[28] In general, I believe the broad comparative work between 'associations' in antiquity should continue to include Jews and Christians in its remit, and, carefully conducted, could help to shed fresh light on what made them socially significant. In the complex social mosaic of antiquity, the continuance of Diaspora Jewish communities, and the emergence of new communities of Christians, are mysterious phenomena which should never be taken for granted. Placing them in the

---

[27] See, for example, the disputes in Ionia reported by Josephus, *Ant.* 16.27–65.

[28] E.g., what was the relative cost of attending meetings? What sort of social interaction took place in such meetings? How comprehensive was the salience of the meeting for the conduct of the rest of one's life?

context of 'associations' may help provide some additional interpretative keys which could help explain how these remarkable phenomena came to establish themselves, with such significant historical results.

6. Deviance and Apostasy

Some Applications of Deviance Theory to First-Century Judaism and Christianity

I. Introduction

Historians of early Christianity are concerned with the phenomenon of deviance in at least two respects. In the first place, we wish to understand the process by which, over a period of a number of generations, this originally Jewish movement was deemed to have deviated sufficiently from Jewish norms to be regarded by its parent community as a distinct social and religious entity. Secondly, we are intrigued by the ways in which the early Christian communities defined their own boundaries, a process which involved excluding those they considered to have deviated from the norms of Christian practice or belief. This double process of definition is central to the phenomenon of early Christianity: its definition as distinct from Judaism and its internal definition of its own identity. The sort of questions which intrigue us are well illustrated by the case of Paul, who was indeed a pivotal figure in the whole process: we want to know how Paul came to be regarded as an apostate by his Jewish contemporaries and how he, in turn, came to reject some adherents of his churches as 'false brothers'.

Sociologists have long been concerned with the processes by which societies define and maintain their boundaries, and special attention has also been accorded to those individuals or groups which deviate from social norms. The 'sociology of deviance' which has flourished under that name since the 1950s (and under other names before that date) might well hold some promise for research focused on the Christian movement as a deviant form of Judaism and on the definition and exclusion of deviants from the early Christian communities. It will not, of course, provide a magic wand with which to solve the many intricate problems of our subject, but we can at least inquire what light, if any, it could shed on the historical processes we struggle to understand. In recent years some attempts have indeed been made to apply deviance theory to the topic of 'the parting of the Ways' between Judaism and early Christianity, notably by Anthony Saldarini and

Jack Sanders.[1] My efforts in this direction will be somewhat more modest than theirs in scope and claim but I hope still fruitful in suggesting avenues for further research.[2]

II. The Sociology of Deviance: The Interactionist Perspective

Many kinds of sociological theory have been employed in the analysis of deviant behaviour, as theoretical approaches go in and out of fashion and as different features of the phenomenon are illuminated.[3] Without making monopolistic claims for its value, I wish here to explore the potential of what has been termed the 'interactionist' or 'societal reaction' perspective (sometimes also, rather loosely, 'labelling theory'). This perspective on deviance suddenly rose to prominence in the early 1960s and became the focus of intense interest (and controversy) through the 1960s and 1970s; the value of its contribution is now widely recognized, though (as we shall see) its limitations are also obvious. Drawing on a theoretical framework known as 'symbolic interactionism' (developed by Mead and Blumer), the interactionist perspective received its programmatic expression in Howard Becker's book *Outsiders* (1963) and fitted the mood of the 1960s so per-

---

[1] A.J. Saldarini, 'The Gospel of Matthew and Jewish Christian Conflict', in David L. Balch, ed., *Social History of the Matthean Community* (Minneapolis: Fortress, 1991) 38–61; J.T. Sanders, *Schismatics, Sectarians, Dissidents, Deviants: The First One Hundred Years of Jewish-Christian Relations* (London: SCM, 1993).

[2] Saldarini combines deviance theory and sect typology in his analysis of the Matthean community, but at a very high level of generality. His conclusions also seem inconsistent: if societies label 'deviants' in defining their boundaries, it makes little sense to insist that 'deviant groups remain part of the whole' ('The Gospel of Matthew', 47). Despite frequent appeals to Erikson (*Wayward Puritans: A Study in the Sociology of Deviance.* [New York: John Wiley and Sons, 1966]; cited as 'Ericson'), Saldarini's thesis runs quite contrary to Erikson's conclusions. Sanders (*Schismatics, Sectarians, Dissidents, Deviants,* 129–151) more accurately reflects the sociological discussion but is inclined to rather sweeping generalizations; see further below (Judaism and Apostasy). Malina and Neyrey have applied deviance theory to the narrative of Matthew and Luke: B.J. Malina and J.H. Neyrey, *Calling Jesus Names: The Social Value of Labels in Matthew* (Sonoma, CA: Polebridge, 1988); B.J. Malina, 'Conflict in Luke-Acts: Labelling and Deviance Theory', in J.H. Neyrey, ed., *The Social World of Luke-Acts: Models for Interpretation* (Peabody: Hendrickson, 1991). But it remains unclear whether their analysis relates to the history of Jesus or to the Gospel narratives; if the latter, it is hard to see what can be achieved beyond renaming the actors and processes in the story.

[3] There are valuable surveys by S.J. Pfohl, *Images of Deviance and Social Control: A Sociological History* (*New* York: McGraw-Hill, 1985); D. Downes and R. Rock, *Understanding Deviance: A Guide to the Sociology of Crime and Rule-breaking* (2nd ed.; Oxford: Clarendon, 1988). Davis' survey is somewhat dense and ideologically biased: N.J. Davis, *Sociological Constructions of Deviance: Perspectives and Issues in the Field* (2nd ed., Dubuque: W.C. Brown, 1980).

fectly as to become the new orthodoxy in an amazingly short time.[4] The basic features of the interactionist perspective can be summarized under two headings: deviance as a social product and the consequences of labelling.

a) Deviance as a social product

The interactionist perspective is essentially a reaction against theories which take deviance to be a particular quality inherent in certain acts or persons; it questions whether deviance is an objectively definable entity at all. If we think we know who or what is deviant and muster quantitative statistics, interactionists insist that the definition of deviance is radically dependent on the societal reaction which behaviour evokes. To quote the now famous words of Becker:

> Social groups create deviance by making the rules whose infraction constitutes deviance, and by applying those rules to particular people and labeling them as outsiders. From this point of view, deviance is not a quality of the act the person commits, but rather a consequence of the application by others of rules and sanctions to an 'offender'. The deviant is one to whom that label has been successfully applied; deviant behavior is behavior that people so label.[5]

The cutting edge of this definition is that deviance cannot be predicated of acts as such, only of acts as they receive a negative social response or reaction. The point here is not simply that in any given society norms and laws define what is or is not deviant (that is true but also trite). The point is that in actual fact societies apply their own norms differentially, selecting and stereotyping those they choose to mark as deviant, so that only some norm-breakers are actually treated as deviant. Moreover, what makes an act socially significant as deviant is not so much that it is *performed*, as that it is *reacted to* as deviant and the actor accordingly labelled. Lots of people drink heavily, but only some are labelled 'alcoholic' and what would make any individual's drinking significant as deviant in the eyes of others is as and when this reaction (and this label) is elicited. In other words, the interactionist perspective focuses not just on the act itself, but on what is made of the act socially, insisting that this social reaction radically affects the nature,

---

[4] Some of the essential elements of the perspective had been outlined by E.M. Lemert (*Social Pathology* [New York: McGraw-Hill, 1951]); but he was somewhat critical of its later expression in the 1960s (*Human Deviance, Social Problems, and Social Control* [2nd ed.; Englewood Cliffs: Prentice Hall, 1972] 14–25).

[5] H.S. Becker, *Outsiders: Studies in the Sociology of Deviance* (New York: Free Press, 1963) 9. Near contemporaneous definitions of this feature of the interactionist perspective can be found in J.I. Kitsuse, 'Societal Reaction to Deviant Behaviour: Problems of Theory and Method' *Social Problems* 9 (1962) 247–256 and K.T. Erikson, 'Notes on the Sociology of Deviance' *Social Problems* 9 (1962) 307–314, both reprinted in H.S. Becker, ed., *The Other Side: Perspectives on Deviance* (New York: Free Press, 1964).

social meaning and implications of the act.[6] Deviance is, in this sense, the product of social interaction.

b) The consequences of labelling

If the deviant act becomes socially significant when it receives a social reaction, interactionists are also interested in the further consequences for the actor when he/she receives such a reaction. Of course, negative reactions can vary in degree of seriousness and not all labels are equally damaging, but interactionists note the ways in which labels generally affect the identity of those who receive them, how, for instance, one considered an 'alcoholic' often adopts a new role in society. Tracing what they have called 'deviant careers' and the grouping of those labelled into 'deviant associations', researchers following the interactionist perspective have often exposed the detrimental effects of labelling and the confirmation of deviant identity leading to what has been called 'secondary deviance'. They therefore insist that, far from being a static phenomenon, deviance is actually a complex process, in which the on-going relationship between the actor and the reacting society defines what counts as deviant.

In the limited space of this essay, I can explore only some features of this perspective and will focus solely on the first and foundational notion of deviance as a social product. It is clear, I hope, that this perspective contains a strong strand of relativism. Its interest is as much in the labellers ('Who is judging this activity to be deviant?') as in the activity so labelled. Since those who create and apply the rules vary in their judgements from one society to another, and differ within the same society at different times and in differing circumstances, 'deviance' appears to be, in an important respect, 'in the eye of the beholder'. In social-scientific parlance, it is an ascribed as much as it is an achieved status. When it analyses cases of deviance, delinquency, criminality, apostasy or the like, the interactionist perspective is always asking 'Whose definitions of deviance are operative here?' and (as a supplementary question) 'Whose interests do these definitions serve?' I am convinced that sensitivity to these questions could clarify some of the historical matters which interest us. However, first I should note some of the limitations of this approach and the criticisms which have been levelled against it. These will help us to see more precisely what we can and cannot do in utilizing this perspective in our research.[7]

---

[6] K.M. Schur, *Labeling Deviant Behaviour: Its Sociological Implications* (New York: Harper and Row, 1971) 16.

[7] Among the most searching critics of this perspective are J.P. Gibbs, 'Conceptions of Deviant Behaviour: The Old and the New' *Pacific Sociological Review* 9 (1966) 9–14 and J. Knutsson, *Labeling Theory: A Critical Examination* (Stockholm: Scientific Research

c) Limitations of the interactionist perspective

Concerning the limitations of this approach, it is important to say at the outset that it is not intended to explain the origins or the motivations of the deviant act as such. Its focus is, as we have seen, on the reaction to the act (and the effects of that reaction), not on the originating causes of the deviation. This peculiar focus has given the impression that the interactionist perspective views the 'deviant' as merely passive, as one whose actions are simply pounced upon by arbitrary labelling authorities, as indeed 'more sinned against than sinning'. When Becker and others paraded their empathy with the 'deviants' they studied in the radical mood of the 1960s,[8] critics suspected them of an anti-establishment bias which sought to blame deviance on the authorities for labelling people and so driving them into crime. In fact, political bias is by no means a necessary consequence of this perspective which properly is concerned neither to excuse nor to blame: it is simply interested in how a society (or an interest group within society) selectively creates its definitions of deviance and how the social significance of an act that deviates from the norms is radically dependent on the sort of reaction which it elicits.[9]

If it does not provide an 'aetiology' of deviant acts, neither does the interactionist perspective in itself explain why societies react as they do to acts they consider 'deviant'. However, it has been allied to various forms of explanation which could shed light on this matter. Becker himself pointed to factors of political and economic power which enable certain individu-

---

Group, 1977). A vulgarized version is sharply rejected by the essayists in W. R. Gove (*The Labelling of Deviance: Evaluating a Perspective* [New York: John Wiley and Sons, 1975]), where, however, Kitsuse and Schur defend its central notions as properly understood. There are also critical discussions in P. Rock, *Deviant Behaviour* (London: Hutchinson, 1973) 19–26; Davis, *Sociological Constructions of Deviance*, 197–234. [Cf. now M. Tellbe, *Christ-Believers in Ephesus* (WUNT 242; Tübingen: Mohr Siebeck, 2009) 141–49; J. M. Marques and D. Abrams et al., 'Social Categorization, Social Identification, and Rejection of Deviant Groups', in M. A. Hogg and R. S. Tindale, eds., *Blackwell Handbook of Social Psychology: Group Processes* (Oxford: Blackwell, 2003) 400–424; L. Pietersen, 'Despicable Deviants: Labelling Theory and the Polemic of the Pastorals', *Sociology of Religion* 58 (1997) 343–52.]

[8] E. g., Becker, *The Other Side*, 1–6.

[9] A careful reading of Becker shows that he is not guilty of suggesting that the deviant act itself is irrelevant to the labelling process, as some have charged: he writes, 'whether a given act is deviant or not depends *in part* on the nature of the act (that is, whether or not it violates some rule) and *in part* on what other people do about it' (*Outsiders*, 9, my emphasis). This led him to some terminological confusion over the use of the word 'deviant' (e. g. he posits a category of 'secret deviant' which critics observe is logically problematic from an interactionist perspective). But so long as one recognizes the distinction between 'deviant' in the weak sense of 'what deviates from social norms' and 'deviant' in the strong sense of 'what elicits the social reaction that "something should be done about it"' (see Schur, *Labeling Deviant Behaviour,* 24–25), this difficulty is not insuperable.

als or groups to enforce their definitions of deviancy.[10] Other sociologists have gone further in exploring the power struggles in which a threatened element in society seeks to identify and label deviants in accordance with its own interests.[11] Such analyses tie deviance theory closely to theories of social control, and even if the complexities of modern society make it exceptionally difficult to trace the influence of competing interest groups, the interactionist perspective certainly invites such an investigation of interests and power where it can be pursued.

On a parallel track, Erikson combined the interactionist perspective with elements of Durkheimian functionalism, in enquiring what functions reactions to deviance serve for society as a whole.[12] He suggested, and sought to illustrate through a study of seventeenth-century New England, that the labelling of deviants can perform an important function in the boundary maintenance of an insecure community.[13] While his thesis (and its functionalist basis) are now considered too simplistic to be applied to modern industrialised societies Erikson's work may be of value in suggesting avenues of enquiry concerning the simpler forms of community which we can study in early Judaism and early Christianity. In particular, his study could shed light on the situation of a simply structured community encountering serious ambiguities in its definition of norms; such ambiguities could arise in situations of novelty or transition, where norms are inconsistently applied or have become controversial, or where activities appear borderline in relation to previous precedents.[14] Here there is a good case to be made that the identification of 'deviants' can serve to give an insecure community clarity and security in its social identity. As we shall see, this has particular relevance to the social situation of early Christianity, but it may also be applicable to certain aspects of first-century Judaism.

---

[10] Becker, *Outsiders*, 17–18.

[11] J. Lofland, *Deviance and Identity* (Englewood Cliffs: Prentice Hall, 1969) 13–19; K. M. Schur, *The Politics of Deviance: Stigma Contests and the Uses of Power* (Englewood Cliffs: Prentice Hall, 1980). Lofland (*Deviance and Identity*, 14) writes: 'Deviance is the name of the conflict game in which individuals or loosely organized small groups with little power are strongly feared by a well-organized, sizable minority or majority who have a large amount of power'.

[12] Erikson, *Wayward Puritans.*

[13] 'The deviant is a person whose activities have moved outside the margins of the group, and when the community calls him to account for that vagrancy it is making a statement about the nature and placement of its boundaries' (Erikson, *Wayward Puritans*, 11). Erikson's thesis has been supported and refined by N. Ben-Yehuda, *Deviance and Moral Boundaries* (Chicago: University of Chicago, 1985) 23–73.

[14] See Schur, *Labeling Deviant Behaviour*, 21 and Lemert, *Human Deviance*, 21–22; the latter insists in this connection that 'no one theory or model will suffice to study the societal reaction; models must be appropriate to the area under study, to the values, norms, and structures identifiable in the area, as well as the special qualities of the persons and their acts subject to definition as deviant' (p. 21).

It would be a mistake to regard the interactionist perspective as a theory operating with clear-cut definitions and testable hypotheses. It is better regarded as a 'sensitizing concept' which suggests an angle of enquiry,[15] rather than a 'theory' or 'model' generating predictive hypotheses. Some of its notions can only be loosely defined (since negative social reactions can take many different forms) and it is misunderstood if it is taken to predict that labelling deviants always and inevitably sets off a 'deviant career'.[16] In certain respects, therefore, the interactionist perspective can never be established by empirical proof, and its resistance to statistical analysis has caused some frustration among sociologists who regard their subject as a natural science. However, rightly employed this perspective can enable us to ask new questions of the historical material we study: it can suggest some interesting directions in which to look, though not, of course, what we will find when we look there.

III. Judaism and Apostasy

It is remarkable how frequently scholars of Judaism appear to regard 'apostasy' as an objectively definable entity, as an inherent quality in certain kinds of behaviour. Discussions of our topic often work on the assumption that we all know what constitutes apostasy: it is only a matter of detecting the cases which crop up here and there in our sources. Yet 'apostasy', like other deviant labels, is essentially a matter of perspective. One may list activities in which Jews were socially assimilated to their gentile environment and thereby abandoned some aspects of their national traditions, but where such assimilation was regarded as 'apostasy' was a matter which different Jews in different locations and times could define in very different ways.[17] A Jew who was assimilated to the extent of attending a Greek school and visiting the Greek theatre might be considered by some Jews as 'apostate' but fully accepted as an observant Jew by others. Given what we know of the diversity of Jewish practice and belief, it is odd how scholars continue to regard the perspective of the Maccabean literature (for instance) as definitive for Juda-

[15] Schur, *Labeling Deviant Behaviour*, 26, 31.

[16] Downes and Rock properly insist that 'interactionism casts deviance as a process which may continue over a lifetime, which has no necessary end, which is anything but inexorable, and which may be built around false starts, diversions and returns' (*Understanding Deviance*, 183).

[17] I have explored this matter in more detail in relation to the Diaspora in 'Who was Considered an Apostate in the Jewish Diaspora?', in G.N. Stanton and G. Stroumsa, *Tolerance and Intolerance in Early Judaism and Christianity* (Cambridge: Cambridge University, 1998) 80–98 [see chapter 7 below]. [See now on the whole topic, S. Wilson, *Leaving the Fold: Apostates and Defectors in Antiquity* (Minneapolis: Fortress, 2004).]

ism as a whole, as if all Jews contrasted 'Judaism' and 'Hellenism' along the lines of 1 and 2 Maccabees, or all regarded the acquisition of Greek citizenship as tantamount to apostasy (as does 3 Maccabees).[18] Where the author of *The Letter of Aristeas* celebrates the social integration of Hellenized Jews in the Ptolemaic court, 3 Maccabees sees only compromise, inevitably entailing idolatry. Given the divergent expressions of Judaism within Palestine before 70 CE and the varieties of Judaism in the Diaspora, we should not be surprised if we find varying definitions or deviants (i. e. sinners, apostates etc.) in our Jewish sources.[19] The interactionist perspective suggests that we should regard 'apostate' as a term defined only in relation to the party issuing the label, and what evidence we have from first-century Judaism bears out the truth of this relativistic observation.

I do not mean to suggest that Jewish communities were invariably disunited in their definition of their boundaries or that the definition of 'apostate' was always negotiated anew in each instance. During periods of stability individual Jewish communities could clearly take some definitions for granted and a certain unity of mind is sometimes perceptible both within individual communities and across geographical and temporal bounds. Philo tells us his own opinion on who has 'deserted the ancestral customs', but also indicates the viewpoint of 'the masses' in the Jewish community in Alexandria with which he is largely in accord.[20] We can also discern certain topics (e. g. engagement in 'idolatrous' worship and eating unclean food) on which there appears to have been a fair degree of unanimity across different Jewish communities in our period. Thus we need not suppose that every case of 'deviating' behaviour had to be negotiated from scratch in the community as to its 'deviant' or 'non-deviant' status. Nonetheless, norms do change over time and even where they are generally upheld and applied, exceptions can be allowed in particular circumstances. A homosexual was a 'pervert' only a generation ago, but is less frequently so labelled today, and although most Americans strongly disapprove of adultery, they are prepared to turn a blind eye in certain notable cases. Thus, as the interactionist perspective suggests, when we find a Jew labelled an 'apostate', it is always

---

[18] A. Kasher is a particularly clear example of this, but by no means the only one (*The Jews in Hellenistic and Roman Egypt. The Struggle for Equal Rights* [Tübingen: Mohr Siebeck, 1985]). For an earlier essay based on the spurious notion of 'orthodoxy' in Judaism see L. H. Feldman, 'The Orthodoxy of the Jews in Hellenistic Egypt' *JSS* 22 (1960) 215–37.

[19] On the varying definitions of 'sinner' in Palestinian Judaism see J. D. G. Dunn, *Jesus, Paul and the Law* (London: SPCK, 1990) 71–77. On diversity in the Diaspora see J. M. G. Barclay, *Jews in the Mediterranean Diaspora from Alexander to Trajan (323 BCE–117 CE)* (Edinburgh: T & T Clark, 1996).

[20] For his own opinion see, e. g., *Jos.* 254; *Virt.* 182; *Mos.* 1.31; *Spec. Leg.* 1.54–58; 3.29. For the opinion of the masses, *Migr. Abr.* 89–93. [See chapter 3 above.]

worth enquiring who is doing the defining and whose interests are involved in this definition.

a) The case of Tiberius Julius Alexander

Let me take one famous example of an 'apostate' and see what might be suggested by this interactionist perspective. My example is Tiberius Julius Alexander, Philo's nephew, who was born into an exceptionally wealthy Jewish family in Alexandria in c. 15 CE.[21] Alexander features as a sceptic in three philosophical treatises written by Philo, but these do not suggest that he was dissociated from the Jewish community or regarded by Philo as an apostate.[22] In his subsequent career we find Alexander prominent in Roman administration, first as *epistratēgos* of the Thebaid (42 CE), then as procurator of Judaea (46–48 CE), as a high-ranking officer in the eastern army (63 CE) and then at the very top of the equestrian ladder as Roman governor of Egypt (66–69 CE). It was during this latter period that he had to suppress a Jewish uprising in Alexandria (Josephus, *Bell.* 2.487–498) and in 70 CK he acted as Titus' advisor and second-in-command at the siege of Jerusalem *(Bell.* 5.45–46; 6.237–242). Thereafter he may have become prefect of the praetorian guard in Rome.

It is striking that when recording these aspects of Alexander's life in his *Jewish War* (late 70s CE) Josephus makes no comment on Alexander's Jewish standing. One can imagine what the members of the Jewish community in Alexandria thought of him when he ordered the Roman troops into their quarter, and from the perspective of the Jewish defenders of Jerusalem he was presumably a traitor and renegade, like Josephus himself *(Bell.* 3.438–442; 5.375). In fact the common fate of Alexander and Josephus as advisors of Titus in the Roman camp and their subsequent honours at Rome may have induced Josephus to omit criticism of Alexander's behaviour, though he presumably knew that his duties involved him in officiating at the worship of Egyptian and Roman deities.[23] If we had only Josephus' *War* we

[21] His biography has been fully detailed by E. G. Turner, 'Tiberius Julius Alexander' *JRS* 44 (1954) 54–64 and V. Burr. *Tiberius Julius Alexander* (Bonn: Habelt, 1955). [Cf. now S. Étienne, 'Réflexion sur l'apostasie de Tibérius Julius Alexander' *Studia Philonica Annual* 12 (2000) 122–42; S. Wilson, *Leaving the Fold*, 29–33.]

[22] In *Prov.* 1 and 2 and in *Anim.* Alexander argues against divine providence, but Philo treats him with warmth and respect and has him retract his doubts at the end of *Prov.* 2. As a caution, note the hesitancy of Hadas-Lebel on the authorship of these treatises and the identity of the Alexander featured in them (*De Providentia I et II: les oeuvres de Philon d'Alexandrie* [Paris: Cerf, 1973] 23–46).

[23] We find Alexander in inscriptions honouring Egyptian deities (and their providence!) in *Orientis Graeci Inscriptiones Selectae* 663 and 669; cf. comparable papyri in *Corpus Papyrorum Judaicarum* 418.

would have no explicit evidence that Alexander was ever regarded as an apostate. It is only in his later work, the *Jewish Antiquities,* that Josephus records that Alexander 'did not remain faithful to his ancestral customs' *(Ant.* 20.100). That was published at a date (93 CE) when Alexander was almost certainly dead. The facts of this case prompt two observations.

First, Alexander's prominent position in Roman government brought no advantage to the Jews either in Alexandria or in Judaea. But if events had turned out differently, if (for instance) he had succeeded in averting violence in Alexandria or had saved Jerusalem, would he still have been castigated as an apostate? To what extent were Jewish communities willing to tolerate compromise among their well-placed members so long as their activities worked to the benefit of Jews? One thinks of the tumultuous welcome accorded to Agrippa I in Alexandria after his enthronement as king by Gaius (38 CE), even though he was well known to be a dishonest bankrupt whose close friendship with Gaius must have involved extensive assimilation (Philo, *Flacc.* 25–30; Jos., *Ant.* 18.143–239). Agrippa could play an important role on behalf of the Jews; Alexander, as it turned out, could not.

Secondly, Josephus may have regarded Alexander as an apostate at the time he wrote the *War,* but refrained from saying so either because it would have reflected badly on himself (he was also somewhat compromised in his role during the war) or because he could not afford to alienate a man of such influence in Rome. Perhaps he named Alexander an apostate in the *Antiquities* because it was safe to do so only when Alexander was dead.[24] This might suggest that charges of apostasy, which could cause offence, were made only when those who levelled them could afford to do so.

These observations on the case of Tiberius Julius Alexander are merely illustrative of the sort of questions which arise when we employ the interactionist perspective on deviance to the phenomenon of apostasy. They suggest that we have to rid ourselves of the notion that everyone knows (and everyone then knew) who was an apostate; we need to watch very carefully who was (or was not) defining and applying the label 'apostate', in what circumstances, from what perspective and in whose interests. Our observations on this particular case also suggest the power factors which could be involved in this process, in which it was easier to label the socially weak than the socially strong.

b) The case of Christians in the first century

Such considerations could be of benefit in investigating the processes by which Christians were edged out of Jewish communities in the course of

[24] Turner, 'Tiberius Julius Alexander', 63.

the first two centuries CE. As I mentioned at the beginning, Jack Sanders has made interesting use of deviance theory in this connection.[25] Sanders' question is: 'Why did the leadership of Roman-period Judaism, normally tolerant of diversity, reject and even persecute the various manifestations of Christianity that it encountered?'.[26] He considers that cultural (i.e. theological) factors are insufficient to answer this question and looks for help from deviance theory,[27] especially that functionalist application developed by Erikson which suggested that the identification of deviants helps to clarify and enforce the boundaries of an insecure community. Taking the early Christians to be a new outcrop of deviants whose status raised difficult questions, Sanders points to the tension-laden years in Judaea both before and after the revolt as the crucial factor in driving the threatened Jewish leadership towards identifying and punishing the Christians as deviants.[28]

Several features of this analysis are suggestive, but it requires, I suggest, much closer definition. In the first place, it is not clear whether the 'social identity crisis' which Sanders discovers in Judaea was as severe in the pre-70 period as he suggests, or prevalent to any degree in those parts of the Diaspora where we can trace the growth of the Christian movement.[29] Second, it is extremely hard to discern, and impossible to generalize about, what were the issues on which Christians were considered 'deviant'. It is even difficult to see to what degree such issues were novel or ambiguous; perhaps some Christians were dismissed without much ado as 'apostates' since they had clearly flouted laws long regarded as tests of loyalty to Judaism.[30] Third, if

[25] Sanders, *Schismatics, Sectarians, Dissidents, Deviants*, 129–151.

[26] Ibid., 129.

[27] Ibid., 99, 139.

[28] Ibid., 136–137.

[29] Ibid., 135. The external threats to Palestinian Jews in the pre-70 period which Sanders lists (p. 137) are not quite equivalent to the identity-threatening features of Puritan New England which he takes from Erikson as his model. Arguably, the threat of the statue of Gaius (39–41 CE) made Palestinian Jews not less but more certain of their unity and the limits of their tolerance. In the Diaspora, the Jewish communities in Egypt and Cyrene were certainly troubled during this century, but we cannot trace the rise of Christianity there; and in the places where our record for Christianity is strong (Rome, Greece, Asia Minor) there is little evidence of 'crisis' in the synagogue communities (except perhaps in Rome in the 40s CE).

[30] Sanders (p. 136) is aware that old and traditional 'crimes' hardly need a social identity crisis to be identified and punished, and thus has to assert that the Christians ('of course') constituted an ambiguous group, a case of 'soft deviance' which either was not or might not have been punished at other times. But this clearly needs to be established in the first place and the situation may have differed greatly between different expressions of Christianity. Sanders is naturally aware of the diversity in early Christianity on such matters as the admission of gentiles, but seems to assume that any welcome of gentiles, even as proper proselytes, was liable to interpretation as deviance (p. 138); that seems to run against the evidence (e.g. Josephus, *Bell.* 2.454).

its social identity crisis even before 70 CE caused mainstream Judaism to reject Christianity 'when it had normally accepted similar deviance',[31] why did it not also reject those other 'deviant' forms of Judaism in this period? Sanders cites comparable examples of deviance as including Philo, the Essenes, John the Baptist and the Pharisaic party, none of which was ostracized in the pre-70 era.[32] In fact, if all of these can be regarded as 'similar' in deviance to each other and to Christianity, it appears that the notion of 'deviance' has become far too large a hammer with which to crack this rather delicate nut.

Rather than adopting any such global hypothesis, we should observe that the interactionist perspective suggests that definitions of 'deviance' could vary somewhat between different parties and interest groups in Judaism, and this could help to explain why Christians were in fact so *variously* assessed during the first century. An activity, we recall, is deviant only to the degree to which others react negatively towards it. To some Jews 'Matthean Christians' may have seemed peculiar but not apostate, while other Jews may have considered them to have crossed a crucial boundary out of Judaism. Other Jewish Christians could have evoked different reactions and their gentile Christian adherents may have been variously judged as valuable sympathizers or dangerous diluters of the faith. In fact, given the relativity which is integral to the subject of deviance and the evidence for varying Jewish definitions of sinners and apostates, it may be unhelpful to look for any single issue on which the early Christians made themselves clearly suspect to contemporary Jews. Rather, since deviance is a matter of definition and since the Christians were deviant only as and when they were reacted to as such, we should imagine there to have been a host of variations in local circumstances and a range of reactions to various kinds of Christianity. As we have seen, some of these variations were probably related to power struggles: where the Christians were politically and socially weak it was far easier to 'deviantize' them than where they had a significant power base in numerical or economic terms. Thus, while general social trends in cultural insecurity probably had some part to play in the whole process, we must be ever alert to the innumerable variables of circumstance and personnel through which the earliest Christians sometimes were and sometimes were not rejected by first-century Jews as deviant. It is unfortunate that we can trace very few actual examples of this deviantizing process. Paul is perhaps the best documented and worth considering in some detail.

[31] Ibid., 136.

[32] Ibid., 86, 133.

c) The case of Paul

From the evidence of his letters it appears that Paul was continually 'endangered' by Jews (2 Cor. 11:26) and felt himself 'persecuted' because of his stance on circumcision (Gal. 5:11). In one passage he mentions being 'banished' and 'prevented from speaking to Gentiles' (1 Thess. 2:15—its authenticity is questioned by some) and in another revealing comment says he has received the synagogue punishment of the thirty-nine lashes on five occasions (2 Cor. 11:24). It appears that even many Christian Jews strongly opposed him; they considered his eating with gentiles sinful (Gal. 2:11–17) and his teaching an invitation to libertinism (Rom. 3:8). In Acts also the theme of Jewish opposition to Paul is prominent, though perhaps somewhat stereotyped. In that narrative Paul is frequently denounced and expelled from synagogues, and sometimes charged with serious offences. When he arrives in Jerusalem he is met by anxious Jewish Christians who have been told that he teaches 'apostasy' from Moses to the Jews who live among the gentiles, telling them not to circumcise their children or to live in accordance with the Jewish customs (Acts 21:21). Paul's previous fears concerning his reception in Jerusalem (Rom. 15:31) are amply fulfilled in his arrest and subsequent trials.

Such evidence suggests that Paul was frequently denounced as an apostate Jew. Such a reaction was not, however, either automatic or immediate. Some Jewish Christians at least some of the time accepted Paul's stance as compatible with their understanding of Judaism (Peter, Barnabas, Prisca and Aquila, for instance), and there is good reason to believe that Paul was initially accepted as a synagogue member in most locations. The thirty-nine lashes were discipline for a synagogue member, not quite the expulsion and ostracism which an officially designated apostate might receive.[33] There were clearly some ambiguities about Paul which elicited varying reactions, and that is not surprising in relation to a man who said he lived as a Jew among Jews, but without reference to the law among gentiles (1 Cor. 9:20–21), and whom we find in his letters sometimes celebrating and sometimes denigrating his Jewish credentials (2 Cor. 11:22; Rom. 11:1; Gal. 1:13–14; Phil. 3:2–11).

Scholars have recently debated whether Paul was or was not an apostate, but usually without reference to how he was actually perceived in his own

[33] See A. E. Harvey, 'Forty Strokes Save One: Social Aspects of Judaizing and Apostasy', in A. E. Harvey, ed., *Alternative Approaches to New Testament Study* (London: SPCK, 1985) 79–96; S. Gallas, '"Fünfmal vierzig weniger einen …" Die an Paulus vollzogenen Synagogalstrafen nach 2Kor 11,24' *ZNW* 81 (1990) 178–91; W. Horbury, 'Extirpation and Excommunication' *VT 35* (1985) 13–38. [Cf. my essay 'Paul among Diaspora Jews: Anomaly or Apostate?' *JSNT* 60 (1995) 89–120.]

day.[34] It should be clear by now that the question requires us to be sensitive to the opinions and judgements of Paul's contemporaries; his deviance, like any other, was in the eye of the beholders. The evidence we have briefly surveyed suggests that many variables could affect their vision of Paul: Jews of different persuasions and in different places reacted differently to this enigmatic figure in their midst. How Paul fared in the Diaspora synagogues perhaps depended on how long he stayed there, what personal animosities he engendered, how his judges at his synagogue trials viewed his defence and what reports (either true or false) they had heard of his behaviour. It is not insignificant that Paul's social position in the Diaspora communities was generally weak: he was a newcomer, of low social status, with no economic or political power base on which to build his defence, and power struggles in the synagogue almost inevitably turned to his disadvantage. Inasmuch as he *was viewed* by his contemporary Jews as an apostate, he *was* (historically speaking) an apostate, and no amount of pleading about the Jewish elements in his theology or the diversity within first-century Judaism can mask or alter that reality.

IV. Early Christianity And The Creation Of Deviants

Here I can add only a few words on that other crucial process of definition which characterizes early Christianity, its internal definition of its own boundaries. We may simply observe here, by way of illustration, a particularly intriguing example of the struggle for the definition of Christian identity in the correspondence of Paul with the church in Corinth. One may read the whole of 1 Corinthians as an attempt by Paul to define the boundaries of the Christian community in Corinth, and an integral part of that effort involves Paul labelling as deviant those he considers should be excluded from the church. Indeed this letter contains a statement which almost precisely summarizes Erikson's thesis on the function of deviance in boundary definition. In 1 Cor. 11:19 Paul introduces his discussion of the Lord's Supper with the stunning comment that 'there must be divisions *(haireseis)* among you in order that those who are genuine *(dokimoi)* among you may be recognized'. That is a proto-sociological statement if ever there was one! Paul recognizes that the creation of distinctions between the 'genuine' *(dokimoi)* and the 'spurious' *(adokimoi,* cf. 1 Cor. 9:27) serves to

[34] See e.g. Dunn, *Jesus, Paul and the Law,* 183–214; H. Räisänen, 'Galatians 2:16 and Paul's Break with Judaism' *NTS* 31 (1985) 543–53; A.F. Segal, *Paul the Convert: The Apostolate and Apostasy of Saul the Pharisee* (New Haven: Yale University, 1990).

give the Christian community definition and identity; he even uses a 'functionalist' purpose clause!

Commentators are surprised at this statement, since earlier in the letter Paul deplores party divisions (1 Cor. 1:10–12).[35] But in fact Paul spends a considerable proportion of this letter indicating where he thinks the proper boundaries of Christian practice lie. Though he does not think the Apollos or Cephas party has deviated significantly from Christian norms, he certainly wants the Corinthians to recognize that the man reported to have had sex with his father's wife (1 Cor. 5:1–13) and those who participate in 'idolatry' (1 Cor. 10:1–22) and those who mishandle the Lord's Supper (1 Cor. 11:17–34) are all to be regarded as 'deviants' who have strayed over the boundary out of the community.[36] Here in this clash between Paul and the Corinthians we see very clearly how 'deviance' is defined by social reaction. The Corinthian Christians do not apparently regard the man mentioned in 1 Corinthians 5 as other than a sexually active brother; Paul insists that he is, and must be publicly labelled as, a *pornos* who is only a 'so-called' brother (5:11). It is fascinating to see here how, in a typical deviance process, Paul selects from this individual's many activities the one feature of which he disapproves and makes that the defining character of his identity: this man does not just *indulge in* some *porneia,* he *is* a *pornos* and must be treated as that, whatever else he might also be in character or behaviour.

In fact a fundamental point of dispute between Paul and the Corinthians is the location of their community boundaries. As I have argued elsewhere,[37] Paul thinks the Corinthians are far too comfortable in their social integration, and he spends much of the letter erecting barriers where the Corinthians presently see none. Conversely, he does not treat as deviant some whom other Christians might well have considered such: he does

---

[35] G. Fee considers this sentence 'one of the true puzzles in the letter' (*The First Epistle to the Corinthians* [NICNT; Grand Rapids: Eerdmans, 1987] 538). C.K. Barrett (*A Commentary on the First Epistle to the Corinthians* [BNTC; London: A & C Black, 1971] 262) significantly tones down its meaning, and J. Munck (*Paul and the Salvation of Mankind* [London: SCM, 1959] 136–137) implausibly relegates its reference to the eschatological future. [For the general topic, see B.J. Oropeza, *Paul and Apostasy: Eschatological Perseverance and Falling Away in the Corinthian Congregation* (WUNT 2.115; Tübingen: Mohr Siebeck, 2000).]

[36] On 1 Corinthians 5 see G. Forkman, *The Limits of the Religious Community* (Lund: Gleerup, 1972) 139–51. On 1 Cor. 11:17–34 see most recently T. Engberg-Pedersen, 'Proclaiming the Lord's Death: 1 Corinthians 11:17–34 and the Forms of Paul's Theological Argument', in D.M. Hay, ed., *Pauline Theology, II: 1 and 2 Corinthians* (Minneapolis: Fortress, 1993) 103–132. [Cf. now A.S. May, *'The Body for the Lord': Sex and Identity in 1 Corinthians 5–7* (London: T & T Clark, 2004); D.R. Smith, *'Hand this Man over to Satan': Curse, Exclusion and Salvation in 1 Corinthians 5* (London: T & T Clark, 2009).]

[37] J.M.G. Barclay, 'Thessalonica and Corinth: Social Contrasts in Pauline Christianity' *JSNT* 47 (1992) 49–74 [reprinted as chapter 9 in this volume].

not want to see excommunicated those who are married to non-Christians, or those who are uncircumcised or those who cannot speak in tongues. Throughout 1 Corinthians Paul is creating insiders and outsiders on his own terms and he does so with regard to so many different issues that it was almost inevitable that some Corinthians would take exception to his rulings. He identifies deviants in order to establish boundaries and solidify the identity of the Corinthian community, precisely as Erikson suggests. Unfortunately, in this case it was a policy which backfired disastrously, for he lacked the authority to get his understanding of deviance accepted. Turning to 2 Corinthians we find that resistance to Paul takes the form of questioning whether *he* is *dokimos* ('genuine') as a Christian (2 Cor. 13:1–7), and Paul has to respond by questioning the Christian status of this whole congregation and by furious invective against opponents whom he castigates as 'false apostles' (2 Cor. 11:13). It is easy to recognize here what we have seen throughout this discussion, that 'deviant' labels are being applied as part of a power struggle, here a fundamental battle for control of the Christian tradition.

We could of course trace this same process in other early Christian conflicts, where we are nowadays conscious of how perspectival terms like 'heretic' and 'apostate' are. Even so, I suspect there is still a tendency to take the views of the New Testament authors as somehow containing an inevitable and objective 'rightness' in their definition of deviance. The advantage of the interactionist perspective in this regard is that it continually reminds us to ask whose definitions we are hearing and whose interests they serve. It certainly suggests, for instance, a thoroughly suspicious reading of the Pastorals, 2 Peter, Jude and other polemical documents from the late first century which react against (and perhaps even invent) those 'deviants' who threaten the social structures which the authors represent. In the Pastorals we can see how practices recognized and tolerated by Paul (e.g. celibacy) have become 'deviantized' in the interests of a particular construction of church policy. In the highly fluid conditions of early Christianity, there were almost no 'taken-for-granted' norms which commanded universal assent, and it was open to each group and party to designate deviance in its own way. That the future of Christianity was determined by power contests between different groups is something no historian can deny, at least none with any sociological awareness: such is the way with all human society.

As I said at the outset, deviance theory is no magic wand with which to solve the many intricate problems which confront the historian of early Christianity. It can only be used in conjunction with minute historical analysis of the sources and cannot fill in the gaps which they leave. Its chief benefit, however, is to call into question our assumptions concerning the objective status of phenomena like apostasy and to invite us to pay close attention to the individuals or groups responsible for the application of deviant labels. If it helps to highlight a degree of relativism in the Judaism of this period, it also suggests that the process of 'the parting of the ways' cannot simply be traced in relation to certain absolute boundary marks, but was radically dependent on the particularities of location, personnel and social context in which early Christianity took root.[38]

[38] I would like to thank my research student Todd Still for his bibliographical assistance and stimulating work on this topic, and the members of the 'Context and Kerygma' conference held in St Andrews in June/July 1994 for their questions and encouragement.

7. Who Was Considered an Apostate in the Jewish Diaspora?

Tolerance has its limits in any community which wishes to preserve its identity. Boundaries which create distinctions between 'insiders' and 'outsiders' have to be established and maintained if a community is to survive, especially a minority community in a pluralist environment.[1] Most Jewish communities in the Diaspora appear to have been successful in preserving their social and religious identity, in many cases over hundreds of years. Where, then, did they fix the boundaries which defined the distinction between members and non-members? This question has often been addressed in enquiring how Gentiles were considered to have crossed the boundary and come into the Jewish community; but remarkably little attention has been paid to the opposite phenomenon, that is, how Jews were considered to have crossed the boundary and passed out of Judaism.[2] Recent studies have rightly emphasized the variety within Second Temple Judaism, its multifarious strands making it difficult to define universal standards of 'acceptability' within Judaism. Yet individual Jewish communities, however diverse they may have been, must have preserved some sense of 'proper' behaviour which made it possible to castigate actual or potential 'apostasy'. To detect where the boundaries lay in this regard would not only shed light on the maintenance of Jewish identity in the Diaspora; it would also provide some hints as to how the fateful division between early Christianity and Judaism took shape in the cities of the Graeco-Roman world.[3]

---

[1] H. Mol, *Identity and the Sacred* (Oxford: Blackwell, 1976) 57–8: 'It is precisely the boundary … which provides the sense of identity'.

[2] For Gentile entry into Judaism see especially S. J. D. Cohen, 'Crossing the Boundary and Becoming a Jew' *HTR* 82 (1989) 13–33. In his massive *Jew and Gentile in the Ancient World: Attitudes and Interactions from Alexander to Justinian* (Princeton: Princeton University, 1993), L. H. Feldman devotes several chapters to the discussion of Gentile proselytes and sympathizers, but only a few pages (79–83) to the question of 'apostasy'. Before him, the longest treatment of this subject in relation to the Diaspora was by H. A. Wolfson, *Philo* (Cambridge, Mass.: Harvard University, 1948) 1:73–85 (largely restricted to passages in Philo). The phenomenon of 'excommunication' in Second Temple Judaism has been explored by W. Horbury, 'Extirpation and Excommunication' *VT* 35 (1985) 13–38.

[3] My focus will be confined largely to the Western Diaspora in the period from Alexander to the second century CE. In relation to the Eastern Diaspora and outside these time-limits our literary sources are minimal (and epigraphic evidence provides little as-

I. Methodological Issues

The wording of my title is carefully chosen: the question is not 'Who *was* an apostate ...?' but 'Who *was considered* an apostate ...?' I stress this distinction to indicate that 'apostasy' (i. e. desertion of Judaism) is in essence not a matter of fact but a matter of perspective; it cannot be measured on any objective scale. Most discussions of our topic appear to work on the assumption that we all know what constituted (or constitutes – modern definitions often creep in here) apostasy; it is only a matter of detecting the cases which crop up in our sources. Yet to charge someone with 'apostasy' is to pin on them a label, to interpret their behaviour within the categories of one's own definition of loyalty to Judaism, which precisely in this matter is likely to be partial. To discuss who were apostates in Judaism is like discussing who were heretics in early Christianity, where, of course, different parties operated with varying definitions of 'heresy' and opposing groups often considered each other 'heretical'. Scholars have recognized that there are dangers in employing terms like 'orthodoxy' and 'heresy' in relation to Second Temple Judaism.[4] We should also acknowledge that we cannot employ the term 'apostate' as if it were an objectively defined category: it always comes loaded with the prejudices of those who use it.

One may measure with a degree of objectivity the extent to which Jews were socially assimilated to their Gentile environment, and the evidence which we shall consider suggests that all charges of 'apostasy' were somehow related to assimilation. But how they were related could vary greatly from one observer to another. A Jew who was assimilated to the extent of attending a Greek school and visiting the Greek theatre might be considered by some Jews an 'apostate', but be fully affirmed as an observant Jew by others. As we shall see, the acquisition of Greek citizenship was regarded by one of our Diaspora witnesses (3 Maccabees) as tantamount to apostasy, but there is reason to believe that this viewpoint was not shared by all Jews in the Diaspora, not even by all Jews in the environment of that witness

---

sistance for this particular quest). Among the studies of boundary-setting in Eretz Israel note G. Forkman, *The Limits of the Religious Community* (Lund: Gleerup, 1972), and F. Dexinger, 'Limits of Tolerance in Judaism: The Samaritan Example' in E. P. Sanders, A. I. Baumgarten and A. Mendelson, eds., *Jewish and Christian Self-Definition*, vol. 2 (London: SCM, 1981) 88–114. J. T. Sanders (*Schismatics, Sectarians, Dissidents, Deviants: The First One Hundred Years of Jewish-Christian Relations* [London: SCM, 1993]) devotes surprisingly little attention to the questions raised in this chapter. [For the general topic, see now S. Wilson, *Leaving the Fold: Apostates and Defectors in Antiquity* (Minneapolis: Fortress, 2004).]

[4] L. L. Grabbe ('Orthodoxy in Judaism: What are the Issues?' *JSJ* 8 [1977] 149–53) rightly insists that 'orthodoxy' is a relative entity and that such a term belongs 'within confessional belief rather than historical investigation' (152–3).

(Alexandria). Yet the judgement of 3 Maccabees has been widely accepted by scholars as a universal norm.[5]

In fact, apostasy, like beauty, is in the eye of the beholder.[6] Jews could and did differ in where they considered other Jews to have 'crossed the boundary' out of Judaism. To observe 'apostasy' in the Diaspora is to observe how Jews in the Diaspora considered other Diaspora Jews to have stepped outside (what they took to be) legitimate Judaism.[7] Thus, the material we shall survey will be discussed, as far as possible, according to the authors in the Diaspora who made the judgements that interest us.[8] We need to note very carefully whose verdict we are hearing when we find Diaspora Jews labelled as 'apostates'. It is only when we have collected all such verdicts that we shall be able to assess to what degree their judgements were commonly held and to what degree they were idiosyncratic.

Our procedure requires, therefore, that we (a) refuse to adopt any predetermined definition of apostasy, and (b) confine ourselves to the cases where we can hear the verdicts of Diaspora Jews about each other. This means that we shall be unable to pass comment on those assimilated Jews who appear in our sources without any indication of their status among their fellow Jews. Thus, for instance, the Jewish actor Aliturus, who was a favourite in the court of Nero and assisted Josephus in his mission there in 64 CE *(Vita* 16),

[5] So, e.g., J.J. Collins (*Between Athens and Jerusalem: Jewish Identity in the Hellenistic Diaspora* [New York: Crossroad, 1986] 105), who reports the view of 3 Maccabees as if it were an objective fact: 'We should also note that the price of this parity [with Alexandrians] is religious apostasy, as was also true for Jews who became full citizens in the Roman era'. A prominent exponent of this mistake is A. Kasher (*The Jews in Hellenistic and Roman Egypt: The Struggle for Equal Rights* [Tübingen: Mohr Siebeck, 1985]), who frequently asserts that only apostates could have been interested in Alexandrian citizenship (e.g. 211–32, 312–13, 335–6).

[6] The study of our subject could benefit from 'labelling' theories of deviance, which I have explored in J. Barclay, 'Deviance and Apostasy: Some Applications of Deviance Theory to First Century Judaism and Christianity', in P.F. Esler (ed.), *Modelling Early Christianity* (London, Routledge, 1995); reprinted as chapter 6 in this volume. See H.S. Becker (*Outsiders. Studies in the Sociology of Deviance* [New York: The Free Press, 1963]), whose work has been employed by Sanders, *Schismatics.*

[7] How such Diaspora Jews viewed themselves and how they were viewed by non-Jews are different matters again. We know of cases where Romans considered Jews to have ceased to practise as Jews (e.g. Josephus, *Ant.* 14.228, 234, 240; Suetonius, *Domitian* 12.2), but we do not know how such Jews were viewed in their own communities. The case of the Jews described in an inscription from Smyrna (early second century CE) as οἱ ποτὲ Ἰουδαῖοι is complex. Are we hearing the vocabulary of the Jews themselves or of the Gentile authority which recorded their donation? And does the phrase mean 'former Judaeans' (i.e. immigrants from Judaea) or 'former Jews'? See P. Trebilco, *Jewish Communities in Asia Minor* (Cambridge: Cambridge University, 1991) 174–5.

[8] I have confined myself here to the verdicts of Jews living in the Diaspora and reacting to other Diaspora Jews. For this reason I have included Josephus (despite his upbringing in Judaea) and excluded 2 Maccabees (which is based on the work of Jason of Cyrene but concerns Palestinian events).

has frequently been regarded as an apostate.[9] But we have no means of knowing how he was regarded by the Jews in Rome and Josephus makes no comment about his Jewish standing. Similarly when we hear of Jewish ephebes in various Greek cities (e. g., Cyrene, Iasos, Hypaepa) or of Eleazar the 'guardian of the law' (νομοφύλαξ) in the civic administration of Cyrene, we cannot leap to conclusions about their status within the Jewish community.[10] Even when we find Jews in lists of donors to Greek gods, we cannot be sure how their Jewish contemporaries would have regarded them.[11]

Thus the only evidence suitable for our assessment is where we find individuals or categories of Jews actually described as 'apostates' from Judaism. This will not exactly match cases of the specific term 'apostate' (ἀποστάτης) or references where the related nouns 'apostasy' (ἀποστασία and ἀπόστασις) and verbs 'to apostatize' (ἀποστατέω and ἀφίστημι) are used. This group of terms is often used in Greek literature in a political sense referring to 'desertion' or 'revolt'. In the LXX we find such words employed also as a metaphor for Israel's religious disloyalty,[12] thus appearing, for instance, in Maccabean literature to describe the Hellenizers at the time of Antiochus IV.[13] Josephus uses the nouns only in the literal political sense of 'desertion' or 'revolt',[14] but he uses the verb ἀφίστημι in a religious as well as a political sense.[15] However, he (and others) have a range of alternative phrases with which to describe disloyalty to the Jewish community and its customs, such as 'abandoning the ancestral laws' or 'neglecting the ancestral customs'. Since many people who were known to have

[9] E. g. E. M. Smallwood, *The Jews under Roman Rule. From Pompey to Diocletian* (2nd ed.; Leiden: Brill, 1981) 281 n. 84: 'he was without doubt an apostate, even if he retained enough national consciousness to befriend Josephus'.

[10] Ephebes in Cyrene: G. Lüderitz, *Corpus jüdischer Zeugnisse aus der Cyrenaika* (Wiesbaden: Reichert, 1983) nos. 6–7 (=SEG 20, 740–1); in Iasos: L. Robert, 'Un corpus des inscriptions juives', *REJ* 101 (1937) 73–86, at 85–6; in Hypaepa: CIJ 755. Eleazar, the 'guardian of the law': Lüderitz, *Corpus* no. 8 (=SEG 20, 737).

[11] See e. g. Niketas son of Jason from Jerusalem who contributed to a Dionysiac festival in Iasos in the second century BCE (CIJ 749); or 'Moschos, son of Moschion, a Jew' who in the third century BCE received instructions in a dream from the gods Amphiaraos and Hygieia, and put up an inscription in Oropus (Boeotia) to record the fact (CIJ vol. 1 [2nd edition] Prolegomenon, 82).

[12] E. g. LXX Jos. 22:18–29; Par. II 28:19; 29:19; Ps. 118 (119):118.

[13] 1 Macc. 1:15; 2:15, 19; 2 Macc. 2:3; 5:8.

[14] See K. H. Rengstorf, *A Complete Concordance to Flavius Josephus* (Leiden: Brill, 1973). I therefore take the reference to the ἀπόστασις of the Jews in Scythopolis at the outbreak of the War *(Bell.* 2.467) as a political comment on their desertion of the Jewish cause, not as a judgement concerning their religious fidelity; cf. the 'revolt' of Tiberias (against Josephus) in *Bell.* 2.632–4. By the same token, the reference to ἀποστάται τοῦ Ἰουδαίων ἔθνους who settled in Shechem in *Ant.* 11.340 appears to be a comment on their political affiliations rather than their religious observances. But see the conclusions (below) on the link between social and religious loyalty in the case of the Diaspora communities.

[15] Besides the examples noted below, see *Ant.* 1.14; 8.229, 313; 13.4

transgressed Jewish laws were not considered apostates, we shall list here only those cases where the verdict concerns what is taken (by the relevant source) to be a *seriously offensive* and *settled* pattern of behaviour which can be *generalized* as a desertion of Judaism. Philo tells of 'Yom Kippur Jews' who attended synagogue in Alexandria only on the Day of Atonement and whose life was not otherwise pious (οἷς κατὰ τὸν ἄλλον βίον εὐαγὲς οὐδὲν δρᾶται, *Spec. Leg.* 1.186); but such Jews, though 'worse' than others, were not (for him) in the same category as those who consistently 'disregarded' their ancestral teaching. It is these latter references to grave and consistent desertion of Judaism which we shall collect in the following survey.[16]

II. A Survey of the Charges of Apostasy

Our evidence from the Diaspora includes four authors who comment on those they consider 'apostate' (the author of 3 Maccabees; the author of Wisdom of Solomon; Philo; Josephus) and one who makes interesting hypothetical remarks on this matter (the author of 4 Maccabees). It also includes one case (Paul) where we can detect a Jew in the Diaspora being thought of as 'apostate'; the Johannine Christians whose situation is reflected in the Gospel of John may be another example of the same phenomenon.

a) 3 Maccabees

The author of 3 Maccabees (end of first century BCE) refers to one individual and a whole group of assimilating Jews whom he considers to be apostate. The individual is Dositheos, son of Drimylos, a trusted courtier of Ptolemy Philopator. He is described as a Jew by birth who later 'rejected the law and was alienated from his ancestral beliefs' (μεταβαλὼν τὰ νόμιμα καὶ τῶν πατρίων δογμάτων ἀπηλλοτριωμένος, 1:3). The author gives no explanation of this verdict but, as we shall see, he appears to regard any close proximity to the royal court as necessitating 'apostasy'. Intriguingly, we have papyri concerning this same Dosithcos (CPJ 127), which indicate that he was the memorandum-writer of Ptolemy Euergetes I and 'the priest of Alexander and the Gods Adelphoi and the Gods Euergetai' (in 222 BCE).

Besides Dositheos, a group of 'apostates' features in the narrative at the point when Ptolemy Philopator gives all Jews the choice of Alexandrian citizenship or death (2:28–33; cf. 7:10–15). Many features of this story are

[16] Feldman, *Jew and Gentile,* 79–83, takes issue with Wolfson's interpretation of the evidence in this matter, but his own distinction between 'apostasy' and 'ceasing to observe the commandments' does not correspond to the perceptions of our sources.

confused (and their relationship to historical fact highly questionable), but it appears that the author considered citizen rights, enlistment in the Dionysiac cult, proximity to the king and the abandonment of Jewish food laws as a 'package' which Jews either accepted or rejected. He describes these apostates as 'deserters of piety' (διέστησαν τῆς εὐσεβείας, 2:32) and transgressors of God's laws (7:10–12) 'for the sake of the stomach' (7:11), who have 'withdrawn' from the Jewish community and are to be considered 'enemies of the nation' (ὡς πολεμίους τοῦ ἔθνους, 2:33). They are to be 'abominated' and shunned (2:33; 3:23), and the author regards it as fitting that at the end of the story these 'defiled' apostates (three hundred of them) were slaughtered by the faithful Jews (7:10–15). It seems that for this author Alexandrian citizenship involves idolatrous worship and neglect of the Jewish food laws and thus an abandonment of Judaism.[17]

b) Wisdom of Solomon

In a lengthy passage on the oppression of the righteous (chapters 2–5), the author of Wisdom of Solomon (100 BCE-30 CE) characterizes the ungodly oppressors with many terms of invective. In this welter of polemic it is difficult to identify 'the wicked', but it is possible that this group includes those he considers Jewish 'apostates'. It is intriguing, for instance, that the ungodly are reproached for 'sins against the law' (2:12) and are described at one point as 'rebels against the Lord' (οἱ τοῦ κυρίου ἀποστάντες, 3:10). This may be simply the application of Jewish terminology to Gentiles (cf. 6:4), but it is possible that the author's target includes those he considers to have abandoned Judaism.[18] If so, their scepticism about justice and their persecution of the righteous indicate what stark effects he considers their desertion of Judaism to have had.

c) Philo

On several occasions Philo criticizes, either directly or indirectly, those he considers to be apostate. Sometimes, in paraphrasing the biblical text, he re-

---

[17] On 3 Maccabees see further Collins, *Between Athens and Jerusalem,* 104–11, and my *Jews in the Mediterranean Diaspora from Alexander to Trajan (323* BCE- *117 ce)* (Edinburgh: T & T Clark, 1996) 192–203. [Also now, E. Gruen, *Heritage and Hellenism: The Reinvention of Jewish Tradition* (Berkeley: University of California, 1998) 222–36; S. Johnson, *Historical Fiction and Hellenistic Jewish Identity: Third Maccabees in its Cultural Context* (Berkeley: University of California, 2004).]

[18] See the discussion of this difficult question by C. L. W. Grimm, *Das Buch des Weisheit* (Kurzgefasstes exegetisches Handbuch zu den Apokryphen des Alten Testaments; Leipzig: Hirzel,1860) 27–30; J. P. Weisengoff, 'The Impious of Wisdom 2' *CBQ* 11 (1949) 40–65; C. Larcher, *Le Livre de la Sagesse* (Paris: Gabalda, 1983) 1:115–17.

veals his observations on contemporary Jewish life in Egypt (early first century CE). Thus in a telling little cameo he represents Jacob's fears for his son Joseph in Egypt, lest he change his customs (ἡ τῶν πατρίων ἐκδιαίτησις):

> for he knew how natural it is for young people to lose their footing and how easy it is for strangers in a land to sin, especially in Egypt which is blind towards the true God because of its deification of created and mortal things; moreover, he knew how wealth and glory could attack minds of little sense and that, left to himself, without an accompanying monitor from his father's house, alone and bereft of good teachers, he would be liable to change to alien ways (πρὸς τὴν τῶν ὀθνείων μεταβολήν). (*Jos.* 254)[19]

Here Philo analyses the factors which, in his view, led to apostasy: youth, desire for wealth and social acceptance, dislocation from the controlling influence of the Jewish home. His comments suggest that he considered there to be more apostasy in Egypt than in the Jewish homeland, perhaps also that the Diaspora in Egypt proved especially prone to leakage from the Jewish community. A similarly generalized comment on the causes of 'apostasy' is to be found in *Virt.* 182, where Philo contrasts with proselytes those he calls 'rebels from the holy laws' (οἱ τῶν ἱερῶν νόμων ἀποστάντες), who have 'sold their freedom' for the sake of food, drink and beauty, pandering to the pleasures of gluttony and sex.

Elsewhere, Philo alludes to three categories of Jew whom he considers to have abandoned their Jewish heritage:[20]

(i) The first category comprises those who are lured by social success into repudiation of their family traditions and Jewish practices. Commenting on Moses' exemplary loyalty even in the Egyptian palace, Philo says that some, puffed up by success, look down on their friends and relations, 'transgressing the laws according to which they were born and bred and subverting the ancestral customs, to which no blame can rightly be attached, by changing their mode of life' (*Mos.* 1.31).

(ii) The second category includes those who marry Gentiles, or at least the offspring of these exogamous alliances. In a comment on the Pentateuchal prohibition of marriage to Canaanite women, he highlights the danger of 'being conquered by conflicting customs' and thus turning aside from the true path to piety. Even if the Jewish spouse remains firm, he declares, 'there is much to be feared for your sons and daughters' lest they forget the honour due to the one God, enticed by 'spurious customs' (*Spec. Leg.* 3.29). He gives a concrete example of this phenomenon elsewhere (*Mos.* 2.193). Also in several passages he discusses the story of the Jewish liaisons with Midianite women (Num. 25), where the 'conversion' (μεταβολή) of the Jewish

[19] Here, as elsewhere, I give my own translation of the texts cited.

[20] See also, though with some differences of emphasis, Wolfson , *Philo,* 73–85.

men took the form of idolatrous worship under pressure from their Gentile wives *(Mos.* 1.295–305; *Spec. Leg.* 1.54–58; *Virt.* 34–44).

(iii) A third type of apostasy in Philo's eyes may be found in his comments on critics of the Jewish Scriptures. Philo defends the Scriptures against many forms of criticism and it is often difficult to discern from his polemic what precisely he is reacting against. At times he talks about those who find in the Scriptures nothing superior to the stories of the Graeco-Roman world: those who consider Abraham's offering of Isaac (Gen. 22) no more significant than comparable stories in the Greek tradition *(Abr.* 178–93), or the story of Babel (Gen. 11) no different from familiar Greek myths *(Conf.* 2–13). While such criticism might have come from knowledgeable Gentiles, it is more likely to represent the views of well-educated Jews whose attitude to their Scriptures was less adulatory than that of Philo. In Philo's view, these critics 'reject the sacred writings' *(Quaest. Gen.* 3.3) and are discontented with the ancestral constitution *(Conf.* 2); they clearly stand, for him, outside the Jewish community.[21]

d) Josephus

Josephus has occasion to comment on a wide range of Jewish practices during the course of his historical works. Several times he refers to transgressors of the law without, apparently, inferring that they had apostasized.[22] What Josephus means by apostasy is made clear in his paraphrase of 1 Maccabees where he describes the Jerusalem Hellenizers: these Jews 'abandoned the ancestral laws and the constitution established by them' (τοὺς πατρίους νόμους καταλιπόντες καὶ τὴν κατ'αὐτοὺς πολιτείαν) and wished, in following Antiochus' laws, to adopt a Greek constitution (τὴν Ἑλληνικὴν πολιτείαν ἔχειν, *Ant.* 12.240).[23] This double aspect (abandoning Jewish ways and adopting those of the Greeks) is present in almost all the cases of 'apostasy' featured by Josephus. We may mention first the four particular cases of apostasy in the Diaspora which he identifies:

(i) Certain offspring of Alexander (descendants of Herod the Great) were brought up in Rome and, says Josephus, 'right from their birth abandoned the native customs of the Jews and transferred to those of the Greeks' (ἅμα τῷ φυῆναι τὴν θεραπείαν ἐξέλιπε τῶν Ἰουδαίοις ἐπιχωρίων

[21] He represents these critics as referring to the Scriptures as 'your so-called holy books' *(Conf.* 2–3); see further J. Daniélou, *Philon d'Alexandrie* (Paris: Fayard, 1958) 107–9.

[22] E.g. the Jewish 'scoundrel' who had fled from Jerusalem to Rome because he was accused of transgressing certain laws *(Ant.* 18.81); he is not referred to in terms suggesting apostasy, perhaps because Josephus knew that he had been accepted in Rome as an interpreter of the law.

[23] Cf. *Ant.* 4.309–10 and 5.113.

μεταταξάμενοι πρὸς τὰ Ἕλλησι πάτρια, *Ant.* 18.141). This comment reveals the importance, for Josephus, of upbringing and family in inculcating the Jewish way of life.[24]

(ii) A different case, of a Jew brought up in an observant family but turning against his tradition, is recorded by Josephus in the story of Antiochus in Antioch *(Bell.* 7.46–62). At the outbreak of the Jewish War, this individual accused fellow Jews, including his own father (the chief magistrate of the Jewish community), of plotting to destroy Antioch by fire. He also tried (says Josephus) to prove his 'conversion' (μεταβολή) from Judaism and his hatred of its customs by offering sacrifice according to Greek custom (τὸ ἐπιθύειν ὥσπερ νόμος ἐστὶ τοῖς Ἕλλησιν, *Bell.* 7.50) and by requiring other Jews to do the same. He proceeded to ban the observance of the sabbath, using military force to compel the Jews to work on that day (7.51–3). We have only Josephus' account of this story, but it is at least clear what Josephus considered to be signs of apostasy: turning against the Jewish community, offering idolatrous worship and disregarding, as a matter of principle, the sanctity of the sabbath.

(iii) A third and famous case of 'apostasy' recorded by Josephus is that of Philo's nephew, Tiberius Julius Alexander. Raised in an immensely wealthy family, Alexander had a glittering career in the Roman administration, acting as *epistratēgos* of the Thebaid in 42 CE and procurator of Judaea in 46–8 CE, and climbing further stages up the equestrian ladder before acquiring the massive responsibility of governor of Egypt (66–9 CE). At the end of the Jewish War he acted as Titus' second-in-command at the siege of Jerusalem and thereafter may have become prefect of the praetorian guard in Rome.[25] His periods of office required him to participate in Egyptian and Roman religion,[26] and, besides his aid to Titus at Jerusalem, he had to suppress a Jewish uprising in Alexandria (Josephus, *Bell.* 2.487–98). Yet it is intriguing to note that Josephus does not refer to him as an 'apostate' in his *Jewish War* (late 70s CE). It is only in the *Antiquities,* published in 93 CE when Alexander was probably dead (he was born around 15 CE), that Josephus refers to his 'apostasy': 'he did not abide by his ancestral customs' (τοῖς πατρίοις οὐκ ἐνέμεινεν οὗτος ἔθεσιν, *Ant.* 20.100).[27]

---

[24] On this particular family see Smallwood, *The Jews under Roman Rule*, 391 n. 8.

[25] His career has been fully described by E. G. Turner, 'Tiberius Julius Alexander' *JRS* 44 (1954) 54–64; and V. Burr, *Tiberius Julius Alexander* (Bonn: Habelt, 1955). [Cf. now S. Étienne, 'Réflexion sur l'apostasie de Tibérius Julius Alexander' *Studia Philonica Annual* 12 (2000) 122–42; S. Wilson, *Leaving the Fold*, 29–33.]

[26] We find Alexander in inscriptions honouring Egyptian deities in *OGIS* 663 and 669; cf. comparable papyri in CPJ 418.

[27] I cannot follow Feldman *(Jew and Gentile,* 81) in taking Josephus' comment to mean anything less than apostasy; the use of the same verb ἐμμένειν in relation to Polemo *(Ant.* 20.146, see below) indicates its meaning clearly enough. Josephus' varied reactions to Al-

(iv) The fourth case of apostasy is that of a proselyte, Polemo, the king of Cilicia, who got himself circumcised in order to marry Berenice, but when deserted by her 'was released from his adherence to Jewish customs' (τοῦ τοῖς ἔθεσι τῶν Ἰουδαίων ἐμμένειν ἀπήλλακτο, *Ant.* 20.145–6). Elsewhere Josephus suggests that there were other cases of proselytes who were unwilling to sustain the Jewish lifestyle: lacking endurance they again 'seceded' (πάλιν ἀπέστησαν, *c. Apion.* 2.123).

Apart from these individual cases, Josephus hints at the deleterious effects of an excess of wealth and pleasure *(Ant.* 5.132–5) and makes explicit warnings about the dangers of apostasy through intermarriage when commenting on the folly of Solomon's behaviour *(Ant.* 8.190–4). He also gives a fascinating analysis of the biblical story of apostasy with the Midianite women (Num. 25; *Ant.* 4.126–55). Dramatizing the story with speeches, he attributes to the women a powerful critique of the peculiar customs of the Jews in matters of food and drink, urging the Hebrew men to be less antisocial and to join in the worship of gods common to all humankind (4.137–8). As the men revel in 'alien foods' and the worship of 'many gods', their representative, Zambrias, confronts Moses with an astonishing critique of his 'tyrannical rule' and a strong statement of personal autonomy in his choice of lifestyle. As van Unnik noted, in this remarkable scene Josephus reflects important debates about the validity of the Jewish way of life, and in Zambrias' speech gives his impression of 'what was thought by his contemporaries who broke away from the ancestral religion and gave their reasons for doing so'.[28]

e) 4 Maccabees

4 Maccabees (end of first century CE) is a story of resistance to the temptation of apostasy, of how first Eleazar, then the seven brothers and their mother, refused to 'renounce Judaism' (4:26) or to 'deny the ancestral laws of their constitution' in 'adopting the Greek way of life and changing their mode of life' (μεταλαβόντες Ἑλληνικοῦ βίου καὶ μεταδιαιτηθέντες, 8:7–8). The test issue here (derived from 2 Macc. 6–7) is 'eating unclean food', specifically pork and 'food offered to idols' (5:2). Faced with the choice of apostasy or death, each martyr refuses to compromise even to the smallest degree. In a subtle speech, Antiochus IV is represented as arguing that God would surely forgive such a small sin, committed under compulsion (5:13),

---

exander suggest his social sensitivity in dubbing important Jews 'apostates', a factor which may also have influenced others in their judgements on assimilated Jews.

[28] W. C. van Unnik, 'Josephus' Account of the Story of Israel's Sin with Alien Women', in M. S. H. G. Heerma van Vos et al., eds., *Travels in the World of the Old Testament* (Assen: Van Gorcum, 1974) 241–61, at 259.

and our author provides a hypothetical speech which an apostasizing Jew might make in these circumstances (8:16–26). The tone of the work suggests that the pressure on the author's generation is not as extreme as that recorded in the narrative (14:9). But, as Klauck has noted, it seems designed to counter the temptations to assimilate among acculturated Jews by parading the example of loyal Jews who resisted offers of social advancement (8:7; 12:5) and remained faithful to the Jewish food laws.[29] It is clear from this narrative what sort of people our author considered to be apostates.

f) Paul[30]

It is not clear whether Paul would have recognized himself to be an apostate Jew or not: in places he vehemently asserts his Jewish identity (2 Cor. 11:22; Rom. 11:1) and his faithfulness to the Scriptures (Rom. 1:1–5; 8:4; 13:8–10; etc.), but elsewhere in his letters he talks about his '*former* life in Judaism' (Gal. 1:13–14) and describes his Jewish privileges as 'loss' and 'dung' (Phil. 3:2–11). In any case, what matters in this context is not what he thought about himself but how other Jews in the Diaspora viewed him.

From the evidence of his letters it appears that he was continually 'endangered' by Jews (2 Cor. 11:26) and felt himself 'persecuted' because of his stance on circumcision (Gal. 5:11; cf. Gal. 4:29; 6:12–13). In one passage he mentions being 'banished' and 'prevented from speaking to Gentiles' (1 Thess. 2:15 – some scholars question its authenticity), and in another (particularly revealing) comment he says he has received the synagogue punishment of the thirty-nine lashes on five occasions (2 Cor. 11:24).[31] It is clear that he was strongly opposed even by fellow Christian Jews who considered his policy on eating with Gentiles sinful (Gal. 2:11–17) and his teaching an encouragement to libertinism (Rom. 3:8). The picture we glean from Acts is consistent with this, even if the theme of Jewish opposition has here become somewhat stereotyped. In Acts Paul meets Jewish opposition in almost every town and is expelled from one synagogue after another (e. g. Acts 14:1–6; 17:1–15; 18:4–7). When he arrives back in Jerusalem, he is met by anxious Jewish Christians who have been told that 'you teach apostasy from Moses (ἀποστασίαν διδάσκεις ἀπὸ Μωϋσέως) to the Jews who live among Gentiles, telling them not to circumcise their children or to live by

[29] H.-J. Klauck, *4 Makkabäerbuch* (*JSHRZ* 3.6; Gütersloh: Mohn, 1989) 664–5.

[30] I have explored this topic further in 'Paul among Diaspora Jews: Anomaly or Apostate?' *JSNT* 60 (1995) 89–120.

[31] See A. E. Harvey, 'Forty Strokes Save One: Social Aspects of Judaizing and Apostasy', in A. E. Harvey, ed., *Alternative Approaches to New Testament Study* (London: SPCK, 1985) 79–96; and S. Gallas, '"Fünfmal vierzig weniger einen ..." Die an Paulus vollzogenen Synagogalstrafen nach 2Kor 11,24' *ZNW* 81 (1990) 178–91.

the [Jewish] customs (μηδὲ τοῖς ἔθεσιν περιπατεῖν)' (Acts 21:21). When he enters the Temple he is recognized and denounced by Jews from Asia who accuse him of bringing Greeks into the inner courts (Acts 21:28).[32]

Thus there is strong evidence to suggest that Paul was treated with very great suspicion in the Diaspora as a Jew who undermined Jewish fidelity to the law; apart from general comments on 'the customs', we find circumcision and food as matters of particular concern. The synagogue beatings suggest that Paul tried to maintain his contact with the Diaspora communities, but was convicted on several occasions for serious breaches of the law. One may presume that, if he maintained his stance on these controversial matters as a point of principle, he may have been considered an apostate who abandoned the Jewish customs.

g) Johannine Christians?

It is reasonably clear from the Gospel of John that the Christians whose experiences it reflects have been expelled from Jewish synagogues (9:22; 12:42; 16:2). Thus they seem to belong to the category of those who were considered to be apostates, but the question in my subheading reflects scholarly uncertainty as to their location, i.e. whether they belong in a discussion of the Diaspora.[33] The degree of polemic in the Gospel makes it clear that the Johannine Christians have been engaged in bitter disputes with synagogue authorities, but renders it difficult to discern the issues which originally brought about their separation.[34] There are echoes of debates over the Temple (2:18–22) and the observance of the sabbath (5:16; 7:19–24), but what stands in the forefront as the issue of dispute with the synagogue is the affirmation of Jesus as the Messiah (9:22; cf. 1:41; 20:31). How precisely this led to expulsion is somewhat obscure, but it is likely that the development of the *birkat ha-minim* had some part to play in the synagogue repudia-

[32] On Jewish-Christian opposition to Paul (including later charges of apostasy) see G. Lüdemann, *Paulus, der Heidenapostel. Band II: Antipaulinismus im frühen Christentum* (Göttingen: Vandenhoeck & Ruprecht, 1983).

[33] J. L. Martyn, who first worked out a detailed hypothesis concerning the social experiences of Johannine Christians, remained non-committal on this question, *History and Theology in the Fourth Gospel* (2nd ed.; Nashville: Abingdon, 1979), 73 n. 100. Early Christian tradition placed John in Ephesus, but some scholars have recently favoured Galilee or Batanea (e.g. K. Wengst, *Bedrängte Gemeinde und verherrlichter Christus* [2nd ed.; Neukirchen-Vluyn: Neukirchener, 1983]). It is a matter of definition whether Batanea should be considered part of the Diaspora.

[34] It is generally acknowledged that the Gospel contains layers of material reflecting different stages of the Johannine community and its theological development; for two slightly different attempts to describe the processes involved see J. L. Martyn, *The Gospel of John in Christian History* (New York: Paulist, 1978); and R. E. Brown, *The Community of the Beloved Disciple* (London: Chapman, 1979).

tion of these Christians.[35] Later evidence (e.g. from Justin, *Dialogue with Trypho* 16, 95–6, 110) may suggest that Diaspora synagogues developed mechanisms for rooting out Christian believers, denouncing them and their faith in Christ as incompatible with synagogue membership. Unfortunately, the precise contours of this repudiation are exceptionally hard to trace.[36]

III. Conclusions

What conclusions can we draw about the boundary-maintenance of Diaspora communities and their judgements concerning who had abandoned Judaism? It is clear that the material we have been able to gather is not very extensive and represents only a few voices. These voices probably all date from between 100 BCE and 100 CE. Some come from Egypt (3 Maccabees; Wisdom of Solomon; Philo), some from Asia/Syria (4 Maccabees; Paul; John?) and one from Rome (Josephus), and we should not presume a unity of perspective in these different locations, where the Jewish communities had very different experiences. Moreover, it is hard to tell how representative any of our voices are: would other Jews in Rome, for instance, have agreed with Josephus' views on this matter? It is clear that not all Jews would have accepted the view of 3 Maccabees that the acquisition of citizenship involved idolatry and laxity in matters of food: probably in Alexandria itself and certainly in other cities, there were Jews who enjoyed both Greek citizenship and good standing in their Jewish communities. Each of the authors we have examined writes with a particular perspective.

However, it is striking that, despite this variety of perspective, certain features recur in many of our disparate sources, and these commonalities *might* be taken to indicate a wider consensus among Diaspora communities. General charges concerning abandoning Jewish customs occur in many of our sources (Philo, Josephus, Acts [re Paul], 4 Maccabees), but two matters in particular are frequently mentioned:

---

[35] So especially Martyn, *History and Theology*, 37–62. For a summary of the evidence and a balanced discussion of this controversial 'benediction' see W. Horbury, 'The Benediction of the *Minim* and Early Jewish Christian Controversy' *JTS* n.s. 33 (1982) 19–61. [For the continuing debate see R. Hakola, *Identity Matters: John, The Jews and Jewishness* (Leiden: Brill, 2005); J. Marcus, *Birkat Ha-Minim* Revisited', *NTS* 55 (2009) 523–51.]

[36] See, for a recent attempt, Sanders, *Schismatics*. I am unable to pursue here the question of methods of excommunication from the synagogue (on which see Horbury, 'Extirpation'). Some who were considered 'apostate' did not need to be expelled: they simply drifted away from the Jewish community of their own volition. Others were socially ostracized (3 Macc. 2:33; 3:23) but not necessarily formally expelled. Perhaps a formal expulsion was only required when the 'apostates' contested their treatment at the hands of the community and when legal issues of authority were at stake.

(i) 'idolatry', i.e. worshipping other gods, or worshipping 'in the Greek manner' (3 Maccabees; Josephus on Antiochus, on the Midianite apostasy and on Solomon; Philo on the offspring of exogamy and on the Midianite apostasy; 4 Maccabees in relation to food offered to idols);

(ii) the Jewish food laws (3 Maccabees; 4 Maccabees; Josephus on the Midianite case (food and drink); Philo on 'the pleasures of the belly' (food and drink); Paul (at the Antioch dispute)).

Of other Jewish customs, circumcision is an issue in the case of Paul, and sabbath in the case of Antiochus (and the Johannine Christians?), but these are not highlighted in other cases; they were of course customs of central importance in the Maccabean story which was well known in certain Diaspora circles.

Otherwise, we find several cases where 'apostates' are accused of criticism of the Scriptures in general and of Moses' laws in particular: this emerges, for instance, in Philo's Scripture-critics, in Josephus' speech by Zambrias and probably in the case of Paul as well (if his letters were known). In several cases there is reference to the social distance which apostates have created between themselves and their fellow Jews, manifested in disdain of Jewish associates (Philo's social climbers) or even in political opposition to the Jewish community (3 Maccabees; Wisdom of Solomon; Antiochus). It seems that the primary basis of charges of apostasy was a process of assimilation, whereby the social ties between the Jew and his/her Jewish community were loosened. This could come about through social advancement (Philo) and the desire not to be thought peculiar (Josephus on the Midianite case) or, for proselytes, through reversion to Gentile company (Josephus' lapsed proselytes). An important feature also here is intermarriage (Philo; Josephus on the Midianite case and on Solomon) and the associated issue of the upbringing of children (Josephus on Alexander's offspring). This latter may be at issue in the attack on Paul regarding circumcision, for failure to circumcise suggests a lack of commitment to bring up one's children as Jews. Presumably also the food issue features so prominently because the Jewish food laws were the major impediment to social integration in the Graeco-Roman world, and compromise here was regarded as the first step towards renunciation of the Jewish community.

Inasmuch as we may generalize about the Diaspora (which is a dangerous thing to do) we may conclude, then, that 'apostates' were those who were considered to have abandoned their commitment to the Jewish community and its way of life through an assimilation most frequently marked by laxity on Jewish food laws and involvement in non-Jewish religion. Naturally, as we have stressed, individual observers and individual communities had different perceptions as to where the boundaries had been crossed even in such matters: an individual regarded as an 'apostate' in some circles or in one place and time could well have been acceptable as a Jew in other circles or in another place and time. I have stressed here this 'perspectival' aspect of 'apostasy' since it has been generally neglected by scholars, and I have arranged my survey of the material by author precisely in order to preserve awareness of the relativism inherent in all judgements on this matter. If my generalizing conclusions have any value, they may help to shed light on how Paul ran into trouble so often in the Diaspora synagogues and thus on the split between the early Christian movement and Judaism in the Diaspora. But the Johannine evidence, if it is relevant, should caution us that special factors may have played a part here which we are unlikely to find paralleled in other material from the Diaspora.

8. Hostility to Jews as Cultural Construct

Egyptian, Hellenistic, and Early Christian Paradigms

In honour of Erich S. Gruen, on his retirement

Josephus' apologetic work, *Contra Apionem*, is our fullest, our clearest and our single most instructive collection of evidence for ancient comments on Jews and their culture. After evaluating and citing a host of 'witnesses' to Jewish antiquity (I 6–218), Josephus responds to a series of derogatory tales concerning the exodus of polluted or leprous Jews from Egypt, as told by Manetho, Chaeremon and Lysimachus (I 219–320), before answering a variety of 'libels' circulated by Apion (II 1–144) and refuting moral and political slurs on the Jewish people cast by Apollonius Molon and others (II 145–286).[1] Many of the authors he cites are otherwise unknown, and several not known for their comments on Jews. Thus, through this apology we are able to trace patterns and paradigms in ancient hostility to Jews that we would otherwise never have known.

But the historian needs to beware. Because Josephus' ethnic apology is unique among ancient sources – because no-one else in antiquity, as far as we know, collected and refuted slurs against their nation – we are inclined to assume that hostility to Jews was unique in antiquity, in degree or kind (or both).[2] Recent scholarship has rightly warned against this assumption.

---

[1] For commentary on this text see my *Flavius Josephus: Translation and Commentary. Vol. 10: Against Apion* (Leiden: Brill, 2007). For book 1, see also D. Labow, *Flavius Josephus Contra Apionem. Buch 1: Einleitung, Text, Textkritischer Apparat, Übersetzung und Kommentar* (Stuttgart: Kohlhammer, 2005). [See now also F. Siegert, ed., *Flavius Josephus, Über die Ursprünglichkeit des Judentums: Contra Apionem* (2 vols.; Göttingen: Vandenhoeck & Ruprecht, 2008).]

[2] In common with many contemporary scholars I am disinclined to employ the term 'anti-Semitism' in relation to antiquity, since it was coined in, and inherently reflects the conditions of 19th-century racial 'science', with its distinction between 'Aryan' and 'Semitic' races. The adjective 'antisemitic' first appears (in German: 'antisemitische') in 1879 (W. Marr), and the term was applied to antiquity in conscious parallel with 19th-century politics; for recent critical discussion of the term, see, e.g., S. J. D. Cohen, '"Anti-Semitism" in Antiquity: The Problem of Definition' in D. Berger, ed., *History and Hate: The Dimensions of Anti-Semitisms* (Philadelphia/New York/Jerusalem: Jewish Publication Society, 1986) 43–47; Z. Yavetz, 'Judeophobia in Classical Antiquity: A Different Approach' *JJS*

Whether we examine Greek stereotypes of Persians and Scythians, Roman disdain of Gauls, or the constant stream of jokes, jibes and insults levelled at Egyptians, the ancient world was full of xenophobic prejudice.[3] If Josephus gathers a large numbers of slanders against Judeans, and Reinach and then Stern could gather still more in their compendia of Greek and Latin literature on Jews and Judaism, one could fill many more volumes with negative comment on Egyptians; Juvenal's few lines on Jews/Judeans, for instance, are heavily outweighed by his satire-length assault on the 'demented Egyptians'.[4] Despite such parallels, it has been argued that there is some factor in ancient hostility to Jews/Judeans, some element in the hatred or the acts of violence against them, which suggests that they were treated not merely like other 'barbarians', but 'a little more so'.[5] But the case is highly questionable: there are unique elements in *all* ancient ethnic stereotypes, and attempts to quantify degrees of hostility are inevitably subjective.[6] What is more, one finds that Josephus himself, despite his rhetorical outrage at the slanders

44 (1993) 1–22. For attempts to hold onto this term, as expressive of something 'unique' about ancient hostility to Jews, see below. Another linguistic conundrum is harder to solve: should one refer to the Ἰουδαῖοι/*Judaei* in ancient sources as 'Jews' or 'Judeans'? The latter preserves what is often an integral component of the term in antiquity – an association with the land of 'Judaea' (by birth or affiliation). But it may also mislead if it is heard to apply only to Jews resident in Judaea, or to residents in the Roman province only (and not, therefore, Galileans). For discussion, see my *Against Apion*, lx-lxi. In what follows, I will use 'Jews' and 'Judeans' interchangeably, and often in conjunction ('Jews/Judeans') to avoid misunderstanding [for fuller discussion, see chapter one, note 19]. The translation issue will become important in discussion of 1 Thess 2:14–16.

[3] See now B. Isaac, *The Invention of Racism in Classical Antiquity* (Princeton: Princeton University, 2004), though the label 'racism' is misleading. Earlier analysis in A. N. Sherwin-White, *Racial Prejudice in Imperial Rome* (Cambridge: Cambridge University, 1967).

[4] G. Bohak, 'The Ibis and the Jewish Question: Ethnic Bias in the Greco-Roman World', in M. Mor, A. Oppenheimer, J. Pastor and D. R. Schwartz, eds., *Jews and Gentiles in the Holy Land in the Days of the Second Temple, the Mishnah and the Talmud* (Jerusalem: Ben Zvi, 2003) 27–43; see also his 'Ethnic Stereotypes in the Greco-Roman World: Egyptians, Phoenicians, and Jews', in *Proceedings of the Twelfth World Congress of Jewish Studies* (Jerusalem: World Union of Jewish Studies, 2000) 7–15.

[5] So Z. Yavetz, 'Judeophobia'; idem, *Judenfeindschaft in der Antike* (München: C.H. Beck, 1997); idem, 'Latin Authors on Jews and Dacians' *Historia* 47 (1998) 77–107. Cf. P. Schäfer's (*Judeophobia: Attitudes toward the Jews in the Ancient World* [Cambridge, Mass./London: Harvard University, 1997] 206) attempt to identify some difference in the extreme of hatred directed against Jews/Judeans, in their identification as 'the "evil incarnate," denying and perverting in their xenophobic and misanthropic hatred all cherished values of humankind, conspiring against the civilized world'.

[6] Schäfer's depiction (see previous note) is itself exaggerated (no ancient source speaks of Jews/Judeans as 'evil incarnate'), and charges of antisocial behaviour, and hostility to others' religion, are levelled against other nations beside Jews (e.g. Cicero, *Font.* 30, on the Celts). It seems particularly precarious to attempt to justify the retention of the term 'anti-Semitism' on the basis of this supposed difference in the degree of hatred directed against Jews/Judeans (contra Schäfer, *Judeophobia*, 197–211; Cohen, '"Anti-Semitism" in Antiquity', 47).

directed against Judeans, does not regard this phenomenon as *sui generis*: he places it squarely alongside other examples of prejudice, especially in the rivalries between city-states (*c. Apion.* I 219–20). This is, of course, not to excuse ancient prejudice or hatred of Jews, just to normalise it: it is only because we care less about the reputation of other ancient peoples that we single out hostility to Jews and misjudge it as unique.

A more serious source of distortion lies in Josephus' tendency to homogenise hostility to Jews/Judeans, to treat it as a single phenomenon whose roots lie in a single cultural tradition. In *c. Apion.* I 223–26 he claims that 'it was the Egyptians who initiated the slanders against us, and certain people who wanted to gratify them attempted to twist the truth' (I 223). As the context makes clear, this concerns in particular the accounts of the exodus from Egypt, on which Josephus proceeds to cite the accounts of Manetho, Chaeremon and Lysimachus (I 227–320). But his response to Apion also centres on the identification of Apion as an 'Egyptian' (e.g., II 28–32, 65–68, 141–44), and when he mentions other authors (Posidonius, Apollonius Molon, Mnaseas, II 79, 112) he makes no attempt to situate their hostile stories within any other cultural tradition. Thus Josephus provides almost no historical and cultural contextualisation for the literary sources he cites, encouraging modern scholars to speak of 'pagan' hostility to Jews as a single and unitary phenomenon (as 'anti-Semitism', a singular '-ism'), arguably distinguishable from subsequent Christian 'anti-Judaism', but not internally divisible or diverse. Since some of the stories and stereotypes he recounts, and others we know from elsewhere, show similarities and traces of continuity, we are inclined to trace ancient hostility to Jews/Judeans diachronically, noting stages in its development from Egyptian origins through the Hellenistic era and into the Roman world. But it is generally assumed that it is *the same* phenomenon we are tracing through these stages and settings, a common and universal disdain or hatred of Jews. Moreover, Josephus' use of psychological explanations (Egyptian envy and feelings of religious inferiority, I 224–26) and his rhetorical depiction of the mental ill-health of his opponents (e.g., I 222, 226; II 132) are echoed in a common scholarly propensity to describe 'anti-Semitism' as an ancient pathology, an infectious psychic aberration passed down through the generations, whose deep impulses forged the 'Jew haters' and 'Jew baiters' we witness in our literature.[7]

---

[7] For the language of 'infection' see, e.g., N. de Lange, 'The Origins of Anti-Semitism: Ancient Evidence and Modern Interpretations', in S. L. Gilman and S. T. Katz, eds., *Anti-Semitism in Times of Crisis* (New York/London: New York University, 1991) 21–37, at 34 ('Prejudices can be infectious'). For the language of 'Jew haters' and 'Jew baiters' see, e.g., Yavetz, 'Latin Authors', 81 and A. Kasher, 'Polemic and Apologetic Methods of Writing in *Contra Apionem*', in L. H. Feldman and J. R. Levison, eds., *Josephus'* Contra Apionem*: Studies in its Character and Context* (Leiden: Brill, 1996) 143–86.

Against such Josephan, but still modern, tendencies, I propose that we can and should identify distinct cultural frameworks within which Jews/Judeans gained a negative reputation, that is, different cultural logics which represented them as the despicable 'other'. While the literary tradition might draw from predecessors of a different time and place, we can understand ancient hostility to Judeans only when we place it within its specific cultural frames – Egyptian, Hellenistic, Christian – and ask what cultural work it is being required to undertake. This suggests that division of our material by topic (e.g., expulsion from Egypt, abstinence from pork) is likely to reinstitute a homogenising approach, even if the material is treated in chronological order.[8] Nor is it likely to be useful to divide the evidence according to the social sources of hostility or opposition (governments, masses and intellectuals).[9] A historical perspective is essential, alert to differences in historical circumstance and context, but above all to the cultural matrices in which expressions of hostility to Jews/Judeans are found.[10] Although this tends towards a 'functionalist' rather than an 'essentialist' account of ancient anti-Judaism,[11] it does not limit its explanation to purely transient historical and social causes. By seeking to identify broader cultural matrices, this analysis attempts to place hostility to Jews within a context narrower than 'paganism' or 'Greco-Roman antiquity', but wider than the specific circumstances of the pogrom in Alexandria or the psychology of any individual author. To identify different varieties of ancient hostility to Jews/Judeans as the product of large socio-cultural forces is not, of course, to excuse them, but it promises to provide a better understanding of what remains an otherwise amorphous and puzzling phenomenon. And the *same* method of analysis could be applied to explanations of *favourable* attitudes towards Jews/Judeans, which are as much a product of cultural prejudices (social, philosophical and religious) as are the negative opinions examined here.[12]

---

[8] So, e.g., Schäfer, *Judeophobia*; cf. J.N. Sevenster, *The Roots of Pagan Anti-Semitism in the Ancient World* (Leiden: Brill, 1975).

[9] So, e.g., L.H. Feldman, *Jew and Gentile in the Ancient World: Attitudes and Interactions from Alexander to Justinian* (Princeton: Princeton University, 1993) chapters 3–5.

[10] The rigorously historical approach was first fully developed by I. Heinemann who identified three contexts of conflict (Syrian-Palestinian; Egyptian; Roman) in which hostility to Jews arose ('Antisemitismus', *PW* Suppl. V, 3–43). My concern is to place these conflicts within wider cultural contexts and to identify the logic by which Jewish/Judean traits were considered unacceptable.

[11] For discussion of Hoffmann's distinction between these two approaches in the work of modern German historians of antiquity, see Schäfer, *Judeophobia*, 2–6.

[12] As E.S. Gruen has argued (*Heritage and Hellenism* [Berkeley: University of California, 1998] 41–43), it makes little sense to divide sources according to the usual binary of 'pro- or anti-Jewish'. Not only are many mixed in their evaluations, but, more fundamentally, this presupposes that their chief purpose is a positive or negative stance towards

Our starting point, therefore, is to normalise ancient hostility to Judeans, to differentiate between its various forms, and to contextualise it within particular historical and cultural configurations. By gathering his materials in one treatise, Josephus gave the impression that they all constituted a single thing, a united barrage of slanders against his people. That impression has remained in scholarly discussions of ancient 'anti-Judaism', and the presence of negative comments about Judeans in early Christianity has induced discussion about whether they are, or are not, the same as their ancient (singular) counterpart in the pagan world.[13] I would like to suggest, by contrast, that we can distinguish at least two different pre-Christian cultural paradigms within which hostility to Judeans was expressed – one Egyptian, the other Hellenistic[14] – and that the New Testament (of which I can discuss here only one text) bears witness to the emergence of a new, third, paradigm, borrowing some elements from the Hellenistic tradition but creating a new cultural logic which generates its own form of hostility to Jews.

I. The Egyptian Paradigm: Typhonian impurity

In *Contra Apionem* Josephus conveys a number of stories – from Manetho, Chaeremon and Lysimachus – which represent a cultural system we can trace also elsewhere in Egyptian sources.[15] The frame within which these

Jews/Judeans. Most have an agenda of their own, to which Jews are sometimes quite peripheral. In any case, it is as necessary to explain why Jews are sometimes favourably depicted as why they are sometimes loaded with negative stereotypes. [For a significant advance in this direction see B. Bar-Kochva, *The Image of the Jews in Greek Literature: The Hellenistic Period* (Berkeley: University of California, 2009).]

[13] A tendency to downplay pre-Christian hostility to Jews, and to identify Christianity as the source of 'anti-Semitism' is evident in the work of J. Isaac, *Genèse de l'Antisémitisme* (Paris: Calmann-Levy, 1956). But even if we acknowledge, as we must, the presence of pre-Christian antipathy and prejudice against Jews, it is another matter to determine to what extent Christianity utilised its predecessors and to what extent it forged it own new cultural logic; the matter has to be decided case by case, not on a global scale. See R. Radford Ruether, *Faith and Fratricide: The Theological Roots of Anti-Semitism* (New York: Seabury, 1974) 23–31, and below, section III.

[14] Is it possible to speak of a specifically Roman cultural paradigm as well? Although there are new elements in the Roman criticism of Jews/Judeans, Roman authors mostly recycle stereotypes of Egyptian and Hellenistic origin, and the cultural logics are not sufficiently different to be able to identify a whole new paradigm. Schäfer's identification of a new Roman element, fear 'born out of the ambivalence between fascination and rejection' (*Judeophobia*, 11) appears exaggerated; see E. S. Gruen, *Diaspora: Jews amidst Greeks and Romans* (Cambridge, Mass.: Harvard University, 2002) 15–53. It is notable that Josephus never cites Roman authors as critics or admirers of Jews/Judeans, despite writing in a context where Judaism was both admired and criticised; see my *Against Apion*, xxxvi – xliv.

[15] This has been widely recognised in the last generation of scholarship, since J. Yoyotte, 'L'Égypte ancienne et les origines de l'antijudaïsme' *RHR* 163 (1963) 133–43.

operate may be described (in simplified form) in the following terms: Egypt is not one nation among others but the focal point of the cosmos, the land that maintains the right order (*Ma'at*) by which not only human society but nature itself is governed and preserved.[16] The Gods oversee this order and ensure its continuity, in constant struggle with the forces of chaos and injustice. It is the role of the king, as the divine representative, to embody this order and enforce the struggle against all that corrupts and pollutes the world, whether foreign armies, insubordinate subjects, or acts that flout (Egyptian) justice and piety. The priests and temples play a critical role in maintaining the equilibrium of the cosmos, and any act of disrespect or violence against them, and against the sacred animals they venerate, is an assault against the nation, the king, and the order of the cosmos. The continual struggle against evil can be represented as the re-enactment of a mythological schema, in which, for our purposes, the most important feature is the perpetual enmity between, on the one side, Isis with her son Horus, and on the other, Seth/Typhon.[17] From the 8th or 7th centuries BCE, Seth had become the epitome of evil within Egyptian mythology, the object of execration and fear: he was associated with foreigners (especially foreign invaders), with the marginal, the impure, the infertile desert, and all that causes disorder or chaos.[18] He was also associated with the ass.

This essentially timeless schema of conflict was repeatedly projected into the sphere of history and experience, so that historical events and figures (foreign invaders, disruptive Egyptians, or whoever is classified as the enemy) take on the archetypal role of Seth/Typhon in their opposition to the Gods and the king.[19] Royal ideology is strongly underpinned by this scheme: the coronation itself enacts the cosmic victory over Seth, and the defeat of foreign enemies is represented as the binding or spearing of the Sethian enemy.[20] The Persian occupation of Egypt after 525 BCE was clearly represented in terms of this paradigm: Cambyses was blamed for devastating Egyptian temples and slaughtering the sacred animals (Herodo-

---

[16] For the concept see J. Assmann, *Ma'at: Gerechtigkeit und Unsterblichkeit im Alten Ägypten* (München: C.H. Beck, 1995).

[17] J.G. Griffiths, *The Conflict of Horus and Seth from Egyptian and Classical Sources: A Study in Mythology* (Liverpool: University of Liverpool, 1960).

[18] H. Te Velde, *Seth, God of Confusion: A Study of his Role in Egyptian Mythology and Religion* (Leiden: Brill, 1977).

[19] D. Frankfurter notes the twin characteristics of this tradition: archaizing (mobilizing ancient paradigms of conflict) and synthesizing (assimilating new characters and events); see 'Lest Egypt's City be Deserted: Religion and Ideology in the Egyptian Response to the Jewish Revolt (116–17 C.E.)' *JJS* 43 (1992) 203–20.

[20] See J.-W. van Henten, 'Antiochus IV as a Typhonian Figure in Daniel 7', in A.S. van der Woude, ed., *The Book of Daniel in the Light of New Findings* (Leuven: Leuven University, 1993) 223–43; J.-W. van Henten and R. Abusch, 'The Jews as Typhonians and Josephus' Strategy of Refutation', in Feldman, ed. *Josephus'* Contra Apionem, 271–309.

tus 3.16–18, 27–29, 37–38; Diodorus 1.46.4; 95.4–5; Strabo 17.1.27; Plutarch, *Mor.* 368 f), and Ochus (Artaxerxes III) was considered "accursed" (ἐναργής) and "polluted" (μιαρός), and appropriately dubbed 'the ass' (Plutarch, *Mor.* 363 c). Such traditions were ever adaptable to new circumstances and new situations of conflict. They were employed by the new Ptolemaic regime,[21] but could also be used in native Egyptian circles to express opposition to the Ptolemies, understood as the newest emergence of the foreign, Typhonian, foe. In the *Demotic Chronicle*, for instance, the Persians are portrayed as 'herds of wild beasts', and the 'Ionians' (Greeks) as foreigners who threaten the rule of law, ideally upheld by the king (probably 3rd century BCE).[22] More dramatically, in the *Potter's Oracle* this native tradition is turned against Alexandria, with bitter criticism levelled against both Persians and Greeks (mysteriously labelled 'girdle-wearers', ζωνόφοροι), who have brought internecine violence, lawless deeds, and terrible damage to the stability of nature (e.g., failure of harvests), and who are repeatedly described as 'Typhonians' (latest version 130 BCE, with older roots).[23]

It is easy enough to recognize the application of these archetypes in both of the narratives of Manetho preserved by Josephus. In the first (*c. Apion.* I 75–90), the dreaded Hyksos, as foreign invaders, play the paradigmatic role in massacring the Egyptian population and razing the temples (I 76). Their base is the city of Avaris, the city of Seth/Typhon (I 78, 86, 237), from which they are eventually expelled by the king. In the second (*c. Apion.* I 228–51), two versions of this same paradigm are stitched together. We find again the cruel foreigners (Solymites), whose impiety extends to mutilating the images of the Gods and roasting the sacred animals (I 248–49); but we find also the polluted figures within the nation, who must be expelled on the order of the Gods in order to purge the land, and whose dangerous, Typhonian character is revealed by their oath to eat sacred animals, and by their occupation of the city of Avaris (I 232–39).[24] In Chaeremon's version, we are not surprised to find reference to the wrath of Isis and damaged temples, together with the divine order to purify the land of its contaminated residents (I 289–90). Echoes of the Isis-Horus myth are also present in Chaeremon (I 292, 300), and the story climaxes, as one would expect,

---

[21] L. Koenen, 'Die Adaptation ägyptischer Königsideologie am Ptolemäerhof', in E. Van't Dack et al., eds., *Egypt and the Hellenistic World* (Leuven: Leuven University, 1983) 143–90.

[22] W. Spiegelberg, *Die sogennante Demotische Chronik* (Leipzig: J.C. Hinrichs, 1914); A.B. Lloyd, 'Nationalist Propaganda in Ptolemaic Egypt' *Historia* 31 (1982) 33–55, with further literature.

[23] L. Koenen, 'Die Prophezіehungen der 'Töpfers" *ZPE* 2 (1968) 178–209; further literature in Frankfurter, 'Lest Egypt's City', 209 n. 32.

[24] For analysis of these and other passages from *Contra Apionem*, see my *Against Apion*.

with the king's return to reclaim the land. In all these versions, the shocking feature of the enemy is their opposition specifically to the Egyptian people and to the Egyptian religious apparatus (not their general unsociability, or their difference from other religious cults).[25] It is also notable that the focus of interest is the outrage caused by the Typhonian characters, and their eventual expulsion. What happens to them after they have left Egypt, on their journey or in their new settlement, is of very little concern; all that matters is that Egypt is cleansed.

Given the adaptability of this archetypal schema, its continual updating and reapplication to new events and persons, we can understand how it is here projected in new directions, the Hyksos legends linked now to Judea and Jerusalem (I 90), the story of the polluted overlaid by reference to Moses (I 250). These are old story-patterns, continually recycled, and such small adjustments and new associations are precisely what we find in parallel texts like the *Potter's Oracle*. None of these stories was originally written (or told) with Jews/Judeans in mind. Thus the significant question is not 'why were stories concocted to depict the Judeans as Typhonians?' but 'why and when were Typhonian archetypes transferred to Judeans?' Because Manetho's stories are obviously composite, and because the reference to Moses in I 250 is clearly superimposed on an original reference to Osarseph, it has been common to argue that the original Manetho made no connection between these tales and the Judeans, with the responsibility shifted to later editors of Manetho's text.[26] But such a hypothesis is unnecessary. Of all the places to which the Hyksos could have gone, Manetho names their destination as Judea and Jerusalem (1.90, 94); it requires unconvincing surgery to remove these details from the text as secondary accretions. Of course, the Hyksos story was originally nothing to do with Judeans/Jews (despite Josephus' spurious claim); but there seems no adequate reason to doubt that Manetho made some link at this superficial level. And he was not the only one of his generation to do so: we know from Diodorus (40.3) that Manetho's contemporary Hecataeus knew an Egyptian tradition that also linked Moses and the origin of the Judean nation with an Egyptian story of plague and expulsion (see further below).

If this traces the link with Jews/Judeans as far back as we can go, it still leaves the question of *why* the Typhonian archetype was transferred to

[25] Even the oath in the second story, to associate with none but their fellow confederates (I 239), concerns specifically their hostility to fellow Egyptians: the rebels make an alliance with foreigners easily enough (I 241). It is a mistake to find here an adumbration of the later quite different and Hellenistic complaint that Jews/Judeans were 'antisocial', contra Schäfer, *Judeophobia*, 11, 167–69.

[26] For discussion of the problems here, see Appendix 1 (pp. 335–37) in my *Against Apion*.

Judeans. As Gruen has argued, there seems nothing to commend the common idea that these stories were created to counter *Judean* versions of the exodus:[27] as we have seen, the shape and most of the details in these Egyptian tales were pre-formed, and had been applied to many others before they were connected to Jews. Our best clue to the rationale for this transferral of the Typhonian archetype may come from an unlikely source – papyri dating from the beginning of the 2nd century CE. In the heat of the Diaspora Revolt (116–17 CE), when, with messianic fervour, Jews/Judeans from Cyrenaica and Egypt were wreaking havoc in the Egyptian countryside and destroying Egyptian temples, we can trace the reaction of the native population. These not only mobilized in force against the Judeans, but employed against them a powerful and ancient ideology, labelling them 'unholy' and 'lawless', identifying them with those once expelled by the wrath of Isis, and thus applying to them the stereotype of the Typhonian foe, the polluting element in the land and the cosmos, who must be eradicated by death or expulsion (*CPJ* 438, 443, 450, 520).[28] Of course, the Diaspora Revolt was an extreme event, in which murderous Jews were naturally understood in this archetypal frame. But it nonetheless suggests the mechanisms by which Typhonian traits could be linked to them, if they were regarded in other, and earlier, circumstances as foreigners, who remained aloof from, or critical towards, the cosmos-sustaining cult, and displayed their hostility to native Egyptians in recognizable ways.

We cannot know when this impression of 'Judean Typhonians' first arose, although Hecataeus and Manetho indicate that it was established by the early 3rd century BCE. It is possible, as has been suggested, that the Judeans' military role in the Persian occupation of Egypt may have been one factor,[29] but our only evidence here is the hostility between Judeans and native Egyptians in the Elephantine garrison (410 BCE). The focal point of that dispute appears to have been the animal sacrifices in the Judean temple in Elephantine,[30] an issue that could hardly arise outside this specific context. But it might be a symptom of the perception that Jews/Judeans were in general hostile to the native religious traditions. We know of an influx of Judeans at the beginning of the Ptolemaic period, some in military roles. They were hardly the only 'foreigners' to arrive at that time, but there is

---

[27] Gruen, *Heritage and Hellenism*, 59–63.

[28] See Frankfurter, 'Lest Egypt's City', on which I draw. Even if he is wrong to place the fragmentary *CPJ* 520 in this historical context, it bears witness to the popular application of the Typhonian archetype to Judeans, which is my larger point.

[29] Yoyotte, 'L'Égypte ancienne'.

[30] *Cowley Papyrus* 33; see discussion in B. Porten, *Archives from Elephantine: The Life of an Ancient Jewish Military Colony* (Berkeley: University of California, 1986); J. Mélèze Modrzejewski, *The Jews of Egypt: From Ramses II to Emperor Hadrian* (Edinburgh: T & T Clark, 1995) 36–44; Schäfer, *Judeophobia*, 121–35.

evidence to suggest that all foreigners in Egypt in that period could be tarred with the Typhonian brush. In Hecataeus' version of the exodus, for instance, the motif of the plague (= pollution), accompanied by divine wrath, is connected not just to Judeans but to 'many strangers of all sorts dwelling in their midst, and practising different rites of religion and sacrifice', to the detriment of Egyptian cult (Diodorus 40.3.1); the result was the expulsion of *all* the aliens, one group of which went to Greece, another to Judea. One can thus imagine a fairly broad application of the Typhonian stereotype at the beginning of the Ptolemaic era, in reaction to the sudden arrival of a large number of foreign Ptolemaic troops in the countryside. Over time, perhaps, this became more narrowly associated with Judeans because, of all the foreigners who settled in Egypt, they remained the most stubbornly unassimilated to Egyptian religious customs. Manetho's reference to Judea and Jerusalem (as the destination of the Hyksos) might also be linked to the campaign of Ptolemy I (Soter), who in 312/11 or 302/1 BCE besieged and captured Jerusalem (see *c. Apion.* I 209–10). It would have been useful propaganda to represent his enemies as the defeated Typhonian foe, and his campaign as a revenge attack on the descendants of the hated Hyksos. None of these hypotheses can be proved, but they would all make sense in the conditions of early Ptolemaic Egypt. And, once established in the public consciousness, Jewish refusal to participate in Egyptian cult could continuously confirm their alien character, threatening the heart of Egyptian culture. There are hints that Jews / Judeans were hated in the cult-centre of Memphis in the 2nd century BCE (*CPJ* 141; cf. *Sib. Or.* 5.60–62, 68–70), and such stereotypes could become fixed if supported by the daily evidence of religious difference. If, as Gruen argues, the Egyptian element in the Alexandrian population was the most important source of violence against Jews / Judeans in the pogrom of 38 CE,[31] this 'Typhonian' framework could have been operative in that context, as it clearly was in the Jewish-Egyptian conflicts of 116–17 CE.[32]

Thus, where it occurred, Egyptian hostility to Jews / Judeans operated within a particular ideological and cultural frame with its own logic applied to Jews / Judeans, but by no means only to them.[33] While traces of this framework can be found in the literary tradition outside Egypt right down to the time of Tacitus (*Hist.* 5.5.3–4), what we find to be central in the Hel-

---

[31] As Philo claims; see Gruen, *Diaspora*, 54–83.

[32] For the probable Egyptian origin of the story that Jews / Judeans worshipped the head of an ass, see Appendix 4 (pp. 350–52) in my *Against Apion*.

[33] It is important to add that some Egyptian stories are quite *positive* in their appreciation of Moses; see Josephus, *c. Apion.* I 279 ('the Egyptians consider this man marvellous and divine'); cf. II 10–11 and the Egyptian legends that appear to lie behind the tales of Artapanus (*apud* Eusebius, *Praep. Ev* IX 27,1–37) and Josephus (*Ant.* II 238–53). Of course these praise Moses also on specifically *Egyptian* grounds.

lenistic tradition represents a quite different cultural logic, a different set of reasons for the disparagement of Judeans.

II. Hellenistic Logics: the sin of misanthropy

A fundamentally different logic drives assessments of Jews/Judeans and their culture which arose within the cultural matrix of Hellenism. Here, even where there are traces of Egyptian motifs, the structure and rationale of the stories and stereotypes are utterly different, because they serve a quite different cultural purpose. The issue here is not whether they are more or less 'anti-Jewish', but what cultural narratives and values they represent.

Our first evidence for this shift comes in the work of Hecataeus, who forms a bridge between the Egyptian and Hellenistic worlds. Although Manetho also worked at the interface between Egyptian and Greek culture, his stories were wholly moulded by an Egyptian structure of thought, even if they were written in Greek. In Hecataeus, on the other hand, there emerges a quite different interest in the exodus, as the point of origin of the Judean nation, and as the story that has the capacity to explain some of the notable characteristics associated with Judean/Jewish culture. In other words, Hecataeus' cultural frame is shaped by *ethnography* and *aetiology*, the Greek attempt to plot the origins of nations on the map of world history and geography, and to provide rational explanation for the fascinatingly (and sometimes alarmingly) different customs practised by the peoples of the known world.[34] To put the matter schematically, where Egyptian stories map the Judeans onto the essentially timeless pattern of cosmic conflict (historicised in particular cases), Hellenistic narratives are concerned to place Judeans in the unrepeatable flow of world history. Where the Egyptian schema is fundamentally dualistic (Egyptian order vs. the chaos created by invasion or impiety), the Hellenistic tradition assumes a kaleidoscope of differing national customs. Where the Egyptian tradition posits Jews/Judeans as essentially the same as others (they are Typhonians, like countless others before them), Hellenistic comprehension expects (and sometimes exaggerates) cultural particularity, interested to explain what makes Judeans different from everyone else.

Hecataeus clearly drew on Egyptian sources: his account of the exodus opens with the traditional Egyptian motifs of the polluted foreigner, the

[34] For foundational work in this area see K. Trüdinger, *Studien zur Geschichte der griechisch-römischen Ethnographie* (Basel: E. Birkhäuser, 1918). For a recent treatment with reference to Tacitus, see R. Bloch, *Antike Vorstellungen vom Judentums: Der Judenexkurs des Tacitus im Rahmen der griechisch-römischen Ethnographie* (Stuttgart: Franz Steiner, 2002).

threat to Egyptian religion and the Gods' punishment of the disordered land (Diodorus 40.3.1–2). But he is not really interested in what these foreigners had done in Egypt, or how they upset its order; his focus shifts, characteristically, to what happened *after* they left. The expulsion of Judeans (alongside others) is now interpreted in quite other terms, as the dispatch of *colonies* from Egypt, to Greece and 'certain other regions' or to Judea – an interpretation which moves in a quite different explanatory framework, derived from the Greek cultural tradition.[35] Now Moses is interpreted not as a renegade Egyptian priest but as a *founder* of a nation, who establishes the physical, legal, and political framework for the new nation of Judeans. Most of the features attributed to him have no connection whatever with Egypt: they reflect what Hecataeus knows about the Judean people (from Greek or Judean sources), tracing contemporary customs and laws back to Moses. What is important about Judean worship is that it is *imageless*, not that it involves the destruction of Egyptian temples or the consumption of sacred animals. The Egyptian origin of the Judeans is used to explain the Judean custom of circumcision (*apud* Diodorus 1.28, 55), by a characteristically Greek understanding of cultural diffusion. Otherwise there is only one connection between the Judeans and their departure from Egypt, and that is the famous comment on their 'somewhat unsocial and inhospitable way of life' (ἀπάνθρωπόν τινα καὶ μισόξενον βίον, Diodorus 40.3.4). Here is the first example of what will become a major theme in Hellenistic accounts of Judean/Jewish culture: the complaint concerning their social aloofness. But it is notable how *unEgyptian* is this implied criticism. In Egyptian logic (whose traditions are hardly hospitable to foreigners), the question was what attitude Judeans took to the Egyptian cults that maintained the natural and social order;[36] for Hecataeus and his successors, it was the inassimilable position of Judeans in the pluralistic world of Hellenistic cities that was the real bone of contention.

The distinction here between Egyptian and Hellenistic thematics is not directly correlated with the ethnicity of the authors concerned: the question is not their ancestry, but the shape of the stories they tell. Nor does it deny that originally and distinctively Egyptian and Hellenistic motifs are often mingled in a variety of composite forms. The aim is rather to clarify the cultural logic by which particular features of Jewish/Judean culture become the

[35] On Hecataeus as a model of ethnography, see D. Mendels, 'Hecataeus of Abdera and a Jewish 'patrios politeia' of the Persian Period (Diodorus Siculus XL, 3)' *ZAW* 95 (1983) 94–119; B. Bar-Kochva, *Pseudo-Hecataeus 'On the Jews': Legitimizing the Jewish Diaspora* (Berkeley: University of California, 1996) 29–39; idem, *Image of the Jews*; further literature in Gruen, *Heritage and Hellenism*, 53 n. 42.

[36] For Egyptian hostility to foreigners, see W. Helck, 'Die Ägypter und die Fremden' *Saeculum* 15 (1964) 103–16. On the logic of the oath of non-co-operation in Manetho's story, see above n. 25.

object of comment (and exaggeration, or even invention), and what cultural agendas are advanced by the blame (or praise) which these draw forth. Thus Diodorus (probably drawing on Posidonius) certainly includes Egyptian motifs in referring to the Jews/Judeans as expelled by a purging of Egypt, being leprous, impious and hated by the gods (Diodorus 34/35.1.1–5). But the weight of the account rests on the vilification of Jews/Judeans as incorrigibly unsociable people who refuse to mix with others and, worse, harbour hatred of others (exhibiting μῖσος, μισοξενία and μισανθρωπία). It is because of this cardinal sin that Antiochus' advisers urge him to 'wipe out' this people, in Diodorus' account. The same combination of Egyptian themes and the central Hellenistic complaint occurs in Pompeius Trogus (*apud* Justin 36.2.15) and Lysimachus (*apud* Josephus, *c. Apion.* I 304–11): an anti-social lifestyle and the refusal to show good-will to anyone are at the heart of these two stories. Similarly, Apollonius Molon accuses the Jews/Judeans of μισανθρωπία and registers a strong complaint that Jews/Judeans do not share fellowship with those who life according to a different life-style (*apud* Josephus, *c. Apion.* II 148, 258).[37] The charge continues to reverberate in the Roman era, where it can be used by Roman authors with particular venom; Tacitus' famous comment (*adversus omnes alios hostile odium*, *Hist.* 5.5.1) indicates the continuing influence of this charge in the second century CE.[38]

The political and philosophical concern for tolerance, sociability and co-operative citizenship is a central feature of the Hellenistic era, when the founding of new cities, the new mobility of populations, and the cultural mixing among the civic elite created new 'virtues' and their corresponding vices. In the ancient Greek tradition, hospitality to strangers (travellers) had become a mark of Greek (and therefore 'civilized') behaviour: although city states had their social and moral boundaries, the fabled inhospitality of the Egyptians was a sign of their feral character (Plato, *Leg.* 953 e). In the Hellenistic era, greatly increased social movement and ethnic interchange favoured ideologies that eased social intercourse. Mutual respect and reciprocal hospitality became social virtues, especially when supported by Stoic notions of a universal humanity.[39] As Josephus himself shows, in this context unfriendly attitudes appear simply 'irrational' (perpetrated by ἀλόγιστοι), while respect for others' customs is a mark of 'gentlemanly' virtue (καλοκαγαθία, *Ant.* XVI 174–78).[40] If Judeans were perceived to flout

[37] For discussion of all such charges against Jews as 'antisocial' see K. Berthelot, *Philanthrôpia Judaica: Le débat autour de la "misanthropie" des lois juives dans l'Antiquité* (Leiden: Brill, 2003) 79–184.

[38] Cf. the contemporary complaints in Juvenal, *Sat.* 14.103–4; Quintilian, *Inst.* 3.7.21.

[39] See Berthelot, *Philanthrôpia Judaica*, 174–79.

[40] Cf. Dionysius of Halicarnassus, *Ant. rom.* 1.41, retrojecting this ethos to the time of Heracles.

basic rules of social reciprocity (by rules against commensality, intermarriage, or religious participation) they could be resented as (uniquely) failing to support a community ethos.

Now there is a new, unpardonable sin, that of social aloofness and the failure to integrate into civic life: Jews/Judeans thus become the antitype of the values of social reciprocity considered necessary for the well-being of civilization as a whole.

III. An emerging Christian paradigm: enemies of the church

If there is no single paradigm of pre-Christian hostility to Judeans, the question is not whether or not Christians adopted 'pagan anti-Judaism', but whether they used either of the paradigms outlined above or developed their own cultural logic in their critical remarks on Jews/Judeans.[41] It seems to me incontrovertible that some New Testament texts, like other early Christian documents, make hostile comments about Jews/Judeans in sufficiently blanket terms to be comparable to the phenomenon of 'hostility to Jews' that we have examined thus far. Although it is inappropriate to call this or any ancient parallel 'anti-Semitism' (see n. 2), such texts evidence a generalised hostility towards Jews/Judeans, spoken either *by* or *to* those who do not place themselves under that label, creating a rhetorical antithesis between 'us' (Christ-believers) and 'them' (Jews/Judeans). If we rid ourselves of the notion that there was a single ancient virus of 'Jew-hatred' that early Christians could have contracted, we are able to ask more nuanced questions concerning the paradigms operative in early Christian texts, and the social and cultural logic which they represent.

Unfortunately, I can treat here only one New Testament text, 1 Thess 2:14–16, but it proves to be peculiarly interesting and perhaps symptomatic of a shift in anti-Judaic paradigms. We may leave to one side here the question of the authenticity of the text;[42] I regard it as almost certainly by Paul

[41] For discussion on the relationship between early Christian and 'pagan' hostility to Jews, see M. Simon, *Verus Israel: A Study of the Relations between Christians and Jews in the Roman Empire (135–425)* (Littman Library of Jewish Civilization; Oxford: Oxford University, 1986) 202–23, stressing both continuities and the distinctive and original theological element in the Christian critique. For emphasis on the discontinuity, see M. Taylor, *Anti-Judaism and Early Christian Identity: A Critique of the Scholarly Consensus* (StPB 46; Leiden: Brill, 1995) 116–21; she stresses the essentially new logic in Christian anti-Judaism. Cf. Ruether, *Faith and Fratricide*, 28–31, 64, 86, 94–95; and, for the larger issue, C. Klein, *Theologie und Anti-Judaismus* (München: Chr. Kaiser, 1975).

[42] For the question, first raised by F.C. Baur, see B.A. Pearson, '1 Thessalonians 2:13–16: A Deutero-Pauline Interpolation' *HTR* 64 (1971) 79–94, with refinement in D.D. Schmidt, '1 Thess 2:13–16: Linguistic Evidence for an Interpolation' *JBL* 102 (1983) 269–79. For a full discussion of the issue, and defence of authenticity, see C.J. Schlueter,

(not an interpolation), but our concern here is less what is attributable to Paul than what patterns we see emerging in early Christianity as a whole. The text reads (in schematic form, to clarify its structure, but with minimal punctuation):

14 ὑμεῖς γὰρ μιμηταὶ ἐγενήθητε, ἀδελφοί, τῶν ἐκκλησιῶν τοῦ θεοῦ τῶν οὐσῶν
ἐν τῇ Ἰουδαίᾳ ἐν Χριστῷ Ἰησοῦ,
ὅτι τὰ αὐτὰ ἐπάθετε καὶ ὑμεῖς ὑπὸ τῶν ἰδίων συμφυλετῶν
καθὼς καὶ αὐτοὶ ὑπὸ τῶν Ἰουδαίων
15 τῶν καὶ τὸν κύριον ἀποκτεινάντων Ἰησοῦν καὶ τοὺς προφήτας
καὶ ἡμᾶς ἐκδιωξάντων
καὶ θεῷ μὴ ἀρεσκόντων
καὶ πᾶσιν ἀνθρώποις ἐναντίων
16 κωλυόντων ἡμᾶς τοῖς ἔθνεσιν λαλῆσαι ἵνα σωθῶσιν
εἰς τὸ ἀναπληρῶσαι αὐτῶν τὰς ἁμαρτίας πάντοτε.
ἔφθασεν δὲ ἐπ' αὐτοὺς ἡ ὀργὴ εἰς τέλος.

Coming from our study of the Egyptian and Hellenistic paradigms, it is immediately noticeable how different this sounds, except in one striking particular. Embedded in the midst of this complex of charges is the claim that Judeans 'are displeasing to God and opposed to all people' (καὶ θεῷ μὴ ἀρεσκόντων καὶ πᾶσιν ἀνθρώποις ἐναντίων, 2:15). The first clause ('not pleasing God') might contain the faintest of echoes of the Hellenistic accusation of Jewish 'irreligion' (ἀθεότης),[43] but the next phrase, 'opposed to all people', without doubt takes us straight to the heart of the Hellenistic complaint of Judean 'misanthropy'. What is striking is how the author of this text *connects* this charge (v. 15 d) with the specifically Christian complaint that they 'prevent us from speaking to the Gentiles' (v. 16 a), that is, Jewish / Judean opposition to the Christian mission. After a series of clauses connected by καί, these two clauses are closely enough linked to have no intervening copula. It appears that the 'opposition to all people' is specifically *demonstrated in* the frustration of the Gentile mission: it is because they are opposed to all people that Jews / Judeans do not want the nations (τὰ ἔθνη) to hear the good news.[44] In other words, a Hellenistic logic is taken up into

Filling up the Measure: Polemical Hyperbole in 1 Thessalonians 2.14–16 (JSNTSup 98: Sheffield: JSOT, 1994); cf. T.D. Still, *Conflict at Thessalonica: A Pauline Church and its Neighbours* (JSNTSup 183: Sheffield: Sheffield Academic, 1999) 24–45.

[43] See, e.g., Apollonius Molon *apud* Josephus, *c. Apion.* II 148, 258. But 'pleasing God' is classic Pauline language (cf. 1 Thess 2:4; Rom 8:8; 1 Cor 7:32).

[44] The close connection between these two clauses is rightly noted by E. Best, *A Commentary on the First and Second Epistles to the Thessalonians* (BNTC; London: A & C Black, 1972) 117; C.A. Wanamaker, *Commentary on 1 and 2 Thessalonians* (NIGTC; Grand Rapids: Eerdmans, 1990) 115. A. Malherbe unnecessarily distances this text from the Hellenistic charge of misanthropy on the basis of the connection between these two clauses ('Pagan criticism was social; Paul's is theological', *The Letters to the Thessalonians* [AB 32B; New York: Doubleday, 2000], 170); cf. M. Bockmuehl, '1 Thessalonians 2:14–16

a new and distinctively Christian frame of reference, which then becomes the dominant ground for complaint against Jews/Judeans as anti-social, anti-Gentile, and specifically anti-Christian-mission.

A parallel phenomenon – the absorption of an older tradition within a new Christian frame – occurs in relation to some other themes in this passage. It is commonly and rightly observed that several of the motifs contained in this text are derived from inner-Jewish polemics, a long rhetorical tradition among Jews/Judeans evidenced from biblical literature through to the Dead Sea Scrolls. The accusation of 'killing the prophets' is one we find elsewhere levelled by Jews against Jews: Elijah complains that the people of Israel have slain the prophets (1 Kings 19:10; cited by Paul in Rom 11:3), and Jeremiah (2:30) and Ezra (in Neh 9:26) repeat the charge.[45] To accuse others of 'filling up the measure of their sins' and drawing down divine 'wrath' is classic Jewish language, usually directed against non-Jews, but sometimes turned against fellow Jews in the bitterness of sectarian disputes.[46] But these Judean motifs are transformed by their new context in this passage. The killing of the prophets is now twinned with, and prefaced by, the killing of the Lord Jesus, a charge that is sure to overwhelm and finally obscure that of prophet-murder, since killing Jesus has such momentous significance for those who call him Lord and Son of God. Similarly, the advent of the wrath εἰς τέλος is predicated on the whole saga of opposition to 'us': it is

---

and the Church in Jerusalem', in M.D. Hooker, ed., *Not in the Word Alone. The First Epistle to the Thessalonians* (St. Paul's Abbey, Rome: Benedictina, 2003) 55–87, at 70 ('even if Paul were consciously echoing contemporary anti-Jewish polemic, here these words have certainly been given a highly particular application, estranged from its usual pagan setting'). Rather, one sees here the social charge taken up into another framework of interpretation, where the accusation of 'misanthropy' is refocused as opposition to the church.

[45] The theme became stock; see Josephus, *Ant.* IX 264–65; X 38; MartJes 5.1–14; VitProph *passim*, and the full treatment by O.H. Steck, *Israel und das gewaltsame Geschick der Propheten* (WMANT 23; Neukirchen-Vluyn: Neukirchener, 1967). The theme was much used in early Christian texts; see (besides ours) Mark 12:5 (implied); Luke 11:47–51; 13:33–34; Acts 7:52; Ignatius, *Mag.* 8.2; Justin, *Dial.* 16, 73, 95 etc.; D.R.A. Hare, *The Theme of Jewish Persecution of Christians in the Gospel according to Matthew* (SNTSMS 6; Cambridge: Cambridge University, 1967) 137–41. For the parallels in Matt 23, see below.

[46] For 'filling up sins', see Gen 15:16 (Amorites); Dan 8:23 (Gentile transgressors); 2 Macc 6:14–15 (Gentiles; πρὸς ἐπλήρωσαν ἁμαρτίων ... πρὸς τέλος); SapSol 19:3–5 (ungodly; Egyptians). On the notion, see R. Stuhlmann, *Das eschatologische Mass im Neuen Testament* (FRLANT 132; Göttingen: Vandenhoeck & Ruprecht, 1983) 103–5. Wrath is a ubiquitous theme in apocalyptic literature, directed against all sin, and therefore potentially inclusive of Jews as transgressors. For Jewish sectarian accusations against fellow Jews, see, e.g., PsSal 8; 1QS and 1QM *passim*; the roots lie at least partly in the invective of the biblical Psalms. The closest verbal parallel to 1 Thess 2:16 is TestLevi 6:11 (retribution from the Lord overtakes Shechem and Hamor εἰς τέλος), though the status of this text (Jewish or Christian?) and its relationship to 1 Thess 2:16 is uncertain.

specifically that opposition which 'fills up the measure of their sins' and constitutes the climactic form of disobedience to God.[47]

In other words, both Hellenistic and Judean traditions are here adopted and adapted in the service of a new logic for hostility to Judeans: that they oppose Christ, hinder his apostles, and prevent the fulfilment of the church's destiny, the preaching of the gospel to the Gentiles. It is not surprising that the new Christian movement, drawing from its Judean roots and Scriptural resources, should express its hostility in forms developed first within inner-Jewish polemics: that gives them all the greater theological weight. Nor is it accidental that the Hellenistic charge of Judean antisocial behaviour should continue to be employed: by placing Jewish/Judean opposition to the Christian mission within the wider framework of their hostility to humanity, Christians can feel that their complaint is not simply partisan, but common to all 'decent-living' residents of the empire. But what we witness here is the emergence of a new reason for hostility to Judeans, a specifically Christian logic arising from Christian history and self-perception, which regards the birth of the church as the climax of God's purpose for the world.

As is often pointed out, the closest parallel to our text within the New Testament is the final of Matthew's 'woes' against the scribes and Pharisees (Matt 23:29–39). There several of the same themes occur: the killing of the prophets (23:29–31, 34–37), the 'filling' of the inherited legacy of sin (23:32: πληρόω), the opposition to Christian mission (killing, scourging in synagogues, persecuting from town to town, 23:34: διώκω), and the descent of God's judgement, in some final or decisive form (23:33, 36, 38). All this stands in the larger context of bitter rivalry between the new Christian communities and the Jewish people (cf. Matt 5:11–12; 10:17–23), the Gentile mission (28:16–20) and, most fundamentally, the laying of blame on the Jewish people for the death of Jesus (27:25, echoing 23:35–36). The similarities between Matt 23 and 1 Thess 2 might suggest some common (pre-synoptic) tradition, or the development in early Christian discourse of a common set of tropes in which the Christian experience of 'persecution' from Judean/Jewish sources was linked to the history of Israel's rejection of prophets, the death of Jesus and the mission to Gentiles.[48]

What both texts illustrate, in their contents and history of reception, is how polemics by Jewish authors (Paul and Matthew) against non-Christ-

[47] We may leave to one side the translation of εἰς τέλος (fully? at last? for ever? to the end?); however this is interpreted, it is clear that opposition to the gospel is the decisive event that brings on the wrath of God in climactic fashion.

[48] For the theme in Matthew, see Hare, *Theme of Jewish Persecution*. There are clearly elements of exaggeration and historical distortion in this tradition, not least in relation to responsibility for the death of Jesus. But Paul himself is witness to some hostile actions against Christian believers from an early date (Gal 1:13, 22; Phil 3:6; cf. his accusations in Gal 4:29; 5:11; 6:12–13).

believing Jews/Judeans become generalised into undifferentiated assaults on 'Jews/Judeans' and thus contribute to a specifically Christian form of anti-Judaism. In the case of our main text, 1 Thess 2:14–16, one might argue whether the Ἰουδαῖοι mentioned in 2:14 are merely the residents in Judea and particularly those who (supposedly) killed the Lord Jesus and the prophets. As I indicated above (see n. 2), Ἰουδαῖος can be used of any Judean/Jew living anywhere in the world (the term conveys some residual connection with the land, but not necessarily residence there); but one might still argue from the context that only Judea-resident Jews/Judeans are in view. After all, the tradition of killing the prophets is particularly associated with Jerusalem (see Matt 23:37; Luke 13:33–34), and it was, on any account, only Judea-resident Judeans who could be charged with killing Jesus. They are also those most obviously in view as opponents of 'the churches in Judea' (2:14). For all these reasons, one might resist the addition of the so-called 'anti-Semitic comma' between v. 14 and v. 15; one might insist, in other words, that all the material in vv. 15–16 relates specifically to Judea-resident Judeans and only to them.[49] But although the complaint undoubtedly starts in that geographical region, I doubt that all the rest of this notorious sentence can truly be restricted in this way. As the text shifts at the end of v. 15 from the past to the present tense (ἐκδιωξάντων ... ἀρεσκόντων), we seem to move into a generalised mode of accusation, and it is not clear how Judea-resident Judeans could be held responsible for hindering Paul and his companions ('us') from speaking to the Gentiles: in fact that Gentile mission takes place primarily, if not exclusively, *outside* the region of Judea.[50] In other words, the charge seems to broaden out to apply to any Judean opposition to the apostle and his Gentile mission, as a symptom of their 'opposition to all people,' a charge levelled at all Judeans everywhere, not only at those in Judea.[51] Just as the charge ranges across time (from those who killed the prophets in the past to those who killed Jesus recently, and to those who oppose the Judean churches now), so it ranges geographically, from the Judea-resident Ἰουδαῖοι to those Ἰουδαῖοι in other places who oppose the Gentile mission. The same generalising move can be detected in the Matthean parallel: woes against 'scribes and Pharisees' extend to include 'this generation' as a whole (23.36), including those who scourge Christian believers in synagogues and persecute them

[49] F.D. Gilliard, 'The Problem of the Anti-Semitic Comma between 1 Thessalonians 2:14 and 15' *NTS* 35 (1989) 481–502.

[50] Even if Paul regards his Jewish-Christian opponents as originating from Judea (cf. Gal 2:4, 11–14; 2 Cor 11:12–14, 22), this can hardly be said of all the opposition he faced in the Diaspora (cf. 2 Cor 11:24).

[51] For recognition that the charge broadens out beyond Judea, see, e.g., Wanamaker, *1 and 2 Thessalonians*, 118–19; E.J. Richard, *First and Second Thessalonians* (SP 11; Collegeville, Minn.: Liturgical, 1995), 120, 125–26.

from town to town (23.34). In both cases, the polemics leak out of their original particularity to form a generalised complaint.

But if Paul is a Jew speaking about other Jews, can this passage be interpreted as inner-Jewish polemic, representative of a pattern of accusation and vitriol internal to the Jewish community and traceable through scriptural and Second Temple texts?[52] As we have seen, several motifs here are paralleled by texts socially located within internal Jewish discourse. But we should also note that some motifs are originally Hellenistic (the slur on opposition to 'all people') and some are distinctively Christian (killing the Lord Jesus and driving out/persecuting 'us'). And, in any case, the whole package of motifs, whatever their origin, is now directed to a predominantly Gentile audience, so that the text has a quite different effect than if it constituted some tract internal to the Jewish/Judean community. If this is from Paul it is indeed a Jew/Judean speaking, but he is speaking not *to* fellow Judeans, but about them. His audience, the ἐκκλησία of the Thessalonians (1.1), does not identify itself as Jewish/Judean, and is made up primarily of non-Judeans who have 'turned from idols to the true and living God' (1:9–10). If Paul endeavours to distance them, rhetorically, from the 'Gentiles who do not know God' (4:5) whose idolatry, persecuting activity, sexual impurity and hopelessness he lambasts in this letter (1:9–10; 2:14; 4:2–8, 13), the present passage serves to distance them also from 'Jews/Judeans', who they can expect, henceforth, to oppose them, and to stand under the wrath of God.[53] As this paragraph circulates among Gentile Christians, it escapes its Judean habitat as surely as is slides from the past Judean death of Jesus to the present Diaspora opposition to Paul.[54]

[52] For internal Jewish polemics, see E. P. Sanders, *Jewish Law from Jesus to the Mishnah: Five Studies* (London: SCM, 1990) 84–89. For the use of hyperbole in ancient vitriol, see Schlueter, 75–110; L. T. Johnson, 'The New Testament's Anti-Jewish Slander and the Conventions of Ancient Rhetoric' *JBL* 108 (1986) 419–41.

[53] On the parallel between statements made in 2:14–16 against Jews/Judeans, and those made elsewhere in the letter against Gentiles, see P. Wick, 'Ist I Thess 2,13–16 antijüdisch? Der rhetorische Gesamtzusammenhang des Briefes als Interpretationshilfe für eine einzelne Perikope' *TZ* 50 (1994) 9–23. I pass over here the question of event(s) referred to in 2:16 c; the statements in this paragraph contain the ingredients of a Christian logic of hostility to Jews, even if the 'wrath' here depicted is not eschatologically final. The same holds true whether they reflect, or do not reflect, particular experiences in Thessalonica, and whether they are, or are not, compatible with Rom 9–11.

[54] Although their situations are not completely parallel, one may compare the careful treatment of this topic by U. Luz in regard to Matthew's gospel, specifically Matt 23: 'Matthew remains a Jew, understands himself not as the representative of a new religion but as an Israelite, and never would have accepted the charge of anti-Judaism. Historically, he and his churches are in transition from Israel to a church dominated by Gentile Christians that to a large extent has already become a reality alongside Israel. However, one can certainly say that when his Gospel is read and represented by Gentile Christians it becomes an anti-Jewish book, for Gentile Christians who are not Jews cannot fail to

We may insist, of course, that this text is directed not against all Jews, and not against Jews as such, but only against those Jews who oppose or persecute the Christian church.[55] But the complaints are articulated in remarkably general terms, and appear to posit such widespread opposition to the Christian message, from the death of Jesus onwards, that they articulate a new and easily universalised logic of hostility to Jews/Judeans, which quickly became integral to Christian discourse. In the book of Acts, Stephen's speech traces a pattern of Jewish/Judean 'stiffnecked' behaviour, culminating in the death of Jesus, for which the Jewish leaders, Jerusalem residents, or 'all the house of Israel' are responsible (Acts 7:51–52; cf. Luke 24:20; Acts 2:23, 26; 3:13–15; 4:10; 5:30; 13:27–28). Similarly, the motif of opposition to Paul and to the Gentile mission is repeated time and again in the narrative of Paul's journeys (Acts 9:23; 13:45–50; 14:2, 19; 17:5, 13 [Thessalonica]; 18:12 etc.); its imprint in this early Christian historiography demonstrates how significant it has become in Christian self-understanding.[56] Of course there are plenty of Jews/Judeans in Luke-Acts who do not oppose the gospel, and in fact become believers; and, despite Acts 28:23–29, the door is perhaps never finally closed in their faces. But time and again the synagogue is the source of hostility towards believers, and inasmuch as Judeans/Jews become stereotyped as mischief-makers, it is because of a specifically Christian complaint, their opposition to the people of Christ. Such development of a new Christian logic for hostility to Judeans is also evident in John's Gospel, where the rejection of the message of Jesus is the chief fault of the Ἰουδαῖοι. Although the referent of this term continues to be the topic of much dispute,[57] there are very few places where it can be confined to the sense 'Judean' in the narrow, geographical sense (resident of Judea), and several indications that Jews/Judeans have become a symptom of the opposition of 'the world', in its blindness to the truth in Jesus.

Thus, for all their differences in nuance and theological frame, these early Christian texts articulate a fundamental antithesis between 'Jews/Judeans'

read it as a foundational book of their new, non-Jewish religion. The canonization of the Gospel of Matthew by the Gentile Christian church was then the final step in making it an anti-Jewish book. For that, however, Matthew himself is not responsible', *Matthew 21–28* (Hermeneia; Minneapolis: Augsburg Fortress, 2005) 173.

[55] See W. Marxsen, *Der erste Brief an die Thessalonicher* (ZBK; Zürich: Theologischer, 1979); Malherbe, *Letters to the Thessalonians*, 169, 174, 178–79; cf. T. Holtz, *Der erste Brief an die Thessalonicher* (EKK; Neukirchen-Vluyn: Neukirchener) 103–4; idem, 'The Judgment on the Jews and the Salvation of All Israel: 1 Thess 2,15–16 and Rom 11,25–26', in R. F. Collins, ed., *The Thessalonian Correspondence* (Leuven: Leuven University, 1990) 284–94.

[56] Among the extensive literature on this topic, see J. T. Sanders, *The Jews in Luke-Acts* (London: SCM, 1987).

[57] See the essays on this topic in R. Bieringer, D. Pollefeyt and F. Vandecasteele-Vanneuville, eds., *Anti-Judaism and the Fourth Gospel* (Assen: van Gorcum, 2001) 229–356.

and the interests of the Christian community, and thus a new but deeply rooted logic for hostility to Jews. In general, the sense of eschatological finality in Christ led Christians to consider the continuing Judean people an anachronism, while the destruction of the temple in 70 CE all too easily solidified this impression. Compared to what we see in Egyptian or Hellenistic paradigms, these are wholly new phenomena, a new paradigm, neither worse nor better than what preceded it, but certainly different.

Josephus is thus potentially misleading but ultimately helpful in handling our topic. His unique collection of ethnic slanders has given readers the misleading impression that hostility to Judeans was *sui generis* in the ancient world, whereas it was only part of a complex web of inter-ethnic prejudice. By gathering all his sources together he has encouraged the sense that there was a single phenomenon we may call 'anti-Judaism' or 'Judeophobia', manifested in varying forms but representative of a single attitude of dislike towards Judeans. It then becomes a question of whether early Christians can be blamed for contracting this ancient virus, or exonerated for using a different discourse, derived from inner-Jewish polemics. But if we use Josephus more carefully, and trace out from his materials (and others he does not cite) the different logics in ancient hostility to Judeans, we find a much more differentiated picture, and are able to identify both what was old and what was new in early Christian discourse. And we can thus understand (not excuse) their opposition to Judeans as a correlate of their own new construction of the world, a cultural framework in which Judeans took a unique place in the story of salvation, encouraging their portrayal sometimes as heroic bearers of the promise but unfortunately more often as stubborn opponents of the Christ and of the truth taught by the church.

III. The Invention of Christian Identity in the Pauline Tradition

9. Thessalonica and Corinth

Social Contrasts in Pauline Christianity

According to the book of Acts, Paul founded five churches during his first mission to Europe: Acts 16–18 records successful evangelism in Philippi, Thessalonica, Beroea, Athens and Corinth. For most of the details of this narrative we have no external check on Luke's account, but in the case of three of these churches – Philippi, Thessalonica and Corinth—we have first-hand historical evidence in the form of Paul's letters; and these provide enough incidental information about the founding of the relevant churches to enable us to question or confirm some parts of the narrative in Acts. In particular, 1 Thessalonians confirms the information given by Luke that Paul arrived in Thessalonica from Philippi, that he was forced to leave the city much earlier than he would have liked, and that he headed south and visited Athens. There is thus sufficient correspondence between Acts and 1 Thessalonians to make it highly likely that when Paul wrote to the Thessalonians a matter of weeks (or, at most, a few months) after his departure from Thessalonica he was already engaged in his mission in Corinth.[1]

We can be reasonably confident, then, that there was only a small interval between the birth of the church in Thessalonica and the establishment by the same evangelist of a Christian community in Corinth. And yet these sibling communities developed remarkably different interpretations of the Christian faith. Any careful reading of Paul's letters to these churches reveals that they had very different characteristics; and any thoughtful analysis of these differences shows how they diverged not just in superficial matters but in their whole perception of the faith they had learned from Paul. The aim of this essay is to explore these divergences in Pauline Christianity and to inquire into their causes. The exploration will highlight one factor in particular which has so far received too little attention, namely the social relations between Christians and non-Christians. Without claiming

---

[1] See E. Best, *The First and Second Epistle to the Thessalonians* (BNTC; London: A & C Black, 1972) 7–13. Despite their differences in the absolute chronology of Paul's life, G. Lüdemann (*Paul: Apostle to the Gentiles: Studies in Chronology* [London: SCM, 1984]) and R. Jewett (*Dating Paul's Life* [London: SCM, 1979]) agree in placing the writing of 1 Thessalonians at this juncture of Paul's mission.

that this is the sole significant factor, I will advance the hypothesis that the presence or absence of conflict in social interaction with outsiders had an important influence on the development of these two churches and on their perception of their Christian identity. In the interests of space, and because they provide our earliest evidence, I will focus almost entirely on the letters known as 1 Thessalonians and 1 Corinthians; but, as the conclusion will indicate, the subsequent letter(s) would not modify but merely confirm our findings here.

I. The Thessalonian Church: Apocalyptic Hope and Social Conflict[2]

a) Paul's Apocalyptic Message and its Reception

We are fortunate to be able to reconstruct with some confidence Paul's gospel message as he preached it in Thessalonica. In 1 Thessalonians Paul refers so many times to the terms of his preaching, and reminds his converts so often of the traditions he had given them, that we can paint a quite detailed picture of his missionary proclamation and his basic instruction of the young church in that city. In its outline and in its central focus that picture is unmistakably apocalyptic. The Thessalonians were told about Jesus, God's Son, how he had died ('for us', 5.10) and been raised (4.14). Most especially, the converts were given instruction about the παρουσία of Jesus, which they were eagerly to await (1.10). The Lord Jesus would suddenly appear with his ἅγιοι (3.13), like a thief in the night (5.1–11), and it was their responsibility always to be ready for his arrival. It is clear that Paul had led his converts to believe that they would live to see the Lord's παρουσία. This is one reason for the shock in the church when some of their number died (4.13–18): it appeared that the deceased had missed the moment which they were all waiting for.

The Thessalonians were also taught to expect that God's wrath would break out on the rest of humanity; although those 'others' imagined that there was 'peace and security', they would soon be overtaken by a sudden and inescapable destruction (5.2–3). Paul's converts, however, would be rescued from such a fate (1.10; 5.9). They had come to know the true and

[2] I have examined the Thessalonian situation in more detail in an article, 'Conflict in Thessalonica' *CBQ* 55 (1993) 512–30, where fuller documentation can be found. [See further T. D. Still, *Conflict at Thessalonica: A Pauline Church and its Neighbours* (Sheffield: Sheffield Academic, 1999); C. van Brocke, *Thessaloniki, Stadt der Kassander und Gemeinde des Paulus: eine frühe christiliche Gemeinde in ihrer heidnischen Umwelt* (WUNT 2.125: Tübingen: Mohr Siebeck, 2001); K.P. Donfried, *Paul, Thessalonica and Early Christianity* (London: T & T Clark, 2002).]

living God in turning from 'idols' (1.9); and, as beneficiaries of his love and his election (1.4), they had been called into his kingdom and glory (2.12). For the present, as Paul warned them, they would experience troubles (προελέγομεν ὑμῖν ὅτι μέλλομεν θλίβεσθαι, 3.4); they should expect their Christian lives to be characterized by suffering. Through it all they should ensure that their behaviour remained holy (4.1–3) and their hearts blameless (3.13): the moment of their vindication was near.

The atmosphere created by this message is heavy with apocalyptic excitement. The standard dualisms of Jewish apocalyptic—between heaven and earth, the present and the future, the elect and the lost—are all present here and given sharp focus through the death and resurrection of Jesus.[3] In this gospel, Christian faith is firmly located within an apocalyptic framework and takes its significance from that special timeframe within which it operates. Moreover, there is every reason to believe that the Thessalonian Christians have been decisively moulded by this structure of belief. Paul is well informed about his converts in Thessalonica following the recent visit by Timothy, but he gives no hint that they have dissented in any significant way from the terms of the gospel which he first preached and now reiterates. The tone of 1 Thessalonians is that of positive reinforcement, not rebuke or correction. The Thessalonians are, in Paul's view, excessively grieved about the deaths of some of their number; but that is because their expectation of the παρουσία is so highly charged that they had not reckoned with the possibility that death might intervene. Paul does not consider that they have given up hope for the παρουσία, only that they have given up hope for their brothers or sisters who had died. Hence the stress in 1 Thess. 4.13–18 is not on the fact that the παρουσία will soon come (he takes for granted that 'we who are alive will be left until his coming', 4.15, 17), but on the hope that the dead in Christ have not been abandoned (4.15–16). This surely indicates that, when Paul addressed the question of 'times and seasons' in 5.1–11, he was led to do so not by a waning of interest in the παρουσία in the Thessalonian church, but precisely by their restless impatience as they daily awaited the signs of the outpouring of God's wrath on unbelievers and their own rescue by the heavenly saviour, Jesus.[4]

---

[3] There are, of course, many definitions of apocalyptic theology, which also had many variations within Judaism. I follow here the working definition of W.A. Meeks, 'The Social Functions of Apocalyptic Language in Pauline Christianity', in D. Hellholm, ed., *Apocalypticism in the Mediterranean World and the Near East* (Tübingen: Mohr Siebeck, 1983) 687–705, in an essay whose observations on 1 Thessalonians are particularly pertinent.

[4] R. Jewett *(The Thessalonian Correspondence* [Philadelphia: Fortress, 1986] 96–100) incorrectly takes 5.1–11 to indicate that the Thessalonians were no longer interested in future events since 'their intense experience of realized eschatology … sustained an unwillingness to live with the uncertainty of a future eschatology' (p. 97). He has been unduly

b) Social Conflict in Thessalonica

If the symbolic world of the Thessalonian church is decidedly apocalyptic, its social context is dominated by conflict. Paul's references to his initial proclamation of the gospel in Thessalonica make clear that his efforts were attended by controversy:

> although we had already suffered (προπαθόντες) and been abused (ὑβρισθέντες) at Philippi, as you know, we had courage in our God to declare to you the gospel of God in the face of great opposition (ἐν πολλῷ ἀγῶνι) (1 Thess. 2.2).

The parallel with Philippi suggests vigorous, possibly physical, opposition—and to this extent Paul's remark supports the account in Acts 17. Indeed, that Paul was the target of at least slanderous attacks from nonbelievers in Thessalonica is the most likely explanation of the painstaking personal defence he mounts in 2.3–12.

But it was not just Paul who came under attack in Thessalonica. It is clear that his converts also have experienced considerable hostility: 'You became imitators of us and of the Lord, having received the word in circumstances of considerable affliction (δεξάμενοι τὸν λόγον ἐν θλίψει πολλῇ) together with joy in the Holy Spirit' (1.6). Moreover, this θλῖψις has continued to affect their lives as Christians. Paul refers to the things they have suffered at the hands of their fellow-countrymen (2.14) and it is evident that he sent Timothy back to Thessalonica out of his deep concern lest they be shaken by such afflictions (3.3). His warning that they were to suffer θλῖψις (3.4) appears to have been entirely accurate.

Although punctuated by these general references to θλῖψις, Paul's letter gives no hint of the forms it took or its causes. θλῖψις can mean merely mental distress (3.7), but the parallel in 1.6 between the Thessalonians' experience and that of Paul and Jesus suggests that at least vigorous social harassment is in view. Elsewhere I have explored the most likely causes of this harassment—in the offensive abandonment by the Thessalonians of traditional religious practices as they turned from 'idols' to 'the true and living God'.[5] The arrogant refusal of Christians to take part in, or to consider as valid, the worship of any God but their own was the cause of deep resentment in the Graeco-Roman world and is probably the root cause of the Thessalonians' troubles. As Acts, 1 Peter and later Christian apologists show, mockery, slander and ostracism were among the many forms of harassment typically employed against such deviant, and threatening, behaviour.

---

influenced by the similar conclusions of W. Lütgert *(Die Vollkommenen im Philipperbrief und die Enthusiasten in Thessalonich* [Gütersloh: Bertelsmann, 1909] 55–81).

[5] See n. 2 above.

It is clear, then, that the relations between Christians and non-Christians in Thessalonica were severely strained. Although the deaths of some of the converts cannot be directly attributed to such θλῖψις (Paul would hardly have missed an opportunity to celebrate the deceased as martyrs), it would certainly be easy for non-Christians to mock those whose faith in a 'saviour' appeared so ineffective. That more than one death occurred so soon after the founding of the church would surely appear more than just coincidental: it is not difficult to imagine hostile comments about the gods' punishment of the impious! There are also signs that the conflict could be heightened by the Thessalonian Christians themselves. Paul has to instruct them not to return evil for evil (5.15) and in 4.11–12 urges them to live quietly, to mind their own affairs and to behave in a seemly fashion towards outsiders. We should probably perceive behind such remarks the dangers of aggressive evangelism which ridicules 'idols' and calls attention repeatedly to the sudden destruction about to fall on all who do not believe in Jesus.[6] Paul knows that the church is already in enough trouble without attracting more through such a public confrontation of outsiders.

c) The Correlation of Apocalyptic and Social Alienation

Thus far I have merely set out side by side the apocalyptic structures of the Thessalonians' beliefs and the social alienation which they have experienced. But it is obvious that there is some correlation here between beliefs and experience which merits investigation.

The symbolic world of apocalyptic is, as we have seen, structured by dualisms; it posits, in particular, a strong distinction between the circle of believers and all the rest of humanity. The Thessalonians were encouraged by Paul to think of all non-believers as 'outsiders' (οἱ ἔξω, 4.12) and to lump them all together in the category of 'the rest' (οἱ λοιποί, 4.13; 5.6). Moreover, such people are described in consistently derogatory terms: they do not know God (4.5); they are 'children of darkness' who merely sleep and get drunk (5.7); and they have no hope (4.13). Although from any 'normal' social perspective Paul is an 'outsider' to Thessalonica, and believers elsewhere in Macedonia, in Achaea and in Judaea are foreigners to the Thessalonian converts compared to their fellow Thessalonians, Paul redraws the social map in order to bind his converts to such comparatively remote people and to loosen their ties to their συμφυλέται nearer to hand (1.7; 2.14–15; 4.10).

---

[6] See E. von Dobschütz, *Die Thessalonicher-Briefe* (Göttingen: Vandenhoeck & Ruprecht, 1909) 180–82, although his suggestion of political involvement is unnecessary and unconvincing. Cf. Best, *Thessalonians,* 175 and W. Marxsen, *Der erste Brief an die Thessalonicher* (Zürich: Theologischer, 1979) 25–26, 62.

Such a dualistic perspective does not rule out the possibility of further conversions; those who have recently been 'children of darkness' themselves might well want to rescue others before it is too late. But it does establish clear boundaries which mark outsiders as alien unless and until they come 'inside'. In some circumstances this fundamental sense of alienation might be mollified or even overruled, where, for instance, close affective bonds tie individuals together across these boundaries. Even apocalyptic symbols can be variously interpreted, according to the interests and circumstances of those who are influenced by them. But where such symbols take a powerful hold in circumstances of social conflict, it is obvious how experience and symbolic world can reinforce each other.

Thus, on the one hand, the Thessalonians' apocalyptic perspective will encourage them to embrace social alienation as normal; indeed, it will sustain their social dislocation by discouraging them from any significant attempt to reduce the conflicts they experience. They will be comforted by the knowledge that their sufferings are only to be expected (they are part of the apocalyptic agenda) and by the assurance that they cannot last for long. The apocalyptic language they have adopted reinforces the social dualism they find operating in practice and injects a strong dose of hostility into their attitudes towards others. All those outside the circle of believers are viewed as actual or potential aggressors. The whole of life is a battle-field and the universe as a whole is caught up in a massive power struggle. Frustration and difficulty is the work of Satan (2.18). The consolation is that those who are responsible for the present troubles will soon themselves be caught up in that sudden destruction due to fall on all objects of God's anger. Thus, every instance of social harassment can be given its 'proper' explanation in this symbolic world structured by oppositions, contrasts and conflicts.

On the other hand, every experience of conflict serves to validate the apocalyptic symbols which the Thessalonian Christians have adopted and to give such symbols vivid and visible meaning. The more they are ridiculed or ostracized, the more clearly is defined the distinction between believers and non-believers, insiders and outsiders; and thus the more obviously correct is the apocalyptic divide between those destined for salvation and those destined for wrath. The more opposition they encounter, the more obviously their opponents are darkened in their understanding, captured by the power of evil forces and justly deserving of the judgment they will shortly face.

Here, then, apocalyptic symbols and social dislocation maintain and reinforce each other. This is, in fact, a classic example of the dialectic between symbolic worlds and social processes in which the symbols suggest a certain interpretation of social events and that construction of events is embraced as confirmation of the 'reality' one believes in. There is no suggestion of determinism intended here: neither their apocalyptic beliefs nor their experiences of harassment determine the development of the Thessalonian church in any simple way.[7] But the coherence of belief and experience in the highly-charged atmosphere of a fledgling community accounts for the special intensity which marked this church and enabled it to survive in a hostile environment.

It will be observed that the focus of this investigation has been on the *social interaction* of the Thessalonian Christians with outsiders rather than their *social status.* These two issues are, to an extent, inseparable: status depends, in part at least, on the value which others place on one's goods and achievements. But I have deliberately departed here from the concentration on the question of status which characterizes most sociological studies of Pauline Christianity in general and the Thessalonian church in particular. In this case we know almost nothing about the social status of the Thessalonian converts,[8] and there is a particular danger of subscribing to the false assumption that an apocalyptic ideology is necessarily founded on, or fostered by, particular economic conditions.[9] For the present investigation we do not need to know about the social origins of Paul's converts or the reasons for their adoption of Christianity. It is only important to observe how their experience as Christians matches and reinforces the apocalyptic symbols which they learned from Paul.

II. The Corinthian Church: Spiritual Knowledge and Social Harmony

We may turn now to examine the church in Corinth, founded so soon after that in Thessalonica. In this case it is harder to be confident about the terms in which Paul preached the gospel when he arrived in Corinth. 1 Corinthians is so intensively focused on developments in the church since its founda-

[7] For a critical discussion of correlations between symbolic and social structures, see B. Holmberg, *Sociology and the New Testament* (Minneapolis: Fortress, 1990) 118–44. He rightly emphasizes that the quest for such correlations must begin from good factual information about social data and must be continually reminded of 'how complex and subtle such relationships typically are' (p. 142). His distinction, drawn from Lampe, between genetic and supportive causality (the latter referring to those factors which enable the continuation of a certain phenomenon) is particularly suggestive for this essay.

[8] Jewett *(Thessalonian Correspondence,* 118–23) argues from 1 Thess. 2.9–12, 4.11 and 2 Thess. 3.6–12 that the Christians were mostly manual workers, and from 2 Cor. 8.2–4 that they suffered extreme poverty. But this is hardly a reliable basis for a social profile of the congregation. 2 Cor. 8 is heavily influenced by rhetorical considerations and it is possible that Paul's injunctions show no more than that *he* assumes that work means work with one's hands.

[9] For the theoretical problems here, see R. L. Rohrbaugh, '"Social Location of Thought" as a Heuristic Concept in New Testament Study' *JSNT* 30 (1987) 103–19.

tion that Paul's pristine preaching and church instruction is no longer in the foreground.[10] In the case of Corinth, then, I will begin the other way round, investigating first the social interaction of the church with Corinthian society, then outlining the dominant understanding of Christian faith among the Corinthians, before exploring what part social factors may have played in the Corinthians' interpretation of Paul's gospel.

a) Social Harmony in Corinth

One of the most significant, but least noticed, features of Corinthian church life is the absence of conflict in the relationship between Christians and 'outsiders'. In contrast to the Thessalonian church, the believers in Corinth appear neither to feel hostility towards, nor to experience hostility from, non-Christians. In writing to the Corinthians, Paul certainly refers to the rejection and harassment which *he himself* experiences. He fought with 'wild beasts' in Ephesus, and claims to be in peril every day (1 Cor. 15.30–32); he is hungry and thirsty, ill-clad, homeless and abused, a public spectacle, like a convict sentenced to die in the arena (4.9–13). But precisely in this passage, where he gives his own catalogue of suffering, Paul notes (with some bitterness) the painless experience of the Corinthians: 'We are fools for Christ's sake, but you are wise in Christ. We are weak but you are strong. You are held in honour, but we in disrepute' (4.10). In the light of Paul's usage of similar terms in 1.26–28, we might be inclined to think that he is referring here only to the minority of Corinthians with relatively high social status. But the ironic rebuke is directed at the whole church and may reflect a consciousness among the Corinthians that, whatever their social origins, their status had been enhanced by their adoption of Christianity.[11]

[10] J.C. Hurd, *The Origin of I Corinthians* (London: SPCK, 1965), is a courageous attempt to excavate through 1 Corinthians to the earliest level of Paul's dealings with the Corinthians; but it is generally acknowledged that his case becomes less convincing the further he goes. [On reconstructions of the Corinthian church and its situation, see now S. Chester, *Conversion at Corinth: Perspectives on Conversion in Paul's Theology and the Corinthian Church* (Edinburgh: T & T Clark, 2003); B.W. Winter, *After Paul Left Corinth: The Influence of Secular Ethics and Social Change* (Grand Rapid: Eerdmans, 2001); E. Adams and D.G. Horrell, eds., *Christianity at Corinth: The Quest for the Pauline Church* (Louisville: Westminster John Knox Press, 2004); S.J Friesen, D.N. Schowalter and J.C. Walters, eds., *Corinth in Context: Comparative Studies on Religion and Society* (Leiden: Brill, 2010).]

[11] The terms in 4.10 do not, then, refer to the original social status of Paul's converts (*pace* G. Theissen, *The Social Setting of Pauline Christianity* [Edinburgh: T. & T. Clark, 1982] 72–73). But neither is it necessary to interpret them as indicating only the Corinthians' spiritual illusions (so G.D. Fee, *The First Epistle to the Corinthians* [Grand Rapids: Eerdmans, 1987] 176–77 and W. Schrage, *Der erste Brief an die Korinther* [EKK, 7.1; Neukirchen-Vluyn: Neukirchener, 1991] 343). Paul's ironic contrast between the Corinthians and the apostles depends on the fact that the Corinthians have good grounds for

It is particularly significant that Paul refers to them as ἔνδοξοι (in contrast to the apostles who are ἄτιμοι) since the context shows that these terms concern their public reputation. Clearly, whatever individual exceptions there may be, Paul does not regard social alienation as the characteristic state of the Corinthian church.[12]

In fact there are plenty of signs suggesting the social acceptability of the Corinthian Christians. That some of them (presumably the wealthier) take their disputes to the civic law-courts (6.1–6) signals their confidence in the legal system; they do not anticipate that believers will receive prejudicial treatment at the hands of non-Christians. Corinthian Christians are invited to meals in the houses of non-believers (10.27) and, conversely, non-believing friends or neighbours might well drop in to the house where the Christian meeting is taking place (14.24–25). Most significant, however, is the fact that some of the leaders of the Corinthian church (whose example others are likely to follow) are to be found as participants in parties and feasts in the dining rooms of the temples (8.10). As Theissen has shown, these people must be not only of some social status, but also sufficiently integrated into Corinthian society to be strongly disinclined to raise any objections on the grounds of religious scruple;[13] it was important for them to retain the social contacts which such temple-dinners provided. Of the individuals named in 1 Corinthians, leaders like Gaius and Stephanas might well have acquired their wealth through that trading and 'dealing with the world' which Paul lists as the occupation of some Corinthian Christians (7.30–31); and, of course, Erastus, as the οἰκονόμος τῆς πόλεως (Rom. 16.23), whether or not he subsequently became aedile, must have sought some tolerable *modus vivendi* with his non-Christian associates at work.[14]

---

considering themselves 'wise, strong and honoured', just as Paul has grounds for describing himself as the opposite.

[12] While there are many opponents in Ephesus (ἀντικείμενοι πολλοί, 16.9) there is no hint of any such opposition in Corinth. The illness and death referred to in 11.30 is divine punishment, and the suffering of individual members in 12.26 is non-specific; there is no indication in either case of the agency of hostile parties. In 7.26 Paul refers in general terms to the 'present distress' (ἐνεστῶσα ἀνάγκη); this may refer to eschatological woes (cf. 7.28–29; Lk. 21.23) or to difficult physical conditions in general (cf. 2 Cor. 6.4; 12.10); there is nothing to indicate an experience of persecution.

[13] Theissen, *Social Setting*, 121–43. [For the extensive recent debates on the social level of Pauline converts, see B. W. Longenecker, 'Socio-Economic Profiling of the First Urban Christians', in T. D. Still and D. G. Horrell, eds., *After the First Urban Christians: The Social-Scientific Study of Pauline Christianity Twenty-Five Years Later* (London: T & T Clark, 2009) 36–59.]

[14] Theissen, *Social Setting*, 69–119. At 7.18 Paul appears to counter the desire of some of the Jewish converts to cover up the marks of circumcision. This indicates a concern to avoid dishonour, but it appears that opprobrium would attach to them not as Christians but as Jews!

It is clear that Paul is somewhat uneasy about the degree of integration which the Corinthian Christians enjoy. To be sure, contacts with 'outsiders' are to be expected, and indeed welcomed, as opportunities for witness (9.19–23; 10.32–33; 7.16?). Paul is concerned that his converts should be able to buy freely in the meat-market and share non-cultic meals with unbelievers (10.25–27). He is careful to show that those married to non-Christians are not thereby polluted (7.12–16) and he recognizes as a general principle that complete separation from the world is impossible (5.9–10). Nonetheless, he has a much more sectarian and separatist expectation of the social standing of the church than the Corinthians. He attacks their recourse to the law-courts not just for pragmatic reasons but on ideological grounds: it is absurd for Christians to submit to the judgment of the ἄδικοι and ἄπιστοι whom they will soon themselves judge, along with the rest of 'the world' (6.1–3).[15] In fact, 'this world' and 'the present age' are spoken of in consistently derogatory terms throughout the letter, for they, together with their rulers, are doomed to imminent destruction (1.18–2.8; 3.18–20; 7.31). In the Corinthians' easy dealings with the world Paul detects a failure to comprehend the counter-cultural impact of the message of the cross (1.18–2.5); the wisdom of the world to which they are so attracted is, he insists, a dangerous enemy of the gospel. Such a consistent stress on the church's distinction from the world would hardly have been necessary in Thessalonica! But in Corinth such things needed to be said, and with heavy emphasis. The Corinthians must be warned against the corrupting influence of 'bad company' (15.33). As the holy temple (3.16), they are a distinct body of 'saints', washed and purified through their baptism (6.11). Their dealings with the world must be controlled by the ὡς μή principle which recognizes its imminent collapse (7.29–31).

In fact there is good evidence to suggest that the Corinthian Christians were quite conscious of their difference from Paul on this matter. Paul's remarks about his earlier letter (5.9–13) indicate that the relationship between believers and non-believers had already been a contentious issue between them. It is possible that the strange outburst in 2 Cor. 6.14–7.1 is a fragment of that earlier letter, with its clarion call to separate from unbelievers.[16] But

[15] What concerns Paul is not just the embarrassment caused by the public display of dirty linen, nor the corruption endemic in Corinthian civil courts (so B. Winter, 'Civil Litigation in Secular Corinth and the Church: The Forensic Background to 1 Corinthians 6.1–8' *NTS* 37 [1991] 559–72). It is the fact that the Corinthian judges are 'unbelievers' and representatives of the 'world' which makes them inappropriate adjudicators of the affairs of believers. If, as appears likely, Paul refers to them as οἱ ἐξουθενήμενοι ἐν τῇ ἐκκλησίᾳ (6.4), the apocalyptic venom is unmistakable.

[16] See the discussion by V.P. Furnish, *II Corinthians* (AB; New York: Doubleday, 1984) 375–83. If, as most concede, this passage does not belong in its present context, it is much more likely that it has been interpolated from another part of Paul's correspondence

even if it is not, and if, as Paul now claims (5.10), his earlier letter urged only separation from wayward Christians, that would still represent an attempt to establish boundaries quite different from those the Corinthians are willing to accept. While allowing a degree of social contact with 'outsiders', Paul still paints the starkest contrast between the church and the world. He understands the church as a community whose rules govern all departments of life and he expects the members to find in it their primary and dominant relationships: their ties to their fellow ἀδελφοί and ἀδελφαί are to be more significant than any others.[17] The Corinthians, however, seem to understand the social standing of the church quite differently. They see no reason to view the world through Paul's dark apocalyptic spectacles and are no doubt happy to enjoy friendly relations with their families and acquaintances.[18] Their reluctance to excommunicate even such a flagrant moral offender as the man discussed in ch. 5 may suggest that they do not see the church as a moral arbiter at all; they may have considered that it had no claim on their lives outside the worship gatherings. The behaviour of the wealthier members at the Lord's Supper and the legal disputes between members are eloquent testimony to the lack of close affective ties within the church; and it is clear, from their continued participation in temple-dinners, that those who are socially well-placed set much more store on the opinions of their non-Christian friends than on the feelings of their 'weaker' Christian ἀδελφοί. Paul's vision is of a church community, where members are open to the world but nonetheless forever conscious of the difference between 'insiders' and 'outsiders', and where the intense relationships among members of the family make belonging to the church the core of their existence. The Corinthian Christians apparently do not see themselves in this light; and their different self-perception is surely not unconnected to the harmony they enjoy in their relationships with non-Christians.[19]

---

with Corinth than from some other Pauline (or non-Pauline) source. The usual objection against the identification with the 'earlier letter' is that it urges separation from unbelievers; but this is precisely how the Corinthians have understood it, and Paul's claim in 1 Cor. 5.10 that he meant otherwise is supported by a suspiciously ambiguous πάντως.

[17] Hence the rule on excommunication in 5.1–13; it is assumed that contact with a 'brother' will corrupt the church in a way that contact with 'outsiders' will not.

[18] N. Walter rightly notes the oddity for Gentiles of the notion that religion could be the cause of suffering, in 'Christusglaube und heidnische Religiosität in paulinischen Gemeinden' *NTS* 25 (1979) 422–42.

[19] On 'boundaries' in general, see W.A. Meeks, *The First Urban Christians* (New Haven: Yale University, 1983) 84–110; cf. M.Y. MacDonald, *The Pauline Churches* (Cambridge: Cambridge University, 1988) 32–45. However, in both cases their description of the boundary-rules of 'Pauline Christians' are generalizations over-dependent on statements made by Paul himself, while MacDonald adopts uncritically Wilson's model of a 'conversionist sect'. The different views and different circumstances of Paul's churches are not adequately explored.

b) The Corinthian Interpretation of Christian Faith

The title of this section is of course over-simplistic. There is no single interpretation of the Christian faith operative in the Corinthian church, but many different perspectives existing alongside or in competition with one another. There are libertines and ascetics, rich and poor, weak and strong—not to mention the four parties whose slogans Paul ridicules in 1 Corinthians 1–4. In contrast to the Thessalonian church, where no major differences of opinion are detectable, the Corinthian church contains a complex tangle of varying interests and opinions.

Yet it is still possible to talk of a dominant ethos in the Corinthian church, a consistent theological pattern which is the recognizable target of Paul's critical comments in most sections of the letter.[20] Judging from Paul's citations of the Corinthian letter in ch. 8, the leading Christians in Corinth are proud of their knowledge (γνῶσις); and this, it seems, is what Paul has in view in his discussion of wisdom (σοφία) in 1.18–3.23.[21] In his concern to disparage 'the wisdom of the world' and to relativize knowledge (1.18–2.5; 3.18–23; 13.8–12), Paul does not clearly describe what content the Corinthians gave to it; but we know that it concerns the understanding of mysteries (13.1–2) and it seems to include some conviction of the oneness of God and the insignificance (or non-existence) of εἴδωλα (8.4–6).

What is sufficiently clear is that the special insight the Corinthians enjoyed was a product of their much vaunted possession of the Spirit. We can legitimately deduce from Paul's ironical remarks in 2.6–3.3 that these Corinthians considered themselves πνευματικοί and τέλειοι in a way which set them apart from the ordinary mass of ψυχικοί.[22] When Paul claims that he too possesses the Spirit of God (7.40), we can be sure that we are picking up echoes of Corinthian claims; indeed Paul directly describes them as ζηλωταὶ πνευμάτων (14.12; cf. 14.1, 37). They had first drunk deeply of the Spirit at baptism (12.13) and they continued to be nourished at the Lord's Supper with the πνευματικὸν βρῶμα and πνευματικὸν πόμα (10.3–4). It

[20] The problems in reconstructing Corinthian theology are fully laid out by Schrage, *Der erste Brief an die Korinther*, 39–47; but he rightly does not despair of the task altogether.

[21] It is possible that Paul deliberately changes the terminology in this passage. While he can only be positive about the possession of γνῶσις, apart from the danger of arrogance (1.5; 8.1–3; 1 Thess. 4.5; Gal. 4.8–9), it is easier to rubbish an attachment to σοφία, whose connotations are more ambiguous. 'The wisdom of the world' can denote mere sophistry and 'the wisdom of words' mere rhetorical ingenuity; it would have been a lot harder to build pejorative associations into a discussion of 'knowledge'.

[22] It is generally recognized that Paul here polemically reuses Corinthian vocabulary (cf. 15.44–46); such terms are not used similarly in other letters. See B. A. Pearson, *The Pneumatikos-Psychikos Terminology in 1 Corinthians* (Missoula, MT: Society of Biblical Literature, 1973).

was in such gatherings for worship that their possession of the Spirit was vividly displayed—first of all in glossolalia (polemically relegated to the end of the list by Paul), but also in prophecy and inspired speech of every kind. 1 Corinthians 11–14 provides a fascinating glimpse of the electric atmosphere of such gatherings; the sparks of the Spirit, in the shape of prophecy, tongues and knowledge (13.8), flew indiscriminately between male and female πνευματικοί (11.4–5).

The confidence provided by this surge of spiritual energy is evident in the slogan of authorization, πάντα ἔξεστιν. The primary context for its use seems to have been in matters of food (6.12–13; 10.23), and, in particular, the consumption of meat imbued with cultic associations. How far this principle of ἐξουσία was extended, it is difficult to know: perhaps as far as the conscious rejection of sexual taboos (5.1–2). The 'knowledge' provided by the Spirit was evidently a versatile commodity; it also provided a sense of immunity and of indifference to apostolic warnings.

Some features of Corinthian practice and belief are not so easily explained. It is unclear, for instance, what motivated the sexual asceticism which prompted a major section of the Corinthians' letter to Paul. Sexual abstinence, in varying degrees, was advocated for so many reasons in early Christianity that the pursuit of parallels could lead us in many different directions.[23] Perhaps the most plausible explanation is the one most closely tied to the Corinthians' passion for πνευματικά. Both in Judaism and in Graeco-Roman religion it was recognized that receptivity to the divine was greatly improved where there was no interference from sexual activity. Perhaps, like Philo's Moses, the πνευματικοί in Corinth wished to hold themselves 'continually in readiness to receive prophetic oracles' and to that end 'disdained sexual intercourse'.[24] Even Paul considers prayer a good reason to abstain from sex (7.5) and it is not unreasonable to surmise that the women who aimed to keep themselves holy in body and spirit (7.34) were those who most desired to act as channels of the Holy Spirit in their prayer and prophecy (11.5).[25]

It is also not entirely clear why some of the Corinthians said there was no resurrection of the dead (15.12). Paul uses such a variety of counter-arguments in ch. 15 that it is not easy to identify his target, and it remains

---

[23] See especially P. Brown, *The Body and Society: Men, Women and Sexual Renunciation in Early Christianity* (London: Faber and Faber, 1989). [Cf. W. Deming, *Paul on Marriage and Celibacy: The Hellenistic Background of 1 Corinthians 7* (2nd edn.; Grand Rapids: Eerdmans, 2004).]

[24] *Mos.* 2.68–69; see Brown, *Body and Society,* 65–82 and, for Judaism, G. Vermes, *Jesus the Jew* (London: SCM, 1973) 99–102. Cf. the decades of celibacy practised by Anna (Lk. 2.36–37) which established her credentials as a reliable prophetess.

[25] M.Y. MacDonald, 'Women Holy in Body and Spirit: The Social Setting of 1 Corinthians 7' *NTS* 36 (1990) 161–81.

possible that he partially misrepresents or misunderstands the Corinthian position.[26] However, if the extensive argument about σῶμα in 15.35–58 is not wholly irrelevant, it would appear that it was the notion of bodily resurrection in particular (rather than continuance beyond death in general) which the Corinthians could not accept. And this again can best be explained in the light of the Corinthians' fascination with πνευματικά. The human person was generally regarded, according to their cultural koine, as a hierarchical dualism of soul and body; few could imagine, or wish for, a bodily existence beyond death. But the gift of the πνεῦμα, with the extraordinary and special powers which it brought, would serve to sharpen this dualism and to throw the body further into the shade of inferiority. In their ecstatic experiences they rose high above the tawdry concerns of the body—indeed, even above the realm of the mind (14.19); in moments of ecstasy it was unclear whether they remained within the body at all.[27] From this perspective the body would obviously seem a hindrance one could well do without (6.13); the notion of a bodily resurrection would be particularly unpalatable to such πνευματικοί.

It has become the scholarly fashion to refer to Corinthian theology as an example of 'realized' or 'over-realized' eschatology. While some dispute continues about the relevance of 2 Tim. 2.18 (those who claim 'the resurrection is past already'), it is widely held, on the basis of 4.8 and Paul's continual references to the future, that the Corinthians considered themselves to have arrived already in the sphere of heavenly glory. But it is important to be aware how Paul's perspective on the Corinthian church tends to control our description of them. *In Paul's view* the freedom, knowledge and spiritual ecstasy enjoyed by the Corinthians constituted a falsely claimed pre-emption of eschatological glory: 'Already you are filled! Already you have become rich! Without us you have come into your kingdom!', he sarcastically remarks (4.8). But did the *Corinthians* see their experience as related to an eschatological time-frame like this? Did they consider that they had already entered the future, or did they simply not operate with Paul's typical contrasts between present and future? Paul downplays present Christian knowledge as partial and imperfect (13.8–12) because he holds an apocalyptic world-view in which the future will be radically new and glorious in contrast to the present (15.42–44): 'if for this life only we have hoped in Christ, we are of all people most to be pitied' (15.19). But

[26] The continuing debate on such matters is most recently reviewed in A.J.M. Wedderburn, *Baptism and Resurrection* (Tübingen: Mohr Siebeck, 1987) 6–37. [Cf. D. Martin, *The Corinthian Body* (New Haven: Yale University Press, 1995).]

[27] Cf. Paul's uncertainty in his competitive account in 2 Cor. 12.1–10. On the possible understandings of ecstasy in the Graeco-Roman world, see Wedderburn, *Baptism and Resurrection*, 249–68.

the Corinthians apparently see nothing pitiable about the present, because their non-apocalyptic perspective anticipates no radical disjunctions in the future. Their Spirit-filled lives are not an early experience of the future; they simply consider themselves to have reached the heights of human potential. If Paul had read Philo's descriptions of the soul's ascent above the concerns of the world to the pure vision of reality or of the wise man's ecstatic and joyous contemplation of divine truths, 'borne aloft into the heights with a soul possessed by some God-sent inspiration', he would no doubt have scribbled in the margin, 'Already you are filled!'[28] It would be misleading to describe Philo's theology as '(over-)realized eschatology'; his theological framework is simply non-eschatological. Perhaps this is also true of the Corinthian Christians.[29]

Unlike the Thessalonians, the Corinthians did not regard their Christian experience as an eager anticipation of a glory ready to be revealed at the coming of Christ. Rather, their initiation in baptism and their receipt of the

---

[28] *Spec. Leg.* 3.1–2; cf. *Op. Mund.* 70–71; *Deus Imm.* 148–51; *Gig.* 31, 53, 60–61; *Somn.* 2.234–36.

[29] This parallel with Philo is not meant to suggest that Corinthian theology is derived from 'Hellenistic Judaism', as has been argued by Pearson *(The Pneumatikos-Psychikos Terminology)* and by R.A. Horsley (in a number of articles, including 'Pneumatikos vs. Psychikos: Distinctions of Spiritual Status among the Corinthians' *HTR* 69 [1976] 269–88 and '"How Can Some of You Say That There Is No Resurrection of the Dead?": Spiritual Elitism in Corinth' *NovT* 20 [1978] 203–31). Their (and other similar) attempts to pinpoint the 'background' to the Corinthians' theology in 'analogies' and 'parallels' from Philo and Wisdom of Solomon are problematic on several counts. [Cf. B. Schaller, 'Adam und Christus bei Paulus. Oder: Über Brauch und Fehlbrauch von Philo in der neutestamentlichen Forschung', in R. Deines and K.-W. Niebuhr, eds., *Philo und das Neue Testament* (WUNT 172; Tübingen: Mohr Siebeck, 2004) 143–53.]

a. They fail to explain what is different and new in Corinth, in particular the heavy emphasis on πνεῦμα (and its associated adjective πνευματικός). In their concern to deny that the Corinthians have adopted a 'Gnostic' package of terms and ideas, they have simply substituted a package from 'Hellenistic Judaism'. The extent to which the Corinthians may be forging new language under the influence of Christian teaching and their experience of the Spirit is not explored [see chapter 10, below].

b. Their thesis puts some weight on the role of Apollos as the mediator of such 'Hellenistic Jewish wisdom speculation'. But one can hardly imagine Paul urging Apollos to return to Corinth (1 Cor. 16.12) if he was responsible for an interpretation of Christianity which so greatly threatened Paul's gospel. In any case, many of the Jewish features of this theology (the oneness of God and nothingness of 'idols', the emphasis on πνεῦμα and its connection with knowledge) could have been as easily derived from Paul and from the LXX as from Apollos!

c. Many of the purported parallels from Philo are from passages where Philo strives to interpret the biblical text in terms drawn from Stoic or Platonic philosophy. It is quite possible that the Corinthians, without any Philonic influence, were engaged in a similar process, combining their Hellenistic theological culture with Jewish terms and traditions taught by Paul. They were forging a form of Judaized Hellenism, parallel to (in the strict sense, not dependent on) Philo's Hellenized Judaism. This would account for the fact that Paul associates their 'wisdom' with the interests of Greeks, not Jews (1.22).

Spirit had signified the grant of a superior insight into divine truths. The regular infusion of the Spirit in the Lord's Supper gave them privileged access to knowledge, and the display of spiritual powers in worship confirmed the superior status which they had attained. They did not daily look up to heaven to await the coming of the Son who would rescue them from the wrath to come, nor did they eagerly search for signs of their impending vindication. Their Christian enlightenment, through the agency of the divine Spirit, was their salvation, and their prophetic, glossolalic and miraculous powers were the proof of its effectiveness.[30]

c) Factors Influencing the Corinthian Interpretation of Faith

We come now to the most difficult stage of this investigation. In the case of the Thessalonian church we saw an obvious correlation between their apocalyptic understanding of Christianity and the social alienation which they experienced from the very beginning. I have now set out the evidence for the notable absence of hostility in the Corinthians' social relations and have sketched in outline their interpretation of Christian faith, with its distinctive emphasis on Spirit and knowledge. The question thus arises: can we posit in this case, too, some correlation between the structure of their symbolic world and the character of their social experience?

We must consider first what other factors might have been at work in shaping the Corinthian hermeneutics.

a. By the time Paul writes 1 Corinthians, there have been other Christian teachers active in Corinth and some would attribute the particular ethos in Corinth to such figures. Attention has focused especially on Apollos, whose name continually recurs through 1 Corinthians 1–4.[31] Now, it would be rash

---

[30] I have resisted referring to this interpretation of Christianity as 'gnostic'. New Testament interpreters in the 20th century (notably W. Schmithals, *Gnosticism in Corinth* [Nashville: Abingdon, 1971 (1956)] and U. Wilckens, *Weisheit und Torheit: Eine exegetisch-religionsgeschichtliche Untersuchung zu 1 Kor 1 und 2* [Tübingen: Mohr Siebeck, 1959]) have so muddied the waters with their loose combination of sources that this term is still liable to mislead (even if one adopts the distinction between *gnosis* and Gnosticism). There are in fact some important similarities between Corinthian theology and that which became popular in educated 'Gnostic' circles in later generations, some of whom found parts of the Corinthian letters extremely congenial. But if 1 Cor. 8.4–6 reflects Corinthian views at all, it is incompatible with that radical pessimism about the material world which is one of the hallmarks of Gnosticism. [On the problems with the label 'Gnostic', see now M.A. Williams, *Rethinking 'Gnosticism': An Argument for Dismantling a Dubious Category* (Princeton: Princeton University, 1996).]

[31] See, e.g., C.K. Barrett, 'Christianity at Corinth', in *Essays on Paul* (London: SPCK, 1982) 1–27; cf. the views of Pearson and Horsley discussed above in n. 29. The reference to the Cephas party in 1.12 has led some to posit the influence of conservative (Palestinian) Jewish voices; so, most recently, M.D. Goulder, 'σοφία in Corinthians' *NTS* 37 (1991)

to deny that Apollos may have had some influence in this connection, but he can hardly bear the sole, or even the chief, responsibility for the theological stance of the Corinthians. In 1 Corinthians Paul nowhere suggests (as he does to the Galatians) that his converts started off running well, but have been misled by subsequent instruction. The burden of the blame lies on the Corinthians themselves, not on Apollos. As far as we know, in the first formative period of the church's life it was Paul alone who had the dominant influence, and there is no clear indication that the Corinthian church has undergone a radical shift since Paul left the scene.

b. That leads us to ask whether Paul himself preached the gospel in Corinth in different terms from those he had used in Thessalonica. Did he abandon apocalyptic language on his way south from Macedonia? We are hampered here by our lack of information about the way Paul first preached in Corinth. Apart from the creed in 15.3–5, the tradition about the Lord's Supper (11.23–26) and his exaggerated claim that he knew nothing among them except Christ crucified (2.1–2), we have no direct evidence to go on.[32] However, I think there are strong reasons to doubt that there was any significant change in Paul's message between Thessalonica and Corinth. When he writes 1 Corinthians Paul has just as much an apocalyptic understanding of the gospel (6.1–3; 7.25–31; 15.20–28) and just as sectarian a view of the church (see above) as in his initial preaching and subsequent letter to the Thessalonians. It is unlikely that Paul has done a double about-turn, first abandoning apocalyptic then taking it up again. Moreover, it is highly probable that Paul wrote 1 Thessalonians precisely while he was on his initial visit to Corinth. The apostle could be all things to all men, but it is doubtful that even he could present such an apocalyptic face in his letter to one church but effectively veil it in his preaching to another!

In fact, one can well imagine how the apocalyptic emphases in Paul's preaching could give rise to a concentration on knowledge as the focus of salvation. An essential element in many forms of apocalyptic thought, including Paul's, is the announcement of secret truths to a select coterie. In

---

516–34. His thesis founders on the distinction he is forced to create between the advocates of σοφία in 1 Cor. 1–4 and of γνῶσις in 1 Cor. 8–10.

[32] Hurd's reconstruction of Paul's original preaching in Corinth *(The Origin of 1 Corinthians)* is subject to criticism on a number of counts. It posits the unlikely influence of the 'Apostolic Decree' on Paul in causing him to undergo a fundamental volte-face in his theology (only to revert towards its original form in 1 Corinthians!). He follows Knox in abandoning the chronology of Acts and thus creates a crucial interval between the mission to Corinth and the composition of 1 Thessalonians. This reordered Pauline chronology has rightly failed to gain wide support. Despite this, I am in general agreement with Hurd's thesis that the Corinthians' theology arises from Paul's own preaching; but instead of Hurd's suggestion of radical changes in Paul's thought, it is only necessary to imagine a particular socially- and culturally-related Corinthian hermeneutic.

Paul's ministry this elite group is defined by initiation through baptism and by receipt of the divine Spirit. It was natural for the Corinthians to conclude that they had been given access in the Spirit to mysteries hidden from others. In other words, the *mode* of revelation was the all-important fact for the Corinthians (not least because it was re-enacted in miraculous ways at each gathering); the *content* of the message could be either ignored or reinterpreted. The possibility of variant interpretations of similar language can be well illustrated from 1 Cor. 2.6–16. Here Paul probably adopts a number of the Corinthians' terms, which emphasized their sense of privilege in the knowledge and communication of 'deep truths'. Paul is able to rework this language and to fill it with apocalyptic content, by stressing the eschatological nature of the truths revealed (2.7, 9). One can imagine, then, a reverse process in which an apocalyptic message is interpreted by the Corinthians in non-apocalyptic terms: the eschatological message could be lost under the impact of its revelatory medium.

c. It seems, then, that the Corinthians' style of faith is not entirely the responsibility of Paul nor wholly the result of later Christian instruction. We need to investigate also the responsibility of the Corinthian Christians themselves. The fact that most were of Gentile origin (12.2) is not a sufficient explanation: so were the Thessalonian believers. Would we come closer to an answer if we focused on their social status? G. Theissen's well-known social investigations of the Corinthian church have certainly demonstrated the importance of the few leading members of relatively high social status; and one would be inclined to think that higher social standing and greater exposure to Hellenistic education might play a significant role in the interpretation of the Christian faith. Those deeply enmeshed in the social networks of Corinthian life at a higher level would certainly have a lot to lose if they adopted too sectarian a mentality; and their Hellenistic training would give them an established mental framework within which to understand Paul's message.

The social status of the dominant minority in the Corinthian church is certainly a factor of some significance. But it would be a mistake to build everything on this foundation alone. In discussing Thessalonica I suggested that there was no necessary correlation between economic deprivation and an apocalyptic world-view; similarly, in Corinth, wealth and its associated social status are not necessarily wedded to a non-apocalyptic and non-sectarian perspective. It is possible for those of high status to undergo major social dislocation and significant resocialization, under the influence of a newly adopted ideology or as a result of social denigration by others. Thus, we cannot rule out the possibility that some of the 'weak' in Corinth—those who had scruples about eating food offered to idols—could have been among the wealthier members of the church; indeed, if they were present at the same dinner parties as the strong (10.27–30) we would have to assume that they were of the same social class.[33] Their unease about such food was, in that case, the product of a strong theological conviction about the dangers of 'idols' which overrode their social convenience. But even if such social dislocation is not self-imposed, it can be imposed by others. The Corinthians' retention of their social status was only possible so long as others did not reject them as 'impious' or 'atheist'. In other words, continuing social interaction with 'outsiders' is at least as significant in determining the Corinthian outlook as initial social status.

When the Corinthian church was founded it did not, apparently, suffer the social ostracism experienced by its sister church in Thessalonica. It is possible that this was because the leading converts deliberately played down the potential offensiveness of their faith, and this may be not unconnected to their social status. But it is intriguing to note that even Paul did not run into trouble in Corinth the way that he did in Thessalonica. Although he lists his woes in 1 Cor. 4.9–13 and 15.30–32, he does not locate any of them in Corinth itself. Indeed, it is striking that the account in Acts 18 has him staying in Corinth more or less peacefully for 18 months. The narrator seems to have felt the need to give some explanation of this unusual phenomenon; he records a specific vision of the Lord which reassures Paul: 'I am with you and no-one shall attack you to harm you; for I have many people in this city' (Acts 18.10). The only opposition comes from some Jews, and their attempt to arraign Paul before Gallio is abortive (Acts 18.6, 12–17). Even after this incident Paul is under no compulsion to leave the city.

The correlation between the harmony of the Corinthians' social context and their particular theology is evident at a number of levels.

a. In the first place, the Corinthian focus on knowledge and possession of the Spirit creates a distinction from the mass of ordinary people, but a *distinction without a sense of hostility.* As πνευματικοί, they are certainly of a superior status, but the rest, the ψυχικοί, are not thereby classed as evil or threatening, merely inferior and unprivileged. The Corinthian symbolic world is structured by contrasts, to be sure, but not such contrasts as represent struggle or conflict. There is no 'present evil age' to be redeemed from, no cosmic warfare against Satan and his powers, no destructive wrath due to fall on all non-believers. That apocalyptic and tension-laden perspective is not characteristic of the Corinthians; their own symbolic world gives them a sufficient sense of superiority to make their conversion worthwhile,

[33] It is crucial to Theissen's argument (*Social Setting,* 121–43) that the 'weak' are socially inferior and that the informant in 10.28 is not a Christian. However, see the contrary opinion on 10.28 in C. K. Barrett, *A Commentary on the First Epistle to the Corinthians* (2nd ed., London: A & C Black, 1971) 239–40; cf. earlier, J. Weiss, *Der erste Korintherbrief* (Göttingen: Vandenhoeck & Ruprecht, 1910) 264–65.

without fostering a sense of hostility towards (or the expectation of hostility from) non-Christians.

b. Secondly, Corinthian theology correlates well with the practice of *differentiation without exclusivity.* The infusion of the divine πνεῦμα at baptism, and its dramatic presence in their midst in worship, were clearly prized features of their Christian existence. They presumably felt that this was in some respects a deeper or richer experience of divine power than they had known before in Graeco-Roman religion (12.2). Yet this did not necessarily annul the claims of others—prophets, poets, seers and philosophers—to similar experiences of ecstasy or inspiration.[34] Their knowledge of the 'oneness' of God was not unlike the monotheistic convictions of those educated in Hellenistic theology. Since others did not define their Christian convictions as alien, there was no reason why they could not accept a kind of theological pluralism, which distinguished their views without discounting all others. This is a theology which both reflects and fosters harmonious relationships.

c. Finally, their religious ethos permits an *involvement in the church which does not entail significant social and moral realignment.* It is important to note the limited context in which the identity of the πνευματικός is displayed: in the worship meetings of the church where the practice of knowledgeable speech, tongues and prophecy fulfils the initiate's calling. Outside these semi-private gatherings in the house of Gaius, the Corinthian Christians might consider their faith of only limited significance. If the church's ecstatic celebrations were the peak of its experience, they could also become its sole focus of interest. Beyond that socially (and temporally) confined context, the πνευματικοί had authority to behave as they wished. They were not bound by a moral tradition which tied them to a distinctive communal lifestyle; indeed, the authority of each individual πνευματικός could not be challenged (2.14). If behaviour is, then, not a matter of ethics but of 'consciousness' and self-understanding, the Christian is not committed in advance to any group norms which might have awkward social implications.[35]

The church is not a cohesive community but a club, whose meetings provide important moments of spiritual insight and exaltation, but do not have global implications of moral or social change. The Corinthians could gladly

---

[34] See Wedderburn, *Baptism and Resurrection,* 249–68.

[35] On the individualism of the Corinthians, expressed through their term συνείδησις, see R.A. Horsley, 'Consciousness and Freedom among the Corinthians: 1 Corinthians 8–10' *CBQ* 40 (1978) 574–89. He rightly suggests that 'for the Corinthians ... the eating of idol-meat and other matters were issues only in an internal personal sense, for one's own individual consciousness, and not in a truly ethical, i.e. relational, sense' (p. 589).

participate in this church as one segment of their lives.[36] But the segment, however important, is not the whole and not the centre. Their perception of their church and of the significance of their faith could correlate well with a life-style which remained fully integrated in Corinthian society.

Once again, then, we have an example of the mutual reinforcement of social experience and theological perspective, which this time involves a major realignment of Paul's apocalyptic symbols. When the first Corinthians became Christians, they did not experience hostility, nor was their apostle hounded out of town. And the more firmly the church got established in conditions of social harmony, the more implausible the apocalyptic content of Paul's message became, with its strong implications of social dislocation. In the face of continuing close and friendly relations with 'significant others' it was hard to sustain an atmosphere of beleaguered hostility. And the more the Corinthians understood their faith as a special endowment of knowledge and a special acquisition of spiritual skills, the less they would expect or embrace hostility: any intimations of conflict would be resolved or minimized. To posit this is not to succumb to some sociological determinism, but simply to note the complex interplay between beliefs and social experience. We must remember how successful the Corinthian church appears to have been, both in its numerical strength and in the intensity of its spiritual experience. The apocalyptic notes in Paul's theology which harmonized so well with the Thessalonians' experience simply failed to resonate with the Corinthians. It is possible that some of them would have felt distinctly uncomfortable in the Thessalonian church and would not indeed have joined, or remained members of, the church in Corinth if it had developed the same ethos as its Thessalonian sibling.

III. Conclusion

This study of the divergent development of these two Pauline churches has shown how misleading it is to generalize about 'Pauline Christians'. It is ironic that it was the church in Corinth which diverged most from Paul's own point of view although he apparently spent much more time there than in Thessalonica! That may be a salutary lesson to us, as it was to Paul, that

[36] This could help explain how the church survived despite its many divisions. The Christians' maintenance of social interests and contacts outside the church prevented them from involving themselves with the internal disputes of the church with such intensity as is typical in more sectarian groups. Those whose participation is more segmental are likely to put less investment into getting their own way in the church; see L. A. Coser, *The Functions of Social Conflict* (London: Routledge & Kegan Paul, 1956) 153.

he had less control than he imagined over the ways his converts interpreted their own conversion.

If we were to follow the development of these churches beyond the point of the writing of 1 Thessalonians and 1 Corinthians, the picture would be enlarged but not substantially altered. If 2 Thessalonians is inauthentic, we can pursue our quest of the Thessalonian church no further. But if, as I am inclined to think, it was written by Paul in close succession to his first letter, it shows a church still undergoing fierce persecution (2 Thess. 1.4–9).[37] There are also signs that the apocalyptic atmosphere in the church has reached a feverish level; there are some who think that 'the day of the Lord' has already arrived (2.2), perhaps interpreting some local or national disaster as the start of that 'sudden destruction' which Paul had prophesied for unbelievers. Paul is sufficiently concerned about this to write another letter, this time with a more frigid and authoritarian tone intended to counter a serious imbalance in the church. Paul's apocalyptic chickens had come home to roost!

The development of the Corinthian church can be more confidently traced, through 2 Corinthians and, much later, *1 Clement.* In 2 Corinthians there is every indication that the church continues to thrive and that its emphasis on spiritual knowledge and power has been reinforced by the authority of 'super-apostles' (11.5) whose 'signs and wonders' create much more impression than Paul's. If there is talk here of the Corinthians suffering ϑλῖψις (1.6–7; 7.8–13), this appears to be caused not by 'outsiders' but by an internal trauma in the church; indeed, if this is connected with Paul's 'sorrowful visit', it is Paul himself who has brought about the only Corinthian ϑλῖψις![38] There are still ironic contrasts in this letter between Paul's weakness and his converts' strength (13.9; cf. 4.12), and 12.21 suggests that serious moral problems remain. If such matters no longer take the foreground in this letter compared to the first, that is because Paul now realizes that he cannot issue correction at all until he can re-establish his authority over the Corinthian church. But his emphasis on the suffering and weakness of his lifestyle (4.7–15; 6.3–10; 11.23–33) suggests that they still declined to accept his counter-cultural vision of the gospel; and the trouble he takes attempting to squeeze money out of them (chs. 8–9) indicates that they still failed to appreciate the significance of their bonds with other Christians. *I Clement* is perhaps too distant chronologically to be of much value, but it may be significant that the author speaks of troubles in Rome but not in Corinth;

[37] I have given a tentative reconstruction of the *Sitz im Leben* of 2 Thessalonians in 'Conflict in Thessalonica'.

[38] A suggestion I owe to Mr [now Dr] Leslie Milton, a research student at Glasgow University.

the church he writes to is not persecuted but torn apart by an internal power struggle over the leadership of the congregation.

It appears, then, that the contrast we have perceived between 1 Thessalonians and 1 Corinthians reveals a genuine divergence in Paul's churches of striking proportions. I have highlighted here one factor which contributes to the explanation of this divergence, the social context of the churches and particularly their social interaction with outsiders. But it should be clear that this only makes sense alongside other factors and that social causes here are not intended to provide total, simple or direct explanations of theological beliefs. Nonetheless the correlation of beliefs with social realities is important and the question of interaction with outsiders is one that has been unduly neglected in sociological studies of early Christianity.[39] After a period of intensive study of the social status of Paul's converts, it is high time to explore further the question of social interaction—and to take care in so doing not to subscribe to the false assumption that all Paul's churches were of the same stamp.[40]

---

[39] A. Schreiber (*Die Gemeinde in Korinth* [Münster: Aschendorff, 1977] 105) cites Mucchielli's comment that 'die Geschichte der Beziehungen einer Gruppe mit anderen Gruppen ihrer Umwelt beeinflußt Meinungen, Beratungen, Gefühle und Tätigkeiten der Gruppenmitgleider'. It is a pity that Schreiber's own work, which focuses on the group dynamics of the Corinthian church, does not address these issues in any detail.

[40] An earlier version of this paper was read at the New Testament Day Conference in King's College London in May 1991. I am grateful for the reactions of those present and for subsequent readers who have helped me in correction and clarification of the argument. [For further explorations of this and similar comparisons between Pauline congregations, see now E. Adams, *Constructing the World: A Study in Paul's Cosmological Language* (Edinburgh: T & T Clark, 2000); C. de Vos, *Church and Community Conflicts: The Relationships of the Thessalonian, Corinthian, and Philippian Churches with their Wider Civic Communities* (Atlanta: Scholars Press, 1999); M. Tellbe, *Paul between Synagogue and State: Christians, Jews and Civic Authorities in 1 Thessalonians, Romans and Philippians* (Stockholm: Almqvist & Wiksell International, 2001). For reflections on the 'correlation' between beliefs and social practices/experiences, see D. Martin, 'Patterns of Belief and Patterns of Life: Correlations in *The First Urban Christians* and Since', in Still and Horrell, eds., *After the First Urban Christians*, 116–33.]

10. Πνευματικός in the Social Dialect of Pauline Christianity

'It was generally recognized within the Pauline mission: that reception of the Spirit was the decisive and determinative element in the crucial transition of conversion; and that the presence of the Spirit in a life was the most distinctive and defining feature of a life thus reclaimed by God'.[1] Thus Professor Dunn sums up one of the characteristic emphases in his research on early Christianity, a theme he has rightly highlighted throughout his extraordinary academic career. In tribute to a scholar from whom I have learned so much, I offer here some reflections on early Christian Spirit-discourse. In particular, I wish to highlight the peculiarity of the adjective πνευματικός in Pauline speech—a lexical oddity which sheds interesting light on the formation of early Christian identity.

I. Language and Social Dialect

Recent studies in the social formation of earliest Christianity have given rather little attention to the significance of its distinctive patterns of language. In analysing 'the language of belonging', Meeks rightly noted that 'not just the shared content of beliefs but also shared forms by which the beliefs are expressed are important in promoting cohesiveness'.[2] Noting some of the distinctive (though not wholly unique) jargon used by Pauline Christians, he remarked that much of this was inherited from Judaism and the 'translation Greek' of the Septuagint, but that 'very quickly the Pauline Christians developed their own slogans and patterns of speech that distinguished them from other Jewish groups as well as from the general environment'.[3] This is an observation which invites much fuller investigation. Crucial to that study would be careful gathering of the linguistic data, but also alertness to *patterns* and *networks* of speech (not isolated items of

[1] J. D. G. Dunn, *The Theology of Paul the Apostle* (Edinburgh: T & T Clark, 1998) 425.
[2] W. A. Meeks, *The First Urban Christians* (New Haven: Yale University, 1983) 93.
[3] Meeks, *First Urban Christians*, 94.

vocabulary); moreover, appropriate analytical tools are needed in assessing the data. Meeks' comments on this topic might suggest a rather straightforward relationship between groups, beliefs and language: distinctive groups develop particular beliefs, and then express these linguistically in forms which serve to reinforce group-distinction.[4] But language can do more than just 'express' beliefs: it can play a critical role in *shaping* ideas and identities, since it does not just reflect, but in important senses *constitutes* the realities which we inhabit. In what follows, I will pursue Meeks' interest in early Christian language, and Dunn's interest in the Spirit, by examining one small, but significant, item in the 'social dialect' of Pauline Christians, the adjective πνευματικός. I will also suggest how this peculiarity of language contributed to the 'construction' of a world with a distinct though highly adaptable configuration, with important consequences for early Christianity.

The notion of 'world-construction' is drawn from the sociology of knowledge as developed by Berger and Luckmann. Among their many contributions to this field is their observation that 'the most important vehicle of reality-maintenance is conversation'.[5] As they point out, this is nowhere more evident than in primary socialization (childhood) and in those examples of 'alternation' (such as religious conversion) in which an individual enters a new world and needs to acquire a new structure of plausibility. As a microsociety somewhat at odds with the taken-for-granted perspectives and practices of its environment (both Jewish and Gentile), early Christianity had to work hard to shape and maintain its own interpretation of reality; and one of its most important tools for this task was the very language it used. Conversation within such a group is of fundamental importance: that its members talk to one another, and how they do so, are both crucial in constituting the 'world' they inhabit. Thus to become a convert was to acquire a new linguistic competence – not, of course, the acquisition of a whole new language, but the ability to comprehend and to participate in the patterns of speech by which the Christian community described itself, its beliefs, its norms, and its social environment.

To this broad conceptual framework supplied by the sociology of knowledge, we may add some features of sociolinguistics.[6] Although early Chris-

[4] Note the statement cited above: 'the beliefs ... expressed are important in promoting cohesiveness'. Meeks adds: 'Every close-knit group develops its own argot, and the use of that argot in speech among members knits them more closely still', (*First Urban Christians*, 93).

[5] P. L. Berger and T. Luckmann, *The Social Construction of Reality* (Anchor Books edition; New York: Doubleday, 1967) 152.

[6] I am grateful to Dr. Edward Adams, of King's College London, for first pointing me in this direction, while he worked on his innovative thesis, now published as *Constructing the World* (Edinburgh: T & T Clark, 2000). His advice has remained invaluable.

tianity was not in all respects, or in all its manifestations, an 'antisociety' equipped with an 'antilanguage',[7] we should expect some early Christian groups to display elements of a 'social dialect' (or 'sociolect') – special forms of speech which both reflect and shape their peculiar interpretations of the world.[8] In its fullest sense, a 'dialect' typically encompasses distinctive patterns of pronunciation, vocabulary and grammar, and we do not have evidence to suggest that Christians developed their own patterns of speech in all these respects: there is no hint, for instance, that they spoke in a distinctive 'accent'. But there were certainly some examples of unusual grammar in their texts (under the influence of the Septuagint), and many peculiarities in their vocabulary, not only in strange idioms like ἐν Χριστῷ ('in Christ'), but also in the novel ways they used standard terms, such as ἐκκλησία ('church'), εὐαγγέλιον ('gospel'), and πνεῦμα ('Spirit'). Indeed, the characteristic linguistic innovation in early Christianity was not the coining of neologisms, but the special frequency and emphasis with which Christians deployed perfectly acceptable terms which were used otherwise quite rarely, or rather differently, outside the circle of believers. As studies of social dialects indicate, what is particularly revealing in this regard is where particular terms come to prominence, and gain a stable meaning, in ways uncharacteristic of their normal usage outside the group.[9] If the in-group language is also in tension with its normal usage, producing meanings which strongly contrast with the usual senses outside the group, this could indicate a site of difference which is one factor in constituting the deviant identity of the group concerned. The adoption of unusual self-labels can be particularly instructive in this regard. Once again, the social dialect does not merely 'reflect' or 'embody' the distinct worldview of the group concerned; it also shapes that distinction since a worldview cannot be conceptualised and thus cannot take shape at all, except through language.[10]

---

[7] M.A.K. Halliday, *Language as Social Semiotic* (London: Edward Arnold, 1978) 164–82.

[8] Halliday, *Language*, 159: 'A social dialect is a dialect – a configuration of phonetic, phonological, grammatical and lexical features – that is associated with, and stands as a symbol for, some more or less objectively definable social group'.

[9] Foundational here are a number of studies conducted in the 1960s and 1970s by Labov and his successors; see W. Labov, *The Social Stratification of English in New York City* (Washington, D.C.: Center for Applied Linguistics, 1966); L. Milroy, *Language and Social Networks* (Oxford: Blackwell, 1987); cf. J. Holmes, *An Introduction to Social Linguistics* (London: Longman, 2002) 144–61, 202–8; J.K. Chambers, *Sociolinguistic Theory* (2nd ed.; Oxford: Blackwell, 2003) 74–115.

[10] The influence of the 'linguistic turn' has certainly been felt in sociolinguistics. See the critique of older scholarship (on the basis of contemporary discourse theory) by G. Williams, *Sociolinguistics: A Sociological Critique* (London: Routledge, 1992). At a theoretical level, the field may be said to be highly unstable, or diversified, at present; see B. Carter and A. Sealey, 'Language, Structure and Agency: What Can Realist Social Theory Offer to Sociolinguistics?' *Journal of Sociolinguistics* 4 (2000) 3–20.

II. The Peculiarity of πνευματικός

Early Christian experience of God did not come self-labelled as 'the Spirit'. While stressing the importance of post-Easter experience, we should note the very particular ways in which early Christians categorised this experience, as a mediation of divine presence or power specifically through 'the Spirit'. As Paige has recently insisted, the description of the personal presence of a deity as πνεῦμα was highly unusual in Greek-speaking antiquity everywhere except in Judaism.[11] Older *religionsgeschichtliche* scholarship appears to have been seriously misguided in its attempts to trace the 'roots' of this language in Greek 'mysticism' or 'Gnosticism': it relied on later texts which were themselves influenced by Christianity, or it grossly exaggerated the significance of only vaguely parallel patterns of vocabulary. In this, as in much else, early Christians were drawing from a biblical and Jewish linguistic reservoir.[12] Even so, the prominence of their Spirit-language is unusual: perhaps only in the Dead Sea Scrolls is the Spirit such a frequent topic of discussion. And nothing that we know of Judaism prepares us for the significance of what we should consider a distinctly Christian adjective, πνευματικός.[13] Since it is in Pauline circles that we can trace the first uses of this term, we will focus our analysis there.[14]

Of the 24 uses of the adjective πνευματικός in the Pauline corpus, 15 occur in one letter alone, the first letter to the Corinthians (also the site of the adverb, πνευματικῶς, 1 Cor. 2.13). In this letter Paul refers to 'Spirit-people' (πνευματικοί) on at least four occasions (1 Cor. 2.13, 15; 3.1; 14.37; possibly also in 12.1), but also uses the neuter plural to refer to 'things of the Spirit' in several places (1 Cor. 2.13; 9.11; 12.1[?]; 14.1). The heaviest use of these terms (1 Cor. 2.6–3.4; 1 Cor. 12–14) occurs in contexts which make clear that the adjective is strongly associated with, even coined from, the noun πνεῦμα, the name used by Paul for the eschatological gift of God's power and grace. Even if a parallel can be drawn with the human 'spirit' at one point (1 Cor. 2.11), it is clear that the adjective πνευματικός is not in

[11] T. Paige, 'Who believes in 'Spirit'? Πνεῦμα in Pagan Usage and Implications for the Gentile Christian Mission' *HTR* 95 (2002) 417–36. He describes the Jewish-Christian usage of πνεῦμα as 'a kind of specialized religious dialect unfamiliar to most Greek speakers' (p. 434).

[12] On the discourse about the Spirit in late second-Temple Judaism see J.R. Levison, *The Spirit in First Century Judaism* (Leiden: Brill, 1997).

[13] For its use in Philo, see below. Compared to its absence from the LXX, and the tiny trickle of examples in Greek-speaking Judaism, the flood of occurrences of this adjective in early Christian literature is striking: see, e.g., G. Lampe, *A Patristic Greek Lexicon* (Oxford: Clarendon, 1961), s.v. πνευματικός.

[14] Cf. J.D.G. Dunn, 'Spirit (NT)', in C. Brown, ed., *New International Dictionary of New Testament Theology, Vol. 3* (Exeter: Paternoster, 1978) 693–707 (esp. 706–7 on 'spiritual').

origin an anthropological but an eschatological term: it describes people not through analysis of their human constitution, but in relation to their new status as graced by the Spirit of God. Thus, the term is self-consciously new – not in the sense that it was wholly unprecedented in the Greek language (we shall note some examples below), but in the sense that Paul employs it to designate a reality not hitherto attested, because it describes a state of affairs believed to be wholly without precedent. If this is true of the adjective as applied to people, it is equally the case with the neuter 'things of the Spirit', which are said to be not generally understood (2.13–14) but which characterise the special work of Paul's preaching (9.11). Thus also, when Paul refers to the πνευματικὸν σῶμα (1 Cor. 15.44, 46), this is a body which can be envisaged only as an eschatological reality. This form of body appears to be so labelled as energised by Christ, 'the life-giving Spirit' (15.45), but the nature of the association with the Spirit is less clear where the adjective is applied to the bread and drink consumed by Israel in the wilderness, and the rock which followed them (namely Christ) in 1 Cor. 10.3–4.[15] Here pre-Christian realities are described in terms which seem self-consciously *transferred* from the Christian era, an exception which thus confirms the rule that Paul employs the adjective to interpret reality in specifically Christian terms. All these uses of πνευματικός derive from and embody a particular Christian hermeneutic.

That Paul can use this language without special explanation suggests that it is not a wholly idiosyncratic phenomenon, an 'idiolect'. Indeed, there are reasonable grounds for suspecting that this might be an item of vocabulary particularly common in the Corinthian church, even a favoured self-label employed by an 'elite' group within it. Huge scholarly attention has been paid to this possibility, in the hope of eliciting the theology of the Corinthian 'enthusiasts' or 'Gnostics'. But much depends here on a subtle 'mirror-reading' which presumes that Paul's unusual vocabulary is explicable only if it is derived from the Corinthians' usage, and we know too little about the Corinthians to go much beyond speculation in these matters.[16] Nonetheless, even if we cannot delineate in detail what the Corinthians meant in employ-

[15] In the first two cases the adjective might be construed in the sense of 'conveying the Spirit', but this is hardly the case with the third; see discussions in G.D. Fee, *The First Epistle to the Corinthians* (NICNT; Grand Rapids, Eerdmans, 1987) 446–49; W. Schrage, *Der erste Brief an die Korinther* (EKK; Neukirchen-Vluyn; Neukirchener, 1995) 2:392–95. We are already alerted here to the elasticity of the term and its potential for adaptation.

[16] For just one, recent, example, see the careful investigation by F.W. Horn, *Das Angeld des Geistes* (Göttingen: Vandenhoeck & Ruprecht, 1992) 180–201. He concludes that πνευματικός was an exclusive self-categorisation of Corinthian glossolalists, who contrasted themselves with ψυχικοί, and may have used the statement of 1 Cor. 2.15 as their watchword. All of this is possible, but it is dependent on a string of hypotheses which remain difficult to establish.

ing these terms, they seem to have shared this vocabulary with Paul (while possibly disagreeing on its connotations). Whoever 'coined' it, the term has become an important item in the social idiom of this particular network. What is more, its usage has set up binary oppositions, which provide an important means to categorise the world. If some people, but only some, are πνευματικοί, others have to be given another category label – either ψυχικοί ('soul-related', 1 Cor 2.14; cf. 15.44, 46), or σαρκινοί/σαρκικοί ('flesh-related', 1 Cor 3.1–3; cf. 9.11). In other words, this Christian network has developed an important linguistic tool by which to interpret social reality, a tool which is fully comprehensible only within its own patterns of discourse.

It was not just Paul and the Corinthians who understood each other when they spoke in these terms. Although Paul uses πνευματικός much less frequently elsewhere, the fact that he does use it, without explanation, in other letters suggests that it had wide Christian currency. It was not only the Corinthians who could appreciate the label πνευματικοί; Paul uses it also in writing to the Galatians (6.1), in line with his instruction on the importance of the Spirit as the defining characteristic of their lives (3.1–5; 5.13–25). Even in writing to the Romans, who had not encountered his speech-patterns before, Paul employs the neuter adjective πνευματικά ('things of the Spirit') in referring to the gospel (Rom. 15.27; cf. the identical metaphor in 1 Cor. 9.11). He also deploys πνευματικός in the context of the Spirit-flesh antithesis (Rom. 7.14, of the law), but also once adjoins it to the noun χάρισμα (Rom. 1.11), in an echo of 1 Cor. 12–14. The adjective has clearly become part of Paul's vocabulary-stock, and he assumes that it was generally comprehensible to other believers, whether or not he had previously met them. It continued to be used by his immediate successors, who referred to 'spiritual' understanding (Col. 1.9), 'spiritual' songs (Col. 3.16; Eph. 5.19), and 'spiritual' blessings (Eph. 1.3; cf. 1 Pet. 2.5, 'spiritual' sacrifices in a 'spiritual' building). The term clearly became common currency in these Pauline circles; but that it could be used in Eph. 6.12 for malign 'spiritual' forces shows how far it could stray from its originally close connection to the 'Holy Spirit'.

All of this stands in stark contrast to the rare and wholly different uses of the adjective in Greek outside early Christianity, both 'pagan' and Jewish. Compared to its heavy usage in the Pauline epistles, πνευματικός is an extremely rare term in non-Jewish Greek. Where it occurs it generally has the sense of 'gaseous' or 'windy', since the normal sense of πνεῦμα is 'wind' or 'air'. Thus, in Plutarch it can be used in reference to the airs or vapours that circulate through the body (e.g., *Moralia* 129c; 290a–b; 978e), while in Athenaeus' dinner talk it means 'flatulent' (e.g., *Deipn.* 2.55b, 69e)![17] In

[17] I am grateful to Terence Paige for sending me the relevant portions of his Ph.D. thesis ('Spirit at Corinth: The Corinthian Concept of Spirit and Paul's Response as Seen in

such cases, even if the adjective has anthropological reference, it is never used in relation to some higher dimension of existence, since πνεῦμα is very rarely employed to designate the highest human capacities.[18] We thus have no precursors to the Christian antithesis between πνευματικός and ψυχικός, and on the rare occasions where πνεῦμα is used in relation to divine influence (e.g. in poetic inspiration or prophecy) it is never prominent or distinctive enough to spawn the adjective πνευματικός for those who receive this divine 'breath'.[19] Indeed, the only context in which the adjective is deployed with frequency in non-Jewish Greek is in Stoic physics, where the significance of the πνεῦμα which circulates throughout and binds together the cosmos makes natural the use of the corresponding adjective to describe those cosmic bonds. Although Stoic physics is also, in the broadest sense, 'religious', the term is never used of *people* or of religious practices, and the Pauline sense of the term seems worlds apart from the Stoic notion that earth and water maintain their unity 'by virtue of participation in a pneumatic and fiery power' (πνευματικῆς μετοχῇ καὶ πυρώδους δυνάμεως, Plutarch, *Moralia* 1085 d).[20] The 'Gnostic' sources sometimes cited as Pauline parallels clearly draw from early Christian usage, and cannot be used to attest an independent linguistic tradition.

Scholarly discussion of the (possible) Corinthian use of the πνευματικός – ψυχικός antithesis turned in the 1970s from a 'Gnostic' to a 'Hellenistic-Jewish' background.[21] Since πνευματικός is absent from the LXX, and occurs nowhere in other Greek-Jewish literature except in Philo, the argument depends entirely on Philonic usage: this is claimed to suggest a stratification within humanity similar to that found in 1 Corinthians, and to rest on an interpretation of Gen 2.7 like that taken to be Paul's target in 1 Cor. 15.44–49. However, closer inspection of the Philo passages indicates that none of the elements of this argument are convincing, and especially not

---

1 Corinthians', University of Sheffield, 1994), based on a TLG search for πνευματκικός; to his material one may add examples from the *Stoicorum Veterum Fragmenta*.

[18] In Epictetus, *Diss.* 3.13.15, for instance, τὸ πνευμάτιον is just one of the four physical elements of the body which dissipates at death: it is not identified with reason, mind or soul.

[19] See the discussion in Paige, 'Who believes in 'Spirit'?'. The denigration of the category ψυχικός also seems to be unprecedented.

[20] Thus, although Celsus tried to make sense of early Christian terminology by reference to Stoic notions of πνεῦμα, Origen rightly highlighted the gulf between the two linguistic traditions (*Contra Celsum* 6.69–75).

[21] The development can be traced in U. Wilckens, *Weisheit und Torheit: Eine exegetisch-religionsgeschichtliche Untersuchung zu 1 Kor 1 und 2* (Tübingen: Mohr Siebeck, 1959); M. Winter, *Pneumatiker und Psychiker in Korinth* (Marburg: Elwert, 1975); B. A. Pearson, *The Pneumatikos-Psychikos Terminology in 1 Corinthians* (Missoula: Society of Biblical Literature, 1973); this remains the explanation of Corinthian vocabulary favoured by Horn, *Angeld*, 194–98.

the supposed parallels to the use of πνευματικός.[22] This adjective occurs no more than nine times in the whole Philonic corpus, in many of which it echoes the Stoic sense of the 'pneumatic bonds' which bind all matter (animate and inanimate) together (e.g., *Heres* 242; *Aet.* 86, 125; *Quaest. Gen.* 2.3?). Where it is used of human beings, it is clear that the 'pneumatic bonds' are not some 'higher' feature, but merely the ligaments which keep the body cohesive, in contrast to the virtues of the soul (ψυχή; e.g., *Praem.* 46). If πνεῦμα represents the life-force, or life-breath, this is not the same as the 'soul' or 'reason' (*Op. Mund.* 67). On the two occasions where the adjective is deployed to represent a superior form of materiality (that of angels), it stands not above but in parallel to the 'soul-like' substance (ψυχοειδὴς οὐσία, *Abr.* 113; *Quaest. Gen.* 1.92). Thus there is nothing in Philo to suggest the prominence of the adjective in the Pauline corpus and the peculiar antitheses it there spawns. Even when Philo interprets Gen 2.7, he gives no special emphasis to the divine πνεῦμα, and appears to take the 'inbreathing' in the account of human creation to represent the installation of the soul (ψυχή); the passage is never taken to signal a particular class of people or things.[23] As Theissen rightly concludes: 'The fact remains that it has up to now been impossible to derive the opposition of *pneumatikos* and *psychikos* from pre-Pauline sources. The interpretation of the two creation accounts with these antonyms is a step beyond the known Hellenistic Jewish exegesis'.[24]

[22] For similar scepticism, see G. Theissen, *Psychological Aspects of Pauline Theology* (Edinburgh: T & T Clark, 1987) 358–67. Note Theissen's conclusion: 'If we read 1 Cor. 2:6–16 against the background of the Jewish Hellenistic wisdom tradition, then it is precisely deviations from this tradition which can best be explained by specifically Christian impulses' (p. 367).

[23] From Josephus, *Ant.* 1.34, it is clear that it was possible to interpret what God breathed into humanity as πνεῦμα (LXX Gen 2.7: πνόη ζώης). But since the result of this inbreathing was to create the human being as a ψυχὴ ζῶσα, it is hard to see how an antithesis can be created from this verse between πνεῦμα and ψυχή. Philo normally cites this verse as the inbreathing of πνόη ζώης, but where he uses πνεῦμα he interprets this 'divine breath' as the soul, even the 'essence of the soul' (*Leg. All.* 1.36; 3.161; *Heres* 55–57; *Spec. Leg.* 4.123; *Det.* 80–84); even in *Opif.* 135 and *Plant.* 18, the 'divine spirit' is not something distinct from, or higher than, the soul which is given to every person. The people Philo admires are those who cultivate the 'soul' and 'reason', not a special class of 'Spirit-people'; and he never uses the adjective πνευματικός in connection with Gen 2.7. It thus greatly confuses the matter for Horn (and others) to use the term 'Pneumatiker' as a label for Philo's highest achievers (*Angeld*, 45–48).

[24] Theissen, *Psychological Aspects*, 363. Only in passing does Horn allow (*Angeld*, 200) that there might lie behind the Pauline usage a specifically Christian interpretation of the effusion of the Spirit.

III. Pauline πνευματικά and their Semantic Potential

The remarkable frequency of πνευματικός in the Pauline epistles is not difficult to explain. Once the new and overwhelming experience of God in early Christianity was interpreted as the presence of 'the Spirit', it was natural that this term, and its adjectival derivate, would play a prominent role in Christian discourse. Since Paul places particular emphasis on 'the Spirit' as the source of eschatological life, the medium of knowledge, and the criterion of morality, it is not surprising that he, and those influenced by his thought, should find themselves speaking of things which characterise their new life as πνευματικά. For those whose lives were dramatically redefined by this new reality, it was natural to consider themselves πνευματικοί. The adjective thus takes on a new and semi-technical sense within a particular religious network, a self-consciously novel family of churches. They did not coin the adjective – it was perfectly good Greek – but they used it with a frequency and an emphasis which mark it out as peculiar to their discourse. They also used it in senses it had not acquired before, since they deployed it within a web of associations (with experience and with other terms) which was unique to this new religious movement.[25] If they employed it in conversation with 'outsiders', it would surely have caused puzzlement; used among themselves, it resonated with other elements in their discourse, notably their special understanding of 'the Spirit'. The term thus creates a linguistic distinction between 'insiders' and 'outsiders'. This does not necessarily correlate with a social separation from non-Christians – indeed, if the Corinthian church used the term, it circulated among Christians who were relatively well-integrated into their social environment.[26] But it is not surprising that this unusual category of 'Spirit-things' and 'Spirit-people' should create a linguistic and conceptual distinction from 'non-Spirit' phenomena, and thus establish novel binary oppositions between πνεῦμα and σάρξ, or πνευματικοί and ψυχικοί. In other words, the use of this linguistic apparatus creates conceptual categorisations which serve to *constitute* the world-view of Pauline Christians: by referring to themselves and the things they held most precious with this adjective, Christians began to define reality in distinctive ways.

---

[25] On the importance of webs of association in determining meaning, as against persistent attempts to 'derive' the meaning of terms from preceding linguistic traditions, see A. Millar and J. K. Riches, 'Interpretation: a Theoretical Perspective and Some Applications' *Numen* 28 (1981) 29–53.

[26] So I have argued in 'Thessalonica and Corinth: Social Contrasts in Pauline Christianity' *JSNT* 47 (1992) 49–74 [see chapter 9, above]. For the self-understanding of the Christians in Corinth, see now S. Chester, *Conversion in Corinth* (Edinburgh: T & T Clark, 2003).

But if πνευματικός is of nodal significance in Pauline discourse, it also displays a degree of semantic indeterminacy which would enable it to be deployed richly, and variously, in later Christianity. As a label for 'spiritual' people, the adjective creates a categorical distinction between Christians and 'others', but the complexities and ambiguities of the key passage on this topic, 1 Cor. 2.6–3.4, leave unclear what it means to label the others as ψυχικοί and σαρκικοί, and indeed whether those are one category or two. Since those adjectives relate to familiar anthropological terms, the passage invites reflection on the constitution of human nature, and what makes Christians distinct.[27] And since there could be doubt whether Paul considered all Christians to be properly labelled πνευματικοί (1 Cor. 3.1; 14.37; even Gal. 6.1), the term could be reserved for an elite, as by Valentinian Christians.[28] Paul's use of the neuter plural in relation to the proclamation of the gospel (1 Cor. 9.11; Rom. 15.27) also stands in an antithesis, with σαρκικά, but leaves unclear what these antonyms designate: does the 'fleshly' realm consist of material things (as against the immaterial), or ordinary human concerns (as against concerns of the 'Spirit'), or 'secular' affairs (as against the affairs of the church)? The flesh-spirit antithesis, so important and so slippery in Paul, could slot into a number of hermeneutical frameworks, in which the Christian realm is variously distinguished from the rest. Much will depend here on what nuance is given to the *relationship* between what is 'fleshly' and what is 'spiritual': are these polar opposites, or complementary realms, and, if complementary, in what sort of hierarchical relationship to each other?[29] Even the Pauline application of the adjective to particular objects leaves many things unclear: if, for instance, some gifts or some songs are 'spiritual', and others (implicitly) not (Rom 1.11; Col. 3.16),

---

[27] For the passage and some chapters in its history of interpretation, see A. Thiselton, *The First Epistle to the Corinthians* (NIGTC; Grand Rapids: Eerdmans, 2000) 276–86.

[28] The label πνευματικός acquired particular significance in Valentinian circles, where it functioned within a three-fold stratification of humanity; see Irenaeus, *Adv. Haer.* 1.5–9 and the *Excerpta ex Theodoto* (F. Sagnard, *Clément d'Alexandrie, Extraits de Théodote* [SC 23; Paris: Cerf, 1970]). Cf. E. Pagels, *The Gnostic Paul* (Philadelphia: Trinity Press International, 1975).

[29] Ignatius' particularly heavy use of the adjective πνευματικός nicely illustrates both the influence and the ambiguity of the Pauline legacy. As soon as he mentions the category distinction between πνευματικοί and σαρκικοί, Ignatius pulls back from allowing the two realms to separate: even what the former do κατὰ σάρκα are πνευματικά (*Eph* 8.2). This, together with his strong emphasis on the 'fleshliness' of Christ's life, passion and resurrection (e.g., *Smyr.* 3.2–3; 5.2; 12.2), reflects Ignatius' anxiety about docetism; cf. W.R. Schoedel, *Ignatius of Antioch* (Philadelphia: Fortress, 1985) 23–24, 64. Ignatius' almost obsessive use of σαρκικός and πνευματικός *together* (e.g. *Pol.* 1.2; 2.2; *Eph.* 10.3; *Mag.* 13.1–2; *Smyr.* 13.2) recognises the difference between the two 'spheres' without allowing them to become separate or in conflict; in the process, the specific connection between πνευματικός and the Spirit is lost, and the meaning of 'spiritual' becomes correspondingly thinned.

does the adjective designate a special quality inherent within them, some special dimension to which they attain, or merely some Christian context in which they are used? Equally ambiguous, though of enormous long-term significance, is the way πνευματικός is used to reinterpret biblical objects (e.g. 1 Cor. 10.3–4; 1 Pet. 2.5; cf. Rom 2.29); when this was combined with Pauline reflection on the role of the Spirit in 'unveiling' Scripture (2 Corinthians 3), it enabled a Christian hermeneutic of Scripture to be termed 'spiritual', and thus spawned a long tradition of allegorical exegesis under this label (cf. already Rev. 11.8).

Both the distinctiveness and the potential ambiguity of the label πνευματικός were thus of pivotal significance for early Christianity. Labelling themselves and their attributes in this unusual way, Pauline Christians constituted themselves a distinct phenomenon in their social and religious environment, and, through their textual legacy, invited early Christianity to both think and act in unprecedented ways. But what precisely it valued as 'spiritual' could be variously understood by Christians of different strands and different epochs. The history of the term 'spiritual' is thus one index of the multiple ways in which Christianity has construed its identity and significance.[30] That it began as a peculiarity in the social dialect of Pauline Christians both grounds and illuminates many aspects of that subsequent history.

---

[30] See the surveys and discussions by J. Leclercq, 'Spiritualitas', *Studi Medievali* 3a, serie 3 (1962) 279–96; L. Tinsley, *The French Expressions for Spirituality and Devotion: A Semantic* Study (Washington, D.C.: Catholic University of America, 1953). (I owe these references to Mr. Alan Brown) The contemporary generalisation of the term (to mean anything 'religious', even anything 'interior') reflects the dissipation of a specifically Christian meaning, and makes Christians themselves uncertain how to use it. In recent discussions of the 'spiritual' role of the elder in the Church of Scotland, it was clear that the term had become so imprecise and polysemous as to be practically valueless. [For recent relevant discussion of the Spirit in Paul, see T. Engberg-Pedersen, *Cosmology and Self in the Apostle Paul: The Material Spirit* (Oxford: Oxford University, 2010); V. Rabens, *The Holy Spirit and Ethics in Paul* (WUNT 283; Tübingen: Mohr Siebeck, 2010).]

11. 'That you may not grieve, like the rest who have no hope' (1 Thess 4.13)

Death and Early Christian Identity

Among the many poignant epitaphs from antiquity, few are so moving as the inscription erected by a Sicilian Christian couple to the memory of their daughter, Julia Florentina, who died aged eighteen months sometime in the fourth century CE. The epitaph (ILCV 1549 = CIL 7112) records the hours of struggle between life and death of this 'dearest and most innocent child'. But it also reveals the peculiar struggle of her parents as they came to terms, as Christians, with the death of their precious daughter. The end of the inscription reads thus:

> While her parents bewailed her death at every moment, the voice of [God's] majesty was heard at night, forbidding them to lament for the dead child. Her body was buried in its tomb in front of the doors of the shrine of the martyrs.[1]

One can surely feel here the rending of the heart, torn in the tension between human grief and the desperate desire to feel (or at least to express) some special Christian conviction that death should not be mourned. Here the normal display of human emotions is suppressed by the peculiar voice of Christian hope, whose abnormality is advertised by this public baring of the soul. As we shall see, the tension is in part relieved by the place of burial: the martyrs' shrine acts as the physical focus of Christian hope, the symbol of victory over death, which the nocturnal voice impressed upon the grieving parents. Nonetheless, the pain of death is here both publicly recognised and publicly overcome, in a combination which illustrates perfectly an extraordinarily potent strategy in early Christian self-definition. Here we see the identification of death as a site on which Christians could

---

[1] 'Cuius occasum cum uterq(ue) parens omni momento fleret, per noctem maiestatis vox extitit, quae defunctam lamen[t]ari prohiberet; cuius corpus pro foribus martyrorum cum loculo suo per prosbiterum humatu(m) e(st)'; I follow the translation by P. Brown, *The Cult of the Saints: Its Rise and Function in Latin Christianity* (London: SCM, 1981) 69, to whom I owe also the reference to this epitaph. [ILCV = E. Diehl, ed., *Inscriptiones Latinae Christianae Veteres* (2 vols., Zürich: Weidmann, 1925, 1961); CIL = *Corpus Inscriptionum Latinarum*].

recognise and display their difference, signalling their peculiarity at a point which, necessarily, touched and troubled everyone. That Christian strategy was inaugurated, I shall argue, in 1 Thessalonians 4.13–5.11.

In recent years scholars have approached this passage with many different interests. As the fullest theological statement in (probably) the earliest extant Christian text, it is bound to attract attention, not least in revealing the apocalyptic atmosphere in which the first Pauline churches were born. Behind the text lies the confusion, anxiety or even despair of the Thessalonian Christians at the death of some of their number. Behind the text lie also earlier Christian traditions, creedal confessions (4.14; 5.10), apocalyptic metaphors (5.2) and miniature portraits of the parousia (4.16–17), which offer a window onto those first explosive years of the Christian movement. Not all of these features can be investigated here. First, I wish to explore some aspects of the crisis in the Thessalonian church insofar as we can reconstruct it. Secondly, I will focus attention on the text itself, tracing, in particular, its theological strategy – asking how Paul's discourse aids the definition of this vulnerable Christian community. Thirdly, since I take the production of this text to be a defining moment not only for the Thessalonian Christians but also for the subsequent development of the Christian movement, our eyes will stray beyond it to the legacy it helped to bequeath.

I. The Crisis in the Thessalonian Church

Since, as a letter, 1 Thessalonians is so evidently responsive in character, it is natural to attempt first a reconstruction of the problems or questions which called forth this section of the letter. Such a task has invited much scholarly industry and ingenuity, but is hampered by the fact that Paul's discourse, which is the only available evidence, is not as straightforward as we might hope. What can we conclude from 4.13? First, that Paul wants to give them instruction: οὐ θέλομεν δὲ ὑμᾶς ἀγνοεῖν, ἀδελφοί. It is not clear (from Pauline parallels) whether this means that what follows is totally new information for the Thessalonians, or whether what is new is the particular interpretation which Paul here gives to familiar apocalyptic teaching.[2] What he wants them to know is περὶ τῶν κοιμωμένων. It appears that some (it is probably more than one)[3] Thessalonian Christians have died, apparently

[2] The Pauline parallels to the expression are 1 Cor 10.1; 12.1; 2 Cor 1.8; Rom 1.13; 11.25. G. Lüdemann's claim that the formula indicates that Paul is introducing something new, or presenting previously unknown information, strains the evidence, *Paul, Apostle to the Gentiles: Studies in Chronology* (London: SCM, 1984) 214.

[3] Unless the plural represents a deliberate generalising: 'on the topic of those who sleep (of which an example has occurred in the Thessalonian church) ...'.

in the interval between Paul's sudden departure from Thessalonica and the writing of this letter. What we do not know is who has died (infants? adults? old people? leaders of the Christian community?), nor under what conditions. It has been suggested that these were 'martyrs', their deaths specifically due to their Christian commitment; but this rests insecurely on the general experience of θλῖψις in the church (which was real enough, but not clearly life-threatening) and on a particular construal of διὰ τοῦ 'Ιησοῦ in 4.14, which, even if it goes with the participle κοιμηθέντας rather than the verb ἄξει, does not clearly indicate a martyr's death 'for the sake of Jesus'.[4] Thus some (to us) unknown Thessalonian Christians have died for (to us) unknowable reasons, although the circumstances of their deaths – whether they were sudden or gradual, whether they could be attributed by hostile observers to the wrath of the Gods on the 'impious' Christians[5] – could have affected the degree of distress which they occasioned.

In fact, what degree of distress was there, and what were its causes? Paul writes, he says, ἵνα μὴ λυπῆσθε καθὼς καὶ οἱ λοιποὶ οἱ μὴ ἔχοντες ἐλπίδα. Does this imply that (he thinks) they already grieve like 'the rest', or is his writing prophylactic, to inoculate them with hope such that they will not end up that way? Even if we conclude that he thinks they are already grieving like the hopeless remainder of humanity, does this construction of their state have to be taken at face value? Paul has a penchant for rhetorical contrasts: you either have hope or you are utterly hopeless, you either know God in Christ or you do not know God at all (4.5). Thus, just as he construes the Corinthian Christians' beliefs about life after death as tantamount to total scepticism (1 Cor 15.30–32),[6] so he might construe the Thessalonians' state of shock as tantamount to (or the first step towards) total despair. Perhaps they had not lost all hope for their deceased fellow believers, but were only upset at their deaths (as was natural, even for those who believed in a resurrection) and perplexed about their participation in the parousia-event; it would not be beyond Paul to represent that as a kind

[4] The thesis of martyr-deaths has been recently revived by K. P. Donfried, 'The Cults of Thessalonica and the Thessalonian Correspondence' *NTS* 31 (1985) 336–56, at 349–50; but see, already, the effective rebuttal by E. von Dobschütz, *Die Thessalonicher-Briefe* (Göttingen: Vandenhoeck & Ruprecht, 1909) 191 (we would expect the Greek διὰ τὸν 'Ιησοῦν; cf. 4 Macc. 16.25). There is a notable lack of commendation, such as Paul accords to those who have risked their lives for the gospel (Phil 2.25–30; Rom 16.4). [For Donfried's essays on 1 Thessalonians, see K. P. Donfried, *Paul, Thessalonica and Early Christianity* (London: T & T Clark, 2002).]

[5] A possibility mooted in my 'Conflict in Thessalonica' *CBQ* 55 (1993) 512–30, at 516.

[6] I cannot enter here into the discussion about what, in fact, the Corinthian Christians did believe about life beyond death, but I consider 15.29 a clue that they were not as hopeless in the face of death at 15.30–32 rhetorically suggests.

of grief parallel to (or leading towards) the sort of hopeless grief he associates with 'the rest' of humankind.

We may be reluctant to attribute to Paul such rhetorical exaggeration, and may prefer to take his statement at face-value; but, if so, we must ask why their grief should be so hopeless. Here scholars, who generally agree on the hopelessness of the Thessalonian church, are divided. A minority line of interpretation, stretching from Lütgert, through Schmithals and Harnisch, to Jewett, takes the shock of the Thessalonians as arising from their realised eschatology: in their 'enthusiasm', they thought death was already defeated and were devastated to find that believers (including potentially themselves) were still mortal.[7] Most scholars suggest that the problem was rather the eagerness of their expectation: they had been led to believe (and Paul in essence still believes, 4.15, 17) that they would be present to witness the glorious parousia of the Lord. That event was, they imagined, so imminent that they did not expect death to intervene. When it did intervene in these cases, it was natural to ask what would become of the deceased; they would clearly not be present at the public vindication of believers, which they all so eagerly awaited. Paul stresses here that God will bring the dead with Jesus (4.14), and emphasises that they will not be left behind (4.15) – in fact will be raised from the first (4.16, πρῶτον). So did the Thessalonian believers think that their deceased would merely be at a disadvantage at the parousia, and perhaps receive their vindication only when the main event was over? Or did they suspect that, by dying before the parousia, their fellow believers were going to miss out on salvation altogether?[8] The latter, more shocking, belief is perhaps more likely, especially if the 'hopeless grief' of 4.13 is an accurate portrayal of their condition. In this case, Paul would be urging: not only are they not going to forfeit their salvation, but God will ensure that they are raised in good time for them to take part in the great parousia procession.

[7] W. Lütgert, *Die Volkommenen im Philipperbrief und die Enthusiasten in Thessalonich* (Gütersloh: Bertelsmann, 1909) 55–81; W. Schmithals, *Paul and the Gnostics* (Nashville: Abingdon, 1972) 128–218; W. Harnisch, *Eschatologische Existenz: Ein exegetischer Beitrag zum Sachanliegen von I. Thessalonicher 4,13–5,11* (Göttingen: Vandenhoeck & Ruprecht, 1973); R. Jewett, *The Thessalonian Correspondence. Pauline Rhetoric and Millenarian Piety* (Philadelphia: Fortress, 1986) 93–100.

[8] The first option is canvassed by J.E. Frame, *A Critical and Exegetical Commentary on the Epistles of St. Paul to the Thessalonians* (Edinburgh: T & T Clark, 1912) 164: 'The brethren were in grief, not because they did not believe in the resurrection of the saints, but because they feared their dead would not have the same advantages as survivors when the Lord came.' Cf. A.F.J. Klijn, '1 Thessalonians 4.13–18 and its Background in Apocalyptic Literature', in M.D. Hooker and S.G. Wilson, eds., *Paul and Paulinism: Essays in Honour of C.K. Barrett* (London: SPCK, 1982) 67–73. The latter option is espoused by most commentators, and supported by R.H. Gundry, 'The Hellenization of Dominical Tradition and the Christianization of Jewish Tradition in the Eschatology of 1–2 Thessalonians' *NTS* 33 (1987) 161–78, at 167–68.

The balance of probability lies with the hypothesis that the Thessalonians feared that their deceased members has slipped, through death, out of the current which was heading for salvation: they would not, and could not, be present when the much-anticipated parousia took place. One could then argue, as scholars still do, about why this fear had taken root. Did they know about a future resurrection of believers, but not know how to integrate this with belief in the parousia? Did they know about it in theory but find their confidence shaken by the shock of the actual events?[9] Or, as many think, did they not know about such a thing as the future resurrection of believers. Perhaps Paul had omitted to tell them about this (although he believed it), or perhaps he had not hitherto formulated this belief himself, so soon did he expect the arrival of the Lord?[10] Here, I sense, we enter so far into the realm of speculation that our steps become very insecure – certainly too insecure to attempt to find here a criterion for the *very* early dating of 1 Thessalonians (Lüdemann), or to be able to reconstruct precisely the stages by which Paul's eschatology developed (Mearns).[11] Who knows what Paul did (or did not) teach in his, apparently truncated, period in Thessalonica, or what did or did not stick in their impressionable but ill-prepared minds, or what image they constructed of the parousia on the basis of his teaching?

Social factors must also be considered here. We should not underestimate, for instance, the emotional shock caused by the death of members in this probably small, and certainly beleaguered, community. It appears that they had sacrificed much in 'turning from idols to the true and living God' (1.9), and had encountered a degree of social harassment sufficient to shake them severely (3.2–3). To lose some of their number, in so short a time, was bound to unsettle them further and to raise the question whether their commitment was worth the cost. All mourners are, as anthropologists say, in a 'liminal state' during the period of mourning,[12] but the Thessalonian Christians, who were already ostracised by their families and friends, now suffered a

[9] The first option is suggested by U. Luz, *Das Geschichtsverständnis des Paulus* (Munich: Chr. Kaiser, 1968) 320–22; the second by, among others, I.H. Marshall, *1 and 2 Thessalonians* (London: Marshall, Morgan & Scott, 1983) 120–22. Note also the thesis of J. Plevnik, 'The Taking Up of the Faithful and the Resurrection of the Dead in 1 Thessalonians 4:13–18' *CBQ* 46 (1984) 274–83, that their parousia-hope was framed in terms of an assumption, and that was conceivable only for those alive at the time.

[10] This latter was argued by W. Marxsen, 'Auslegung von 1 Thess 4,14–18' *ZTK* 66 (1969) 22–37, and is supported by many others.

[11] Lüdemann, *Paul*, 201–38; C. Mearns, 'Early Eschatological Development in Paul: The Evidence of I and II Thessalonians' *NTS* 27 (1980–81) 137–57.

[12] The classic study remains A. Van Gennep, *The Rites of Passage* (Chicago: University of Chicago, 1960); see also R. Hertz, *Death and the Right Hand* (Glencoe, Ill.: Free Press, 1960) 27–86.

double liminality.[13] It may be that their normal processes of mourning were in fact disrupted by the social tensions their faith had engendered. Moreover, the intensity of their mutual reliance and φιλαδελφία (4.9–12) would render these deaths especially debilitating: as the anthropologist, Loring Danforth, comments in another context, 'the more the bereaved defined themselves in terms of their relationship to the deceased, the more death threatens their socially constructed world.'[14] In other words, the crisis which they (and Paul) faced was perhaps as much to do with their self-belief as with their beliefs about the deceased. Were they really as special and as 'beloved by God' (1.4) as Paul made them out to be? On the present evidence, and by the normal criterion that God protects those whom he loves, it was hard to see how that could be so. Were they really plucked out from the mass of humanity, chosen for salvation and delivered from the wrath to come (1.4, 10)? Or was their destiny no different from anyone else's?[15]

That these questions were real, or at least perceived by Paul to be likely, is indicated, I believe, by the expansion of his discourse from the immediate question concerning the deceased (4.13–16) into the larger portrayal of the destiny of the elect (5.1–11). Already in 4.17 one senses that Paul wants to give assurance to the Thessalonians about *themselves*, not only about the dead: καὶ οὕτως πάντοτε σὺν κυρίῳ ἐσόμεθα. If he then encourages them to comfort one another (4.18), the 'comfortable words' concern themselves (the still alive) as well as the dead. And this is the springboard for the extended discussion of their future destiny which follows (5.1–11). The repetition of the exhortation to comfort in 5.11 is designed to match that in 4.18, and serves to tie the two paragraphs, 4.13–18 and 5.1–11, closely together. It is easy to be misled by the περὶ δέ formula in 5.1 into believing that 5.1–11 tackles a new and different problem from that raised in 4.13–18, and some scholars have speculated whether the Thessalonians pressed Paul for accurate information on the timing of the parousia.[16] But even if they did, what is significant is that Paul does not satisfy them on that point (5.1–2), but still spends eleven verses giving what seems to some a non-reply. The reason

---

[13] On the nature and cause of this conflict in Thessalonica see my 'Conflict in Thessalonica' and T. Still, *Conflict at Thessalonica* (JSNTSup 183; Sheffield: Sheffield Academic, 1999).

[14] L.M. Danforth, *The Death Rituals of Rural Greece* (Princeton: Princeton University, 1982) 138; the point is practically a sociological truism.

[15] The threat of these deaths to the whole faith-structure of the Thessalonians is well emphasised by W. Marxsen, *Der erste Brief an die Thessalonicher* (Zürich: Theologischer, 1979) 63–66. [Cf. R.S. Ascough, 'A Question of Death: Paul's Community-Building Language in 1 Thessalonians 4:13–18' *JBL* 123 (2004) 509–30.]

[16] See the discussion of this point in, e.g., E. Best, *A Commentary on the First and Second Epistles to the Thessalonians* (BNTC; London: A & C Black, 1972) 203–4; T. Holtz, *Der erste Brief an die Thessalonicher* (EKK, Neukirchen-Vluyn: Neukirchener, 1986) 209–11.

is that he has other, and more important, things to do than to delineate an eschatological timetable. His portrayal of the future, and of the contrasting destinies of believers and 'the rest', is, in fact, of cardinal significance for the strategy of the letter. Here he exposes the fault-line which separates the 'children of the day' from 'the children of darkness': believers are here encouraged to recognise their contrasting destinies, and to celebrate and affirm their future salvation precisely in the face of death.[17]

II. The Great Divide

One of the most striking structural features of 1 Thess 4.13–5.11 is its reiterated dualism, as Paul repeatedly spotlights the distinction between believers and 'the rest'. The strategy is immediately apparent in 4.13: 'that you might not grieve, like the rest who have no hope'. 'The rest' (οἱ λοιποί) dismissively lumps the whole world outside the church into a single category, a tactic repeated and reinforced in 5.6. Paul's rhetoric here refuses to acknowledge the ethnic or cultural distinctions between Jews and Gentiles which he recognises elsewhere (1 Cor 1.22–24; Rom 1.14); rather, he agglomerates all non-Christian humanity into a single, nameless lump. What is more, the rest are defined, in a wholly undifferentiated manner, as those 'who have no hope'. Commentators are apt to stumble at this point. Most assume that Paul can only here be talking about Gentiles: after all, he knew at first hand how important were Jewish hopes for an afterlife, at least as held in Pharisaic and apocalyptic circles (cf. Acts 26.5–8).[18] But I see no reason for taking Paul's rhetoric as other than straightforward. As he shows elsewhere (e.g., in this letter at 4.5), he *can* distinguish 'Gentiles' from 'Jews' when he so wishes. It seems his rhetoric here is deliberately blunt: there can be only two categories in this discourse, not (even implicitly) three. Thus *all*, Jews and Gentiles (whatever their actual, and highly variegated, beliefs about the afterlife) are draped in the all-enveloping shroud of hopelessness: there are no exceptions to 'the rest who have no hope'.[19]

---

[17] This explanation of the relevance of 5.1–11 renders still less plausible G. Friedrich's proposal that this paragraph is a post-Pauline interpolation, '1 Thessalonicher 5,1–11, der apologetische Einschub eines Späteren' *ZTK* 10 (1973) 288–315.

[18] J.B. Lightfoot comments: 'had St. Paul been addressing a Jewish population he could not have spoken so strongly' (*Notes on Epistles of St. Paul* [London: Macmillan, 1904] 64). Most commentators assume his comments refer only to the 'pagan' world.

[19] We should not miss the boldness of this move, from the perspective of the history of religions. Almost all the eschatological motifs in this letter are fruits from the soil of Judaism, especially Jewish apocalyptic: the climactic 'Day of the Lord', the 'wrath to come', the trumpets, the angels and even the resurrection of the dead are the stock-in-trade of Jewish apocalyptic expectation. But Paul has fused them so fully to distinctively Christian

Again, commentators with knowledge of the ancient world are inclined to choke: is there not plenty of evidence that some people in antiquity held strong hopes of life beyond death, in one form or another? Indeed there is, but Paul is not offering an anthropological observation, but a rhetorical, and pejorative, generalisation. Thus it is mistaken to attempt to defend Paul here by claiming that, at least 'in general' or 'on average', the pagan world was characterised by hopelessness in the face of death.[20] There are for Paul only two, massively stereotyped, categories: the grieving mass of humanity, and the non-grieving, because hope-filled, believers.

I say 'non-grieving believers' because it seems to me difficult to strain Paul's language to mean 'that you should not grieve as much, or in the same way, or for the same reasons, as the rest'. Humane as this may sound, and even (today) homiletically necessary, it is not, I think, what the text means. Commentators have been divided on this issue from an early date, but for linguistic and contextual reasons I would side with Frame who insists (by appeal to the parallel in 4.5) that

> καθὼς καί here does not mean that the Christians are indeed to grieve, but not in the same manner or degree as the unbelievers ... Paul speaks absolutely, for death has a religious value to him, in that after a short interval the dead are brought to the goal of the Christian hope, σὺν αὐτῷ. In view of this glorious consummation, present grief, however natural, is excluded.[21]

themes that their realisation is claimed to apply *only* to Christian believers. The 'Day' now belongs to the Lord *Jesus*, by whom alone one can hope to be delivered from 'the wrath to come'; the trumpets will announce *Jesus*' descent from heaven, and the resurrection is here specifically of 'the dead *in Christ*' (4.16). By this appropriation, Paul implicitly *disqualifies* even Jewish (non-Christian) bearers of these traditions. Light is denied to exist anywhere except in the tiny circles of radiance made up of 'the children of the day'; and their brightness serves to sharpen the surrounding darkness.

[20] As is argued by, for instance, F.F. Bruce, *1 and 2 Thessalonians* (Waco: Word, 1982) 104 ('There is ample evidence that among pagans generally there was a sad sense of hopelessness in the face of death'); I.H. Marshall, *1 and 2 Thessalonians*, 119 ('All that the average pagan could do was to mourn'). That Paul has overstated the matter is rightly recognised by E. Best, *Epistles to the Thessalonians*, 185–85, and C. Wanamaker, *Commentary on 1 & 2 Thessalonians* (NIGTC; Grand Rapids: Eerdmans, 1990) 167. To put the matter another way, Paul's definition of hope is specifically Christian and thus disqualifies all other hopes (cf. Eph 2.12); see P. Hoffmann, *Die Toten in Christus* (Münster: Aschendorff, 1966) 209.

[21] Frame, *Epistles of St. Paul to the Thessalonians*, 167; the parallel in 4.5 καθάπερ καί clearly does not mean 'in the same manner or degree of πάθος' as Gentiles, but sets a sharp contrast between Gentile 'passion' and Christian 'passionlessness'. Von Dobschütz insists on this point (*Thessalonicher-Briefe*, 187–88), against the moderating interpretations which go back as far as Theodoret, and were supported by Luther and Calvin. Cf. A. Malherbe, *The Letters to the Thessalonians* (AB 32B; New York: Doubleday, 2000) 204: 'Paul is making an absolute prohibition' (at least, in this context, in reply to the Thessalonians' specific question). On the other side, B. Gaventa (*First and Second Thessalonians* [Louisville: John Knox, 1998] 67) goes so far as to say: 'Paul does not discourage grief with pious nonsense to the effect that Christians should not grieve because they know their

In other words, the nocturnal voice which forbade the parents of Julia Florentina to grieve could plausibly be considered an echo of Paul's.[22]

If 4.13 marks the chasm which separates faith from unbelief, 5.1–11 forces the reader to gaze at and internalise that yawning gulf. The structure of this passage reflects Paul's train of associative thought, rather than any strict sequence of logic, but it is relatively easy to follow nonetheless.[23] The issue of 'times and seasons' (5.1) leads Paul to remind the Thessalonians of a simile apparently already familiar in Christian circles: the 'Day of the Lord' will come as unexpectedly as 'a thief in the night' (5.2; cf. Mt 24.43//Lk 12.39; 2 Pet 3.10). But that simile also bears threatening connotations, which Paul expands in 5.3, warning of 'sudden destruction', and utilising the common apocalyptic image of the woman in labour. It is important to note how Paul here dwells on this dark threat, and then immediately assures the Thessalonians (with an emphatic ὑμεῖς δέ) that it does not apply to them (5.4). The thief is no threat to those who are not 'in darkness'; so, with a clever play on the term ἡμέρα (signifying both 'the Day of the Lord' and 'daytime'), Paul paints an absolute contrast between 'the children of light/the day' and those who belong to 'the night/darkness' (5.5). Those metaphors naturally lead to another: the night is the time of sleep, and such is the condition of 'the rest' (οἱ λοιποί again), while 'we', Paul exhorts, should keep awake and sober

---

loved ones will be with God. Instead he recognises the reality of grief, but distinguishes the Christian's grief from that of others who do not know the hope of the Lord's return.' I suspect Paul promotes precisely what is here dubbed 'pious nonsense'. See further next note.

[22] The point remains controversial and elicited much debate with colleagues at the Colloquium Paulinum (and with a dialogue partner at Yale Divinity School, Glenn Snyder). I am grateful to them all for pressing me on this issue. Linguistic parallels (the use of καθὼς καί and equivalents) strongly suggest an absolute contrast: 1 Thess 4.5 is unambiguous in this matter (cf. 1 Cor 10.6–10 and Matt 6.2–7; Eph 4.17 is not a real exception to this pattern). There are several passages in the Pauline letters where a kind of λύπη is recognised as necessary, even beneficial (Rom 9.2; 2 Cor 2.2–5; 6.10; 7.8–11), and there are examples of permissible weeping (κλαίειν, 1 Cor 7.30; Rom 12.15). Paul does not repress emotions in general, but none of these other passages concern death. In the one case where death is at issue, Paul is relieved that Epaphroditus' brush with death has not brought him λύπη ἐπὶ λύπην (Phil 2.27). In the light of Phil 1.21, the grief here must be for Paul himself in his loss, not for Epaphroditus. So would Paul allow, even expect, Christian grieving by the bereaved on their own behalf, if not on behalf of the deceased (for the distinction, cf. Josephus, *Bell.* 7.356)? One cannot rule out this possibility, but it hardly fits the rhetoric of this passage, which deals in absolute, not comparative, contrasts, and whose purpose is not to clarify different kinds of grief but to overcome grief with comfort (4.18). Whatever parallels Christian piety might draw with Jesus' weeping at the tomb of Lazarus (John 11.35), the closest rhetorical and theological parallel in the gospels is Mark 5.39. If later interpreters of Paul developed a particularly rigorous ban on mourning at funerals (see further below), one can hardly accuse them of misreading this text.

[23] B. Rigaux, *Saint Paul: Les Épitres aux Thessaloniciens* (Paris: Gabalda, 1956), sets out a four-part partition of the passage (vv. 1–3; vv. 4–8 a; vv. 8 b–10; v. 11), which is in danger of placing over-neat divisions within a continuous flow of text.

(5.6). Once again Paul dwells on the negative side of this contrast – on those who sleep at night and get drunk at night (5.7) – echoing his earlier emphasis on how 'the Day' will catch others unawares and unprepared (5.3). He then repeats the exhortation for the sobriety of day-dwellers (5.8 a), and moves from there to another, but not unrelated metaphor, of the soldier bearing arms, in which he metaphorically combines the breastplate and helmet of Isaiah 59.17 with the triad of faith, love and 'the hope of salvation' (5.8, echoing 1.3). This last expression is then the springboard for the following statement of assurance: that God has destined us, not for ὀργή but for περιποίησις σωτηρίας (5.9; cf. 1.3). The agent of this salvation, the Lord Jesus (Christ), is identified, and his agency portrayed by a creedal formula concerning his death 'for us' (5.9–10); then the whole paragraph is wrapped up and linked back to 4.13–18 by the assurance that 'whether we are awake or asleep' (that is, whether we stay alive or die), we shall live together with him.[24] It is this assurance, of a secure salvation attained either during life or after death, that forms the ground for the mutual encouragement and upbuilding in which Paul encourages them to continue (5.11, echoing and expanding 4.18).

What I wish to emphasise about this passage is its insistent contrasts between the two categories of humanity. On the one side lie 'you' or 'us' (Paul keeps to the inclusive form from 5.5 b through to 5.10), that is, the 'brothers' (5.1, 4), who live in a community circle of mutual encouragement and support (5.11). They are hailed as 'children of the day' (twice, 5.5, 8) and 'children of light' (5.5); they already know about 'the times and seasons' and therefore understand the fate of humanity, of which all others are completely unaware. Their identity is thus continually defined by its negative foil. 'You' are not like the (nameless and naive) 'them' (5.3), as 'children of light'; you stand in antithesis to those who are 'of darkness' and 'of night'; you remain awake while 'the rest' are asleep (5.6); and you are destined emphatically '*not* for wrath' but 'for the attaining of salvation' (5.9). What is more, this negative stereotyping of 'the rest' is more than just a rhetorical scaffold. One cannot fail to sense the satisfaction with which Paul here lingers over their fate – the 'sudden destruction' from which they

[24] The verbs used here, γρηγορῶμεν and καθεύδωμεν, differ from the sleep terminology of 4.13–15 (κοιμάω), while matching the vocabulary of 5.6–7. But it is practically impossible to take Paul's meaning here to be ' whether we stay alert (as children of the day) or fall asleep (like children of darkness)': that form of sleep (being morally and spiritually unaware) is the characteristic of 'the rest' and Paul could hardly undermine his exhortation with a hint that it doesn't really matter after all! The clear echo in 5.10 of 4.17 indicates clearly enough that 'the sleep' in view here is that of death. The terminology for the death-sleep has changed under the influence of 5.6–7 (the semantic slippage occurs because Paul's vocabulary is as associative as his processes of thought), but the meaning remains the same. See, e. g. Holtz, *erste Brief*, 230–31; Best, *Epistles to the Thessalonians*, 218.

will emphatically *not* escape (οὐ μὴ ἐκφύγωσιν, 5.3), the scene made all the more delicious by their ignorant assertion of security.[25] It is precisely their ignorance of their fate – their naivety and foolhardy self-confidence – which makes the Christians' knowledge so sweet.

Thus Paul here reinforces the boundary which separates believers from 'outsiders' (4.12), drawing the line at the point where eschatology reaches back into the present and divides humanity according to their ultimate fate. It was not easy for the Thessalonian Christians to define who they were. They were a new community, an odd species of 'family' fathered by Paul, a controversial, and now crucially absent, figure. They did not fit into any known social or religious category, and their abnormality was no doubt emphasised by those who harassed and ostracised them. Paul cannot, or will not, slot them comfortably into a local synagogue community, even though his boundary-definitions so often match those employed by Jews. What distinguishes the Thessalonian Christians from 'the rest'? In this letter Paul explicitly places three boundary markers. First, they have 'turned from idols to the true and living God' (1.9). Such renunciation of 'idolatry' was no doubt behind much of the ostracism they experienced. Secondly, according to Paul, their distinctiveness lies also in their moral conduct: even their intimate sexual behaviour is distinguished in character from 'the Gentiles who do not know God' (4.5). And here in 4.13–5.11 we find the third trench, perhaps even deeper and more fundamental than the others. Here Christians are distinguished from 'the rest', as clearly as day differs from night, in terms of their eschatological fate and confidence for the future.

The crucial move that Paul makes here is to adjust this differentiation so as to take account of death, indeed to direct believers into making death itself – how they mark it and how they view it – a symbol of their distinction. As the decades, and then the centuries, rolled by, it was to become less and less possible to live in the immediacy of expectation by which one imagined one might be caught up any moment, alive, to 'meet the Lord in the air'. But it could still make sense to look beyond death ('whether we are awake or asleep', 5.9) to the salvation to which believers were destined, and it was possible to find ways to express at, and in the face of death, this hope which was felt uniquely to characterise the believing community. Here Paul's 'that you may not grieve like the rest' could point the way: it was the first clue that one could, and should, mark the event of death itself in a distinctively Christian way, that a public signal could here be placed point-

[25] It is possible that Paul here deliberately echoes, and ridicules, the imperial slogan 'pax et securitas'; so H.L. Hendrix, 'Archaeology and Eschatology at Thessalonica', in B.A. Pearson, ed., *The Future of Early Christianity* (Minneapolis: Fortress, 1991) 107–18; cf. E. Bammel, 'Ein Beitrag zur paulinischen Staatsanschauung' *ThLZ* 85 (1960) 838–39. [See further below, chapter 19.]

ing to that fundamental division of humanity between the hopeful and the hopeless. In other words, by dealing theologically and pastorally with these first deaths in the history of this Christian community, Paul was providing the mechanism by which the power released in the early rush of parousia-enthusiasm could be transmitted into a longer-lasting momentum, which could still mark, death by death, and generation by generation, its hope of an ultimate salvation.

III. Christianising Death

Our passage, I am arguing, represents the first move towards making the death of a Christian a Christian death. But we could still ask to what degree and in what respects this differentiation could make itself felt in this and subsequent generations. Taking their cue from 1 Thess 4.13, scholars are apt to make generalised contrasts between Christian hope and the hopelessness of 'the pagan world', as illustrated by epitaphs and burial customs. The great New Testament historian George Milligan is one in a long line who considers 'the general hopelessness of the pagan world in the presence of death' as 'almost too well-known to require illustration'; he demonstrates the point by a selection of tags from literature and nihilistic epitaphs.[26] Similarly, Alfred Rush begins his pioneering study of *Death and Burial in Christian Antiquity* with reference to epitaphs in which, he asserts,

> people manifest what they really feel and believe concerning the inevitable reality of death. From a study of pagan inscriptions, the conclusion is unavoidable that their chief characteristic is a dreary outlook, an utter lack of prospect of anything beyond the grave; and once they venture to look beyond the grave, all is dark and gloomy.[27]

It is important to be much more cautious at this point concerning what our sources do, or do not, reveal. The vast majority of tombs in antiquity bore no inscription at all, and the vast majority of those with epitaphs make no reference to afterlife hopes, either positive or negative; they are generally

[26] G. Milligan, *St. Paul's Epistles to the Thessalonians* (London: Macmillan, 1908) 56; the same tactic is employed by Lightfoot, *Notes*, Bruce, *1 and 2 Thessalonians*, and others ad loc.

[27] A. Rush, *Death and Burial in Christian Antiquity* (Washington, D.C.: Catholic University of America, 1941) 8. A similar tone pervades the chapter by B. Ramsey, *Beginning to Read the Fathers* (London: Darton, Longman and Todd, 1985) on 'Death and Resurrection' (213–28). Here the inscriptions are taken to show that 'by and large' pagans 'regarded death as something terrible', with no expectation of life after death, or, if there is such belief, it contains 'no gladness'. The 'typical response' is 'despair or rebellion, or an irreparable sense of loss'. By contrast, Christian grave inscriptions are taken to 'betray a different spirit' with emphasis on peace and light and 'a wonderful serenity and even joy' (213–14).

very brief and their main function was to commemorate the deceased and their achievements in life. Thus a silence here about the fate of the deceased need not imply despair or agnosticism.[28] Where we do find references to death and its prospects (or finality), they are often so standardised as to suggest that stonecutters used common clichés, which may have had very little to do with the personal beliefs of the deceased or their commemorators.[29] What is more, many of these commonplaces are decidedly ambiguous: metaphors of 'sleep' and references to 'peace' could convey several meanings.[30] Where we do encounter expressions of a definite expectation (of annihilation, or some kind of after-life), it is impossible to know how 'typical' or representative these are, and it would certainly be inaccurate to characterise them as 'generally' lacking in hope.[31]

We should exercise the same caution in relation to burial customs (inhumation, cremation or secondary ossuary-burial), grave-side rites (e.g. the 'feeding' of the dead with libations of wine) and funerary art: as historians and anthropologists remind us, such customs are notoriously conservative or may reflect practical convenience, with little or no relation to the actual beliefs of those who practise them.[32] In general, it is the hardest thing to know how people experience and make sense of death, particularly in past generations and in different cultures. Even mourning rituals may express despair to a greater degree than its participants actually feel.[33]

---

[28] See the helpful note of caution on this topic in L. Rutgers, *The Hidden Heritage of Diaspora Judaism* (Leuven: Peeters, 1998) 157–68. A very large percentage of Christian inscriptions also make no reference to the afterlife at all.

[29] On this feature of ancient epitaphs, see R. Lattimore, *Themes in Greek and Latin Epitaphs* (Urbana: University of Illinois, 1962) 17–20. Of course a stereotypical formula may reflect widespread current opinion, but it may also represent a near-meaningless platitude, such as jovial defiance in the face of death, which represents public facade more than personal belief.

[30] The problem besets the interpretation even of Jewish inscriptions, where we have good literary evidence for variant Jewish beliefs; see the discussion by P. van der Horst, *Ancient Jewish Epitaphs* (Kampen: Kok Pharos, 1991) 114–26. [Cf. N.T. Wright, *The Resurrection of the Son of God* (London: SPCK, 2003) 129–206; C.D. Elledge, *Life after Death in Early Judaism: The Evidence of Josephus* (WUNT 2.208; Tübingen: Mohr Siebeck, 2006).]

[31] See the survey by Lattimore, *Themes*, esp. 21–86.

[32] See in general I. Morris, *Death-Ritual and Social Structure in Classical Antiquity* (Cambridge: Cambridge University, 1992). The over-interpretation of funerary art (e.g. by Cumont and Goodenough) was effectively criticised by A.D. Nock, 'Sarcophagi and symbolism', in J. Stewart, ed., *Essays on Religion and the Ancient World* (Oxford: Oxford University, 1972) 2.606–41.

[33] See the discussion of this problem by K. Hopkins, *Death and Renewal* (Cambridge: Cambridge University, 1983) 217–26, and the perspective of a comparative anthropologist, N. Barley, *Dancing on the Grave: Encounters with Death* (London: John Murray, 1995) 13–45.

Literary sources are also uncertain witnesses to popular beliefs since, even when they comment on general convictions, their perspective is often skewed. Plutarch claims that few, apart from 'mothers and nurses', believe in the old myths about the underworld (*Moralia* 1104 a–1107 c), but Lucretius' attack on fear of death (*De Rerum Natura*, 3.850–1094) presupposes that fear of death and of the horrors of Hades was widespread. Similarly, for his satirical purposes, Lucian suggests that 'the common herd ... trust Homer and Hesiod and the other myth-makers in these matters' and takes the placing of a coin in the mouth of the deceased to demonstrate belief in the Charon-myth (*De Luctu*, 2–11). We have to allow for an enormous range of beliefs, many ill-formed or self-contradictory, ranging from nihilism, through agnosticism, to beliefs in the continuance of the soul in some form (in the underworld, among the stars, or re-absorbed into the world-soul), and, at the other end of spectrum, hopes of personal survival in a blessed afterlife.[34] The picture is as variegated as the mosaic of peoples, traditions and social levels in the Graeco-Roman world.

However, we can clearly observe within the Christian tradition a concern to approach death in a distinctive way, both in inculcating certain beliefs about death and the after-life, and in instantiating those beliefs in the rites of mourning and burial. Christians knew, and were generally prepared to acknowledge, that they were not the only ones who believed in some form of existence after death: their distinctiveness lay not in the notion of post-mortem existence *per se*, but in the peculiar form in which they envisaged it, the resurrection of the body. Here Paul's discussion of this topic in 1 Corinthians 15 was to have an enormous impact: it is remarkable how frequently the topic of the resurrection of the body occurs in early Christian apologetics, and how, precisely because it is regarded by non-Christians as ridiculous and distasteful, this article of belief becomes central to early Christian self-definition.[35] In a parallel development, the very concreteness of Christian beliefs in the judgement of the damned and the bliss of the saved could take on special prominence: as Robin Lane Fox observes, it is impossible to imagine anywhere outside Christianity the intense inner-communal debate

[34] The standard discussion of this matter by F. Cumont, *After Life in Roman Paganism* (reprint; New York: Dover, 1922) badly needs updating. There is isolated, but clear, evidence of afterlife hopes fostered in some 'mystery-cults' (e.g. some versions of the Eleusinian and Dionysiac cult), but scholars dispute how widespread or significant this phenomenon was; see R. MacMullen, *Paganism in the Roman Empire* (New Haven: Yale University, 1981) 55–57, and H.-J. Klauck, *The Religious Context of Early Christianity* (Edinburgh: T & T Clark, 2000) 81–152.

[35] Two notable examples are Tertullian's treatise *De Resurrectione Carnis* and the treatise *On the Resurrection of the Dead* attributed to Athenagoras.

concerning the sequence and shape of millenarian expectations.[36] In this way, the early parousia hope and the vivid expectation of salvation from 'the wrath to come' continued to exert its influence long after that first expectant generation had died.

But equally noticeable and important are the efforts developed in early Christianity to embed beliefs about death and salvation in the practice and experience of death. Here, as elsewhere, Christianity could not, and did not, make a wholly fresh start. One can trace clearly enough in much early Christian practice the *continuation* of death rituals from their cultural environment: both at Christian and at non-Christian deaths there took place the gathering of the last breath, the closing of the eyes, the laying out and washing of the body, the wake, the funeral cortège, the disposal of the body (cremation or inhumation), the funeral speech, the importance of the third day after death, and of set periods of mourning thereafter (nine, thirty and forty days) – all these are, as far as we can tell, common to early Christian and non-Christian funerals.[37] Even today one can trace in the Greek (Orthodox) rural context ritual laments and mourning customs which have come down unchanged from classical antiquity.[38] Of course, even the same rites can be made to 'feel' different by the social context in which they are performed, and in this sense Christian burials could be transformed by the presence and participation of the Christian community and (later) the conduct of funerals by a priest in a church.[39]

However, what is perhaps most revealing is the (selective) effort to inscribe Christian difference in the performance of mourning. The most significant examples are where Christians omitted to follow normal practice.[40]

---

[36] R. Lane Fox, *Pagans and Christians* (Harmondsworth: Penguin 1986) 265–66; cf. the contrasts he draws between the range of pagan opinions about the afterlife and the 'coherence' apparent in Christian teaching (95–98). This had its negative as well as its positive side: 'Terrors in the next world were not unfamiliar to pagans, but Christians insisted on their certainty and imminent realization' (327).

[37] On ancient funerary customs, see D. C. Kurtz & J. Boardman, *Greek Burial Customs* (London: Thames & Hudson, 1971); R. Garland, *The Greek Way of Death* (London: Duckworth, 1985). For the early Christian marking of days after death see E. Freistedt, *Altchristliche Totengedächtnistage und ihre Beziehung zum Jenseitsglauben und Totenkultus des Antike* (Münster: Aschendorff, 1928). [Cf. K. E. Corley, *Maranatha: Women's Funerary Rituals and Christian Origins* (Minneapolis: Fortress, 2010).]

[38] See the classic study by M. Alexiou, *The Ritual Lament in Greek Tradition* (Cambridge: Cambridge University, 1974) esp. 36–51; cf. Danforth, *Death Rituals*.

[39] Even so, Christians were often buried in common cemeteries, and we often lack in such cases convincing criteria by which to distinguish Christian from non-Christian burials; see R. MacMullen, *Christianizing the Roman Empire, A. D. 100–400* (New Haven: Yale University, 1986) 153 n. 22. Lattimore, *Themes*, 301–40 shows the continuance of 'pagan elements' in Christian epitaphs.

[40] Although our focus here is primarily on distinction from 'pagan' practice, we may note the strenuous effort in *Didascalia Apostolorum* 26 to distinguish Christian attitudes

Thus Justin, in his *First Apology* (24.2) notes that Christians were criticised for not offering libations, fat-offerings or other sacrifices for the dead, referring perhaps to memorial meals at the graveside.[41] In the same passage he refers to the non-use of garlands, and this omission is also commented on by Tertullian and Minucius Felix, in the latter case again as a subject of criticism.[42] It is not entirely clear why Christians made a point of this differentiation (Tertullian associates it with idolatry) but the token, though small, was clearly significant.

More clearly representative of the Christian sense of hope were the efforts by some church fathers to tone down, or even banish, traditional expressions of grief.[43] Both Cyprian and Chrysostom criticise the wearing of black mourning clothes (black and purple being the colours of death), while Basil instructs Christians to cease tearing their clothes and covering themselves with dust.[44] More generally, we find repeated pleas that the wailing, dirges and loud cries which were the traditional accompaniment of death (sometimes with the aid of hired mourners) should be banished from Christian funerals and replaced by the joyful chanting of psalms.[45] This is frequently

---

to the corpse from 'Jewish' notions of corpse-uncleanness (R. H. Connolly, *Didascalia Apostolorum* [Oxford: Oxford University, 1929] 250–54). It is not clear how far this rhetoric was carried through in practice, since corpse-impurity was, in fact, a universal notion in antiquity (see R. Parker, *Miasma. Pollution and Purification in early Greek Religion* [Oxford: Clarendon, 1983] 32–48). However, later evidence of the veneration of martyr-relics indicates that Christian practice here did, at least in these cases, deliberately flout accepted custom; see Lane Fox, *Pagans and Christians*, 447–48 and Brown, *Cult of the Saints*, 6–8.

41 Other sources refer to such memorials as deliberately timed by Christians to coincide with the death-anniversary, rather than the birthdays, of the deceased (e. g. Ambrose, *De Excessu fratris sui Satyri* 2.5). But this may refer specifically to martyrs, whose deaths were often commemorated as their *dies natalis* in an effort to signal death as the start of (real) life; see Rush, *Death and Burial*, 72–87. That custom starts as early as the date of the *Martyrdom of Polycarp* (18.3).

42 Tertullian, *De Corona Militis* 10; Minucius Felix, *Octavius* 12.6; 38.3–4. See the full discussion in Rush, *Death and Burial*, 133–49, though his material is not all equally relevant. On garlanding the dead, see Lucian, *De Luctu*, 12.

43 The distinction which may be drawn between grief for oneself and grief for the deceased could hardly serve to differentiate Christians in public; observers could hardly tell on what basis the mourning took place. The tendency to banish grief altogether is therefore fully comprehensible.

44 Cyprian, *De Mortalitate* 20; John Chrysostom, *De Consolatione Mortis* 2.6 (Migne, *PG* 56.303); Basil, *De Gratiarum Actione* 6 (*PG* 31.229): 'They should show moderate distress in their affliction, with only a few tears, shed quietly and without moaning, wailing, tearing of clothes and grovelling in the dust, or committing any other indecency commonly practised by those uneducated in heavenly matters' (translation by Alexiou, *Ritual Lament*, 28, altered).

45 On the normal mourning practice see Alexiou, *Ritual Lament*, 4–23 and the vivid depiction in Lucian, *De Luctu*, 12: 'Next come cries of distress, wailing of women, tears on all sides, beaten breasts, torn hair, and bloody cheeks. Perhaps, too, clothing is rent and dust sprinkled on the head, and the living are in a plight more pitiable than the dead; for they roll on the ground repeatedly and dash their heads against the floor ...' (Loeb

insisted upon as a *necessary* mark of difference from 'the world'. Chrysostom insists that the use of hired mourners ('this disease of females') would be 'fatal to the church'.[46] Cyprian claims that without this distinction at death Christians could rightly be accused of rank hypocrisy.[47]

The fact that this exhortation required constant repetition shows how brutally it collided with the solid reality of human grief. In this context, particular significance came to devolve onto the deaths of Christian martyrs, since at least these provided clear proof of the Christian ability to conquer death. In the deaths of the martyrs, Christians acclaimed not only exemplary courage, but also the power to stare down death, so that the commemoration of these deaths could serve as a focal point for the affirmation of life beyond death. Peter Brown has traced how the martyrs' tombs became sites of special celebration and holiness (such that burial near their tombs was highly prized), how the accounts of their deaths took on symbolic value as exemplars of Christian death-defiance, and how the martyrs themselves, crowned in the presence of Christ, became the channels of special grace, points of contact with eternity. Thus, in the celebration of these 'very special dead', we have:

> a consistent imaginative determination to block out the lurking presence of … "black death" … the working of an imaginative dialectic which led late-antique men to render their beliefs in the afterlife palpable and directly operative among the living by concentrating these on the privileged figure of the dead saint.[48]

In other words, if it was too difficult not to mourn at the funeral of one's own loved ones, at least the joyful celebration of the martyrs' 'birthdays' (anniversaries of their deaths) could mark in the Christian calendar, and

---

translation). For Christian authors banning such laments see, e. g., Tertullian, *De Patientia* 9; Gregory of Nyssa, *Vita S. Macrinae* (Migne, *PG* 46.985–88); John Chrysostom, *Homily 62 on John*, 4 (*PG* 59.346); *Homily 31 on Matthew*, 3 (*PG* 57.374); Jerome, *Epistle* 108.29–30. Aristides, *Apology* 15, makes a special point of claiming that 'if any righteous man among them [Christians] passes from the world, they rejoice and offer thanks to God; and they escort his body as if he were setting out from one place to another near' (translation, *ANF* X.277).

[46] Chrysostom, in Migne, *PG* 59.346; 63.44.

[47] Cyprian, *De Mortalitate* 20: 'our brethren who are freed from this world by the Lord's summons are not to be lamented, since we know that they are not lost but sent before; … occasion should not be given to the Gentiles for them deservedly and rightly to reprehend us, that we mourn for those, who, we say, are alive with God, as if they were extinct and lost … We are prevaricators of our hope and faith; what we say appears to be simulated, feigned, counterfeit' (translation *ANF* V.474). We may compare Ambrose, *De Excessu fratris sui Satyri* 1.70: 'quia debet aliquid inter fidos et perfidos interesse … Intersit inter Christi servulos idolorumque cultores; ut illi fleant suos quos in perpetuum existimant interiisse.' See further Rush, *Death and Burial*, 174–86.

[48] Brown, *Cult of the Saints*, 71.

impress deep into Christian consciousness, the sense that the Christian faith had uniquely triumphed over death.

This process of 'Christianising death' was of profound significance.[49] As Metcalf and Huntingdon show, in their comparative anthropology of death,

> the issue of death throws into relief the most important cultural values by which people live their lives and evaluate their experiences. Life becomes transparent against the background of death, and fundamental social and cultural issues are revealed.[50]

To maintain the integrity of its vision of salvation, the church needed to help believers organise their experience of death in a religiously significant way, and to provide rites, or interpretations of rites, which maintained its sense of 'reality' and fostered its sense of difference from the rest of humanity. As a community which made a special point of being destined to salvation, the successful negotiation of the obstacle of death was of pivotal significance. Here the Pauline legacy (often cited in later Christian literature) had a special part to play. Not only did Paul successfully mould the apocalyptic resources of Judaism into a distinctive Christian form, but he also guided the Christian mind through the barrier of death and showed ways in which precisely the deaths of believers could become markers of Christian difference. Theologically, his achievement was to show how the notion of participation in Christ could and should be extended through death: if believers exist 'in Christ', and if Christ died and rose for them, then it was natural and necessary that the dead 'in Christ' should also be raised (1 Thess 4.16), that God should bring them 'with him' at the parousia (σὺν αὐτῷ , 4.14).[51] Thus the hope for all believers, whether alive or dead at the parousia, should be that they continue their life σὺν κυρίῳ (4.17; 5.10). By tying Christian hopes for the dead so tightly to the core beliefs of the Christian confession, Paul ensured that the future Christian treatment of death would remain forever at the centre of its theological attention and could not be relegated to the margins as a matter of uncertainty or indifference.

As we began with grieving Christian parents, we may end with the stifled grief of a Christian son. In a moving section of his *Confessions*, Augustine records the death of his mother, Monica, and his struggle to contain, indeed

---

[49] I borrow this phrase from F.S. Paxton, *Christianizing Death. The Creation of a Ritual Process in Early Medieval Europe* (Ithaca: Cornell University, 1990), though the period of his interest is later than that under consideration here. See also G. Rowell, *The Liturgy of Christian Burial (*London: SPCK, 1977). Remarkably little attention has been paid to this element of early Christian self-definition.

[50] P. Metcalf and R. Huntingdon, *Celebrations of Death. The Anthropology of Mortuary Ritual* (2nd ed.; Cambridge: Cambridge University, 1991) 25.

[51] I have not been able here to develop this theological aspect of Paul's response. Christ's death ὑπὲρ ἡμῶν enables participation both in his death and in his resurrection, the foundation of the more developed theology of Rom 6.4–8 and 14.7–9.

suppress, his grief. As he closed her eyes, a great wave of sorrow surged into his heart and he wanted to cry 'like a child'.

> But a more mature voice within me, the voice of my heart, bade me keep my sobs in check, and I remained silent. For we did not think it right to mark my mother's death with weeping and moaning, because such lamentations are the usual accompaniment of death when it is thought of as a state of misery or as total extinction. But she had not died in misery, nor had she wholly died.[52]

Augustine's struggle with his emotions in fact proved unsuccessful: after a night's rest 'it was a comfort to weep for her and for myself and to offer my tears to you [God] for her sake and for mine' (9.12 [33]). But he confesses these tears as a weakness, indeed a 'sin', a sign of 'too much worldly affection' (9.13 [34]).[53] Today we may judge this struggle as misguided, indeed 'unnatural',[54] but for Augustine it represented the test of whether he could look past the human horizon of death to the 'eternal Jerusalem' to which he and all believers were bound (9.13 [37]). It thus stands, alongside the struggle of Julia Florentina's parents, as impressive testimony to the intensity with which early Christians understood their calling as 'children of the day' and the lasting significance of Paul's call to distinguish themselves by hope, not only in life, but also – indeed, especially – in death.

---

[52] Augustine, *Confessions* 9.12 (29); translation by R. S. Pine-Coffin (Penguin Classics).

[53] In a very helpful email exchange, Glenn Snyder pointed out to me the contrast between Augustine's reaction to his mother's death and his pre-Christian mourning of a friend as described in *Confessions* 4.4 (7) – 12 (19). It is true that Augustine goes to some lengths to excuse his tears for his mother (they were private and brief, and both he and his mother rested in God); but he still portrays them as a sin, even if a pardonable one.

[54] The Christian demand is here parallel to, and perhaps not uninfluenced by, the Stoic call for the extirpation of the passions (see M. Nussbaum, *The Therapy of Desire* [Princeton: Princeton University, 1994] 359–401). As with the Stoics, there is an element of 'de-feminising' in this demand, since 'weeping' at death was culturally constructed as a pre-eminently female characteristic (see, e.g., the 'feminising' effect of tears noted in Josephus, *Bell.* 7.339). [Cf. R. Sorabji, *Emotion and Peace of Mind: From Stoic Agitation to Christian Temptation* (Oxford: Oxford University, 2000); M. R. Graver, *Stoicism and Emotion* (Chicago: University of Chicago, 2007).]

12. Ordinary but Different

Colossians and Hidden Moral Identity

I. A Christocentric Theology

Visitors to the remarkable church of San Clemente in Rome are immediately struck by its shimmering 12th-century apse, whose mosaic depicts the meaning of salvation in a rich complex of theological art. At its focal point, visually and theologically, is the cross, upon which the hand of God descends from above bestowing the victor's crown on the crucified Jesus. From the base of the cross spring the shoots of the tree of life, spreading to cover the whole apsidal surface. At the bottom graze animals, domestic and wild, representing the created order, while alongside them, as well as encircled by the tendrils of the tree, are vignettes depicting scenes of work and everyday life – scribes, tenders of flocks, dressers of vines – which represent the human sphere of activity. The cross of Christ is thus the centre and the integrating focus of the whole of creation; it fructifies the natural world and gives meaning and purpose to human life in all its dimensions.

It would be hard to imagine a better illustration of the theology of Colossians. Here, too, not only in the 'hymn' (1.15–20) but also in the theology which develops its themes, the focal point is Christ, whose victorious death reintegrates the creation (1.20; 2.14–15). And here, too, the significance of the Christ-event spreads to cover the entire surface of the world: *all things* (τὰ πάντα) are made through him and for him (1.16), *all things* hold together in him (1.17) and by his death he has reconciled *all things* (1.20). Indeed, the most distinctive feature of Colossians is precisely its placement of Christ at the core of the cosmos, where he determines the shape of all reality and the course of all eternity: one could speak here of a 'creation Christology' and a 'Christology of time'.

The main contours of this Christology may be sketched here briefly.[1] Famously, the hymn portrays Christ not only as the agent of all creation, but also as its goal and inner meaning: all things were created both 'through

[1] I have discussed aspects of the theology of Colossians in more detail in *Colossians and Philemon* (New Testament Guides; Sheffield: Sheffield Academic, 1997) 75–96.

him' (δι' αὐτοῦ) and 'for him' (εἰς αὐτόν , 1.16), and this totality includes all heavenly and earthly reality. From every angle, Christ is first: the 'firstborn of all creation' (1.15), the first principle by which all things cohere (1.17), the head and beginning of the church (1.18), the first-born from the dead (1.18): in truth, he comes first in everything (ἵνα γένηται ἐν πᾶσιν αὐτὸς πρωτεύων).[2] And, as the first, he determines the character and destiny of the rest, so that there is nothing in the whole of creation, or in the history of creation and redemption, which does not derive from him its origin and rationale. Notably emphatic here is the inclusion of 'the powers', in their multiple guises, within this Christocentric cosmos. Of the 'things in heaven and things on earth' which were created in, through and for Christ, the hymn lists 'thrones', 'lordships', 'powers' and 'authorities' (εἴτε θρόνοι εἴτε κυριότητες εἴτε ἀρχαὶ εἴτε ἐξουσίαι, 1.16); the scope of reconciliation is equally broad: 'whether things on earth or things in heaven' (1.20). In a notable ambiguity, Colossians leaves ill-defined what this reconciliation entails. What looks in 1.20 like restoration to an original unity is elsewhere (2.14–15) portrayed as the public humiliation of the powers and authorities (αἱ ἀρχαὶ καὶ αἱ ἐξουσίαι), in a conflict metaphor which looks more like subjugation (pacification?) than reconciliation. The theological metaphors may not entirely cohere, but Christ's supremacy, whether grounded in creation or won by redemption, is clear: whichever way one looks at it, he is 'head of every power and every authority' (κεφαλὴ πάσης ἀρχῆς καὶ ἐξουσίας, 2.10).

If 'all things' thus connect with Christ at their centre, it may truly be said that he constitutes the 'mystery' of all reality. Colossians repeatedly celebrates Christ as 'the mystery of God' (2.2), in whom may be found 'all the treasures of wisdom and knowledge' (2.3). To preach the gospel is thus to proclaim 'the mystery which is Christ' (4.3), a truth not recently invented but built into the fabric of time – 'the mystery which has been hidden throughout the ages and generations but has now been revealed to his saints' (1.26–27). Thus the ultimate reality (God), the eternal secrets (of all time) and the deepest truths (of wisdom and knowledge) are all revealed in Christ. Cognitive metaphors accordingly pervade this letter: if in Romans faith is characterised by obedience, here it is most closely associated with

[2] The possible prehistory of the Colossian 'hymn' is not our topic here, and may be, in fact, of only marginal importance for understanding the theology of the letter: even if we could trace with confidence the author's additions or modifications (in truth, a somewhat speculative task), what counts for our purposes is the final form of the text, the totality of the hymn as he chooses to cite and use it. I also deliberately bypass here the question of the identity of the author, which has typically distracted attention from the more theologically significant questions concerning the *content* of the letter; on the authorship issue see my *Colossians and Philemon*, 18–36. I use the male pronoun given the greater probability that the household code was composed by a man.

'knowledge' (1.6, 9, 10, 27; 2.2, 3; 3.10), 'wisdom' (1.8, 28; 2.3, 23; 3.16; 4.5) and 'understanding' (1.9; 2.2). To know the secret of reality is to know Christ, the first principle and thus the inner meaning of all that is true.

A variety of factors may have shaped this Colossian Christocentricity. If the 'hymn' existed in a pre-Colossian form, it may have inspired the author to develop this theme, while the competition he senses from the 'philosophy and empty deceit' (2.8, the context of 2.10) may have encouraged its development in a polemical vein.[3] In broader historical terms, the burgeoning of the Christian church, 'bearing fruit and growing throughout the whole world' (1.6), may have led the Pauline movement to self-conscious reflection on its Christological confession and its implicit universal claim. Whatever its roots, the Christology of Colossians is as confident and broad in scope as is to be found anywhere in the New Testament. While there may lurk yet a 'power of darkness' from which believers are redeemed (1.13), and while the term κόσμος itself still stands in notable antithesis to Christ (2.8, 20), there is in principle no sphere of life where Christ's rule cannot be brought to bear: it is fitting that the Colossian baptismal formula (3.11) proclaims that Christ is 'everything and in everything' (τὰ πάντα καὶ ἐν πᾶσιν).

It is evident from a very early point that the author expects this Christological cosmology to shape not just the minds of his addressees but also their lives.[4] His first prayer-request is that they be filled with knowledge, accompanied by 'all wisdom and spiritual understanding' – but this is not just knowledge of truth abstractly conceived, but specifically 'knowledge of his will', so they might 'walk worthily of the Lord, pleasing to him in every way, bearing fruit in every good work' (1.9–10). The comprehensiveness implied by these expressions is matched elsewhere: Paul's aim is to warn and teach everyone 'in all wisdom, that we might present every man perfect [or, mature] in Christ' (1.28; cf. 1.22), while Epaphras' prayer-goal is 'that you might stand perfect and complete in all the will of God' (4.6). Thus the letter covets and contends for the total orientation of the whole person to Christ (or to 'the will of God'). Indeed, its central polemical section (2.6–20)

[3] I bypass here the problematic, and perhaps insoluble, task of reconstructing this Colossian 'heresy', whose shifting profile may reflect scholarly fashion more than solid advance in the discovery or interpretation of evidence (see my *Colossians and Philemon*, 37–55). In any case, it is not clear to me that the theology of Colossians is wholly determined by this conflictual context and, given the difficulty of reconstruction, it seems better to read the theology of Colossians in its own right, not simply as a foil to another.

[4] This is a point rightly emphasised by W. A. Meeks, '"To Walk Worthily of the Lord": Moral Formation in the Pauline School Exemplified by the Letter to the Colossians', in E. Stump and T. P. Flint, eds., *Hermes and Athena: Biblical Exegesis and Philosophical Theology* (Notre Dame: University of Notre Dame, 1993) 37–58; see, e.g., p. 39: 'If the writer is concerned with correcting the beliefs of the Colossian Christians, it is not for the sake of beliefs as such, but in order to shape the audience's moral dispositions and behavior'.

is founded on the appeal to 'walk in Christ', 'as you have received Christ Jesus as Lord' (2.6). The practices which are here proscribed are disqualified primarily because they are not 'according to Christ' (2.8): their rites are a shadow of the substance to be found in Christ (2.16), their visions cause a fatal disconnection from Christ the head (2.19), and their rules constitute a pattern of life now passé for those who have died with Christ (2.20). Hence the ethical vision of this letter (which surfaces well before the turn from indicative to imperative at 3.1) appears to be as thoroughly Christological as its cosmology: it is entirely natural that this letter should contain the injunction that 'everything you do, in word or in deed, should be done in the name of the Lord Jesus, giving thanks to God the Father through him' (3.17).

II. Are the Ethics of Colossians Thoroughly Christian?

Given the consistent Christological focus of Colossians, we should expect its portrayal of the moral life to reflect a thorough Christianisation of motive, norm and practice, and to a degree we are not disappointed. When the author turns to delineate his positive injunctions (3.1 ff.), they are presented on the premise that believers, as now raised with Christ, should 'seek the things that are above' (τὰ ἄνω ζητεῖτε, 3.1, 2), since their life, in all its dimensions, is 'hid with Christ in God'. The 'with Christ' thematic that pervades these introductory verses (it occurs three times in 3.1–4) encourages an expectation that everything will now be thought through on the basis of the Christ event. It accords with this that the opening moral exhortation, with its lists of vices and virtues (3.5–14), revolves around the baptismal imagery of disrobing and reclothing, by which the old ἄνθρωπος is discarded, together with its deeds, while a new person is donned 'which is being renewed in knowledge according to the image of its creator' (3.10). Attentive readers cannot fail to hear the echo of 1.15, where Christ is described as that image (εἰκών); and the baptismal formula of 3.11 confirms that this new person is so redefined in identity that previous ethnic or status labels are displaced by the overwhelming new reality of Christ, who 'is everything and in everything (or everyone)'. The new life is so redefined by Christ that it may be said to be Christ himself. In this sense Christ is indeed 'our life' (3.4).

Consistent with this sense of newness is the author's portrayal of vices as the *past* way of life ('in which you once walked, when you lived in them', 3.5). To be sure, the vices named (in two lists of five, 3.5, 8) include some common targets of moral censure in the ancient world (ἐπιθυμία κακή, πλεονεξία, ὀργή), but even such standardised lists of vices bear some traces of creative moral reflection, as when greed is analysed as a form of 'idolatry' (3.5). The Christian movement could hardly be expected, perhaps, to *invent* many new vices: the real test of its moral refashioning will be in the positive virtues it inculcates. Here, whatever the overlap one might detect between Christian and non-Christian notions of 'kindness' and 'long-suffering' (3.12), there are many indications of a specifically Christian moral profile (3.12–17). Not only do believers now act out of a special sense of being chosen and loved by God (3.12), they also let the character of divine grace determine their relations with others: 'just as the Lord has forgiven (or, been gracious to) you, so you also must behave' (3.13; cf. 2.13). It is thus no real surprise to find such an unusual value placed on ταπεινοφροσύνη (3.12), or to find the chief virtue identified as 'love, which is the bond of perfection' (3.14). The creation of a gracious, peaceful and worshipping community (3.15–16) is, in fact, the appropriate outcome of that great act of reconciliation which the hymn celebrated (1.15–20): this is precisely the new (or restored) creation taking social shape (cf. 3.10). Here every word and deed is offered up in thanks to God, in the name of the Lord Jesus, the integrating focus of all reality (3.17).

Thus in foundation, form and content there is much in the moral vision of Colossians which suggests that it is as Christocentric as the rest of the letter. But then we strike upon the household code (3.18–4.1). The change in form from the previous material is immediately obvious: unlike anything that has come before, here we find specific instructions to designated groups, arranged in pairs, in a standardised form (address, instruction and, usually, motivating reason). The unique formulation of this segment, its inner coherence but lack of explicit connection with its context at either end (between 3.17 and 3.18, or between 4.1 and 4.2), leads to the common conclusion that this is a self-contained block of material, unassimilated to the rest of the letter. This impression is, of course, strengthened by the many parallels between these household instructions and the moral traditions of both Jewish and Graeco-Roman cultures. Without entering here into the long scholarly debate concerning the closest parallels (in form, theme or content) to the NT household codes, we may safely concur with the well-founded consensus that, as regards both its theme and its contents, very little in this Colossian code represents a specifically Christian creation: almost all of it could have been, and indeed was, taught by moralists in both the Jewish and the non-Jewish Hellenistic traditions of the first century.[5] The author is not

[5] A useful survey of research may be found in D.L. Balch, 'Household Codes', in D.E. Aune, ed., *Greco-Roman Literature and the New Testament: Selected Forms and Genres* (Atlanta: Scholars Press, 1988) 25–50. [Cf. J.P. Hering, *The Colossian and Ephesian* Hausafeln *in Theological Context* (New York: Peter Lang, 2007); J. Woyke, *Die neutestamentlichen Haustafeln: Ein kritischer und konstruktiver Forschungsüberblick* (Stuttgart: Katholishes Bibelwerk, 2000); M.Y. MacDonald, 'Beyond Identification of the Topos of Household Management: Reading the Household Codes in the Light of Recent

quoting verbatim a pre-formed code, but he is certainly propounding moral sentiments of widespread currency in his ambient culture.

The difficulty which this causes is twofold. In the first place, the near-wholesale adoption of moral assumptions from outside the Christian tradition seems to sit awkwardly with the otherwise Christocentric focus of the letter. Colossians elsewhere *contrasts* living 'according to Christ' with living 'according to human tradition' (2.8), but, with our knowledge of the ancient world, the household code looks uncannily like common 'human tradition'. In the first four segments of this code (the instructions to wives and husbands, to children and fathers, 3.18–21), the only indication that this is a Christian code is the use of the phrase ἐν κυρίῳ, which actually only occurs twice, in the instruction to the subordinate partners (wives and children). At first sight this looks rather paltry – a superficial Christianisation of a code which has thus undergone no substantial adaptation by its rapid 'baptism' into Christian moral discourse.[6] If rather more Christian references occur in the extended section concerning slaves and masters (3.22–4.1), these appear to provide the *motivation* for the required conduct rather than determining the *character* of the conduct itself. There seems to be remarkably little here which is distinctly or genuinely Christian.[7]

The second problem resides in the further nuance of this term 'genuine'. Not only is this material not originally Christian, but it also seems to clash with what seem (to us) fundamental Christian values. The subordination required of the submissive partners in each relationship (wives to husbands, children to fathers, slaves to masters) clearly perpetuates the hierarchical and patriarchal assumptions of antiquity, while the endorsement of slave-obedience, as an unproblematic requirement, grates against all that we have come to associate with the Christian gospel. Here, then, the social and domestic *status quo* is not only unchallenged but, worse, legitimated by the addition of a Christian rationalisation. From this perspective, Colossians has simply wrapped a fundamentally non-Christian product in a thin layer of Christian packaging, and thus successfully smuggled these dangerous goods into Christian territory, where their justification of inequality and

---

Methodologies and Theoretical Perspectives in the Study of the New Testament' *NTS* 57 (2011) 65–90.]

[6] M. Dibelius and H. Greeven speak of a 'leichte Verchristlichung', and take both ἀνῆκεν (3.18) and εὐάρεστον (3.21) to be originally non-Christian formulations, which have been elevated to a Christian level by the addition of ἐν κυρίῳ (*An die Kolosser, Epheser und Philemon* [HNT 12; 3rd ed.; Tübingen: Mohr Siebeck, 1953] 46).

[7] The latter phrase is used, and implicitly ruled inapplicable, by E. Schüssler Fiorenza, *In Memory of Her* (2nd ed.; London: SCM, 1994) 254: 'While a few scholars think that the demands for the obedience and submission of wives, children, and slaves are genuinely Christian, the majority sees the domestic code as a later Christian adaptation of a Graeco-Roman or Jewish-Hellenistic philosophical-theological code'.

even brute exploitation 'in the Lord' has done untold damage ever since. Not surprisingly this code, and by extension this letter (in which such a code makes its first Christian appearance), have become the butt of hefty theological and ideological critique.[8]

The expression of moral outrage here is both understandable and justified, especially if it comes from those who have suffered at the hands of this text.[9] However, my task here is, in the first place, neither critical nor apologetic, but an attempt to discern to what degree, or in what ways, this erratic block on the Colossian landscape can be associated with its Christological environment. To be sure, this question is not without hermeneutical implications: to minimise the Christological colouring of this section might assist its swifter ejection from Christian discourse, while to maximise the significance of the motif 'in the Lord' could result in deepening our theological embarrassment. Nonetheless, I wish for now to contain the influence of such considerations, while recognising that these hermeneutical issues lurk not far beneath the surface of all exegesis.

III. A New Hermeneutic: Life 'in the Lord'

In what respects, then, and to what degree, are the ethics of the Colossian household code influenced by the Christocentric theology of the letter as a whole? And what conclusions could we draw from this about the way our letter forges a Christian moral identity?

To begin with, some common false trails should be identified. It is sometimes asserted, for instance, that there is special Christian significance in the giving of instructions to both sides of each paired relationship: to both husbands and wives, both children and fathers, both masters and slaves. This reciprocity has been claimed as a 'balancing' of duties and responsibilities, giving the superordinate duties as well as rights, and the subordinate rights as well as duties.[10] To be sure, it is important to note that each relationship

---

[8] The theological animus is evident not only in feminist criticism (as, for instance, in Schüssler Fiorenza) but across a broad spectrum of interpretative opinion. Wedderburn asks whether this code is 'any more than lending a Christian endorsement to the thoroughly patriarchal norms of society of the day' (A. T. Lincoln and A. J. M. Wedderburn, *The Theology of the Later Pauline Letters* [Cambridge: Cambridge University, 1993] 56). J. T. Sanders is only slightly more explicit in declaring that 'the *Haustafeln* must therefore be seen as completely worthless for Christian ethics' (*Ethics in the New Testament* [London: SCM, 1975] 75).

[9] See the fine essay by W. A. Meeks, 'The "Haustafeln" and American Slavery: The Hermeneutical Challenge', in E. H. Lovering and J. L. Sumney, eds., *Theology and Ethics in Paul and his Interpreters* (Nashville: Abingdon Press, 1996) 232–53.

[10] So, e. g., C. F. D. Moule, *The Epistles to the Colossians and to Philemon* (Cambridge: Cambridge University, 1957) 127–28 (with qualifications) and N. T. Wright, *Colossians*

is reciprocal, but it is hard to see how this could justify talk of 'balance' or 'rights' in the relationships here named. In relation to one another, the persons here addressed remain stubbornly *unequal*: only one side is required to 'submit' or 'obey', and, unlike Ephesians 5.21, there is no call for mutual submission. Thus, the ἰσότης which masters are required to give their slaves (4.1) looks more like 'equity' than 'equality' – or if the latter, it is of a kind that does not seriously threaten their ownership and control of their slaves.[11] One feature of this final verse (4.1) is, however, of greater significance: here masters (κύριοι) are told to remember that they too have a Master in heaven (κύριος ἐν οὐράνῳ). This word-play on κύριος – between human masters and the heavenly Master – is, as we shall see, an important rhetorical strategy in this household code, but we may simply note here its effect in the master-slave relationship. On the human level they remain to one another master and slave, but in the broader perspective of their status before Christ, they are all equally slaves of a heavenly κύριος. This implies that what is said of slaves in their service of the Lord Christ (3.22–25) could therefore equally apply to masters, who are also answerable (as slaves) to the Master, and under his constant supervision.

A second false trail finds particular significance in the fact that the subordinate members in each pairing are addressed, as well as their superiors. A long line of interpreters have found this a notable, even unprecedented, feature of this code. Here inferior members of the family (wives, children) are treated as morally responsible agents in their own right, while slaves are addressed as if competent to exhibit moral value; such has seemed to many an 'unusual conscientisation'.[12] The point is convincing, it seems to me, only if one limits one's attention to comparison with Stoic and other codes, which are typically addressed to the male *paterfamilias*. But there is plenty of evidence, in both moral tracts and everyday life, that wives, children and slaves were routinely given instructions implying moral effort and responsibility, and there is nothing especially remarkable or ennobling in the use of such direct address in this Colossian code. More remarkable, in fact, might be the *identical tone* of the address to both superior and subordinate partners: both are given direct, apodictic, commands on the assumption that all are under the same type of obligation. Once again, the explanation may lie

and Philemon (Leicester: IVP, 1986) 147–48 (unqualified).

[11] Cf. Philo's claim in *De Decalogo* 167 that a master's kindness and gentleness can 'equalise inequality' (δι' ὧν ἐξισοῦται τὸ ἄνισον). This passage (165–67) is also structured by the notion of reciprocal duties, which is hardly a Christian innovation.

[12] See most recently J.J. Meggitt, *Paul, Poverty and Survival* (Edinburgh: T & T Clark, 1998) 182; also Meeks, 'To Walk Worthily', 51 and many commentators. E. Schweizer, *Colossians* (London: SPCK, 1982) goes so far as to say that in the non-Christian codes 'the idea that women, children and slaves could also act in an ethically responsible way is scarcely even considered' (213).

in the last verse of the code, where even masters (who were also often the husbands and fathers in the household) are placed under the Master above.

These preliminary investigations suggest that if this code is integrated at all into the Christological framework of the letter, it is so primarily in its orientation, rather than its specific rules. Whatever might be our impatience to find the 'difference in practice', we should attend first to the signs of this structural Christianisation, which may turn out to be less superficial than it seems.[13]

Our first observation must be the heavy concentration of κύριος-language within this household code. The term appears, with reference to Christ, no less that seven times in these 9 verses, in the formula ἐν κυρίῳ (twice, 3.18, 20), in reference to 'fearing the Lord' (3.22), in the notion of working for, or serving, the Lord (3.23, 24), in the expectation of receiving a reward from the Lord (3.24), and in the reminder to human κύριοι that they too have a κύριος (4.1). This degree of repetition can hardly be accidental, and the play on words, between human and heavenly 'masters', is evident not only in 4.1 but also in the careful delineation of the human masters (always in the plural) as κατὰ σάρκα κύριοι (3.22). But this is neither the only nor the first time that Colossians has drawn attention to the Lordship of Christ. The title had been used, in fact, two or three times in the verses immediately preceding the household code: with reference to the Lord's forgiveness (3.13), possibly with reference to the 'word of the Lord' (3.16 – so א* and others; Nestlé-Aland follow the reading Χριστοῦ in P^{46}), and certainly in the important reference to performing all actions, whether word or deed, 'in the name of the Lord Jesus' (3.17). (Given the prominence of the term κύριος in the household code, one might even consider 3.17 as its heading, even if there is no syntactical connection between 3.17 and 3.18.) But the term κύριος has also appeared at crucial points earlier in the letter, and at precisely those places where we earlier identified the author's interest in ethics. Thus, at 1.10, the point of knowing the will of God is to walk 'worthily of the Lord in all that is pleasing to him' (περιπατῆσαι ἀξίως τοῦ κυρίου εἰς πᾶσαν ἀρεσκείαν), a phrase which chimes in remarkably closely with the command to children to do 'what is pleasing in the Lord' (εὐάρεστον

---

[13] The impatience with a (mere) difference of orientation is evident in Schweizer's complaint that 'merely to use a form of words expressing subordination to the "Lord" does not amount to much, if it does not effect a corresponding change in the content as well' *Colossians*, 217. R. MacMullen's essay, 'What Difference did Christianity make?' *Historia* 35 (1986) 322–43 is explicitly pragmatist in approach: to answer this question requires a test 'which must show Christians not just talking but doing; and it must show them in some opposition to evidently accepted standards. Without that opposition they cannot have produced any difference' (324). This is an understandable requirement, but also somewhat crude, since it cannot take into account the more intangible differences in worldview and ethos.

ἐν κυρίῳ, 3.20). Similarly, the strategic command to 'walk in him' (2.6) is premised on the affirmation that 'you have received the Christ Jesus (as) the Lord' (παρελάβετε τὸν Χριστὸν Ἰησοῦν τὸν κύριον).[14]

Thus the whole letter has drawn attention to the Lordship of Christ – and not just through the title κύριος. As we saw earlier, one of the leading themes of Colossians – pre-eminently in the hymn but not only there – is the authority, headship and priority of Christ, in all creation and through all time. Thus to submit to the Lordship of Christ is hardly a new or extraneous motif, but belongs to the core of this letter.[15] If the code concentrates this motif in the term κύριος, this has an important effect: not only does it enable the double-entendre which is exploited in the slave-master section, but it also, as Gielen has demonstrated, places all believers (whatever their social status) in the position of slaves (of Christ).[16] This metaphor is indeed alluded to elsewhere in the letter (1.7; 4.7 [σύνδουλος ἐν κυρίῳ]; cf. 4.17), but its explicit use in the code implies that, if even masters have a Master in heaven (4.1), so also do husbands, fathers, wives and children. Thus, the ἐν κυρίῳ formula in 3.18, 20 is no thoughtless piece of packaging, but a reminder, indeed an insistence, that the subordination here required is in ultimate service to the Master whom all serve. From this perspective, we can make good sense of the special concentration on the obligations of slaves in 3.22–25, for they become, as it were, the paradigm case of Christians who fulfil their household obligations within the context, and as an expression, of their ultimate allegiance to Christ. For slaves, the task of obeying their human masters (3.22) can be redefined as the task of serving Christ (τῷ κυρίῳ Χριστῷ δουλεύετε, 3.24)[17] – and so also can *all* Christian duties within the household. What is said here of slaves is easily applied by extension to all the other categories mentioned (cf. again 4.7, and the parallel instruction, universally applicable, in Rom 12.11); after all, pleasing the Master, rather than human authorities (ἀνθρωπάρεσκοι, 3.22), is what the author expects of them all (1.10).

---

[14] The word order suggests that 'Lord' is an apposition to 'the Christ Jesus'; see the discussion of alternative construals of this phrase in J. D. G. Dunn, *The Epistles to the Colossians and to Philemon* (Grand Rapids: Eerdmans, 1996) 139–40; cf. the earlier usage of the title in 1.3.

[15] Cf. P. Pokorný, *Colossians. A Commentary* (Peabody: Hendrickson, 1991) 177–78.

[16] M. Gielen, *Tradition und Theologie neutestamentliche Haustafelethik* (BBB 75, Frankfurt a. M.: Anton Hain, 1990) 107–21. This is an extremely valuable discussion of the structural features of 3.18–4.1, which is also noted and effectively employed by A. Lincoln, 'The Household Code and the Wisdom Mode of Colossians' *JSNT* 74 (1999) 93–112; at several points the present essay runs along lines parallel to those drawn by Lincoln.

[17] Most commentators take this sentence as an imperative, in which case, as Gielen notes, it matches and redefines the imperative of 3.22 (*Tradition*, 109, 112–13).

Thus the household code represents a consistent attempt to apply the Christology of the letter to the realm of household duties, or, to put it the other way around, to bring even the mundane duties of everyday relations under the Lordship of Christ. It is thus entirely consistent with the universalising thrust of the letter as a whole, in which the tendrils of the Christ-event spread out, as it were, to cover the whole surface of life. This *theological* explanation of the presence of the code somewhat lessens (though it does not disqualify) the desire to find immediate *historical* explanations for its first appearance in this letter. Explanations abound. Is the author trying to counter a radical 'enthusiasm' within the church, which took Gal 3.28 as its charter of freedom?[18] Is he countering the otherworldly asceticism of the 'heresy' with a 'good worldliness' of commitment to the household?[19] Is there an apologetic purpose here, to show that the Christian movement poses no threat to the stability of the household (cf. 4.5)?[20] Or is the extended section on slaves written with special reference to Onesimus (4.9) and the problems revealed in the letter to Philemon?[21] If none of these explanations are entirely convincing, I would also judge none of them truly necessary. The author of Colossians lived in a social world structured by households, with their standard expectations of how their members would behave. It was his special concern to show that the one whom Christians confess as Lord/Master is not some local deity, or private cult hero, but the agent and rationale for all creation and all human existence. It is surely natural that he would press this point by specifying how 'doing everything in the name of the Lord Jesus' (3.17) would change the meaning of life in the household, the primary context in which practically all believers lived and where they needed to know how to 'please the Master'.

Thus the achievement of the Colossian household code is to interpret household relations within the framework of allegiance to the Lord. This

[18] So J.E. Crouch, *The Origin and Intention of the Colossian Haustafel* (Göttingen: Vandenhoeck & Ruprecht, 1972); however there are no signs of such a 'revolutionary' spirit in the context addressed by Colossians (if indeed they existed at all in early Christianity), nor can the instructions to children make sense on this score.

[19] So E. Schweizer in his commentary and associated essays (e.g. 'Traditional Ethical Patterns in the Pauline and post-Pauline letters and their development (lists of vices and house-tables)', in E. Best and R. McL. Wilson, eds., *Text and Interpretation.* [Cambridge: Cambridge University, 1979] 195–209; 'Die Weltlichkeit des neuen Testaments: die Haustafeln', in *idem*, *Neues Testament und Christologie im Werden: Aufsätze* [Göttingen: Vandenhoeck & Ruprecht, 1982] 194–210). However, there is no sign that the 'ascetic' rules of the 'heresy' (as we see them reflected in 2.16–23) involved any significant withdrawal from household obligations or responsibilities.

[20] This is D.L. Balch's thesis with regard to the code in 1 Peter (*Let Wives be Submissive. The Domestic Code in 1 Peter* [Chico: Scholars Press, 1981]); it is applied to the Colossian code by Lincoln, 'Household Code', 110–11.

[21] So J. Knox, *Philemon among the Letters of Paul* (Nashville: Abingdon, 1959).

is more than just a change in motivation (though it alters that too): it re-describes and thereby re-evaluates how Christians act in the household, providing a distinctively Christian life-hermeneutic by reconceiving their roles, their actions and their purposes. The believer who loves his wife, or the child who obeys her parents, does so now not simply as a husband or a child; they are servants of the Lord, whose status ἐν κυρίῳ gives them a new identity which encompasses all their household roles. Their duties are now performed to, and for, the Lord, whatever proximate purposes they may also serve. Hence the act itself gains a new moral significance, a new meaning: a Christian slave now attends to his master's affairs *as an act of service to the (true) Master*, placing ordinary tasks in a different interpretative framework. As Geertz shows, this enclosing of routine human activity in a religious worldview is not an innocent or insignificant move: 'it alters, often radically, the whole landscape presented to common sense, alters it in such a way that the moods and motivations induced by religious practice seem themselves supremely practical, the only sensible ones to adopt given the way things "really" are'.[22]

The best illustration of this practical effect is in the paradigmatic instructions given to slaves in 3.22–25. Here slaves are encouraged to work with integrity, not just from a general sense of the fear of the Lord (3.22), but because they are to reconceive their work as being, in fact, for the Master himself, not for their human masters (ἐκ ψυχῆς ἐργάζεσθε ὡς τῷ κυρίῳ καὶ οὐκ ἀνθρώποις, 3.23). The instruction to obey their masters (3.22) is thus restated in other, and more appropriate terms in 3.24: serve the Master, Christ. This transforms the sense that slaves (and by extension, other members of the household) can give to their lives. Its many tasks appear on the surface to serve only human needs and requests, but in answering a master's request, they can now think of themselves as obeying the commands of their (heavenly) Master. Thus all of life becomes an unseen transaction between believer as slave and Jesus as Master; what is truly going on may be invisible to others, but is none the less real for that. To conceive of life ἐν κυρίῳ is thus to place it within a different framework: far from being empty, the formula is a verbal and conceptual symbol which, like many sacred symbols, evokes a whole worldview and invests a routine act or object with profound religious significance. It is in this sense that believers are to 'seek the things above' (3.1) or 'think on the things above' (3.2) precisely in the

[22] C. Geertz, 'Religion as a Cultural System', in *The Interpretation of Cultures* (New York: Fontana, 1993) 87–125, at 122. He also notes, however, the variations in the degree to which a religious worldview colours people's sense of reality: the effect may be more or less pervasive or profound (124). In a similar vein, Meeks notes that ethics (not least in Colossians) 'is a hermeneutical process' ('To Walk Worthily', 47).

performance of their household tasks. There is no real paradox in the placing of the household code under the rubric of 'seeking the things above', since our author does not call members of the household simply to fulfil their responsibilities, but to fulfil them to, or in, the Lord: they seek the things above precisely by serving their Master in heaven (4.1). In this sense all of everyday life is decisively changed, not only in those instances where Christian practices stand out visibly from the rest, but also where Christians appear to behave no differently from others. It is possible to do something quite different in performing the routine and the conventional, because it is possible in performing these acts to serve the Master.

It is clear that, to preserve this sense of 'reality', believers are going to need continual reinforcement of their distinctive worldview. It is not easy to sustain the conviction that every act is a hidden transaction with one's Master unless one is repeatedly reminded of this 'real reality' and unless it is internalised so powerfully as to displace the competing 'commonsense' alternative. It is thus no accident that, as we noted above, this letter is replete with references to knowledge, wisdom and understanding. To receive the gospel is here to 'know' and 'learn' it (1.6–7), and its truth is what the author feels continually obliged to 'teach in all wisdom' (1.28; cf. 2.7). When he prays that they be perfected in 'the knowledge of [God's] will, in all wisdom and spiritual understanding' (1.9), this is not just the wisdom to know what is right to do, but also the cognitive resources to interpret themselves and their lives aright. Slaves can only work with the right disposition if they know (εἰδότες) that they will receive their reward from the Master (3.24), just as human masters need to know (εἰδότες) that they have a Master in heaven (4.1). Hence an important part of Christian responsibility to one another is that 'the word of Christ [or, the Lord] dwell in you richly, as you *teach and admonish one another*' (3.16). Without that teaching and its constant reality-reinforcement, it would be easy to lose one's hold on that special dimension which makes ordinary life so different.

In the same context there is particular mention of the community life of worship, 'singing psalms, hymns and spiritual songs, with gratefulness in your hearts to God' (3.16). Thanksgiving is, in fact, a very prominent theme in this letter, the verb εὐχαριστεῖν and its cognate noun appearing no less than six times (1.3, 12; 2.7; 3.15, 17; 4.2). It is noticeable that these occurrences cluster precisely where the author provides underpinning for the practical commitments of believers – and understandably so. Not only does the act of thanksgiving reorientate the believer to the divine reality, it also implies the acceptance of present conditions as those in which Christ can be worshipped and served. Thus to 'do everything in the name of the Lord Jesus, *thanking God through him*' (3.17) is to reaffirm the reality of the Lordship of Christ, in creation and redemption, and thus to reinforce the sense that it is possible and glorious to serve Christ in what is truly his own domain. Thankfulness makes life both purposeful and hopeful.[23]

In thus transforming the purpose and meaning of ordinary life, the Colossian household code also inculcates some special character traits. The phrase 'whatever you do' in 3.17 is repeated in 3.23, where the quality of this action is given some definition: whatever you do, you should work 'from the heart' (ἐκ ψυχῆς), since you are really serving the Master, not a human owner. In the same way, the slave should perform his tasks 'not with eye-service' (ὀφθαλμοδουλία – a Colossian neologism), but with simplicity (or integrity) of heart (ἐν ἁπλότητι καρδίας, 3.22). This not only gives special dignity to the Christian slave (who serves no less than the Master of the universe); it also induces a particular self-discipline, as the slave (and, by extension, every believer) finds every act an opportunity for service, and can find no excuse to shirk or make do with the minimum. This is an extraordinarily strenuous demand, which requires the commitment of the whole person, and underlines the moral seriousness of even 'mundane' activities. It is not fanciful to detect here an embryonic sense of that 'Protestant ethic' which Weber illuminated.[24] Here, as in the Reformation, religion penetrates to all spheres of life, private as well as public, and endues all kinds of work with a sanctity and moral earnestness which requires maximum concentration and commitment. Although Colossians lacks that special Calvinist sense of the need to prove one's election in the fulfilment of one's 'calling', there is a clear connection in the concern to Christianise the whole of life, and in the discipline and 'innerweltliche Askese' which this requires. A peculiar wholeheartedness is required of those who take even domestic duty as the testing ground of their service to their true Master.

IV. An Ambiguous Legacy

We may conclude, then, that the Colossian household code is profoundly 'Christianised' even if, to an outside observer, Christian wives, children and slaves performed no differently to their non-Christian counterparts, beyond taking their (conventional) duties with the utmost seriousness. The new Christian rationale for, and comprehension of, domestic roles does not necessarily result in visible difference. This is not, I think, an accidental feature in a letter which also celebrates the fact that its 'circumcision' is 'made without hands' (2.11), since there is now neither Jew nor Greek, cir-

[23] Cf. Lincoln, 'Household Code', 109.

[24] M. Weber, *The Protestant Ethic and the Spirit of Capitalism* (reprint; London: Routledge, 1992).

cumcision nor uncircumcision (3.11). This culture-spanning consciousness has given to the early Christian movement a certain reluctance to tie the expression of Christian faith too tightly to any single, culturally particular, practice. Simultaneous with the desire to express faith in the practical business of everyday life is the concern not to let human δόγματα disqualify one expression of Christian faith in favour of another (2.16–23). Whatever the believer does or says must be done in the name of the Lord (3.17), and this induces some real changes of conduct (3.9); but the primary significance of the act lies less in its content than in its orientation – the fact that it is done to and for the Lord. In this sense the author may truly affirm that 'your life is *hidden* with Christ in God' (3.3): he is not denying that they should express that life in their daily conduct, but suggesting that its value will only become evident when it comes to be assessed not by human observers but by the Lord (3.4, 24). Thus, while it is crucial that believers live out their service to Christ *in* their present conditions, it is equally important that they are living not *for* those conditions but for the Lord. It is therefore possible to serve the Lord, and equally well, either as Jew or as Greek, indeed even in the cultural conditions of 'barbarians' and 'Scythians', since within each sphere one can turn one's particular responsibilities and duties into acts of service to the heavenly Master (3.11).

Such a moral strategy leaves an ambiguous legacy, containing both radical and conservative elements. On the one hand, since the believers' ultimate commitments are to their Master not to their social conditions, this weakens any impulse to change those conditions, to which Christians can exercise almost Stoic-like indifference. Any amelioration of conditions would not, in fact, guarantee their ultimate value, since what counts is how one lives to the Lord, not the conditions in which one does so. If even the worst conditions (e.g. of slavery) can be made purposeful, as an arena for serving Christ, they are also made endurable – much to the master's relief. What is more, the household code comes extremely close to sanctioning the present hierarchical structures as if they were supervised and supported by the ultimate Master, Christ. If all the power structures of the cosmos (εἴτε θρόνοι εἴτε κυριότητες εἴτε ἀρχαὶ εἴτε ἐξουσίαι, 1.16) were created by and for Christ, and if that creation-order has been restored and redeemed by the cross of Christ, one could easily conclude that the κύριοι in the master-slave relationship were fulfilling their Christ-sanctioned role in the hierarchical pattern of the universe. Indeed, it is but a short step from the Colossian code to identifying service to the human master as service to Christ. Although the author is careful to distinguish between human masters (κύριοι κατὰ σάρκα) and the Master above, to serve the latter *while* serving the former gets perilously close to serving the latter *in* serving the former. Before long, unquestioning service to the master can be presented as essential for the good reputation of the faith (Tit 2.9–10), and the master himself can be taken to stand as God's representative (ὑποταγήσεσθε τοῖς κυρίοις ὡς τύπῳ θεοῦ, Did 4.11; cf. Barn 19.7). And we can hardly ignore the fact that to make slaves responsible for pleasing not their human masters but the Lord (3.22) is to extract from them service of a far higher standard than any master could dream of obtaining by ordinary sanctions. If their work is no longer merely 'eye-service' (3.22), they are made conscious of the continuous, penetrating surveillance exercised by the heavenly Master. Slaves are thus placed in a perfect Benthamite Panopticon, and the greatest beneficiary is the master they serve.[25]

However, the moral strategy of the Colossian code is not simply a reactionary charter. If believers are to live to the Lord *in* these domestic conditions, they are not committed *to* them as the only or absolute expression of the Lord's will: it might be possible to adopt a complex stance of 'detached involvement', not unlike the ὡς μή policy of 1 Cor 7.29–31. If slaves find in their slavery an arena for serving the Lord, there is nothing to say that they can *only* serve Christ in that condition, since the freed and free also serve the Master in their own way (4.1; cf. 1 Cor 7.20–24). Indeed, since slavery is, primarily, an arena for serving Christ, it is possible to put a critical distance between the merely earthly masters (κύριοι κατὰ σάρκα, 3.22) and the heavenly Master, even to the extent of refusing the one for the sake of the other. To be sure, the blanket instruction, ὑπακούετε κατὰ πάντα (3.22), hardly encourages such a critical stance, but the reference to 'fearing the Lord' (3.22) and the commitment to justice (3.25; 4.1) make it possible to justify what the household code of 1 Peter presupposes: that Christian slaves, in serving the Lord, can deliberately *disobey* their human masters, and thereby suffer for the sake of righteousness (1 Pet 2.19–25).[26] In the same way, it might be possible to interpret the requirement of wives to submit to their husbands ὡς ἀνῆκεν ἐν κυρίῳ (3.18) as implying a Christian *qualification* of that submission.[27] Again, 1 Peter shows that a Christian household code can simultaneously encourage wifely submission while

---

[25] On Bentham's Panopticon and its perfection of surveillance see especially M. Foucault, *Discipline and Punish. The Birth of the Prison* (London: Penguin, 1991) 195–228. One may also observe, however, that masters are here situated in the same spiritual Panopticon.

[26] An obvious point of conflict might be the sexual demands of their owners (where 3.5 sets a high moral standard); it is not clear, however, how far Christian slaves could or did withstand the advances of their owners, who knew they had a right to their bodies, not just their work. See the discussion of this issue by J. A. Glancy, 'Obstacles to Slaves' Participation in the Corinthian Church' *JBL* 117 (1998) 481–501. [Cf. J. Glancy, *Slavery in Early Christianity* (Oxford: Oxford University, 2002); J. A. Harrill, *Slaves in the New Testament: Literary, Social and Moral Dimensions* (Minneapolis: Fortress, 2006).]

[27] So Dunn, *Epistles*, 247–48.

encouraging her to maintain her faith *despite* the evident disapproval, even threats, of her non-Christian spouse (1 Peter 3.1–6). Whether such a critical stance could be maintained within a solidly 'Christian' household is, of course, another matter.

It may be possible to find in the Colossian code the first signs of a realisation that the fulfilment of domestic duties and responsibilities should be performed not just 'to the Lord' but also in a specifically Christian way. The instructions to husbands not to be harsh with their wives (3.19), and to fathers not to provoke their children (3.21), may be influenced by the virtues of kindness, gentleness and forgiveness which were advocated in 3.12–13 and given there a distinctively Christian flavour. Similarly, the promise to slaves of a reward from the heavenly Master (3.24), and the threat of punishment from the same source (3.25), suggest the application of a moral standard of which Christ alone is the judge; and since the slave's accountability here is paradigmatic of that applicable to all the members of a household, it could be said that a Christian morality is implicitly imposed on all. Thus it is possible that the love which is required of husbands in regard to their wives, although not uniquely Christian in this verbal expression, is expected to derive its character from the love received and experienced in Christ.[28] If so, these are no more than hints and suggestions in the Colossian code, and it is only in the later developments of this tradition that the quality of behaviour in the household is given explicitly Christian colouring. The Ephesian code, apparently based on that in Colossians, indicates the sort of directions this could take, with the husband's love, for instance, given a Christian rationale and an exacting Christ-like standard (Eph 5.21–33).

Thus the Colossian code bears the potential for a more thorough Christianisation of its rules of conduct, which might help shape the quality of relations and even the nature of authority within the household. But we must not overestimate the strength of this 'reforming' potential, for its capacity to ameliorate household conditions does not entail the power to challenge its structures. It is hard to find anything in the Colossian household code which provides the resources to confront the structure of slavery itself; indeed, by giving meaning to the slave's service, and by setting standards for the master's behaviour, it gives every appearance of confirming slavery as a social condition fully compatible with Christian morality. We may contrast with this Philo's instructions on the conduct of the Sabbath rest within the household (*Spec. Leg.* 2.65–70). Here the provision of rest for slaves is taken to represent for them 'the ember or spark of freedom' as they look forward

[28] The majority of commentators take ἀγαπᾶν in this special Christian sense, although Crouch, *Origin* 111–13, vigorously contests this on the basis of non-Christian linguistic parallels.

to their possible manumission, a reward for loyal service (2.67). Colossians raises no such hope on the earthly level: slaves may look forward to an inheritance (κληρονομία) from Christ, not from their human masters, since a merely worldly inheritance – the ownership of property which accompanies or results from manumission – is presumably of no ultimate significance. But Philo also goes much further. In the same context he notes that even animals are exempt from Sabbath work, even though one might expect the law to make a fundamental distinction between animals and slaves. For the latter, says Philo, are free by nature (φύσει ἐλεύθεροι), since no human being is by nature a slave (ἄνθρωπος γὰρ ἐκ φύσεως δοῦλος οὐδείς, 2.69). The comment is made in passing, and is not used by Philo to question the practice of slavery, but one cannot miss its radical potential, and its unusual expression of the principle of human equality.[29] History has shown that Philo's principle had far more potential to destabilise social structures than the formula of Col 3.11, and it is not difficult to see why. Where Colossians relativises human differences from the perspective of 'the things above', its investment lies not in human status or condition but in the use of those conditions for the service of the Lord. Philo's principle, on the other hand, draws attention to nature, and thus points to the earthly sphere as the locus where the human problematic is to be resolved. The course of western history makes it arguable that, without this humanistic impulse, the Christian tradition would never have been able to free itself from the assumption that slavery (and, correlatively, gender inequality) was compatible with a Christian ethos.

Thus the legacy of the Colossian code is neither inherently radical nor straightforwardly conservative. If it has no *principled* commitment to the patriarchal conditions of the household in antiquity (they are only the conditions *in which* one serves the Lord), it also presents no *principled* opposition to them. It represents that 'Christian patriarchalism' which Troeltsch analysed, in which 'conservative and revolutionary elements in Christian thought were united to and conditioned by each other'.[30] The reason it could combine both in this complex interplay is because it developed a comprehensive life-hermeneutic which was not dependent on the attainment or enjoyment of any particular life-conditions. In the Colossian moral strategy it was possible (and necessary) to 'serve the Lord' in all the different household roles, in all sorts of cultural conditions, and whether that service did, or did not, create a visible difference in the character of Christian action. Rather than a social revolution, Colossians represents a cognitive

[29] For the degree to which this was unusual see P. Garnsey, *Ideas of Slavery from Aristotle to Augustine* (Cambridge: Cambridge University, 1996).

[30] E. Troeltsch, *The Social Teaching of the Christian Churches* (London: G. Unwin, 1931) 1:69–89, here at 84.

revolution, by which the whole of life is brought under the authority of 'the Master', and every act and word, whether recognisably 'Christian' or not, is internally Christianised by being offered up in thanks to God and in service to Christ. Despite our moral reservations, we should not underestimate this ambitious programme, in which the reconciliation effected by the Christ event is applied in order truly to unite all things in Christ. Colossians, too long sidelined as a 'deutero-Pauline' letter, thus represents a considerable theological achievement, whose capacity to stimulate Christian theology continues to this day.[31]

[31] [Cf. R. Roitto, 'Act as a Christ-Believer, as a Household Member or as Both? A Cognitive Perspective on the Relation between the Social Identity in Christ and Household Identities in Pauline and Deutero-Pauline Texts', in B. Holmberg and M Winninge, eds., *Identity Formation in the New Testament* (WUNT 227: Tübingen: Mohr Siebeck, 2008) 141–61.]

13. There Is Neither Old nor Young?

Early Christianity and Ancient Ideologies of Age

Considerable research has been focused in recent decades on gender differentials in early Christianity, alongside differences in ethnicity, wealth, legal status, and social location. By contrast, very little attention has been paid to differentials in age, despite the fact that several early Christian texts make explicit comment on generational divides. The instructions in these texts, both within and outwith the New Testament, refer to 'the older' and 'the younger' in terms loaded with moral and political assumptions; and although such age-group relations clearly had structural significance for early Christian communities, it is rarely discussed how they participated in larger cultural systems of value and power. Recent discussion of the development of offices in the early church, including Alastair Campbell's book on *The Elders*, has re-opened the question of the relationship between office, honour and seniority in age,[1] but there is still much to be learned in this area, not least from the recent outpouring of classical scholarship on the life-cycle in antiquity and on the place of the 'older' generation within it.[2] Given the breadth of this topic, I shall confine myself to literature broadly in the Pauline tradition, but the results could be relevant to those working in other fields.

---

[1] R. A. Campbell, *The Elders: Seniority within Earliest Christianity* (Edinburgh: T & T Clark, 1994). Among other things, this succeeded in overturning the old consensus that early Christians took over the 'office' of 'elder' specifically from Judaism. His survey of 'the status of older people in the Graeco-Roman world' (79–90) is suggestive, though the focus of his study is on how the title of 'elder' developed within early Christian churches.

[2] On the life-cycle approach, see, e. g., M. Harlow and R. Laurence, *Growing Up and Growing Old in Ancient Rome* (London: Routledge, 2002). The upsurge of interest in old age in Western societies has helped spawn a new focus on the representations and realities of old age in both Greek and Roman antiquity. See, e. g., K. Cokayne, *Experiencing Old Age in Ancient Rome* (London: Routledge, 2003); T. G. Parkin, *Old Age in the Roman World: A Cultural and Social History* (Baltimore: Johns Hopkins University, 2003). On age in early Christianity, see C. Gnilka, 'Greisenalter' *RAC* 12 (1983) 995–1094 and idem, *Aetas Spiritualis: die Überwindung der natürlichen Altersstufen als Ideal frühchristlichen Lebens* (Bonn: Hanstein, 1972). For bibliography (up to 1989) see E. Eyben, 'Old Age in Greco-Roman Antiquity and Early Christianity', in T. M. Falkner and J. de Luce, eds., *Old Age in Greek and Latin Literature* (Albany, NY: SUNY, 1989) 230–51.

We may start with some observations and a few simple questions. By the end of the first century, leaders of the Christian movement, in many of its branches, were called πρεσβύτεροι, as witnessed by texts as diverse as James (5.14), 1 Peter (5.1, 5), Acts (11.30; 14.23; 15.2, 4, etc.), the Pastorals (1 Tim 5.17; Titus 1.5–9), and, perhaps, the shorter Johannine epistles (2 John 1; 3 John 1). What is more, in a range of texts (1 Peter; the Pastorals; *1 Clement*; Polycarp, *Philippians*), instructions are given to adult members of the church using the simple polarity of 'older' and 'younger' (usually πρεσβύτεροι and νεώτεροι; see below). Normally in such texts the comparative adjective is used, but sometimes the positive form is found (νέαι or the noun πρεσβῦται; cf. Titus 2.2–4); in either case it is implied that, between them, these labels embrace the whole adult congregation.[3] What do such apparently vague terms mean and why is this binary sufficient to cover everyone? How did one know whether one was in the 'older' or 'younger' category? Was it possible to be neither, but something in between? Just as importantly, what ideological freight do such terms carry – what moral and social expectations would have clustered around them, and what ideological work are they being required to perform in Christian texts? And if these were, as we shall see, common terms for the totality of an adult population, why do we *not* find them within the authentic Pauline letters – neither the term πρεσβύτερος nor indeed any reference to people's age, beyond the mention of the centenerian Abraham (Rom 4.19) and Paul's reference to himself, in Philemon 9, as a πρεσβύτης?[4] Is this absence of age vocabulary

[3] The comparative πρεσβύτεροι is used in the NT as follows: a) on its own, with reference to: the 'elders' of the Jews (e.g. Matt 26.3); the 'elders' of the church (e.g. Acts 14.23; 1 Tim 5.17; 2 John 1 [singular]; Jas 5.14); 'elders' as general figures of authority (e.g. Matt 15.2); the 'elders' in the heavenly courtroom (e.g. Rev 4.4); b) in conjunction with νεώτεροι: in address to congregations: 1 Pet 5.1–5; 1 Tim 5.1–2 (both male and female forms); with reference to 'older' and 'younger' brothers (Luke 15.12, 25); c) in conjunction with νεανίσκοι (Acts 2.17). The noun πρεσβῦται / πρεσβύτιδες is used in conjunction with νεώτεροι / νέαι in instructions to the church (Titus 2.2–6), or on its own (Phlm 9, singular). The comparative νεώτεροι / νεώτεραι is found sometimes in a comparative context (in contrast to πρεσβύτεροι, Luke 15.12; 1 Pet 5.5; 1 Tim 5.1–2; or simply to πρεσβῦται / πρεσβύτιδες, Titus 2.2–6; or in implicit contrast with the widows aged 60 and over, 1 Tim 5.11, 14; cf. John 21.18 [ὅτε ἦς νεώτερος in contrast to ὅταν γηράσῃς]), but sometimes not (Acts 5.6, identical in meaning to νεανίσκοι, Acts 5.10). νέαι has a comparative sense, though not a comparative form, in Titus 2.4 (juxtaposed with νεώτεροι, Titus 2.6). These facts suggest that the terms 'young' and 'younger' are in most contexts synonymous (as are 'old man' and 'older man'); in other words, even the non-comparative forms generally carry an implicit comparative sense, since such age labels are almost always defined *by comparison with* one another.

[4] Bentley's emendation (to πρεσβεύτης) has been rightly dismissed by Birdsall; see J.N. Birdsall, 'πρεσβύτης in Philemon 9: A Study in Conjectural Emendation' *NTS* 39 (1993) 625–30. It is still just possible that πρεσβύτης could be interpreted to mean 'ambassador' (so J.B. Lightfoot, *The Epistles of St. Paul to the Colossians, to Philemon* [5th ed.; London: Macmillan, 1880] 338–39; M. Barth and H. Blanke, *The Letter to Philemon*

a purely accidental phenomenon, or does Paul's silence on age differentials suggest a different social configuration, even a different theological anthropology?

I. The Binary of 'The Old' and 'The Young'

Let us begin with some demographic facts – or at least reconstructions.[5] In the most recent estimates, the high rates of infant mortality put average life-expectancy at birth in the range of 20–30 years. Of course, for those who survived into their teens, the future looked better, but the number of people living beyond the age of 60 was still, compared to the modern Western world, extremely low. According to estimates used by Parkin, if we set average life-expectancy at birth at 25, and if we take a cross section of the population of the early Roman empire, we would find about 60 % of the population to be under the age of 30; about a third (33 %) between the ages of 30 and 59; and only about 7 % over the age of 60 (dropping to 4 % over the age of 65).[6] Of course, some individuals are known to have lived into their 70 s, even their 80 s and 90 s, but plenty of sources indicate that people who died in their 60 s would be considered to have lived a full

[Grand Rapids: Eerdmans, 2000] 321–3), but there is no difficulty in giving the term its normal meaning 'old man', which makes sense as a ground for Paul's appeal and should probably be preferred (so, e.g., P. Stuhlmacher, *Der Brief an Philemon* [EKK; Zürich: Benziger, 1975] 37–8).

[5] The demography of ancient societies – based on the sparse record of tombstones, census returns from Egypt, and the analysis of skeletons – is a precarious science, which depends in large part on the slightly fuller record of pre-industrial societies in parallel conditions; see T. G. Parkin, *Demography and Roman Society* (Baltimore: Johns Hopkins University, 1992) and R. P. Saller, *Patriarchy, Property and Death in the Roman Family* (Cambridge: Cambridge University, 1994) 9–69. These utilise the model life tables of Coale and Demeny which assess age-distributions of stable populations according to varying estimates of life-expectancy at birth. It is generally accepted that the closest model to the conditions of the ancient world is Coale-Demeny[2] West Level 3 (female), with life-expectancy at birth averaged at 25; see Parkin, *Old Age*, 36–56, 280 (table 3); Saller, *Patriarchy*, 22–25. But the field is fraught with difficulty; see the critique by W. Scheidel, 'Roman Age Structure: Evidence and Models' *JRS* 91 (2001) 1–26; idem, ed., *Debating Roman Demography* (Leiden: Brill, 2001). Scheidel doubts the value of the Coale-Demeny models (except for highly schematic calculations of kinship structures), and emphasises the likelihood of greater adult mortality (due to disease and malnutrition). The following figures may, thus, overestimate the percentage of the population who lived to and beyond the age of 60.

[6] Parkin, *Old Age*, 280, Table 3; the aggregation of the relevant percentage figures at Level 3 (life expectancy at birth of 25) is more precisely: 59.64 %; 33.38 %; and 6.98 %, dropping to 4.07 % over 65. But the precise figures give a spurious sense of accuracy, and if these tables are of any value at all (see previous note), they are useful only for giving a very rough sense of possible age profiles. We should perhaps be content with a rough sense that only 5 % – 8 % of the population was over the age of 60.

life.[7] If we think this through in terms of generations, the results are interesting. Parkin reckons that the average age of marriage for men in the Roman world was 30, for women 15.[8] That would mean that by the time he reached 10, a boy would have a father aged 40 and a paternal grandfather, if he was very lucky, aged 70. When the boy reached 20, his father would be 50, and his paternal grandfather would be alive only if he had survived till the age of 80. Even if we reduce the average age at marriage for men to 25, the paternal grandfather would have to live to 70 to witness his grandson's twentieth birthday – only likely, as we have seen, for a tiny percentage of the population.[9] Thus by the time a young male began to become socially and politically active, he would have had, for all intents and purposes, only one generation above him – even his *maternal* grandfather would be in the thin bracket of 60-year olds.[10] Adult life was, for practically everyone, a two generation phenomenon.[11] To put this in other terms, there were too few people in the 60+ age-bracket for them to constitute a socially significant age-class of their own.

This already alerts us to the fact that age-categories, in antiquity as today, are the product of history and culture. While we may each count our own age in years (with more or less accuracy or honesty),[12] the age-categories into which we place ourselves, or are placed by others, are manifestly social constructs. In the Greek and Roman worlds, at puberty a boy became a 'youth' (νεανίας; *adulescens*) and a girl, in most cases, a wife; thereafter there

---

[7] Livy (*apud* Seneca *Suas.* 6.22) considered Cicero's death at 63 not premature, while Statius thought his father's death (at 65) neither early nor late (*Silv.* 5.3.252–4).

[8] Parkin, *Old Age*, 51–52. There is some evidence that in elite Roman families men may have married earlier (ca. 25). For the average age of marriage for Roman men, see R.P. Saller, 'Men's Age at Marriage and its Consequences in the Roman Family' *CP* 82 (1987) 20–35.

[9] It is possible that the marriage age for Jewish men was lower (as young as 18: see *m. Aboth* 5.21 and the anecdote of the married 18 year-old in *b. Ber.* 28a, cited below; cf. 1QSa 1.9–11 [not below 20]. I am grateful to Dr. Roger Aus for advice on this point and for reference to the rabbinic sources gathered in Strack-Billerbeck 2.373–5). But it is not clear if this was so in the Diaspora; and, in any case, most of the churches addressed in the texts here studied were predominantly Gentile.

[10] Saller's tables for senatorial families (*Patriarchy*, 54–9, Table 3.2) give precise figures using Coale-Demeny^2 Level 3 West: only 13 % of men aged 20 would have had a living grandfather of either sort, only 3 % a living paternal grandfather.

[11] This was complicated, of course, by the different ages at marriage of men and women: a man's father-in-law was likely to be in the generation space between himself and his father; see Harlow and Laurence, *Growing Up*, 92–103. The point here is that there was no significant presence of a generation *above* that of his father or father-in-law.

[12] There is evidence in antiquity that individuals were likely to know their birthdays (for celebrations or astrological calculations) better than the exact year of their birth (Parkin, *Old Age*, 33–4); it is common in epitaphs for ages to be rounded to the nearest five; see R.P. Duncan-Jones, 'Age-Rounding, Illiteracy and Social Differentiation in the Roman Empire' *Chiron* 7 (1977) 333–53.

were no *physiological* transitions which demarcated the remaining course of a human life.[13] In the midst of the gradual and constant process of ageing, stages in life, if they are marked at all, have to be culturally imposed.[14] In ancient narratives – histories and novels – the age of characters is often, in fact, *unmarked*; it is either unknown or irrelevant to the story being told. Where it is marked, it bears some narrative significance, and it is striking how those individuals whose age is noted are generally labelled either 'young' or 'old'. In Xenophon's *Ephesiaca*, where 15 of the 45 characters are classified in age, all these are identified as either 'young' or 'old': 'young' where they are beautiful, marriageable or full of passion (e.g., 1.2: Habrocomes and Anthia; 1.13: Corymbus; 2.3: Manto and Rhode), and 'old' where they are soon to die or in stereotypical roles, such as the elderly tutor, the retired soldier, or the garrulous old woman (e.g., 1.14: Habrocomes' elderly τροφεύς; 3.9: the garrulous Chrysion; 3.12: Araxus, the former soldier).[15] There are no 'middle-aged' people noted here: *their* age would contribute nothing to the narrative or to their character profile. In Chariton's *Callirhoe*, the same is true (the young hero and heroine, 1.1; the half-dead elderly father, 3.5; the wise elderly philosopher, 8.3) – or, rather, the one exception, Dionysius, proves the rule: he is introduced as a man 'in the prime of life' (ἡλικίᾳ καθεστώς, 1.12.6), only so that when he falls madly in love with Callirhoe he chides himself for being immature, behaving like an adolescent (2.3–4). In Luke-Acts the narrative profile is similar: children, 'youths' and 'old people' are noted, very occasionally with their exact age (e.g., Anna: Luke 2.36–7); but most people remain unmarked in age.[16] Not everyone has to be put into

[13] The menopause is a possible exception for women. Though it is never explicitly noted as a moment of category-transition, there are some indications of changes in attitude to women once they were considered infertile (Harlow and Laurence, *Growing Up*, 127–9). The rules on the support of widows over 60 in 1 Tim 5.3–16 may be a case in point ('younger widows' are expected to marry and bear children, 5.11–15); although 60 seems a high threshold for the menopause, it is not unparalleled in antiquity (Soranus *Gyn*. 1.6.20).

[14] The point is widely recognised in the sociology and anthropology of ageing. For a study of African social systems, in which physiological and 'structural' age are clearly distinct phenomena, see B. Bernardi, *Age Class Systems: Social Institutions and Politics Based on Age* (Cambridge: Cambridge University, 1985).

[15] I am grateful to Prof. Tomas Hägg for pointing me to the Greek novels for evidence of the marking, or non-marking, of age.

[16] How old were Joseph, Herod, Pilate, Stephen, Barnabas, Philip? The question is of no interest to Luke. The advanced ages of Zechariah and Elizabeth (Luke 1.7, 18, 36) are important to the narrative, as is the youthfulness of the son of the widow of Nain (Luke 7.12–14) and of the boy Jesus (Luke 2.42). Anna's great age (2.36–7), with her long period of widowhood, demonstrates her purity in reception of prophecy; the age of the lame man healed by Peter and John indicates how miraculous is his healing (Acts 4.23). It is not entirely clear why Luke marks the age of Jesus as 'about 30' at the start of his ministry (Luke 3.23); there may be echoes of Joseph (Gen 41.46) or David (2 Sam 5.4), or an allusion to the age of Moses (32) 'when he began to instruct Israel in Egypt' (*Num. Rabbah* Naso 14.18 on Num 7.85 [suggested to me by Dr. Aus]; but cf. *Exod. Rabbah* 1.27, 30).

an age bracket, but when they are, the terms 'young' and 'old' are the ones most frequently used and most culturally significant.

This conclusion is largely corroborated elsewhere. Certain specialised discourses might divide the lifespan into precise units, or mark exact age for the sake of legal entitlement or obligation. Medical and astronomical calculations, for instance, might divide a life into 7-year or 9-year units;[17] enrolment in the army operated with lower and upper age-limits;[18] taxation sometimes operated in age-bands, deftly manipulated by the tax-payers;[19] and for the holding of political office an age-qualification might be legislated, and an upper limit (for 'retirement') discussed, though not necessarily applied.[20] But outside these special arenas, and, it seems, for most spheres of ordinary life, a simple binary was sufficient: after childhood and a loosely defined 'youth' (for men until their mid 20s), the free population (both male and female) was divided into two categories, the 'young(er)' and 'old(er)', with no clearly defined boundary between them, or rather, only such demarcation as fitted the rhetorical or political interests of those who created it.[21]

It may strike us as odd that there are only these two categories: it was very rare for either Greeks or Romans to talk of a 'middle age' of mature adulthood before one became 'old'.[22] Aristotle did advance something like this notion, but only because he wanted to define a golden mean between the excesses of youth, on the one hand, and the miseries of old age, on the other (*Rhet.* 2.12–14 [1388b31–1390b13]). In the course of this definition Aristotle distinguishes between the maturity of the body (at the age of 30–35) and the maturity of the soul (at the age of 49); but using two different ages in the definition of 'maturity' (ἀκμή) makes the schema practically

[17] E. g., Hippocrates' seven ages of humankind (*apud* Philo *Op. Mund.* 105, with a 21-year period for the age of 'manhood' [ἀνήρ]); on similar divisions see Parkin, *Old Age*, 16–19, noting their marginal significance.

[18] Aulus Gellius *Noct. Att.* 10.28, recording Roman practice (enrolment at 17; entering the status of *seniores* at 46).

[19] For the evidence from Roman Egypt regarding liturgy-obligations and the poll tax, see Parkin, *Old Age*, 138–72.

[20] For the rules and their application regarding the Roman senate, see Parkin, *Old Age*, 96–128.

[21] Thus, although Philo knows Hippocrates' scheme (*Op. Mund.* 105), he generally refers to the adult population in these two categories (see below). It is therefore mistaken to assume that one may use Hippocrates' (or others') life-stage schemas as means to determine precisely when Paul or others could classify themselves as 'old' (*pace* J. Murphy-O'Connor, *Paul: A Critical Life* [Oxford: Oxford University, 1996] 1–4, on Phlm 9). Slaves can also be marked in literature as both old and young, though in a social sense they have the marginal status of a 'child' (παῖς); see T. Wiedemann, '*Servi senes*: the role of old slaves at Rome' *Polis* 8 (1996) 275–93.

[22] On Greek usage of just these two categories, see R. Garland, *The Greek Way of Life* (London: Duckworth, 1990) 205–6, 242–3.

unworkable.[23] Elsewhere adult society was divided, in a neat polarity, into 'the young' and 'the old', with 'old' (or 'older') applicable to parents or senior politicians in their 40 s and 50 s as well as to the tiny percentage of those who lived into their 60 s or beyond. Occasionally the term *senium* is used by Roman authors, in distinction from *senectus*, to describe what we might term 'senility'.[24] But in general when our texts talk about 'the old' or 'the older', we should resist thinking of those considered in the West (until recently) 'of retirement age'; the term could apply to anyone distinguishable from a younger generation.[25]

The categories are interestingly flexible and uncertain. When did men or women become 'old'? Only when the next generation so defined them, or when it suited the 'older' to categorise themselves in this way.[26] According to Xenophon (*Mem*. 1.2.35), when Socrates was accused of corrupting 'the young', he had to ask his critics who counted as 'young' (νέοι); anyone, he was told, not yet wise enough to serve on the Council (βουλή), that is anyone under the age of 30. The fact that he had to ask the question shows that the term was ill-defined, and it is this very lack of definition, together with the neat polarity of the two opposing categories, young and old, that makes these labels so rhetorically useful. Precisely because they were ambiguous, such terms were malleable and could be put to all kinds of prejudicial use. And that leads us to enquire into the politics of these categories: if 'older' and 'younger' do not have a precise physiological sense, but are nonetheless in frequent use, what ideologies are they being made to serve?

---

[23] Aristotle's categories are νεότης, ἀκμή and γῆρας. The young are over-passionate, over-heated and naïve; the old are cold, suspicious, cowardly and mean; in between, by the principle of μηδὲν ἄγαν, are those 'in their prime'. But the contrasts are artificially schematic, and the paucity of comment on 'middle age' (beyond its falling between the opposite extremes) suggests it was a category of limited value. Artemidorus sometimes uses a four-age scheme (child; youth; grown man [ἀνήρ]; old man, 1.50; cf. 2.44; 4.10), but not always (cf. 1.78), and it is striking that the third category (ἀνήρ) does not itself signify age. Terms for middle age (*constans aetas*; *aetas virilis*; *medium tempus*) are notably rare in Latin, even when the lifespan is divided into four or more stages; see E. Eyben, 'Die Einteilung des menschlichen Lebens im römishen Altertum', *Rheinisches Museum* 116 (1973) 150–90; Parkin, *Old Age*, 21–2.

[24] T. G. Parkin, 'Out of Sight, Out of Mind: Elderly Members of the Roman Family', in B. Rawson and P. Weaver, eds., *The Roman Family in Italy* (Oxford: Clarendon, 1997) 123–48, esp. 141–8.

[25] This is true even of the Latin term *senex*: as Parkin insists, 'one cannot and should not define general terms like *senex* by a minimum number of years' (*Old Age*, 25); on the distinction in Roman law between *minores* and *maiores* see *idem*, *Old Age*, 93–5.

[26] According to Livy (30.30.10–11), Hannibal at the age of 44 called himself a *senex* in contrast to the *adulescentia* of Scipio (aged 34); but Cicero, looking back, can call himself at the time of the Catalinarian conspiracy (when he was 44) an *adulescens* (*Phil*. 2.46.118).

II. Ideologies of Age

In antiquity, as today, youth and age carried their own particular stereotypes, both positive and negative. Old age is notoriously easy to ridicule. The stock image of the decrepit old man, deaf and losing his memory, with tottering limbs, bald head, and drivelling nose – or the old woman, bent over, wrinkled and with toothless gums – is common in literature and art (most memorably in Aristophanes' plays and Juvenal's *Satire* 10.188–288).[27] Besides these physical traits, the older generation are often depicted as long-winded, opinionated, carping, slow-witted, miserly, and ridiculous when they pursue love-affairs.[28] The old or older of course see things differently: from their perspective – and this is a notion ubiquitous in the ancient world – with age come prudence, moderation, and the wisdom of experience.[29] The young, who can be portrayed in certain contexts as vigorous, beautiful, and bursting with sex-appeal, can also be viewed, by the older, as wilful, greedy, ambitious, sex-crazed and emotionally unstable. And because the population divides into two groups, one can charge men even in their 30 s with the immaturity and indiscretions of 'youth', or conversely, label a 45-year old a *senex*, and load against him all the associated negative connotations.

Such stereotypes are not socially or politically innocent: they enter into the structuring of power, providing rationalisations for its unequal distribution across the generations. In the domestic sphere, the appeal for the young to respect their elders is as common as, and frequently tied to, the expectation that children obey their parents. Summarising the Jewish law, but in line with all ancient moralists, Josephus twins the honouring of parents with the instruction that the young should honour everyone who is older (πᾶς ὁ πρεσβύτερος), 'since God is oldest' (*c. Apion.* 2.206).[30] For Philo there is an obvious symmetry in the hierarchical relationships which demand respect (*Spec. Leg.* 2.224–41): between children and parents, juniors and elders, pupils and teachers, beneficiaries and benefactors, subjects and rulers, slaves

[27] On the latter, with literary parallels, see Parkin, *Old Age*, 80–6. On the depiction of the old in statuary, see Cokayne, *Experiencing*, 11–33; with the Roman fashion for 'verism', the wrinkled face of an older man can become a symbol of dignity, solemnity and authority.

[28] See Parkin, *Old Age*, 76–89; the last case signifies the sense that each age has its own proper pattern of behaviour.

[29] The topos of the wise old counsellor is familiar in Greek literature from Homer onwards; for examples, Parkin, *Old Age*, 335 n. 18, to which add Sir 25.4–6 among other examples in the Jewish tradition.

[30] For discussion, see my *Flavius Josephus, Translation and Commentary. Vol 10: Against Apion* (Leiden: Brill, 2007) ad loc. Elsewhere, Josephus' narrative assumes that the young are lower in ἀξία and thus take lower places at the table (*Ant.* 12.210); the same assumption is present in Luke 22.26 (the νεώτερος is normally in the humble role of the διακονῶν). Cf. Sir 32.3–9 on the right to speak at banquets.

and masters. The parallel with parents is particularly stressed: to disrespect an older man or woman would be an indirect, but gross, dishonour to one's parents (*Spec. Leg.* 2.237–8). More generally, Philo links older age with wisdom, virtue, maturity and reason, while the youth (νέοι) are an inherently dangerous phenomenon, associated with upheaval and revolution (νεωτεροποιία; νεωτερίζειν, *Sob.* 6–29).[31] Such political terms alert us to the cross-over between the household and the state. In politics, the division between the two generations, the old and the young, is as old as Homer, whose portrait of the wise (but garrulous) old Nestor constituted a stock figure (*Il.* 1.247–51; 2.369–72, etc.). The famous Athenian debate on the Sicilian Expedition (Thucydides *Hist.* 6.8–23) is turned by Nikias into a contest between the older and wiser generation (the γεραίτεροι or πρεσβύτεροι), led by himself, against the young, headstrong and madly ambitious youngsters (νέοι, led by Alcibiades, aged 35); needless to say, the political victory of the young led to military disaster. The ideological ramifications of age are spelled out even more clearly in Plutarch's treatise 'Whether an old man should engage in public affairs' (*Mor.* 783 b–797 f). Here Plutarch argues than an older politician should not 'retire' from public life (all the alternatives are dishonourable and 'womanish'), but should continue to offer to the rest of society, and particularly to the young, the benefits of their superior experience, prudence and wisdom. The young may be physically stronger, but they are addicted to honour, to competition and to show, and are ruled by strong impulses (790 c–d). The older, by contrast, have an established advantage in experience and thus in good sense (φροντίς); they are by definition οἱ νοῦν ἔχοντες (788 a–e; 789 d; 797 e). And this distinction makes the power differential wholly *natural*: it is of the essence of youth to obey, of old age to rule (πειθαρχικὸν ἡ νεότης, ἡγεμονικὸν δὲ τὸ γῆρας, 789 e).[32]

The philosophical discussion of this topic is equally revealing. Cicero's famous treatise *De Senectute* carefully counters four arguments that old age is an unhappy and burdensome period of life (namely, that it removes us from active pursuits; that it weakens our bodies; that is deprives us of almost every pleasure; and that it brings us nearer to death). Cicero (through his mouthpiece Cato) will not allow any of these claims to devalue old age: they are either half truths or, from the perspective of philosophy, describe conditions which are positively advantageous – after all, with the passions

[31] According to Philo, the Essenes do not admit young men, 'since the character of such are unstable with a waywardness corresponding to the immaturity of their age' (*Hyp.* 11.3); they sit in rows in their synagogues, the younger below the older (*Prob.* 81). Cf. the ideal community of the Therapeutae, where the younger members serve the older (*Contempl.* 70–2).

[32] Plato would have strongly approved: he takes it for granted that the 'older' will rule the 'younger' in any just political system (*Resp.* 412 c, 465 a; *Leg.* 659 d, 690 a).

dimmed, there is more room for virtue! Although Cicero knows the stereotype of old men as morose and irascible (*Sen.* 65), he disputes its universal application. More positively, he associates old age with *auctoritas*, *consilium* and *sententia* (*Sen.* 17). Busy in their own (more intellectual) ways, old men can offer the young wisdom and good sense, a *maturitas* (*Sen.* 33) like that of ripe fruits on a tree, just before they fall (*Sen.* 5, 71).[33] Sometimes in this treatise (written age 62), Cicero deploys a four-age schema of 'boyhood' (*pueritia*), 'youth' (*adulescentia*), 'settled age' *(aetas constans* or *media*) and 'old age' (*senectus*; e.g., *Sen.* 33, 76) but generally this resolves to a simpler scheme of 'young' and 'old', in which the wisdom of age can be contrasted to the immaturity and wild *voluptates* of youth (*Sen.* 17–26, 39–50).[34] For a Stoic, or indeed anyone in a philosophical tradition where mind is valued over body, older age provides the perfect conditions for the full display of virtue; it is a period not of decline but of ever greater moral development.

We should note here the ideological work of such texts ('ideological' in the strong sense of sustaining asymmetrical relations of power): age and youth are carefully defined to maintain the status quo as both *natural* and *morally necessary*. In the simple polarity of 'younger' and 'older', an older man can never be classed as 'too old'; if there is no final category of 'senile' into which to decline, the 'old' can continue to compare themselves advantageously with the 'young' for as long as it suits them to do so. The right of the older to rule is vigorously asserted: that is the reward (γέρας) that goes with old age (γῆρας, Plutarch *Mor.* 789f). I am not claiming that this is the perspective of everyone in the Roman world: the fact that the philosophers have to work to extol the benefits of age indicates that the subject is contestable and contested.[35] But it is clear that where age, however loosely defined, becomes a criterion for power – and there is good evidence that in the political sphere most men in power were definable as 'older,' that is

[33] As one might expect, little positive attention is given by Cicero or other ancient authors to older women, who are quite frequently (though unflatteringly) depicted in statuary. The old woman still desperate for sex, or addicted to drink, is a common object of scorn or satire; see O. Musso, 'Anus ebria' *Atene e Roma* 13 (1968) 29–31; Cokayne, *Experiencing*, 134–52.

[34] In the same vein, Seneca admits only a simple bipolarity: 'youth' (*adulescentia*, sometimes twinned with *pueritia*) and 'seniority' (*senectus*). The latter is the time when the mind is at its full bloom (*Ep.* 26.2), when the apple is perfectly ripe (*Ep.* 12.4). Although the body may be comparatively weak, so are its vices, while the mind enjoys *tranquillitas* and *modestia* (*Ep.* 26.3).

[35] There are certainly cases in antiquity where those considered 'too old' are dismissed as 'stupid' or 'useless'; see e.g., Josephus *Ant.* 12.172–3; Thucydides *Hist.* 2.44.4. In CD 10.4–10 the office of judge is removed from anyone over the age of 60, 'for on account of man's sin his days were shortened, and because of God's wrath against the inhabitants of the earth, he decided to remove knowledge from them before they completed their days'; cf. CD 14.6–11; 1QSa 2.7 (the tottering aged are excluded from the congregation).

in their 40s and 50s[36] – it has developed a structural significance which requires continual legitimation and reinforcement. Since age could be used as a mechanism for the distribution, and eventual rotation, of power, discourse about it is by no means politically innocent; we should expect its presence or absence in early Christian texts to be similarly significant.

III. Age Instructions in the Pauline Tradition

Space does not permit more than a survey of four texts which lie broadly in the Pauline tradition. They are strikingly similar in their assumptions and ideologies of age, illuminated by the context we have just set.

i) *1 Peter*: Despite its language about charismatic endowment (1 Pet 4.7–11), the opening verses of 1 Pet 5 indicate that respect is due to age in the Christian community. It is πρεσβύτεροι who are exhorted to 'shepherd' the flock, and not from greed (5.2).[37] Even if the term πρεσβύτερος refers to an 'office', it is clear that only 'older' people are expected to wield this authority, for the corresponding injunction is to 'the younger' (νεώτεροι, 5.5) – which is not a junior 'office', but an age-category, the younger people in the churches.[38] They are issued with one simple instruction: ὑποτάγητε πρεσβυτέροις (5.5); as normal, youth defers to age. The unequal distribution of power is hardly qualified by the following instruction that all should show humility to one another; in terms of 'submission' there is no ethos of reciprocity. What we find here is precisely what we noted in the ideologically driven literature: vagueness in definition of the categories 'older' and 'younger', accompanied by the firm smack of order.

ii) *1 Clement*: Clement's letter to Corinth displays the outrage caused when this proper hierarchy is not observed. Although the details are unclear, it appears that there has been some 'revolt' (στάσις) against the πρεσβύτεροι (47.6); whether this comes from within their ranks, or from outside, the strategy of Clement throughout is to reinforce the authority of the duly constituted 'elders' (οἱ καθεσταμένοι πρεσβύτεροι, 54.2).[39]

---

[36] Parkin, *Old Age*, 100: 'we might say as a generalization that most power (as opposed to less tangible respect) lay not with those over the age of 60, but with those in their 40s and 50s.'

[37] On the avarice or meanness of the older generation, see above, n. 23.

[38] See discussion by E. G. Selwyn, *The First Epistle of St. Peter* (London: Macmillan, 1955) 227, 233; N. Brox, *Der erste Petrusbrief* (Zürich: Benziger, 1979) 226–7, 233–5. The latter argues that πρεσβύτεροι both in 5.1 and 5.5 means 'elders' (as an office); but even if so, the age connotations of the term are clear in the contrast of 5.5.

[39] On this revolt and its social causes, see B. E. Bowe, *A Church in Crisis: Ecclesiology and Paraenesis in Clement of Rome* (Minneapolis: Fortress, 1988); D. G. Horrell, *The Social Ethos of the Corinthian Correspondence* (Edinburgh: T & T Clark, 1996) 238–80.

One means to this end is to construct a chain of contrasts, each shocking in its implication that order has been overturned: the factionalism that has broken out in Corinth is conducted by the ἄτιμοι against the ἔντιμοι, the ἄδοξοι against the ἔνδοξοι, the ἄφρονες against the φρόνιμοι, and the νέοι against the πρεσβύτεροι (3.3). Although these four antitheses are not precise equivalents, the associations are telling: the 'young' are classed alongside the 'disreputable' and the 'senseless' – presumably because they lack the age-entitlement to honour and wisdom.[40] A second tactic is to reinforce obedience to the 'elders' by placing them in a network of relationships requiring proper submission to the κανὼν ὑποτάγης (1.3). Thus in *1 Clement* 1 the Corinthians are praised for their previous orderly conduct, and in *1 Clement* 21 exhorted, in very similar terms, to renew this order. In both cases obeying their leaders and 'paying proper honour' (τιμὴ ἡ καθήκουσα) to their 'elders' is juxtaposed with expectations that the young (νέοι) are taught to 'think moderate and respectful thoughts' (μέτρια καὶ σεμνὰ νοεῖν, 1.3), and are instructed in the discipline of the Lord (21.6). The hierarchical relationship between 'the older' and 'the young' is closely allied to that presupposed in the family, with the normal assumption that the young tend to excessive and irresponsible behaviour.[41] It is not quite clear here whether the πρεσβύτεροι represent an informal age-group or a formal office.[42] But that suits Clement's rhetoric well: respect for the office of 'elder' is boosted by its association with 'old age', while respect for the older members of the congregation is boosted by their association in nomenclature with the emerging office of 'elder'. In either case, age proves if not a prerequisite at least a distinct advantage for aspiring leaders in communities who share Clement's ideology.

iii) *The Pastorals*: A similar set of assumptions, and rhetorics, is to be found in the Pastoral epistles. There is the same ambiguity about the label πρεσβύτεροι, which in some cases seems to designate an age-group (1 Tim 5.1–2; cf. Titus 2.2–6), and in others an office (1 Tim 5.17, 19; Titus 1.5; cf. τὸ πρεσβυτέριον, 1 Tim 4.14). The term may be in transition, or the subject of subtle political redescription;[43] but all its uses build upon the

[40] Since Clement's phraseology is partially drawn from Isa 3.5, we should be cautious in reading historical reality from his description of the parties; see Horrell, *Social Ethos*, 247 n. 58.

[41] Cf. *1 Clement* 63.3, where there is praise for faithful and 'temperate' (σώφρονες) men, 'who have lived blamelessly among us from youth to old age.' The advantage of the old is apparent; they have a life-long Christian commitment to prove their worth in the community.

[42] See Campbell, *Elders*, 211–6.

[43] See F. Young, *The Theology of the Pastoral Epistles* (Cambridge: Cambridge University, 1994) 104–11; Campbell, *Elders*, 176–205; I.H. Marshall, *The Pastoral Letters* (ICC; London: T & T Clark, 1999) 170–81.

special respect accorded to age. Titus 2.1–5 represents many of the classic cultural assumptions about age. Older men (πρεσβῦται) are to be sober, serious and moderate – the virtues one would expect in those who have left behind what the Pastor elsewhere terms 'youthful passions' (νεωτερικαὶ ἐπιθυμίαι, 2 Tim 2.22). Older women are to control their tongues and their appetite for drink.[44] Such women, however, have a crucial role to play in socialising the younger generation of wives (αἱ νέαι) into the proper family ethos, to ensure that they are domestic, motherly and obedient to their husbands (Titus 2.4–5). Younger men (νεώτεροι) are to be moderate in everything (σωφρονεῖν περὶ πάντα), learning to shed youthful excess so they are fit to be, in turn, the wise older generation. In 1 Timothy, where the addressee is presented as young (4.12; see below), care is to be taken as to how the older generation are exhorted and corrected. Just as slaves are not to be insolent to their Christian masters (1 Tim 6.1–2), so older men must not be rudely rebuked (πρεσβυτέρῳ μὴ ἐπιπλήξῃς), but exhorted 'as fathers' (1 Tim 5.1), older women 'as mothers' and the younger generation (νεωτέρους and νεωτέρας) as brothers and sisters. Again, we note, there are only two categories (older and younger), no 'middle-aged'. And the family metaphor is significant:[45] it indicates that in a community which thinks of itself as 'the household of God' (1 Tim 3.15), the patterns of respect for the older generation in the family are likely to be replicated in social relations within the church.

iv) *Polycarp*: In his letter to the Philippians, Polycarp includes a number of comments about the generational divide which tally precisely with what we have discovered thus far, but add a further moral tone. In *Phil.* 5–6 he first instructs the 'younger men' (νεώτεροι) to exercise self-control. The dangers here are 'impurity' and 'the desires of the world', and, considering what was generally believed about young men's libido, it is not surprising that the following list of vices – a shortened version of 1 Cor 6.9–11 – is entirely focused on *sexual* misdemeanour. To avoid this, or any other such 'aberrant behaviour' (ἄτοπα), the young must be subject to 'the elders and deacons' (τοῖς πρεσβυτέροις καὶ διακόνοις), as to God and Christ; one could hardly devise a stronger legitimation of the authority of the leaders, who are simply presumed to be of the older generation. Meanwhile, the 'elders', who have the power to correct and care for the rest of the congregation, are warned to avoid the usual vices of age – the tendency to be cantankerous and money-grubbing (6.1; cf. 11.1–4). Rather, they are to be merciful, generous, unprejudiced, free from anger, and mild in their judge-

[44] For the stereotype of the drunken old woman, see above, n. 33.

[45] For parallels in inscriptions and literature, where older people are to be honoured as parents, contemporaries as siblings, see M. Dibelius – H. Conzelmann, *The Pastoral Epistles* (Hermeneia; Philadelphia: Fortress, 1972) 72.

ment of others. We have the impression of a community where leadership is more or less neatly aligned with age, and where the younger generation will have to prove their ability to 'rein themselves in' (5.3) over a protracted period before they, in turn, can fill the role of 'elders'.

IV. Two Exceptions that Prove the Rule

Lest the picture appear over-simple, we should note two passages which suggest that, on occasion, leaders in the churches might be comparatively young. In both cases it is clear that this is problematic and exceptional, and words are carefully chosen to validate this unusual phenomenon. The fact that it happens at all indicates that early Christian practice did not always match its age-presumptions; but the justification provided for these exceptions proves that they did little to disrupt the normal assumptions concerning the authority of age.

In the first of these texts, 1 Tim 4.12, instruction is given to 'Timothy' not to let anyone 'despise' him because of his youth (μηδεὶς σου τῆς νεότητος καταφρονείτω). The notice may go back to early memory of Timothy, or serve as an interpretation of Pauline fears on his behalf (1 Cor 16.11; cf. Titus 2.15). In this pseudonymous letter, such a fictionalised instruction has been taken by Brox to suggest that young leaders were not untypical in the circles addressed by the Pastorals.[46] To counteract this disadvantage, Timothy must make himself an 'example' to others (examples are normally expected in the older generation), and, as we have seen, he must be specially careful to address older men and women with respect (5.1–2). He is also reminded of the χάρισμα which was given to him through prophecy (4.14) – but given through the laying on of hands by the council of elders (τὸ πρεσβυτέριον)! In other words, Timothy's youthful authority is not an example of 'charisma' which escapes or challenges the 'traditional' authority of the older generation. What at first sight appears to circumvent the due process of age-qualification turns out to be authentic, and authenticated, only when the elders have appointed him to his task. That they might appoint such a young person indicates that age is not a *sine qua non* for leadership in such churches; but in the context of the Pastorals as a whole, this disregard of the age criterion is clearly an exception.

Our second text offers a real case of a youthful leader, in the role of overseer (ἐπίσκοπος). In his letter to the *Magnesians* (3.1), Ignatius urges

[46] N. Brox, *Die Pastoralbriefe* (4th edition; Regensburg: Pustet, 1969) 178–9; cf. J. Roloff, *Der erste Brief an Timotheus* (EKK; Zürich: Benziger, 1988) 251; but the inference is not wholly secure. Cf. N. Brox, 'Pseudo-Paulus und Pseudo-Ignatius. Einige Topoi altchristlicher Pseudepigraphie' *VC* 30 (1976) 181–8.

the church not to take advantage of Damas because of his age: they are to accord him all proper respect (as if he were 'old'), as even the 'holy elders' have done (overriding their natural scorn of the young). The crucial justification for this unusual phenomenon is then presented: his youthful status/condition (νεωτερικὴ τάξις) is only an outward appearance (φαινομένη),[47] and the elders, seeing through this deceptive exterior, have honoured Damas 'as one who is wise in God' (ὡς φρονίμῳ ἐν θεῷ).[48] Wisdom is, of course, precisely what one would *not* expect in a young man, but would naturally associate with the old, and it is Damas' 'wisdom in God' which equips him to play his unusual role. Heavy sanctions are added: one must defer to Damas as if to God, and not with hypocrisy, for that would be detected by the divine ἐπίσκοπος (3.2). One has the impression that Damas' job would have been a lot easier if his hair had been that little bit greyer and his brow a little more wrinkled.[49]

V. The Silence of Paul

Finally, we may return to our question about Paul. Is it significant that, in comparison with these later texts written in his name or in his tradition, and despite the depiction in Acts (14.23), Paul did not appoint πρεσβύτεροι in his churches? Leadership was indeed appointed, or at least emerged (1 Thess 5.12–13; 1 Cor 16.15–16; Phil 1.1), but it was not characterised by terms depicting age. Age differentials are not included in the formula of Gal 3.28, alongside the nullified labels of ethnicity, gender and legal status; but are they implicitly ignored in Pauline anthropology?

As always, silence can be interpreted in more than one way. We might conclude that Paul really thought no differently from everyone else on this matter. As we have seen, one did not have to speak of people's ages in every context (age often goes unmarked), but the fact that Paul did once pull rank, or evoke pity, as a πρεσβύτης (Phlm 9) might suggest that he associ-

[47] For the translation of τάξις see J. B. Lightfoot, *Apostolic Fathers. Part II. S. Ignatius, S. Polycarp*, vol. II (2nd ed.; London: Macmillan, 1889) 113–4; *BAGD* s. v.

[48] Following the reading in A, rather than φρονίμους in G and L; so Lightfoot, *Apostolic Fathers*, 114; B. Ehrman, *The Apostolic Fathers* vol 1 (LCL; Cambridge, Mass.: Harvard, 2003) 244. For the notion of a young man as wise as an elder, cf. Susanna 44–50 (Theodotion), regarding Daniel; *Apostolic Constitutions* 2.1 (a man under 50 may be appointed bishop 'if he has behaved from his youth like a much older person').

[49] I am grateful to Dr. Joel Kaminsky for pointing me to an apposite anecdote in the Babylonian Talmud. When Rabbi Eleazar ben Azaraiah was only 18 years only he was appointed head of the Sanhedrin and there was concern that the masses would not respect him because of his youthful appearance; so a miracle occurred and his beard turned white overnight (*b. Ber.* 28 a).

ated authority with age.[50] His appeal to his converts to think no longer as παιδία but as τέλειοι (1 Cor 14.20; cf. 1 Cor 2.6; 13.11; Phil 3.12–15; Col 1.28; 4.12) could be taken to indicate that he linked Christian maturation to experience and age. Moreover, it has been argued that in churches founded by Paul leadership would naturally gravitate to householders and hosts, and thus to the *paterfamilias* or equivalent – in any case (given the importance of age in the domestic context) to the oldest generation.[51]

On the other hand, there are both sociological and theological indications of a quite contrary conclusion. As a first-generation conversionist sect, the Pauline movement could hardly afford to limit leadership to an older generation (there might be few among the converts in any particular place), and its charismatic features could break with the traditional structures of authority associated with age. Just as Luke, citing Joel, can imagine both young men seeing visions and old men dreaming dreams (Acts 2.17), spiritual gifts in Pauline theology are not distributed by age. There is no indication that prophecy or teaching, or even apostleship, must be in the hands of the older generation (1 Cor 12–14), and this not by accidental omission but because the structures of power in the Pauline churches escape both legal and traditional frameworks.[52] Theologically, one may relate this to the emergence in Paul of an alternative, apocalyptic anthropology. If the wisdom of the world is made foolish by the message of the cross, and if the form of this world is passing away (1 Cor 1.18; 7.31), one can hardly expect the normal associations between age, wisdom and authority to remain intact. In the καινὴ κτίσις (Gal 6.15; 2 Cor 5.17) the believer is reconstituted by dependence on the Spirit, who is the source of wisdom and of the moral qualities that constitute growth in Christ. It is not clear that an older person must be necessarily wiser 'in Christ', and if a believer goes astray, it is the πνευματικοί who are to correct him, not the πρεσβύτεροι (Gal 6.1). Experience of life in 'the present evil age' (Gal 1.4) can hardly qualify one for leadership in the emerging new creation, while the gifts and fruits of the Spirit are acquired not by the passage of time but by the distribution of grace.

Thus, from related sociological and theological angles, it is possible to find traces in Paul of an alternative ideology, challenging the structuring

[50] Cf. the presumption that the first-born son (Jesus) has a higher rank than his brothers (Rom 8.29); as father (or mother) of his churches, Paul assumes authority over them (e.g., 1 Cor 4.14–15), but this lies more in his parentage than in his superior 'age'.

[51] So Campbell, *Elders*, 97–140, arguing that 'elder' (a general term of honour) does not emerge in Pauline times, since each church had its own leader. It emerges only later when churches are collectively represented by groups of leaders, called elders. But it is still unclear whether Paul would have accepted an age-term as a label of leadership.

[52] The issue is more complex than can be discussed here; see B. Holmberg, *Paul and Power: The Structure of Authority in the Primitive Church as Reflected in the Pauline Epistles* (Lund: Gleerup, 1978).

assumptions of Roman society. But if so, one can understand why this did not last. As soon as time began to pass, and converts could be expected to mature in the faith, the typical links between seniority, experience and wisdom would naturally emerge. If Christians conceived of themselves as 'growing into salvation' (1 Pet 2.2), they could plot a path of increasing spiritual maturation through the life-cycle; and via the normal processes of routinization, leadership would be largely restricted to those qualified by their social standing, domestic or otherwise. Thus in time 'the young' are told to knuckle down and respect their 'elders'. But, arguably, there remains within the Christian tradition a trace of an earlier, alternative, vision of a social structure that is Spirit-led and age-blind.[53]

[53] Gnilka traces in subsequent Christian literature the discussion of 'age' as a spiritual, rather than a physical, phenomenon, and thus the capacity to recognise the spiritual maturity of the young. This discourse has its roots more in philosophy (e.g., the topos of the *puer senex*) than in charismatic freedom, but the exception texts noted above (1 Tim 4.12; Ignatius *Mag*. 3.1) played their part in this discussion (*Aetas Spiritualis*, 170–3, 244).

IV. Josephus, Paul and Rome

14. The Politics of Contempt

Judaeans and Egyptians in Josephus' *Against Apion*

I. Introduction

Among the literary monuments of Roman imperialism, there are none more skilfully crafted than Virgil's depiction of Aeneas' shield in *Aeneid* Book 8 (626–731). At the climax of this celebration of Roman history stands the battle of Actium (671–728) in which Caesar (Octavian), supported by the Italians, the Senate and the people, is opposed by Anthony, whose 'barbarian' resources are symbolised by his shockingly 'Egyptian' wife: *sequiturque (nefas) Aegyptia coniunx* (688). The fact that Cleopatra was in truth of pure Macedonian descent does not deter the propagandist: as queen of Egypt and therefore 'Egyptian', she summons the troops with her native *sistrum* (696). Octavian's victory thus represents the triumph of Roman civilisation over the barbarian East, an antithesis whose profundity is nowhere more conspicuous than in its religious dimensions. Here religious monstrosity – the Egyptian cult of animals – confronts the sanity and familiarity of the Roman deities:

omnigenumque deum monstra et latrator Anubis
contra Neptunum et Venerem contraque Minervam
tela tenent. (698–700)[1]

The poetry is exquisitely carved in contempt: like her terrain, her populace and her dignity, Egypt's religion is crushed by the superior power of Rome.

Virgil's scorn for the troublesome but defeated foreigner represents a deep vein of Roman xenophobia in the late Republic and early Empire, which often borders on racism. If the only good Egyptian is one subject to the sobering and civilising influence of Roman power, the same may be said of Gauls, Judaeans, Syrians and many others. Cicero could count on such prejudices in a Roman jury when he needed to discredit foreign witnesses: 'is any of the most honourable natives of Gaul to be set on the same

[1] 'Barking Anubis, a whole progeny of grotesque deities are embattled against Neptune and Minerva and Venus' (trans. C. Day Lewis). The translations of *Against Apion* given below are my own.

level with even the meanest citizen of Rome?' (*Pro Fonteio* 27). Here too, political or military resistance to Rome is twinned with outrageous religion. These Gauls who once threatened the city of Rome, who have 'repeatedly attacked this city and its empire' (35), are notorious, Cicero claims, for their 'monstrous and barbarous custom of sacrificing humans' (31). Who can trust their oaths by the immortal Gods when their barbarity renders them so contrary to all humanity? 'Other nations wage war in defence of their religion; they do so against the religion of every people' (30).

Military superiority and religious disdain forge a powerful circularity which is all but mentally unassailable: just as the crushing of nations which have the effrontery to challenge Roman might demonstrates their gross or pathetic contrariety to all religious decency, so Roman piety is proven by her incessant success. The same nexus could be employed to discredit Judaeans. Cicero overturns Judaean complaints against Flaccus simply enough by reference to Pompey's victory in Jerusalem. Even when there was peace, Judaean religion was at variance with 'the glory of our empire, the dignity of our name'. But 'now it has shown by its armed resistance what it thinks of our rule', and the result indicates how little the Gods care for them (*Pro Flacco* 28.69). The same logic undergirds Tacitus' disdain more than 150 years later: the Judaean Revolt is consistent with the fact that 'they regard as profane all that we hold sacred; on the other hand, they permit all that we abhor' (*Histories* 5.4.1).[2] From this political perspective the 'otherness' of Judaean religious tradition is nothing but outright hostility, their indigenous customs simply 'depraved'.

The arrogance of this imperial ideology could co-exist with a selective admiration, even adoption, of 'native customs'. As the Roman empire became increasingly conscious of its own cultural diversity, 'Roman' identity could embrace a variety of non-Italian religious customs – although always within limits, under imperial patronage, or as 'exotica'. With regard to Egyptian religion, the practices which Juvenal satirises among the élite (*Sat.* 6.511–42) indicate some fashionable interests in Egyptian deities, while the Flavian rulers, and especially Domitian, seem to have accorded especial honours to Isis.[3] The phenomenon is familiar in colonial contexts as a species of 'Orientalism': interest and admiration for certain features of an 'exotic' cultural tradition can go hand-in-hand with a deep disdain for the actual populace

[2] E.S. Gruen (*Diaspora: Jews Amidst Greeks and Romans* [Cambridge: Harvard University, 2002], 41–52) questions such a link between Tacitus' invective and the Judean Revolt, but his excursus on the Judeans is offered in the context of an account of that Revolt.

[3] On the scandal of the Roman matron seduced by 'Anubis' in 19 CE (Josephus 18.65–80), with illuminating discussion of Domitian's interest in Isis, see now S. Matthews, *First Converts: Rich Pagan Women and the Rhetoric of Mission in Early Judaism and Christianity* (Stanford: Stanford University, 2001), 10–28.

among whom those traditions have been preserved.[4] But the ideology which maintained that disdain was never seriously threatened by fads for Egyptian or Judaean customs, or even by their subtle incorporation into the 'Roman' way of life: when politically expedient or militarily necessary the Roman élite could draw on a long strain of contempt for the nations they had benevolently 'pacified'.[5]

We possess understandably few remnants of the ways in which subject nations responded to such Roman disdain. In most cases only the ambiguous witness of material culture gives us access to the voices of the colonised. All the more precious, therefore, is Josephus' *Contra Apionem*, where a knowledgeable spokesman for the Judaean tradition is bold enough to answer back to his cultural critics and skilful enough to do so in terms calculated to win Roman attention. In this essay I wish to explore one facet of Josephus' apologetic, a strategy which simultaneously exploits and counters Roman contempt for her subjects. In observing how Josephus deploys negative Roman stereotypes of Egyptians I hope to unearth some facets of his rhetorical strategy and to illuminate thereby the cultural and political stance he adopts in re-presenting the Judaeans to his Roman or Romanised readers.[6]

II. Egyptians and Judaeans in Contra Apionem[7]

An overview of *Contra Apionem* reveals Josephus' varied deployment of the category 'Egyptian', in accordance with the differing aims of his rhetoric.

[4] The classic discussion remains E. Said, *Orientalism: Western Representations of the Orient* (London: Routledge & Kegan Paul, 1978). Plutarch endeavours to prove that the Isis and Osiris mythology is highly philosophical (*Isis and Osiris*, passim), but is scathing of the Egyptian populace who need Roman force to stop their stupid quarrels (*Isis and Osiris* 72 [380 a–c]).

[5] Earlier studies of Roman imperial attitudes to other races (e.g., A.N. Sherwin-White, *Racial Prejudice in Imperial Rome* [Cambridge: Cambridge University Press, 1967]) can now be supplemented by perspectives drawn from post-colonial theory (e.g., D.J. Mattingly, ed., *Dialogues in Roman Imperialism* [Portsmouth, RI: Journal of Roman Archaeology, 1997]). [Cf. B. Isaac, *The Invention of Racism in Classical Antiquity* (Princeton: Princeton University, 2004), with discussion of ancient attitudes to Egyptians (352–70) and Jews (440–91). On Alexandrian Jewish attitudes to Egyptians, see S. Pearce, *The Land of the Body: Studies in Philo's Representation of Egypt* (WUNT 208; Tübingen: Mohr Siebeck, 2007).]

[6] I have outlined some reasons to interpret Josephus' strategy and readership along such lines in J.M.G. Barclay, 'Judaism in Roman Dress', in J.U. Kalms and F. Siegert, eds., *Internationales Josephus-Kolloquium Aarhus 1999* (Münster: LIT, 2000), 231–45. Of course, both Roman opinions on Judaeans and many of Josephus' counter-strategies had their roots in the Hellenistic era, but Josephus' apology is also closely related to his own historical and political context.

[7] At some points my observations here run parallel to those of K. Berthelot, 'Josephus'

For his opening gambit (1.6–56), in which he subverts the appeal to 'famous Greek historians' and their damaging lack of reference to Judaeans, it suits Josephus to divide ancient historiography into two camps. On the one side lie Greeks, whose lack of ancient records and endemic disagreements disqualify their historiographical pretensions; on the other are 'Egyptians, Chaldaeans and Phoenicians', with whom Josephus aligns Judaeans, whose antiquity and care for the preservation of ancient records is legendary (1.8–14, 28–29). This division into 'Greek' and 'barbarian' historiography (1.58) is a massive over-simplification, but it enables Josephus to gain from the prestige of others' acknowledged antiquity and, in particular, from the famous preservation of records in Egypt.[8] Whatever they thought about contemporary Egyptians, the Roman reading public were inclined to respect the marvellous antiquity of records housed in Egyptian temples, and Josephus is eager to let that prestige seep across to the less recognised terrain of the Judaean scriptures.

The nations singled out for this respect are the ones whose records Josephus will use in 1.69–160 for their witness to Judaean antiquity. For this purpose it is important that the ancient Egyptians be treated with respect, since Josephus needs Manetho to be unimpeachable: the Hyksos story, which Josephus presses into his service (1.73–104), is validated as a translation from the 'sacred records' (1.73). Josephus' position is awkward, however, since Manetho also supplies the first example of the 'Egyptian slanders' which he will set himself to combat in 1.219–2.144. Hence the effort which Josephus expends on keeping the two Manetho stories apart, separated not only by a large section of text but also by a heavily reinforced distinction between sources: when Manetho demonstrated Judaean antiquity he was drawing on ancient Egyptian writings, but when he talked about the departure of the lepers he was following 'anonymous fables' (1.105, repeated in 1.228–29 and 1.287). The distinction is almost certainly artificial: whatever the mixture of sources from which Manetho drew, there are as many legendary elements in the Hyksos story as in that about the lepers, and the two obviously belonged together in Manetho's narrative (despite Josephus' claim in 1.230–32). But since the one story is to be affirmed and the other repudiated, the first is validated by its origin in the Egyptian ancient records, the other traced to untrustworthy legend, whose falsity is attributable to Egyptian hate (1.287).

It is significant that when he turns to this new section of his work (1.219–2.144) Josephus dubs all his opponents as 'Egyptian' either by origin or

Use of Graeco-Roman Stereotypes of the Egyptians', in J.U. Kalms and F. Siegert, eds., *Internationales Josephus-Kolloquium Aarhus 1999* (Münster: LIT, 2000) 185–221.

[8] The extreme antiquity of Egyptian records had been a topos since Herodotus (2.100); Cicero, *De Re Publica* 3.14 shows its continuing influence in Roman discourse.

by orientation: 'It was Egyptians who began the libels directed against us, and certain people who wanted to gratify them attempted to twist the truth' (2.223). The identity and motivation of these others who 'wanted to gratify' the Egyptians is left deliberately vague: Josephus clearly hopes by this means to sweep into the 'Egyptian' category not only Manetho and Chaeremon, whose ethnicity probably was Egyptian, and not only Apion, whom he will falsely represent as such, but also Lysimachus and even perhaps Apollonius Molon (see below, section IV). In any case, 1.223 marks the transition from a positive to a negative stereotype of Egyptians, signalled immediately by abuse of their 'stupid' religion (1.224–25). From this point on, the label 'Egyptian' is uniformly dirty and, in a rhetorical climax, gleefully stuck all over the testimony of Apion. By the time he has finished with him (with his gruesome and somewhat 'Egyptian' death, 2.142–44), Josephus has finished with the Egyptian strategy altogether: it plays no part in his encomium for the Judaean constitution in 2.145 ff. Like any skilled orator, Josephus has selected and manipulated ethnic stereotypes to suit his argumentation, allowing as little interference as possible between positive and negative images. 'Egyptian' is malleable enough to serve his rhetoric in various ways.[9]

It is noticeable, however, that wherever he positions Judaeans in relation to Egyptians, as historiographical allies or religious foes, Josephus insists on one point: whatever else Judaeans are, they are not Egyptian by origin. The prominence of this theme is not so clearly signalled in the preface to the work (1.1–5) as one might expect: although Josephus there asserts that he has previously established both the antiquity of the Judaean nation and its own original nature (1.1), it is the antiquity topic alone which he signals as presently contested (1.2–3), and which is the theme of the historiographical debate (1.6–56) and of the various witnesses in 1.69–218 (e.g., 1.59, 69, 93, 215, 217). Nonetheless, when he summarises his achievements at the end of the work (2.287–92), Josephus places as much emphasis on his refutation of false claims that the Judaeans' ancestors were Egyptian as on the proof that they were ancient (2.288–89), and this accurately reflects the fact that the issue of Jewish non-Egyptian ancestry emerges repeatedly throughout the treatise.

It is striking, for instance, that when Josephus summarises what can be learned from Manetho, who had been introduced to prove Judaean antiq-

---

[9] The one cross-over of positive and negative stereotypes occurs in 2.140–41 where Josephus needs wise and pious Egyptian priests to establish Apion's wicked abandonment of his 'native' traditions. Josephus would not wish his readers to consider what cultic functions these priests might serve. The label 'Greek' is also used with varying valence in *Against Apion*, and the only unambiguously positive labels are, significantly, 'Judaean', 'Chaldaean' and 'Roman'.

uity (1.69, 93), the *first* conclusion drawn is that ‘we came to Egypt from elsewhere’ (1.104; cf. 1.228). As this reference shows, Josephus is willing to endorse (or create) a preposterous identification between the Hyksos and the Israelites: he quotes Manetho’s derogatory account of the Hyksos’ reign of terror (1.75–90) without apology or correction, since this ‘proves’ not only the Judaeans’ antiquity but also, and equally importantly, their foreign origin. Manetho’s reference to ‘some people of an obscure race from eastern parts’ (1.75) will serve Josephus’ purposes well enough – even his speculation that they were Arabs (1.82) – just so long as this story, certified by the Egyptian records, makes clear that ‘we are not Egyptian’. In fact, Josephus insists on this point when discussing Manetho’s leper-story no less that five times (1.228–29, 252–53, 270, 278, and 279–86 re Moses); it appears that what he fears most is not just the association of Jews with lepers but also, and in particular, the association with *Egyptian* lepers. He cannot allow any such ‘mixing’ (1.229, 253, 278).

The same concern recurs throughout Josephus’ response to Chaeremon, Lysimachus and Apion. Josephus’ reply to Chaeremon puts greatest emphasis on questions of identity: ‘The absolute gem is this: he has not said who these large numbers of soldiers were [the 380,000 at Pelusium], and where they were from – whether they were of Egyptian descent or had come from elsewhere’ (1.298). Similarly ‘the most remarkable thing is one cannot discover from him whom he calls “Judaeans”’ (1.302). The same issue arises with regard to Lysimachus, who had apparently labelled those who suffered leprosy and scabies ‘Judaeans’ (1.305). ‘Who are these people?’, Josephus asks: ‘were they foreign or native by descent? So why, if they were Egyptians, do you call them Judaeans? And if they were foreigners, why do you not say where they came from?’ (1.314; cf. 1.316 re Moses).

By the time he gets to Apion, the exodus-theme is just about done to death, but Josephus still reminds his readers that ‘our fathers were neither Egyptian by descent nor expelled from there due to physical disfigurement or any other such misfortune’ (2.8, cf. 2.28, 122). It seems as if Josephus has read these accounts of the leper-exodus with as much concern about the confusion of ‘Judaean’ and ‘Egyptian’ as about the attribution of sacrilege, God-forsakenness and impurity. His rhetoric displays an almost frantic concern to place as clear a distinction as possible between ‘Egyptian’ and ‘Judaean’. The expression ‘Egyptian Judaeans’ which he had allowed himself to use in *War* 1.190 would have been disastrous here!

We are entitled to ask why Josephus adopts this stance with such rigour. It does not seem sufficient to reply that this is because the biblical records (for him ‘the truth’) stood against this association. There are many things in the biblical record he does not bother to defend here, and, as we have noted, many features in Manetho’s story about the Hyksos which contradict the biblical account concerning the identity of the Hebrews and their sojourn in Egypt. Yet Josephus happily *endorses* Manetho's Hyksos story, just as he somewhat absurdly accepts Choerilus' account of the tonsured Solymi as a reference to inhabitants of Jerusalem (1.172–75). Thus rhetorical strategy, and not just biblical authorisation, determines what Josephus will or will not accept, and his repeated insistence that Judaeans are not Egyptians must have more at stake than simply its discord with the biblical account. In fact, he makes no effort here to establish a counter-claim that the Judaeans had Chaldaean ancestry; the point is mentioned once (1.71) but never argued (cf. *Ant.* 1.158–60). All the emphasis falls on the negative point: whatever they were, they were *not Egyptian*. It seems he had a formidable presumption to negate and a large strategic investment in destroying it.[10]

III. The Popular Association of Judaeans and Egyptians

A broad range of evidence suggests that it was commonly believed in the Hellenistic-Roman era that the Judaeans were originally of Egyptian stock. While Tacitus lists a number of different theories about Judaean origins (*Histories* 5.2–3), two out of the six narrate an element of the Egyptian population migrating to Judaea, either voluntarily or by expulsion (5.2.2; 5.3); indeed, he indicates that in his day 'most authors' followed some version of the leper-expulsion narrative (5.3.1). In fact, if we survey other authors, it is clear that there were at least three ethnographical models which traced the Judaean nation to its roots in Egypt. In one model, the Judaeans are depicted as an Egyptian colony;[11] in a second, an exodus from Egypt is led by Hierosolymus and Juda (in some versions with Typhonian associations);[12] in a third, there is an expulsion or voluntary exodus led by Moses, typically associated with a plague and the divinely ordained removal of diseased or accursed inhabitants of Egypt. This last version is the one best known to us, both from Tacitus' full account and from the variant versions which Josephus cites from Manetho, Chaeremon and Lysimachus. It is also evident in varied forms in Diodorus (following Hecataeus) and Pompeius Trogus,

[10] Josephus' concern on this matter featured already in *Ant.* 2.177. This suggests that his emphasis in our text is not just a particular rhetorical stratagem, but the expression of a broader cultural anxiety.

[11] This model takes its inspiration from Herodotus' link between Egyptian circumcision and the 'Syrians in Palestine' (2.104), and is found in Diodorus 1.28, 55 (possibly derived from Hecataeus), in Strabo 18.2.5 (cf. Strabo apud Josephus, *Ant.* 14.118) and in Celsus apud Origen, *Contra Celsum* 1.22; 3.5–6; 4.31; 5.41. Strabo also has a different version (16.2.34–39), in which circumcision is a later degradation; but that account is otherwise similar to this tradition, with no reference to a plague.

[12] Tacitus, *Histories* 5.2.2; Plutarch, *Isis and Osiris* 31 (363 c–d).

and appears to have been utilised by Apion.[13] But the notion of the Judaeans as Egyptian colonists, who left Egypt as a surplus population or in revolt against Egyptian religious practices, was also of widespread currency, so one did not have to adopt the 'leper' story to consider the Judaeans originally Egyptian. Even those who associated Judaeans with other points of origin ('the east', for example, or Damascus) seem to have linked such accounts to one or another version of the Egyptian exodus, thus reinforcing the popular conception that the Judaeans were really (that is, by origin) a variant, rebellious or polluted offshoot of the Egyptian race.[14]

The popularity of this linkage to Egypt, and of its multiple narrative versions, can be easily explained: it made excellent aetiological sense. Just as the Judaeans attributed the Passover, Unleavened Bread, the leadership of Moses and the giving of the law to the circumstances of their escape from Egypt and its aftermath, so Greek and Roman authors gave historical explanations for the distinctive customs of the Judaeans. Why, for instance, did Judaeans observe the seventh-day rest? A narrative explanation could easily be found: they crossed the desert from Egypt in six days and rested from their exertions on the seventh.[15] Why were they somewhat unsociable in their habits? Because they had suffered the hostility of others in their expulsion from Egypt and learnt to trust no-one else.[16] Why was their religion aniconic and monotheistic? Obviously in reaction to the Egyptian animal cults and the multiplicity of deities they had grown up with in Egypt.[17] Why did they observe fasts? Because of their hunger in the desert.[18] Why were they so devoted to Moses? Because they had sworn an oath of undying

[13] Tacitus, *Histories* 5.3; Manetho apud Josephus, *c. Apion.* 1.227–250; Chaeremon apud Josephus, *c. Apion.* 1.288–92; Lysimachus apud Josephus, *c. Apion.* 1.304–11. In Diodorus 40.3 (derived from Hecataeus) the Judaeans are already 'foreigners' who are expelled because of a plague, but not themselves diseased; in another account (34/35.1.1–2) they are lepers and accursed. Pompeius Trogus (apud Justinus 36.2) has the Judaeans originate in Damascus, but also expelled from Egypt because of a plague. Apion probably followed some such account as we find in Chaeremon and Lysimachus (see *c. Apion.* 1.122), though he supplemented the 'disease' element with the groin-tumours suffered in the desert (2.20–27). In many of these accounts, Moses is represented as an Egyptian (specifically, Heliopolitan) priest (*c. Apion.* 1.250, 290; 2.10).

[14] Thus Manetho and Pompeius Trogus, cited above.

[15] Apion in *c. Apion.* 2.20–27; Tacitus, *Histories* 5.4.3; Pompeius Trogus (Justinus 36.2.14) refers to a seven-day fast in the desert; Plutarch, *Isis and Osiris* 31 (363 c–d) mentions a seven-day flight.

[16] Hecataeus in Diodorus 40.3; Manetho in *c. Apion.* 1.239; Lysimachus in *c. Apion.* 1.309; Pompeius Trogus in Justinus, *Epitome* 36.2.15; Diodorus 34/35 1.1–2.

[17] Diodorus (following Hecataeus) 40.3.4; Strabo 16.2.35; Celsus apud Origen, *Contra Celsum* 1.23–24; 3.5.

[18] Tacitus, *Histories* 5.4.3; Lysimachus apud *c. Apion.* 1.308.

loyalty as he led them out of Egypt.[19] Why did they worship an ass? Because an ass showed them the way to a spring as they struggled across the desert.[20] The list could go on, but is long enough already to indicate how readily the popular imagination could link known or imagined, but puzzling, Judaean characteristics with some element or other of the exodus drama, which was linked in turn to the original Egyptian ethnicity of the Judeans. If the aetiologies look to us extraordinarily simplistic, that simplicity is what made them attractive. Tacitus' heavy use of this mode of explanation indicates that he could rely on such aetiologies being taken seriously in élite circles.

The evidence suggests that two of the most widely known Judaean peculiarities – circumcision and food-abstentions – served especially to link them in the popular imagination with Egypt. Circumcision, that self-disfigurement which amused or shocked both Greeks and Romans, was widely known to be a Judaean habit, but also one observed by Egyptians, or at least by Egyptian priests. Herodotus' claim that the Colchians, Phoenicians and 'Syrians in Palestine' (2.104) had learned this practice from the Egyptians (2.104) all but invited the application to Judaeans. In accordance with the current diffusionist theories of culture, it was widely believed that the Judaeans had inherited or borrowed this custom from the Egyptians: Hecataeus (?), Diodorus, Strabo, Celsus and even Philo follow this line of thought.[21] Indeed, Josephus, who is anxious to find notable Greek witnesses to Judaeans, thinks Herodotus was actually referring to Judaeans, and thus is forced to agree with him that the 'Syrians in Palestine' (for Josephus, the Judaeans) learned this custom from Egypt (*c. Apion.* 1.168–71).[22] He also uses the commonality of circumcision between Judaeans and Egyptian priests as evidence with which to indict Apion (2.141–44). By so doing, he bears testimony to, and unwittingly reinforces, the common perception of 'Judaeans as Egyptians'.

[19] Moses' leadership is emphasised in nearly all the accounts; the loyalty motif is stressed by, for instance, Manetho (apud *c. Apion.* 1.238) and Tacitus (*Histories* 5.4.1).

[20] Tacitus, *Histories* 5.3.2; 5.4.2; Plutarch, *Quaest Conviv* 4.5.2 (670d–e).

[21] See above note 11 and Berthelot, 'Josephus' Use of Graeco-Roman Stereotypes', 207. Philo, *Spec Leg* 1.2 admits circumcision is shared with Egyptians, but not that it is borrowed from them. For the Egyptian habit (variously ascribed to all Egyptians, or just to priests) see, e.g., Diodorus 1.28.3 (all Egyptians) and Athenaeus, *Deipnosophistae* 299f (priests); cf. A. Burton, *Diodorus Siculus, Book 1. A Commentary* (Leiden: Brill, 1972), 121. Josephus relies on it being recognised as a practice of Egyptian priests (*c. Apion.* 2.141).

[22] There is good reason to think that Herodotus is not thinking of, and did not know about, a people called 'Judaeans', but Josephus needs to read him that way. Since normally Josephus wants to show how others have learned from (i.e. imitated) the Judaeans, this admission is striking, but necessary if he is to use Herodotus at all; see my commentary, *Flavius Josephus: Translation and Commentary. Vol. 10: Against Apion* (Leiden: Brill, 2007) ad loc. Not surprisingly, circumcision does not feature in the account of the Judaean way of life in 2.145ff.

Judaean food-abstentions strengthened the association. Those who read Herodotus (2.47–48) knew that Egyptians would not sacrifice a pig (except at the full moon), so it was easy to link Jewish abstention from pork with Egyptian scruples.[23] In fact, since these were the only two nations known to abstain from pork – and how peculiar! What else was a pig for, except to be eaten?[24] – it was obvious that one should bracket them together. More generally, it was widely thought that Judaean abstention from certain animals and fish was a sign that they honoured, revered, or even divinised such creatures, and here the obvious parallels (besides that with the Syrians and fish) were the animal cults, and associated food-taboos, of the Egyptians. We find such misconceptions being vigorously denied by Ps.-Aristeas (144–71 re mice etc.), but it is striking how frequently we find Judaean food-taboos being discussed in parallel with those of the Egyptians: the two nations were in a common category.[25] Where it was noticed that Judaeans actually ate some of the animals which Egyptians regarded as sacred (e.g. cows), this could be explained on the premise that they deliberately instituted this reversal in their revolt from their Egyptian roots.[26]

Thus whether as borrowing from Egypt, paralleling her strange taboos, or flouting her customs, the explanation of Judaean practices frequently linked them with Egypt. As geographical neighbours with so much in common, and such remarkable shared differences from Hellenistic-Roman culture, Egyptian-Judaean culture could easily be conflated. Endless recycling of old and erroneous stereotypes, and the skin-deep curiosity of the élite, ensured that such 'barbarian' nations had little chance of correcting such misperceptions. It is not entirely surprising that Tiberius should lump Judaeans and Egyptians together in his expulsion of foreign elements from Rome in 19 CE.[27] It is probable, indeed, that Judaeans were sometimes mistaken for Egyptians: even such a high-profile (though admittedly non-

[23] Egyptian abstention from pork is still being discussed by Aelian, *De Natura Animalium* 10.16. The link with Judaeans is noticed by Sextus Empiricus, *Pyr* 3.223: a Judaean or an Egyptian priest would die rather than eat pork. Josephus depends on this perception in *c. Apion.* 2.141.

[24] The question is raised as a genuine puzzle in Cicero, *De Natura Deorum* 2.160; Porphyry, *De Abstinentia* 1.16. Most other animals had an obvious utility to humanity.

[25] See, e.g., Plutarch, *Quaest Conviv* 4.5 (669c–670e4), where it is discussed whether the Judaean abstention from pork arises from respect for the pig, parallel to Egyptian respect for field mice, crocodiles, cats or hares; cf. the parallel between Egyptians and Judaeans in food-taboos in Philo, *Legatio* 361–2; Epictetus 1.11.12–13; 1.22.4; Porphyry, *De Abstinentia* 2.26, 61; Erotianus apud *Vocum Hippocraticarum Collectio* frag. 33.

[26] E.g., Tacitus, *Histories* 5.4.2.

[27] Josephus, *Antiquities* 18.65–84; Suetonius, *Tiberius* 36; Tacitus, *Annals* 2.85.4. However, caution is required concerning the interpretation of this episode (cf. Gruen, *Diaspora*, 29–36), and the simultaneous expulsions of Judeans and Egyptians does not necessarily indicate their perception as identical. In this context, Tacitus' use of the singular *ea superstitione* may cover both Egyptian and Judaean rites, though it may refer to the latter alone.

practising) Judaean as Tiberius Julius Alexander could be described, by a well-informed Roman, as an Egyptian (Tacitus, *Histories* 1.11).

This widespread view of Judaean Egyptian origins, its cementation by aetiological reasoning, and the common observation of parallel cultural phenomena, provides an historical context for Josephus' insistence that Judaeans are *not* in origin Egyptians. The immediate literary context for many of these pleas is his attempt to discredit versions of the leper-exodus, but I doubt whether that can provide the whole explanation. It was open to him, for instance, to counter the leper-stories with a milder version of the exodus – for instance, Strabo's positive account of Moses' disgust with Egyptian religion, his advance on Greek anthropomorphism and his leadership of the 'most thoughtful' Egyptians to Judaea (16.2.34–36). Perhaps Josephus felt that *any* account which made Judaeans an offshoot, and therefore culturally derivative, from the Egyptians, would have conceded too much. Although it might have been possible to argue that whatever they derived from Egypt they *improved*, he perhaps invested too much in the notion of Moses as the *first* inventor of piety and constitutional virtue to be able to allow cultural second-handedness at this crucial point.[28]

But it seems that the overriding concern for Josephus, in distinguishing Judaeans from Egyptians, was to set them in contrast, in fact in the sharpest possible antithesis, in their placement on the prevailing *honour scale*. In the last resort, the Judaeans are not, and cannot be, Egyptians because Josephus has staked so much on a rhetoric of antithesis, which both facilitates his apologetic task and permits him to exploit popular denigration of Egyptians while boosting the reputation of Judaeans. It is to these aspects of his strategy that we now turn.

IV. Dishonourable Egyptians: Slandering the Slanderers

At the opening of the first book of *Contra Apionem*, Josephus mounts a sustained attack on Greek historiography, aligning Judaeans, as we have observed, with Egyptians, Phoenicians and Chaldaeans (1.6–56). In this fine specimen of cultural retaliation, he punctures the arrogance of those who care only about 'renowned Greek historians' (1.2) and even offers the Greeks a taste of their own medicine (1.69). From this vantage-point it

[28] Celsus (apud Origen, *Contra Celsum* 1.2) overcame the perception of Greek inferiority by insisting that Greeks were better able to judge the value, and practise the virtues, of what 'barbarians' had discovered! Josephus presumes Mosaic priority in *c. Apion.* 2.168, 281, 293–95. For the topic see P. Pilhofer, *Presbyteron Kreitton: Der Alterbeweis der jüdischen und christlichen Apologeten und seine Vorgeschichte* (Tübingen: Mohr Siebeck, 1990).

might have been possible for Josephus to mount a defence of Judaeans *in consort with* other 'barbarian' nations, including the Egyptians, countering the insufferable snobbery with which they were routinely treated. In fact, as we have noted, he does no such thing. Having utilised the Egyptian reputation for antiquity, he turns against them with a vehemence explicable only by the requirements of his rhetoric. In short, he chooses to represent the 'slanders' he counters as coming from an Egyptian source, and chooses the perfect weapon of an orator in countering this opposition: ethos denigration.[29]

As we have observed, when Josephus turns to that part of his agenda dealing with 'those slanders and slurs which certain people have aimed at our nation' (1.219), he identifies their authors as 'Egyptians' and those who sympathise with them (1.223). However one may judge the historical plausibility of this claim, its role in his rhetoric is clear.[30] Under this label he can include Manetho, Chaeremon and Lysimachus, but also Apion, whose 'Egyptian' identity is one of Josephus' most emphatic themes. What is more, while refuting Apion, Josephus includes a number of other scurrilous stories about the Judaeans, such as the discovery of the ass head in the temple, the annual sacrificial feast on a Greek, and the Idumaean theft of the head of a pack-ass (2.79–124). Whether or not Apion used these stories, as Josephus claims, it is essential to Josephus' rhetoric to reply to them *in responding to Apion*, rather than dealing directly with 'those who supplied Apion with this fodder' (2.79), Posidonius, Apollonius Molon and Mnaseas. To respond directly to these authors would be to clarify that such legends were not specifically Egyptian (even if the ass-stories had Typhonian echoes). Such legends are far easier to answer if they are thought of as 'Egyptian' and associated with Apion, since Josephus can reply in kind, using the Egyptian animal cults as an easy target (e.g. 2.81, 85–86). To recognise these slanders as authentically Greek or Idumaean would unravel the loose claim of 1.223 and would require Josephus to recognise a source of opposition to Judaeans with quite different cultural roots. When he does move on to the criticisms of Apollonius Molon (2.145, 148, 258), he associates him vaguely with Lysimachus (2.145, 236) and Apion (2.295). Indeed, Molon had been listed with 'Egyptian' authors giving the date of the exodus (2.18), and later Josephus claims he was an admirer of the Persians (2.270). Thus it seems that, even if he cannot be entirely 'Egyptianised', Apollonius Molon can be allowed

[29] See J. M. May (*Trials of Character: The Eloquence of Ciceronian Ethos* [Chapel Hill: North Carolina Press, 1988]) for an analysis of Cicero's techniques in this sphere.

[30] On the origins of anti-Judaean stories see recently P. Schäfer, *Judeophobia: Attitudes towards the Jews in the Ancient World* (Cambridge, Mass.: Harvard University, 1997). [See further, chapter 8 above.]

no clear ethnicity of his own; and it must by no means be revealed that he had been a teacher of notable Romans (Plutarch, *Cicero* 4.4–5; *Caesar* 3.1).

Thus Josephus sustains, or at least takes care not to disrupt, the impression that Judaeans have only the Egyptians ranged against them, and if he can establish that presumption his task is infinitely easier. For the Egyptians can be presented not only as inveterate enemies of the Judaeans, and thus clearly prejudiced and unreliable in their 'slander', but also as consumed by *envy* (1.224). As Bertholet has noted, this latter motif is crucial, since it constructs a hierarchy in the relationship between Egyptians and Judaeans: one only envies those in a position superior to oneself.* Judaean superiority is in fact cleverly maintained in a comment which Josephus inserts into his response to Apion:

> In relation to us, Egyptians are swayed in one of two directions: they either boost themselves by claiming common ancestry with us, or they drag us down by association with their poor repute. (2.31)

The argument depends on the premise of Egyptian κακοδοξία ('poor repute'), never demonstrated, but always assumed. It implies, by contrast, that Judaeans are honourable: *they* would never want to associate with mean Egyptians, but the latter, either from envy or from spite, will claim the association. Here there comes to the surface the tactic which undergirds Josephus' whole strategy in relation to the Egyptians: to affirm and then utilise their negative reputation as a foil against which to place Judaean honour.

Before exploring this strategy in further detail, we should note its prevalence throughout Josephus' response to Apion (2.1–144). Despite his frequent claims about Apion's imbecility, Josephus has clearly found his multi-faceted case against the Judaeans formidable, and perhaps judges his influence in Rome to be of continuing significance.[31] But he has found a simple way of dealing with him: just characterise him as 'Egyptian'. The label here is almost as absurd as Virgil's dubbing of Cleopatra an *Aegyptia coniunx*. Although he was not apparently an Alexandrian citizen by birth, Apion had been granted this citizenship (2.32) and benefited from an enormously advanced Greek education to become famous as an orator and γραμματικός; indeed, he proved to be of such significance to the Alexandrian citizenry that he was accorded the leadership of the delegation to Gaius after the riots of 38 CE (Josephus, *Antiquities* 18.257–60). It is thus almost inconceivable that he was a native Egyptian by ancestry; in any case, his Alexandrian citizenship automatically negated that label. The fact that he

* Berthelot, 'Josephus' Use of Graeco-Roman Stereotypes'

[31] See further J. M. G. Barclay, 'Josephus v. Apion: Analysis of an Argument', in S. Mason, ed., *Understanding Josephus: Seven Perspectives* (Sheffield: Sheffield Academic, 1998) 194–221.

was born at the Oasis does not make him, as Josephus claims, 'an Egyptian par excellence' (2.29): plenty of 'Hellenes' were born in towns other than Alexandria. We may be practically certain, therefore, that Josephus has falsified Apion's ethnicity and it is not hard to see why. This deception gives Josephus his most valuable weapon in responding to Apion, one which he will utilise in practically every counter-argument and which will in some cases constitute the only argument he cares to deploy.

Two examples of Josephus' strategy must suffice as illustration here. Apion's polemic against Judaeans arose out of the Alexandrian crisis, and one of its themes was the 'illegitimacy' of the claim of some Judaeans to Alexandrian citizenship. As he begins his reply (2.38–42), Josephus claims that it is natural that early settlers in a colony should be named after the city, and makes vague claims that Judaeans elsewhere are called 'Antiochenes' etc. (2.38–39). He then confuses the issue by reference to Roman citizenship: 'Has not the generosity of the Romans ensured that their name has been shared with practically everyone, not only with individuals but with sizeable nations as a whole?' (2.40). As Josephus must have known, Roman citizenship was hardly parallel, in legal or political terms, to citizenship of a *polis*, but the argument enables both this gratuitous praise of the Romans and a sly counter-polemic against Apion:

> And if Apion discounts this type of citizenship, let him cease to call himself an 'Alexandrian'. For he was born, as I said above, in the depths of Egypt; so how could he be an 'Alexandrian' if he discounts this type of citizenship, as he sees fit to do in our case? In fact it is only to Egyptians that the Romans, who are now rulers of the world, have refused to grant any form of citizenship. Such was Apion's nobility of character that he considered himself worthy of acquiring privileges from which he was debarred, and tried to bring false charges against those who justly obtained them. (2.41–42)

The argument, which will hardly bear close scrutiny, depends on the depiction of Apion as an 'Egyptian' whose Alexandrian status is suspect and whose proper (in)dignity is revealed by *Roman* opinion: it is the judgment of those who 'rule the world' (and therefore determine honour) which indicates how one ought to consider an 'Egyptian' like this.

The same tactic of contempt is deployed in relation to religion. Where Apion had asked, 'Why, if they are citizens, do they not worship the same Gods as the Alexandrians?' (2.65), Josephus evades a full reply by issuing a counter-charge:

> Why, in your case, although you are Egyptians, do you wage among yourselves huge, implacable, battles over religion? Is it not indeed for this reason that we do not call you all 'Egyptians' – nor even collectively 'human beings', since you worship beasts hostile to our nature, nurturing them with great care – while our nation at least is clearly single and thus uniform? (2.65–66)

Again the argument would not work if Apion had not been identified as a representative of the Egyptians. In this case Josephus can exploit the bafflement with which non-Egyptians viewed the diverse animal cults in Egypt (see below, section V) and takes care to represent these not simply as strange but as gross, and their Egyptian practitioners as sub-human. Once again an honour-scale is erected: the Egyptians are at the bottom, along with their wild animals, while the Judaeans by contrast display the virtues the Egyptians lack. As this section of the argument develops (2.67–72), it swings back into politics (with which the religious question was always connected) and places the blame for the Alexandrian troubles on the infiltration of 'Egyptians' (2.69); it closes, significantly, with another appeal to *Roman* opinion:

> For none of the kings seems to have bestowed citizen rights on Egyptians, nor now do any of the emperors, while in our case Alexander brought us into the city, the kings augmented our rights and the Romans have seen fit to preserve our privileges for all time. (2.72)

Such abuse of the 'Egyptian' Apion is ubiquitous, giving Josephus ready ammunition with which to turn defence into attack, while spicing his rhetoric with the humour of ethnic ridicule. Josephus would deny, of course, that he resorts to counter-slander: he is not slandering the Egyptians, simply telling the truth. But the 'truth' he is telling is one established by the cultural dynamics of the Roman empire, and it is his alignment with this discourse in the twinned spheres of religion and politics that we will now investigate in a little more depth.

V. Egyptian Religion and Roman Values

It is significant that as soon as he turns against 'Egyptians' for their various slanders of Judaeans, Josephus highlights the *religious* contrast between the two nations:

> The contrast between the two peoples has inspired in them a great animosity, since our form of piety differs from what they practise to the same degree that the nature of God stands removed from irrational animals. It is their common ancestral tradition to consider these animals as Gods, although they differ from one another on a local basis in the honours they accord them. Empty-headed and utterly stupid people, they were inured from the beginning to erroneous opinions about Gods, and so did not succeed in imitating the lofty character of our theology but envied us when they saw us emulated by others. (1.224–25)

Encapsulated here are most of the themes to which Josephus will return in his denigration of Egyptian religion (cf. 1.254; 2.86, 128, 139, besides the polemic of 2.65–66 cited above). He insists on taking the Egyptian theriomorphic cults at face value: the Egyptians really are stupid enough to worship animals. Although he once alludes to a mythological explanation of these cults (2.128), he never refers to long-established rational explanations, based on the utility of these animals for human well-being, nor to the allegorical or 'mystical' interpretations of Egyptian religion.[32] What is more, it is not just ordinary, or friendly, animals that Egyptians treat as Gods: they nurture *savage* animals (2.139), wild beasts 'contrary to our nature' (2.66), such as crocodiles and asps (2.86). This not only rules out any rationale for these cults based on their value for humanity, it demonstrates how low the Egyptians sink in finding objects of worship and how stupid they are to revere things which damage themselves: to Josephus' amusement, they even consider those bitten by asps or seized by crocodiles blessed and worthy of God (2.86).[33] Equally important are their internal localised differences (1.225), their 'huge, implacable battles' (2.65; cf. *Ant* 1.166; 13.66). Such internal splintering of the Egyptian nation demeans them all, but it also suggests an instability, a volatility, which damages their political reputation. A religion which is so harmful to humanity and so socially divisive is an easy target.

The *contrast* with Judaeans in the passage cited above (1.224–25) is crucial to Josephus' strategy. It presupposes a hierarchy of being, which we find universally represented in the Hellenistic-Roman world. At the bottom is inanimate nature (stones, plants etc.) and just above that level are the animals, which are sentient but 'irrational'. Above the animals is humanity, endowed with reason; and above humans, the stars and/or 'daemons', which are themselves inferior to the supreme level of being, God(s). To worship animals is thus to sink from the highest to almost the lowest end of the chain of being: to conceive of the Gods in anthropomorphic terms was at least better than this! Of course, it was possible to represent iconic worship as a still inferior religion, since the statues and portraits were themselves made of inanimate material, and thus the polar opposite of God. Josephus exploits this antithesis once in *Contra Apionem*, in explaining why Judaeans do not use images in worship (2.75; cf. 2.190–92). But it is noticeable that he makes less of this than he does of Egyptian animal cults, and it is particularly significant that his critique of those who use statues in worship is directed

[32] Rational explanations, stressing the value of such animals for humanity, are found as early as Herodotus (e.g. 2.75 re the ibis) and became popular in the Hellenistic and Roman eras (e.g. Cicero *De Natura Deorum* 1.101). The notion of a mysterious but secret theology was also encouraged by Herodotus (2.65) and was advanced by apologists of many sorts (e.g. Plutarch, *Isis and Osiris* 74–76 [380f–382c]; Celsus apud Origen, *Contra Celsum* 1.20; 3.19). Josephus' refusal to countenance allegorical explanations of 'Greek' myths (*c. Apion.* 2.255) suggests he would have had little sympathy with this approach. Contrast Philo, *Mos* 1.23.

[33] This topos also derives from Herodotus (2.90), but Herodotus had expressed no disdain; even Aelian (*De Natura Animalium* 10.21) expresses more amazement than scorn.

against 'Greeks and some others' (2.74), as if he is going out of his way to *avoid* any criticism of the Romans.[34]

Thus Josephus' critique of Egyptian religion is employed both to denigrate those whose stories could damage the reputation of Judaeans and to set off Judaean religion by contrast. This is so evidently superior and 'lofty' that it is naturally emulated and admired by many (1.225; cf. 1.166; 2.280–86). That Josephus needs to do so little to establish the 'stupidity' of Egyptian religion is an indication of how widespread and how culturally embedded this verdict had become.[35] Where Herodotus had expressed his amazement at Egyptian animal cults, without showing disdain, Diodorus and Plutarch were obviously embarrassed by the cults they tried to explain; in Josephus' day, and in Roman circles, Egyptian theriolatry was a topic of widespread amusement.[36] This is clear not only from the work of satirists like Lucian and Juvenal, whom one can expect to pounce on anything capable of ridicule, but also from a number of general comments which note that Egyptian cults are 'laughed at' by 'the majority' of people.[37] Plutarch knows he has an uphill struggle in his attempt to find uplifting symbolism in the animal cults, and it seems that few Romans were willing to make the effort, however much they may have admired and even adopted the worship of Isis.

Two comments by élite Romans indicate the sort of disdain which Josephus could count on. According to Dio, Augustus on his annexation of Egypt refused to visit the Apis bull, despite its significance in Egyptian national consciousness and the respect with which the Apis tradition had been upheld by the Ptolemies. His dismissive comment, that he was accustomed to worship Gods not cattle (Dio 51.16.5), indicates the stance of the new rulers of Egypt; we noted at the outset Virgil's supercilious attitude to the 'monstrous' Gods of Egypt. A century and a half later Juvenal could count on the willingness of his readers to share his laughter at the 'monsters' worshipped by 'mad Egypt', and, like Josephus, could build on that presumption to ridicule their mutual intolerance. In his powerful *Satire 15* he displays the impatience of the Roman ruling class at those subjects obstinate enough to consider their Gods the only ones worth worshipping (*solos credat habendos / esse deos quos ipse colit*, 15.37–38) and dramatises

[34] See further J. M. G. Barclay, 'Snarling Sweetly: Josephus on Images and Idolatry', in S. C. Barton, ed., *Idolatry: False Worship in the Bible, Early Judaism and Christianity* (London: T & T Clark, 2007) 73–87; reprinted as chapter 17 in the current volume.

[35] Of course, Josephus was also drawing on a long Jewish tradition, represented in the Diaspora by, e. g., Ps.-Aristeas 138; Wisdom of Solomon 11.15; 15.18–19; *Sib Or* 3.29–30; 5.276–80; Philo, *Decal.* 76–80; *Contempl.* 8–10. Artapanus is the striking exception.

[36] See the full survey of material in K. A. D. Smelik and E. A. Hemelrijk, 'Who knows not what monsters demented Egypt worships?', *ANRW* 2.17.14: 1852–2000.

[37] Cicero, *De Natura Deorum* 1.101; Aelian, *De Natura Animalium* 12.5. Cf. Lucian, *De Sacrificiis* 15; *Deorum Concilium* 10–11; *Jupiter Tragoedus* 42.

Egyptian fractiousness in a gruesome account of a local feud. In his appeal to a Roman or Romanised reading-public Josephus could count on such a set of stereotypes, and a tradition of cultural contempt, which renders his victory over his 'Egyptian' opponents remarkably straightforward. Cicero would have been proud of him.

What would have surprised Cicero was Josephus' use of this ridicule of Egyptians precisely in order to defend another 'barbaric' race, the Judaeans. The contrasts which Josephus sets up – between animal-worshipping stupidity and the σεμνότης (one can almost hear the Latin *gravitas*) of Judaean 'theology' (1.225), between the volatility of Egyptian religious disputes and the harmoniousness of Judaean unanimity (2.65–68) – are designed to establish Judaean religion as an honourable, safe religion, entirely compatible with the Roman ethos. In fact, throughout this apology Josephus is concerned to present Judaean religion as consonant with the noblest and highest philosophy (1.175; 2.168, 239, 255–57, 281). The Judaean conception of God is parallel to, in fact the source of, the best in the whole philosophical tradition (2.168, 281) and its freedom from 'Greek' mythology indicates how far it rises above such demeaning conceptions of God (2.239–54). Even its controversial imagelessness indicates how lofty its theology really is (2.73–75).

The main problem for Josephus was in explaining why this noble Judaean religion was so intolerant as to appear 'antisocial' towards those with other religious practices and beliefs. Juvenal's impatience with those who thought only their Gods worth worshipping (*Satire* 15.37–38, cited above) indicates how serious was the sort of criticism which Josephus cites here from Apollonius Molon: that the Judaeans were misanthropic (2.148), in fact the most worthless specimens of humanity (2.236) because they did not admit those who had other conceptions of God and did not share fellowship with those who preferred a different lifestyle (2.258). Of course this criticism of Judaeans had a long pedigree. The originally Hellenistic sense of shock, that in the 'civilised' world there should be those so 'unfriendly' as to refuse ordinary decency to other 'Greeks', was inherited and maintained by the Roman ruling class for whom such religious exclusivism was unwelcome, since it could cause serious social tensions in an empire which required smooth inter-cultural co-operation. Josephus' defence of Judaeans on this count appeals, in the end, to the right of Judaeans to preserve their ancestral customs (2.259–75), even against the critical demands of philosophy (2.262–68). This appeal was well-made: in the sphere of religion, élite Romans typically fell back on the inherited *mos maiorum* when questioned by philosophy, and cultural conservatism was a trait Romans had to respect.[38] And here Josephus' double-standard is particularly glaring. Where Judaean religion

[38] See, e.g., Cicero, *De Natura Deorum* 3.5–6.

was noble, lofty and philosophical – or, where it was open to philosophical criticism, at least traditional and thus respectable – Egyptian religion was nothing but stupid, its philosophical interpretation not worth the barest mention and its practices, however immensely ancient, simply ridiculous.[39]

VI. Egyptians and Judaeans under Roman Hegemony

As we noted in the introduction, Roman ridicule of Egyptian religion went hand in hand with disdain of the (contemporary) Egyptian people: it was a central tenet of imperial propaganda that subject peoples were lesser beings who could only be improved by Roman governance. It was simple enough to draw direct conclusions from the 'absurdity' of the animal cults: people with a religion like that must be very gullible, excessively 'superstitious', if not entirely mad. The fact that they actually fought over such animal-worship, the people of one nome deliberately provoking another by eating their sacred animals, only shows what a hot-headed and uncivilised people they are. Juvenal contrasts such barbarity with the spread of Graeco-Roman culture throughout the empire: even Britain is civilised now (*Satire* 15.110–12), and only in Egypt could such horrors still prevail. Plutarch records the feud between the dog-worshipping Cynopolites and the fish-worshipping Oxyrhynchites, which led the people of the two nomes to war; he concludes, significantly, by noting that they were finally brought to order only through the 'punishment' applied by the Romans (*Isis and Osiris* 72 [380 a–c]). Such are the benefits of Roman control. The Egyptian people as a whole might be characterised as 'useless and unwarlike' (e. g., Juvenal, *Satire* 15.126), or alternatively as reckless, impudent and insubordinate (e. g., Tacitus, *Histories* 1.11).[40] Dio presents an illuminating example of Roman condescension towards the province: a populous place with rich resources of importance to Rome, its people had a facile, fickle character, while the Alexandrians had an alarming capacity for revolution (50.24; 51.17.1–3). The humiliations which Augustus inflicted on this justly proud city caused, as we know, deep and long-lasting indignation, but Dio saw nothing but the proper exercise of imperial power: 'thus was Egypt enslaved' (51.17.4).

Josephus uses a number of such stereotypes in *Contra Apionem*, and he needed them. One can make out from Josephus' reply that Apion had denied the right of Judaeans to be citizens of Alexandria. According to Apion, they were insignificant residents in the city who had been disloyal to the

[39] At *Ant.* 18.65–84 Josephus is at pains to distinguish between the sexually dangerous Egyptian cult and the noble (if exploited) Judean religion, although both were implicated in scandals in 19 CE; see Matthews, *First Converts*, 10–28.

[40] See further Smelik and Hemelrijk, 'Who knows not', 1920–54.

Ptolemies and even challenged Roman power at a critical moment in history (2.50). He had accused them of stirring up trouble in Alexandria; they were a troublesome and unassimilated element in the population (2.65, 68), who were brazen enough not to accord Roman emperors the usual honours (2.73). In fact, the wickedness of their culture and the impiety of their religion were proved by their perpetual 'slavery' to other nations and by the repeated capture of their city; we may suspect he made special mention of Pompey's capture of Jerusalem in 63 BCE (2.125). These were powerful accusations, whose special barb lay in their presentation of Judaeans as hostile to their Roman overlords.[41] Josephus' sensitivity to such charges suggests that they continued to resonate in his day, when they could acquire additional force from the Jewish Revolt.

As we have noted, Josephus' typical response is to turn such accusations back against his 'Egyptian' prosecutor. It is Egyptians like Apion who are debarred from citizenship (2.38–42), and it was not Judaeans who stirred up trouble in Alexandria, but Egyptian-Alexandrians of Apion's sort (2.68–70).[42] What else can one expect from 'fickle and empty headed' Egyptians (1.225) with their 'evil habits' (2.70)? The tactic serves to distract the reader from the significance of the charge against the Judaeans, but it also involves a concerted campaign to present Judaeans as politically honourable from the perspective of Roman power. In terms of their history in Egypt, Josephus insists that Judaeans supported the rightful Ptolemaic line, and makes great capital out of Apion's point that Cleopatra refused to grant them grain: agglomerating several aspects of Augustan anti-Cleopatran propaganda he takes it as an *honour* that the Judaeans were slighted by her (2.56–60). The emperors, he insists, have always had a good opinion of Judaeans in Egypt (2.61–64), and if the Judaeans do not set up their images, that is cause to admire the *magnanimitas* and *mediocritas* of the Romans (2.73). Thus at no point does Josephus allow Judaean and Roman interests to come into conflict, while the Egyptians are always at fault or in disgrace.

The crowning example of this tactic comes in 2.125–34 when Josephus responds to Apion's claim about Judaean political weakness. His first and main response is simply to return the compliment: 'they, obviously, belong to the most dominant city, and have become accustomed from the beginning to ruling, rather than serving, the Romans!' (2.125). The sarcasm continues: 'So it is only the Egyptians ... who have the special privilege of not having

[41] On Philo's response, also Romanised, see M. Niehoff, *Philo on Jewish Identity and Culture* (Tübingen: Mohr Siebeck, 2001) 111–36.

[42] Josephus here reflects the polemical use of ethnic labels in the Alexandrian crisis, in which both Judaeans and Alexandrians called the other 'Egyptian'; see K. Goudriaan, 'Ethnical Strategies in Graeco-Roman Egypt', in P. Bilde et al., eds., *Ethnicity in Hellenistic Egypt* (Aarhus: Aarhus University, 1992) 74–99.

been subservient to any of those who conquered Asia or Europe – these who throughout time have not had a single day of freedom, not even at the hands of their indigenous masters!' (2.129; cf. again 2.130, 133). Such rhetoric suitably demeans the Egyptians under the heel of their Roman 'masters', but the *tu quoque* is clearly not a sufficient reply. Interestingly, Josephus adds that most nations experience changes of fortune (2.127), and insists that one cannot blame pious victims if their temples were impiously destroyed:

> I pass over the kings who were famed for their piety (for example, Croesus) and the disasters they experienced in their lives; I pass over the burning of the Athenians' acropolis, of the temple in Ephesus, and that in Delphi, and thousands of others. No-one has used these events to reproach the victims, but the perpetrators. (2.131)

One can hardly read this argument without a certain frisson: among those 'thousands of others' is, of course, the Judaeans' famous temple in Jerusalem, an example which cannot have been absent from Josephus' mind, even if it could not have been present in Apion's. Josephus here comes within an ace of a devastating criticism of Rome: who else, after all, 'perpetrated' this destruction? To develop this argument would be to destroy that circularity which tied Roman piety to Roman military might and thus subvert the self-congratulation of Roman imperialism. Josephus, however, prefers to 'pass [this] over' – a silence as strategic as his contorted efforts in the *War* to exonerate Titus for the burning of the temple. Elsewhere in *Contra Apionem* he mentions Titus' 'occupation' of the temple (2.82), but not the destruction; in fact, he insists on speaking of the temple as a continuing reality (e.g. 2.193–98). The Judaeans who, in Josephus' lifetime, were butchered in theatres all over the Roman empire did so for their defiance of Rome during that war, and no doubt with curses of Rome on their lips. Josephus alludes to such deaths in theatres and he will honour them, but only for their bravery in dying 'for the law' (e.g. 1.43; 2.232–34); he never lets us enquire who tortured them, and why.

By shying away from any hint of criticism, Josephus indicates that his apologetic strategy depends on an alignment of the interests of Judaeans and Romans. He finishes this section (2.125–34) by insisting that 'when all monarchs on all sides made war on the Romans, ours alone were maintained as allies and friends due to their loyalty' (2.134). The example is well out of date: thanks to the Romans, Judaeans no longer had 'monarchs', and 'loyalty' was the not first thing to spring to the mind of anyone contemplating the events of 66–73 CE! Josephus' silences and diplomatic manoeuvres indicate that his apology is written under the constraints of Roman power. The denigration of 'enslaved' Egyptians is again the foil for the portrayal of Judaean 'friends', but it is clear that such an honour is in the gift of Rome. If the emperors have the right to determine the recounting of history (1.50–52),

Josephus cannot challenge their right to apportion honour on their terms. At every turn Josephus is confronted by this political constraint.[43]

VII. Conclusions

In exploring Josephus' use of the category 'Egyptian' I hope to have illuminated some parts of his rhetorical strategy, but also, and at the same time, some aspects of his cultural and political stance. It can now be seen that his insistence that Judaeans are not in any way 'Egyptian' serves to counter a common contemporary association between the two nations, but is also part of a strategy to set the two in polar opposition, constructing Judaean honour against the backdrop of Egyptian disgrace. Labelling his opponents as 'Egyptian' not only enables Josephus to dispose of them swiftly; it also helps him insert Judaeans into the honour-codes of Roman discourse, as exemplars of reasonable and traditional piety and as loyal friends to Rome. Josephus thus utilises Roman disdain of one subservient people in order to redeem the honour of another; he laughs with them at the 'barking Anubis' in order to silence their criticism of an 'antisocial' religion.

Such an analysis suggests we view Josephus as an ambivalent figure, caught in the dilemma of an apologist: he needs to speak in the terms of the dominant culture if he is to win respect, but he speaks on behalf a culture not entirely aligned to that mainstream. If we examine the power-relations which underlie this apologetic stance, we find a figure who has been given permission to speak for Judaeans against their contemporary detractors but who can afford to do so only in terms which, on the surface at least, are fully complimentary to his Roman masters. This stance is complex and can be variously assessed. From one angle, Josephus' achievement is to use the tools of the Hellenistic-Roman tradition, and the value-system most relevant to his Roman(ised) readers, in order to represent and advocate his own Judaean tradition: if the effort shows how far he has been acculturated in his Roman environment, it also displays what might be termed reverse acculturation, the use of Hellenistic-Roman culture to render honourable a stubbornly particularist tradition. From another angle, Josephus' evasions and delicate tip-toeing around Roman sensitivities look like the capitulation of the colonised to the terms imposed by the colonisers, unable any longer to hear, or at least to represent, the voices of those who had suffered at the

[43] For an analysis of these cultural and political power-relations, and the possibility of reading a different message at places 'between the lines', see J. M. G. Barclay, 'The Empire Writes Back: Josephan Rhetoric in Flavian Rome', in J. Edmondson, S. Mason and J. Rives, eds., *Flavius Josephus and Flavian Rome* (Oxford: Oxford University, 2005) 315–32; reprinted as chapter 15 in the current volume.

hands of the 'magnanimous' Romans. I do not wish to adjudicate between these two perspectives or to find some mediating position between them: neither can be easily dismissed. But I suppose we might have hoped that he had shared less heartily in the Romans' jokes at others' expense or, better, dropped some hint that their sense of humour was racially and culturally demeaning.[44]

[44] My evaluative language makes explicit the political perspective from which I write, influenced by post-colonial sensitivities and contemporary cultural and religious problematics on a global scale; other perspectives (pro-Roman, anti-Jewish, anti-Egyptian, uncritically pro-Josephan) would read the evidence differently. All historiography is contingent in varying ways and I do not regard the restrained deployment of that perspectival contingency as historically irresponsible. Cf. Hill: 'That is why history has to be rewritten in each generation: each new act in our human drama necessarily shifts our attitude towards the earlier acts ... We ourselves are shaped by the past; but from our vantage point in the present we are continually reshaping the past which shapes us' (*Change and Continuity in Seventeenth Century England* [London: Weidenfeld and Nicholson, 1974] 284).

15. The Empire Writes Back

Josephan Rhetoric in Flavian Rome

Scholarship on Josephus is now more than even conscious that all his literary projects – his histories as well as his apologetics – are shaped by rhetoric; every work is an act of persuasion, and each demonstrates, in varying ways, his mastery of rhetorical forms and techniques.[1] One can analyse this rhetoric at one level as a matter of technical competence: Josephus' use of tropes, his deployment of arguments, his *ethos*-attacks on his opponents and *pathos* appeals to his readers/listeners – all such techniques can be identified and mapped in comparison with culturally contiguous parallels. But at another level Josephus' rhetoric demonstrates more than technique: it reveals his ideological commitments. In deploying his rhetoric Josephus displays the norms and honour-codes to which he is committed. His narrative-structures and syllogisms show what counts, for him, as honourable or dishonourable behaviour, and the norms and values by which events and cultures should be judged. Rhetoric is never value-free: it depends on a set of assumptions, often unspoken but easily enough deduced by analysis of its discourse-structures. Moreover, in the case of Josephus' rhetoric we may watch an accomplished writer handle the complexities of unequal power-relations, in which an elite foreigner in Rome carefully shapes his discourse in order to win maximal advantage for himself and for his people, within the constraints of his social and political environment. Thus, even when it is not overtly political, Josephus' rhetoric invites us to consider his politics, the strategies by which his cultural tools are made to serve particular political ends.

Josephus' *Against Apion* is a blatantly rhetorical work, whose argumentative techniques can be analysed simply enough by reference to ancient rhetorical conventions.[2] But it is also, as a number of scholars have noted, a

[1] For two very recent examples of this trend in Josephus scholarship, see G. Mader, *Josephus and the Politics of Historiography: Apologetic and Impression Management in the* Bellum Judaicum (Leiden: Brill, 2000) and S. Mason, *Flavius Josephus. Translation and Commentary Vol 9: Life of Josephus*. (Leiden: Brill, 2001).

[2] For preliminary steps in this direction see, for instance, R. G. Hall, 'Josephus' *Contra Apionem* and Historical Inquiry in the Roman Rhetorical Schools', in L. H. Feldman and J. R. Levison, eds., *Josephus'* Contra Apionem: *Studies in its Character and Context with a Latin Concordance to the Portion Missing in Greek* (Leiden: Brill, 1996) 229–49; J.-W. van

subtly Romanised piece of argumentation, which transposes Jewish thematics into a specifically Roman key.[3] At this point the rhetorical and cultural contours of the text map onto each other: Josephus' rhetoric is moulded to appeal to Roman standards of honour, and his discourse is variously confined or developed according to the cultural presumptions of his environment. Here our analysis will be enriched if we pay attention to the dynamics of power which flow around and through this presentation of a Romanised Judaism. For such an analysis I have found it helpful to utilise some aspects of current 'post-colonial theory', which is particularly well attuned to the phenomenon of power and how subordinate groups can (or cannot) represent themselves. Since this is, to my knowledge, a new angle of approach to Josephus, I wish to outline first the potential value of this perspective, before turning to one text, *Against Apion* 2.125–34, which emerges in this light as a particularly suggestive example of Josephus' rhetoric.

I. Josephus and Post-Colonial Theory

Despite its label, the theoretical paradigms which are grouped under the name of 'post-colonial theory' are not only concerned with the cultural after-effects once a colonial or imperial system has withdrawn. Their subject-matter is, in fact, the power-relations between dominant (or colonising) cultures and the subordinated cultures which were once, or still are, under their political or economic power.[4] Broadly speaking, post-colonial

Henten and R. Abusch, 'The Jews as Typhonians and Josephus' Strategy of Refutation in *Contra Apionem*', in L.H. Feldman and J.R. Levison, eds., *Josephus'* Contra Apionem: *Studies in its Character and Context with a Latin Concordance to the Portion Missing in Greek* (Leiden: Brill, 1996) 271–309; J.M.G. Barclay, 'Josephus v. Apion: Analysis of an Argument', in S. Mason, ed., *Understanding Josephus. Seven Perspectives* (Sheffield: Sheffield Academic Press, 1998) 194–221.

[3] See, e.g., M. Goodman, 'Josephus as a Roman Citizen', in F. Parente and J. Sievers, eds., *Josephus and the History of the Graeco-Roman Period* (Leiden: Brill, 1994) 329–38; G. Haaland, 'Jewish Laws for a Roman Audience: Toward an Understanding of *Contra Apionem*', in J.U. Kalms and F. Siegert, eds., *Internationales Josephus-Kolloquium Brüssel 1998* (Münster: LIT, 1999) 282–304; J.M.G. Barclay, 'Judaism in Roman Dress: Josephus' Tactics in the *Contra Apionem*', in J.U. Kalms, ed., *Internationales Josephus-Kolloquium Aarhus 1999* (Münster: LIT, 2000) 231–45.

[4] The literature in this sphere is now vast. For a valuable overview see A. Loomba, *Colonialism/Post-Colonialism* (London: Routledge, 1998), and for a collection of seminal essays P. Williams and L. Chisman, eds., *Colonial Discourse and Post-Colonial Theory: A Reader* (London: Harvester Wheatsheaf, 1993). A useful introduction to the key concepts in this field may be found in B. Ashcroft, G. Griffiths and H. Tiffin, *Key Concepts in Post-Colonial Studies* (London: Routledge, 1998). [See also now the excellent survey and analysis by S. Moore, *Empire and Apocalypse: Postcolonialism and the New Testament* (Sheffield: Phoenix Press, 2006).]

theory seeks to analyse the power of the dominant in the sphere of ideology, that is the 'hegemony' with which superior nations or classes control not only the economic and material lives of their subordinates, but also the terms in which they are described and defined, even the terms in which they think and speak. There is an acute consciousness here of the problem of representation: who has the power to represent the lives and cultures of the subordinate, and, if the colonised themselves take that role, under what constraints and in what terms are they able to make themselves heard? If Said's *Orientalism* focused attention on the ways in which the dominant creators of knowledge stereotype, essentialise and patronise the cultures they describe, more recent attention has focused on the ways in which once or still colonised cultures acquire the voice with which to answer back.*

Since post-colonial theory has been developed first in English-language departments, the most important objects of analysis have been post-colonial literature, especially on how, to borrow one book-title, *The Empire Writes Back*.** At an early stage, scholars' main object was to detect strategies of *resistance*, noting how in the colonial or post-colonial era the literature authored by the subordinate managed to evade, twist or even subvert the cultural authority under which it was written. More recently, particularly under the influence of Homi Bhabha,[5] it has been recognised that the immensely complex relations between colonised and coloniser are not best analysed by the binary antithesis of assimilation/antagonism, but typically take subtle and ambivalent forms of 'in-between-ness', which serve to complicate and even destabilise the two cultures concerned. One key concept here is that of 'hybridity', which refers not simply to a conflation or syncretism of two cultures, but to the ambivalence of the new cultural formation which results from cultural contact in conditions of unequal power. The hybrid results of this contact not only alter the 'original' native culture but also challenge the solidity of the coloniser's cultural system, since the new product is both like and unlike the dominant culture (Anglicised, if you like, but not English).[6] The important point is that this potential instability is open to exploitation by the colonised themselves. Although it is impossible for them to resurrect an 'authentic'or 'original' culture – indeed the search

---

* E. Said, *Orientalism: Western Representations of the Orient* (London: Routledge & Kegan Paul, 1978).

** B. Ashcroft, G. Griffiths and H. Tiffin, eds., *The Empire Writes Back: Theory and Practice in Post-Colonial Literature* (London: Routledge, 1989).

[5] His seminal essays are collected in H. K. Bhabha, *The Location of Culture* (London: Routledge, 1994).

[6] See especially Bhabha, *The Location of Culture*, 102–122, and for an elucidation of this complex notion, adapted from Derrida, see Loomba, *Colonialism/Post-Colonialism*, 178–83. There is a valuable analysis of Bhabha's work by B. Moore-Gilbert, *Postcolonial Theory: Context, Practices, Politics* (London/New York: Verso, 1997) 114–151.

for 'authenticity' is itself an artificial endeavour – they can nonetheless creatively employ the dominant culture for their own ends. Here strategies of 'resistant adaptation' can be adopted, in which post-colonial authors neither simply succumb to, nor simply subvert, the colonial culture but negotiate complex paths of self-expression through the adapted medium of the dominant discourse.[7]

Could such perspectives assist in analysing the power-relations between Romans and the subordinate cultures within the Roman empire? Of course there are numerous social, political and economic differences between the power-dynamics of the Roman empire and those of modern imperialisms and neo-colonialisms. We cannot expect, and should not create, precise parallels in political relationships or cultural strategies between ancient and modern times. But I am convinced that some of the basic questions raised by post-colonial theory, concerning ideology, representation and power, are worth posing to the ancient phenomena as well, and some Roman archaeologists are now exploring this terrain. For instance, with regard to the provinces of Gaul and Britain, fruitful questions can be asked about the meaning of the architecture and religious artefacts generated in Gallo-Roman cultures, in which we may enquire, for instance, to what extent Romanised Gauls reconstructed and advanced their own Gallic culture even while partially adopting the material and religious expressions of their Roman overlords. The use of Roman artefacts within a British burial, or the presence of a Roman-origin deity within Gallic religious statuary, might indicate a process of cultural supervention by the dominant Roman power. But they could also be examples of 'transculturation', that process by which members of subordinated or marginal groups select or invent from the materials transmitted by a dominant culture, recycling themes, genres, images and artefacts for their own use, sometimes with subtly subversive effects.[8] In such cases, archaeologists are apt to bemoan the fact that we have no native Gallic or British literature in which to view how the indigenous cultures understood, or at least represented, themselves within the terms of their Romanising environment. And here students of ancient Judaism have a massive, but underexploited, advantage. Here we

---

[7] For an example from South America, see S. Stern, *Peru's Indian Peoples and the Challenge of the Spanish Conquest* (Wisconsin: University of Wisconsin, 1982).

[8] See, for instance, the collection of essays in J. Webster and N. Cooper, eds., *Roman Imperialism: Post-Colonial Perspectives* (Leicester: Leicester University School of Archaeological Studies, 1996) and D.J. Mattingly, ed., *Dialogues in Roman Imperialism: Power, Discourse and Discrepant Experience in the Roman Empire* (Journal of Roman Archaeology Supplement Series 23; Portsmouth, RI: JRA, 1997), as well as the issue of *World Archaeology* 28 (1996–97). A highly nuanced analysis of 'Romanisation' in Gaul has been offered by G. Woolf, *Becoming Roman: The Origins of Provincial Civilization in Gaul* (Cambridge: Cambridge University, 1998).

have exactly what the post-colonial Roman archaeologists are looking for: expressions by a subordinate group of their own traditions and values, but under the constraints, and to some degree within the terms, of the dominant Hellenistic-Roman culture.

From this perspective, Josephus is a perfect example of 'the empire writing back'. In response to alternative and generally derogatory accounts of the Jewish Revolt, Josephus dares to present his own version of the War, and then, at great length, his own account of Jewish history and the place of Jews within the world-history of the Hellenistic and early Roman periods. In analysing South American responses to Spanish imperialism, Mary Louise Pratt has termed this sort of activity 'auto-ethnography'. Typical of such texts are the ways 'they involve a selective collaboration with and appropriation of idioms of the metropolis or conqueror. These are merged or infiltrated to varying degrees with indigenous idioms to create self-representations intended to *intervene* in metropolitan modes of understanding'.[9] The openness to complexity (even ambiguity) in this approach, and the awareness of power-relations and constraints, is precisely what is needed in analysis of Josephus, where evaluations of his stance towards the Romans have frequently been conducted in simplistic or psychological terms. Understandably enough, his statements on his role in the Revolt, his relationship to Vespasian and Titus and the destruction of the Temple have elicited strong suspicion, and he has frequently been pilloried as an imperial stooge and self-serving sycophant. In reaction to such verdicts, others have sought to exonerate Josephus, or at least to maintain that he consistently served what he thought were the interests of his fellow Jews.[10] But much more is at play in Josephus' works than his personal agenda. His careful restatements of Jewish history and culture, under the cultural and political constraints of the post-70 CE era, should draw us to examine the complexity of his Jewish self-representation. The issue here is not simply how he melds Jewish tradition with Hellenistic cultural forms and Romanised value-systems, but how the product, in its 'hybridity', not only changes the character of Judaism but also contributes to the ever-changing discussion of what it means to be 'Roman'. Once again, the power-dynamics are crucial, imposing limits on what Josephus can say openly. But in such a situation, as James Scott has demonstrated, the 'public transcript' can be heard differently by different audiences: while those in power may hear only compliance, others who

[9] M. L. Pratt, 'Transculturation and Autoethnography: Peru 1615/1980' in F. Barker, P. Hulme and M. Iversen, eds., *Colonial Discourse/Postcolonial Theory* (Manchester: Manchester University, 1994) 24–46, at 28; cf. her monograph, *Imperial Eyes: Travel Writing and Transculturation* (London: Routledge, 1992).

[10] The long debate, frequently highly-charged, is surveyed in P. Bilde, *Flavius Josephus between Jerusalem and Rome* (Sheffield: JSOT, 1988).

know, or suspect, a hidden transcript can detect the oblique and circumspect strategies by which the subordinate maintain an alternative discourse.[11]

To approach Josephus from this perspective would direct our angle of vision in at least these ways:

1. We should recognise, and take for granted, that Josephus is operating under considerable constraints in his writing projects. His position in Rome, and his desire to reach and persuade a Roman or Romanised elite make it impossible for him to voice overt criticism of Roman policy to the Jews. This affects not only what he says about Vespasian and Titus in the conduct of the war against the Jews, but also, more broadly, his statements on Roman cultural characteristics. It is, for instance, both necessary and diplomatic to praise Roman φιλανθρωπία in affording Roman citizenship to so many non-Romans (*c. Apion*. 2.40), but also, when commenting on the distinctive Jewish aniconic religious tradition, to steer away from direct comment on Roman culture by noting simply that 'the Greeks and some others think it right to make statues' – a practice Josephus condemns as 'profitable neither to God nor to humanity' (2.74–75; cf. below, chapter 17). As a political subject in Rome, and as an apologist, Josephus cannot afford to allow his discourse to clash openly or directly with Roman sensibilities.

2. Given such constraints, we should expect Josephus' most effective advocacy for the Jews to emerge not in confrontation with Roman cultural values, but in the ways he turns and shapes those values to his own interests. Like every other culture, the norms, values and beliefs of the Roman elite did not constitute a monolithic unity, but were a complex composite of traditions, inevitably filled with tensions and gaps, and in constant process of adaptation and reconfiguration. Such plasticity was what made it possible for Roman moralists, satirists, orators and historians to turn their own 'Roman' traditions against fellow Romans, and to redeploy them creatively for their own political and social interests. It was thus equally possible for a non-Roman like Josephus to turn that complex Roman tradition to the interests of his own cultural tradition. In *Against Apion* we can see Josephus working on Roman terms, but manipulating Roman values and norms to include, as exemplars, the Jews themselves – appropriating Roman cultural symbols, sometimes subtly redefined, for the greater glory of Judaism. Although his use of the Roman tradition in some respects consolidates the

[11] Scott has written two brilliant monographs on this theme: J. C. Scott, *Weapons of the Weak: Everyday Forms of Peasant Resistance* (New Haven: Yale University, 1985); idem, *Domination and the Arts of Resistance* (New Haven: Yale University, 1990). See, e.g., ibid., 34: 'What may look from above like the extraction of a required performance can easily look from below like the artful manipulation of deference and flattery to achieve its own ends'.

legitimacy of Roman discourse, it also empowers him to find a persuasive medium in which to re-express Judaism.

3. What we might also find in Josephus, suitably concealed or partial in expression, are hints of a cultural defiance which refuses to let Judaism merely mirror back to the Romans their own cultural mores. This is not a necessary or inevitable feature of writers under colonial conditions: some have simply erased their native cultural pride. But Josephus has not rested content with showing that the Jews are simply, as it were, 'Romans' from Judaea. By insisting on the extreme antiquity of Judaism and the originality of Moses' constitution (which has been imitated and envied by all other peoples), and by inserting under Roman moral categories his own Jewish customs (e.g., the Jewish ban on abortion, *c. Apion.* 2.202), Josephus, as it were, infiltrates Roman discourse with his own distinctively Jewish traditions. The comparison with Roman culture is always indirect: it is typically 'the Greeks' with whom Josephus favourably compares the Jewish constitution. But his claim that Judaism is really the best, and most pious, constitution ever invented has indirect and unspoken implications for its position in relation to the Romans themselves. In this light, we might be open to consider whether Josephus uses ambiguous or veiled statements which could suggest to some readers a counter-current to his own public deference towards the Romans.

II. A Sample of Josephus' Rhetoric: Against Apion 2.125–34

I wish to illustrate some features of Josephus' rhetoric by examination of a passage in *Against Apion* which I find fascinatingly complex and suggestive. Towards the end of his response to Apion, Josephus turns to an accusation of considerable political and cultural importance, the Jews' history of political subordination and military failure. The issue was clearly important at the time when Apion voiced this criticism in the aftermath of the Alexandrian riots (38–41 CE), but Josephus is surely aware of its still greater salience in his own day. I cite the text in my own translation:[12]

---

[12] There are minor textual problems in a few places, in which I follow most recent editors: e.g. at 125 insert τὸ μὴ ἄρχειν before δουλεύειν (with ed. pr. and recent editors); at 126 read ἀνάσχοιτο μεγαλαυχίας with B. Niese (*Flavii Iosephi Opera edidit et apparatu critico instruxit* [vol. 5; Berlin: Weidmann, 1889]) et al.; at 127 read διὰ καίρου τινος with T. Reinach (*Flavius Josèphe contre Apion: Texte établi et annoté* [Paris: Société d'édition "Les belles lettres", 1930]); at 131 the square brackets indicate an uncertain text (without support from the Latin), which might be better omitted or radically emended; on 134, see below. [See now the translation and commentary in my *Flavius Josephus, Translation and Commentary. Volume 10: Against Apion* (Leiden: Brill, 2007); cf. F. Siegert, ed., *Flavius*

125. One should also be particularly amazed at the great intelligence in what Apion goes on to say. For he says that it is proof of the fact that we do not follow just laws or worship God as we should that, rather than govern, we are subservient to other nations, one after another, and we have experienced some misfortunes affecting our city – while they, obviously, belonging to the most dominant city, have become accustomed from the very beginning to ruling, rather than serving, the Romans! *126.* Perhaps someone on the Roman side might sustain such a boast. But of the rest of humanity, there is no-one who would deny that this argument of Apion turns precisely against himself. *127.* It has fallen to few to gain sovereignty over a period of time, and changes have again brought even these under the yoke to serve others; most peoples have been subject to others on many occasions.

128. So it is only the Egyptians – because the Gods, so they say, fled to their country for refuge and were saved by changing into the form of animals – who have the special privilege of not having been subservient to any of those who conquered Asia or Europe – these who throughout time have not gained a single day of freedom, not even at the hands of their indigenous masters! *129.* The way in which the Persians treated them – who not only once but on many occasions sacked their cities, razed their temples to the ground and slaughtered what they consider to be 'Gods' – I would not reproach them for that. *130.* For it is not fitting to imitate Apion in his ignorance: he has not considered the misfortunes of the Athenians or the Lacedaemonians, the latter universally agreed to be the most courageous of the Greeks, the former the most pious. *131.* I pass over the kings who were famed for their piety [for example, Croesus] and the disasters they experienced in their lives; I pass over the burnt Athenian acropolis, the temple in Ephesus, that in Delphi, thousands of others. No-one has blamed these things on the victims, but on the perpetrators. *132.* Our novel accuser, Apion, turns out to have forgotten his own disasters affecting Egypt: Sesostris, the mythical king of Egypt, has blinded him!

On our side, could we not speak of our kings, David and Solomon, who mastered many nations? *133.* Let us pass over them – although Apion was ignorant of the universally-known fact that the Egyptians were subservient to the Persians, and to the Macedonians who ruled Asia after them, with a status no different from slaves, *134* while we, being free, used to rule in addition over the surrounding cities for about 120 years up till the time of Pompey the Great; and when all the monarchs, on all sides, were hostile to the Romans,[13] ours alone were maintained as allies and friends due to their loyalty.

Apion's charge is relatively simple: that history is proof of the insignificance or inferiority of the Jews, or rather, still stronger, that it proves the moral deficiencies in the structure of their culture ('that we do not have just laws') and the inadequacy, even impiety, inherent in their religion ('or worship God as we should'). These are serious and far-reaching criticisms, and Apion's argument is based on a cultural logic generally accepted through-

---

Josephus, Über die Ursprünglichkeit des Judentums (Contra Apionem) (2 vols.; Göttingen: Vandenhoeck und Ruprecht, 2008).]

[13] I follow Niese, who probably correctly here emends the text to ἐκπολεμωθέντων πρὸς Ῥωμαίους.

out the ancient world: that military and political success is proof of moral excellence and piety while, conversely, defeat or disaster are attributable to the moral and religious inferiority of the losers.[14] This is a logic which the Romans themselves consistently supported, not least because it enabled them to interpret their own habit of victory as a proof of their cultural and religious superiority. Roman military prowess and religious disdain thus created a powerful circularity which was all but mentally unassailable: just as Roman success was proof of her greater piety, so the crushing of nations which had the effrontery to challenge her might demonstrated their gross or pathetic contrariety to all religious decency. It was a logic easily employed by the Romans to discredit the Jews (although not only them). Cicero, for instance, overturned Jewish complaints about the governor Flaccus simply enough by reference to Pompey's recent victory in Jerusalem. When they dared to show by their armed resistance what they thought of Roman rule, the result – slavery, taxation, humiliation – shows how dear their city is to the Gods (*quam cara dis immortalibus esset docuit, quod est victa, quod elocata, quod serva facta est*, *Pro Flacco* 28.69).[15]

Apion's charge simply applied this logic on a larger scale: no doubt he reminded his readers about Antiochus Epiphanes' despoiling of the temple (2.80) and about Pompey's 'subjugation' of Judaea. How much further he ranged in history we cannot tell, but Josephus is surely aware that this sort of charge has particular resonance in his own day, after the Roman crushing of the Revolt, the destruction of Jerusalem and the razing of the temple. The Flavian dynasty was, as we know, hungry for propaganda, and the supression of the Jewish revolt provided a rich source of self-legitimation.[16] Inevitably, Flavian self-congratulation was at the expense of Jewish honour: the display of Temple spoils in the triumphal procession, the diversion of the Temple tax to the *fiscus Iudaicus*, the issue of 'Judaea Capta' coins, the triumphal arches and the derogatory depiction of the Jews in accounts of the War circulating in Rome – all these indicate the salience of the cultural logic which Josephus confronts here. What is more, this is a logic which he himself subscribes to throughout his earlier works. As his preface to the *Antiquities* makes clear, the whole of that narrative is meant

---

[14] Regarding Egypt, a topic of significance for our passage, Diodorus (1.69.5–6) reckons her very long period of self-rule (4700 years, by his count) as proof of the value of her laws and customs.

[15] Cf. Celsus' verdict on the Jews and Christians: 'See how much help God has been to both them and you. Instead of being masters of the world they have been left no land and no home of any kind!' (apud Origen, *Contra Celsum* 8.69).

[16] See the essays by Millar, Barnes, Rives and Goodman in J. Edmondson, S. Mason, and J. Rives, eds., *Flavius Josephus and Flavian Rome* (Oxford: Oxford University Press, 2005).

to illustrate that God rewards the pious and brings disaster on those who disregard his laws (*Ant.* 1.10–14); consistent with this conviction, Josephus indicates that where the Jewish people have suffered, and when Jerusalem has been occupied or its temple destroyed, this has been because of their own impiety.[17] In the case of the recent disaster in the war against Rome he had to put the blame not on all Jews, but on that party of 'bandits' and 'tyrants' whose lunacy led Jews into war, and whose impiety and cruelty brought down God's judgement on his now polluted sanctuary.[18] Thus Apion's charge represents a sore and extremely difficult point for Josephus to deal with, and had greater contemporary relevance in Josephus' day than Apion could have guessed.

Josephus knows that what is at stake here is the meaning of history, and in this struggle it will be crucial not only to cite the 'facts' with due selectivity but also to define and interpret those 'facts' in a way that leaves Jewish honour intact. In general, there are two interpretative strategies open to Josephus: to admit the cultural logic (that subjugation signals inferiority) but deny the applicability of the charge (we were not truly subjugated), or to admit the charge (we were subjugated) but challenge the logic (that does not mean we are inferior). In this passage we find Josephus trying both strategies, at some cost to the logical consistency of this passage but with considerable rhetorical skill. We will trace each in turn.

1. One side of Josephus' argumentation depends on admitting the cultural logic that military defeat and the loss of national autonomy is a sign of cultural or religious inadequacy. His main tactic here, as so often in his response to Apion, is to turn the charge back against his accuser. Although Apion would undoubtedly have considered himself a 'Greek', who had been legitimately accorded Alexandrian citizenship, Josephus' tactic, here as elsewhere, is to treat him as an 'Egyptian' and thus to throw back at him as much prejudice about the 'Egyptians' and their history as he can muster. In this short passage, Josephus returns to the topic of Egyptian disgrace again and again, with as many as six separate points, fixing in particular on their chequered political history and (a favourite topic) their animal cults. He could be sure that these would gain recognition and approval in his audience, as it was well known in Rome that Egypt was a proud country which had nonetheless been ruled by the Persians for several centuries and had been subdued by absorption into the Roman empire after 31 BCE.[19] (The

[17] See, on the general point, H. Attridge, *The Interpretation of Biblical History in the Antiquitates Judaicae of Flavius Josephus* (Missoula: Scholars, 1976). For this pattern as determining the fate of the temple see *Ant.* 4.313; 20.166.

[18] The strategy permeates the *War* (e.g. 1.10; 6.94–95, 124–128, 250).

[19] Dio 51.17 exults in the humiliation of Alexandria and views the annexation of Egypt with pride: 'thus was Egypt enslaved' (51.17.4).

Egyptian animal-cults were also a topic of guaranteed amusement among the Roman elite.[20]) Josephus' tactic is to treat all these events as examples of 'slavery' – indeed even to add the glorious Ptolemaic era as another period of slavery, when the Egyptians were subservient to 'the Macedonians' with 'a status no different from slaves' (133)! He also rubs in the ignominy of the Persian period, by reference to their well-known intolerance of the Egyptian animal cults (129) – claiming at the end of that long description that this is not a matter of reproach (though of course it is, otherwise he would not have dwelt on it)![21] Thus by the tactic which especially delights him (cf. 2.5), Josephus makes the accuser the accused, and in this way distracts attention from the seriousness of the charge directed against the Jews. After mentioning the charge in 125 it is not until midway through 132 that Josephus picks it up directly, and by that time we have almost forgotten what this is all about!

That Josephus should turn on the Egyptians in this connection is typical of his strategy throughout this work, which I have elsewhere analysed as part of 'the politics of contempt'.[22] Trading on the disdain which the Romans generally showed towards Egypt, especially her theriomorphic religion, Josephus can deflect criticism of his subordinate culture by transferring it onto another. In one sense, of course, this plays straight into the hands of the Romans: there is nothing more convenient for the dominant than to have the dominated exploit one another! From another perspective, it shows the skills with which Josephus can manipulate the Romans' own cultural values into denigration of the critics of Judaism, his vituperation of the Egyptians aligning him with the common views of history and religion held by the Romans. It is thus not surprising that he should start this section with reference to the Romans, sarcastically commenting on the Egyptians' 'most dominant city' (Alexandria) as 'accustomed from the very beginning to ruling rather than serving the Romans!' (125). Unchallengeable Roman rule is a theme he can safely and wisely deploy for rhetorical advantage.

Thus this section begins with an emphatic affirmation of the logic that victory indeed signals cultural and religious value. It finishes with the same too, but here, in the final paragraph, whilst retaining the logic, Josephus denies the charge. Where Apion had charged that the Jews had persistently been subservient to other nations and suffered humiliating defeats (125), Jo-

---

[20] The topos is well-known: see K. A. D. Smelik and E. A. Hemelrijk, 'Who knows not what monsters demented Egypt worships?', *ANRW* 2.17.14, 1852–2000.

[21] For the Persian hostility to the Egyptian cults see, e. g., Strabo 17.1.27, 46; Plutarch, *Isis and Osiris* 355 c, 363 c, 368 f.

[22] J. M. G. Barclay, 'The Politics of Contempt: Judaeans and Egyptians in Josephus' *Against Apion*' in J. M. G. Barclay, ed., *Negotiating Diaspora: Jewish Strategies in the Roman Empire* (London: T & T Clark, 2004) 109–207; reprinted as chapter 14 in this volume.

sephus insists on a different account of history. It is perhaps a sign of his desperation that he has to go all the way back to David and Solomon in order to find a period of Jewish autonomy and supremacy (132 b). It is noticeable that he does not date these kings' rule, nor refer back to his earlier accounts of their somewhat mixed fortunes. Nor does he say here, for obvious reasons, what he records elsewhere, that the first time the Jerusalem temple was sacked it was captured by an *Egyptian* king (Isokos, taken to be Sesostris), who removed David's and Solomon's temple treasures (*Ant.* 8.253–62)! Josephus' discourse is often as revealing for what it omits as for what it says, but his 'let us pass over them' cleverly gives the impression that he could have said much more on this tack which he has kept deliberately vague. Once again, he distracts our attention by a comparison with the Egyptians (133), while implying, misleadingly, that all through the Persian and Macedonian period the Jewish nation was autonomous. The one recent period of 'freedom' he can point to is that '120 years' before the time of Pompey – though if we go by his own calculations elsewhere (*War* 1.53, dating freedom from the Macedonians to 142 BCE) this should actually be reduced to no more than 80 years!

It is not clear that Apion had claimed that Jews had *always* been under foreign rule, only that they had repeatedly been so, and suffered multiple captures of their city. It is notable that Josephus has managed to change the subject, ignoring the five occasions on which the temple was captured (listed in *War* 6.435–37) and conveying the impression that Jewish dignity was salvaged by the fact that they were at least *sometimes* free! By contrast, it was necessary to suggest, by hint and generalisation, that Egypt had never been free, not even for a single day, thus not even under her own indigenous rulers (128)!

But what could be said about the Jewish period post-Pompey? Here, we may note, Josephus subtly changes the terms of the discourse. Up to this point there have been only two categories, slavery or submission on the one hand, and freedom or rulership on the other.[23] Unable to claim that after Pompey the Jews were 'free', but unwilling to concede 'slavery', the language suddenly changes to the face-saving vocabulary of 'allies and friends' (134). This is a crucial rhetorical move. Throughout the *War*, Josephus had been content to employ the language of freedom and slavery: the rebels were fighting for 'freedom' from Rome, but, as Agrippa's speech in *War* 2.345–401 makes clear, that struggle is hopeless since all the world is enslaved to Rome. Here Josephus shies away from such blunt recognition of political reality and takes refuge in the very euphemisms which the Romans

[23] Thus, on the one hand, δουλεύειν (125, 127, 133), ὑπακούειν (127), or ὑποζεύγειν (127) and, on the other, ἄρχειν (125, 133) or ἐλευθερία (128, 133).

themselves preferred to adopt: their client kings, whom they appointed, controlled and employed as proxy tax-collectors, were rather to be termed 'allies' and 'friends'. The hint here that Jews were in a special position was largely unfounded.[24] Once again, by generalisation and strategic silence (there is no mention, of course, of the Revolt!) Josephus manages to turn 'history' to his advantage, and his complicity in Roman euphemism helps suggest that Jews and Romans have identical political interests.

2. Thus far, as we have seen, Josephus works within and exploits the cultural logic that military success is proof of moral virtue and divine favour: he has turned that logic against the Egyptians, to denigrate his accuser, and he has denied that the Jews are a case in point, by suppressing examples of their defeat while profiling samples of their success and 'alliance' with Rome. Without denying outright the applicability of Apion's charge, he has rendered it insignificant compared to the contrary facts he chooses to highlight. But now we must also note, embedded within our section of text, two passages which hint at an alternative rhetorical strategy, and threaten to undo not only Josephus' own argumentation in this passage but also basic Roman convictions about power and success. In these two passages, the tactic is opposite to that we have traced thus far: here the cultural logic underlying Apion's charge is itself brought into question, so that defeat is treated as no necessary basis for moral or religious stigma, and questions can be raised about the perpetrators, not the victims, of national disasters. These counter-currents are comparatively weak – undeveloped, generalised, and indirect suggestions – but we should at least notice them.

The first passage which at least qualifies, if it does not undermine, Apion's cultural logic, is Josephus' statement in 127 that 'it has fallen to few to gain sovereignty over time, and changes have again brought even these under the yoke to serve others; most peoples have been subject to others on many occasions'. At one level this is simply an observation on history: empires come and go. It thus serves at least to blunt the force of the presumption that subservience to other nations is a proof of unjust laws or improper piety. If this were said of the Jews, it would have to be said of most nations, and the more universally it is said the less bite the axiom can retain. But at another level, in the power-dynamics of empire, no 'observation on history' is ever that simple, especially if made by the subordinate.[25] If 'it has fallen to few

[24] Josephus' account of Claudius' decree (*Ant.* 19.287–291) similarly suggests a special Jewish 'loyalty' to Rome; but our papyrus copy of Claudius' judgement on affairs in Alexandria (*CPJ* 153) tells a very different story!

[25] Scipio's famous warning that one day Rome would fall like Carthage (Polybius 38.22.3) is sometimes cited in this regard: but the same warning made by a Carthaginian would have a very different ring. Titus' observation that 'no human affairs are secure' (*War* 3.396) is similarly safe on his lips.

to gain sovereignty over a period of time', the example which would spring immediately to mind would be the Roman empire. Thus to say that 'changes have again brought even these under the yoke to serve others' is, by this generalisation, not to say anything about Rome in particular, and not to say anything about the future, but also, by this generalisation, not to exclude possible application to Rome. Scholars[26] have poured over statements which Josephus makes elsewhere about the 'changes in fortune' which have taken place during history, although this one has not been noted in this connection. Frequently in the *War* Josephus comments on the 'fortune' favouring the Romans, and puts both in his own mouth and in Titus' the expression that God was on the side of the Romans (e. g. 2.390–391; 3.484; 5.412; 6.411). At one famous point, when talking about changes in fortune, he says that God goes the rounds of the nations in history and has given rulership now to Italy (*War* 5.367; cf. *c. Apion.* 2.41). 'Now' could, of course, be an entirely innocent observation on the present state of affairs, but it could also hint (no more than hint) that the future might be very different. In the *Antiquities* Josephus is notoriously coy about that future. Balaam's prophecy of future success for Israel (4.114–17, 125) is notably vague, and Josephus leaves the vision of Daniel, with the stone predicted to smash the iron empire, tantalisingly uninterpreted: my task, he says, is to recount the past, not to predict the future (10.210).[27] Thus, even though he elsewhere suggests, without directly saying so, that this iron empire is that of the Romans (10.276), Josephus always speaks on this topic partially and indirectly, with the aid of generalisation or allusion.[28] Here, in our passage, Josephus resorts to a generalisation that is spoken in the context of Roman rule, but makes no explicit reference to the present Roman empire. But the observation that even world rulers have been reduced to slavery, while couched in the past tense, could easily seep into the present and future.

Our second passage is fuller, but even more indirect. As we have noticed, at the end of 129 Josephus suddenly changes tack from denigration of the

---

[26] E. g., M. de Jonge, 'Josephus und die Zukunftserwartungen seines Volkes', in O. Betz et al., eds., *Josephus-Studien* (Göttingen: Vandenhoeck & Ruprecht, 1974) 205–19.

[27] I am grateful to Paul Spilsbury for discussion of this point, and his unpublished paper 'Flavius Josephus on the Rise and Fall of the Roman Empire'. He rightly draws attention to Balaam's remarkable promise of Jewish resurgence and vengeance, after a period of abasement (*Ant.* 4.127); could this be heard as relevant in Josephus' own day?

[28] Mason's insistence that Josephus is simply sticking to his task as a historian seems to underplay the way Josephus tantalises his readers, hinting at a future that he self-consciously leaves unspoken ('Josephus, Daniel and the Flavian House', in F. Parente and J. Sievers, eds., *Josephus and the History of the Graeco-Roman Period* [Leiden: Brill, 1994] 161–91, at 170–73). Mason's judgement that 'Josephus' remarks seem … to fall into the category of harmless philosophical reflection, not revolutionary aspiration' (173) leaves unconsidered a large number of possible intermediate stances.

Egyptians for their sorry history of occupation, to a refusal to attribute shame on that basis. With a swipe at Apion's ignorance (cf. 2.26, 38), he then begins to list a number of 'misfortunes' in Greek history which were widely known, but which had not dented the reputation of the victims. Once again, Josephus is vague: he does not record what events he has in mind in 130, and when he becomes more specific in 131 he does not recount the circumstances of these various temple destructions: the reader cannot assess, independently of his verdict, where the blame might be apportioned. The general tenor of this line of argument is clear. A national disaster, even the destruction of a temple, is not necessarily proof of unjust laws or inappropriate worship: it might only prove the impiety of the conquerors! Thus here Josephus actually unpicks the conceptual seam which holds the rest of his argument together, the conviction that victory and virtue are intrinsically linked. At this point his argument begins to unravel altogether.[29]

But what is even more striking about this passage is its implication for the assessment of Jewish history in particular. Although Josephus had not mentioned the Jewish temple in 125 (whereas Apion probably had, cf. 2.80), the fate of the Jerusalem temple was clearly the most sensitive spot in the assessment of Jewish dignity. Josephus very specifically names temples in 131, and finishes his catalogue with the notable generalisation: 'thousands of others'. Could he have *avoided* thinking of his own temple in this connection? And if so, what is implied by that potentially devastating comment that 'no-one has blamed these things on the victims, but on the perpetrators' (οἱ δράσαντες)?

Now, in the *War*, Josephus was notoriously careful not to blame the Romans for the destruction of the Jerusalem temple. He could not afford to attribute 'impiety' to the Romans in general or to Titus in particular, and he needed to grapple with the question of theodicy, how God could allow such a catastrophe to take place.[30] While it was the Romans who, in the end, burned the temple down, Titus had not wanted this result (1.10; 6.266), had argued against it in the council of war (6.236–43), and had consistently offered the Jews the chance to fight on other territory (6.95). Thus the blame largely falls on the Jewish rebels themselves, whose pollution of the temple required the judgement of God to cleanse it (6.108–10).[31] In our passage, if

[29] It is a sign of his rhetorical skill that only very close observation of his text reveals this contradiction.

[30] See T.D. Barnes, 'The Sack of the Temple in Josephus and Tacitus', and J. Rives, 'Flavian Religious Policy and the Destruction of the Temple', in Edmondson et al., eds., *Flavius Josephus and Flavian Rome*, 129–44, 145–66.

[31] Note, however, that Josephus puts on Eleazar's lips the complaint that the temple had been uprooted 'in such a profane manner' (οὕτως ἀνοσίως, *War* 7.379). The complaint is rendered safe since it is uttered by a discredited rebel, but it is still spoken!

he had mentioned the Jerusalem temple explicitly, Josephus could hardly have admitted that it was the impiety of Jews themselves that was chiefly to blame: that would have proved Apion's point, however much Josephus had claimed that these were only some, unrepresentative, Jews. Nor could he describe this destruction as a necessary act of divine wrath. It was better not to mention the Jerusalem temple at all, and thus not invite questions on the identity of the perpetrators who should be blamed. But Josephus is acutely aware that his temple has been destroyed, and just a few pages earlier he had mentioned Titus in a list of those who 'occupied' it (2.82). Thus nothing is said that could lead explicitly to the suggestion that the Romans are 'the perpetrators' to be blamed. But it does not take much for that conclusion to be drawn, and the advertised 'passing over' of those 'thousands of others' leaves many options open for the reader.

By this silence Josephus does not destroy that circularity which linked Roman piety to Roman military might and thus does not subvert the self-congratulation of Roman imperialism. But is this 'passing over' a subtle way of making mention, a hint that an alternative reading of Jewish history is possible? I doubt that we can answer this question with confidence at the level of Josephus' intention, but the case may illustrate what post-colonial theory rightly brings to our attention: that in a melody apparently composed of complicity and cultural subservience, there can sound soft notes of self-assertion and resistance, at least for some ears.

This brief survey of a complex passage is perhaps enough to indicate that Josephus' rhetoric is necessarily a political phenomenon. Not every passage, of course, bears directly on political matters, and few are as intricate as this in their rhetorical stance. But none stands outside the power-constraints of Josephus' social and cultural position, and most demonstrate, at the same time, Josephus' own empowerment as he deploys his new intellectual resources in the interests of his fellow Jews. That paradoxical result, which is characteristic of the colonial and post-colonial condition, assuredly generates its own ironies and ambiguities, but I venture to suggest that the study of Josephus might benefit from such sensitivity to the complexities of this Flavian Jew.[32]

[32] I am most grateful to fellow members of the York University (Toronto) Conference for feedback on this paper both during and after the event, and to Stephen Moore for advice on its postcolonial dimensions. [For further explication and further examples of postcolonial readings of Josephus, see my commentary, *Flavius Josephus, Translation and Commentary: Against Apion*.]

16. Who's the Toughest of Them All?

Jews, Spartans and Roman Torturers in Josephus' *Against Apion*

Josephus, the Judean general, Roman captive and Flavian protégé, devoted the last twenty-five years of his life, as a privileged resident in Rome, to the redescription of Jewish identity and to the strategic placement of his cultural tradition on the controverted map of the late first-century empire. After writing his delicately poised account of the *Judean War*, and the large-scale 'autoethnography' known as the *Jewish Antiquities*, his final and most intricate literary endeavour is his apologetic work, *Against Apion*. Here Jewishness is constructed and positioned in carefully nuanced dialectic with images of 'Egyptian', 'Chaldean', 'Greek' and (to some degree) 'Roman' cultural tradition.[1] The rhetorical flamboyance of this piece and its predominantly polemical tone give Josephus considerable license to manipulate the tropes that suit his argumentative needs. His eye-catching exordium and the opening vilification of 'Greek' historiography (1.1–56) start this treatise with a familiar antithesis between Eastern antiquity and the comparative youth and fickleness of the Greeks. But as the discourse develops we find Josephus deploying his considerable knowledge of the Greek literary and historical tradition to place his Jewish tradition both outside and inside 'Greekness', indeed also above (superior to) and behind (historically earlier than) what may be variously labelled 'Greek'.[2] What gives this manipulation of Greek historical and literary tropes particular interest is not only that Josephus writes explicitly as a Jew, and in defence of his own Jewish tradition, but that he does so in Rome, aware of how 'Greekness' may be variously bought and sold in the Roman market-place, 'displayed or excoriated for its decadence'.[3] It is within this triangulation of Jewish, Greek and Roman –

[1] For recent introduction, translation and commentary on *c. Apion.*, see J. M. G. Barclay, *Flavius Josephus, Translation and Commentary. Vol. 10: Against Apion* (Leiden: Brill, 2007).

[2] For Josephus' literary indebtedness to the Greek tradition in this work, see C. Schäublin, 'Josephus und die Griechen' *Hermes* 110 (1982) 316–41; for his rhetorical directions and misdirections regarding Jews and Greeks, see E. S. Gruen, 'Greeks and Jews: Mutual Misperceptions in Josephus' *Contra Apionem*', in C. Bakhos, ed., *Ancient Judaism in its Hellenistic Context* (Leiden: Brill, 2005) 31–51.

[3] T. Whitmarsh, *Greek Literature and the Roman Empire. The Politics of Imitation* (Oxford: Oxford University, 2001) 15.

the last always implicit if not explicit in Josephus' text – that the subject of Sparta becomes a particularly interesting topic of discussion.

The Lycurgan constitution of Sparta and the peculiar character of Spartans – both Greek and oddly, in certain respects, untypical of Greeks – provided a set of tropes easily pressed into Josephus' service. In *Contra Apionem* passages that we will not discuss here, he plays on the contrast between Athenian verbosity and Spartan practical training to insist that Jewish *paideia* exhibits the best of both worlds – both Athenian words (written laws) and Spartan practice (2.171–74). In a delicate discussion of Jewish attitudes to foreigners, he both praises and criticises the Spartan 'expulsions of foreigners' (ξενηλασίαι), using the comparison, of course, to bring credit to the Jews (2.259–61).[4] The myths surrounding Sparta's special disciplines had for centuries provided a model of austerity, simplicity and military training, and Josephus is not alone among his contemporaries in turning once again to the 'mirage spartiate'.[5] His redeployment of this ideal bears some interesting points of comparison with his near contemporary, Plutarch, to whom we will refer below. Both find in an idealised Lycurgan past a model usable as a critical tool, though where Plutarch deploys it against a luxurious present, Josephus turns it against itself, in its alleged inconsistency, in order to surpass it with his own Jewish exemplars. But his image of the Jews as 'super-Spartans' also has a contemporary Roman edge, indeed an edginess that one could interpret as a form of colonial 'mimicry'.[6] In acclaiming and trumping Spartan 'toughness', the Spartan attribute most universally acclaimed by Rome, Josephus, as we shall see, presents Jews in heroic contempt of death, and in precisely that context (under Roman torture) where their bravery 'outendures' and thus outsmarts Rome itself.

The Spartan comparison on which we will focus here occurs within the last section of *Against Apion*, a final refutation of slanders (attributed to Apollonius Molon, Lysimachus and others), structured around Josephus' presentation of the Jewish constitution (2.145–286). Among the slanders

---

[4] Josephus does not use in this treatise the tradition of the political (and even ethnic) link between Sparta and the Jews that he had deployed in his *Antiquities*; see E.S. Gruen, 'The Purported Jewish-Spartan Affiliation', in R.W. Wallace and E.M. Harris, eds., *Transitions to Empire. Essays in Greco-Roman History, 360–146 B.C., in honor of E. Badian* (Norman/London, University of Oklahoma, 1996) 254–69.

[5] See F. Ollier, *Le Mirage Spartiate: Étude sur l'Idealisation de Sparta dans l'Antiquité grecque de l'Origine jusqu'aux Cyniques* (reprint; New York: Arno, 1972; originally, 1933, 1943); E.N. Tigerstedt, *The Legend of Sparta in Classical Antiquity* (3 vols., Stockholm: Almqvist & Wiksell, 1965–1978).

[6] On colonial mimicry, see H.K. Bhabha, *The Location of Culture* (London: Routledge, 1994), a collection of essays of which 'Sly Civility' and 'Signs Taken for Wonders' are especially significant in this connection. Bhabha's notion of mimicry suggests an ambivalence in which the copying of the dominant culture both affirms its power and subtly undermines its claim to be special and superior.

listed at the start of this section, alongside the claim that Jews are 'atheists' and 'misanthropes', Josephus notes Apollonius' charge that Jews display 'cowardice' (δειλία) and (at the same time, or in other contexts) 'rashness' (τόλμα) or 'recklessness' (ἀπόνοια, 2.148). Josephus pre-empts these charges by listing, at the outset, six Jewish virtues: piety, fellowship with one another, universal benevolence, justice, endurance in labours (ἡ ἐν τοῖς πόνοις καρτερία), and contempt for death (θανάτου περιφρόνησις, 2.146). In the subsequent description of the structure of the constitution (2.150–89) and the summary of key laws (2.190–218), many of these virtues are amply illustrated, but the last two are under-represented and evidently required fuller treatment. Thus Josephus finishes his summary of the laws with reference to those who 'keep the laws, and should it be necessary to die for them, meet death eagerly' (2.218) and appends a short section (2.219–35) on Judean endurance for the law. Here, after general claims about the length of time Jews have been faithful to their laws, Josephus offers a comparison with Spartans and their Lycurgan constitution in the following terms:[7]

2.225 But there are some who think that Plato's works are empty verbiage, written in a florid style and with great arrogance; of the legislators, they most admire Lycurgus, and everyone sings the praises of Sparta, since she stuck to his laws (ἐνεκαρτέρησεν) for the longest time. *226* So, let this be granted, that obedience to the laws is proof of virtue. But let those who admire the Lacedaemonians compare their time-span with the more than two thousand years of our constitution, *227* and let them consider, in addition, that for as long as they had their freedom the Lacedaemonians were of a mind to keep the laws scrupulously, but when changes of fortune came to affect them, they completely forgot almost all the laws! *228* As for us, although we have undergone countless different fortunes, thanks to the changes among the kings who ruled Asia, we have not betrayed the laws even in the most extreme crises, fostering them not for the sake of idleness or luxury[8] but, if anyone would care to examine, [he would find] imposed on us ordeals and labours (ἄθλους καὶ πόνους) far greater than the endurance (καρτερίας) supposedly required of the Lacedaemonians. *229* They neither worked the land nor laboured in a craft, but were released from all work and used to spend their time about the city looking sleek and exercising their bodies for the sake of beauty, *230* using others as servants for all the business of daily life and getting their food from them, ready prepared, exercising endurance (ὑπομένοντες) in doing and suffering anything purely for this one fine and benevolent task: to conquer everyone against whom they went to war. *231* I pass over the fact that they did not succeed even in this; for not only singly, but many of them on many occasions and en masse ignored the commands of the law and surrendered, with their weapons, to the enemy.

[7] My own translation, based on the Münster text, as in Barclay, *Against Apion*. [Cf. now F. Siegert, ed., *Flavius Josephus, Über die Ursprünglichkeit des Judentums (Contra Apionem)* (2 vols.; Göttingen: Vandenhoeck und Ruprecht, 2008).]

[8] οὐκ ἀργίας οὐδὲ τρυφῆς ... χάριν (τρυφῆς is Dindorf's conjecture rightly followed by modern editors).

232 As for us, then, has anyone known – not to pitch the number so high – even two or three who have been traitors to the laws or afraid of death (θάνατον φοβηθέντας), and I mean not that easiest of deaths, which comes to those in battle, but that accompanied by physical torture (τὸν μετὰ λύμης τῶν σωμάτων), which has the reputation of being the most hideous of all? *233* I myself think that some of our conquerors have applied this to those in their power not out of hatred but because they wanted to see, as an amazing spectacle (ὡς θαυμαστόν τι θέαμα), if there were any people who believed that the only evil they faced was to be forced either to do something contrary to their laws or to say a word in contravention of them. *234* One should not be amazed if we face death on behalf of the laws more courageously (ἀνδρείως) than everyone else. For others cannot easily endure (ὑπομένουσιν) even what seem the easiest of our customs: I mean working for oneself, a simple diet, not eating or drinking anything thoughtlessly or according to the whims of individual desire,[9] nor in connection with sexual relations or extravagance, and, on the other hand, enduring (ὑπομεῖναι) an unchangeable regime in abstention from work. *235* But those who fight with swords, hand to hand, and rout the enemy by their attack could not face the rules about daily life. In our case, by contrast, from our glad obedience to the law in these matters issues our display of nobility there also.

The passage opens by comparing the length of time for which the respective constitutions have lasted: in the Spartan case an unspecified time, but one now presumed to be over; in the case of Jews, two thousand years (and counting). This forms the first category of Jewish 'endurance' (καρτερία, 2.225), the stickability of Jews in faithfulness to their constitution. The rest of the text concerns the second sense of καρτερία, endurance or toughness, and is structured in chiastic fashion in relation to two possible contexts for the display of this virtue – the domestic regime and warfare. Thus Josephus here discusses:

A The Spartan domestic conditions (2.228–30)
  B Spartans facing death in war (2.230–31)
  B' Jews facing death in war – and torture (2.232–33)
A' The Jewish domestic regime (2.234–35)

What is immediately evident from this structure is the centrality of Jewish faithfulness to the laws in the face of death, and particularly under torture. The space given to this theme in 2.232–33, together with authorial comment ('I myself think'), also give it special prominence, while the vague reference to 'some of our conquerors' (τινὰς κρατήσαντας ἡμῶν, 2.233) leaves space for readers to fill this scenario with historical figures of their choosing.[10]

[9] The phrase contains some textual uncertainty (ἐπιτεθυμηκώς is Hudson's conjecture, followed by all modern editors), but is clearly about the control of desire.

[10] For a similar vagueness concerning the destruction of temples, see 2.131; and for argument concerning its applicability to Roman conquerors, see J. M. G. Barclay, 'The Empire Writes Back: Josephan Rhetoric in Flavian Rome', in J. Edmondson, S. Mason, and J. Rives, eds., *Flavius Josephus and Flavian Rome* (Oxford: Oxford University, 2005) 315–32 (reprinted as chapter 15, above).

In what follows we will examine the three most important Spartan-Jewish contrasts in this passage, keeping for last this motif of spectacular physical toughness under torture.

I. Toughing it out for two thousand years

Josephus' opening comments about Lycurgus lay emphasis on the longevity of the Spartan constitution: it is because they have stuck to his laws 'for the longest time' (or 'for a very long time', ἐπὶ πλεῖστον) that 'everyone sings the praises of Sparta' (2.225). This is an old trope: it was on such grounds that Polybius had compared Sparta favourably with Thebes and Athens (6.10–11, 43–48). Opinions differed quite widely about precisely how long Lycurgus' constitution had lasted, not only because of the wide variation in the dating of Lycurgus, but also because it was a matter for argument when Lycurgus' system could be said to have lapsed – or indeed, if its subsequent revivals could be claimed to be its genuine continuation. Polybius considered it had lapsed only at the time of Cleomenes III (235–222 BCE; Polybius 2.47.3; 4.18.12–14), Plutarch that it had remained unchanged only until Agis (5th century BCE), when it had broken down with the influx of wealth (*Lyc.* 29, 1, 6). For him it was a mark of Lycurgus' immense success that he had so engrained the constitutional norms within the education of Spartan boys that 'the chief and greatest features of the legislation endured for more than five hundred years', while Numa's had not lasted a moment beyond his death (*Numa* 26.5). Nonetheless, it was generally recognised that it had faltered at some point in history, and if it was now in part restored, its history was not continuous. To be sure, Cicero could claim, in a rhetorical flourish, that Sparta had kept a single set of customs unaltered for seven hundred years (*Flac.* 63), but this, he knew, was true only because Rome had herself 'preserved' (i.e. restored) them (*Mur.* 74). Whether the breakdown of the Lycurgan system was dated to the reign of Agis, the battle of Leuctra (371 BCE), or the reign of Cleomenes III, it was generally recognised that it was only when Rome dissolved the Achaean League and restored (a reduced) Sparta to the status of an 'independent' city (146 BCE) that the Lycurgan 'ancestral customs' were revived.[11] Thus Josephus can trade on a common perception that the Spartan political tradition had been at least interrupted, and his vague reference to 'changes of fortune' leaves it open to readers to choose from several options in identifying its moment(s) of rupture.

[11] For the history, and the Roman invention of tradition, see P. Cartledge and A. Spawforth, *Hellenistic and Roman Sparta. A Tale of Two Cities* (2nd ed.; London: Routledge, 2002) 190–211.

Sparta's failure to 'endure' (καρτερεῖν) is here connected to her loss of 'freedom' (2.227): her people, it is suggested, kept her laws only when it was convenient and easy to do so, not when she lost her sovereignty or suffered the rule of foreigners. The Jews, by contrast, have maintained their constitution (according to Josephus) for two thousand years (2.226), a figure apparently traditional in Jewish self-understanding of the period.[12] What is more, they have done so despite 'countless different fortunes' including multiple changes of rule in 'Asia' (and thus over Jews).[13] Thus Jews maintained their laws even under foreign rule, and even when that rule altered in nature and demand. The hugely impressive span of time is meant to draw admiration: if Plutarch thought Sparta was amazing for its Lycurgan continuity over 500 years, Josephus' claim is quite stupendous.[14] It rests not only on his (largely unproven) dating of the life of Moses, and not only on granting that all the Jewish laws derived from him, but also on his strategic vagueness regarding 'the laws', since many aspects of the constitution (such as rule by kings or priests) had, on Josephus' own admission (in his *Antiquities*) changed more than once in the course of that time.[15] Here, in *Against Apion*, he admits only a single and unchanging structure of the constitution ('theocracy', 2.165), and in this context his focus is, in any case, on the daily and domestic regimen of the law, not its larger political framework. Thus defined (and his rhetoric typically requires some such strategic redefinition or limitation of terms), the Jews had 'toughed it out' in their faithfulness to their laws 'even in the most extreme crises' (ἐν τοῖς ἐσχάτοις τῶν δεινῶν, 2.228).

II. Macho Jews and Softie Spartans

If there was one thing for which Spartans were known and admired in the Roman era, it was their austerity and discipline. Plutarch makes this one of the central themes in his depiction of Lycurgus' system (*Lyc. passim*), with its

[12] Cf. *Ant.* 1.16 and Philo (?), *Hyp.* 6.9; one could calculate the same figure from *c. Apion.* 1.1, 39. For Josephus' assumption that Moses was of an era much earlier than Lycurgus, see 2.154.

[13] By a loose definition of 'Asia', the reference could be to Assyrians, Babylonians, Persians and Seleucids (cf. 2.128, 133).

[14] For Jewish deployment of the ancient presumption that good things prove their value by long usage and continuity, see P. Pilhofer, *Presbyteron Kreitton: Der Alterbeweis der jüdischen und christlichen Apologeten und seine Vorgeschichte* (Tübingen: Mohr Siebeck, 1990).

[15] See *Ant.* 20.224–51. Although Strabo thought that Moses' laws had been altered (by the Hasmonean 'bandits', 16.2.34–39), that perception was rare among non-Jews; normally, without any special reflection on their longevity, it was assumed (for aetiological convenience) that current Jewish customs originated in the circumstances of the Jews' departure from Egypt.

admiring description of the Spartan ἀγωγή. The training of boys for feats of hardship, the frugal food shared in the famous *syssitia*, the bare decoration of homes, the Lycurgan currency that did not allow the accumulation of wealth, the sexual restraint and military discipline – all such traditions elicit his highest praise, and form the foil for tirades against contemporary luxury or decadence (*Lyc.* 10.1–3; 13.4; 15.5). The Spartan use of Helots in agriculture and crafts is hailed by Plutarch as an example of Lycurgus' foresight: absorbing the men in communal concerns, he made it unnecessary for them to work for individual sustenance, and impossible for them to devote themselves to moneymaking (and therefore greed): 'when they were not on military campaigns', he concludes, 'all their time was taken up with choral dances, festivals, feasts, hunting expeditions, physical exercise (γυμνάσια) and conversations' (*Lyc.* 24.2). Thus while business was apportioned to slaves and Helots, the free Spartan citizens 'knew and cared for nothing other than to obey their leaders and conquer their enemies' (ἄλλο δὲ οὐδὲν εἰδότας οὐδὲ μελετῶντας ἢ πείθεσθαι τοῖς ἄρχουσι καὶ κρατεῖν τῶν πολεμίων, *Numa* 24.3). As Plutarch surely knew, this was precisely the image of Sparta that chimed with Roman ideals of *gravitas* and *disciplina* (Cicero, *Pro Flacco* 28.63; Valerius Maximus 2.6); it was not for nothing that Roman tourists visited Sparta and witnessed the spectacle of 'floggings' that now epitomised Spartan training in endurance to the point of death (see below).[16]

Josephus plays off precisely these traditions, and this reputation, but cleverly manipulates them to depict the Spartans as, in relative terms, effete and work-shy spongers! He combines three different phrases to indicate their abstention from 'work' (2.229), and turns their use of others (Helots) for the daily needs of life into a sign of laziness or luxury: their ready-cooked meals (2.230) are here taken to suggest decadence, not total focus on more manly pursuits. Indeed their very manliness is brought into question by Jo-

[16] For Plutarch's relationship to Romans and to Rome, see C.P. Jones, *Plutarch and Rome* (Oxford: Clarendon, 1971); R. Preston, 'Roman questions, Greek answers: Plutarch and the construction of identity', in S. Goldhill, ed., *Being Greek under Rome: Cultural Identity, the Second Sophistic and the Development of Empire* (Cambridge: Cambridge University, 2001) 86–119; for the purpose and ideology of the *Lives*, see T. Duff, *Plutarch's Lives. Exploring Virtue and Vice* (Oxford: Oxford University, 1999), esp. 287–309. Plutarch's comparison of Lycurgus and Numa finishes with critical comments on Numa's attitude to education; for their relationship to recent debates in Rome on this topic, see P. Desideri, '*Lycurgus*: The Spartan Ideal in the Age of Trajan', in P.A. Stadter and L. van der Stockt, eds., *Sage and Emperor: Plutarch, Greek Intellectuals, and Roman Power in the Time of Trajan (98–117 A.D.)* (Leuven: Leuven University, 2002) 315–27. Whitmarsh's general comments on the uses of Greek identity in this period are clearly relevant to both Plutarch and Josephus: 'The central points, however, are two: first , that this imaginary 'Greece' was always circumscribed by the Roman empire (and this is the case even when the Roman present seems most explicitly ignored); secondly, that Greekness was not a self-evident essence, but a locus of conflict between multiple, at times exclusive, definitions' (*Greek Literature and the Roman Empire*, 29).

sephus, who describes them as merely hanging about the city (a suspiciously decadent location) looking 'sleek' (λιπαροί). This is precisely the term that Plutarch had used in relating Lycurgus' encouragement of the Spartiates to grow their hair long for the purposes of warfare (*Lyc.* 22.1; cf. *Lys.* 1). Josephus wilfully reads such body language in a negative sense; even their exercise (ἀσκεῖν) was for no higher goal than 'beauty' (κάλλος, 2.229)! And even if he does (and must) admit that these 'effeminate' Spartans were (also) training for war, he skilfully denigrates their achievements with a double rhetorical blow: this one goal of conquering their opponents (2.230; cf. Plutarch, *Numa* 24.3) is treated with sarcasm as a 'fine and benevolent' task (τὸ καλὸν ἔργον καὶ φιλάνθρωπον, 2.230), and one in which they repeatedly failed (2.231).

If the fabled Spartan hardness is here rendered distinctly flaccid, Josephus presents Jews as tougher and stronger in every respect. Not only do they work for themselves (αὐτουργία, 2.234),[17] but in relation to both food and sex they control desires and avoid all extravagance (2.234; cf. 2.173–4). Indeed, Josephus even makes Sabbath observance – always open to criticism as a sign of Jewish 'sloth' – a symbol of Jewish virility: ἀργία here is an unchangeable 'regime' (τάξις) which Jews alone are able to 'endure' (ὑπομεῖναι).[18] Here is a Jewish ἀγωγή far tougher than the Spartans'. If the Jews' military record could hardly be dressed up in more glorious terms than that of the Spartans, in the domestic sphere, at least, they could be made to appear both leaner and meaner.[19]

III. The Spectacle of Torture

The scene to which Josephus draws the reader's eye, by its placement at the centre of his tableau, is the locus at which he explicitly invites visualisation: the 'amazing spectacle' (θαυμαστόν τι θέαμα) of Jews under torture, willing to give their lives rather than say or do anything against the law

[17] Josephus' idealised portrait of Jewish agricultural work (cf. *c. Apion.* 1.60; 2.234, 291, 294) may owe something to old-fashioned Roman ideals, just as his critique of Spartans in this regard is paralleled by Tacitus' complaint about German fighters who do not also till the land (*Germ.* 14.3–4).

[18] The same verb is used earlier in relation to Greek proselytes who abandoned Judaism, being unable to 'endure' its laws (2.123). ἀργία can, of course, carry negative connotations, but Josephus manages to turn it here into a difficult discipline.

[19] As I write, British newspapers report a similarly 'shocking' inversion of stereotypes: it has taken an Italian (!) manager to instil discipline into the English football team. 'Under Steve McClaren, it was do as you please. Wake up when you fancy, amble downstairs when it suits, eat what you like, take as long as you like ... Under Capello, it's quick march down to the dining room in formation, eat what you're told, chew the regulation number of times, eat together, leave together ...' (*The Independent*, 8th February 2008).

(2.232–33). The whole passage draws our eyes away from the glories of victory in war. Although the Spartans can be criticised for surrendering when they were meant never to do so (2.231), their very ambition to 'conquer' everyone against whom they went to war is here devalued by sarcasm, as we have just seen (2.230). Later Josephus will insist that Jews 'have not trained our courage (ἀνδρεία) for warfare for the sake of self-aggrandizement (or 'greed', χάριν πλεονεξίας) but for the preservation of the laws' (2.272). The phraseology leaves nicely ambiguous whether *all* warfare can be characterized in such negative terms, but it is no accident that Josephus' tract makes the same association between war and greed no less than three times (cf. 1.62; 2.292).[20] In any case, he insists, the courage and contempt of death to which he draws attention is of far higher quality than any that might be displayed in the battle-field, since it surmounts a far greater challenge: 'not that easiest of deaths which comes to (τὸν συμβαίνοντα) those in battle but that accompanied by physical torture, which has the reputation of being the most hideous of all' (2.232).

At one level, Josephus' concern here is to show that this superior fearlessness in the face of death is not, as some allege, mere bravado or recklessness (cf. 2.148). Three times in 2.232–33 he insists that the courage he here illustrates is exercised on behalf of the laws: it is a reasonable and rational decision, not, as might appear, simply stubbornness and foolish impetuosity. Philo, defending the Jews' notorious willingness to die for their laws, insists that this is not, as some allege, evidence of a 'barbarian mindset', but the product of a free and rational choice (*Legatio* 215). The identical slur hangs around the Jews in Josephus' account of the *Judean War*: Vespasian charges that 'incautiousness in warfare and mad impetuosity are alien to us Romans, who owe all our success to skill and discipline: they are a barbarian fault, and one to which the Jews mainly owe their defeats' (*Bell.* 4.45). Since this claim comes in the aftermath of the Romans' own inglorious behaviour at Gamala, one may suspect Josephus of some irony in putting this simplistic

[20] A highly ambiguous assessment of warfare also hangs around Plutarch's comparison between Lycurgus and Numa: while Lycurgus' virtues were clearly military, his goals, Plutarch insists, were not imperialistic (*Lyc.* 30–31). Numa is praised for keeping the early Rome at peace for so long (with the doors of the temple of Janus shut). But his system of peace and justice did not last, for soon after his death 'Italy was filled with the blood of the slain' (*Numa* 26.6). Did not Rome therefore gain improvement (ἐπὶ τὸ βέλτιον) by warfare? Plutarch notably refuses to answer: 'That is a question that would need a long answer for people who hold that improvement consists in wealth, luxury and empire, rather than safety, gentleness and independence (αὐταρκεία) accompanied by justice' (*Numa* 26.7). The comment is by no means straightforwardly 'anti-Roman' (an assessment too crude for a complex and in many respects Romanised figure like Plutarch), but it plays on Rome's own anxieties that her military success is, in moral terms, an ambiguous phenomenon. On Plutarch's cultural self-positioning in his *Lives*, see Jones, *Plutarch and Rome*, 88–109, 122–23.

stereotype into the mouth of Vespasian at just that juncture. But the image in our *Contra Apionem* passage of Jews under torture staying faithful to the law while reckoning up (like Stoic philosophers) whether torture was indeed 'the only evil they faced' (2.233) certainly works to dispel the impression of a thoughtless disregard of their own lives.

At another level, Josephus is simply illustrating the virtue so highly prized in Rome, contempt of death. Although its roots, of course, run deep in the philosophical, and especially Stoic tradition, the deliberate facing of death, and the strenuous endurance of ordeal to the point of death, had become central to the Roman notion of *honor*.[21] Josephus knows very well how central this was to Roman conceptions of warfare: at the siege of Jerusalem he has Titus rouse his troops with exhortations and promises designed to induce 'forgetfulness of danger' and 'contempt of death' (*Bell.* 6.33). He is therefore proud to display Jewish combatants displaying this selfsame 'contempt of death' and even being admired by the Romans for doing so (e.g., *Bell.* 3.356; 5.315, 458; 6.42). Famously, for all the hostility which he displays towards the Zealots, he wrings from the reader an ounce of admiration for Eleazar and his fellows in their mass suicide at Masada. However he may view Eleazar's justification for suicide, he records that the Romans' discovery that their enemies had committed the ultimate self-sacrifice impressed the besiegers and even deprived them of some satisfaction in their victory: 'instead of exulting as over enemies, they admired the nobility (γενναιότης) of their resolve and their contempt of death in its remorseless execution' (*Bell.* 7.406).

In our *Contra Apionem* passage the bravery to which Josephus draws attention contains no moral ambiguity: the deaths which Jews here undergo are neither in warfare nor in suicide, but take place under torture where the only choice is between death and infidelity to the laws. Josephus is no doubt drawing on the Maccabean martyr-tradition, whose formulation in 2 Maccabees 6–7 was taken up and greatly developed in the extraordinary text we know as 4 Maccabees.[22] Here those rendered most powerless as victims display a mastery over themselves which is given a higher valuation than domination over others; by their self-control they not only master their own passions but outman the tyrant himself, for all that he may think

[21] See especially C.A. Barton, *Roman Honor: The Fire in the Bones* (Berkeley: University of California, 2001). Cicero famously made the gender connotations explicit: 'the *virtus* ('virtue') proper to a man is *fortitudo* ('courage'), for which there are two main tasks: scorn of death and scorn of pain (*mortis et doloris contemptio*). We must practise these if we wish to possess *virtus*, or rather if we wish to be *viri* ('men').' (*Tusc.* 2.18.43). Cf. Quintilian, *Inst.* 12.3.30.

[22] On the tradition, see especially J.-W. van Henten, *The Maccabean Martyrs as Saviours of the Jewish People: A Study of 2 and 4 Maccabees* (Leiden: Brill, 1997); for the gender dynamics of 4 Maccabees, see S.D. Moore and J. Capel Anderson, 'Taking It like a Man: Masculinity in 4 Maccabees' *JBL* 117 (1998) 249–73.

he controls their bodies and their fate. Josephus is highly conscious of this tortured-martyr tradition as still current in his own day. The conduct of the Essenes during the war, for instance, elicts a passage of fulsome praise:

> The war with the Romans tested their souls in every kind of way: racked and twisted, burned and broken, and made to pass through every instrument of torture to induce them to slander their legislator or eat some forbidden thing, they refused to yield to either demand, or even cringe once to their torturers or shed tears. Smiling in their agonies and adopting an ironic stance (κατειρωνευόμενοι) towards those who applied the tortures, they gladly gave up their souls, since they would receive them back again. (*Bell.* 2.152f.)

This motif is prominent in *Contra Apionem* and not just in our passage. Already in 1.42–43 Josephus, contrasting Jews with Greeks in their attitude to their literature, emphasised that

> it is innate in every Jew, right from birth, to regard them [the Jewish scriptures] as decrees of God, to remain faithful to them and, if necessary, gladly to die on their behalf. Thus to date many have been seen, on many occasions, as prisoners of war undergoing torture and all kinds of deaths in theatres for not letting slip a single word in contravention of the laws and the records associated with them.

The theme recurs: a citation from (pseudo-) Hecataeus refers to 'those who face tortures and the most terrible of all deaths rather than deny their ancestral laws' (1.190–91), while the theme of dying for the law is repeatedly highlighted by Josephus himself (1.212; 2.218, 272). Josephus suggests he could tell many a tale of tortures gladly undergone at the hands of 'our conquerors' (2.233).

As we have noted, our passage places notable stress on such torture as spectacle: Josephus imputes to 'our conquerors' the desire to *see* Jews hold out under torture, as a θαυμαστόν τι θέαμα (232). If the Spartans had, in Josephus' day, their famous spectacles of endurance, where tourists came to watch Spartan youths undergo floggings at the altar of Artemis Orthia, even to the point of death, Jews too had spectacular feats of bravery, under the instruments of torture.[23] Of course, if it had been designed as a spectacle, such torture would have been intended to demonstrate the absolute power of those who inflicted this physical violence: the spectacle of the body in pain was an extremely effective communication of the mastery of the torturer.[24] Josephus, however, imagines it as a spectacle of something else: a stage specially prepared by the 'conquerors' to display not their own power but

---

[23] Plutarch had witnessed the famous 'floggings' (*Lyc* 18.1), and the rite remains a topic of fascinated comment for generations thereafter: see, e.g., Lucian, *Anach*. 38 (paralleled with torture); Philostratus, *Vit. Apoll.* 6.20; Libanius, *Orat*. 1.23.

[24] For Josephus' awareness of such semiotics, see M. Gleason, 'Mutilated Messengers: Body Language in Josephus', in S. Goldhill, *Being Greek under Rome*, 50–85.

the moral, intellectual and physical courage of those they tortured to death. In other words, Josephus wrests power out of what was apparently the most powerless situation of all: the 'conquerors' (κρατοῦντες) end up displaying the mastery exercised by their own victims. And if, as Seneca says, 'whoever despises his own life is master of yours' (*quisquis vitam suam contempsit, tuae dominus est*, *Ep.* 4.8), the victims could even be seen to outmaster their 'conquerors'. As we know from his comment on the Essenes, Josephus readily sees irony in the torture chamber.

But who is this irony directed against? If the 'spectacle' (θέαμα) here is related to treatment of prisoners in the 'theatres' (θέατρα) mentioned in 1.43, we do not have far to look. Several times at the end of his *Judean War*, Josephus had given examples of this phenomenon. The majority of the prisoners of war, he related, were 'presented by Titus to the various provinces to be destroyed in the theatres by sword or by wild beasts' (*Bell.* 6.418). At Caesarea Philippi, Titus used the prisoners for all sorts of 'spectacles' (θεωρίαι): some were thrown to wild beasts, many were compelled to fight each other in opposing groups; in this location alone, 2500 were killed in such contests (7.23 f., 37 f.). Eleazar's speech refers, in quite credible terms, to others who died on the rack at the hands of the Romans, tortured by fire or whips, or half-eaten by wild beasts (7.373 f.). We might think that such 'tortures' had little to do with 'being forced either to do something contrary to the laws or to say a word in contravention of them' (*c. Apion.* 2.233), but Josephus clearly thought otherwise. The last example he gives, at the close of his *Bell.*, is of Sicarii captured in Egypt who amazed everyone with their καρτερία ('endurance'). Under every form of torture, devised to make them acknowledge Caesar as Lord (Καῖσαρ δεσπότης), they would not utter even these words, however much their bodies were wracked with pain; even children managed this quite astounding feat (*Bell.* 7.416–19). Thus the 'conquerors' whom Josephus imagines displaying their torture victims for public admiration most certainly include the Roman victors in the *Bell.*, and Jewish endurance suddenly takes on, in this light, a remarkable political hue. Although in *Contra Apionem* he does not explicitly name those responsible for the torture (either in 1.42 f. or in 2.232 f.), the implication is not hard to trace. Here we have Josephus, the captured general of the conquered Jewish nation now writing in Rome, celebrating the endurance of Jews under (Roman) torture, an endurance displayed in defiance of their Roman captors, resisting Roman imperial claims in the name of Jewish law-observance, and displaying a quintessentially 'Roman' contempt of death in the face of the Romans themselves.[25]

---

[25] Whom is he writing this for? On the ever-controverted question of Josephus' audience(s), see Barclay, *Against Apion*, xlv-liii.

Josephus' rhetorical stance is fascinatingly complex. He is educated enough in the 'mainstream' Greek tradition to be able to select, deploy and twist the Spartan legend to his own purposes: he knows both where Sparta's reputation is admired, and where it is vulnerable to critique or rhetorical outflanking. The Jews emerge not just as Spartans from the East, but as tougher than the toughest Spartan ideal, able to endure a domestic regime no Spartan could live with. Such a comparison is being played out in Rome, in a treatise written by a military failure (a Jewish general who did not have the guts to commit suicide) who uses his adopted education to strengthen and empower his national tradition, turning the always over-determined image of Sparta, so admired by Rome, into a platform for Jewish self-pride. In the course of this, while skilfully subordinating the mastery of others in warfare to the mastery of oneself in domestic routine or pain, Josephus illustrates the Jewish display of an old but now recognisably 'Roman' trait, the contempt of death, and hints at its display, under torture, not in accordance with Roman political interests, but in defiance of Roman imperial power. There are traces here of a colonial 'mimicry' that is characteristically ambivalent: this tamed, 'civilized' and partially Romanised Jew mirrors back the ideals that had become central to the maintenance of empire, but re-sites them within a Jewish framework of commitments that in certain conditions flies directly against the interests of Rome. And, paradoxically, it is on the torture rack where this contest of powers is most vividly displayed: at the very point of victory, where the 'conquerors' maim, torture and kill their victims to make spectacular display of their power, a smiling Jewish victim, super-Spartan in his manliness, and eerily Roman in his contempt of death, threatens to outmanoeuvre the Roman master, dying out of commitment to a cause and a cultural tradition that can never quite be assimilated or safely absorbed.

17. Snarling Sweetly

A Study of Josephus on Idolatry

'Idolatry' is a portmanteau word into which many different concepts can be conveniently packed. The range of possible senses is large. It can mean, in the first place, the deflection of worship to a spurious 'deity' (worshipping a being not properly constituting a 'god'); also, secondly, improper representation of the true God (for instance, in the Jewish and Christian traditions, creating an image of God); and, thirdly, by extension, 'idolatry' can be used to refer to erroneous concepts of God (thinking of God in 'idolatrous' ways). Recently, of course, the range of meaning of this flexible term has been increased to include anyone or anything which receives adulation (such as a 'pop idol'). In this contemporary, secular, usage the term's negative valence has been largely lost, but historically it has always conveyed a polemical tone. 'Idolatry' was employed in the Jewish tradition as a boundary sign, a pejorative characterisation of the religious traditions of non-Jews, the negative foil for the aniconic and exclusive monotheism which came to characterise Judaism, and hence Christianity and Islam. Greeks and Romans did not call their deities, or the images which represented them, εἴδωλα; in normal Greek usage, the word denotes 'phantoms' or 'insubstantial phenomena'. In Jewish polemics, the term conveys a sneer, a claim to superior piety or truth. It thereby stakes out a terrain on which Jewish self-definition was (and still is) constructed.[1]

Self-definition, however, is a complex, historically contingent and ever-shifting phenomenon, even when a culture considers itself to be merely maintaining its traditions. The history of the concept of 'idolatry' thus maps the ways in which Judaism and its offshoots have understood themselves within their religious contexts. At the same time, the history of the ways in which Jews have talked to non-Jews about their 'idolatry' illustrates particularly clearly their politics of communication. By the first century CE Jews had developed a large register of terms and a complex set of categories

[1] For a philosophical analysis of this topic from a Jewish perspective, see M. Halbertal and A. Margalit, *Idolatry* (Cambridge, Mass.: Harvard University, 1992). The history of the debate about images in Western culture is surveyed by A. Besançon, *The Forbidden Image. An Intellectual History of Iconoclasm* (Chicago: University of Chicago, 2000).

with which to characterise the 'idolatry' of Gentiles; they had also learned to adopt a variety of tones in which to speak on this topic, ranging from sheer scorn to gently ironic debate.[2] In this paper I wish to explore the strategies adopted by Josephus on this matter in his apologetic work *Against Apion*, which he wrote at the end of the first century CE. In particular, I hope here to trace how Josephus places Jewish aniconic peculiarity on the map of Greek and Roman culture, and in so doing will highlight his rhetorical subtlety, as he skilfully conveys his disdain of non-Jewish religious practices without offending his Roman (or Romanised) audience.

I. Entering Graeco-Roman Debates

Judging from a distance, and listening to some Jewish polemics, we might gain the impression that the Jewish tradition stood in stark antithesis to the discourse on religion among Greeks and Romans. It seems like a straightforward clash of cultures: the Jewish monotheistic and aniconic tradition simply collided with a radically different pattern of religious practice and belief. In fact, the intercultural relationship could be far more complex. Jews who knew something about Greek and Roman religion were not compelled simply to assault it, as a unitary system, from the outside. Rather, they could insert themselves into the internal debates among their pagan contemporaries, positioning themselves not outside the Graeco-Roman tradition, but at least partially within it, as contributors to long-running internal discussion about the appropriate means to represent, worship and speak about the divine.

The most obvious example of this strategy is the Jewish reaction to Greek 'myths' and associated anthropomorphic representations of the gods. In his *Against Apion* Josephus has a fine passage lambasting the myths concocted by poets, attacking their scurrilous and demeaning representation of the gods, the tales of family conflict and outrageous sexual behaviour, the gods' monstrous sins and pathetic vulnerabilities (2.236–49). But as he himself points out, this is not a new criticism concocted by Jews. Allying himself with 'those of superior intelligence' (2.242), Josephus leads off his critique with the comment: 'who of those admired by Greeks for their wisdom has not censured the most famous poets and the most trusted lawgivers for originally sowing such notions among the masses?'

[2] The range is evident even in a single author such as Philo, who enjoys invective against 'gods made of wood and stone' (*Decal.* 66–76), but also gives a careful philosophical analysis of the faults of polytheism (e.g. *Ebr.* 108–110; *Spec. Leg.* 2.164–67); in a different context he makes only subtly ironic comments about 'so-called demigods' and 'the greater ones' (Hermes, Apollo and Ares, *Legatio* 78–113).

(2.239). What follows are, in fact, precisely the criticisms of Homeric myth which we can trace back as far as Xenophanes in the sixth century BCE, and which Plato had made the basis of his refusal to allow poets into his model city-state.[3] Indeed, one might say it was this very stand-off between philosophy and poetry which had exercised Greek, and subsequently Roman, reflection on 'theology' for centuries, and had encouraged the well-known philosophical attempts to 'purify' the myths by means of allegory (as Josephus knows, 2.255).

In other words, Jews were neither the only ones, nor the first, to object to the 'indecent theology' of the Greek myths: in voicing their criticisms they were insinuating themselves into a long debate *within* the Greek tradition, whether or not, like Josephus, they acknowledged this tactic. They were not the first to recognise the theological problems of anthropomorphism. Indeed, one might say, they learnt from Greek philosophy the problem of anthropomorphism within their own Scriptures, and took the philosophical high ground against Greek myth only after receiving a helping hand from Greeks themselves.[4]

As this example already illustrates, Greek (and Roman) religious belief and practice was neither a simple nor a unitary system. In their broad and somewhat ramshackle cultural traditions, Greeks and Romans cultivated many different ways of conceptualising and speaking about the divine, many different practices for dealing with God(s), and many different forms of representing divine presence and power. The closer one looks at Greek and Roman religious culture, the more one realises its internal complexities: cultural systems of varied origin and function overlapped, interacted and competed. In its rich diversity lay multiple tensions and contradictions.

One of the most influential attempts to make sense of this inner complexity was developed in Stoic philosophy, and is known to us from the Roman scholar Varro, who wrote in the first century BCE. According to Varro (as we know him via Augustine), discourse on religion operates according to 'three kinds' of theology. First, there is 'mythical' theology, created by poets and dramatised in the theatre, in which the Gods are represented in anthropomorphic forms. Secondly, there is (what Stoics termed) 'natural' theology, developed by philosophers, in which the divine is identified or associated with the powers and properties of nature, as the immanent world-soul. Thirdly, there is 'civic' theology, the ways of addressing and appeasing the

---

[3] Xenophanes of Colophon, fragments 19–20; Plato, *Rep* 3.377 d–392 b.

[4] A clear case in point, much influenced by Stoic philosophy, is the work of Aristobulus; see N. Walter, *Der Thoraausleger Aristobulos* (Berlin: Akademie, 1964), and my *Jews in the Mediterranean Diaspora from Alexander to Trajan (323 BCE – 117 CE)* (Edinburgh: T & T Clark, 1996) 150–58.

Gods practised by citizens, and especially by priests, in the interests of the civic community (including prayers, sacrifices, oracles and temple-rituals).[5]

This 'tripartite theology' was utilised in antiquity as a way of comprehending the bewildering variety of ways in which religion functioned and was discussed. It also appeals to many present-day analysts of Greek and Roman religion, who note that these very different systems of discourse and practice could coexist, despite their different rationalities, in the thinking and practices of Greeks and Romans.[6] Thus a representative of the Roman elite who, as a member of a college of priests, inspected the entrails of a sacrificed animal, might in another context, as philosopher, employ Stoic discourse on the nature of the Gods, and yet elsewhere, as a spectator of plays or reader of literature, enjoy the anthropomorphic tradition of poetry. To us, such compartmentalisation of thought – what Veyne once called 'brain-balkanisation' – may appear extraordinary, but it was neither unusual nor problematic in antiquity. In other words, Greek and Roman religion is not a single bounded system, but a 'system of systems' whose conglomeration was the source of much invention, creativity and cultural reflection.

In a culture where different modes of belief could criss-cross, intersect and collide, it was possible for knowledgeable Jews to exploit the internal tensions between these different discourses. Josephus is, I think, well-attuned to this possibility. He is probably cognisant of the 'tripartite' schema mentioned above, since in the context of his attack on mythology he takes pains to ally himself with one kind of discourse, the philosophical, against poetry and the patterns of religion permitted by 'lawgivers' (that is, 'civic' theology, *Apion* 2.239, 250–252). Josephus had learned that the most effective form of apologetic was not an unremitting blast against a putatively unified religious system, but precisely the exploitation of its inconsistencies, the wedging open of the gaps that lay between one system of religion and another.

Josephus' general strategy is to align himself with 'philosophy', though not with any particular school within it. This enables him to take the intellectual and moral high ground, but also to utilise the tradition of disdain which philosophy had long cultivated towards the gullibility of the masses

---

[5] Varro *apud* Augustine, *Civ. Dei* 4.27, 31; 6.5–6. See B. Cardauns, 'Varro und die römische Religion: Zur Theologie, Wirkungsgeschichte und Leistung der *Antiquitates Rerum Divinarum*,' *ANRW* II.16.1, 80–103; G. Lieberg, 'Die "theologia tripertita" in Forschung und Bezeugung', *ANRW* I.4 , 63–115. I am grateful to James Rives of York University, Toronto, for his advice on this topic.

[6] M. Beard, J. North and S. Price, *Religions of Rome, Volume 1: A History* (Cambridge: Cambridge University, 1998) 30–41, 211–44; D.C. Feeney, *Literature and Religion at Rome: Cultures, Contexts and Beliefs*, (Cambridge: Cambridge University, 1988) 14–18, 92–97. [Cf. J.B. Rives, *Religion in the Roman Empire* (Oxford: Blackwell Publishing, 2007) 21–41.]

and the compromises of legislators. Josephus is clearly conscious of the peril of engaging in religious invective: in the introduction to his ridicule of myths he insists that Moses 'prohibited us from mocking or blaspheming those whom others consider to be Gods for the sake of the very name "God"' (2.237, alluding to LXX Exod 22.27).[7] Of course he carries on, nonetheless, in his gleeful scorn of Greek mythology, but only after pointing out that he shared the perspective of 'many extremely illustrious people' (2.238). Thus as we examine Josephus' comments on 'images', we should expect him to position himself carefully within the cultural debates of his environment, and to exploit their cracks and crevices for his own advantage. We should also observe the tone with which he handles this topic, alert to the careful concealments which his rhetorical strategy might require.

II. The Response to Apion on Imperial Images

In the course of his reply to Apion (2.1–144), Josephus raises a topic which had been of great significance in the Alexandrian crisis of 38 CE. During the riots in Alexandria of that year, imperial statues or busts had been maliciously placed in Jewish synagogues, and Apion, the leader of the Alexandrian Greeks, had apparently exploited Jewish embarrassment on this matter and claimed that their failure to pay due honour to these images proved their fundamental hostility to Rome. The issue was clearly difficult for Jews to handle, and of enormous political significance. Philo expended huge effort exonerating his fellow Jews in his two tractates on this affair (his *In Flaccum* and *Legatio ad Gaium*), having led a delegation to Rome to counter Apion's accusations. That subjects in the Roman empire should openly *refuse* to pay religious respect to images of the emperor was, for Roman politicians, a shocking phenomenon, easily exploited by those who wished Jews to be portrayed as actual or potential subversives. Tacitus' seemingly respectful comment on the Jewish aniconic tradition is artfully ambivalent: *non regibus haec adulatio, non Caesaribus honor* (*Hist*. 5.5.4).

Josephus knows he is on dangerous ground. In his *Antiquities* (18.257–60) he had given a fuller description of Apion's charges, but had not presented the Jewish reply. Instead he had chosen to conflate the Alexandrian issue with Gaius' project to erect a statue in the Jerusalem temple, thus enabling the whole to be represented as a monumental act of impiety by an emperor who had opted to fight against God. In fact, the topic of imperial images

[7] Cf. Philo, *Spec. Leg*. 1.53; P. van der Horst, '"Thou shalt not revile the Gods": The LXX Translation of Ex. 22.28 (27), its Background and Influence', in *Hellenism – Judaism – Christianity. Essays on their Interaction* (Kampen: Kok Pharos, 1994) 112–21.

had arisen on a number of occasions in Josephus' narrative in both *War* and *Antiquities*, though with important differences between the two works. In *The Jewish War* the topic of religious images is handled with some circumspection; Josephus records the issue a limited number of times and Jewish objections to images are stated indirectly, not in a direct authorial voice (*Bell.* 1.403–14, 648–55; 2.169–74, 184–203). In the *Antiquities*, on the other hand, Josephus includes many more episodes concerning religious images, is more outspoken in his criticism of both Herod and Gaius, and gives fuller and more direct explanations of the Jewish taboo (e.g., *Ant.* 15.267–91, 328–41; 17.149–63; 18.55–59, 256–309; 19.299–311). Thus Josephus turns to this topic in *Against Apion* 2.73–78 with a practised hand, but also with a mental and rhetorical flexibility which equips him to craft his response with as much attention to what he leaves out as to what he says and how he says it.

Josephus' response to Apion runs like this (my own translation):[8]

> [73] Likewise, Apion has attempted to denounce us because we do not set up images of the emperors – as if they did not know this or needed Apion to mount their defence! He ought rather to have admired the magnanimity and moderation of the Romans, since they do not compel their subjects to transgress their ancestral laws, but accept such honours as it is pious and legitimate for their donors to give; they are not grateful for honours conferred under compulsion or force. [74] The Greeks and some others consider it good to erect statues. Indeed they take pride in painting portraits of their fathers, wives and sons. Some indeed acquire statues of people with whom they have no connection, others do the same even for favourite slaves. So what is surprising if they are seen to render such an honour also to their rulers and masters? [75] On the other hand, our legislator – not as if he were prophesying that Roman power should not be honoured, but because he disdained a means which brought no benefit either to God or to human beings, and because an inanimate object proves to be inferior to every living creature, and much more to God – forbade the making of statues. [76] He did not prohibit that good men be paid homage with honours, secondary to that due to God: with such expressions of respect we give glory to the emperors and to the Roman people. [77] We offer on their behalf continual sacrifices, and not only do we conduct such rites every day at the public expense of all Judaeans, but we perform no other such sacrifices at public expense, not even for our own children. It is only for the emperors that we jointly exhibit this exceptional honour, which we confer on no other human being. [78] Let these remarks together provide a sufficient rebuttal of Apion's statements on the topic of Alexandria.

This reply to Apion is a masterpiece of rhetorical deflection: as spin-doctors go, Josephus is one of the best. Although Apion's charges specifically concerned Alexandria in the reign of Gaius, Josephus chooses to broaden the issue to the relationship of Jews to imperial power in general. This may look

---

[8] For this portion of *Apion* we rely on a Latin translation from the 6th century CE; at 75, I read (with Boysen) 'inanimatum' (LBP: 'inanimatu'); see my commentary ad loc. The translation offered here is provisional.

foolhardy: he had developed an effective strategy of vituperation of Gaius in his *Antiquities*, and it might have seemed safer to confine the issue to Gaius' reign and to exploit Roman anxieties on the topic of imperial deification. But Josephus and his readers knew that the issue did not disappear after Gaius' death, and he has chosen not to open up the highly sensitive topic of the religious status of the emperor.[9] In fact, Josephus senses here an opportunity to reaffirm in general terms Jewish loyalty to Rome. Hence the instant flattery of Roman 'magnanimity' and 'moderation', the ready recognition that Jews are Roman subjects and the appeal to the Roman perception of themselves as tolerant respecters of others' religious traditions (73). In those few phrases Josephus conjures up Rome's flattering self-image, her imperial desire to be known as merciful, generous and pious.

But the portrait of happy cultural cohabitation between Jews and Romans will surely break down on the issue of imperial images and, in general, the place of visual representation in religion. How can Josephus avoid their diametrical difference on this point? As you will observe, by a series of ingenious side-steps. Rather than enter the intricate debate among Romans as to religious rites which should be offered to or for the emperors (living or dead), Josephus drops the specific topic of imperial images to focus on images in general. Indeed, he broadens the theme from religious representation to visual representation in general: we are suddenly talking about family portraits and the erection of statues of famous men or favourite slaves, none of which have religious connotations. And to cap it all, these habits from which Josephus now distances himself are attributed not to Romans, but to 'the Greeks and some others'! Not even at this point will Josephus allow an explicit statement of Jewish cultural difference from Rome.

This reference to 'the Greeks and some others' is a fine example of circumspection. As James Scott has shown, the politically subordinate can rarely afford to voice overt criticism of their superiors; their real views are either kept unspoken or carefully concealed in patterns of 'indirectness' which speak at different levels to different hearers.[10] Josephus knows that the practice of which he here speaks was ubiquitous in Roman society: both private and public spaces in Rome were full of portraiture and statuary, both secular and religious.[11] But he does not here name 'Romans', and his careful foregrounding of 'Greeks' exploits a particular Roman consciousness that

---

[9] The issue was of special sensitivity in the Domitianic era (during, or soon after which, *c. Apion.* was written), with the increased Flavian emphasis on imperial religious honours.

[10] James Scott, *The Weapons of the Weak: Everyday Forms of Peasant Resistance* (New Haven: Yale University, 1985); *Domination and the Arts of Resistance: Hidden Transcripts* (New Haven: Yale University, 1990).

[11] At *War* 7.158–59, Josephus records, without negative comment, Vespasian's huge store of paintings and sculpture. Cicero complained that Rome was overcrowded with sculptures, *Tusc.* 5.102.

most of what they appreciated in art and sculpture was originally 'Greek'. More than that, it hints at a specifically Roman discourse which considered an interest in art, and especially sculpture, as a species of 'Greek luxury' or 'decadence'.[12]

Thus the threatened cultural clash is deflected, and Josephus is careful to complete this section with a series of strong assertions about Jewish compliance with Roman power. Twice he insists that Moses did not intend to ban the paying of proper honour to Roman authority (2.75 a, 76), while injecting the crucial Jewish distinction between honours to 'humans' and those due to 'God'. At the end he emphasises the daily sacrifices as evidence of Jewish loyalty to Rome (2.76–77). That was a tactic he had used before in relation to Gaius' statue (*Bell.* 2.197), though it seems somewhat artificial to repeat it now when the temple no longer stood and the Jerusalem sacrifices had been discontinued! Josephus simply glosses over that problem, in the interests of parading a practical proof of Jewish religious respect for the emperors; in the process he probably exaggerates, if he does not invent, the Jews' financial contribution to these sacrifices, which Philo says were paid for by the emperors themselves![13]

Embedded in all this intricate 'spin' is the real heart of the matter: the Jewish refusal to admit images in a religious context. Josephus allows himself just two phrases to explain this taboo (2.75). The first is that images 'bring no benefit either to God or to human beings'. At first sight that does not look like a strong argument. 'Benefit' is difficult to measure, and is largely determined by cultural context; a Roman could find 'beneficial' what a Jew did not. But the suggestion that images also bring no benefit to God is a significant hint at a philosophical critique of popular religion: according to this, the common assumption that religious rites bring benefit to God is ridiculous, given that God, who by definition is self-sufficient, needs no 'benefits' at all. The hint is not developed here (it will be strengthened in 2.190), but it is supplemented by the second, more explicit, explanation for Moses' ban: that an inanimate object is inferior to a living creature, and thus still more to God. In the present context, no more is said to indicate why images are therefore inappropriate: they are not here dubbed a token of impiety. In this sensitive political context Josephus can afford only to suggest that Jews have a rational objection to images and leave it at that. But he does allow himself one small barb. Moses, he says, banned the use of images because he 'disdained' them (Latin: *despiciens*, 2.75). There is venom in that term, a cultural snarl: but so sweet is the smile on this Jewish face turned towards Rome that the sneer can pass almost unnoticed.

---

[12] E.g., Cicero, *Tusc.* 1.4; *In Verrem* 2.4.132–34 and *passim*; Livy 25.40.1–3.

[13] Philo, *Legatio*, 157; cf. Josephus, *War* 2.197.

III. Philosophical Objections to Making Images of God

Let us return to Josephus' comment that 'an inanimate object proves inferior to every living creature, and much more to God' (2.75). At one level this is an obvious statement of fact: no one could deny that an image, whatever its materials and however great its beauty, is lifeless, and thus, in that respect, inferior to the person or deity it represents. But why should this matter? Why cannot an inferior object represent a superior being? (After all, a flag represents a country and a badge an organisation, although both are clearly 'inferior' to the complex social entities they represent.) Implicit in Josephus' argument are a number of premises in an enthymeme which seems to run something like this (unspoken lines in italics):

A. Images are meant to be similar to the reality they represent.
B. Images are lifeless and therefore inferior to what they represent.
C. But the inferior cannot be adequately similar to the superior.
D. What is not wholly adequate in religion is wholly inadequate, indeed impious.
E. Therefore: image-representation of God was rightly banned by Moses.

If lines B and E are explicit in Josephus' reasoning, the others are only implicit, but it seems that they, or something like them, are necessary to make sense of the fact that Moses *banned* the use of images. Together, the unspoken lines (A, C and D) constitute two crucial aspects of Josephus' aniconic logic:

1. a presumption that images function on the basis of similarity-representation (line A); and
2. an extreme 'adequacy'-requirement, such that the partially adequate is, in the sphere of religion, judged wholly inadequate (lines C and D).

Let me now illustrate from later passages in *Against Apion* that this is how Josephus' reasoning operates.

The presumption that images function on the basis of similarity-representation naturally fits the artistic representation of human beings, and by running together the representation of human *and divine* subjects, Josephus makes it easy to apply the same logic to religious representation. Later in this work Josephus discusses the Jewish constitution, naming it a 'theocracy', by which he means the all-seeing supervision and sovereignty of God (2.165–66). He immediately supplements this with a definition of God (2.167):[14]

[14] For the opening words I follow Eusebius' citation (*Praep.ev.* 8.3), which omits the ἕνα ('one') read in L and reproduced in the Latin translation.

> But God he represented as uncreated, immutable through all eternity, more beautiful than any mortal form, made known to us by his power, but as to what he is like in essence, unknown.

Although nothing explicit is said here about images of God, the heavy concentration of negatives clearly suggests their inappropriateness. Since he is 'uncreated' and 'immutable' God is, by definition, in a category wholly other than the materials from which an image could be made. As 'more beautiful than any human form', he shares with human art the property 'beauty', but wholly surpasses it in degree, As 'unknown in essence' God defies any attempt to create a similarity-representation. Not only can we not adequately represent what we *do* know about God; we cannot begin to make something similar to what we *do not* know. It is striking that at this point Josephus takes care to claim as allies in this conception of God (although they were first taught by Moses!) 'the wisest among the Greeks', including in this category a short roll-call of philosophers, Pythagoras, Anaxagoras, Plato and the Stoics (2.168). In other words, he here aligns himself broadly with the philosophical tradition, and suggests that Judaism is the original and truest philosophical discourse on God. That he can cite such philosophers together indicates the level of generality at which he is operating. But it is also notable that, while citing them as supporters of his exalted view of God, he cannot claim that they practised what he takes to be its logical correlate: that no-one should create or employ an image of God.

This last point, implicit in 2.167, is made explicit soon thereafter at the start of the section on the laws of the constitution (2.190–218). Partly mirroring the decalogue, Josephus begins this section with statements about God and the inadmissibility of images:

> [190] The first, at the head, is a statement about God, that God encompasses all things, perfect and blessed, self-sufficient and sufficing for all, that he is the beginning, middle and end of all things; he is visible through his works and acts of grace and more evident than anything else, but in form and greatness beyond our description. [191] All materials, however costly, are too cheap to represent his image, and all artistry is incapable of designing his likeness. We have not seen nor can we imagine anything like him, nor is it pious to portray him.

In the course of this passage Josephus suggests that God actually has an 'image' (εἴκων, 191), but it is clear that it is neither possible nor proper to attempt to reproduce it. The presumption in the earlier passage on Moses' ban is now explicit: a proper image would have to be a 'likeness' (Josephus uses the terms μίμησις and ὅμοιον). But this is simply impossible in the case of God, because even the best materials would be inadequate and because, in any case, we can neither describe his 'form' nor conceive his 'likeness'. What is more, to attempt this task is not simply, for Josephus, a doomed enterprise. Anything less than God demeans him (any material would be ἄτιμος, 191): any image is, on this understanding, an act of impiety (οὔτε ... ὅσιον, 191).

Josephus' critique of images is clear and strong enough, but it is far milder and more subtle than an alternative Jewish strategy on this topic. Taking their cue from the prophetic ridicule of idols, many other Jews in the Graeco-Roman world accused their pagan contemporaries of a cruder and more basic mistake: that they considered the objects they made as images not just to *resemble* Gods but actually to *be* Gods. Patterns of cultic practice in the Graeco-Roman world may have encouraged this perception: worshippers routinely offered gifts to the Gods by placing them in front of images, they addressed statues in prayer and worship, attended to their beauty and paraded them through the streets as if the Gods themselves were present in their midst.[15] Influenced by this or by their own prophetic tradition, Jews typically scorned their contemporaries for the error of *substitution*, for treating the images (blind, deaf and lifeless) as if they were Gods themselves.[16] Even Philo enjoys repeating this pattern of ridicule (*Decal.* 66–81). By contrast, Josephus refrains from any such scorn. He never says that Gentiles take their images *to be* Gods.[17] For him, the basic fault in the making of images is not the attempt to create and then worship a *substitute* God, but the attempt to represent God through *similarity*. He assumes that images are created with this rationale, denies the possibility of the task and then quietly remarks that failure in adequate representation is 'not pious'.

IV. Exploiting the Cracks in Contemporary Religious Discourse

In taking this stance, Josephus was able to enter and exploit current debates concerning the adequacy of religious images within the Graeco-Roman tradition itself. To have lambasted 'idolatry' as the senseless creation of *substitute 'gods'* might have made cheap rhetoric, but would have made little intellectual impact: it was easy enough for non-Jews to reply that their images were media to represent the Gods, and not themselves the objects of worship. But to press the question of similarity relations between image and reality, and to align oneself with 'philosophy', was to open up a crack

[15] Feeney, *Literature and Religion*, 92–97; cf. R. L. Gordon, 'The Real and the Imaginary: Production and Religion in the Graeco-Roman World' *Art History* 2 (1979) 5–34. [Cf. J. Elsner, 'Image and Ritual: Reflections on the Religious Appreciation of Classical Art', *Classical Quarterly* 46 (1996) 513–31.]

[16] See, e. g., the polemics in *Wisdom of Solomon* 13–15 and the *Sibylline Oracles*.

[17] He also employs the term 'idol' only in very restricted contexts, in reference to biblical history: *Ant.* 9.99, 205, 243, 273; 10.50, 65, 69. In *War* the term is only used in its normal Greek sense of 'phantoms' (5.513; 7.452).

between philosophical and other forms of religious discourse, a fissure fully acknowledged in Josephus' educated circles. We may mention here just three examples.

The late-Republican scholar Varro, the celebrated authority on Roman religion, questioned whether there could be *vera simulacra* of the Gods, and suggested that at their origins, and for their first 170 years, the Romans had worshipped the Gods without using images. If that tradition had been maintained, Varro suggested, the Gods would have been cultivated more piously (*castius*). In fact, those who had set up images 'for the people' had introduced error and diminished reverence for the Gods (*apud* Augustine, *Civ. Dei* 4.27, 31). In another place (*Civ. Dei* 7.5) Varro justified the use of anthropomorphic images on the grounds that the human form contains the soul, and thus points to the world-soul, the divine. But if he were founding Roman religion anew, Varro said, he would have named the Gods according to the principles of nature. Still, one has to keep to traditional conceptions, since it is better for the masses to worship the Gods, even if some of their beliefs are false (4.31).

Varro's evident unease on this issue, and his self-conscious acceptance of compromise, expose the tensions between popular and philosophical discourse. Varro would not oppose a deeply ingrained cultural sensibility which by convention and long tradition had associated anthropomorphic images with the Gods. Such images were woven into both 'civic' religious practice and 'mythical' religious discourse by webs of association which it was simply impossible – in fact, religiously dangerous – to break. Thus philosophical standards of 'error' and 'truth' could not be, and should not be, rigorously pursued in practice. But interestingly, Varro knew and approved of the Jewish practice of imageless worship (4.31), and the structures of his thought could give Jews the right to claim that they embodied the consistent practice of philosophy.[18]

Varro's awareness of compromise is even more acute in what we know of Seneca's work *On Superstition*.[19] Seneca's critique of images even turns into satire: after complaining of the oddities concocted by religious imagination and carved in *materia vilissima atque inmobilis*, Seneca ridicules the rituals enacted in front of the image of Jupiter, as attendants introduce him to worshippers, tell him the time of day, or pretend to bath or anoint him. But just when we expect logic to compel Seneca to urge non-compliance with this whole iconic tradition, he declares that 'wise men will observe all these rites as instructed by the laws, not as gratifying to the Gods' (*tamquam*

[18] Cf. at a later date, Numenius' apparent approval of the Jews' belief in an incorporeal God (*apud* Origen, *Contra Celsum* 1.15).

[19] Unfortunately, this is known to us only via Augustine, *Civ. Dei* 6.10.

legibus iussa, not tamquam diis grata). Here again is the recognition that law and tradition coexist, by necessity, with philosophy: even if cultic practice pertains more to custom than to reality (*magis ad morem quam ad rem*), it is still better that it be performed.

A similar tension pervades Dio Chrysostom's 12th *Oration*, the most extended discussion of religious imagery in our classical sources. Dio raises nearly all the questions that occur to Josephus: are images helpful or harmful to piety? Can we ever adequately represent the divine? Is philosophy a truer form of discourse than artistic tradition and myth? Dio is well aware that one cannot adequately portray 'the highest and most perfect nature' (55). But he will not press the logic to Josephus' extreme. Even if it be finally inadequate, religious art can still be fitting, as it is the best that humans can do: if we cannot represent 'reason' or 'mind' alone (it is inaccessible to sight and inquiry), we can, through the human form in which such reason resides, portray the invisible through the visible, using art as *symbol* of truth (55–59). Throughout Dio recognises the force of convention, the power of the poetic tradition, and the desire to worship the Gods in accessible forms. Even if philosophy is the truest form of discourse on the Gods, philosophers are nothing like as popular as sculptors and poets (48), and philosophical rationality has to content itself with being one among several ways of representing the divine. In any case, Dio claims, no-one would think it better to do away with statues and images of Gods and worship only the heavens (60): the Jewish option is here presumed to be impossibly austere.

These three voices witness to the complexity and inner tension in the relationship between diverse forms of religious discourse. Josephus' tactic is quietly, without invective, to prize open the gaps between them, to align himself with 'philosophy' and to insist on the radical application of the philosophical option. Of course he did not reach this conclusion by philosophical reasoning. He is drawing on his own aniconic tradition whose roots lie elsewhere, and is answerable to a set of Jewish expectations every bit as conventional as those with which most pagan philosophers complied. But his skill is in representing Judaism not as an alien alternative to the Graeco-Roman tradition, but as the radical and consistent application of its own 'wisest' concepts.

V. Conclusions

By aligning himself with 'philosophy' in criticism of 'myths' and images, Josephus assumes he will be granted the high ground. But he also seems aware of possible criticisms which could be levelled against a culture directed purely by philosophy, for in antiquity philosophy was ever vulnerable to the charge that it was narrowly élitist and hopelessly contentious. Josephus knows both these criticisms (e.g. 2.180, 224), but takes care to show that neither apply to the 'philosophy' represented by Judaism. Among Jews, he insists, there is complete unanimity in both practice and belief (2.179–81), and a conscious and successful effort to ensure that the truths about God are known by the masses and embedded in the life of every Jew (2.169–78).

Josephus thus enters contemporary debates about appropriate forms of religion, but he also alters the terms of that debate. By pushing for a unitary, totalising, system of religious discourse, he marks a difference that distinguished Judaism, and later Christianity and Islam, in their persistent efforts to cut away from non-philosophical discourse on religion, in their fear of 'myth', and in their anxious reflex against visual representations of God. The drive for a consistent, over-arching and integrating system of thought, matched to practice, shifts decisively away from the Graeco-Roman plurality of discourses. Roman thinkers, while aware of their cultural inconsistencies, were never excessively troubled by them and, with the partial exception of Epicureans, felt little pressure to unify or purify their clashing systems of thought and practice. Jews, however, precisely in their engagement with Hellenistic and Roman culture, found themselves drawn to imagine their tradition as purist, radical, coherent, and unitary, and, whatever its internal inconsistencies, to consider these a matter of weakness and not of strength.

If we cast an eye beyond Josephus, we find Christians such as Tertullian and Eusebius well-equipped by their Jewish heritage to place themselves above pagan culture, at the same time as they employ pagan patterns of thought. Both writers employ the schema of the 'tripartite theology' which we have found alluded to by Josephus, but in greater depth and with a marked difference of tone.[20] Tertullian and Eusebius speak with open disdain of the Graeco-Roman religious tradition, ridiculing Roman custom and scorning Roman rites. By contrast, Josephus, as we have seen, snarls more sweetly. He never attacks Roman religion directly, and what he says in criticism of the Greeks is safely allied to that Roman perception which contrasted Greek 'decadence' to their own 'frugality'. Perhaps Josephus could not afford to be as blunt as his Christian successors, but perhaps he did not wish to be. The result is a finely-composed apologetic, in which ears differently attuned may hear – or may entirely miss – some of its subtler polemical undertones.[21]

[20] For Tertullian, see *Ad Nationes* 2.1, 8–15. Eusebius uses the 'tripartite' theology to structure the opening 6 books of his *Praeparatio Evangelica*.

[21] I have clearly not covered all that could be said on the subject of Josephus and idolatry. For instance, it is striking that Josephus never refers to humanity as made 'in the image' (Gen 1.26 LXX: κατ᾽ εἰκόνα) of God.

18. Paul, Roman Religion and the Emperor

Mapping the Point of Conflict

Recent years have witnessed the revival of the hypothesis that Paul and his converts placed themselves and their Lord (Christ) in direction opposition to the Roman emperor, and specifically to 'the imperial cult'.[1] Influenced by the contemporary flurry of research on the place of the emperor in Roman religion, New Testament scholars have emphasised the prominence of the imperial cult in the social, political and religious context of the early Christian churches.[2] Those well schooled by classical scholarship have learned to beware generalisations. 'The imperial cult' was no single entity, but constituted a large range of practices which related the emperor, his family or his predecessors to the divine in a variety of ways: different patterns of speech, and various forms of cultic honour or celebration were practised by different kinds of people, varying across time and place around the empire.[3]

[1] See, for instance, N.T. Wright, *Paul: Fresh Perspectives* (London: SPCK, 2005); for analysis and critique, see the following chapter in this volume.

[2] Among the most important treatments by classicists are S.R.F. Price, *Rituals and Power: The Roman Imperial Cult in Asia Minor* (Cambridge: Cambridge University, 1984); S.J. Friesen, *Twice Neokoros: Ephesus, Asia and the Cult of the Flavian Imperial Family* (Leiden: Brill, 1993); D. Fishwick, *The Imperial Cult in the Latin West* (3 volumes, with multiple parts; Leiden, Brill, 1987–2005); I. Gradel, *Emperor Worship and Roman Religion* (Oxford: Clarendon, 2002); H. Cancik and K. Hitzl, eds., *Die Praxis der Herrscherverehrung in Rom und seinen Provinzen* (Tübingen: Mohr Siebeck, 2003). For studies by scholars of early Christianity, see H.-J. Klauck, *The Religious Context of Early Christianity: A Guide to Graeco-Roman Religions* (E.T. by B. McNeil: Edinburgh: T & T Clark, 2003) 250–330; A. Brent, *The Imperial Cult and the Development of Church Order: Concepts and Images of Authority in Paganism and Early Christianity before the Age of Cyprian* (VC Sup 45; Leiden: Brill, 1999); idem, *A Political History of Early Christianity* (London: T & T Clark, 2009). Cf. the programmatic essay by J.J. Meggitt, 'Taking the Emperor's Clothes Seriously: the New Testament and the Roman Empire', in C.E. Joynes, ed., *The Quest for Wisdom. Essays in Honour of Philip Budd* (Cambridge: Orchard Academic, 2002) 143–69.

[3] For emphasis on the variety masked by the term 'the imperial cult', see M. Beard, J. North and S. Price, *Religions of Rome* (2 vols.: Cambridge: Cambridge University, 1998) 1.348–65 (distinguishing between different social contexts: *coloniae*, *municipia*, ordinary towns, groups of Roman citizens, the army, and ordinary subjects of the empire); J.B. Rives, *Religion in the Roman Empire* (Oxford: Blackwell, 2007) 148–56 (emphasising the range of ways the emperor was treated as a god, or as a mortal for whom prayers were

In relation to Paul, the focus has understandably been concentrated on locations associated with his mission in the Greek East.[4] Here I will focus on the city of Tarraco in Spain (modern Tarragona), a Roman colony, the provincial capital, and Paul's most likely destination if he ever succeeded in extending his mission to Spain (Rom 15.28).[5] Although the political and religious conditions in the West were not identical to the Greek East, in most crucial respects the function and expression of the imperial cult in a Roman *colonia* such as Tarraco was closely similar to that in eastern colonies such as Corinth, Pisidian Antioch or Philippi.[6] By imagining Paul in this context, we may examine, firstly, the place of the emperor in relation to Roman (and other) religion, and, secondly, Paul's attitude to this religious matrix, including 'the imperial cult'; in conclusion, we may hope to map as accurately as possible the point of conflict between Pauline Christianity and Roman religion. The fact that Tarraco was the location of the martyrdom of Bishop Fructuosus and two deacons, Augurius and Eulogius, in the imperial persecutions of 259 CE makes this a particularly appropriate site for such inquiries.

I. Tarraco, Religion and the Imperial Cult

In a charming introduction to a dialogue on Virgil (now mostly lost), a popular Roman author of the early second century CE named Publius Annius (or Lucius Annaeus) Florus sets the scene in Tarraco, a city he clearly knew well.[7] After travelling around many parts of the Mediterranean, he

offered to the gods, or ambiguously on the margin between the two spheres). All are clear that there was no coherent or organised system of worship directed to the emperor as god.

[4] See especially P. Oakes, *Philippians: From People to Letter* (SNTSMS 110; Cambridge: Cambridge University, 2001); J.K. Hardin, *Galatians and the Imperial Cult* (WUNT 2.237; Tübingen: Mohr Siebeck, 2008); for the Apocalypse, see S. Friesen, *Imperial Cults and the Apocalypse of John: Reading Revelation in the Ruins* (New York: Oxford University, 2001).

[5] Whether he ever did is of course a disputed issue. See the essays by R. Riesner, H. Omerzu and A. Puig i Tàrrech in J.M. Gavaldà Ribot et al., eds., *Pau, Fructuós I El Cristianisme primitiu a Tarragona (Segles I–VIII)* (Tarragona: Fundació Privada Liber, 2010) 101–55. This chapter is an expanded version of my essay in that volume, which arose out of a splendid conference at Tarragona in June 2008, marking 750 years since the martyrdom of Bishop Fructuosus and his deacons.

[6] In the Greek East, divine honours to the emperors and their families were normally grafted onto an urban Greek tradition; in the West, there was sometimes no pre-existent urban culture as a substratum for Roman religion. But the difference is least in respect to Roman *coloniae*, where a strongly Romanised ethos was imported into the local environment; see Beard-North-Price, *Religions of Rome*, 339, 342, 352–53.

[7] Text and French translation in P. Jal, *Florus, Oeuvres* (Budé edition, 2 vols.;Paris: Société d'Édition "Les Belles Lettres", 1967) 2.111–15.

reports, he has chosen to settle in Tarraco. The climate is wonderful and the people honest, frugal and hospitable, enjoying a gentle pace of life (2.7–8). Although the town may seem provincial compared to the bustle of Rome, it has, Florus insists, its own dignity. Its very name speaks glory (it had been refounded as a colony by Julius Caesar as *Colonia Urbs Triumphalis Tarraco*), and as the seat of the Roman governor of the province *Hispania citerior* (or *Tarraconensis*) it housed the imperial military standards. At this point, writing in about 122 CE (with a dramatic date just after 102 CE), we expect Florus to wax lyrical about the spectacular temple to Augustus in the remodelled Flavian upper Forum. It is possible that this is indeed the temple in whose groves the dialogue takes place (in the shade of the trees, 1.1),[8] but Florus draws attention rather to the city's 'ancient temples' (*vetera templa*), and in particular the temple of Jupiter Ammon, associated with a mythological tale of an abducted virgin (2.9). Like other places he had visited on his Mediterranean tours (Crete, Sicily, Egypt), the identity and the fame of Tarraco are bound up with religion: temples and altars, festivals and processions, sacrifices, priests and myths are, as in any city of the Mediterranean world, essential to the fabric of civic life.

Florus' reference to Jupiter Ammon (the 'horned god'), illuminated by a beautiful marble roundel found in Tarraco,[9] illustrates well the character of religion in this world. Ammon was an Egyptian god, with the head of a ram, known to Greeks especially through his oracle at Siwa, famously visited by Alexander the Great. Associated with Zeus by the identification of deities common in antiquity, Ammon was then 'Romanised' as Jupiter Ammon, just as the Phoenician deity Melkart, introduced by Carthaginian settlers in the south of Spain, became associated with Greek Heracles, and thus Roman Hercules. The Spanish peninsula was, indeed, a melting-pot of cultures and religious traditions. Indigenous cults survived into the Roman era especially in the myths and rituals of the countryside, Phoenician and Greek deities were introduced into coastal cities by settlers and traders from the seventh century BCE onwards, and Roman cults were strongly represented in Roman colonies and sites of Roman settlement, together with all the other deities which spread across the Mediterranean world from the East. Thus, in Tarraco itself, there is evidence for everything from a pre-Roman cult in a cave sanctuary (Cova de Font Major de L'Espluga de Francoli) to the worship of Isis (*RIT* 35).[10] Since Tarraco became a Roman military base from the end of the third century BCE, and then a Roman colony under Julius Caesar in the 40 s BCE, it is nor surprising that Roman traditions are most in

[8] So J.S. Richardson, *The Romans in Spain* (Oxford: Blackwell, 1996) 222.

[9] See S.J. Keay, *Roman Spain* (Berkeley: University of California, 1988) 146.

[10] *RIT* = G. Alfödy, *Die römischen Inschriften von Tarraco* (2 vols; Berlin: de Gruyter, 1975).

evidence in the epigraphical remains.[11] There is evidence here for a temple of Minerva, restored by one Q. Assius Messor in the second century CE (*RIT* 39), while inscriptions indicate dedications and vows to Jupiter (*Iovi Optimo Maximo*; *RIT* 32, 33, etc.) or to the Capitoline triad, Jupiter, Juno and Minerva (*RIT* 34). As one would expect in a military base, there are statues or altars to Mars (*RIT* 38), while the religious dimension of other spheres of life are illustrated by phallic statuettes of Priapus.[12] A painting of Nemesis, the Greek goddess of fate, found in the basement of the amphitheatre of Tarraco, may illustrate the hopes and fears of gladiators getting ready to hazard their lives in the arena above (*RIT* 45–46). What is evident, even in this relatively quiet corner of the Roman world, is the presence of multiple non-exclusive cultic traditions, co-existing in a pluralism that represented the multifaceted lives of a multicultural city. In such a context, Roman deities are merged with or added to other and earlier religious traditions. Their predominance represents the fact that Tarraco was, first and foremost, a Roman provincial capital, the seat of the provincial governor and the centre for the provincial *conventus* whose members, the leading families of the province, were keen to express their Roman identity and their loyalty to the empire from which they derived their status.

The political significance of religion in Tarraco is well illustrated by the arrival and growth of cultic practices associated with the emperor. As soon as Octavian had become established as undisputed *princeps* of the Roman world, and was granted by the Senate the religious-sounding title *Augustus*, it was inevitable that his power would be recognised in religious forms. On his first extended visit to Spain, he spent more than a year in Tarraco (26–25 BCE), recuperating from an illness contracted during the 'Cantabrian War' in the north-west of Spain. During that period (Suetonius, *Aug.* 26.3), Tarraco became the centre of imperial power, on which the eyes of the empire were focused. It appears that a delegation from Mytilene arrived in Tarraco, bringing news to Augustus of a decree according him honours equal to the gods, which he was happy to accept.[13] The citizens of Tarraco were quick to follow suit. From both literary sources (Quintilian 6.3.77) and coins,[14] we know that Tarraco set up an altar to Augustus (probably to both Roma and Augustus), displaying on its front the imperial insignia

---

[11] On the use of specifically Roman religious traditions in *coloniae*, see Beard-North-Price, *Religions of Rome*, 1.328–34. For Roman religion in Spain as a whole, see J. Mangas, 'Die römische Religion in Hispanien während der Prinzipatszeit', *ANRW* II.18.1, 276–344.

[12] Keay, *Roman Spain*, 151.

[13] *OGIS* 2.456; see R. Étienne, *Le Culte Impérial dans la Péninsule Ibérique d'Auguste à Dioclétien* (Bibliothèque des Écoles Françaises d'Athènes et de Rome 191; Paris: de Boccard, 1958) 365–67.

[14] Fishwick, *Imperial Cult*, 1.1, plate xxxviib.

which had been awarded to Augustus by the Senate. At some point, whether by accident or design, a palm tree was found to take root on this altar, and since the palm was the symbol of victory, the people of Tarraco were quick to inform Augustus of this excellent omen (Quintilian records his ironic retort: 'that shows how often you kindle fire on it!', 6.3.77). The altar did not involve a temple building or cult statue, and some ambiguity surrounds what was implied regarding Augustus' status in this regard, but the niceties of ontological definition were less important than the symbolic significance of the altar. Here the élite of Tarraco, many of whom probably considered themselves 'Romans in Spain' rather than 'Spaniards', could express their commitment to Augustus' imperial rule in cultic form.[15]

The strength of this commitment, and the anxiety to express it, is evidenced by a notice in Tacitus that immediately after the death of Augustus (14 CE), when the deceased was declared *divus Augustus*, the 'people of Spain' (*Hispani*) requested Tiberius that a temple to Augustus should be constructed in the colony of Tarraco (Tacitus, *Ann.* 1.78). The initiative probably came from the leading figures in the province of Tarraconensis, rather than all three provinces of Spain: although there is evidence for a similar temple in Lusitania, the province of Baetica does not appear to have had an equivalent. Tiberius duly gave his permission, and coins from his era (14–37 CE) indicate the design of the intended temple which was apparently dedicated to *Aeternitas Augusta*, the divinised quality of 'eternity' attributed to Augustus (and perhaps to the Augustan dynasty).[16] The temple, it seems, was built on an upper terrace, on a site overlapping that of the present Cathedral, attached to a new Forum complex which was subsequently redesigned and made more magnificent under Flavian rule. If Paul came to Tarraco, this temple was either already built or close to completion, and stood out prominently as a massive statement of loyalty to Rome. Within it was a statue of Augustus depicted as Jupiter, seated and holding in his right hand a globe, topped by a winged victory. One can hardly imagine a stronger association between the power that established and pacified the Roman empire, and the power that rules the universe, variously identifiable as Jupiter, Zeus or Ammon.[17]

---

[15] Fishwick, *Imperial Cult*, 1.1, 171–79; cf. Étienne, *Culte Impérial*, 368–78.

[16] Fishwick, *Imperial Cult*, 1.1, 150–58, with plates xxvii-xxxv; cf. D. Fishwick, 'Four Temples at Tarraco', in A. Small, ed., *Subject and Ruler: The Cult of the Ruling Power in Classical Antiquity* (Journal of Roman Archaeology Supplement 17; Ann Arbor: University of Michigan, 1996) 165–84.

[17] On the site, see X. Dupré i Raventós, "Un gran complejo provincial de época flavia en Tarragona; aspectos cronologicos", in W. Trimmlich and P. Zanker, eds., *Stadtbild und Ideologie* (Munich: Verlag der Bayerischen Akademie der Wissenschaften, 1990) 319–25; J.M. Macias et al., 'Excavaciones en la Catedral de Tarragona y su Entorno: Avances y Retrocesos en la Investigación sobre el Culto Imperial', in T. Nogales and J. González,

Tacitus suggests that Tarraco set the trend in offering to build a temple to *divus Augustus*, providing a precedent for others (*Ann.* 1.78). In time, some form of the imperial cult (normally temples, sacrifices and festivals) became central to the identity of each province in Spain, with the provincial *conventus* gathering for this purpose. The imperial priesthood thus became a highly coveted honour, as witnessed by the lavish inscriptions set up by imperial *flamines* in the vicinity of the temple to Augustus in Tarraco (e.g., *RIT* 290–328).[18] Thus, if Paul arrived in Tarraco he would have found an ethnically and religiously mixed population living in a 'Romanised' environment similar to what he had encountered in eastern colonies like Philippi or Pisidian Antioch: this included a strong political and religious orientation to Rome, expressed in the prominence of Roman deities, a Roman religious calendar, and a massive temple complex dedicated to the divine Augustus.[19] The initiative for such religious veneration of imperial deities came here, as often elsewhere, from local representatives, rather than by order from Rome, and it functioned at least as much to distinguish the Roman or Romanised elite from the 'barbarian' population, and the city of Tarraco from lesser cities, as to bind the city into the empire-wide web of Roman power.[20] As Florus hints, the fame of Tarraco was thus bound up with the fame and glory of Rome, and religion functioned both to express and to cement the tight nexus of human and divine power that constituted the Roman order.[21]

---

eds., *Culto Imperial: política y poder* (Hispania Antigua, Serie Arqueológica, 1; Rome: 'L'erma' di Bretschneider, 2007) 763–87. For the Roman character of Tarraco and the local expression of the imperial cult, see further I. Rodà de Llanza, 'La Tarragona de mitjan segle I dC', in J. M. Gavaldà Ribot et al., *Pau, Fructuós*, 73–100.

[18] G. Alföldy, *Flamines Provinciae Hispaniae Citerioris* (Madrid: Instituto Español de Arqueologia, 1973). For the abiding social prestige which an imperial priest might hope to gain, see Epictetus 1.19.26–29; for a study of imperial priests and priestesses in Ephesus, see Friesen, *Twice Neokoros*, 76–113. On the flourishing of the imperial cult in Spain in the second century, see Étienne, *Culte Impérial*, 461–96.

[19] On Roman colonies as 'mini-Romes', replicating Roman religion, see Beard-North-Price, *Religions of Rome*, 1.328–34.

[20] On the question of initiative, often impossible to detect, see Price, *Rituals and Power*, 65–75; Beard-North-Price, *Religions of Rome*, 356–57. For the role of the cult in fostering the interests of the local elite, and advantaging their city in rivalry with others, see ibid., 336, 358–59.

[21] See K. Hopkins, *Conquerors and Slaves* (Cambridge: Cambridge University, 1978) 210: 'The processions, dedications and sacrifices were the symbolic forms by which the local elite and the local populace of free men and slaves, townsmen and peasants, reaffirmed their relative positions and their subordination, however they perceived it, to their distant emperor. How else would anyone have known that he ruled?'

II. The Emperor and the Gods

The Augustan revolution ensured that the emperor, as the figurehead and representative of Roman power, was everywhere received with honours that integrated his person at an elevated level into the cosmic hierarchy. Imperial images were ubiquitous, not only on coins, but on innumerable busts and statues in public places. These were not always or by definition cult-images (objects of ritual), but they had to be treated with the utmost respect, except in the rare cases of disgraced emperors, such as Gaius, Nero and Domitian, after their deaths.[22] Emperors exercised an equal influence on the organisation of time: the Roman calendar (observed by Roman citizens, but also strongly influential on public urban life) was rearranged around the birthdays, victories or deaths of emperors and their families, with local variations. Of widest impact here were the annual *vota* at the start of the year (3rd January), where sacrifices were offered to the gods (normally the Capitoline Triad) for the wellbeing of the emperor and the eternity and safety of the empire.[23] As in Tarraco, so throughout the empire the first century witnessed an explosion of temple-building associated with the emperors, transforming public space with huge edifices that remoulded civic architecture. Provincial centres, like Tarraco, would be particularly shaped by this new expression of Roman religion, and we may imagine here (as we find elsewhere) imperial festivals, complete with processions, garlanded door-posts, sacrifices, feasts and games, which punctuated the calendar and structured civic life. Whatever variable practice one might find at a private level (e.g. domestic shrines with imperial images), and in clubs or associations which might devote religious attention to imperial deities (e.g. the *Augustales*), at the civic level imperial rituals and celebrations made a very large impact on the social life not just of the elite but of every inhabitant of significant cities throughout the empire.

Typically 'imperial' temples were dedicated to deceased emperors, accorded the epithet *divus*, as was the case with Augustus in Tarraco. Colossal statues, portraying deified past emperors with the attributes of Jupiter or another of the Olympian or Roman gods, are common; members of the imperial family (mothers and sons) often accompanied these figures in receiving divine honours. In relation to the present (living) emperor, matters were more complex and more varied. Sometimes (as in Rome itself) publically

---

[22] On imperial images, and distinctions in their status and role, see Price, *Rituals and Power*, 1.170–206; C. Ando, *Imperial Ideology and Provincial Loyalty in the Roman Empire* (Berkeley: University of California, 2000) 206–73.

[23] See Price, *Rituals and Power*, 214–15. For a typical formula (vowing the gods a sacrifice the following year if the emperor is kept safe in the intervening period), see Gradel, *Emperor Worship and Roman Religion*, 370–71.

sponsored honours for the emperor explicitly stopped short of treating him as a god (Gaius' reign was a partial exception)[24]; sometimes no such inhibition was practised and in both language and rite the reigning emperor was incorporated among the immortal deities. Often a certain ambiguity was practised, with sacrifices made to the *genius* or *numen* (or in Greek contexts, τύχη) of the emperor, not to the emperor himself, or formulae and statuary were employed that placed the emperor at the very meeting point of the human and divine, assigning him ambiguously to both spheres at once.[25] In this connection it was very common to offer sacrifices and prayers *to* the gods *on behalf of* the emperor (or his family, or Rome): thus, for instance, in the army sacrifices were made to the Capitoline triad and the emperor's deified predecessors *for* the emperor, and in numerous other instances, even at the annual *vota* and at the provincial festivals presided over by 'imperial priests', sacrifices were made to the traditional gods on behalf of the emperor and the empire.[26] A living emperor, like a deified ancestor, might be portrayed as Jupiter himself, or addressed alongside a traditional deity, or he might be portrayed in a traditional Roman pose offering sacrifices to the gods, or in an ambiguous mixture of the two styles.[27] In all such cases, he formed a hinge-point connecting the Roman empire with the divine, and channelling the religious devotion of Roman citizens and subjects into a form that expressed social and political commitment to the Roman empire.

It is important to stress here that 'cults of the emperor were not an independent element of religious life',[28] but were generally incorporated into

---

[24] For the details, see Gradel, *Imperial Worship*, 109–61.

[25] See discussion in Price, *Rituals and Power*, 210–20; J.B. Rives, *Religion in the Roman Empire*, 153–56. On the distinction between the provinces and Rome (where official public cults were not offered to living emperors), see Dio 51.20.8. Even outside Rome, the Julio-Claudian emperors were generally reluctant to *claim* divinity, although they might accept divine honours if they were offered.

[26] For a discussion of the evidence, see Price, *Rituals and Power*, 209–14, 226, 232–33. As he points out, 'in only one instance is a sacrifice *to* the emperor known to have been performed by an imperial priest. In all other cases their sacrifices were on behalf of the emperor' (211).

[27] Prayers might also reflect this ambiguity; Aelius Aristides, in panegyrical mood, claims that at the mere mention of the emperor's name people rise to 'pray to the gods on the emperor's behalf, and to the emperor for his own affairs' (*Oration* 26.32). No-one prayed to a god on behalf of a god, but on the other hand no-one prayed to anyone but a god. Cf. the comments on this passage in Friesen, *Twice Neokoros*, 146–52; he rightly insists that the 'ambiguity' would be less felt in antiquity where questions of ontology were relatively unimportant in the context of imperial cult: what mattered was the unique place of emperors in the divine care of human affairs.

[28] Beard-North-Price, *Religions of Rome*, 1.348. Elsewhere they note: 'the incorporation of the emperor into the traditional cults of provincial communities, his association with other deities, was often just as important as worship which focussed specifically and solely on him. Nor was imperial cult necessarily the most important marker of Romanization in religion: in specifically Roman communities abroad (*coloniae* and *municipia*)

already existing traditions (Roman or local) or linked with traditional deities in location, name or practice. Thus it was common to house imperial statues and the rites attached to them within a temple to another god or goddess: alongside the principal deity there would be niches for statues or altars dedicated to imperial (or other) gods, or separate imperial temples might be erected within an already existing sanctuary.[29] In such cases it was clear that the emperor did not rival or supplant traditional deities: he was fitted into a traditional religious matrix of practice and belief. In the same way, it is common to find nomenclature that indicates the merging of imperial and other deities. In Tarraco, just as we find a temple that seems to identify Augustus with Jupiter (and Ammon?), so it became common to dedicate altars to *Isis Augusta* (*RIT* 35) or *Juno Augusta* (*RIT* 36). Similarly, elsewhere we find imperial names inscribed on the architrave of the Parthenon, or cults devoted to such figures as *Mars Augustus*. Here it is difficult to say whether an imperial deity has been imposed upon a pre-existing Greek or Roman tradition, or whether that tradition has simply incorporated an additional dimension: both perspectives are possible, and perhaps equally true.[30] But it is clear again that imperial cult is not usually self-standing, or a replacement for other religious traditions, but is made traditional precisely by its incorporation within older religious customs.[31] Similarly, as we have seen, prayers were typically made *on behalf of* the emperor *to* other deities (especially in a Roman context, to the Capitoline Triad) such that the figure of the emperor was woven deeply into the fabric of a religious cloth of long and resonant antiquity. The ancient traditions of Rome or of the local environment were the context into which the emperor was fitted, and, as Beard et al. insist, this is true even in western provinces like Spain, where it has been tempting to regard the imperial cult as an isolated phenomenon. Here the imperial cult may not have been so fully integrated into local existing traditions as in the Greek East, but it was certainly embedded within a wider Roman matrix and 'was part of something bigger'. 'Analyses of the imperial cult in the Latin west which examine only the imperial cult itself suffer from

imitations of the transformed system of Augustan Rome were often a far more important aspect of religious Romanization than any direct worship of the emperor' (1.318).

[29] For evidence, see Price, *Rituals and Power*, 146–56, 179, 189, 212, 232.

[30] As Beard-North-Price comment on the case of the Parthenon: 'we can easily understand how the Roman presence could have seemed to some like an outrageous intrusion of the imperial power into one of the most holy cult places of Greece; or, equally, like the incorporation of Rome within the venerable traditions of Greek religion. 'Continuity' or 'change' can be matters of interpretation' (*Religions of Rome*, 1.344); on the inscriptions combining the name of a god with *Augustus/a*, see ibid., 1.352.

[31] For the local modulations of the imperial cult in the West, in line with local traditions and political conditions, see J.B. Rives, 'Imperial Cult and Native Tradition in Roman North Africa', *The Classical Journal* 96 (2001) 425–36.

a serious case of scholarly tunnel vision and simply fail to grapple with the problem of the relationship of the new forms of imperial rituals to the local religious context'.[32]

One reason for this 'tunnel vision' is the long-established Christian tradition of positioning the imperial cult as the main threat to Christianity, and as *the* focus of religiosity in the 'pagan' world.[33] Although all scholars have now rightly given up some Christianizing prejudices (e.g. that the traditional cults were in terminal decline, and that the imperial cult was 'political' rather than 'religious'), the legacy of this tradition lives on in the fascination of New Testament scholars with the imperial cult, in isolation from its wider religious matrix. John's Apocalypse and a partial reading of the accounts of martyrdom (see below) have encouraged this sense of a religious single-combat between devotion to Christ and the cult of Caesar; it is certainly much easier for Christian apologists to lampoon 'paganism' once its defining feature becomes the deification of human beings.[34] But Simon Price, the scholar who has done the most recently to recover the significance of the imperial cult (in Asia) warns against 'the consistent misrepresentation by Christian scholars of the persecution of the Christians, which inflates the importance of the imperial cult and posits a stark choice between Christ and the Caesars'.[35] As the same author insists, in fact 'both supporters and detractors of the imperial cult set it firmly in the context of traditional religious practices'.[36]

The reason why the imperial cult sits firmly within a larger context of religious tradition and practice is that the emperors were not independent deities, but were enmeshed in a cosmic order that preserved the balance of the universe. Whether as pious worshippers, as recipients of favours from the gods (in answer to their subjects' prayers), or as themselves installed among (or as) universal divine powers, the imperial family, alive and dead, was part of a larger divine matrix – a prominent part but in no way isolatable from the divine machinery by which the world was rightly governed. In Tarraco as elsewhere, the worship of the divine Augustus (and Roma) indicated the recognition that the Roman imperial order was the guarantor and mediator of the favour of the gods, and that Roman emperors, with

[32] Beard-North-Price, *Religions of Rome*, 1.361.

[33] For this Christianising perspective and its distorting effect, see the critical remarks in Price, *Rituals and Power*, 10–19, 125–26; Beard-North-Price, *Religions of Rome*, 1.359–61.

[34] For the current political interest in portraying early Christianity as chiefly opposed to the imperial cult, and thus to the ideology of 'the Roman empire', see the following chapter.

[35] Price, *Rituals and Power*, 15.

[36] Price, *Rituals and Power*, 202. Although his book has refocused attention on the imperial cult, Price himself insists that 'the incorporation of the emperor into the traditional religious system has formed the theme of much of this book', 235.

their unique and superhuman capacities, were endowed with divine powers to benefit human society. It was precisely because it was incorporated into local interpretations of this pervasive divine order that the imperial cult became so successful so quickly. One did not choose between worshipping 'the gods' and worshipping the imperial house; one worshipped the imperial house because of its central role within the cosmic order sponsored and sustained by the whole panoply of gods.

III. Paul and Roman Religion

How should we imagine Paul responding to all this if he came to Spain, crossing from Italy by the standard route between Ostia and Tarraco? We can judge only, of course, by what he said in letters to other places in other circumstances, but when we examine those letters we find some remarkable phenomena. Although he had met many different kinds of cult, in many different contexts, Paul never differentiates between one cult and another, and never names the various deities which he undoubtedly encountered. He recognizes that there are 'many gods' and 'many lords' (1 Cor 8.5), but he shows no interest in their differing identities, lumping them together into a single category. His converts in Thessalonica, he says, have 'turned from idols (εἴδωλα) to serve the true and living God' (1 Thess 1.10); likewise believers in Corinth were once led astray to 'voiceless idols' (τὰ εἴδωλα τὰ ἄφωνα, 1 Cor 12.2; cf. 2 Cor 6.16). Both the Corinthians and the converts in Galatia are warned against a generic sin labelled 'idolatry' (εἰδωλολατρία, 1 Cor 5.11; 6.9; Gal 5.20), while the latter are told that at one time (before their 'calling') they did not know God, but were enslaved to 'beings that by nature are not gods' (οἱ φύσει μὴ ὄντες θεοί, Gal 4.8). By questioning the ontological status of these beings – he elsewhere calls them 'so-called gods (λεγόμενοι θεοί), whether in heaven or on earth' (1 Cor 8.5) – Paul leaves unclear precisely what they are, and elsewhere fills this gap in various ways. In Galatians they are referred to as 'weak and impoverished στοιχεῖα' (Gal 4.9; cf. 4.3), leaving commentators still unsure quite what he means by this term, although it is used again, in a different context, by himself or his imitator, in Col 2.8, 20 ('the στοιχεῖα of the κόσμος').[37] In 1 Corinthians, having declared that an εἴδωλον is nothing in the world (1 Cor 8.4), he warns his converts that if they get involved in sacrifices they will make themselves partners not of Christ but of δαιμόνια (1 Cor 10.20–21). But in Romans, where he notes with approval how Jews 'abhor idols' (ὁ βδελυσσόμενος τὰ

[37] See M. C. de Boer, 'The Meaning of the Phrase τὰ στοιχεῖα τοῦ κόσμου in Galatians' *NTS* 53 (2007) 204–24.

εἴδωλα, 2.22), he implies that there is nothing involved in 'idol-worship' beyond a vain and foolish exercise in honouring images of mortal men or animals (Rom 1.18–23).

Anyone at home in the richly diverse and sophisticated world of Roman religious practice and belief would be quite startled by this Pauline rhetoric. Not only does he homogenize all the different forms of religiosity, treating them as a single phenomenon, but he is relentlessly negative in his verdict upon them. They are εἴδωλα (phantoms, or phantasms, the mere appearance of reality), they are dumb and lifeless, they are falsely labelled 'gods', and they are quite properly 'abhorred'. Although Paul knows the proper label for something offered in sacrifice (ἱερόθυτον, 1 Cor 10.28), he prefers the obviously pejorative label εἰδωλόθυτον (1 Cor 8.1; 10.19); in every context in which he speaks of these things, there is aggression in his voice. And despite the obvious importance of the imperial cult in practically every city he visited, there is no special mention made by Paul of the cult of the emperors. Although emperors may be among the 'gods in heaven or on earth' of 1 Cor 8.5, and their cult-statues included in the anthropomorphic images of Rom 1.23, their cult falls into the same negative category as every other, dismissively labelled 'idolatry'.

One obvious explanation for this blanket dismissal of Roman religiosity is of course Paul's Jewish heritage. Paul's discourse on this topic is derived from the rhetorics and polemics of Jews, who had learned thereby to define themselves in ideological and social antithesis to other ethnic and religious traditions. The biblical tradition was already steeped in such polemics, which were sharpened and simplified by their translation into Greek.[38] Jews in the Diaspora developed a composite set of indicators to define what was illegitimate religion. At its simplest, any worship that was conducted by non-Jews was by definition wrong: as both Philo and Josephus maintain, there can only be one Temple for the one God, and that temple is in Jerusalem (Philo, *Spec. Leg.* 1.67; Josephus, *c. Apion.* 2.193). More specifically, criticism was levelled at any implication that there was or could be more than one deity. But since non-Jews, too, could affirm the existence of one Supreme Deity, Jewish purism in this respect was twinned with a purity of practice: no image or representation of the deity must be used in worship.[39] This latter stipulation was, of course, open to interpretation (what constituted an image and what constituted worship?), but it provided the necessary

[38] For Septuagintal use of εἴδωλον see R. Hayward, 'Observations on Idols in Septuagint Pentateuch', in S. C. Barton , ed., *Idolatry. False Worship in the Bible, Early Judaism and Christianity* (London: T & T Clark, 2007) 40–57.

[39] For the Diaspora Jewish reaction to alien, pluralist and iconic cult, see J. M. G. Barclay, *Jews in the Mediterranean Diaspora from Alexander to Trajan (323 BCE–117 CE)* (Edinburgh: T & T Clark, 1996) 428–34.

ammunition for countless Jewish tirades against the use of images, either as representations of God or (worse) as substitutes for God.[40]

The Alexandrian Jewish tractate, *The Wisdom of Solomon*, gives us a good sense of the Jewish polemical tradition in Paul's day, in its extended digression on the folly of non-Jews (chapters 13–15). There are some who suppose that the natural elements – fire, or wind, or the stars – are divine beings, but they stupidly fail to see beyond this created world to the Creator who made them (Wis 13.1–9). More wretched are those who make from wood or clay the images that are then worshipped: they are guilty of crass ignorance in thinking that these dumb and lifeless objects are worth decorating or addressing in prayer (13.10–15.17). And off the scale of stupidity are the Egyptians, as degraded as the animals they worship (15.18–19).[41] Within the second category *Wisdom* includes the making of images for a distant 'king' which, by exaggerating his image, induces people to address the objects themselves as gods (14.17–21). This is certainly a reference to the imperial cult, interpreted as a crude substitution of image for reality and as an impious claim on the 'name [of God] that cannot be shared' (14.21). Undergirding this critique is the principle of the transcendence of God, beyond the material universe and thus beyond any material similarity (cf. Josephus, *c. Apion.* 2.191). From this vantage point, every variety of non-Jewish cult in the Mediterranean world can be dismissed as inadequate, misleading or positively impious. Such rhetoric helps preserve Jewish distinctiveness, for there is a close correlation between the 'otherness' of the deity whom Jews worship, above the created order, and the 'otherness' of the Jews who alone worship this true God aright. As the *Letter of Aristeas* puts it: 'the wise lawgiver ... hedged us about with impenetrable fences and iron walls to prevent us from mixing in any way with people of other nations, being preserved pure in body and soul, separated from false beliefs, honouring the one God who is powerful above the whole creation' (παρ' ὅλην τὴν πᾶσαν κτίσιν, 139). The logic is clear: just as God is powerful above/beyond the whole creation, so Jews are necessarily distinct from 'other nations' and their 'false beliefs'.

Paul's Jewish convictions were, of course, modified and expanded by his understanding of the Christ event, whose influence we can trace in at least two respects. In the first place, the Jewish antithesis between 'idols' and 'the true and living God' is now modified by the acclamation of Jesus as 'Lord', so that 'one God' and 'one Lord' stand together on one side of the antithesis,

---

[40] For this distinction and a wider analysis of Jewish modes of critique, see M. Halbertal and A. Margalit, *Idolatry* (Cambridge, Mass.: Harvard University, 1992).

[41] For full analysis see M. Gilbert, *La critique des dieux dans le Livre de la Sagesse (Sg 13–15)* (Rome: Biblical Institute, 1973). Cf. the similar three-part schema in Philo, *Decal.* 52–81.

against the many 'so-called gods and lords' on the other (1 Cor 8.4–6). Since κύριος is a common title for deities in the Mediterranean world, the primitive Christian confession, κύριος Ἰησοῦς, as an *exclusive* claim, provided a strong reason to dismiss the pretensions of any other 'divinity' who claimed this label. By the same theological dynamic, when Paul warns the Corinthian believers against 'idolatry', he insists that one cannot drink from the cup of the Lord and the cup of δαιμόνια; one cannot share in the table of the Lord and the table of δαιμόνια (1 Cor 10.21). Here the new Christian ritual of the Lord's Supper has become a defining mark of Christian difference, participation in which becomes the 'impenetrable fence and iron wall' of the Christian community, as it keeps itself free of contamination by idols.[42]

Secondly, the Christ event has reinforced and sharpened Paul's apocalyptic convictions to the point where he believes that the crucifixion of Christ has dealt the death-blow to the κόσμος, while the resurrection has signalled the beginning of the new creation (Gal 6.14–15; 2 Cor 5.17). The dividing-line between the Christian community and 'idolatry' does not run on ethnic lines (between Jews and non-Jews), but it is freighted with equal if not greater meaning, since outside the sphere of God's re-creative activity lies 'the world', the sphere of 'the flesh', and 'the present evil age' (Gal 1.4). If reality is structured by this dualism, 'idolatry' can be numbered among the numerous 'works of the flesh' (Gal 5.19–21), in contrast to the fruit of the Spirit (Gal 5.22–23), and there is no reason, within Paul's epistemology, to give special attention to the imperial cult.[43] Moreover, if the world is viewed in such straightforward contrasts, it is easy to see how the 'idols' which Paul excoriates can also be associated with the malevolent powers that populate the apocalyptic cosmos. Such an association is suggested by the parallel contrasts Paul draws in 2 Cor 6.15–16 between Christ and Beliar, believer and unbeliever, the temple of God and idols. But it is made more explicit in the antithesis noted above between 'the table of the Lord' and 'the table of δαιμόνια' (1 Cor 10.21). The term δαιμόνιον is derived by Paul from a passage in Deuteronomy (32.17, cited in this context). It *could* be heard as a relatively neutral term referring to the semi-divine beings, situated between gods and humanity, which Greeks normally called δαίμονες. But in Paul's apocalyptic cosmos, where the world is at war until Christ puts all his enemies under his feet (1 Cor 15.20–28), there are no neutral beings, and

[42] Paul's subtle argumentation regarding 'idols' and 'idol-food' in 1 Corinthians 8–10 has elicited a voluminous scholarly literature. Of recent contributions, see especially D. Newton, *Deity and Diet: The Dilemma of Sacrificial Food in Corinth* (JSNTSup 169; Sheffield: Sheffield Academic, 1998); D.G. Horrell, 'Idol-Food, Idolatry and Ethics in Paul', in Barton, ed., *Idolatry*, 120–40.

[43] See the argument of the following essay, on why the Roman empire was insignificant to Paul.

if these entities form an alternative to Christ, they must be ranged *against* him. Thus we have here a hint, of immense significance to later Christianity, that the beings who were ordinarily worshipped at the altars and temples of a town such as Tarraco were actually demonic powers, not just phantoms but powerfully malevolent forces on the opposite side in the cosmic war.[44]

IV. Mapping the Point of Conflict

The events in Tarraco in the year 259 CE are a good indication of the clash of commitments that was taking place all over the empire at the height of the conflict between Christians and the Roman authorities. In Decius' demand for universal sacrifice (249–251 CE; repeated by Valerian, 253–260 CE), there was for the first time an empire-wide centrally ordained assault on the Christian community, but it is clear that what was required by the emperors was not participation in the imperial cult as such, but sacrifice to 'the gods' in general.[45] According to the Christian record, bishop Fructuosus of Tarraco and two deacons were brought before the governor in January 259 and confronted with the emperors' orders.[46] When he professes ignorance of these orders, Fructuosus is told: 'they have ordered you to worship the gods' (*praeceperunt deos coli*, 2.3). Fructuosus refuses to recognise the existence of any god apart from 'the God who has made heaven and the earth, the sea and all that is in them' and provocatively begins to pray to this God (2.4–5), at which the governor insists, 'these [the gods] are obeyed, these are feared, and these are adored (*hi audiuntur, hi timentur, hi adorantur*)';[47] he then adds the rider, 'if the gods are not worshipped, then the images of the emperors are not adored' (*si dii non coluntur nec imperatorum vultus adorantur*). This makes clear that the central issue in the charge against the Christians is that they do not worship 'the gods'; one facet of that worship, of special concern to the governor, is the imperial cult, but this was neither the presenting nor the central issue in the trial. The argument works

[44] On the significance of this notion of cosmic war, see J.B. Rives, 'Christian Expansion and Christian Ideology', in W.V. Harris, ed., *The Spread of Christianity in the First Four Centuries* (Leiden: Brill, 2005) 15–41; see also R. Lane Fox, *Pagans and Christians* (London: Penguin, 1986) 325–30.

[45] See Ando, *Imperial Ideology*, 206–9; J.B. Rives, 'The Decree of Decius and the Religion of Empire' *JRS* 89 (1999) 135–54.

[46] *Passio Sanctorum Martyrum Fructuosi Episcopi, Auguri et Eulogi Diaconorum*; text in R. Knöpf, G. Krüger and G. Ruhbach, *Ausgewählte Märtyracten* (4th edn.; Tübingen: Mohr Siebeck, 1965) 83–85; cf. H. Musurillo, *Acts of the Christian Martyrs* (Oxford: Clarendon, 1972) 176–85. For discussions of the text see the essays by G. Luongo and J. Torra i Bitlloch in J.M. Gavaldà Ribot et al., *Pau, Fructuós*, 255–292.

[47] Knöpf et al. *Märtyrakten*, 83 print *qui audiuntur, qui timentur, qui adorantur*, as a question; the sense remains the same.

a maiore ad minus (if they don't worship the gods, the imperial cult will be neglected) and our impression is confirmed that the imperial cult is not viewed, by either the Romans or the Christians, as a self-standing entity, but as enmeshed within the much larger structure of Roman religion.[48] The Christian refusal to take part in the imperial cult is just one aspect of their offensive disregard of the whole Roman religious system; as Tertullian puts it, what they face is 'the accusation of treason most of all against Roman religion' (*crimen laesae maxime Romanae religionis*, *Apol.* 24.1).

Our conclusions from the trial of Fructuosus are supported by other evidence from the early Christian centuries. Suspicions against the Christians in Rome in the 60s concerned their alleged criminality and anti-social behaviour: Nero's persecution has, as far as we can tell, no specific connection to the imperial cult (Tacitus, *Ann.* 15.44). 1 Peter indicates that criminal charges were brought against Christians (4.15–16) and that their desertion of ancestral tradition was deeply offensive (1.18; 4.1–3); their threat to normal social life was on a much broader front than their attitude to the imperial cult. In the trials conducted before Pliny (Pliny, *Letters* 10.96–97), the accusations (by members of the public) concerned being a Christian (which Pliny associated with crimes and with the neglect of the local temples in general); it was only once they were in court that he asked them to sacrifice, and then in a double test, 'to repeat a formula of invocation to the gods and to make offerings of wine and incense to your [Trajan's] statue' (10.96.5). He understood that true Christians could not do such things (along with reviling Christ), but it is noticeable that the imperial image is incorporated into the larger issue of their attitudes to 'the gods'. Similarly, in the Martyrdom of Polycarp, the crowd's chief accusation against Christians is that they are 'atheists': the hostile mass is represented as crying out against Polycarp, 'This is the teacher of impiety, the father of the Christians, the destroyer of our own gods, the one who teaches many not to sacrifice or worship the gods' (*M. Polycarp* 12.2). It is once he is in court that the proconsul, trying to make life easy for Polycarp, urges him to swear 'by the fortune (τύχη) of Caesar and say "away with the atheists"' (9.2; cf. 8.2, on pronouncing 'Caesar is κύριος'). For the proconsul, religious devotion to Caesar (even in a form which does not treat him unambiguously as a god) is the most obvious way to clear Polycarp of the suspicion of 'atheism', but Caesar-devotion is clearly also for him part of a much larger religious matrix.

Indeed, in his thorough survey of all the authentic martyrdom accounts, Millar has noted how rare it is for concern specifically with the imperial cult

[48] Cf. Ando, *Imperial Ideology*, 393: 'if the emperor's *felicitas* made him a mediator between the gods of the state and the state itself, then ... piety towards the gods who ensured the well-being of the state could and should be expressed in piety towards the emperor'.

to emerge in the popular concerns against Christians or even in the actions of local magistrates; where it occurs in the trials (and it often does not), it is a matter raised by Roman officials, and usually 'in close conjunction with the wider question of pagan worship in general'.[49] Canvassing material up to and including the Great Persecution, he notes how thoroughly the imperial cult was integrated into the local cults of the provinces and that it is 'precisely this integration of the Imperial cult into the wider spectrum of pagan cults which is the first reason why it plays only a modest role in the persecutions'.[50] It appears that it was acknowledged on all sides that the battle-line was drawn not at the imperial cult as such (or alone) but at the point of the fundamental, general Christian antagonism to the entire religious structure of the Roman world. By refusing allegiance to the gods who supported the whole fabric of life, including the fabric of the Roman empire under imperial rule, the Christians certainly disregarded whatever religious claims were made for the emperor, but only because of their 'atheism' in general, not because of their special resistance to that cult.[51]

If what one side regarded as 'atheism' the other considered the height of piety we have evidence for a fundamental clash in the construction of reality and its divine order. Since religion defined relationships of power,

> not to place oneself within the set of relationships between emperor, gods, élite and people was effectively to place oneself outside the mainstream of the whole world and the shared Roman understanding of humanity's place within that world. Maintenance of the social order was seen by the Romans to be dependent on maintenance of this agreed set of symbolic structures, which assigned a role to people at all levels.[52]

What we find already adumbrated in Paul is not a critique of this or that cult for overstepping the mark, nor the demotion of pagan religiosity to the status of a half-truth relativized but embraced by a larger reality, but a thoroughgoing rejection of the mental and practical fabric of these symbolic structures, in the name of a new reality which has restructured the co-ordinates of existence. It is this radical, totalising stance which made Christianity so 'intolerant' of alternative perspectives, since the 'truth',

---

[49] F. Millar, 'The Imperial Cult and the Persecutions', in W. den Boer, ed., *Le culte des souverains dans l'empire romain* (Fondation Hardt Entretiens 19; Geneva: Fondation Hardt, 1972) 145–65, at 151.

[50] Millar, 'Imperial Cult', 164. For the same conclusion, see Price, *Rituals and Power*, 124–26, 221–22; Beard-North-Price, *Religions of Rome*, 1.239–44, 361. C.K. Rowe's carefully nuanced portrait of the Christian position with regard to imperial claims (*World Upside Down:Reading Acts in the Graeco-Roman Age* [Oxford: Oxford University, 2009] 92–116) is still, to my mind, too narrowly focused on the status of the emperor himself.

[51] Cf. Price, *Rituals and Power*, 124–25: 'The difficulties which the Christians posed for their contemporaries lay firstly with their threat to traditional cults in general and only secondarily with an allegedly subversive attitude to the emperor'.

[52] Beard-North-Price, *Religions of Rome*, 1.361.

centred on Christ, exposed every alternative as at best an illusion, at worst a demonic insurgency. As Rives has argued, it was not just its aggressive 'intolerance' that was decisively novel about Christianity; it was the combination of such exclusivity with the Christian drive towards homogeneity, and its creation of a totalising ideology (uniting myth, ritual and philosophy), that created something genuinely new in the Roman world, not just a new cult, competing for adherents on the same terms as others, but 'a new social and conceptual system, a new ideology of religion'.[53] This new ideology did not just challenge Caesar's divine claims, it offered a radical alternative to the structures of Roman religion and thus of Roman civilisation as a whole. In the words of Keith Hopkins, 'Christianity subverted the whole priestly calendar of civic rituals and public festivals on which Roman rule in the provinces rested. Christianity was a revolutionary movement'.[54] Paul has a good claim to be the founding ideologue of that revolution, and it was because of the loyalty of Fructuosus and his church in Tarraco to this fundamentally different vision of the world that both the common people and the Roman authorities were to sense in them such a significant threat.

---

[53] Rives, 'Christian Expansion', 16.

[54] K. Hopkins, *A World Full of Gods. Pagans, Jews and Christians in the Roman Empire* (London: Phoenix, 1999) 78.

19. Why the Roman Empire Was Insignificant to Paul

Over the past two decades there has arisen a new surge of interest in the specifically Roman context of the New Testament – that is, in placing the documents of the early Christian movement in the political context of Roman imperial power, its modes of control and its 'religious' expression in cultic devotion to the emperors. Within this interpretative frame Paul's letters have acquired a new set of resonances, and there has emerged the thesis (in many permutations) that Paul took the Roman empire and / or the imperial cult as a particular target of his theological polemics. After sketching the outlines of this thesis in its current expression, I will scrutinise in particular the contributions of N. T. Wright, whose influence is far-reaching.[1] While agreeing with the general trend of current research that Paul's theology is not 'apolitical', the title of this chapter indicates my counter-thesis, that to give the Roman empire particular significance is to misconstrue the terms with which Paul addressed the political (and other) dimensions of human life.[2]

---

[1] This essay is a heavily reworked version of my contribution to a debate with N. T. Wright on this issue, held at the San Diego meeting of the Society of Biblical Literature in November 2007; the original debate is available online as taped on the occasion and subsequently transcribed. I am grateful to the British Academy for financial support to enable attendance at the conference and to many friends (not least Dale Martin) for comments on my original paper.

[2] A persistent problem in this debate is the varying use of the terms 'politics' and 'political'. Usage ranges across a spectrum from a narrow (politics as statecraft) to an extremely broad sense (politics as communal organisation or the exercise of social power). To dub Paul's theology 'apolitical' is normally taken to mean that it is individualistic, pietistic or socially unengaged. I here use the term 'politics' in a broad sense to denote the sphere of social relations and the exercise of social power, and these in relation both to the church as a community and to society as a whole, though I shall argue that Paul's integrated perception of reality fuses the political with the personal (and the cosmic) from an angle of vision quite different from ours, and is suggestive, but underdeveloped, in relation to many dimensions of 'politics' in the modern Western sense. Current discussions of Paul's 'theopolitics' or 'biopolitics' relate Paul to politics in a contemporary European sense, which includes the operation of state power but encompasses also a wider vision of the well-functioning society. See, e. g., J. Taubes, *The Political Theology of Paul* (Stanford: Stanford University, 2004); D. Harink, ed., *Paul, Philosophy and the Theopolitical Vision: Critical Engagements with Agamben, Badiou, Žižek, and Others* (Eugene: Cascade Books, 2010); J. Milbank, 'Paul against Biopolitics', in J. Milbank, S. Žižek and C. Davis, *Paul's New Moment: Continental Philosophy and the Future of Christian Theology* (Grand Rapids: Brazos, 2010) 21–73. Milbank draws on a 'political Paul' very different

I. Current Research on Paul and Empire

While the relationship between Paul and the Roman empire (or 'the Caesars') has been a topic of repeated debate over many centuries, with particular reference to his famous statements on 'the governing authorities' (Rom 13.1–7), one of the roots of current research lies in Adolf Deissmann's observations on the 'polemical parallelism between the cult of the emperor and the cult of Christ'. Based on extensive research in non-literary sources, Deissmann noted that very many terms used in the imperial cult stood in parallel with early Christian vocabulary: besides the obvious examples of θεός, θεοῦ υἱός, θεῖος and κύριος, he noted the use of βασιλεύς, σωτήρ, and ἀρχιερεύς as titles for the emperor, and εὐαγγέλιον, παρουσία and ἐπιφάνεια as special imperial terminology.[3] Although he considered the *origin* of the Christian use of such terms to be, in many cases, pre-Roman and Septuagintal, such that the overlap with Roman use did not usually represent a genealogical relation, he also considered that 'mere chance coincidences might later awaken a powerful sense of contrast in the mind of the people' (343), and conjectured that in some cases not only would hearers find in Paul's preaching of Jesus Christ as 'Lord' 'a silent protest against other "lords," and against "the lord," as people were beginning to call the Roman Caesar', but that 'St. Paul himself may have felt and intended this silent protest' (355). Key features of the current debate are here adumbrated: the overlap of early Christian and 'imperial' vocabulary, explanations for this overlap, its meaning in the minds of early Christian hearers, and the extent to which an anti-Roman polemical intent can be attributed to Paul himself, even if muted ('silent') in expression.

If Deissmann forms a distant inspiration for the current debate about Paul, two German contributions of the 1980s, by Klaus Wengst and Dieter Georgi, opened up afresh the political implications of Paul's theology.[4] The latter, who presents Paul's theology as a directly antithetical reaction to Roman ideology, was taken up into American scholarship from the 1990s by

from that here discussed, as projected onto a Hellenistic political background by B. Blumenfeld, *The Political Paul: Justice, Democracy and Kingship in a Hellenistic Framework* (Sheffield: Sheffield Academic, 2001).

[3] A. Deissmann, *Light from the Ancient East* (trans. by L.R.M. Strachan from the 4th revised German edition [1922]; London: Hodder and Stoughton, 1927) 338–78.

[4] K. Wengst, *Pax Romana and the Peace of Jesus Christ* (trans. by J. Bowden; London: SCM, 1987), ranging over the whole New Testament and beyond (German original, 1986); D. Georgi, *Theocracy in Paul's Practice and Theology* (trans. by D.E. Green; Minneapolis: Fortress, 1991), originally a contribution to a collection of essays on political theology edited by J. Taubes (German original, 1987). Among notable discussions of Paul's theological relationship to the Roman empire in the intervening decades, see O. Cullmann, *The State in the New Testament* (London: SCM, 1955).

Richard Horsley, who brought together classical and New Testament scholarship in an influential collection of essays,[5] and then edited further collections of fresh essays where a variety of interpreters engaged with Pauline themes from a loosely defined 'political' perspective.[6] The broad coalition here created embraces a wide range of liberationist, feminist, postcolonial, historical and theological perspectives: they are unified less by theory than by a sense that Paul's theology is radically subversive at some social or political level, and that regnant interpretative paradigms, which place Paul in critical engagement with Judaism, have to be supplemented, if not replaced, by analysis of his antagonism towards 'Rome'. Besides Horsley, a leading figure in this trend is Neil Elliott, whose liberationist readings of Paul, beginning in the 1990 s, have moved towards a Marxist critique of power (as exercised in the Roman empire, but also by Paul himself).[7] Amongst the significant works spearheading this suddenly widespread scholarly trend,[8] there are notable readings of Pauline letters, such as Peter Oakes' study of Philippians,[9] Robert Jewett's commentary on Romans,[10] and new readings of Galatians by Justin Hardin and Brigitte Kahl.[11] The development of postcolonial readings of Paul (noted in the introduction to this volume) has also contributed to this trend.[12]

[5] R. A. Horsley, ed., *Paul and Empire: Religion and Power in Roman Imperial Society* (Harrisburg: Trinity Press International, 1997). For a parallel (and more wide-ranging) interdisciplinary collection, predating Horsley, see L. C. A. Alexander, ed., *Images of Empire* (Sheffield: Sheffield Academic, 1991).

[6] R. A. Horsley, ed., *Paul and Politics: Ekklesia, Israel, Imperium, Interpretation* (Harrisburg: Trinity Press International, 2000); idem, ed., *Paul and the Roman Imperial Order* (Harrisburg: Trinity Press International, 2004).

[7] N. Elliott, *Liberating Paul: The Justice of God and the Politics of the Apostle* (Maryknoll, NY: Orbis, 1994); idem, *The Arrogance of Nations: Reading Romans in the Shadow of Empire* (Minneapolis: Fortress, 2008); idem, 'Ideological Closure in the Christ-Event: a Marxist Response to Alain Badiou's Paul', in Harink, ed., *Paul, Philosophy and the Theopolitical Vision*, 135–54.

[8] E. g., B. J. Walsh and S. C. Keesmaat, *Colossians Remixed: Subverting the Empire* (Downers Grove, Ill.: InterVarsity, 2004); J. D. Crossan and J. L. Reed, *In Search of Paul: How Jesus' Apostle Opposed Rome's Empire with God's Kingdom* (New York: HarperSanFrancisco, 2005); W. Carter, *The Roman Empire and the New Testament: An Essential Guide* (Nashville: Abingdon, 2006).

[9] P. Oakes, *Philippians: From People to Letter* (Cambridge: Cambridge University, 2001).

[10] R. Jewett, *Romans* (Hermeneia; Minneapolis: Fortress, 2007).

[11] J. K. Hardin, *Galatians and the Imperial Cult* (WUNT 2.237; Tübingen: Mohr Siebeck, 2008); B. Kahl, *Galatians Re-Imagined: Reading with the Eyes of the Vanquished* (Minneapolis: Fortress, 2010). For parallel work on 1 Thessalonians (by Donfried, Koester, Harrison et al.), see the summary in S. Kim, *Christ and Caesar: The Gospel and the Roman Empire in the Writings of Paul and Luke* (Grand Rapids: Eerdmans, 2008) 3–10.

[12] See, e. g., J. Marchal, *The Politics of Heaven: Women, Gender and Empire in the Study of Paul* (Minneapolis: Fortress, 2008); F. F. Segovia and R. S. Sugirtharajah, eds., *A Postcolonial Commentary on the New Testament Writings* (London: T & T Clark, 2007).

This refocusing of scholarly interest on the Roman (as opposed to the Jewish) context of early Christianity is typically concerned to integrate its social, political and 'religious' dimensions as the seamless fabric of ancient life. Drawing from fresh classical scholarship, New Testament interpreters have been intrigued by the literary and non-literary expressions of Roman ideology in the early imperial period – its claims to bring the blessings of peace and prosperity to the world, its brutal suppression of dissent or disturbance, its focus on the status and achievements of the emperors themselves, and its religious expression in multiple forms of imperial cult, especially in those cities where Pauline churches were founded.[13] By pressing the ubiquity, the prominence and the social significance of such phenomena, it is stressed that early Christians, including Paul and his hearers, must have been aware of such Roman ideology as a (or even the) primary feature of their cultural context: in Deissmann's words, 'it must not be supposed that St. Paul and his fellow-believers went through the world blind-folded, unaffected by what was then moving the minds of men in great cities'.[14] It is thus claimed (with some justification) that New Testament scholars have generally underestimated the importance of specifically Roman politico-religious features for the life of the first Christians.

Building on this historical research, a crucial second step is the claim that Paul's gospel must be heard in direct antithesis to the Roman ideology with which he and his hearers were familiar. The parallels in vocabulary, discussed by Deissmann, have been much rehearsed in recent scholarship, and supplemented with suggestions that Paul's discussions of 'peace', 'righteousness'/'justice', and 'faith'/'loyalty' also echo distinctively Roman themes. It is generally claimed that Paul's hearers 'must' have heard the parallelism between his language and the language of Roman propaganda, and it is frequently (though not always, or so confidently) claimed that Paul must have intended such a pointed juxtaposition. Moreover, the juxtaposition is assumed to be antithetical: if the gospel preaches peace, this is directly counter to, and subversive of, the claim of the imperial 'gospel' to pacify the Mediterranean world. Whether Paul opposes primarily and precisely the 'imperial cult' (the multiform association of the emperors with the sphere of the divine), or more broadly the propagandistic claims and power-ideologies of the Roman empire, is one point of difference between

[13] For discussion of the 'imperial cult', see the previous chapter. Particularly influential on New Testament scholars have been S. R. F. Price, *Rituals and Power: The Roman Imperial Cult in Asia Minor* (Cambridge: Cambridge University, 1984); P. Zanker, *The Power of Images in the Age of Augustus* (Ann Arbor: University of Michigan, 1988); and C. Ando, *Imperial Ideology and Provincial Loyalty in the Roman Empire* (Berkeley: University of California, 2000).

[14] Deissmann, *Light from the Ancient East*, 340.

scholars in this broad coalition: for some (e.g. Kahl) the imperial cult is just one characteristic of a broader oppressive ideology opposed by Paul, for others (e.g. Wright) it is the chief point of Paul's attack, for others again (e.g. Oakes) it is of no independent significance for Paul within his broader critique of 'idolatry'. But it is generally assumed that any parallelism of terms or concepts carries a directly negative charge (if Jesus is Lord, Caesar is not), and, conversely, that the antithetical structures that run through Pauline theology can be taken to express direct opposition to central aspects of the Roman empire.

A number of factors fuel this scholarly movement and energise the passion with which it is pursued. For some it is attractive, even ideologically necessary, to interpret Paul's polemics as directed primarily (if not solely) against an imperial power, rather than against 'Judaism'; at the very least, this offers a fresh frame for Pauline interpretation beyond both traditional and 'new' perspectives, free of any possible hint of 'supersessionism'. For many this reading of Paul, in challenging the modern distinction between 'religion' and 'politics', offers a means of relating Paul to social and political issues in a newly 'post-secular' world, in contrast to the individualised (or privatised) readings common in theologically conservative traditions. In some cases (e.g. Horsley), Paul's opposition to 'empire' provides immediate resources for contemporary critique of empires, particularly (in American discourse) the forms of 'empire' subtly enforced by the global power of the United States or the West.[15] This 'socio-kerygmatic' agenda by no means discredits this scholarly enterprise, even if it influences its results: every reading of Paul is bound to carry 'political' implications.[16] However, we clearly need to beware of distortions that may arise from situating Paul's theological politics within the categories and theoretical frameworks which shape our own (post)modern understanding of 'politics'; if there is a danger of modernisation in separating 'religion' from 'politics', there is also a danger of allowing the fusion of these domains to be governed by modern expectations and perceptions.

---

[15] See, e.g., R. Horsley, *Jesus and Empire* (Minneapolis: Fortress, 2002) 3–5; cf. the Prologue by H. Taussig to the essays collected in *USQR* 59 no. 3–4 (2005): 'this volume … means to mark a break with New Testament scholarship's complicity with the imperial and imperious cultural domination of the West' (2).

[16] For the label 'socio-kerygmatic', see G. Theissen, *Social Reality and the Early Christians* (Edinburgh: T & T Clark, 1993) 17–19.

II. The Contribution of N.T. Wright

In a number of essays and chapters, and in his commentary on Romans, N.T. Wright has added his voice to the chorus of interpreters who take Paul's theology to be directly opposed to 'Caesar's empire', though he also strikes some distinctive notes, especially in his attempt to incorporate imperial topics within the central themes of Pauline theology .[17] Wright's reading of Paul may be summarised in the following eight points:

1. Wright emphasises, in common with recent research, the pervasiveness of the imperial cult in the Mediterranean world, its integration into other aspects of 'paganism', and its prominence in all the cities evangelised by Paul. The massive presence of this cult – in statues, temples, festivals, calendars, coins, inscriptions and sundry other social phenomena – was so much a part of the fabric of society that it was bound to impress itself forcefully on the minds of all who inhabited such cities. As the capstone of the ideology which legitimated Roman power, the imperial cult united the (inseparable) religious and political dimensions of the Roman empire. That Paul should say nothing about the imperial cult thus seems, to Wright, inconceivable: for Paul, politics were not just an implication of his theology, but integral to it, and driven by it.[18]

2. In fact, Wright finds plenty of 'echoes' of Roman imperial ideology in the vocabulary used by Paul. Following the findings of Deissmann (expanded in recent years), Wright draws out the parallels between common Pauline terms for Christ (Lord, Saviour, etc.) and for soteriology ('salvation', 'gospel', etc.) and the vocabulary used for Roman world-wide benefits associated with the emperors or the imperial cult. Pauline texts of particular importance for Wright include: the opening of Romans (Rom 1.3–17, describing Jesus' Messianic status as 'son of God' and the institution of divine 'justice' through the 'gospel'), a text which anticipates the climactic promise of the Davidic rule of the nations (Rom 15.7–13); the language of royal or imperial 'arrival' in 1 Thess 4.13–18; the allusion to an apparently Roman slogan, 'peace and security', in 1 Thess 5.3; the implicit contrast between Jesus' story (Phil 2.5–11) and the common narratives of imperial accession

[17] His views may be traced in N.T. Wright, 'Paul's Gospel and Caesar's Empire', in Horsley, ed., *Paul and Politics*, 160–83; 'Gospel and Theology in Galatians', in L.A. Jervis and P. Richardson, eds., *Gospel in Paul: Studies on Corinthians, Galatians and Romans for Richard N. Longenecker* (Sheffield: Sheffield Academic, 1994) 222–39; 'Paul and Caesar: A New Reading of Romans', in C. Bartholemew et al., ed., *A Royal Priesthood? The Use of the Bible Ethically and Politically* (Carlisle: Paternoster, 2002) 173–93; *Paul: Fresh Perspectives* (London: SPCK, 2005) 59–79; 'The Letter to the Romans: Introduction, Commentary and Reflections', in *The New Interpreter's Bible. Volume X* (Nashville: Abingdon, 2002) 395–770.

[18] 'Paul's Gospel', 161, 164, 182.

and rule; the use of political language (πολίτευμα) in association with the coming of a 'saviour' and 'Lord' in Phil 3.20–21 (cf. 1.27); and suggestions of a political background to Galatians, if certain verses suggest a pressure to confirm to the imperial cult (Gal 6.12–13).[19]

3. From such evidence, Wright concludes that Paul's message 'could not but be construed as deeply counterimperial, as subversive to the whole edifice of the Roman Empire; and there is in fact plenty of evidence that Paul intended it to be so construed'.[20] The inevitability of this reading is a frequent point of emphasis: 'Paul's declaration that the gospel of King Jesus reveals God's *dikaiosunē* must also be read as a deliberate laying down of a challenge to imperial pretension [of providing *Iustitia*]. If justice is wanted it will be found not in the *euaggelion* that announces Caesar as Lord but in the *euaggelion* of Jesus.'[21] While Paul's notion of 'gospel' drew extensively on the Isaianic declarations of monotheism, 'politically, it cannot but have been heard as a summons to allegiance to "another king", which is of course precisely what Luke says Paul was accused of saying (Acts 17:7).'[22] Moreover, this reading is attributed not just to Paul's hearers, but to Paul himself: 'Paul intended it to be so construed'.[23] Time and again Wright finds that Paul's words 'must be read as a deliberate challenge to the imperial pretension'.[24] Indeed the text may be said to declare its own meaning. On Phil 3.20 Wright comments: 'These are Caesar-titles. The whole verse says: Jesus is Lord, and Caesar isn't. Caesar's empire, of which Philippi is a colonial outpost, is the parody; Jesus' empire, of which the Philippian church is

---

[19] For this last, Wright appeals to B. W. Winter, *Seek the Welfare of the City: Christians as Benefactors and Citizens* (Grand Rapids: Eerdmans, 1994) 134–42; cf. B. W. Winter, 'The Imperial Cult and Early Christians in Pisidian Antioch (Acts XIII 13–50 and Gal VI 11–18)', in T. Drew-Bear et al., eds., *Actes du Ier Congrès International sur Antioche de Pisidie* (Lyon: Kocaeli, 2002) 67–75. The case has been made in detail by Hardin, *Galatians and the Imperial Cult*, 85–115.

[20] 'Paul's Gospel', 162; cf. *Fresh Perspectives*, 76–77 on the opening of Romans: 'the whole introduction to the letter contains so many apparently counter-imperial signals that I find it impossible to doubt that both Paul and his first hearers and readers – in Rome of all places! – would have picked up the message, loud and clear. Jesus is the world's true Lord, constituted as such by the resurrection. He claims the whole world, summoning them to 'the obedience of faith', that obedient loyalty that outmatches the loyalty Caesar demanded.'

[21] 'Paul's Gospel', 172. Equal emphasis on what 'cannot be other than subversive' or what 'must be seen' as such pervades the essay 'Paul and Caesar' (e.g., pp. 176–77, 180, 188–89).

[22] 'Paul's Gospel', 165; cf. *Paul: Fresh Perspectives*, 70.

[23] 'Paul's Gospel', 162; cf. 'Paul and Caesar', 178: 'at least at some points Paul is consciously parodying and subverting imperial ideology'; cf. 185: 'at the symbolic level, as well as at the level of praxis and narrative, [Paul's] challenge to Caesar was central and decisive.'

[24] 'Romans', 404: 'the rest of Romans will show that this meaning is indeed in Paul's mind at point after point' (405).

a colonial outpost, is the reality.'[25] Text, authorial intention and the implied audience are here taken to be at one in the construction of a single, clearly anti-Roman meaning.

4. Wright is, of course, aware that all the 'and Caesar is not' clauses, with which he augments Paul's text, are never made explicit: they lie underneath the text, not on its surface. The chief theoretical tool he uses to explain this phenomenon is that of literary 'echo'. Drawing on Hays' method in detecting 'echoes of Scripture in Paul', Wright detects 'echoes of Caesar' throughout the Pauline text: cultural allusions, he insists, are frequently implicit rather than explicit.[26] He also cites as parallels some ancient contemporary examples of 'coded critique' of the political regime: Goodenough argued that Philo's *De Somniis* contains veiled critique of the Roman governor of Egypt, while there is plenty of evidence that public figures and artists in Rome had to be extremely careful lest their work was heard to make cryptic negative comments on the reigning emperor.[27] One may thus be alert to the possibility that Paul's discourse in his letters is subtly 'coded'. The parade example, for Wright, is Paul's re-evaluation of his Jewish loyalties in Phil 3.2–11: in calling for imitation, Paul here subtly encourages the Philippians to 'rethink their Roman allegiance', using his own example to issue a 'coded challenge to Caesar's empire', which becomes more overt in 3.20–21. Hence Paul's notice that he is writing what is 'safe' (Phil 3.1): 'Why "safe"? Because nobody reading verses 2–16 would at once deduce that the recipients of the letter were being encouraged to be disloyal to Caesar. This is the coded message of subversive intrigue'.[28]

5. Wright defines the target of Paul's polemics sometimes in broad terms as 'Caesar's empire' or 'the ideology of the Roman empire', but more often in ways that highlight 'paganism' and, in particular, 'the Caesar-cult'. This partly distinguishes Wright from the bulk of 'Paul and Empire' scholars, at least in his emphasis on the Caesar-cult as a form of 'paganism'. Like others he sometimes identifies Paul's target as 'imperial pretensions' to provide justice, peace, security etc., or more broadly as 'Caesar's empire' and 'Caesar's system'. But he insists that Paul 'was not opposed to Caesar's empire primarily because it was an empire, with all the unpleasant things we have learned to associate with that word, but because it was Caesar's, and because Caesar was claiming divine status and honors which belonged only to the

[25] 'Paul's Gospel', 173.

[26] *Paul: Fresh Perspectives*, 61–62, 70–71. Cf. R.B. Hays, *Echoes of Scripture in the Letters of Paul* (New Haven; Yale University, 1989).

[27] Wright here cites the work of E. Champlin on the reign of Nero (*Nero* [Cambridge, Mass.: Harvard University, 2003]) and E. Goodenough on Philo (*The Politics of Philo Judaeus: Practice and Theory* [New Haven: Yale University, 1938] 21–41).

[28] 'Paul's Gospel', 175; the discussion of Phil 3 covers pp. 174–81.

one God.'[29] This means, on the one hand, that Paul is not opposed 'entirely to everything to do with the Roman empire', and, on the other, that the main target of his critique is the imperial cult and its associated ideology. These distinctions are painted with broad brush-strokes, but Wright's emphasis suggests that Paul reacts primarily to the 'paganism' of the Roman empire, rather than its social, economic or military characteristics as empire.[30]

6. Wright puts Paul's reaction to the Roman empire or the imperial cult on the map of the Jewish tradition in its reaction to 'paganism': he traces biblical (prophetic) roots for the antithesis between monotheism and pagan pretensions of absolute power, and compares Paul with a variety of Second Temple Jewish authors in their responses to Hellenistic or Roman rulers (Wisdom of Solomon; Psalms of Solomon; Josephus; Qumran; 4 Ezra, etc.). This leads him to conclude that Paul's reaction to the Roman world should not be divorced from his (complex) relation to the Jewish tradition, since Paul's critique of Roman 'paganism' lies within 'the mainstream Jewish monotheistic critique of paganism', which 'found in Paul's day a more focused target and in Paul's theology a sharper weapon'.[31]

7. The Lordship of Christ, which is integral to Paul's monotheism, makes particularly clear the necessary antithesis between allegiance to God/Christ and allegiance to the false claims of imperial worship. With the enthronement of Christ (Phil 2.10–11; 3.20–21; 1 Cor 15.20–28), it is revealed who is the true Lord of the universe, including the earthly realm claimed by Caesar. Paul's churches are opposed to the 'principalities and powers', which include or are associated with 'Caesar's system';[32] they represent 'the true empire of the true Lord', since they form 'colonial outposts of the empire that is to be: subversive little groups when seen from Caesar's point of view'.[33] Given this apocalyptic theology, 'at every point ... we should expect what we in fact find: that, for Paul, Jesus is Lord and Caesar is not'.[34] The

---

[29] 'Paul's Gospel', 164.

[30] The term 'paganism' seems to have a broad range of meaning in Wright's usage, though its definition is not always clear: see e.g., 'Gospel and Theology', 228: 'The more Jewish we make Paul's "gospel", the more it confronts directly the pretensions of the Imperial cult, and indeed all other paganisms whether "religious" or "secular".'

[31] 'Paul's Gospel', 170. Paul thus articulates 'an essentially Jewish political theology' (*Paul: Fresh Perspectives*, 70) and we may 'locate Paul credibly both within the standard Jewish views of how to live within pagan empire and within the new world inaugurated by the gospel of the crucified and risen Messiah' (79).

[32] The relationship between the Roman empire and the 'principalities and powers' is not fully clarified in Wright's work: see, e.g., 'Paul's Gospel', 173, 179; 'Gospel and Theology', 229–33; *Paul: Fresh Perspectives*, 76; 'Paul and Caesar', 180; since Wright considers Colossians and Ephesians to be by Paul, there is the added complication that all such powers are said to be created in Christ.

[33] 'Paul's Gospel', 174, 182–83.

[34] *Paul: Fresh Perspectives*, 69.

fact that the true Lord was crucified on a Roman cross, the very means by which Rome expressed her power in the world, reinforces the sense of a total antithesis between the two 'Kingdoms'.[35]

8. Finally, what of Romans 13.1–7? Because he has not presented Paul as opposed in every respect to Roman power, Wright is less embarrassed by this (in)famous paragraph than many other 'Paul and Empire' scholars;[36] and since he considers Paul in many respects to continue a Jewish tradition of political submission alongside religious critique of 'pagan' empires, he can point to the many parallels between Paul's sentiments and Jewish texts regarding divine control of non-Jewish authorities.[37] Like some others, Wright insists that the statements about divine appointment of the powers implicitly challenge the inflated claims of Roman emperors: against their arrogant assertion of divine status, Paul demotes them to being merely the servants of God.[38] But since Paul could not support anarchy, he appreciates the role of the authorities in maintaining social stability (they are the proper alternative to private vengeance, Rom 12.19–21), and as a Roman citizen, who was to appeal in due course to Caesar, he is hardly opposed to all features of Roman authority. Nonetheless, Wright's reading requires that there is a dialectical tension between Rom 13.1–7 and the rest of Romans. The divine appointment of such authorities to rule has to be emphasised by Paul precisely because of all the 'counter-imperial hints Paul has given not only in this letter and elsewhere but indeed by his entire gospel';[39] it stands as a dialectical counterpart to such 'hints', lest believers think that loyalty to Jesus means civil disobedience or revolution.[40] Thus the whole paragraph, according to Wright, carries within it a large, but implicit 'Nevertheless':[41] despite all that Paul has said to undermine 'Caesar's empire' in the rest of the letter, believers in Rome should respect Roman authority, as appointed (at least temporarily, Rom 13.11–14) by God. The strong assertion of the divine authorization of Roman rule is the rhetorical counterweight to Paul's own subversion of Rome's 'imperial ideology'.

---

[35] *Paul: Fresh Perspectives*, 73.

[36] See, for instance, Elliott's struggles in 'Romans 13:1–7 in the Context of Imperial Propaganda', in Horsley, ed., *Paul and Empire*, 184–204; idem, *The Arrogance of Nations*, 152–56. Cf. Jewett, *Romans*, 780–803.

[37] 'Romans', 718.

[38] 'Paul's Gospel', 172; 'Paul and Caesar', 190–91.

[39] *Paul: Fresh Perspectives*, 78.

[40] 'Romans', 719: 'it is important that his readers do not take his covert polemic against the imperial ideology as a coded call to a Christian version of the so-called fourth philosophy'.

[41] 'Romans', 722; the commands of this paragraph are otherwise too obvious to have been necessary: what makes them such are possible (but wrong) deductions from Paul's own anti-Roman hints throughout the letter.

III. Response to N.T. Wright

Wright's main claims are best answered by a reframing of the issues. In what follows I will pick up each of the above eight points by considering the peculiarity of Paul's perception of reality (Rome and Pauline Epistemology), the interpretation of parallel terminology ('Political' Vocabulary in Paul), the choice of appropriate reading strategies (Reading between the Lines?), and Paul's theopolitical construal of conflicting powers (Paul's Political Theology).

a) Rome and Pauline Epistemology

We may grant Wright (and others) that the imperial cult was an increasingly prominent part of the civic landscape experienced by Paul. Although its manifestations were varied and geographically patchy, Paul lived in an era when statues, festivals, inscriptions and temples attached to one or another form of devotion to the imperial family were growing in number and significance in the Greek east, and many other forms of cultic devotion were redefined or redirected in honour of Rome.[42] Not all forms of 'honour' to the emperors were interpreted, even by Jews, as entailing worship: Paul no doubt knew of the prayers and sacrifices offered daily in the Temple for (not to) the emperor, and probably encountered monuments of Jewish respect for the emperors in the synagogues of the Diaspora.[43] But, like Philo, he would certainly have baulked at the direct offering of worship to imperial deities, and to the extent that this was regularly expected of civic officials and Roman citizens, we may be sure that his reaction was wholly negative.[44]

[42] See chapter 18 in this volume for full discussion of this matter, via a case study (Tarraco).

[43] On the Temple sacrifices, see Josephus, *c. Apion.* 2.76–77; *Bell.* 2.197; Philo, *Legatio* 157, 291, 317. Gaius is reported as complaining that such sacrifices were offered for, but not to, him (Philo, *Legatio* 357). For synagogue inscriptions, shields and crowns in honour of emperors, see Philo, *Legatio* 133.

[44] The extent to which participation in the imperial cult was expected of ordinary city residents (perhaps only at festivals) and the degree to which that participation constituted (in Jewish or Christian eyes) idolatrous worship are matters of dispute among scholars; see, for instance, the cautionary remarks of P. Oakes, 'Remapping the Universe: Paul and the Emperor in 1 Thessalonians and Philippians', *JSNT* 27 (2005) 301–22 (at 311–15), with reference to the differing views of Price and Fishwick on popular participation in the imperial cult. At a later time, it seems that many Christians took part in the activities of imperial festivals (attending shows, receiving handouts, wearing festival garlands, etc.) without considering themselves to be committing 'idolatry': the strict Tertullian complains about Christians festooning their gates with laurel-wreaths and lamps on such days (*De Idololatria* 15). It is a mistake to take the exceptional court-room scenarios, where Christians were required to offer sacrifice or to swear oaths to the gods, including the emperors-as-deities (Pliny, *Letters* 10.96; *Martyrdom of Polycarp* 4, 8–9) as typical of

But the question is not the prevalence of the imperial cult but how Paul perceived this phenomenon. We may agree with Deissmann that Paul was hardly 'blindfolded' as he travelled around the Roman world; but there is more than one way of seeing. *We* may perceive the imperial cult as the dominant mode of 'pagan' religiosity, and as an insidious expression of Roman hegemony, but it is another matter how *Paul* perceived the religio-political context in which he lived; his interpretative frame may have been different from our late-modern modes of historical interpretation and ideological analysis. If everywhere we look we see 'Rome' as the stand-out feature of Paul's landscape, it is not necessarily the case that Paul saw likewise (and *must* therefore have referred to Rome, in code if not in plain speech). Perhaps he saw his world no less well than we do, but differently – as a world structured by powers permeating the political realm (and other realms) on an axis other than that constituting the power sphere of 'the Rome empire'.

The main reason for mooting this alternative is the pattern of reference and non-reference in Paul's letters. Paul, of course, refers repeatedly to 'idolatrous' cult, as his converts have 'turned to God from idols' (1 Thess 1.9), have ceased to serve 'beings that by nature are non-Gods' (Gal 4.8), having once been led astray to 'dumb idols' (1 Cor 12.2). No special reference is made here to the imperial cult (or indeed to any named deity), not because Paul was ignorant of the names of Jupiter, Isis or Dionysus or of the imperial family, but because their named identities are not what is (to him) salient. In 1 Cor 8.4–5 he recognises that there are 'so-called Gods in heaven and on earth', since there are many 'Gods' and many 'Lords'. The Gods 'in heaven and on earth' might well include the objects of the imperial cult, but if so, Paul is not concerned to spell out their Roman profile, nor does he give this form of idolatry any special emphasis or heightened attention.[45]

The letters of Paul evidence an equal and parallel non-specification of Rome: Paul seems to show no interest (as we do) in the Roman empire *as Roman*. Although his name is Latin and although (according to Acts) he had Roman citizenship,[46] and although much of his mission was conducted in cities which were either Roman colonies or had strong Roman allegiances,

---

the pressures under which most Christians lived their everyday lives. Oakes concludes, 'For most Christians, the imperial cult was probably a less pressing issue than other cults in which they had previously participated' ('Remapping', 313). See the previous chapter for further discussion.

[45] For discussion of the Pauline logic and of the ways in which the imperial cult was embedded in older and wider patterns of cultic behaviour, see the previous chapter in this volume.

[46] Although the Lukan claim is regarded with scepticism in some quarters, Paul's citizenship is by no means implausible, as M. Hengel has shown (*The Pre-Christian Paul* [London: SCM, 1991] 5–16). It is all the more striking that, despite many passages of self-description, Paul never mentions this feature of his identity.

Paul never describes the world he inhabits in terms that allude to its Roman character. Paul never refers to Roman governors, or to any Roman emperor by name, though he does once refer to King Aretas and is clearly not averse to naming rulers (2 Cor 11.32). Although he speaks frequently of the death of Christ, and very often of the cross, he never identifies this as a *Roman* punishment or relates this to *Roman* agents: it is the nameless 'rulers of this age' who crucified the Lord of glory (1 Cor 2.6, 8), and at one place (if the text is from Paul) 'the Jews/Judeans' (1 Thess 2.15). The cross is certainly a world-defying scandal, but its offence is drawn out in relation to Jews and Greeks, or undifferentiated 'nations' (τὰ ἔθνη), never in relation to Romans in particular. Paul's own imprisonments and punishments, including his incarceration in the praetorium and his beating with rods (Phil 1.13; 2 Cor 11.25), are never attributed to *Roman* authorities: he is endangered by his own γένος and by τὰ ἔθνη in 2 Cor 11.26, but never specifically by *Romans*. When Paul appears to allude to what we label a 'Roman' boast of 'peace and security' (1 Thess 5.3), he attributes this not to a *Roman* source, but to those who 'belong to the night and the darkness' (1 Thess 5.1–5), that is, 'the rest' outside the Christian community (5.6): it represents for him a general, not a specifically Roman, delusion. Although Paul speaks frequently about powers, authorities and rulers (Rom 8.35–39; 1 Cor 2.6–8; 15.24–28; Rom 13.1–7; and, if we include such evidence, Col 1.15–20 and 2.14–15), these are always anonymous, and never specifically identified with Rome. Lest we think that all this silence is suspicious, and that there is an unnamed 'you know who' or 'you know where' that Paul cannot dare to name, we should note that he can speak openly about Rome (though only in Rom 1.7, 15), and that he does refer to Caesar (though only when speaking of believers in Caesar's household, Phil 4.22). In other words, there is no conspiracy of silence, but also no specification of Rome on the countless occasions when Paul *could have* spoken of her empire, her rulers and her cult. All those 'and especially Caesar' clauses that Wright employs to exegete the target of Paul's polemics, are supplements to the text, additions and specifications not made by Paul himself.

If Paul's descriptions of his world indicate the terms in which he viewed it – his particular epistemology – we should take seriously the fact that his angle of perception on the Roman world was different from ours, and different from the frameworks of description employed by other New Testament authors. The question is not whether Paul noticed the power of Rome – he clearly did to the extent of feeling its physical impact on his body; the question is what power he saw to be operative in such experiences. Before we rush to make the identifications with Rome that Paul conspicuously does not make, we should ask if he knows the world differently – not, as he would put it, κατὰ σάρκα, but according to the co-ordinates of a reality redefined by the new creation (2 Cor 5.16–17).[47] If Rome is not specifically named from this angle of vision, this does not mean that Paul's theology was apolitical, only that the political is for him enmeshed in an all-encompassing power-struggle which covers every domain of life, including but not limited to the religio-political domain we call 'the Roman empire', and not neatly divisible into a battle between forces 'for' and 'against' Roman rule.

b) 'Political' Vocabulary in Paul

As we have seen, from Deissmann to Wright a good deal of capital is made of the overlap of vocabulary between Pauline terms for the church, for salvation and for Christ, and the politico-religious terminology current in the Roman empire. Although this overlap is not always as exact as claimed,[48] it is certainly true that (whatever the sources for such terms) there is much common 'political' vocabulary. The question is whether this overlap of vocabulary implies an *antithetical* relationship between the two domains, and, conversely, whether Paul's antithetical constructs place Christ or the church in opposition to the Roman empire in the way suggested by Wright and others.

As a general principle we should note that the use of common language, even common political language, does not in itself entail a competitive, or antithetical, relationship between the entities using the same terms. Numerous clubs and associations used 'political' terms of themselves and of their leaders without challenging the larger civic bodies that used identical terminology.[49] Paul can speak of ecclesial leaders as διάκονοι and λειτουργοί of God (1 Cor 3.5; Rom 15.16), but can also label political authorities διάκονοι and λειτουργοί θεοῦ (Rom 13.4, 6) without the one challenging or cancelling out the other. Both figures serve God under identical labels; if Paul is a διάκονος θεοῦ there is no implication 'and Caesar is not'. To describe the church (or individual believers) as 'the temple of God' (1 Cor 3.16; 6.19) does not imply that the Jerusalem building is no longer to be considered a temple: the ecclesial metaphor develops out of, and is arguably founded on, the continuing recognition of the temple in Jerusalem.[50]

---

[47] See J. L. Martyn, 'Pauline Epistemology at the Turn of the Ages', in his *Theological Issues in the Letters of Paul* (Edinburgh: T & T Clark, 1997) 89–110.

[48] It is frequently overlooked, for instance, that the Pauline εὐαγγέλιον is consistently singular, the imperial 'good news' (εὐαγγέλια) consistently plural; for the pecularity of the Pauline (and early Christian) usage, see S. Mason, *Josephus, Judea, and Christian Origins* (Peabody, MA: Hendrickson, 2009) 285–86. For fuller discussion, see G. Stanton, *Jesus and Gospel* (Cambridge: Cambridge University, 2004) 25–49.

[49] See, e.g., F. Poland, *Geschichte des griechischen Vereinswesens* (Leipzig; B. G. Teubner, 1909) 363–66.

[50] See F. W. Horn, 'Paulus and der herodianische Tempel', *NTS* 53 (2007) 184–203.

By the same token, to describe groups of believers in political language as 'assemblies' (ἐκκλησίαι) and to use a political metaphor of the Christian life (πολιτεύεσθαι, Phil 1.30; cf. 3.20) does not of itself challenge the validity of the local civic 'assemblies', or subvert Paul's converts' usual political behaviour: we need explicit evidence of an antithesis to be sure that Paul sets the one *in contrast to* the other. In relation to Christological titles, precisely this sort of antithesis is present in 1 Cor 8.4–6: whatever beings other people may honour as 'Lords' and 'Gods', 'for us there is one κύριος and one θεός' (1 Cor 8.6). Given this evidence it is no surprise that Paul does not refer to political authorities as κύριοι. But we know of his sensitivity regarding this title only because he explicitly marks this antithesis. This is not the case with regard to some other terms (διάκονος), and we cannot assume it to be the case elsewhere. Everything depends on precise analysis of the linguistic and rhetorical contexts in which such terms are used.[51]

This is not to deny that Paul's language for salvation and his other Christological titles *could have been heard* to imply a challenge to other (political) uses of such terms; the question is whether this would constitute a good hearing/reading of his letters. Wright's claim that Paul's statements 'could not but be construed' in such antithetical terms is strikingly short of examples indicating that this did in fact take place, and it is crucial to identify under what conditions such a hearing was likely to occur. Acts 17.7 records that hostile hearers of Paul could interpret reference to Jesus as βασιλεύς as a threat to the 'king/emperor' status of Caesar. But this is *Luke*'s construction of a hearing of 'Paul', and one he considers mistaken; moreover, it concerns a Christological title that Paul himself does not use (though cf. cognate terms in 1 Cor 15.24–25), and hardly constitutes evidence for how Christian hearers/readers construed Paul's letters.[52] In a depiction of the martyrdom of Paul now contained in *The Acts of Paul* (2nd century CE), a cupbearer in the imperial court is imagined declaring his allegiance to Jesus as 'King of the ages' who 'destroys all kingdoms under heaven'; he shocks the emperor Nero, and is accordingly tortured and imprisoned.[53] One sees here that in contexts when Christian allegiance clashed directly with the demands of Roman authorities, it was possible to place Christ and Caesar in antithesis as rival claimants to the same title (though again here in non-

---

[51] For similar observations, cf. C. Bryan, *Render to Caesar: Jesus, the Early Church and the Roman Superpower* (Oxford: Oxford University, 2005) 82–92. For the importance of literary context (as well as 'context of situation') in determining meaning, see M. Silva, *Biblical Words and their Meaning: An Introduction to Lexical Semantics* (Grand Rapids: Zondervan, 1983) 138–48.

[52] For a nuanced discussion of Luke's Christology and the status of Jesus as κύριος in relation to Caesar, see C. K. Rowe, *World Upside Down: Reading Acts in the Graeco-Roman Age* (Oxford: Oxford University, 2009) 103–16.

[53] J. K. Elliott, *The Apocryphal New Testament* (Oxford: Clarendon, 1993) 386.

Pauline terms; cf. *Martyrdom of Polycarp* 9.3). But in most contexts and at most times, it appears, such a clash was neither experienced nor anticipated. Thus the author of 1 Timothy, a direct interpreter of the Pauline tradition, finds no embarrassment in attributing the title βασιλεύς to human rulers (1 Tim 2.2), although the same title can be used also of Christ (6.15); there is no antithesis, because Christ is the 'King of kings' (and Lord of lords, 1 Tim 6.15). In other words, the relationship between two holders of the same title need not be antithetical; it might be that one is the *supreme* holder of a title that others share, at a subordinate rank.[54] Overlaps in terminology (between the divine and human spheres of power or between human possessors of the same title) do not of themselves indicate a competitive relationship.[55] Unless this is signalled in the text itself (e.g. 1 Cor 8.4–6), readers/hearers are only likely to construct such an antithetical relationship in socio-political contexts of acute tension.[56]

Wright, as we have seen, is confident that he can detect not only what 'must have been heard' in Paul's letters, but also what Paul himself intended. Those hermeneutically less committed to (or confident about) authorial intention, may still approximate this strategy in offering a responsible (as opposed to an arbitrary) reading of the text. If individual terms by themselves do not define their meanings, a good reading requires close attention

[54] This is strikingly the case, for instance, in Philo's *Legatio*: in a text that particularly stresses Jewish monotheistic abhorrence of the imperial cult (here Gaius' self-deification), Philo uses extremely elevated titles of the emperors, in some cases terms that are also used of God. Thus while God is the one benefactor of all (118), the saviour of Israel (196), the father and king of all (3) who gives universal blessings of peace, justice and providence (306, 318, 336), Philo is lavish in his praise of the emperors (especially Augustus): he and the Jewish actors in the drama refer to the emperor as 'Master' (δεσπότης, 271, 276, 290) and 'Lord' (κύριος, 286, 356), the 'benefactor' (148–49) and 'saviour' (22), who has brought great blessings to the world, including peace (8–13, 141, 143–54) and civilization (20). Jews are thus represented here as implacably opposed to imperial worship, and strongly critical of certain emperors and certain Roman governors, but nonetheless consistently φιλοκαίσαρες (280) – a combination that seems impossible to many current interpreters of the Jewish Paul.

[55] Even Tertullian is willing to call the emperor 'Lord', but 'in the common sense of the term and not when I am forced to call him Lord as in God's place'; he insists he has one true Lord, who is Lord of the emperor as well (*Apology* 34.1). This sensitivity to the range of meaning of labels, and the context of usage, contrasts with the flat reading of vocabulary parallels conducted by Wright and others. In place of the simple alternatives of 'support' or 'subversion', the evidence requires a set of nuanced categories, including that of limited, contextually defined but wholehearted honour.

[56] For early Christian perspectives influenced by the Pauline tradition, which advocate prayer for and obedience to 'those who rule and govern us here on earth', see, e.g., 1 Pet 2.13–17; Titus 3.1; 1 Clement 61. Tertullian, while robustly refusing to accord emperors divine honours, insists that Christians pray for the welfare of the imperial house and the security of the empire, citing 1 Tim 2 in support (*Apology*, 30–33). None of these exhibit the 'challenge to Caesar's empire' that Wright thinks 'must have been heard' in Paul's letters.

to their rhetorical and literary contexts: links with other terms, explications, antithetical relations, and practical consequences all help to define the range of nuances implied by the text. Paul never places the terms 'good news', 'salvation', or 'faith/loyalty' in antithesis with a Roman form of the same; the righteousness/justice of God is contrasted with that of the Torah, not of Rome.[57] As we have seen, some other terms, such as κύριος and θεός, are placed in antithetical contexts (1 Cor 8.4–6), though even here the antithesis does not run along a fault-line between Christ and Rome. Christ is 'Lord' over against *all other lords* (1 Cor 8.4–6), and is eventually to receive homage from all things in heaven, on earth and under the earth (Phil 2.11): there is here no special attention to Caesar or to any specific divine or human entity. Paul would certainly deny the Lordship of Caesar but the text gives no rhetorical clues that he identified Caesar's claims as of particular significance or threat. If the Philippians are to 'conduct themselves sociopolitically' (πολιτεύεσθαι, Phil 1.27), this is certainly mapped in contrast to an alternative, but there is nothing to indicate that the alternative is 'Rome'. The antithesis to the church is 'the world' with its 'crooked and perverse generation' (Phil 2.15); it contains 'adversaries' (1.28) but there is no textual clue to encourage a construal of these enemies as specifically or even primarily 'Roman'. And if, as Paul asserts, 'our πολίτευμα is in heaven', this statement is placed in antithesis not to a civic πολίτευμα (in Philippi or Rome), but to the conceptual and psychological commitment to 'earthly things' (οἱ τὰ ἐπίγεια φρονοῦντες, Phil 3.19–20). Elsewhere, Paul can contrast a heavenly city with an earthly one (the two Jerusalems, Gal 4.25–26) but he does not do so here; the contrast is not with a civic entity but with an 'earthly' sphere of preoccupation. There is therefore no contextual reason to find Rome specifically implicated in this text, and every reason to suggest that the text evokes a broader reality which may encompass the political but is not limited to it. Of course, modern hearers may find an echo of 'Rome' in this text, with the noise of 'the Roman empire' dominating their sensory perception. The question is whether they have listened well to Paul's text, with its peculiar labels and antithetical constructs; perhaps when *he* listened to his world he heard rather different sounds.

c) Reading Between the Lines?

As we have noted, a key strategy for Wright (and others) in positing that Paul's theology targeted the Roman empire is the suggestion that there is

[57] Wright does not claim, as do some others (e. g. Kahl, *Galatians Re-imagined*, 227–29), that Paul refers to Roman law as well as the Mosaic law when he speaks of νόμος. Again, the context usually makes clear that the law in question belongs to Moses/Israel and is embodied in the Jewish Scriptures.

much beneath the text that Paul does not and cannot allow to rise to its surface, since for political reasons it would have been unsafe to make his critique of Rome explicit. As we have seen, Wright justifies this interpretative strategy by reference to Hays' method (and success) in detecting echoes of Scripture in Paul's letters; by the same means, he finds 'echoes' of the Roman empire in places where Rome is not explicitly mentioned. But the parallel is hardly valid. Hays' intertextual methodology proceeds from the said to the unsaid, from numerous and explicit citations of Scripture to echoes that surround and supplement that solid sound of citation; Wright is working from nothing explicit in the text, from thin air to even thinner. From the massive evidence of citation, no-one could doubt that Paul's theology is closely engaged with his Scriptures; to posit a similar engagement with the Roman empire would require a similar evidential base.

From Valentinus onwards, many interpreters of Paul have succumbed to the temptation to find a second or additional meaning in Paul's text, beneath or beyond its surface; only so can Paul be made to speak on subjects that such interpreters hope or expect him to address. But there is no indication that the text gestures beyond itself to a hidden meaning; 1 Cor 4.6 indicates the way Paul might make such a gesture (ταῦτα μετασχημάτισα ...), but to find Rome implicit where it is nowhere named one would have to posit that this strategy pervaded all his letters. Other Jewish and early Christian texts employed a range of symbols in referring to Rome – as Babylon (1 Pet 5.13; Rev 18), or Kittim (1QM etc.), or an eagle (4 Ezra 11–12). Paul uses no such symbolic devices,[58] nor does he write differently when he approaches 'sensitive' topics or addresses certain locations (e.g. Rome).[59] Indeed, it is hard to envisage the conditions in which Paul's letters would endanger either himself or his converts any more than his preaching which, on Wright's thesis, must have made clear that the Lordship of Jesus stood in direct opposition to the authority of Caesar. There is no indication, for instance, that early Christian letters were likely to be intercepted by Roman secret agents, and the notion that Paul should find it necessary to mask his meaning, lest he expose himself or his converts, exaggerates the political importance of the earliest Christian groups and underrates Paul's courage. To be sure,

[58] The one exception could be 2 Thess 2.3–12, which employs prophetic language (from Daniel, Ezekiel et al.) to describe the arrogance of a 'man of lawlessness' who establishes himself in God's temple. But numerous questions surround this passage (regarding meaning, reference and authorship), whose register is very different from the undisputed Pauline texts; in any case, the text appears to refer to a future apocalyptic event, not a present political reality.

[59] The notice that he is writing what is 'safe' (Phil 3.1) indicates the attempt to make his point rhetorically secure (and hence repeated) not immune from political danger; I know no commentary that would support Wright's reading of this text or of Phil 3.1–11 in general.

prominent citizens in Rome had to be careful what they said or implied regarding the reigning emperor, and there were acute political sensitivities in the metropolis to what was said in public (e.g. on the stage) or through rumours circulated by soothsayers. But the Roman empire was not a police state and, even where voluntary associations were under suspicion, it did not take steps to monitor the written communications of comparatively small groups incapable of launching a political insurrection.[60] Moreover, it is hard to imagine Paul, whose preaching frequently landed himself and his converts in trouble, being afraid to speak his mind in his letters; since he expects believers to face 'persecution' (Phil 1.27–30), he is hardly going to shade the gospel to avoid it. Indeed, if he thought the letter to the Philippians might be read by hostile authorities, he foolishly blows the cover of Christians (in Rome?) by sending greetings from believers in the household of Caesar (4.22)!

Paul's greatest religious offence to Rome – his denial of the gods who were believed to shield and support the emperors and the empire – is perfectly explicit on the surface of his letters. Since he was known to be a Jew, what would he need to bury beneath the surface that would not be well known already as a Jewish opinion? That Caesar is neither God nor son of God? Philo said so at length in a document addressed to a wide audience (his *Legatio*), indeed more or less directly to the emperor's face (*Legatio* 357). That one should not take part in the imperial cult? That was a well-known Jewish stance, and Paul says it clearly enough in his blanket ban on worshipping 'idols'. If his Gentile converts were notorious for abandoning 'pagan' cultic activity in general, it would hardly surprise a hostile reader that they were disinclined to worship the emperors. Josephus, who tiptoed carefully round this subject in his tractate *contra Apionem*, still found it possible to castigate the imperial cult as 'a means that is useful neither to God nor to human beings' (2.75).[61] That Roman governors and their agents, such as Pilate, were responsible for miscarriages of justice? Josephus, like Philo,[62] says that time and again, in documents that were genuinely pub-

[60] Tertullian refers to the *curiosi* who monitor the low-life of the city (and complains that Christians are so regarded, *De Fuga* 13); but there is no indication that Christian letters were liable to be intercepted.

[61] See my essay 'Snarling Sweetly: Josephus on Images and Idolatry', in S. Barton, ed., *Idolatry: False Worship in the Bible, Early Judaism and Christianity* (London: T & T Clark, 2007), 73–87 [reprinted above, chapter 17].

[62] Philo is relentlessly critical of Pilate, Flaccus and other governors in his *In Flaccum* and *Legatio ad Gaium*. Goodenough's suggestion (*The Politics of Philo Judaeus*, 21–41, adopted by Wright) that Philo's critical remarks on Joseph in *De Somniis* were a coded attack on the current Roman governor are implausible, and have rightly been criticised by e.g. R. Barraclough, 'Philo's Politics, Roman Rule and Hellenistic Judaism', *ANRW* II.12.1 (1980) 417–553 (at 491–506).

lic, and even presented to emperors.[63] That the Roman empire consists of 'plundering, butchering and stealing' in the name of 'peace'? Even Tacitus, in the heart of the establishment, can see and say that, with typical irony (*Agricola* 30.3–31.2, a speech attributed to Calgacus). In other words, the notion that Paul found it necessary to write in code is without historical foundation; and since the text itself gives no indication of any such thing, we may dismiss the suggestion as a fantasy.

A common tactic in this connection (though one not, to my knowledge, adopted by Wright) is to appeal to the notion of a 'hidden transcript', as coined by James Scott.[64] Thus it is frequently claimed that Paul's letters bear one meaning on the surface but contain also traces of a 'hidden transcript' which was more directly critical of Rome.[65] In Scott's analysis, the 'public transcript' is to be found 'onstage', in the face of the dominant parties and under the constraints of power. The 'hidden transcript' takes place 'offstage' in the safety of internal discourse among 'the weak', and 'beyond direct observation by powerholders'; it is generally inaccessible outside the circle of the subordinate themselves.[66] As an intermediate phenomenon, Scott identifies examples of disguise, doubleness or anonymity which take place in public view ('onstage') but bear double meanings, for instance in codes, jokes or euphemisms that can be variously heard by different groups.[67] These discourses of disguise are not themselves 'the hidden transcript', but they bear traces of it in a dissembled form.

If we are to apply Scott's taxonomy to Paul's letters we have to decide whether they are to be located 'onstage' or 'offstage', that is, in the public domain, or in private circulation among insiders. Since they are not addressed to outsiders (unlike Josephus' texts, which are certainly open to Scott's analysis),[68] Paul's letters are not public documents in any obvious sense: they are not addressed to non-believers, nor do they anticipate fall-

[63] As is shown by these examples, along with countless petitions from Egyptian peasants, if one was dissatisfied with one layer of (Roman) officials, one could always appeal above them to the layer above, eventually (for Roman citizens, as in Luke's story of Paul) all the way to the emperor. If the current emperor was regarded as corrupt, one could appeal to the example of his predecessors. It is only if one regarded the whole Roman empire as, in principle, evil, that one would be driven to root-and-branch critique of Rome – an opinion which it is hard to attribute to the Paul who wrote Rom 13.1–7.

[64] J. C. Scott, *Domination and the Arts of Resistance: Hidden Transcripts* (New Haven: Yale University, 1990).

[65] See, e. g., R. A. Horsley, ed., *Hidden Transcripts and the Arts of Resistance: Applying the Work of James C. Scott to Jesus and Paul* (Semeia Studies 48; Atlanta: Society of Biblical Literature, 2004). The notion is frequently appealed to by N. Elliott (e. g. in his *Arrogance of Nations*) and others; cf. Kahl, *Galatians Re-imagined*, 48, 253.

[66] Scott, *Domination*, 4–5, 18, 25, 27.

[67] Scott, *Domination*, 18–19, 136–82.

[68] See chapters 15–17 above.

ing into such hands. There is every reason to think that we have here, in pure form, a Christian 'hidden transcript' – that is, what they said among themselves 'offstage' in freedom and without fear. Thus we should not expect here the kind of dissimulation or disguise associated with Scott's intermediate category; we should find here not coded traces of the hidden transcript, but its full expression, precisely that open and frank language that takes place 'offstage' among those without political power. But if we have access here to the undisguised 'hidden transcript' (i. e., if this is more or less how Paul would talk to his converts if he were in a private house), it is striking that Paul makes no openly subversive statements about Caesar or Rome as one might expect if the gospel stood in direct opposition to the Roman empire. In other words, Scott's analysis argues directly *against* those who would regard Paul's letters as a coded discourse which masks what he or other early Christians really thought.

For all these reasons, the case for tracing a hidden 'code' in Paul's letters appears extremely implausible. Rather than reading between the lines, or supplementing Paul's text with 'and especially Caesar' additions, proper exegetical method requires us to read precisely what is on the lines. If this does not fit what we imagine Paul *must have* said, it is not Paul's texts that need revision, but our preformed expectations of his political theology.[69]

d) Paul's Political Theology

Reading Paul's letters with responsible attention to their own dynamics, we find that his theology concerns the subversive and redemptive power of divine grace in Christ, which creates and empowers new communities of social (and therefore broadly political) significance. These communities (inadequately) represent the advance of the gospel on a conflicted world stage, where the main players are what Paul calls 'powers' (ἀρχαί and δυνάμεις, e. g. Rom 8.38): on the one side, the Spirit and grace, on the other, Sin, Death and the Flesh (and sometimes, Satan or δαιμόνια). The Roman empire is not itself one of these powers, because they operate across all levels simultaneously – individual, social, political, and cosmic; like any empire, it may be co-opted, in whole or in part, into the ranks of 'the sons of darkness', but only within an undifferentiated mass whose identity is determined not by its current political configuration but by its alignment with powers of far greater influence. In fact, Paul's most subversive act, vis-à-vis the Roman

[69] As I indicated in the oral debate with N. T. Wright, in the current wave of enthusiasm for reading Paul's gospel as directly targeted at Caesar, I feel like the little boy in the fable. When the boy saw the emperor parading in what were supposedly 'new clothes' he was bold enough to say, 'but the emperor is naked'. In this case, when I am bidden to watch the emperor walking around Paul's letters, I am rude enough to object, 'but I see no emperor!'.

empire, was not to oppose or upstage it, but to relegate it to the rank of a dependent and derivative entity, denied a distinguishable name or significant role in the story of the world.

Interpreters who take Paul's theology to oppose 'Caesar', 'the Roman empire' or 'imperial ideology' are apt to find themselves trapped within the political categories created by Rome itself or by modern political analysis. But Paul uses different categories and maps the world in different terms. If we ask about *imperium*, Paul certainly makes use of the language of 'reigning' (βασιλεύω), but employs it for the overthrow of the reign of Sin by the reign of Grace (Rom 5.12–21), and for the 'kingdom' being established by Christ, who is engaged in deactivating every 'rule', every 'authority' and every 'power', the last of which is Death (1 Cor 15.24–28). The Pauline classifications and their related antinomies here cut across the categories normally employed by historians and social analysts. Where we divide the world into historical periods and ethno-political units (the Hellenistic or Roman eras; the Seleucid kingdom or the Roman empire), Paul sees no significant differences between Romans and Greeks, only a categorical distinction between the κόσμος and the καινὴ κτίσις which was created by the cross (Gal 6.14–15): in shattering other classifications of culture and power, the world is divided anew around the event of Christ.[70] 'The world' or 'this age' (1 Cor 1–2; Gal 1.4) is a Pauline category that can be used to characterize both political rulers (1 Cor 2.6–8) and the cultural systems by which they operate ('wisdom' and 'power', 1 Cor 1.20): it is sufficiently comprehensive to include Roman power, but its defining characteristics are by no means 'Roman'. Thus the 'principalities' and 'powers' discussed by Paul are entities which defy our normal taxonomies. They are not simply 'anthropological' since they cover the whole gamut of existence, from death to social disintegration to the corruption that infests the whole cosmos (1 Cor 15.26; Rom 8.18–39); to call them 'cosmic' might suggest that they hover in some extra-human sphere, and not (also) in human lives on the earthly stage.[71] Paul's language of 'powers' thus denotes comprehensive features of reality which penetrate (what we call) the 'political' sphere, but only as it is enmeshed in larger and more comprehensive force-fields.

[70] Where Wright places Paul in ideological continuity with the biblical/Jewish tradition of monotheistic critique of paganism, I would place stronger emphasis on the new division of the cosmos created by the Christ-event (cf. Gal 1.4; 1 Cor 1.18–2.16), which strongly reshapes and reapplies the biblical categories themselves.

[71] The hermeneutical difficulty in handling this Pauline category has long been recognised: see G.B. Caird, *Principalities and Powers: A Study in Pauline Theology* (Oxford: Clarendon, 1956); W. Wink, *Naming the Powers: The Language of Power in the New Testament* (Philadelphia: Fortress, 1984); idem, *Engaging the Powers: Discernment and Resistance in an Age of Domination* (Minneapolis: Fortress, 1992).

Paul's theology is thus by no means 'apolitical' – neither privatised, confined to the level of individual piety, nor spiritualised, detached from the social and political realities of everyday life. His failure to name 'Rome' springs not from naivety or pietism (nor from fear of political openness), but because his systemic analysis of the world differs from ours: for him the 'political' is fused with other realities whose identity is clarified and named from the epistemological standpoint of the Christ-event. In this sense the Roman empire is not significant to Paul *qua the Roman empire*: it certainly features on his map, but under different auspices and as subservient to more significant powers.

Because Paul does not recognise the Roman (or any other) empire as an autonomous or self-contained political system, he does not assign it to one side or other of the battle-lines created by the Christ-event: different persons, facets, or events which *we* merge under the label 'the Roman empire' Paul could disaggregate according to their position in the *real* power-struggle of the cosmos. There were undoubtedly numerous aspects of Roman power that Paul would castigate as energised by the Flesh, by Sin or by Death, but since he was not opposed to Caesar or Rome *as such*, he could also recognise aspects of Roman rule that were at least compatible with the rule of God. His many different experiences of Roman power did not have to be aligned into straightforward opposition or support for 'the empire'. Because his criteria for evaluation derived from outside Rome's self-expression or self-definition, he was able to traverse the political conditions of the Roman world at a 'diagonal', orientated neither for nor against Rome in political terms. Inasmuch as the Roman empire operated by the power and wisdom of 'this world', opposed Christ and his people, or arrogated to itself false pretensions of significance, it was a manifestation of 'the present evil age' doomed to destruction (1 Cor 1–2; 1 Thess 5.1–11; Phil 1.27–30; Rom 8.31–39). Inasmuch as its authority was subservient to God's and it was capable of preserving and rewarding 'the good', it could be recognised and honoured accordingly (Rom 13.1–7). In this sense Romans 13 is no Pauline aberration, nor even under the hidden rubric of 'nevertheless' (Wright): it expresses Paul's judgment that political authorities can be subsumed under divine power, as well as under the power of Sin. Although this passage is not theologically integrated into Paul's Christology (and is hardly adequate as it stands as a 'political theology' in the modern sense), its juxtaposition with Rom 8.31–39 indicates that Paul can simultaneously offer highly differentiated evaluations of Roman power according to its context and expression.[72] What unifies these evaluations is not a political stance for

[72] On the place of Rom 13.1–7 (in its context) as offering a 'bifocal' reading of politics (engagement, but within a total other engagement), see the suggestive observations of T.

or against Rome, but a perspective which reads political history according to a different script. Just as Paul can be under the Torah or outside the Torah according to the demands of the gospel (1 Cor 9.20–21), so his stance towards the Roman empire is neither simple opposition nor obedience: it is a field of human reality criss-crossed and contested (like all others) by the opposing forces of Flesh and Spirit, and is subject to powers far greater than itself in the battle created by the gospel.

For these reasons, Paul's gospel is subversive of Roman imperial claims precisely by not opposing them within their own terms, but by reducing Rome's agency and historical significance to just one more entity in a much greater drama. To oppose the Roman empire *as such* would be to take its claims all too seriously: to upstage or outdo Rome would be to accept its terms of reference, even in surpassing them. Even turning Roman values on their head entails a form of confinement within the ideological system in which those values are defined.[73] Paul, more radically, reframes reality, including political reality, mapping the world in ways that reduce the claims of the imperial cult and of the Roman empire to comparative insignificance. Confronted by temples and statues of Caesar (as he undoubtedly was), Paul makes no special mention of them, not because he was politically naïve but because they represent for him the power of δαιμόνια (1 Cor 10.14–21) – the same δαιμόνια operative in other cults, with the same delusion and bankruptcy and the same incompatibility with the Lordship of Christ. From Paul's perspective, the Roman empire never was and never would be a significant actor in the drama of history: its agency was derived and dependent, co-opted by powers (divine or Satanic) far more powerful that itself. There was nothing significant about it being Roman – nothing new, nothing different, and nothing epoch-making. If Paul does not name or spotlight Rome, it was not because he thought it harmless or irrelevant, but because Rome did not rule the world, or write the script of history, or constitute anything unique. Its grand claims have been most effectively denied (and subverted) by Paul not by direct challenge, but by subsuming Rome into the undifferentiated crowd of 'the rest' (1 Thess 5.6), and by placing her, even in her supporting role for 'the good', under the anonymous title διάκονοι θεοῦ (Rom 13.4). At the deepest level Paul undermines Augustus and his succes-

---

Engberg-Pedersen, 'Paul's Stoicizing Politics in Romans 12–13: The Role of 13.1–10 in the Argument', *JSNT* 29 (2006) 163–72.

[73] In this sense, Kahl's deeply researched and moving reading of Galatians against the backdrop of the Pergamene altar (*Galatians Re-Imagined*) ends up confined to the mythic-political terms of the altar, even in reversing its dynamics of power. Paul sees the Galatians as subject to the power not of Rome, but of Sin (3.22) and of the στοιχεῖα τοῦ κόσμου (4.8–10), and these not as apolitical entities, but as powers that infiltrate and corrupt every sphere of human activity.

sors not by confronting them on their own terms, but by reducing them to bit-part players in a drama scripted by the cross and resurrection of Jesus.

We thus reach the paradoxical conclusion that Paul's theology is political precisely in rendering the Roman empire theologically insignificant. For Paul to accord the Roman empire the kind of significance imagined by Wright (and others) would not only grant Rome excessive respect but would reduce Paul's theology to the political terms that Rome herself was accustomed to use (and we are accustomed to repeat). Rather than adding a fresh dimension to Pauline theology, Wright's interpretation diminishes the range and significance of Paul's remapping of the cosmos. This Pauline cartography includes the 'political', but so fuses and enmeshes it with other realities within a broader frame of analysis that it refuses to interpret Rome (or any other empire) on its own terms. Since the Lordship of Christ is destined to operate in every sphere of existence (Phil 2.11), the Pauline gospel penetrates every dimension of life, including what we label 'political', but it declines to separate the political from the personal, the state-power of Sin from the interpersonal-power of Sin. In an age when 'politics-as-state-power' is proving increasingly inadequate as a framework in which to analyse the corruption, oppression and degradation of our world, it may in fact be a theological advantage that Paul does not oppose Rome *as Rome*, but opposes anti-God powers wherever and however they manifest themselves on the human stage.[74] The Roman empire was insignificant to Paul precisely because his peculiar epistemology placed politics on this wider and more complex stage; to interpret him otherwise is not only to reduce and misshape his theology, but to abandon a precious tool of analysis drawn from his distinctive theopolitics.

---

[74] One thinks, for instance, of the power wielded by international finance quite beyond state control, the prevalence of financial corruption operative through all levels of society, the multidimensional forces of evil active in the drug trade and sex-trafficking, the depletion of the world's resources caused by factors ranging from national arrogance to personal greed, and the forms of oppression that operate at every level from the neo-colonial slanting of the rules of trade to patriarchal systems of power and the domestic abuse of women and children. In the power of the Spirit and under the sign of the cross, those who belong to Christ are driven to oppose all these manifestation of the Flesh, operative in both political and non-political spheres (Gal 5.19–25). In forming communities which embody an alternative social and political configuration, they serve to counteract the power of the Flesh in its multiple and subtle operations.

Bibliography

Adams, E., 'First Century Models for Paul's Churches', in T.D. Still and D.G. Horrell, eds., *After the First Urban Christians: The Social-Scientific Study of Pauline Christianity Twenty-Five Years Later*. London: T & T Clark, 2009, 60–78.

–, *Constructing the World: A Study in Paul's Cosmological Language*. Edinburgh: T & T Clark, 2000.

Adams, E., and D.G. Horrell, eds., *Christianity at Corinth: The Quest for the Pauline Church*. Louisville: Westminster John Knox, 2004.

Alexander, L.C.A., ed., *Images of Empire*. Sheffield: Sheffield Academic, 1991.

Alexiou, M., *The Ritual Lament in Greek Tradition*. Cambridge: Cambridge University, 1974.

Alföldy, G., *Flamines Provinciae Hispaniae Citerioris*. Madrid: Instituto Español de Arqueologia 1973.

Amir, Y., 'Θεοκρατία as a Concept of Political Philosophy: Josephus' Presentation of Moses' *Politeia*' *SCI* 8–9 (1985–88) 83–105.

Ando, C., *Imperial Ideology and Provincial Loyalty in the Roman Empire*. Berkeley: University of California, 2000.

Ascough, R.S., 'A Question of Death: Paul's Community-Building Language in 1 Thessalonians 4:13–18' *JBL* 123 (2004) 509–30.

–, *Paul's Macedonian Associations: The Social Context of Philippians and 1 Thessalonians*. WUNT 2.161. Tübingen: Mohr Siebeck, 2003.

–, *What Are They Saying about The Formation of Pauline Churches?*. New York: Paulist, 1998.

Ashcroft, B., G. Griffiths and H. Tiffin, *Key Concepts in Post-Colonial Studies*. London: Routledge, 1998.

–, *Post-Colonial Studies: The Key Concepts*. 2nd ed. London: Routledge, 2001.

–, eds., *The Empire Writes Back: Theory and Practice in Post-Colonial Literature*. London: Routledge, 1989.

Assmann, J., *Ma'at: Gerechtigkeit und Unsterblichkeit im Alten Ägypten*. München: C.H. Beck, 1995.

Attridge, H., *The Interpretation of Biblical History in the Antiquitates Judaicae of Flavius Josephus*. Missoula: Scholars Press, 1976.

Balch, D.L., 'Household Codes', in D.E. Aune, ed., *Greco-Roman Literature and the New Testament: Selected Forms and Genres*. Atlanta: Scholars, 1988, 25–50.

–, *Let Wives be Submissive: The Domestic Code in 1 Peter*. Chico: Scholars, 1981.

Balsdon, J.P.V.D., *Life and Leisure in Ancient Rome.* London: The Bodley Head, 1969.

Bammel, E., 'Ein Beitrag zur paulinischen Staatsanschauung' *ThLZ* 85 (1960) 838–39.

Barclay, J.M.G., 'Conflict in Thessalonica' *CBQ* 55 (1993) 512–30.

–, 'Deviance and Apostasy: Some Applications of Deviance Theory to First Century Judaism and Christianity', in P.F. Esler, ed., *Modelling Early Christianity*. London: Routledge, 1995, 114–27; reprinted as chapter 6 in this volume.

–, 'Josephus v. Apion: Analysis of an Argument', in S. Mason, ed., *Understanding Josephus: Seven Perspectives*. Sheffield: Sheffield Academic Press, 1998, 194–221.

–, 'Judaism in Roman Dress', in J.U. Kalms and F. Siegert, eds., *Internationales Josephus-Kolloquium Aarhus 1999*. Münster: LIT, 2000, 231–45.

–, 'Paul among Diaspora Jews: Anomaly or Apostate?' *JSNT* 60 (1995) 89–120.

–, 'Snarling Sweetly: Josephus on Images and Idolatry', in S.C. Barton, ed., *Idolatry: False Worship in the Bible, Early Judaism and Christianity*. London: T & T Clark, 2007, 73–87; reprinted as chapter 17 in this volume.

–, 'The Empire Writes Back: Josephan Rhetoric in Flavian Rome', in J. Edmondson, S. Mason and J. Rives, eds., *Flavius Josephus and Flavian Rome*. Oxford: Oxford University, 2005, 315–32; reprinted as chapter 15 in this volume.

–, 'The Family as the Bearer of Religion in Judaism and Early Christianity', in H. Moxnes, ed., *Constructing Early Christian Families*. London: Routledge, 1997, 66–80.

–, 'The Politics of Contempt: Judaeans and Egyptians in Josephus' *Against Apion*', in J.M.G. Barclay, ed., *Negotiating Diaspora: Jewish Strategies in the Roman Empire*. London: T & T Clark, 2004, 109–207; reprinted as chapter 14 in this volume.

–, 'Thessalonica and Corinth: Social Contrasts in Pauline Christianity' *JSNT* 47 (1992) 49–74; reprinted as chapter 9 in this volume.

–, 'Who was Considered an Apostate in the Jewish Diaspora?', in G.N. Stanton and G. Stroumsa, eds., *Tolerance and Intolerance in Early Judaism and Christianity*. Cambridge: Cambridge University, 1998, 80–98; reprinted as chapter 7 in this volume.

–, *Colossians and Philemon*. New Testament Guides. Sheffield: Sheffield Academic, 1997.

–, *Flavius Josephus: Translation and Commentary. Vol. 10: Against Apion*. Leiden: Brill, 2007.

–, *Jews in the Mediterranean Diaspora from Alexander to Trajan (323 BCE–117 CE)*. Edinburgh: T & T Clark, 1996.

–, *Obeying the Truth. A Study of Paul's Ethics in Galatians.* Edinburgh: T & T Clark, 1988.

Bar-Kochva, B., *Pseudo-Hecataeus "On the Jews": Legitimizing the Jewish Diaspora*. Berkeley: University of California, 1996.

–, *The Image of the Jews in Greek Literature: The Hellenistic Period.* Berkeley: University of California, 2009.

Barley, N., *Dancing on the Grave: Encounters with Death*. London: John Murray, 1995.

Barraclough, R., 'Philo's Politics, Roman Rule and Hellenistic Judaism', *ANRW* II.12.1 (1980) 417–553.

Barrett, C.K., 'Christianity at Corinth', in *Essays on Paul.* London: SPCK, 1982, 1–27

–, *A Commentary on the Epistle to the Romans.* London: A & C Black, 1971.

–, *A Commentary on the First Epistle to the Corinthians.* 2nd ed. London: A & C Black, 1971.

Barth, M., and H. Blanke, *The Letter to Philemon*. Grand Rapids: Eerdmans, 2000.

Bartlett, J.R., ed., *Jews in the Hellenistic and Roman Cities*. London/New York: Routledge, 2002.

Barton, C.A., *Roman Honor: The Fire in the Bones*. Berkeley: University of California, 2001.

Barton, S.C., and G.H.R. Horsley, 'A Hellenistic Cult Group and the New Testament Churches' *JAC* 24 (1981) 7–41.

Beard, M., J. North and S. Price, *Religions of Rome*. 2 vols.: Cambridge: Cambridge University Press, 1998.

Becker, H.S., *Outsiders. Studies in the Sociology of Deviance*. New York: Free Press, 1963.

–, ed., *The Other Side: Perspectives on Deviance*. New York: Free Press, 1964.

Benko, S., 'The Edict of Claudius of A.D. 49 and the Instigator Chrestus' *TZ* 25 (1969) 406–18.

Ben-Yehuda, N., *Deviance and Moral Boundaries*. Chicago: University of Chicago, 1985.

Berger, K., 'Almosen für Israel' *NTS* 23 (1977) 180–204.

Berger, P.L., and T. Luckmann, *The Social Construction of Reality*. Anchor Books edition. New York: Doubleday, 1967.

Berkley, T.W., *From a Broken Covenant to Circumcision of the Heart: Pauline Exegesis in Rom 2:17–29*. Atlanta: Society of Biblical Literature, 2000.

Bernardi, B., *Age Class Systems: Social Institutions and Politics Based on Age*. Cambridge: Cambridge University, 1985.

Berthelot, K., 'Josephus' Use of Graeco-Roman Stereotypes of the Egyptians', in J.U. Kalms and F. Siegert, eds., *Internationales Josephus-Kolloquium Aarhus 1999*. Münster: LIT, 2000, 185–221.

–, *Philanthrôpia Judaica: Le débat autour de la "misanthropie" des lois juives dans l'Antiquité*. Leiden: Brill, 2003.

Besançon, A., *The Forbidden Image. An Intellectual History of Iconoclasm*. Chicago: University of Chicago, 2000.

Best, E., *A Commentary on the First and Second Epistles to the Thessalonians*. BNTC. London: A & C Black, 1972.

Bhabha, H.K., *The Location of Culture*. London: Routledge, 1994.

Bieringer, R., D. Pollefeyt and F. Vandecasteele-Vanneuville, eds., *Anti-Judaism and the Fourth Gospel*. Assen: van Gorcum, 2001.

Bilde, P., *Flavius Josephus between Jerusalem and Rome*. Sheffield: JSOT, 1988.

Binder, D.D., *Into the Temple Courts: The Place of the Synagogues in the Second Temple Period*. Atlanta: Society of Biblical Literature, 1999.

Birdsall, J.N., 'πρεσβύτης in Philemon 9: A Study in Conjectural Emendation' *NTS* 39 (1993) 625–30.

Bloch, R., *Antike Vorstellungen vom Judentums: Der Judenexkurs des Tacitus im Rahmen der griechisch-römischen Ethnographie*. Stuttgart: Franz Steiner, 2002.

Blumenfeld, B., *The Political Paul: Justice, Democracy and Kingship in a Hellenistic Framework*. Sheffield: Sheffield Academic, 2001.

Bockmuehl, M., '1 Thessalonians 2:14–16 and the Church in Jerusalem', in M.D. Hooker, ed., *Not in the Word Alone. The First Epistle to the Thessalonians*. St. Paul's Abbey, Rome: Benedictina, 2003, 55–87.

Bohak, G., 'Ethnic Stereotypes in the Greco-Roman World: Egyptians, Phoenicians, and Jews', in *Proceedings of the Twelfth World Congress of Jewish Studies*. Jerusalem: World Union of Jewish Studies, 2000, 7–15.

–, 'The Ibis and the Jewish Question: Ethnic Bias in the Greco-Roman World', in M. Mor, A. Oppenheimer, J. Pastor and D. R. Schwartz, eds., *Jews and Gentiles in the Holy Land in the Days of the Second Temple, the Mishnah and the Talmud*. Jerusalem: Ben Zvi, 2003, 27–43.

Borgen, P., 'Philo of Alexandria: A Critical and Synthetic Survey of Research since World War II', in *ANRW* II.21.1, 98–154.

–, *Philo, John and Paul. New Perspectives on Judaism and Early Christianity*. Atlanta: Scholars, 1987.

Bourdieu, P., *Outline of a Theory of Practice*. Cambridge: Cambridge University, 1977.

–, *The Logic of Practice*. Stanford: Stanford University, 1990.

Bowe, B. E., *A Church in Crisis: Ecclesiology and Paraenesis in Clement of Rome*. Minneapolis: Fortress, 1988.

Boyarin, D., *A Radical Jew. Paul and the Politics of Identity*. Berkeley / London: University of California, 1994.

–, *Border Lines: The Partition of Judaeo-Christianity*. Philadelphia: University of Pennsylvania, 2004.

–, *Carnal Israel: Reading Sex in Talmudic Culture*. Berkeley: University of California, 1993.

–, *Dying for God: Martyrdom and the Making of Judaism and Christianity*. Stanford: Stanford University, 1999.

Brent, A., *A Political History of Early Christianity*. London: T & T Clark, 2009.

–, *The Imperial Cult and the Development of Church Order: Concepts and Images of Authority in Paganism and Early Christianity before the Age of Cyprian*. VC Sup 45. Leiden: Brill, 1999.

Brown, P., *The Body and Society: Men, Women and Sexual Renunciation in Early Christianity.* London: Faber and Faber, 1989.

–, *The Cult of the Saints: Its Rise and Function in Latin Christianity*. London: SCM, 1981.

Brown, R. E., *The Community of the Beloved Disciple.* London: Chapman, 1979.

Brox, N., 'Pseudo-Paulus und Pseudo-Ignatius. Einige Topoi altchristlicher Pseudepigraphie' *VC* 30 (1976) 181–8.

–, *Der Erste Petrusbrief*. Zürich: Benziger, 1979.

–, *Die Pastoralbriefe*. 4th ed. Regensburg: Pustet, 1969.

Bruce, F. F., *1 and 2 Thessalonians*. Waco: Word, 1982.

Bryan, C., *Render to Caesar: Jesus, the Early Church and the Roman Superpower*. Oxford: Oxford University, 2005.

Bultmann, R., *Theology of the New Testament*. London: SCM, 1952.

Burr. V., *Tiberius Julius Alexander.* Bonn: Habelt, 1955.

Burtchaell, J. T., *From Synagogue to Church: Public Services and Offices in the Earliest Christian Assemblies*. Cambridge: Cambridge University, 1992.

Burton, A., *Diodorus Siculus, Book 1. A Commentary*. Leiden: Brill, 1972.

Caird, G. B., *Principalities and Powers: A Study in Pauline Theology*. Oxford: Clarendon, 1956.

Cameron, A., *Christianity and the Rhetoric of Empire: The Development of Christian Discourse*. Berkeley: University of California, 1991.
Campbell, R.A., *The Elders: Seniority within Earliest Christianity*. Edinburgh: T & T Clark, 1994.
Campbell, W.S., *Paul and the Creation of Christian Identity*. London: T & T Clark, 2006.
–, *Paul's Gospel in an Intercultural Context.* Frankfurt am Main: Peter Lang, 1992.
Cancik, H., 'Theokratie und Priesterherrschaft: Die mosiasche Verfassung bei Flavius Josephus, c. Apionem 2, 157–198', in J. Taubes, ed., *Religionstheorie und politische Theologie*. München/Paderborn/Wien/Zürich: Wilhelm Fink/Ferdinand Schöningh, 1987, 3.65–77.
Cancik, H., and K. Hitzl, eds., *Die Praxis der Herrscherverehrung in Rom und seinen Provinzen*. Tübingen: Mohr Siebeck, 2003.
Cardauns, B., 'Varro und die römische Religion: Zur Theologie, Wirkungsgeschichte und Leistung der *Antiquitates Rerum Divinarum*', *ANRW* II.16.1, 80–103.
Carroll, R.P., *Jeremiah*, OT Library. London: SCM, 1986.
Carter, B., and A. Sealey, 'Language, Structure and Agency: What Can Realist Social Theory Offer to Sociolinguistics?' *Journal of Sociolinguistics* 4 (2000) 3–20.
Carter, W., *The Roman Empire and the New Testament: An Essential Guide*. Nashville: Abingdon, 2006.
Cartledge, P., and A. Spawforth, *Hellenistic and Roman Sparta. A Tale of Two Cities*. 2nd ed. London: Routledge, 2002.
Catto, S.K., *Reconstructing the First-Century Synagogue: A Critical Analysis of Current Research*. London: T & T Clark, 2007.
Chadwick, H., 'St. Paul and Philo of Alexandria' *BJRL* 48 (1966) 286–307.
Chambers, J.K., *Sociolinguistic Theory*. 2nd ed. Oxford: Blackwell, 2003.
Champlin, E., *Nero.* Cambridge, Mass.: Harvard University, 2003.
Chester, S., *Conversion at Corinth: Perspectives on Conversion in Paul's Theology and the Corinthian Church*. Edinburgh: T & T Clark, 2003.
Christiansen, I., *Die Technik der allegorischen Auslegungswissenschaft bei Philon von Alexandrien*. Tübingen: Mohr Siebeck, 1969.
Claussen, C., *Versammlung, Gemeinde, Synagoge: das hellenistisch-jüdischer Umfeld der frühchristlichen Gemeinden*. Göttingen: Vandenhoeck & Ruprecht, 2002.
Cohen, S.J.D., 'Crossing the Boundary and Becoming a Jew' *HTR* 82 (1989) 13–33.
–, '"Anti-Semitism" in Antiquity: The Problem of Definition', in D. Berger, ed., *History and Hate: The Dimensions of Anti-Semitisms*. Philadelphia/New York/Jerusalem: Jewish Publication Society, 1986, 43–47.
Cokayne, K., *Experiencing Old Age in Ancient Rome*. London: Routledge, 2003.
Collins, J.J., 'A Symbol of Otherness: Circumcision and Salvation in the First Century', in J. Neusner and E.S. Frerichs, eds., *"To See Ourselves as Others See Us". Christians, Jews, "Others" in Late Antiquity*. Chico: Scholars, 1985, 163–86.
–, *Between Athens and Jerusalem: Jewish Identity in the Hellenistic Diaspora.* New York: Crossroad, 1986.
–, *Between Athens and Jerusalem: Jewish Identity in the Hellenistic Diaspora*. 2nd ed. Grand Rapids: Eerdmans, 2000.
Colson, F.H., *The Week.* Cambridge: Cambridge University, 1926.
Connolly, R.H., *Didascalia Apostolorum*. Oxford: Oxford University, 1929.

Corley, K. E., *Maranatha: Women's Funerary Rituals and Christian Origins*. Minneapolis: Fortress Press, 2010.

Coser, L. A., *The Functions of Social Conflict*. London: Routledge & Kegan Paul, 1956.

Cranfield, C. E. B., *The Epistle to the Romans*. ICC. Edinburgh: T & T Clark, 1979.

Crossan, J. D., and J. L. Reed, *In Search of Paul: How Jesus' Apostle Opposed Rome's Empire with God's Kingdom*. New York: HarperSanFrancisco, 2005.

Crouch, J. E., *The Origin and Intention of the Colossian Haustafel*. Göttingen: Vandenhoeck & Ruprecht, 1972.

Cullmann, O., *The State in the New Testament*. London: SCM, 1955.

Cumont, F., *After Life in Roman Paganism*. Reprint. New York: Dover, 1922.

Danforth, L. M., *The Death Rituals of Rural Greece*. Princeton: Princeton University, 1982.

Daniélou, J., *Philon d'Alexandrie*. Paris: Fayard, 1958.

Davis, N. J., *Sociological Constructions of Deviance: Perspectives and Issues in the Field*. 2nd ed. Dubuque: W. C. Brown, 1980.

Dawson, D., *Allegorical Readers and Cultural Revision in Alexandria*, Berkeley: University of California, 1992.

de Boer, M. C., 'The Meaning of the Phrase τὰ στοιχεῖα τοῦ κόσμου in Galatians' *NTS* 53 (2007) 204–24.

de Jonge, M., 'Josephus und die Zukunftserwartungen seines Volkes', in O. Betz et al., eds., *Josephus-Studien*. Göttingen: Vandenhoeck & Ruprecht, 1974, 205–19.

de Lange, N., 'The Origins of Anti-Semitism: Ancient Evidence and Modern Interpretations', in S. L. Gilman and S. T. Katz, eds., *Anti-Semitism in Times of Crisis*. New York / London: New York University, 1991, 21–37.

de Vos, C. S., *Church and Community Conflicts: The Relationships of the Thessalonian, Corinthian and Philippian Churches with the wider Civic Communities*. Atlanta: Scholars, 1999.

Deissmann, A., *Light from the Ancient East*. Trans. by L. R. M. Strachan from the 4th revised German edition (1922). London: Hodder and Stoughton, 1927.

Deming, W., *Paul on Marriage and Celibacy: The Hellenistic Background of 1 Corinthians 7*. 2nd edn. Grand Rapids: Eerdmans, 2004.

Desideri, P., '*Lycurgus*: The Spartan Ideal in the Age of Trajan', in P. A. Stadter and L. van der Stockt, eds., *Sage and Emperor: Plutarch, Greek Intellectuals, and Roman Power in the Time of Trajan (98–117 A. D.)*. Leuven: Leuven University, 2002, 315–27.

Dexinger, F., 'Limits of Tolerance in Judaism: The Samaritan Example', in E. P. Sanders, A. I. Baumgarten and A. Mendelson, eds., *Jewish and Christian Self-Definition*. vol. 2. London: SCM, 1981, 88–114.

Dibelius, M., and H. Greeven, *An die Kolosser, Epheser und Philemon*. HNT 12. 3rd ed. Tübingen: Mohr Siebeck, 1953.

Dibelius, M., and H. Conzelmann, *The Pastoral Epistles*. Hermeneia. Philadelphia: Fortress, 1972.

Dillon, J., *The Middle Platonists: A Study of Platonism 80 B. C. to A. D. 200*, London: Duckworth, 1977, 146–48.

Dodd, C. H., *The Epistle of Paul to the Romans*, London: Hodder & Stoughton, 1932.

Doering, L., *Schabbat: Sabbathalacha und -praxis im antiken Judentum und Urchristentum*. TSAJ: Tübingen: Mohr Siebeck, 1999.
Donfried, K. P., 'The Cults of Thessalonica and the Thessalonian Correspondence' *NTS* 31 (1985) 336–56.
–, *Paul, Thessalonica and Early Christianity*. London: T & T Clark, 2002.
–, ed., *The Romans Debate*. rev. ed. Edinburgh: T & T Clark, 1991.
Donfried, K. P., and P. Richardson, eds., *Judaism and Christianity in First-Century Rome*. Grand Rapids: Eerdmans, 1998.
Downes, D., and R. Rock, *Understanding Deviance: A Guide to the Sociology of Crime and Rule-breaking*. 2nd ed. Oxford: Clarendon, 1988.
Duff, T., *Plutarch's Lives. Exploring Virtue and Vice*. Oxford: Oxford University, 1999.
Duncan-Jones, R. P., 'Age-Rounding, Illiteracy and Social Differentiation in the Roman Empire' *Chiron* 7 (1977) 333–53.
Dunn, J. D. G., 'Spirit (NT)', in C. Brown, ed., *New International Dictionary of New Testament Theology*. Exeter: Paternoster, 1978, 3:693–707.
–, *Jesus, Paul and the Law*. London: SPCK, 1990.
–, *Romans 1–8*. WBC 38A, Waco: Word, 1988.
–, *Romans 9–16*. WBC 38B. Waco: Word, 1988.
–, *The Epistles to the Colossians and to Philemon*. Grand Rapids: Eerdmans, 1996.
–, *The Partings of the Ways*. London: SCM, 1991.
–, *The Theology of Paul the Apostle*. Edinburgh: T & T Clark, 1998.
–, ed., *Jews and Christians: The Parting of the Ways AD 70–135*. WUNT 66. Tübingen: Mohr Siebeck, 1992.
Dupré i Raventós, X., 'Un gran complejo provincial de época flavia en Tarragona; aspectos cronologicos', in W. Trimmlich and P. Zanker, eds., *Stadtbild und Ideologie*. Munich: Verlag der Bayerischen Akademie der Wissenschaften, 1990.
Ebel, E., *Die Attraktivität früher christlicher Gemeinden: Die Gemeinde von Korinth im Spiegel griechisch-römischer Vereine*. WUNT 2.178. Tübingen: Mohr Siebeck, 2004.
Ehrman, B., *The Apostolic Fathers*. LCL. Cambridge, Mass.: Harvard, 2003.
Eilberg-Schwartz, H., *The Savage in Judaism*. Bloomington: Indiana University, 1990.
Elledge, C. D., *Life after Death in Early Judaism: The Evidence of Josephus*. WUNT 2.208. Tübingen: Mohr Siebeck, 2006.
Elliott, J. H., *Social-Scientific Criticism of the New Testament*. London: SPCK, 1993.
Elliott, J. K., *The Apocryphal New Testament*. Oxford: Clarendon, 1993.
Elliott, N., 'Ideological Closure in the Christ-Event: a Marxist Response to Alain Badiou's Paul', in Harink, ed., *Paul, Philosophy and the Theopolitical Vision*, 135–54.
–, 'Romans 13:1–7 in the Context of Imperial Propaganda', in Horsley, ed., *Paul and Empire*, 184–204.
–, *Liberating Paul: The Justice of God and the Politics of the Apostle*. Maryknoll, NY: Orbis, 1994.
–, *The Arrogance of Nations: Reading Romans in the Shadow of Empire*. Minneapolis: Fortress, 2008.
Elsner, J., 'Image and Ritual: Reflections on the Religious Appreciation of Classical Art' *Classical Quarterly* 46 (1996) 513–31.

Engberg-Pedersen, T., '1 Corinthians 11:16 and the Character of Pauline Exhortation' *JBL* 110 (1991) 679–89.

–, 'Paul's Stoicizing Politics in Romans 12–13: The Role of 13.1–10 in the Argument' *JSNT* 29 (2006) 163–72.

–, 'Proclaiming the Lord's Death: 1 Corinthians 11:17–34 and the Forms of Paul's Theological Argument', in D.M. Hay, ed., *Pauline Theology, II: 1 and 2 Corinthians.* Minneapolis: Fortress, 1993, 103–132.

–, 'The Gospel and Social Practice According to 1 Corinthians' *NTS* 33 (1987) 557–84.

–, *Cosmology and Self in the Apostle Paul: The Material Spirit.* Oxford: Oxford University, 2010.

–, ed., *Beyond the Judaism/Hellenism Divide.* Louisville/London: Westminster John Knox, 2001.

Erikson, K.T., 'Notes on the Sociology of Deviance' *Social Problems* 9 (1962) 307–314.

–, *Wayward Puritans: A Study in the Sociology of Deviance.* New York: John Wiley and Sons, 1966.

Esler, P.F., 'Models in New Testament Interpretation: A Reply to David Horrell' *JSNT* 78 (2000) 107–113.

–, *Conflict and Identity in Romans: The Social Setting of Paul's Letter.* Minneapolis: Fortress, 2003.

–, *Galatians.* New Testament Readings. London/New York, 1988.

Étienne, R., *Le Culte Impérial dans la Péninsule Ibérique d'Auguste à Dioclétien.* Bibliothèque des Écoles Françaises d'Athènes et de Rome 191. Paris: de Boccard, 1958.

Étienne, S., 'Réflexion sur l'apostasie de Tibérius Julius Alexander' *Studia Philonica Annual* 12 (2000) 122–42.

Eyben, E., 'Die Einteilung des menschlichen Lebens im römishen Altertum' *Rheinisches Museum* 116 (1973) 150–90.

–, 'Old Age in Greco-Roman Antiquity and Early Christianity', in T.M. Falkner and J. de Luce, eds., *Old Age in Greek and Latin Literature.* Albany: SUNY, 1989, 230–51.

Fee, G.D., *The First Epistle to the Corinthians.* NICNT. Grand Rapids: Eerdmans, 1987.

Feeney, D.C., *Literature and Religion at Rome: Cultures, Contexts and Beliefs.* Cambridge: Cambridge University, 1988.

Feldman, L.H., 'The Orthodoxy of the Jews in Hellenistic Egypt' *JSS* 22 (1960) 215–37.

–, *Jew and Gentile in the Ancient World. Attitudes and Interactions from Alexander to Justinian.* Princeton: Princeton University, 1993.

Feldman, L.H., and J.R. Levison, eds., *Josephus'* Contra Apionem: *Studies in its Character and Context with a Latin Concordance to the Portion Missing in Greek.* Leiden: Brill, 1996.

Fishwick, D., 'Four Temples at Tarraco', in A. Small, ed., *Subject and Ruler: The Cult of the Ruling Power in Classical Antiquity.* Journal of Roman Archaeology Supplement 17. Ann Arbor: University of Michigan, 1996, 165–84.

–, *The Imperial Cult in the Latin West.* 3 volumes, with multiple parts. Leiden: Brill, 1987–2005.

Fitzmyer, J. A., *Romans.* Anchor Bible 33. New York: Doubleday, 1993.

Forkman, G., *The Limits of the Religious Community.* Lund: Gleerup, 1972.

Foucault, M., *Discipline and Punish. The Birth of the Prison*. London: Penguin, 1991.

Frame, J. E., *A Critical and Exegetical Commentary on the Epistles of St. Paul to the Thessalonians*. Edinburgh: T & T Clark, 1912.

Frankfurter, D., 'Lest Egypt's City be Deserted: Religion and Ideology in the Egyptian Response to the Jewish Revolt (116–17 C.E.)' *JJS* 43 (1992) 203–20.

Fredriksen, P., 'Judaizing the Nations: the Ritual Demands of Paul's Gospel' *NTS* 56 (2010) 232–52.

Freistedt, E., *Altchristliche Totengedächtnistage und ihre Beziehung zum Jenseitsglauben und Totenkultus des Antike*. Münster: Aschendorff, 1928.

Fridrichsen, A., 'Der wahre Jude und sein Lob' *Symbolae Arctoae* 1 (1922) 39–49.

Friedrich, G., '1 Thessalonicher 5,1–11, der apologetische Einschub eines Späteren' *ZTK* 10 (1973) 288–315.

Friesen, S. J., *Imperial Cults and the Apocalypse of John: Reading Revelation in the Ruins*. New York: Oxford University, 2001.

–, *Twice Neokoros: Ephesus, Asia and the Cult of the Flavian Imperial Family*. Leiden: Brill, 1993.

Friesen, S. J., D. N. Schowalter and J. C. Walters, eds., *Corinth in Context: Comparative Studies on Religion and Society*. Leiden: Brill, 2010.

Furnish, V. P., *II Corinthians.* AB. New York: Doubleday, 1984.

Gager, J. G., *Reinventing Paul.* Oxford: Oxford University, 2000.

Gallas, S., '"Fünfmal vierzig weniger einen …" Die an Paulus vollzogenen Synagogalstrafen nach 2Kor 11,24' *ZNW* 81 (1990) 178–91.

Garland, R., *The Greek Way of Death*. London: Duckworth, 1985.

–, *The Greek Way of Life*. London: Duckworth, 1990.

Garnsey, P., *Ideas of Slavery from Aristotle to Augustine*. Cambridge: Cambridge University, 1996.

Gaventa, B., *First and Second Thessalonians*. Louisville: John Knox, 1998.

Geertz, C., 'Religion as a Cultural System', in *The Interpretation of Cultures*. New York: Fontana, 1993, 87–125.

Georgi, D., *Theocracy in Paul's Practice and Theology*. Trans. by D. E. Green. Minneapolis: Fortress, 1991.

Gerber, C., *Ein Bild des Judentums für Nichtjuden von Flavius Josephus. Untersuchungen zu seiner Schrift Contra Apionem*. Leiden: Brill, 1997.

Gibbs, J. P., 'Conceptions of Deviant Behaviour: The Old and the New' *Pacific Sociological Review* 9 (1966) 9–14.

Gielen, M., *Tradition und Theologie neutestamentliche Haustafelethik*. BBB 75. Frankfurt a. M.: Anton Hain, 1990.

Gilbert, M., *La critique des dieux dans le Livre de la Sagesse (Sg 13–15)*. Rome: Biblical Institute, 1973.

Gilliard, F. D., 'The Problem of the Anti-Semitic Comma between 1 Thessalonians 2:14 and 15' *NTS* 35 (1989) 481–502.

Glancy, J. A., *Slavery in Early Christianity*. Oxford: Oxford University Press, 2002.

–, 'Obstacles to Slaves' Participation in the Corinthian Church' *JBL* 117 (1998) 481–501.

Gleason, M., 'Mutilated Messengers: Body Language in Josephus', in S. Goldhill, ed., *Being Greek under Rome: Cultural Identity, the Second Sophistic and the Development of Empire*. Cambridge: Cambridge University, 2001, 50–85.

Gnilka, C., 'Greisenalter' *RAC* 12 (1983) 995–1094.

–, *Aetas Spiritualis: die Überwindung der natürlichen Altersstufen als Ideal frühchristlichen Lebens*. Bonn: Hanstein, 1972.

Goldhill, S., ed., *Being Greek Under Rome: Cultural Identity, the Second Sophistic and the Development of Empire*. Cambridge: Cambridge University, 2001.

Goodenough, E., *The Politics of Philo Judaeus: Practice and Theory*. New Haven: Yale University, 1938.

Goodman, M., 'Josephus as a Roman Citizen' in F. Parente and J. Sievers, eds., *Josephus and the History of the Graeco-Roman Period.* Leiden: Brill, 1994, 329–38.

–, 'Modeling the "Parting of the Ways"', in his *Judaism in the Roman World: Collected Essays*. Leiden: Brill, 2007, 175–8.

–, 'Nerva, the *Fiscus Judaicus* and Jewish Identity' *JRS* 79 (1989) 40–44.

–, 'The *Fiscus Judaicus* and Gentile Attitudes to Judaism in Flavian Rome', in J. Edmondson, S. Mason and J. Rives, eds., *Flavius Josephus in Flavian Rome*. Oxford: Oxford University, 2005, 167–77.

–, 'The Persecution of Paul by Diaspora Jews', in his *Judaism in the Roman World*. Leiden: Brill, 2007, 145–52.

–, *Rome and Jerusalem: The Clash of Ancient Civilizations*. London: Allen Lane, 2007.

–, ed., *Jews in a Graeco-Roman World*. Oxford: Oxford University, 1998.

Gordon, R. L., 'The Real and the Imaginary: Production and Religion in the Graeco-Roman World' *Art History* 2 (1979) 5–34.

Goudriaan, K., 'Ethnical Strategies in Graeco-Roman Egypt', in P. Bilde et al., eds., *Ethnicity in Hellenistic Egypt*. Aarhus: Aarhus University, 1992, 74–99.

Goulder, M. D., 'σοφία in Corinthians' *NTS* 37 (1991) 516–34.

Gove, W. R., ed., *The Labelling of Deviance: Evaluating a Perspective*. New York: John Wiley and Sons, 1975.

Grabbe, L. L., 'Orthodoxy in Judaism: What are the Issues?' *JSJ* 8 (1977) 149–53.

–, *Etymology in Early Jewish Interpretation: The Hebrew Names in Philo*. Atlanta: Scholars, 1988.

Gradel, I., *Emperor Worship and Roman Religion*. Oxford: Clarendon Press, 2002.

Graver, M. R., *Stoicism and Emotion*. Chicago: University of Chicago, 2007.

Griffiths, J. G., *The Conflict of Horus and Seth from Egyptian and Classical Sources: A Study in Mythology*. Liverpool: University of Liverpool, 1960.

Grimm, C. L. W., *Das Buch des Weisheit.* Kurzgefasstes exegetisches Handbuch zu den Apokryphen des Alten Testaments. Leipzig: Hirzel,1860.

Gruen, E. S., 'Greeks and Jews: Mutual Misperceptions in Josephus' *Contra Apionem*', in C. Bakhos, ed., *Ancient Judaism in its Hellenistic Context*. Leiden: Brill, 2005, 31–51.

–, 'The Purported Jewish-Spartan Affiliation', in R. W. Wallace and E. M. Harris, eds., *Transitions to Empire. Essays in Greco-Roman History, 360–146 B. C., in honor of E. Badian*. Norman / London, University of Oklahoma, 1996, 254–69.

–, *Diaspora: Jews Amidst Greeks and Romans*. Cambridge, Mass. Harvard University, 2002.

–, *Heritage and Hellenism: The Reinvention of Jewish Tradition*. Berkeley: University of California, 1988.

Gundry, R. H., 'The Hellenization of Dominical Tradition and the Christianization of Jewish Tradition in the Eschatology of 1–2 Thessalonians' *NTS* 33 (1987) 161–78.

Guterman, S. L., *Religious Toleration and Persecution in Ancient Rome*. London: Aiglon, 1951.

Gutsfeld, A., and D.-A. Koch, eds., *Vereine, Synagogen und Gemeinden im kaiserzeitlichen Kleinasien*. Tübingen: Mohr Siebeck, 2006.

Haaland, G., 'Jewish Laws for a Roman Audience: Toward an Understanding of *Contra Apionem*', in J. U. Kalms and F. Siegert, eds., *Internationales Josephus-Kolloquium Brüssel 1998*. Münster: LIT Verlag, 1999, 282–304.

Hadas-Lebel, M., *De Providentia I et II: les oeuvres de Philon d'Alexandrie.* Paris: Cerf, 1973.

Hafemann, S., *Paul, Moses and the History of Israel*. Tübingen: Mohr Siebeck, 1995.

Hakola, R., *Identity Matters: John, The Jews and Jewishness*. Leiden: Brill, 2005.

Halbertal, M., and A. Margalit, *Idolatry*. Cambridge, Mass.: Harvard University, 1992.

Hall, J., *Ethnic Identity in Greek Antiquity*. Cambridge: Cambridge University, 1997.

Hall, R. G., 'Josephus' *Contra Apionem* and Historical Inquiry in the Roman Rhetorical Schools', in L. H. Feldman and J. R. Levison, eds., *Josephus'* Contra Apionem: *Studies in its Character and Context with a Latin Concordance to the Portion Missing in Greek.* Leiden: Brill, 1996, 229–49.

Halliday, M. A. K., *Language as Social Semiotic*. London: Edward Arnold, 1978.

Hardin, J. K., *Galatians and the Imperial Cult*. WUNT 2.237. Tübingen: Mohr Siebeck, 2008.

Hare, D. R. A., *The Theme of Jewish Persecution of Christians in the Gospel according to Matthew*. SNTSMS 6. Cambridge: Cambridge University, 1967.

Harink, D., ed., *Paul, Philosophy and the Theopolitical Vision: Critical Engagements with Agamben, Badiou, Žižek, and Others*. Eugene: Cascade Books, 2010.

Harland, P. A., *Dynamics of Identity in the World of the Early Christians: Associations, Judeans and Cultural Minorities*. New York / London: T & T Clark, 2009.

–, *Associations, Synagogues, and Congregations*. Minneapolis: Fortress, 2003.

Harlow, M., and R. Laurence, *Growing Up and Growing Old in Ancient Rome*. London: Routledge, 2002.

Harnisch, W., *Eschatologische Existenz: Ein exegetischer Beitrag zum Sachanliegen von I. Thessalonicher 4,13–5,11*. Göttingen: Vandenhoeck & Ruprecht, 1973.

Harrill, J. A., *Slaves in the New Testament: Literary, Social and Moral Dimensions*. Minneapolis: Fortress, 2006.

–, *The Manumission of Slaves in Early Christianity*. Tübingen: Mohr Siebeck, 1995.

Harris-Shapiro, C., *Messianic Judaism*. Boston: Beacon, 1999.

Harvey, A. E., 'Forty Strokes Save One: Social Aspects of Judaizing and Apostasy', in A. E. Harvey, ed., *Alternative Approaches to New Testament Study.* London: SPCK, 1985, 79–96.

Hatch, E., *The Organization of the Early Christian Churches*. 2nd ed. London: Rivingtons, 1882.

Hay, D.M., 'Philo's References to Other Allegorists' *Studia Philonica* 6 (1979–80) 41–75.

Hays, R.B., *Echoes of Scripture in the Letters of Paul.* New Haven: Yale University, 1989.

Hayward, R., 'Observations on Idols in Septuagint Pentateuch', in S.C. Barton, ed., *Idolatry. False Worship in the Bible, Early Judaism and Christianity.* London: T & T Clark, 2007, 40–57.

Hecht, R.D., 'The Exegetical Contexts of Philo's Interpretation of Circumcision', in F.E. Greenspahn et al., eds., *Nourished with Peace. Studies in Hellenistic Judaism in Memory of Samuel Sandmel.* Chico: Scholars, 1984, 51–79.

Heemstra, M., *The* Fiscus Judaicus *and the Parting of the Ways.* WUNT 2.277. Tübingen: Mohr Siebeck, 2010.

Helck, W., 'Die Ägypter und die Fremden' *Saeculum* 15 (1964) 103–16.

Hendrix, H.L., 'Archaeology and Eschatology at Thessalonica', in B.A. Pearson, ed., *The Future of Early Christianity.* Minneapolis: Fortress, 1991, 107–18.

Hengel, M., *The Pre-Christian Paul.* London: SCM, 1991.

Hering, J.P., *The Colossian and Ephesian* Hausafeln *in Theological Context.* New York: Peter Lang, 2007.

Hertz, R., *Death and the Right Hand.* Glencoe, Ill.: Free Press, 1960.

Hill, C., *Change and Continuity in Seventeenth Century England.* London: Weidenfeld and Nicholson, 1974.

Hochschild, R., *Socialgeschichtliche Exegese. Entwicklung, Geschichte und Methodik einer neutestamentlichen Forschungsrichtung.* NTOA 42. Göttingen: Vandenhoeck & Ruprecht, 1999.

Hoffman, L., *Covenant of Blood: Circumcision and Gender in Rabbinic Judaism.* Chicago: University of Chicago, 1996.

Hoffmann, P., *Die Toten in Christus.* Münster: Aschendorff, 1966.

Holladay, C.R., *Fragments from Hellenistic Jewish Authors.* 3 vols. Chico/Atlanta: Scholars, 1983, 1989, 1995.

Hollis, A.S., *Ovid: Ars Amatoria Book One.* Oxford: Clarendon, 1977.

Holmberg, B., 'Early Christian Identity – Some Conclusions', in B. Holmberg, ed., *Exploring Early Christian Identity.* WUNT 226. Tübingen: Mohr Siebeck, 2008, 173–78.

–, 'Jewish *versus* Christian Identity in the early Church?' *Revue Biblique* 105 (1998) 397–425.

–, 'Understanding the First Hundred Years of Christian Identity', in B. Holmberg, ed., *Exploring Early Christian Identity.* WUNT 226. Tübingen: Mohr Siebeck, 2008, 1–32.

–, *Paul and Power: The Structure of Authority in the Primitive Church as Reflected in the Pauline Epistles.* Lund: Gleerup, 1978.

–, *Sociology and the New Testament.* Minneapolis: Fortress, 1990.

Holmberg, B., and M. Winninge, eds., *Identity Formation in the New Testament.* WUNT 227. Tübingen: Mohr Siebeck, 2008.

Holmes, J., *An Introduction to Social Linguistics.* London: Longman, 2002.

Holtz, T., 'The Judgment on the Jews and the Salvation of All Israel: 1 Thess 2,15–16 and Rom 11,25–26', in R.F. Collins, ed., *The Thessalonian Correspondence.* Leuven: Leuven University, 1990, 284–94.

–, *Der erste Brief an die Thessalonicher*. EKK. Neukirchen-Vluyn: Neukirchener, 1986.

Hopkins, K., *A World Full of Gods. Pagans, Jews and Christians in the Roman Empire*. London: Phoenix, 1999.

–, *Conquerors and Slaves*. Cambridge: Cambridge University, 1978.

–, *Death and Renewal*. Cambridge: Cambridge University, 1983.

Horbury, W., 'Extirpation and Excommunication' *VT 35* (1985) 13–38.

–, 'The Benediction of the *Minim* and Early Jewish Christian Controversy' *JTS* n.s. 33 (1982) 19–61.

Horbury, W., and D. Noy, eds., *Jewish Inscriptions of Graeco-Roman Egypt*. Cambridge: Cambridge University, 1992.

Horn, F. W., 'Paulus and der herodianische Tempel' *NTS* 53 (2007) 184–203.

–, *Das Angeld des Geistes*. Göttingen: Vandenhoeck & Ruprecht, 1992.

Horrell, D. G., 'Idol-Food, Idolatry and Ethics in Paul', in Barton, ed., *Idolatry*, 120–40.

–, 'Between Confirmity and Resistance: Beyond the Balch-Elliott Debate: Towards a Postcolonial Reading of 1 Peter', in R. L. Webb and B. Bauman-Martin, ed., *Reading First Peter with New Eyes*. London: Continuum, 2007, 111–43.

–, 'Models and Methods in Social-Scientific Interpretation: A Response to Philip Esler' *JSNT* 78 (2000) 83–105.

–, 'Pauline Churches or Early Christian Churches? Unity, Disagreement, and the Eucharist', in A. Alexeev et al., eds., *Einheit der Kirche im Neuen Testament*. WUNT 218. Tübingen: Mohr Siebeck, 2008, 185–203.

–, 'Social Sciences Studying Formative Christian Phenomena: A Creative Movement', in A. J. Blasi, J. Duhaime and P.-A. Turcotte, eds., *Handbook of Early Christianity: Social Scientific Approaches*. Walnut Creek: Altamira, 2002, 3–28.

–, 'The Label Χριστιανός: I Pt 4:16 and the Formation of Christian Identity' *JBL* 126 (2007) 361–81.

–, 'Whither Social-Scientific Approaches to New Testament Interpretation? Reflections on Contested Methodologies and the Future', in Still and Horrell, eds., *After the First Urban Christians*, 6–20.

–, *The Social Ethos of the Corinthian Correspondence: Interests and Ideology from 1 Corinthians to 1 Clement*. Edinburgh: T & T Clark, 1996.

Horsley, R. A., '"How can Some of you Say that there Is no Resurrection of the Dead?": Spiritual Elitism in Corinth' *NovT* 20 (1978) 203–31.

–, 'Consciousness and Freedom among the Corinthians: 1 Corinthians 8–10' *CBQ* 40 (1978) 574–89.

–, 'Pneumatikos vs. Psychikos: Distinctions of Spiritual Status among the Corinthians' *HTR* 69 (1976) 269–88

–, *Jesus and Empire*. Minneapolis: Fortress, 2002.

–, ed., *Hidden Transcripts and the Arts of Resistance: Applying the Work of James C. Scott to Jesus and Paul*. Semeia Studies 48. Atlanta: Society of Biblical Literature, 2004.

–, ed., *Paul and Empire: Religion and Power in Roman Imperial Society*. Harrisburg: Trinity Press International, 1997.

–, ed., *Paul and Politics: Ekklesia, Israel, Imperium, Interpretation*. Harrisburg: Trinity Press International, 2000.

–, ed., *Paul and the Roman Imperial Order*. Harrisburg: Trinity Press International, 2004.

Huddart, D., *Homi K. Bhabha*. London: Routledge, 2006.

Hurd, J. C., *The Origin of I Corinthians.* London: SPCK, 1965.

Isaac, B., *The Invention of Racism in Classical Antiquity*. Princeton: Princeton University, 2004.

Isaac, J., *Genèse de l'Antisémitisme*. Paris: Calmann-Levy, 1956.

Jal, P., *Florus, Oeuvres*. Budé edition, 2 vols. Paris: Société d'Édition "Les Belles Lettres", 1967.

Jenkins, R., *Pierre Bourdieu*. London: Routledge, 1992.

–, *Social Identity*. London: Routledge, 2004.

Jewett, R., *Dating Paul's Life.* London: SCM, 1979.

–, *Romans*. Hermeneia. Minneapolis: Fortress, 2007.

–, *The Thessalonian Correspondence.* Philadelphia: Fortress, 1986.

Johnson Hodge, C., *If Sons, Then Heirs: A Study of Kinship and Ethnicity in the Letters of Paul*. Oxford: Oxford University, 2007.

Johnson, L. T., 'The New Testament's Anti-Jewish Slander and the Conventions of Ancient Rhetoric' *JBL* 108 (1986) 419–41.

Johnson, S., *Historical Fiction and Hellenistic Jewish Identity: Third Maccabees in its Cultural Context*. Berkeley: University of California Press, 2004.

Jones, C. P., *Plutarch and Rome*. Oxford: Clarendon, 1971.

Judge, E. A., 'Contemporary Political Models for the Inter-Relations of the New Testament Churches' *RTR* 22 (1963) 65–75.

–, 'The Social Identity of the First Christians: A Question of Method in Religious History', in D. M. Scholer, ed., *Social Distinctives of the Christians in the First Century: Pivotal Essays by E. A. Judge*. Peabody, MA: Hendrickson, 2008, 117–36.

–, *The Social Pattern of Christian Groups in the First Century*. London: Tyndale, 1960; reprinted in D. M. Scholer, ed., *Social Distinctives of the Christians in the First Century: Pivotal Essays by E. A. Judge*. Peabody, MA: Hendrickson, 2008, 1–56.

Juster, J., *Les Juifs dans l'Empire Romain*. Paris: P. Geuthner, 1914.

Kahl, B., *Galatians Re-Imagined: Reading with the Eyes of the Vanquished*. Minneapolis: Fortress, 2010.

Karris, R. J., 'Romans 14:1–15:13 and the Occasion of Romans', in K. P. Donfried, ed., *The Romans Debate.* rev. ed. Edinburgh: T & T Clark, 1991, 65–84.

Käsemann, E., 'The Spirit and the Letter', in *Perspectives on Paul.* London: SCM, 1971, 138–66.

–, *An die Römer*. HNT 8 a. 4th ed. Tübingen: Mohr Siebeck, 1980.

–, *Commentary on Romans*. Trans. by G. Bromiley. London: SCM, 1980.

Kasher, A., 'Polemic and Apologetic Methods of Writing in *Contra Apionem*', in L. H. Feldman and J. R. Levison, eds., *Josephus'* Contra Apionem: *Studies in its Character and Context*. Leiden: Brill, 1996, 143–86.

–, *The Jews in Hellenistic and Roman Egypt. The Struggle for Equal Rights.* Tübingen: Mohr Siebeck, 1985.

Keay, S. J., *Roman Spain*. Berkeley: University of California, 1988.

Kim, S., *Christ and Caesar: The Gospel and the Roman Empire in the Writings of Paul and Luke*. Grand Rapids: Eerdmans, 2008.

Kimber Buell, D., *Why This New Race: Ethnic Reasoning in Early Christianity*. New York: Columbia University, 2005.

Kitsuse, J.I., 'Societal Reaction to Deviant Behaviour: Problems of Theory and Method' *Social Problems* 9 (1962) 247–256.

Klauck, H.-J., 4 *Makkabäerbuch*. JSHRZ 3.6. Gütersloh: Mohn, 1989.

–, *The Religious Context of Early Christianity: A Guide to Graeco-Roman Religions*. E.T. by B. McNeil: Edinburgh: T & T Clark, 2003.

Klein, C., *Theologie und Anti-Judaismus*. München: Chr. Kaiser, 1975.

Klijn, A.F.J., '1 Thessalonians 4.13–18 and its Background in Apocalyptic Literature', in M.D. Hooker and S.G. Wilson, eds., *Paul and Paulinism: Essays in Honour of C.K. Barrett*. London: SPCK, 1982, 67–73.

Kloppenborg, J.S., 'Collegia and *Thiasoi*: Issues in function, taxonomy and membership' in J.S. Kloppenborg and S.G. Wilson, eds., *Voluntary Associations in the Graeco-Roman World*. London: Routledge, 1996, 16–30.

–, 'Edwin Hatch, Churches and *Collegia*', in B.L. McLean, ed., *Origins and Method: Towards a New Understanding of Judaism and Christianity*. Sheffield: Sheffield Academic, 1993, 212–38.

Kloppenborg, J.S., and S.G. Wilson, eds., *Voluntary Associations in the Graeco-Roman World*. London: Routledge, 1996.

Knox, J., *Philemon among the Letters of Paul*. Nashville: Abingdon Press, 1959.

Knutsson, J., *Labeling Theory: A Critical Examination*. Stockholm: Scientific Research Group, 1977.

Koenen, L., 'Die Adaptation ägyptischer Königsideologie am Ptolemäerhof', in E. Van't Dack et al., eds., *Egypt and the Hellenistic World*. Leuven: Leuven University, 1983, 143–90.

–, 'Die Prophezіehungen der 'Töpfers'' *ZPE* 2 (1968) 178–209.

Kurtz, D.C., and J. Boardman, *Greek Burial Customs*. London: Thames & Hudson, 1971.

la Piana, G., 'Foreign Groups in Rome during the First Centuries of the Empire' *HTR* 20 (1927) 183–403.

Labov, W., *The Social Stratification of English in New York City*. Washington, D.C.: Center for Applied Linguistics, 1966.

Labow, D., *Flavius Josephus Contra Apionem. Buch 1: Einleitung, Text, Textkritischer Apparat, Übersetzung und Kommentar*. Stuttgart: Kohlhammer, 2005.

Lampe, G., *A Patristic Greek Lexicon*. Oxford: Clarendon, 1961.

Lampe, P., 'The Eucharist: Identifying with Christ on the Cross' *Interpretation* 48 (1994) 36–49.

Lane Fox, R., *Pagans and Christians*. London: Penguin, 1986.

Larcher, C., *Le Lime de la Sagesse*. Paris: Gabalda, 1983.

Lattimore, R., *Themes in Greek and Latin Epitaphs*. Urbana: University of Illinois, 1962.

Leclercq, J., 'Spiritualitas' *Studi Medievali* 3 a, serie 3 (1962) 279–96.

Lemert, E.M., *Human Deviance, Social Problems, and Social Control*. 2nd ed. Englewood Cliffs: Prentice Hall, 1972.

–, *Social Pathology*. New York: McGraw-Hill, 1951.

Levine, L.I., *The Ancient Synagogue: The First Thousand Years*. New Haven: Yale University, 2000.

Levison, J.R., *The Spirit in First Century Judaism*. Leiden: Brill, 1997.

Lieberg G., 'Die "theologia tripertita" in Forschung und Bezeugung' *ANRW* I.4, 63–115.

Lieu, J., 'I am a Christian: Martyrdom and the Beginning of Christian Identity', in J. Lieu, *Neither Jew nor Greek*, 211–32.

–, *Christian Identity in the Jewish and Graeco-Roman World*. Oxford: Oxford University, 2004.

–, *Neither Jew nor Greek: Constructing Early Christian Identity*. Edinburgh: T & T Clark, 2002.

Lieu, J., J. North and T. Rajak, eds., *The Jews among Pagans and Christians in the Roman Empire*. London/New York: Routledge, 1992.

Lifschitz, B., *Donateurs et Fondateurs dans les synagogues juives*. Paris: Gabalda, 1967.

Lightfoot, J.B., *Apostolic Fathers. Part II. S. Ignatius, S. Polycarp*, vol. II. 2nd ed. London: Macmillan, 1889.

–, *Notes on Epistles of St. Paul*. London: Macmillan, 1904.

–, *The Epistles of St. Paul to the Colossians, to Philemon*. 5th ed. London: Macmillan, 1880.

Lincoln, A.T., 'The Household Code and the Wisdom Mode of Colossians' *JSNT* 74 (1999) 93–112.

Lincoln, A.T., and A.J.M. Wedderburn, *The Theology of the Later Pauline Letters*. Cambridge: Cambridge University, 1993.

Lloyd, A.B., 'Nationalist Propaganda in Ptolemaic Egypt' *Historia* 31 (1982) 33–55.

Lofland, J., *Deviance and Identity*. Englewood Cliffs: Prentice Hall, 1969.

Longenecker, B.W., 'Socio-Economic Profiling of the First Urban Christians', in T.D. Still and D.G. Horrell, eds., *After the First Urban Christians: The Social-Scientific Study of Pauline Christianity Twenty-Five Years Later*. London: T & T Clark, 2009, 36–59.

–, *Remember the Poor: Paul, Poverty and the Greco-Roman World*. Grand Rapids: Eerdmans, 2010.

Loomba, A., *Colonialism/Postcolonialism*. London: Routledge, 1998.

Lopez, D.C., *Apostle to the Conquered: Reimagining Paul's Mission*. Minneapolis: Fortress, 2008.

Lüdemann, G., *Paul: Apostle to the Gentiles: Studies in Chronology*. London: SCM, 1984.

–, *Paulus, der Heidenapostel. Band II: Antipaulinismus im frühen Christentum*. Göttingen: Vandenhoeck & Ruprecht, 1983.

Lüderitz, G., *Corpus jüdischer Zeugnisse aus der Cyrenaika*. Wiesbaden: Reichert, 1983.

Lütgert, W., *Die Vollkommenen im Philipperbrief und die Enthusiasten in Thessalonich*. Gütersloh: Bertelsmann, 1909.

Luz, U., *Matthew 21–28*. Hermeneia. Minneapolis: Augsburg Fortress, 2005.

–, *Das Geschichtsverständnis des Paulus*. Munich: Chr. Kaiser, 1968.

MacDonald, M.Y., 'Beyond Identification of the Topos of Household Management: Reading the Household Codes in the Light of Recent Methodologies and Theoretical Perspectives in the Study of the New Testament' *NTS* 57 (2011) 65–90.

–, 'Women Holy in Body and Spirit: The Social Setting of 1 Corinthians 7' *NTS* 36 (1990) 161–81.

–, *The Pauline Churches: A Socio-Historical Study of Institutionalisation in the Pauline and Deutero-Pauline Writings*. Cambridge: Cambridge University, 1988.

Macias, J. M., et al., 'Excavaciones en la Catedral de Tarragona y su Entorno: Avances y Retrocesos en la Investigación sobre el Culto Imperial', in T. Nogales and J. González, eds., *Culto Imperial: política y poder*. Hispania Antigua, Serie Arqueológica, 1. Rome: 'L'erma' di Bretschneider, 2007, 763–87.

MacMullen, R., 'What Difference did Christianity Make?' *Historia* 35 (1986) 322–43.

–, *Christianizing the Roman Empire, A. D. 100–400*. New Haven: Yale University, 1986.

–, *Paganism in the Roman Empire*. New Haven: Yale University, 1981.

Mader, G., *Josephus and the Politics of Historiography: Apologetic and Impression Management in the* Bellum Judaicum. Leiden: Brill, 2000.

Malherbe, A. J., 'Determinism and Free Will in Paul: The Argument of 1 Corinthians 8 and 9', in T. Engberg-Pedersen, ed., *Paul in his Hellenistic Context*. Edinburgh: T & T Clark, 1994, 231–55.

–, *Social Aspects of Early Christianity*. Philadelphia: Fortress, 1977.

–, *The Letters to the Thessalonians*. Anchor Bible 32B, New York: Doubleday, 2000.

Malina, B. J., 'Conflict in Luke-Acts: Labelling and Deviance Theory', in J. H. Neyrey, ed., *The Social World of Luke-Acts: Models for Interpretation.* Peabody: Hendrickson, 1991.

Malina, B. J., and J. H. Neyrey, *Calling Jesus Names: The Social Value of Labels in Matthew*. Sonoma, CA: Polebridge, 1988.

Mangas, J., 'Die römische Religion in Hispanien während der Prinzipatszeit', *ANRW* II.18.1, 276–344.

Marchal, J. A., *The Politics of Heaven: Women, Gender, and Empire in the Study of Paul*. Minneapolis: Fortress, 2008.

Marcus, J., '*Birkat Ha-Minim* Revisited' *NTS* 55 (2009) 523–51.

–, 'The Circumcision and the Uncircumcision in Rome' *NTS* 35 (1989) 67–81.

Marques, J. M., and D. Abrams et al., 'Social Categorization, Social Identification, and Rejection of Deviant Groups', in M. A. Hogg and R. S. Tindale, eds., *Blackwell Handbook of Social Psychology: Group Processes*. Oxford: Blackwell, 2003, 400–424.

Marshall, I. H., *1 and 2 Thessalonians*. London: Marshall, Morgan & Scott, 1983.

–, *The Pastoral Letters*. ICC. London: T & T Clark, 1999.

Martin, D., 'Patterns of Belief and Patterns of Life: Correlations in *The First Urban Christians* and Since', in Still and Horrell, eds., *After the First Urban Christians*, 116–33.

–, *The Corinthian Body*. New Haven: Yale University, 1995.

Martyn, J. L., 'Pauline Epistemology at the Turn of the Ages', in his *Theological Issues in the Letters of Paul*. Edinburgh: T & T Clark, 1997, 89–110.

–, *History and Theology in the Fourth Gospel*. Nashville: Abingdon, 1968.

–, *History and Theology in the Fourth Gospel.* 2nd ed. Nashville: Abingdon, 1979.

–, *The Gospel of John in Christian History.* New York: Paulist, 1978.

Marxsen, W., 'Auslegung von 1 Thess 4,14–18' *ZTK* 66 (1969) 22–37.

–, *Der erste Brief an die Thessalonicher*. ZBK. Zürich: Theologischer, 1979.

Mason, S., 'Jews, Judeans, Judaizing, Judaism: Problems of Categorization in Ancient History' *JSJ* 38 (2007) 1–56, reprinted in his *Josephus, Judea, and Christian Origins*. Peabody: Hendrickson, 2009, 141–84.

–, 'Josephus, Daniel and the Flavian House' in F. Parente and J. Sievers, eds. *Josephus and the History of the Graeco-Roman Period.* Leiden: Brill, 1994, 161–91.
–, *Flavius Josephus. Translation and Commentary Vol 9: Life of Josephus.* Leiden: Brill, 2001.
–, *Josephus, Judea, and Christian Origins.* Peabody, MA: Hendrickson, 2009.
Matthews, S., *First Converts: Rich Pagan Women and the Rhetoric of Mission in Early Judaism and Christianity.* Stanford: Stanford University, 2001.
Mattingly, D.J., ed., *Dialogues in Roman Imperialism: Power, Discourse and Discrepant Experience in the Roman Empire.* Journal of Roman Archaeology Supplement Series 23. Portsmouth, RI: JRA, 1997.
May, A.S., *'The Body for the Lord': Sex and Identity in 1 Corinthians 5–7.* London: T & T Clark, 2004.
May, J.M., *Trials of Character: The Eloquence of Ciceronian Ethos.* Chapel Hill: North Carolina, 1988.
McEleney, N.J., 'Conversion, Circumcision and the Law' *NTS* 20 (1974) 319–41.
Mearns, C., 'Early Eschatological Development in Paul: The Evidence of I and II Thessalonians' *NTS* 27 (1980–81) 137–57.
Meeks, W.A., '"To Walk Worthily of the Lord": Moral Formation in the Pauline School Exemplified by the Letter to the Colossians', in E. Stump and T.P. Flint, eds., *Hermes and Athena: Biblical Exegesis and Philosophical Theology.* Notre Dame: University of Notre Dame, 1993, 37–58
–, 'Breaking Away: Three New Testament Pictures of Christianity's Separation from the Jewish Communities', in J. Neusner and E.S. Frerichs, eds., *"To See Ourselves as Others See Us." Christians, Jews, "Others" in Late Antiquity.* Chico: Scholars, 1985, 93–115.
–, 'Judgment and the Brother: Romans 14:1–15:13', in G.F. Hawthorne and O. Betz, eds., *Tradition and Interpretation in the New Testament. Essays in Honor of E. Earle Ellis.* Grand Rapids: Eerdmans, 1987, 290–300.
–, 'The "Haustafeln" and American Slavery: The Hermeneutical Challenge', in E.H. Lovering and J.L. Sumney, eds., *Theology and Ethics in Paul and his Interpreters.* Nashville: Abingdon, 1996, 232–53.
–, 'The Polyphonic Ethics of the Apostle Paul' *Annual of the Society of Christian Ethics* (1988) 17–29; reprinted in W. Meeks, *In Search of the Early Christians.* New Haven: Yale University Press, 2002, 196–209.
–, 'The Social Functions of Apocalyptic Language in Pauline Christianity', in D. Hellholm, ed., *Apocalypticism in the Mediterranean World and the Near East.* Tübingen: Mohr Siebeck, 1983, 687–705.
–, *In Search of the Early Christians.* New Haven: Yale University, 2002.
–, *The First Urban Christians: The Social World of the Apostle Paul.* New Haven: Yale University, 1983.
Meggitt, J.J., 'Taking the Emperor's Clothes Seriously: the New Testament and the Roman Empire', in C.E. Joynes, ed., *The Quest for Wisdom. Essays in Honour of Philip Budd.* Cambridge: Orchard Academic Press, 2002, 143–69.
–, *Paul, Poverty and Survival.* Edinburgh: T & T Clark, 1998.
Mélèze Modrzejewski, J., *The Jews of Egypt: From Ramses II to Emperor Hadrian.* Edinburgh: T & T Clark, 1995.
Mendels, D., 'Hecataeus of Abdera and a Jewish 'patrios politeia' of the Persian Period (Diodorus Siculus XL, 3)' *ZAW* 95 (1983) 94–119.

Metcalf, P., and R. Huntingdon, *Celebrations of Death. The Anthropology of Mortuary Ritual*. 2nd ed. Cambridge: Cambridge University, 1991.

Michel, O., *Der Brief an die Römer.* KEK 6. 14th ed. Göttingen: Vandenhoeck & Ruprecht, 1978.

Milbank, J., 'Paul against Biopolitics', in J. Milbank, S. Žižek and C. Davis, *Paul's New Moment: Continental Philosophy and the Future of Christian Theology*. Grand Rapids: Brazos, 2010, 21–73.

Millar, A., and J.K. Riches, 'Interpretation: a Theoretical Perspective and Some Applications' *Numen* 28 (1981) 29–53.

Millar, F., 'The Imperial Cult and the Persecutions', in W. den Boer, ed., *Le culte des souverains dans l'empire romain*. Fondation Hardt Entretiens 19. Geneva: Fondation Hardt, 1972, 145–65.

Milligan, G., *St. Paul's Epistles to the Thessalonians*. London: Macmillan, 1908.

Milroy, L., *Language and Social Networks*. Oxford: Blackwell, 1987.

Minear, P.S., *The Obedience of Faith*. London: SCM, 1971.

Mitchell, M., *Paul and the Rhetoric of Reconciliation*. Louisville: Westminster/John Knox, 1991.

Mol, H., *Identity and the Sacred.* Oxford: Blackwell, 1976.

Momigliano, A., *The Emperor Claudius and His Achievement.* rev. ed. Oxford: Oxford University, 1961.

Moore, S.D., *Empire and Apocalypse: Postcolonialism and the New Testament*. Sheffield: Sheffield Phoenix, 2006.

Moore, S.D., and J. Capel Anderson, 'Taking It like a Man: Masculinity in 4 Maccabees' *JBL* 117 (1998) 249–73.

Moore-Gilbert, B., *Postcolonial Theory: Context, Practices, Politics*. London/New York: Verso, 1997.

Morris, I., *Death-Ritual and Social Structure in Classical Antiquity*. Cambridge: Cambridge University, 1992.

Moule, C.F.D., *The Epistles to the Colossians and to Philemon*. Cambridge: Cambridge University, 1957.

Moxnes, H., *Constructing Early Christian Families: Family as Social Reality and Metaphor*. London: Routledge, 1997.

Munck, J., *Paul and the Salvation of Mankind.* London: SCM, 1959.

Murphy-O'Connor, J., *Paul: A Critical Life*. Oxford: Oxford University, 1996.

Murray, M., *Playing a Jewish Game: Gentile Christian Judaizing in the First and Second Centuries CE*. Waterloo, Ontario: Wilfrid Laurier University, 2004.

Musso, O., 'Anus ebria' *Atene e Roma* 13 (1968) 29–31.

Musurillo, H., *Acts of the Christian Martyrs*. Oxford: Clarendon, 1972.

Naber, S.A., *Flavius Iosephus. Opera Omnia*. Leipzig: Teubner, 1896.

Nanos, M.D., *The Irony of Galatians: Paul's Letter in First-Century Context*. Minneapolis: Fortress, 2002.

–, *The Mystery of Romans: The Jewish Context of Paul's Letter*. Minneapolis: Fortress, 1996.

Newton, D., *Deity and Diet: The Dilemma of Sacrificial Food in Corinth*. JSNTSup 169. Sheffield: Sheffield Academic, 1998.

Neyrey, J.H., *Paul in Other Words: A Cultural Reading of his Letters*. Louisville: Westminster John Knox, 1990.

–, ed., *The Social World of Luke-Acts: Models for Interpretation.* Peabody: Hendrickson, 1991.

Nickle, K. F., *The Collection: A Study in Paul's Strategy*. London: SCM, 1966.

Niebuhr, K.-W., 'Identität und Interaktion. Zur Situation paulinischer Gemeinden im Ausstrahlungsfeld des Diasporajudentums', in J. Mehlhausen, ed., *Pluralismus und Identität*. Gütersloh: Chr. Kaiser, 1995, 339–59.

Niehoff, M., *Philo on Jewish Identity and Culture*. Tübingen: Mohr Siebeck, 2001.

Nielsen, I., and H. S. Nielsen, *Meals in a Social Context*. Aarhus: Aarhus University, 1998.

Niese, B., *Flavii Iosephi Opera edidit et apparatu critico instruxit.* vol. 5. Berlin: Weidmann, 1889.

Nock, A. D., 'Sarcophagi and symbolism', in J. Stewart, ed., *Essays on Religion and the Ancient World*. Oxford: Oxford University, 1972, 2.606–41.

Noethlichs, K.-L., *Das Judentum und der römische Staat:Minderheitenpolitik im antiken Rom*. Darmstadt: Wissenschaftliche Buchgesellschaft, 1996.

Nolland, J., 'Uncircumcised Proselytes?' *JSJ* 12 (1981) 173–94.

Noy, D., ed., *Jewish Insciptions of Western Europe.* 2 vols. Cambridge: Cambridge University, 1993, 1995.

Noy, D., W. Ameling et al., eds., *Inscriptiones Judaicae Orientis.* 3 vols. Tübingen: Mohr Siebeck, 2004.

Nussbaum, M., *The Therapy of Desire*. Princeton: Princeton University, 1994.

Oakes, P., 'Remapping the Universe: Paul and the Emperor in 1 Thessalonians and Philippians' *JSNT* 27 (2005) 301–22.

–, *Philippians: From People to Letter.* SNTSMS 110. Cambridge: Cambridge University, 2001.

Ollier, F., *Le Mirage Spartiate: Étude sur l'Idealisation de Sparta dans l'Antiquité grecque de l'Origine jusqu'aux Cyniques*. reprint, New York: Arno, 1972, originally, 1933, 1943.

Olsson, B., and M. Zetterholm, eds., *The Ancient Synagogue from its Origins until 200 C. E.* Stockholm: Almqvist & Wiksell International, 2003.

Oropeza, B. J., *Paul and Apostasy: Eschatological Perseverance and Falling Away in the Corinthian Congregation*. WUNT 2.115. Tübingen: Mohr Siebeck, 2000.

Osiek, C., and D. L. Balch, *Families in the New Testament World: Households and House Churches*. Louisville: Westminster John Knox, 1997.

Osiek, C., and M. Y. MacDonald, *A Woman's Place: House Churches in Earliest Christianity*. Minneapolis: Fortress, 2006.

Pagels, E., *The Gnostic Paul*. Philadelphia: Trinity Press International, 1975.

Paige, T., 'Spirit at Corinth: The Corinthian Concept of Spirit and Paul's Response as Seen in 1 Corinthians', Ph.D. Thesis, University of Sheffield, 1994.

–, 'Who believes in 'Spirit'? Πνεῦμα in Pagan Usage and Implications for the Gentile Christian Mission' *HTR* 95 (2002) 417–36.

Parente, F., and J. Sievers, eds., *Josephus and the History of the Graeco-Roman Period.* Leiden: Brill, 1994.

Parker, R., *Miasma. Pollution and Purification in early Greek Religion*. Oxford: Clarendon, 1983.

Parkin, T. G., 'Out of Sight, Out of Mind: Elderly Members of the Roman Family', in B. Rawson and P. Weaver, eds., *The Roman Family in Italy*. Oxford: Clarendon, 1997, 123–48.

–, *Demography and Roman Society*. Baltimore: Johns Hopkins University, 1992.

–, *Old Age in the Roman World: A Cultural and Social History*. Baltimore: Johns Hopkins University, 2003.

Passio Sanctorum Martyrum Fructuosi Episcopi, Auguri et Eulogi Diaconorum. text in R. Knöpf, G. Krüger and G. Ruhbach, *Augewählte Märtyracten*. 4th edn. Tübingen: Mohr Siebeck, 1965.

Paxton, F.S., *Christianizing Death. The Creation of a Ritual Process in Early Medieval Europe*. Ithaca: Cornell University, 1990.

Pearson, B.A., '1 Thessalonians 2:13–16: A Deutero-Pauline Interpolation' *HTR* 64 (1971) 79–94.

–, *The Pneumatikos-Psychikos Terminology in 1 Corinthians.* Missoula, MT: Scholars, 1973.

Pfohl, S.J., *Images of Deviance and Social Control: A Sociological History*. New York: McGraw-Hill, 1985.

Pietersen, L., 'Despicable Deviants: Labelling Theory and the Polemic of the Pastorals' *Sociology of Religion* 58 (1997) 343–52.

Pilhofer, P., *Presbyteron Kreitton: Der Alterbeweis der jüdischen und christlichen Apologeten und seine Vorgeschichte*. Tübingen: Mohr Siebeck, 1990.

Pinter, D.L., 'Divine and Imperial Power: A Comparative Analysis of Paul and Josephus'. Ph.D. thesis, Durham University, 2009.

Plevnik, J., 'The Taking Up of the Faithful and the Resurrection of the Dead in 1 Thessalonians 4:13–18' *CBQ* 46 (1984) 274–83.

Pokorný, P., *Colossians. A Commentary*. Peabody: Hendrickson, 1991.

Poland, F., *Geschichte des griechischen Vereinswesens*. Leipzig: Teubner, 1909.

Porten, B., *Archives from Elephantine: The Life of an Ancient Jewish Military Colony*. Berkeley: University of California, 1986.

Pratt, M.L., 'Transculturation and Autoethnography: Peru 1615/1980', in F. Barker, P. Hulme and M. Iversen, eds., *Colonial Discourse/Postcolonial Theory.* Manchester: Manchester University, 1994, 24–46.

–, *Imperial Eyes: Travel Writing and Transculturation.* London: Routledge, 1992.

Preston, R., 'Roman questions, Greek answers: Plutarch and the construction of identity', in S. Goldhill, ed., *Being Greek under Rome: Cultural Identity, the Second Sophistic and the Development of Empire*. Cambridge: Cambridge University, 2001, 86–119.

Price, S.R.F., *Rituals and Power: The Roman Imperial Cult in Asia Minor*. Cambridge: Cambridge University, 1984.

Pucci ben Zeev, M., *Jewish Rights in the Roman World*. Tübingen: Mohr Siebeck, 1998.

Rabens, V., *The Holy Spirit and Ethics in Paul.* WUNT 283. Tübingen: Mohr Siebeck, 2010.

Radford Ruether, R., *Faith and Fratricide: The Theological Roots of Anti-Semitism*. New York: Seabury, 1974.

Räisänen, H., 'Galatians 2:16 and Paul's Break with Judaism' *NTS* 31 (1985) 543–53.

Rajak, T., 'The *Against Apion* and the Continuities in Josephus's Political Thought', in S. Mason, ed., *Understanding Josephus. Seven Perspectives*. Sheffield: Sheffield Academic, 1998, 222–46.

–, *The Jewish Dialogue with Greece and Rome: Studies in Social and Cultural Interaction*. Leiden: Brill, 2001.

Ramsey, B., *Beginning to Read the Fathers*. London: Darton, Longman and Todd, 1985.

Rauer, M., *Die "Schwachen" in Korinth und Rom nach den Paulusbriefen*. Freiburg: Herder, 1923.

Reasoner, M., *The Strong and the Weak: Romans 14.1–15.13 in Context*. SNTSMS 103. Cambridge: Cambridge University Press, 1999.

Reinach, T., *Flavius Josèphe contre Apion: Texte établi et annoté*. Paris: Société d'édition "Les belles lettres", 1930.

Rengstorf, K., *A Complete Concordance to Flavius Josephus*. Leiden: Brill, 1973.

Reynolds, J., and R. Tannenbaum, *Jews and Godfearers at Aphrodisias*. Cambridge: Cambridge Philological Society, 1987.

Richard, E.J., *First and Second Thessalonians*. SP 11. Collegeville, Minn.: Liturgical, 1995.

Richardson, J.S., *The Romans in Spain*. Oxford: Blackwell, 1996.

Riches, J., and D. Sim, eds., *The Gospel of Matthew in its Roman Imperial Context*. London: Continuum, 2005.

Rigaux, B., *Saint Paul: Les Épitres aux Thessaloniciens*. Paris: Gabalda, 1956.

Rives, J.B., 'Christian Expansion and Christian Ideology', in W.V. Harris, ed., *The Spread of Christianity in the First Four Centuries*. Leiden: Brill, 2005, 15–41.

–, 'Imperial Cult and Native Tradition in Roman North Africa' *The Classical Journal* 96 (2001) 425–36.

–, 'The Decree of Decius and the Religion of Empire' *JRS* 89 (1999) 135–54.

–, *Religion in the Roman Empire*. Oxford: Blackwell, 2007.

Robert, L., 'Un corpus des inscriptions juives' *REJ* 101 (1937) 73–86.

Rock, P., *Deviant Behaviour*. London: Hutchinson, 1973.

Rodà de Llanza, I., 'La Tarragona de mitjan segle I dC', in J.M. Gavaldà Ribot, et al., *Pau, Fructuós*, 73–100.

Rohrbaugh, R.L., '"Social Location of Thought" as a Heuristic Concept in New Testament Study' *JSNT* 30 (1987) 103–19.

Roitto, R., 'Act as a Christ-Believer, as a Household Member or as Both? A Cognitive Perspective on the Relation between the Social Identity in Christ and Household Identities in Pauline and Deutero-Pauline Texts', in B. Holmberg and M. Winninge, eds., *Identity Formation in the New Testament*. WUNT 227: Tübingen: Mohr Siebeck, 2008, 141–61.

Roloff, J., *Der Erste Brief an Timotheus*. EKK. Zürich: Benziger, 1988.

Rowe, C., and M. Schofield, eds., *The Cambridge History of Greek and Roman Political Thought*. Cambridge: Cambridge University, 2000.

Rowe, C.K., *World Upside Down: Reading Acts in the Graeco-Roman Age*. Oxford: Oxford University, 2009.

Rowell, G., *The Liturgy of Christian Burial*. London: SPCK, 1977.

Runesson, A. 'Inventing Christian Identity: Paul, Ignatius and Theodosius I', in B. Holmberg, ed., *Exploring Early Christian Identity*. WUNT 226. Tübingen: Mohr Siebeck, 2008, 59–92.

–, *The Origins of the Synagogue: A Socio-Historical Study*. Stockholm: Almqvist & Wiksell International, 2001.

Runesson, A., D.D. Binder and B. Olsson, eds., *The Ancient Synagogue from its Origins to 200 C.E: A Source Book*. Leiden: Brill, 2008.

Rush, A., *Death and Burial in Christian Antiquity*. Washington, D.C.: Catholic University of America, 1941.
Rutgers, L.V., *The Hidden Heritage of Diaspora Judaism*. Leuven: Peeters, 1998.
–, *The Jews in Late Antique Rome: Evidence of Cultural Interaction in the Roman Diaspora*. Leiden: Brill, 1995.
Said, E., *Orientalism: Western Representations of the Orient.* London: Routledge & Kegan Paul, 1978.
Saldarini, A.J., 'The Gospel of Matthew and Jewish Christian Conflict', in David L. Balch, ed., *Social History of the Matthean Community*. Minneapolis: Fortress, 1991, 38–61.
Saller, R.P., 'Men's Age at Marriage and its Consequences in the Roman Family' *CP* 82 (1987) 20–35.
–, *Patriarchy, Property and Death in the Roman Family*. Cambridge: Cambridge University, 1994.
Sanders, E.P., 'Jewish Association with Gentiles and Galatians 2.11–14', in R.T. Fortna and B.R. Gaventa, eds., *The Conversation Continues. Studies in Paul and John in Honor of J. Louis Martyn*. Nashville: Abingdon, 1990, 170–88.
–, *Jewish Law from Jesus to the Mishnah: Five Studies*. London: SCM, 1990.
Sanders, J.T., 'Paul between Jews and Gentiles in Corinth' *JSNT* 65 (1997) 67–83.
–, *Ethics in the New Testament*. London: SCM, 1975.
–, *Schismatics, Sectarians, Dissidents, Deviants: The First One Hundred Years of Jewish-Christian Relations*. London: SCM, 1993.
–, *The Jews in Luke-Acts*. London: SCM, 1987.
Schäfer, P., *Judeophobia: Attitudes toward the Jews in the Ancient World*. Cambridge, Mass.: Harvard University, 1997.
Schaller, B., 'Adam und Christus bei Paulus. Oder: Über Brauch und Fehlbrauch von Philo in der neutestamentlichen Forschung', in R. Deines and K.-W. Niebuhr, eds., *Philo und das Neue Testament*. WUNT 172. Tübingen: Mohr Siebeck, 2004, 143–53.
Schäublin, C., 'Josephus und die Griechen' *Hermes* 110 (1982) 316–41.
Scheidel, W., 'Roman Age Structure: Evidence and Models' *JRS* 91 (2001) 1–26.
–, ed., *Debating Roman Demography*. Leiden: Brill, 2001.
Schlier, H., *Der Römerbrief*. HTKNT VI. Freiburg: Herder, 1977.
Schlueter, C.J., *Filling up the Measure: Polemical Hyperbole in 1 Thessalonians 2.14–16*. JSNTSup 98: Sheffield: JSOT, 1994.
Schmeller, T., *Hierarchie und Egalität: eine sozialgeschichtliche Untersuchung paulinischer Gemeinden und griechisch-römischer Vereine*. Stuttgart: Katholisches Bibelwerk, 1995.
Schmidt, D.D., '1 Thess 2:13–16: Linguistic Evidence for an Interpolation' *JBL* 102 (1983) 269–79.
Schmithals, W., *Der Römerbrief als historischer Problem*. Gütersloh: Gütersloher Verlagshaus Gerd Mohn, 1975.
–, *Gnosticism in Corinth.* Nashville: Abingdon, 1971 (1956).
–, *Paul and the Gnostics*. Nashville: Abingdon, 1972.
Schoedel, W.R., *Ignatius of Antioch*. Philadelphia: Fortress, 1985.
Schrage, W., *Der erste Brief an die Korinther*. EKK. Neukirchen-Vluyn: Neukirchener, 1991–1995.
Schreiber, A., *Die Gemeinde in Korinth.* Münster: Aschendorff, 1977.

Schröder, B., *Die 'väterlichen Gesetze'. Flavius Josephus als Vermittler von Halachah an Griechen und Römer*. Tübingen: Mohr Siebeck, 1996.
Schur, K.M., *Labeling Deviant Behaviour: Its Sociological Implications*. New York: Harper and Row, 1971.
–, *The Politics of Deviance: Stigma Contests and the Uses of Power*. Englewood Cliffs: Prentice Hall, 1980.
Schüssler Fiorenza, E., *In Memory of Her*. 2nd ed. London: SCM, 1994.
Schwartz, D.R., '"Judean" or "Jew": How should we translate *ioudaios* in Josephus?', in J. Frey, D.R. Schwartz and S. Gripentrog, eds., *Jewish Identity in the Greco-Roman World*. Leiden: Brill, 2007, 3–28.
–, 'Josephus on the Jewish Constitutions and Community' *SCI* 7 (1983–84) 30–52.
–, *Studies in the Jewish Background of Christianity*. Tübingen: Mohr Siebeck, 1992.
Schwartz, S., *Imperialism and Jewish Society, 200 B.C.E. to 640 C.E.* Princeton: Princeton University, 2001.
Schweizer, E., '"Der Jude im Verborgenen ..., dessen Lob nicht von Menschen, sondern von Gott kommt." Von Röm 2,28f und Mt 6,1–18', in J. Gnilka, ed., *Neues Testament und Kirche. Für Rudolf Schnackenburg*. Freiburg: Herder, 1974, 115–24.
–, 'Traditional Ethical Patterns in the Pauline and post-Pauline Letters and their Development (Lists of Vices and House-tables)', in E. Best and R. McL. Wilson, eds., *Text and Interpretation*. Cambridge: Cambridge University 1979.
–, *Colossians*. London: SPCK, 1982.
–, *Neues Testament und Christologie im Werden: Aufsätze*. Göttingen: Vandenhoeck & Ruprecht, 1982.
Scott, J.C., *Domination and the Arts of Resistance: Hidden Transcripts*. New Haven: Yale University, 1990.
–, *The Weapons of the Weak: Everyday Forms of Peasant Resistance*. New Haven: Yale University, 1985.
Segal, A.F., *Paul the Convert: The Apostolate and Apostasy of Saul the Pharisee*. New Haven/London: Yale University, 1990.
Segovia, F.F., and R.S. Sugirtharajah, eds., *A Postcolonial Commentary on New Testament Writings*. London: T & T Clark, 2007.
Seland, T., *Establishment Violence in Philo and Luke. A Study of Non-Conformity to the Torah and Jewish Vigilante Reactions*. Leiden: Brill, 1995.
Selwyn, E.G., *The First Epistle of St. Peter*. London: Macmillan, 1955.
Sevenster, J.N., *The Roots of Pagan Anti-Semitism in the Ancient World*. Leiden: Brill, 1975.
Sherwin-White, A.N., *Racial Prejudice in Imperial Rome*. Cambridge: Cambridge University, 1967.
Siegert, F., ed., *Flavius Josephus, Über die Ursprünglichkeit des Judentums: Contra Apionem*. 2 vols. Göttingen: Vandenhoeck & Ruprecht, 2008.
Silva, M., *Biblical Words and their Meaning: An Introduction to Lexical Semantics*. Grand Rapids: Zondervan, 1983.
Simon, M., *Verus Israel: A Study of the Relations between Christians and Jews in the Roman Empire (135–425)*. Littman Library of Jewish Civilization. Oxford: Oxford University, 1986.
Sinclair, T., *A History of Greek Political Thought*. London: Routledge & Kegan Paul, 1951.

Slingerland, H. D., *Claudian Policymaking and the Early Imperial Repression of Judaism in Rome*. Atlanta: Scholars Press, 1997.

Smallwood, E. M., *The Jews under Roman Rule: From Pompey to Diocletian.* 2nd ed. Leiden: Brill, 1981.

Smelik, K. A. D., and E. A. Hemelrijk, 'Who knows not what monsters demented Egypt worships?', *ANRW* 2.17.14, 1852–2000.

Smith, D. R., *'Hand this Man over to Satan': Curse, Exclusion and Salvation in 1 Corinthians 5*. London: T & T Clark, 2009.

Smith, J. Z., *Drudgery Divine: On the Comparison of Early Christianities and the Religions of Late Antiquity*. London: School of Oriental and African Studies, 1990.

Sorabji, R., *Emotion and Peace of Mind: From Stoic Agitation to Christian Temptation*. Oxford: Oxford University, 2000.

Spiegelberg, W., *Die sogennante Demotische Chronik*. Leipzig: J. C. Hinrichs, 1914.

Stanton, G. N., *Jesus and Gospel*. Cambridge: Cambridge University, 2004.

–, *A Gospel for a New People. Studies in Matthew*. Edinburgh: T & T Clark, 1992.

Steck, O. H., *Israel und das gewaltsame Geschick der Propheten*. WMANT 23. Neukirchen-Vluyn: Neukirchener, 1967.

Stern, M., *Greek and Latin Authors on Jews and Judaism*. Jerusalem: The Israel Academy of Sciences and Humanities, 1974, 1980.

Stern, S., *Peru's Indian Peoples and the Challenge of the Spanish Conquest.* Wisconsin: University of Wisconsin, 1982.

Still, T. D., *Conflict at Thessalonica: A Pauline Church and its Neighbours*. JSNTSup 183. Sheffield: Sheffield Academic, 1999.

Still, T. D., and D. G. Horrell, eds., *After the First Urban Christians: The Social-Scientific Study of Pauline Christianity Twenty-Five Years Later*. London: T & T Clark, 2009.

Stowers, S. K., 'Does Pauline Christianity Resemble a Philosophical School?', in Engberg-Pedersen, ed., *Beyond the Judaism/Hellenism Divide*, 81–102.

Stuhlmacher, P., *Der Brief an Philemon*. EKK. Zürich: Benziger, 1975.

Stuhlmann, R., *Das eschatologische Mass im Neuen Testament*. FRLANT 132. Göttingen: Vandenhoeck & Ruprecht, 1983.

Taubes, J., *The Political Theology of Paul*. Stanford: Stanford University, 2004.

Taussig, H., *In the Beginning was the Meal: Social Experimentation and Early Christian Identity*. Minneapolis: Fortress, 2009.

Taylor, M., *Anti-Judaism and Early Christian Identity: A Critique of the Scholarly Consensus*. StPB 46. Leiden: Brill, 1995.

Te Velde, H., *Seth, God of Confusion: A Study of his Role in Egyptian Mythology and Religion*. Leiden: Brill, 1977.

Tellbe, M., 'The Temple Tax as a Pre-70 CE Identity Marker', in J. Ådna, ed., *The Formation of the Early Church*. WUNT 183. Tübingen: Mohr Siebeck, 2005, 19–44.

–, *Christ-Believers in Ephesus: A Textual Analysis of Early Christian Identity Formation in a Local Perspective*. WUNT 242. Tübingen: Mohr Siebeck, 2009.

–, *Paul between Synagogue and State: Christians, Jews, and Civic Authorities in 1 Thessalonians, Romans, and Philippians*. Stockholm: Almqvist & Wiksell International, 2001.

Thackeray, H. St. J., *Josephus*. LCL. Cambridge, Mass.: Harvard University, 1926.

Theissen, G., 'Legitimation und Lebensunterhalt: Ein Beitrag zur Soziologie urchristlicher Missionare' *NTS* 21(1974/75) 192–221; E.T. in *The Social Setting of Pauline Christianity*. Edinburgh: T & T Clark, 1982, 27–67.

–, 'Sociological Research into the New Testament', in *Social Reality and the Early Christians: Theology, Ethics and the World of the New Testament*. Edinburgh: T & T Clark, 1993, 1–29.

–, 'Soziale Integration und sakramentales Handeln. Eine Analyse von 1 Cor. XI 17–34' *NovT* 16 (1974) 179–206; E.T. in *The Social Setting of Pauline Christianity*. Edinburgh: T & T Clark, 1982, 145–74.

–, *Psychological Aspects of Pauline Theology*. Edinburgh: T & T Clark, 1987.

–, *Social Reality and the Early Christians*. Edinburgh: T & T Clark, 1993.

–, *Studien zur Soziologie des Urchristentums*. WUNT 19. Tübingen: Mohr Siebeck, 1979.

–, *The Social Setting of Pauline Christianity*. Trans. by J.H. Schütz. Edinburgh: T & T Clark, 1982.

–, *Theorie der urchristlichen Religion*. Gütersloh: Gütersloher Verlag, 1999. ET: *A Theory of Primitive Christian Religion*. Trans. by J. Bowden. London: SCM, 1999.

Thiselton, A., *The First Epistle to the Corinthians*. NIGTC. Grand Rapids: Eerdmans, 2000.

Tigerstedt, E.N., *The Legend of Sparta in Classical Antiquity*. 3 vols. Stockholm: Almqvist & Wiksell, 1965–1978.

Tinsley, L., *The French Expressions for Spirituality and Devotion: A Semantic Study*. Washington, D.C.: Catholic University of America, 1953.

Tomson, P.J., *Paul and the Jewish Law*. Compendia Rerum Iudaicarum ad Novum Testamentum III.1. Assen/Maastricht: Van Gorcum, 1990.

Trebilco, P., *Jewish Communities in Asia Minor*. Cambridge: Cambridge University, 1991.

–, *The Early Christians in Ephesus from Paul to Ignatius*. WUNT 166. Tübingen: Mohr Siebeck, 2004.

–, *Self-Designations and Group Identity in the New Testament*. Cambridge: Cambridge University, 2011.

Troeltsch, E., *The Social Teaching of the Christian Churches*. London: G. Unwin, 1931.

Trüdinger, K., *Studien zur Geschichte der griechisch-römischen Ethnographie*. Basel: E. Birkhäuser, 1918.

Turner, E.G., 'Tiberius Julius Alexander' *JRS* 44 (1954) 54–64.

Urman, D., and P.V.M. Flesher, eds., *Ancient Synagogues: Historical Analysis and Archaeological Discovery*. Leiden: Brill, 1995.

van Brocke, C., *Thessaloniki, Stadt der Kassander und Gemeinde des Paulus: eine frühe christiliche Gemeinde in ihrer heidnischen Umwelt*. WUNT 2.125: Tübingen: Mohr Siebeck, 2001.

van der Horst, P.W., '"Thou shalt not revile the Gods": The LXX Translation of Ex. 22.28 (27), its Background and Influence', in *Hellenism – Judaism – Christianity. Essays on their Interaction*. Kampen: Kok Pharos, 1994, 112–21.

–, *Ancient Jewish Epitaphs*. Kampen: Kok Pharos, 1991.

van Gennep, A., *The Rites of Passage*. Chicago: University of Chicago, 1960.

van Henten, J.-W., 'Antiochus IV as a Typhonian Figure in Daniel 7', in A. S. van der Woude, ed., *The Book of Daniel in the Light of New Findings*. Leuven: Leuven University, 1993, 223–43.

–, *The Maccabean Martyrs as Saviours of the Jewish People: A Study of 2 and 4 Maccabees*. Leiden: Brill, 1997.

van Henten, J.-W., and R. Abusch, 'The Jews as Typhonians and Josephus' Strategy of Refutation in *Contra Apionem*', in L. H. Feldman and J. R. Levison, eds. *Josephus'* Contra Apionem: *Studies in its Character and Context with a Latin Concordance to the Portion Missing in Greek*. Leiden: Brill, 1996, 271–309.

van Unnik, W. C., 'Josephus' Account of the Story of Israel's Sin with Alien Women in the Country of Midian (Num. 25.1ff)', in M. S. H. G. Heerma von Voss et al., eds., *Travels in the World of the Old Testament: Studies Presented to Professor M. A. Beek*. Assen: Van Gorcum, 1974, 241–61.

Vermes, G., *Jesus the Jew*. London: SCM, 1973.

von Dobschütz, E., *Die Thessalonicher-Briefe*. Göttingen: Vandenhoeck & Ruprecht, 1909.

Walsh, B. J., and S. C. Keesmaat, *Colossians Remixed: Subverting the Empire*. Downers Grove, Ill.: InterVarsity, 2004.

Walter, N., 'Christusglaube und heidnische Religiosität in paulinischen Gemeinden' *NTS* 25 (1979) 422–42.

–, *Der Thoraausleger Aristobulos*. Berlin: Akademie, 1964.

Waltzing, J. P., *Etude historique sur les Corporations professionelles chez les Romains*. Reprint. Bologna: Forni, 1968.

Wanamaker, C. A., *Commentary on 1 and 2 Thessalonians*. NIGTC. Grand Rapids: Eerdmans, 1990.

Watson, F., *Paul and the Hermenueutics of Faith*. London: T & T Clark, 2004.

–, *Paul, Judaism and the Gentiles: A Sociological Approach*. SNTSMS 56. Cambridge: Cambridge University, 1986.

–, *Paul, Judaism, and the Gentiles: Beyond the New Perspective*. 2nd edn. Grand Rapids: Eerdmans, 2007.

Weber, M., *The Protestant Ethic and the Spirit of Capitalism*. reprint. London: Routledge, 1992.

Webster, J., and N. Cooper, eds. *Roman Imperialism: Post-Colonial Perspectives*. Leicester: Leicester University School of Archaeological Studies, 1996.

Wedderburn, A. J. M., *Baptism and Resurrection*. Tübingen: Mohr Siebeck, 1987.

–, *The Reasons for Romans*. Edinburgh: T & T Clark, 1988.

Weisengoff, J. P., 'The Impious of Wisdom 2' *CBQ* 11 (1949) 40–65.

Weiss, J., *Der erste Korintherbrief*. Göttingen: Vandenhoeck & Ruprecht, 1910.

Wengst, K., *Bedrängte Gemeinde und verherrlichter Christus*. 2nd ed. Neukirchen-Vluyn: Neukirchener, 1983.

–, *Pax Romana and the Peace of Jesus Christ*. Trans. by J. Bowden. London: SCM, 1987.

Westerholm, S., 'Letter and Spirit: The Foundation of Pauline *Ethics*' *NTS* 30 (1984) 229–48.

White, L. M., *Building God's House in the Roman World*. Baltimore: Johns Hopkins University, 1990.

Whitmarsh, T., *Greek Literature and the Roman Empire. The Politics of Imitation*. Oxford: Oxford University, 2001.

Wick, P., 'Ist I Thess 2,13–16 antijüdisch? Der rhetorische Gesamtzusammenhang des Briefes als Interpretationshilfe für eine einzelne Perikope' *TZ* 50 (1994) 9–23.

Wiedemann, T., '*Servi senes*: the role of old slaves at Rome' *Polis* 8 (1996) 275–93.

Wilckens, U., *Der Brief an die Römer*. EKK. Neukirchen-Vluyn: Neukirchener, 1982.

–, *Weisheit und Torheit: Eine exegetisch-religionsgeschichtliche Untersuchung zu 1 Kor 1 und 2*. Tübingen: Mohr-Siebeck, 1959.

Wilken, R. L., *The Christians as the Romans Saw Them*. New Haven: Yale University, 1984.

Williams, G., *Sociolinguistics: A Sociological Critique*. London: Routledge, 1992.

Williams, M., 'Being a Jew in Rome: Sabbath Fasting as an Expression of Romano-Jewish Identity', in J. M. G. Barclay, ed., *Negotiating Diaspora: Jewish Strategies in the Roman Empire*. London: T & T Clark, 2004, 8–18.

–, *The Jews among Greeks and Romans: A Diasporan Sourcebook*. London: Duckworth, 1988.

Williams, M. A., *Rethinking 'Gnosticism': An Argument for Dismantling a Dubious Category*. Princeton: Princeton University, 1996.

Williams, P., and L. Chisman, eds. *Colonial Discourse and Post-Colonial Theory: A Reader.* London: Harvester Wheatsheaf, 1993.

Wilson, S. G., *Leaving the Fold: Apostates and Defectors in Antiquity*. Minneapolis: Fortress, 2004.

–, *Related Strangers: Jews and Christians 70–170 CE*. Minneapolis: Fortress, 1995.

Wink, W., *Engaging the Powers: Discernment and Resistance in an Age of Domination*. Minneapolis: Fortress, 1992.

–, *Naming the Powers: The Language of Power in the New Testament*. Philadelphia: Fortress, 1984.

Winter, B. W., 'Civil Litigation in Secular Corinth and the Church: The Forensic Background to 1 Corinthians 6.1–8' *NTS* 37 (1991) 559–72.

–, 'The Imperial Cult and Early Christians in Pisidian Antioch (Acts XIII 13–50 and Gal VI 11–18)', in T. Drew-Bear et al., eds., *Actes du Ier Congrès International sur Antioche de Pisidie*. Lyon: Kocaeli, 2002, 67–75.

–, *After Paul Left Corinth: The Influence of Secular Ethics and Social Change*. Grand Rapid: Eerdmans, 2001.

–, *Seek the Welfare of the City: Christians as Benefactors and Citizens*. Grand Rapids: Eerdmans, 1994.

Winter, M., *Pneumatiker und Psychiker in Korinth*. Marburg: Elwert, 1975.

Wolfson, H. A., *Philo*. Cambridge, Mass.: Harvard University, 1948.

Wolter, M., 'Ethos und Identität in paulinischen Gemeinden' *NTS* 43 (1997) 430–44.

–, 'Identität und Ethos bei Paulus', in M. Wolter, ed., *Theologie und Ethos im frühen Christentum*. WUNT 236. Tübingen: Mohr-Siebeck, 2009, 121–69.

Woolf, G., *Becoming Roman: The Origins of Provincial Civilization in Gaul.* Cambridge: Cambridge University, 1998.

Woyke, J., *Die neutestamentlichen Haustafeln: Ein kritischer und konstruktiver Forschungsüberblick*. Stuttgart: Katholishes Bibelwerk, 2000.

Wright, N. T., 'Gospel and Theology in Galatians', in L. A. Jervis and P. Richardson, eds., *Gospel in Paul: Studies on Corinthians, Galatians and Romans for Richard N. Longenecker*. Sheffield: Sheffield Academic, 1994, 222–39

–, 'Paul and Caesar: A New Reading of Romans', in C. Bartholemew et al., ed., *A Royal Priesthood? The Use of the Bible Ethically and Politically*. Carlisle: Paternoster, 2002, 173–93.

–, 'Paul's Gospel and Caesar's Empire', in Horsley, ed., *Paul and Politics*, 160–83.

–, 'The Law in Romans 2', in J. D. G. Dunn, ed., *Paul and the Mosaic Law*. Tübingen: Mohr Siebeck, 1996, 131–50.

–, 'The Letter to the Romans: Introduction, Commentary and Reflections', in *The New Interpreter's Bible. Volume X*. Nashville: Abingdon, 2002, 395–770.

–, *Colossians and Philemon*. Leicester: IVP, 1986.

–, *Paul: Fresh Perspectives*. London: SPCK, 2005.

–, *The Resurrection of the Son of God*. London: SPCK, 2003.

Yavetz, Z., 'Judeophobia in Classical Antiquity: A Different Approach' *JJS* 44 (1993) 1–22.

–, 'Latin Authors on Jews and Dacians' *Historia* 47 (1998) 77–107.

–, *Judenfeindschaft in der Antike*. München: C. H. Beck, 1997.

–, *Julius Caesar and his Public Image*. London: Thames and Hudson, 1983.

Young, F., *The Theology of the Pastoral Epistles*. Cambridge: Cambridge University, 1994.

Young, R. J. C., *Postcolonialism: An Historical Introduction*. Oxford: Blackwell, 2001.

–, *White Mythologies: Writing History and the West*. London: Routledge, 1990.

Yoyotte, J., 'L'Égypte ancienne et les origines de l'antijudaïsme' *RHR* 163 (1963) 133–43.

Zanker, P., *The Power of Images in the Age of Augustus*. Ann Arbor: University of Michigan, 1988.

Zetterholm, M., *The Formation of Christianity at Antioch: A Social-Scientific Approach to the Separation between Judaism and Christianity*. London: Routledge, 2003.

Ziesler, J., *Paul's Letter to the Romans*. TPI New Testament Commentaries. London: SCM, 1989.

Acknowledgements

All the following essays are published with permission, gratefully acknowledged:

'"Do We Undermine the Law?": A Study of Romans 14.1–15.6', in J. D. G. Dunn, ed., *Paul and the Mosaic Law* (Tübingen: Mohr Siebeck, 1996) 287–308.

'Paul and Philo on Circumcision: Romans 2.25–29 in Social and Cultural Context' *New Testament Studies* 44 (1998) 536–56. By permission of Cambridge University Press.

'Matching Theory and Practice: Josephus' Constitutional Ideal and Paul's Strategy in Corinth', in T. Engberg-Pedersen, ed., *Paul Beyond the Judaism/Hellenism Divide* (Louisville/London/Leiden: Westminster John Knox, 2001) 139–63. Used by permission of Westminster John Knox Press.

'Money and Meetings: Group Formation among Diaspora Jews and Early Christians', in A. Gutsfeld and D.-A. Koch, eds., *Vereine, Synagogen und Gemeinden im kaiserzeitlichen Kleinasien* (Tübingen: Mohr Siebeck, 2006) 113–27.

'Deviance and Apostasy: Some Applications of Deviance Theory to First Century Judaism and Christianity', in P. F. Esler, ed., *Modelling Early Christianity* (London: Routledge, 1995) 114–27. By kind permission.

'Who was Considered an Apostate in the Jewish Diaspora?', in G. N. Stanton and G. Stroumsa, *Tolerance and Intolerance in Early Judaism and Christianity* (Cambridge: Cambridge University, 1998) 80–98. By permission of Cambridge University Press.

'Hostility to Jews as Cultural Construct: Egyptian, Hellenistic, and Early Christian Paradigms', in C. Böttrich and J. Herzer, eds., *Josephus und das Neue Testament* (Tübingen: Mohr Siebeck, 2007) 365–85.

'Thessalonica and Corinth: Social Contrasts in Pauline Christianity' *Journal for the Study of New Testament* 47 (1992) 49–74. By permission of SAGE Publications.

'Πνευματικός in the Social Dialect of Pauline Christianity', in G. N. Stanton, B. W. Longenecker, and S. C. Barton, eds., *The Holy Spirit and Christian Origins. Essays in Honor of James D. G. Dunn* (Grand Rapids: Eerdmans, 2004) 157–67. Reprinted by permission of the publisher, all rights reserved.

'"That you may not grieve like the rest who have no hope" (1 Thess 4.13): Death and Early Christian Identity', in M. D. Hooker, ed., *Not in the Word Alone: The First Epistle to the Thessalonians* (St. Paul's Abbey, Rome: 'Benedictina' Publishing, 2003) 131–53. By kind permission.

'Ordinary but Different: Colossians and Hidden Moral Identity', in *Australian Biblical Review* 49 (2001) 34–52. By kind permission.

'There is Neither Old nor Young? Early Christianity and Ancient Ideologies of Age' *New Testament Studies* 53 (2007) 225–41. By permission of Cambridge University Press.

'The Politics of Contempt: Judeans and Egyptians in Josephus' *Against Apion*', in J. M. G. Barclay, ed., *Negotiating Diaspora: Jewish Strategies in the Roman Empire* (London: T & T Clark, 2004) 109–27. Reproduced by kind permission of Continuum International Publishing Group.

'The Empire Writes Back: Josephan Rhetoric in Flavian Rome', in J. Edmondson, S. Mason, and J. Rives, eds., *Flavius Josephus and Flavian Rome* (Oxford: Oxford University, 2005) 315–32. By permission of Oxford University Press

'Who's the Toughest of Them All? Jews, Spartans and Roman Torturers in Josephus' *Against Apion*' *Ramus* 36 (2008) 39–50. By kind permission.

'Snarling Sweetly: Josephus on Images and Idolatry', in S. C. Barton, ed., *Idolatry: False Worship in the Bible, Early Judaism and Christianity* (London: T & T Clark, 2007) 73–87. Reproduced by kind permission of Continuum International Publishing Group.

'Paul and Roman Religion: Graeco-Roman Divinities and Cult to the Emperor', in J. M. Gavaldà Ribot, A. Muñoz Melgar, and A. Puig i Tàrrech, eds., *Pau, Fructuós i el Christianisme Primitiu a Tarragona (Segles I–VIII)* (Tarragona: Fundació Privada Liber, 2010) 59–71 (from which some materials in chapter 18 are derived). By kind permission.

Index of Sources

Old Testament

Jewish Texts (Excluding Philo and Josephus)

New Testament

Philo

Josephus

Early Christian Texts

Greek and Roman Texts

Index of Authors

Index of Selected Topics